Chesterton on War and Peace

In Flanders Fields

In Flanders fields the poppies blow
Between the crosses, row on row,
That mark our place; and in the sky
The larks, still bravely singing, fly
Scarce heard amid the guns below.

We are the Dead. Short days ago
We lived, felt dawn, saw sunset glow,
Loved, and were loved, and now we lie
    In Flanders fields.

Take up our quarrel with the foe:
To you from failing hands we throw
The torch; be yours to hold it high!
If ye break faith with us who die
We shall not sleep, though poppies grow
    In Flanders fields.

Major John A. McCrae, M.D. (1872–1918) was a Canadian field surgeon in World War I. He wrote this poem on May 3, 1915, after the death of a friend, Lt. Alexis Helmer, in the Second Battle of Ypres. He continued to serve at the field hospital until his death of pneumonia and meningitis on January 28, 1918.

This book is dedicated to all those who fought, suffered and died in the war they once called the Great War.

Chesterton on War and Peace

Battling the Ideas and Movements that Led to Nazism and World War II

G. K. Chesterton

Michael W. Perry, Editor

With these Contributors:

Thomas Aquinas, "Is It Always a Sin to Go To War"

Winston Churchill, "The Balkan Situation"

Norman Angell, "The Great Illusion"

Bernard Shaw, "Common Sense about the War"

Bertrand Russell, "The Ethics of War"

Mahatma Gandhi, "Soul-Force and Tapasya"

H. G. Wells, "In the Fourth Year"

Inkling Books　　Seattle　　2008

Description

This book is a collection of articles on war and peace written by G.K. Chesterton before, during and just after World War I. In those articles, Chesterton, one of best-known writers of that day, warned something had gone tragically wrong with Germany that, if left uncorrected, would lead within few decades to a far more horrible war with Germany. His opponents spanned the political spectrum and included militarists who thought might made right, internationalists who trusted in international institutions to keep the peace, liberals lacking the persistence to work for a victory that would ensure lasting peace, and pacifists who, for all their condemnations of war in the abstract, were strangely reticent about condemning Germany for the war it had begun.

All these articles were written for the prestigious *Illustrated London News* between 1905 and 1922, and all but one are from "Our Note-Book," his weekly column in that magazine. One hundred and eleven of the best were selected for their relevance to today's debates about war and peace. Since he was writing for a well-educated contemporary audience, introductions, and over seven hundred footnotes have been added to provide a helpful biographical and historical background.

Included are seven appendices, two by writers with whom Chesterton was in general agreement on this topic (Aquinas and Churchill, although he loathed the latter's zeal for the British Empire), and five by contemporaries whose ideas about war and peace he considered foolish or dangerous enough to take on in public debate (Angell, Shaw, Russell, Gandhi, and Wells).

Copyright Notice

Library Cataloging Data

Chesterton on War and Peace: Battling the Ideas and Movements that Led to Nazism and World War II

Author: G.K. Chesterton (1874–1936). Editor: Michael W. Perry (1948–).

Additional contributions by Thomas Aquinas (1225–1274), Winston Churchill (1874–1965), Norman Angell (1872–1967), Bernard Shaw (1856–1950), Bertrand Russell (1872–1970), Mahatma Gandhi (1869–1948), and H.G. Wells (1866–1946).

448 pages; 6.14 x 9.21 x 0.9 inches, 234 x 156 x 23 mm; 1.4 lb, 625 gm.

Detailed index, seven appendices, one graphic, article introductions, and footnotes.

BISAC Subject Headings: HIS037070 HISTORY/Modern/20th Century; HIS027090 HISTORY/Military/World War I; HIS027100 HISTORY/Military/World War II; HIS015000 HISTORY/Europe/Great Britain.

Library of Congress Control Number: 2007937169

Paperback—ISBN-13: 978-1-58742-061-0 ISBN-10: 1-58472-061-9
Hardback—ISBN-13: 978-1-58742-062-7 ISBN-10: 1-58742-062-7

Published in the United States of America on acid-free paper.
First Edition, Second Printing, April 2008.

Contents

Foreword

My initial plan for this book was to include between two covers virtually everything Chesterton wrote about war before 1923. That soon proved impractical, if not impossible. Chesterton was a prolific writer and during the First World War he focused his enormous energy on writing about the fighting from almost every angle. A draft of this book was approaching a thousand pages, without many clarifying notes, when good sense dictated I narrow the focus.

Once that decision was made, the next step was obvious. I would pick the best of the best. This book is built around a careful selection from the articles Chesterton wrote for "Our Note-Book," his weekly column in the *Illustrated London News*. Before radio and television, the *Illustrated London News* was highly influential, reaching a large audience throughout Britain, across Europe, and in the United States. The articles you see here were chosen for their historical importance and their lasting relevance to today's debates about war and peace. That's precisely how Chesterton intended for them to be taken. In his first article after the war, Chesterton told his readers what his guiding principle had been during the war.

> I have my own opinions about those internal political quarrels, but I have deliberately kept them out of the notes it has been my business to jot down on this page for the last four years. Though the form of them has been in the crudest sense journalistic, I have tried to keep the philosophy of them in some sense historic. I have tried to think of the great war as it would have appeared to our remote ancestors if they had known it was coming, as it will appear to our remote descendants when they consider how it came.

As I edited, I kept a key principle in mind—to allow Chesterton to speak as clearly to this generation as he did to his own. That's the reason for the chapter introductions and the many footnotes. Chesterton was writing at a particular moment in history—that's what he meant by "in the crudest sense journalistic." When he mentions people, places and events, he typically alludes to them, knowing his contemporaries had read about them in newspapers, or that they were common knowledge among the well-informed. Through these notes, you'll learn what his readers knew.

There's another reason why these articles matter. Chesterton was present at the birth of the modern age. Many issues we debate today had their coming out party in London during the first two decades of the twentieth century. Just before the war, disarmament, internationalism and pacifism were being offered as enlightened solutions to the problem of war. Chesterton's experience with those ideas could not have been better. Many were championed by people who were his friends, including H.G. Wells and Bernard Shaw. Almost all came from people he personally knew. Most important of all, when he debated those ideas with his usual good sense, humor and eloquence, they were as fresh as a morning breeze. Today, when many of those debates have grown stale and predictable, it helps to visit that earlier debate and recapture some of its excitement and vividness.

With only a few breaks for health or travel, Chesterton wrote for the *Illustrated London News* from 1905 to 1936—an incredible 31 years. When the war began in August 1914, he had been writing his column for almost nine years. He would continue to write for it until his death on June 14, 1936, with his last article appearing on the following Saturday, June 20.

Chesterton's first article, published on September 30, 1905, was a light-hearted look at a time (still with us) in late summer when the government takes a holiday and so little seems to happen that reporters become desperate for stories. Using the paradoxical style for which he was famous, Chesterton flipped the issue around.

> I cannot imagine why this season of the year is called by journalists the Silly Season: it is the only season in which men have time for wisdom. This can be seen even by glancing at those remarkable documents, the daily papers. As long as Parliament is sitting, the most minute and fugitive things are made to seem important. We have enormous headlines about the vote on a coastguard's supply of cats' meat, or a scene in the House over the perquisites of the butler of the Consul at Port Said. Trivialities, in a word, are made to seem tremendous, until the Silly Season, or the season of wisdom, begins. Then, for the first time, we have a moment to think.... We begin to discuss "The Decay of Home Life," or "What is Wrong?" or the authority of the Scriptures, or "Do We Believe?" These really awful and eternal problems are never discussed except in the Silly Season.... Yes; it is only during this fleeting time that we can really think of the things that are not fleeting. The time of our holidays is the only time in which we can really manage to turn our minds to these grave and everlasting riddles that abide behind every civilisation.... The Silly Season is the only time when we are not silly.

Chesterton's first war article appeared two weeks later, when he spoke against the "scientific" nonsense that Europe had outgrown war. It was vintage Chesterton, bucking fashionable opinion in a way that would later be proved right. He believed complexities such as war are often best seen as paradoxes. On one hand, he hated war for all the pain and suffering it brought. He began his public writing career as one the few who opposed the popular Boer War, and he did so with obvious sympathy for the out-gunned Boer farmers. That illustrates something exceptional about him. He was intensely patriotic, but his patriotism was as broad as the world. Imagine a happily married man who wants other men to be happy in their marriages. That's his love for England and the world.

But it's also true that few modern writers have as unabashedly praised the reasons why men go to war as avidly as Chesterton. You can it see in his best known novel, *The Napoleon of Notting Hill*. It's a tale that delights in London's rich colours and traditions, and those who would replace that richness with a grey and soulless efficiency soon find themselves under attack. In an early poem Chesterton hinted at why Notting Hill fought: "There is one sin: to call a green leaf grey."

In an era when most English, whatever their politics, worshiped their Empire, he was a leading champion of the right of little nations, such as Ireland, Poland, and the future Israel, to be free rather than puppets of powerful nations or pawns in a so-called march of progress. As his brother would write, "he denied the right of any nation or Empire, on the pretence of being more civilized, more progressive, more democratic, or more efficient, to take away from another nation its birthright of independence."[1] To those who gloated about being part of an empire on which the sun never set, he replied that he "had no use for an empire that had no sunsets."

Along with his love for nations came a dislike for those who would destroy them, putting in their place something not in keeping with human nature. He criticized the *cosmopolitan*, that alleged citizen of the world, for being so wrapped up in himself he gives his heart to no country. He believed the best answer to the hatreds that fuel wars did not lie in eliminating patriotic feelings. When patriotism is crushed, he warned, something unhealthy appears. He believed that the way to peace lay in teaching people to appreciate the love others feel for their country. Wells might see nationalities as mere raw material for a scientifically run World State, but Chesterton saw in them something enduring and uniquely human. As a Christian, he agreed with the last chapter in the Bible, where, at the end of history, nations not only exist, they have their wounds healed by a Tree of Life (Revelation 22:2). Our nationalities are to be as eternal as our personalities.

Chesterton warned of the dangers posed by *internationalists,* who would create a mockery of peace by concentrating all power in the hands of a chosen few. Chesterton believed Europe's peace depended on the larger democracies helping to protect smaller nations from a recognized aggressor. When German militarism emerged again, he believed it would turn east, as indeed it did, so Britain and France should help Poland and its neighbours remain free. Once Germany dominated Eastern Europe, its two-front problem would be solved. It could turn west to attack Britain and France, precisely as it did in 1940. After World War II, Chesterton's idea became the North Atlantic Treaty Organization, a sensible alternative to a League of Nations that was too weak and unfocused or a World State that was too strong and rigid.

German *militarism,* which Chesterton often called Prussianism, was another danger he understood perhaps better than anyone else. When you see Prussianism in this book, think of militarism with an accompanying racial justification in the once respectable idea of Teutonism. Chesterton fiercely loathed both. His contempt for Teutonism in the international arena and eugenics within a society made him one of Nazism's earliest foes.

Finally, there was no affection lost between Chesterton and *pacifists.* He poked gentle fun of the older Quaker pacifists, regarding them as harmless. But he was disturbed by a new pacifism growing more powerful in his day. He believed its leaders were vain and its followers too simple-minded to think beyond clichés. He

1. Cecil Chesterton, *G.K. Chesterton: A Criticism* (Seattle: Inkling, 2007), 43–44.

pointed out a key fact—that these new pacifists often argued alongside militarists. Both claimed Germany wasn't responsible for the war, so it shouldn't be punished. Pacifists might argue that man was outgrowing nature's struggle of 'tooth and claw,' while militarists might link war to progress, since it ensured that the 'fit' ruled, but both made the same mistake. Both believed might made right. That, Chesterton repeatedly warned, was pure folly. An unpunished Germany would be an unrepentant Germany that would repeat its aggressions. History has shown just how correct he was. It took the disgrace and destruction of World War II to get Germany to abandon its fascination with militarism and the "Strong Man."

When Chesterton wrote about war, he often drew a sharp distinction between civilization and barbarism. A civilized society, such as Europe's historic Christendom, had not outgrown war. It had learned how to fight properly, respecting a chivalry so little understood today that the word carries an unmistakable medieval air. Civilizations, he stressed, believe that societies and individuals are responsible for their deeds and hold them accountable. In contrast, barbarians place the blame for events on external forces, whether primitive demons haunting a stream or abstract, scientific forces such as race (Nazism) or class (Marxism). No matter how technologically advanced, a society dominated by fatalism and determinism is barbarian, because it places some 'thing' above human decisions and personal bravery.

Now a few technical details. There's always a problem handling tense in a collection like this. Everything happened in the past, so some purists may insist I write in the past tense. I disagree. If we are to experience these issues as Chesterton's readers did, we must read them as if we were living back then, with each article fresh off the press, smelling of ink and new paper. That's why I slip into the past tense only to look back. Of course in a book this long, sometimes I'll get that wrong, but I feel that's better than covering these wonderful articles with the dust of ages. There are also differences between British and American spelling. You'll find both here. Everyone knows "civilization" is the same word as "civilisation." This book also has the usual problem with capitalizing terms such as pacifism and my solution to that was to muddle through in spite of inconsistencies. Finally, keep in mind that the semi-bold text you see wasn't in the original articles. I've added it to make it easier to find memorable, quotable passages.

One final remark. As a writer, Chesterton has great depth. Read this book several times, and each time you'll gather more insights into how our sad and troubled world works and what might be done about that. The issues he deals with here are a part of the permanent human condition and are matters from which we cannot escape, however hard we might try. War is merely the most obvious example of situations when we must face with courage, persistence and wisdom an evil that some would deny and others would bend before. Chesterton was an honest and brave man. He did not lie and would not bend. We can learn much from him.

—Michael W. Perry, Seattle, February 25, 2008

1

Battling Illusions

1905–1913

A Time of Illusion — Editor

Despite the passage of over a century and enormous advances in manufacturing, technology, and world trade, the words with which Charles Dickens opened his classic on the French Revolution, *A Tale of Two Cities* (1859), continued to ring true as our story begins.

> It was the best of times, it was the worst of times, it was the age of wisdom, it was the age of foolishness, it was the epoch of belief, it was the epoch of incredulity, it was the season of Light, it was the season of Darkness, it was the spring of hope, it was the winter of despair, we had everything before us, we had nothing before us, we were all going direct to Heaven, we were all going direct the other way — in short, the period was so far like the present period, that some of its noisiest authorities insisted on its being received, for good or for evil, in the superlative degree of comparison only.
>
> There were a king with a large jaw and a queen with a plain face, on the throne of England; there were a king with a large jaw and a queen with a fair face, on the throne of France. In both countries it was clearer than crystal to the lords of the State preserves of loaves and fishes, that things in general were settled for ever.

Outside a now republican France, much of Europe on the eve of World War I differed little from France on the eve of the French Revolution. In the words of A.G. Gardiner, Chesterton's editor at the *Daily World*, it was a world divided between, "a small select aristocracy born booted and spurred to ride and a large dim mass born saddled and bridled to be ridden."

"It was the best of times" for those who were European, rich, and of noble birth. As "lords of the State," most high political offices were in their hands and many felt that this top-down social structure was "settled for ever." Britannia ruled the waves and an immense empire upon which the sun never set. France's colonial empire might have been smaller, but it had one of the largest land armies on earth. Germany, although far behind in empire and trying desperately to catch up with the Royal Navy on the sea, nevertheless had the continent's leading industrial economy and, as the war would show, an army at least equal to that of France.

Nothing captured that now lost world better than the May 1910 funeral for England's Edward VII, a man often called the "uncle of Europe," because he was related by blood or marriage to virtually all the crowned heads on the continent. In fact, Europe's royalty had intermarried for so long, they'd begun to look alike — hence

Dickens' "large jaw" above, a reference to a protruding chin common in the Hapsburg dynasty. This was Old Europe's supreme moment in the sun. The historian Barbara Tuchman brilliantly captured the moment.

> So gorgeous was the spectacle on the May morning of 1910 when nine kings rode in the funeral of Edward VII of England that the crowd, waiting in hushed and black-clad awe, could not keep back gasps of admiration. In scarlet and blue and green and purple, three by three the sovereigns rode through the palace gates, with plumed helmets, gold braid, crimson sashes, and jeweled orders flashing in the sun.... Together they represented seventy nations in the greatest assemblage of royalty and rank ever gathered in one place and, of its kind, the last. The muffled tongue of Big Ben tolled nine by the clock as the cortege left the palace, but on history's clock it was sunset, and the sun of the old world was setting in the dying blaze of splendor never to be seen again.[1]

Strange as it may sound today, in that era kings and queens were regarded as necessary for the stability of society, much as a policeman is necessary for controlling crime. There was also the awe factor Tuchman described — the need some feel to regard a certain class as superior to themselves, a belief it seems that no amount of royal incompetence, folly, or sheer perversity can alter.[2]

As you'll see in the articles that follow, before World War I royalty played a role in international politics that was more than ceremonial. What a German prince said to the German Kaiser was still being repeated in the English press years later. (See the October 20, 1906 article in this chapter.) The main benefit this expensive-to-maintain class provided flowed from their close family ties. "How could the nations of Europe go to war," some would say, "when the Kings of England, Germany and Russia are such close relatives? They vacation together. They call each other by 'pet' first names. Surely, if war were about to break out, they would intervene in what is for them a family squabble." It was a powerful argument. Since the Napoleonic Wars a century earlier, the continent had experienced an almost unprecedented period of relative peace.

But it was a sham. In her monumental *The Origins of Totalitarianism* (1951), Hannah Arendt described this deceptive calm, pointing out that Chesterton was one of the few wise enough to see through the illusion.

> Only two decades separated the temporary decline of the antisemitic movements from the outbreak of the first World War. This period has been adequately described as a "Golden Age of Security" because only a few who lived in it felt the inherent weakness of an obviously outmoded political structure which, despite all prophecies of imminent doom, continued to function in spurious splendor and with inexplicable, monotonous stubbornness. Side by side, and apparently with equal stability, an anachronistic despotism in Russia, a corrupt bureaucracy in Austria, a stupid militarism in Germany and a half-hearted Republic in continual crisis in France — all of them still under the shadow of the world-wide power of the British Empire — managed to carry on. None of these governments was especially popular, and all faced growing domestic opposition; but nowhere did there seem to exist an earnest political will for radical change in political conditions. Europe was much

1. Barbara Tuchman, *The Guns of August* (New York: Ballantine, 1962), 1.

2. A century ago this misplaced worship focused on royalty, and their every activity was news. Today that same obsession focuses on entertainment celebrities. Perhaps that's why they now make 'pronouncements' on affairs about which they know even less than Europe's old royalty, who were at least reared to rule from the cradle.

too busy expanding economically for any nation or social stratum to take political questions seriously. Everything could go on because nobody cared. Or, in the penetrating words of G.K. Chesterton, "everything is prolonging its existence by denying that it exists."[3]

The lie was exposed in the summer of 1914, when a hurried exchange of personal telegrams between "Willie" (Kaiser Willhelm II of Germany, also known as William II) and "Nickie" (Czar Nicholas II of Russia) failed to halt the slow slide toward one of history's bloodiest wars. In fact, orders issued by both monarchs are on any historian's list of the steps that led to war. Even less was accomplished by the close ties between the British and German royal families. (Queen Victoria's eldest daughter was the mother of the German Emperor.) Europe's monarchies had failed in the worst possible way. The Great War, as people once called it, would stamp "Finished" on their rule.

In the first article we examine, written nine years before the war, Chesterton warns that Europe's faith in its ability to maintain the peace was unjustified. The European civilization to which he belonged, which he often calls Christendom, was tilting out of balance and would bring unhealthy exaggerations and violent conflict.

Because this book is about war, the exaggerations discussed here focus on relations *between* nations and include cosmopolitanism, militarism, pacifism, and a once academically respectable form of racism called Teutonism. Some of those disorders are bipolar in the sense that ideologies that seem radically different share a common fault. In the case of militarism and pacifism, it's the belief that might makes right, that the nation most willing to arm and resort to force ought be able to impose its will on others. Near the end of the war, Chesterton points out that English pacifists were displaying the same hostility toward punishing Germany as German militarists. For both, German might ranked higher than Belgian rights.

Cosmopolitanism and isolationism form another bipolar disorder. Cosmopolitanism (also called internationalism) believes that wars are caused by nations and patriotism. Weaken the independence of nations with powerful international institutions and crush patriotic feelings through schools and culture, and the world will become peaceful. It's apparent opposite is isolationism, a self-obsessed nationalism that sees no need to be involved in a war that does not directly threaten one's own country. Because this book focuses on what Chesterton wrote around the time of

3. Hannah Arendt, *The Origins of Totalitarianism* (New York: Harcourt Brace Jovanovich, 1951–1973), 50–51. In the footnote to that Chesterton quote she wrote: "For a wonderful description of the British state of affairs, see G. K. Chesterton, *The Return of Don Quixote,* which did not appear until 1927 but was 'planned and partly written before the War.'" (See also his July 20, 1907 article.) Her quote is from Michael Herne in Chapter 12 of that book.

"I know what he means," said Braintree grimly, "and it's not true. Do you really believe yourself, Mr. Herne that all that mysticism is true? What do you mean exactly by saying that this old society of yours was sane?"

"I mean that the old society was truthful and that you are in a tangle of lies," answered Herne. "I don't mean that it was perfect or painless. I mean that it called pain and imperfection by their names. You talk about despots and vassals and all the rest; well, you also have coercion and inequality; but you dare not call anything by its own Christian name. You defend every single thing by saying it is something else. You have a King and then explain that he is not allowed to be a King. You have a House of Lords and say it is the same as a House of Commons. When you do want to flatter a workman or a peasant you say he is a true gentleman; which is like saying he is a veritable Viscount. When you want to flatter the gentleman you say he does not use his own title. You leave a millionaire his millions and then praise him because he is 'simple,' otherwise mean and not magnificent; as if there were any good in gold except to glitter! You excuse priests by saying they are not priestly and assure us eagerly that clergymen can play cricket. You have teachers who refuse doctrine, which only means teaching; and doctors of divinity disavowing anything divine. It is all false and cowardly and shamefully full of shame. Everything is prolonging its existence by denying that it exists."

WWI, Isolationism isn't as important as it would become in the 1930s. Whether Britain could have isolated itself from a German attack on France is for historians to debate. In August 1914, events develop too quickly for that to be an issue. During the war, the conflict lay between those who wanted a *hard* allied victory so overwhelming Germany would learn not to make war, and those who wanted an earlier and less clear-cut *soft* victory, because they believed that after the war international institutions such as the League of Nations would keep the peace. In that context, Chesterton criticizes cosmopolitans for showing the same indifference to what happened in Belgium or Poland as isolationists. Both share the same failing, an indifference to the fate of those patriotic smaller nations on which Chesterton believes peace ultimately depends.

Elsewhere, Chesterton condemns unhealthy exaggerations *within* a nation. Domestically, socialism and unrestrained capitalism are as unhealthy as militarism and pacifism. There a similar bipolar disorder exists. Although the two appear to be different, each concentrates too much economic power in the hands of a few. Finally, the domestic equivalent of Teutonism is eugenics, which applies the same Darwinian fit versus unfit criteria within a nation that Teutonism applies between nations, although eugenics found a rationale in biology that Teutonism found in history.[4]

A Warning Sign

October 7, 1905 (excerpt)

The arguments by which the scientific persons attempt to prove that men must become more mechanical or more peaceful always ignore one not unimportant factor — the men themselves.

Editor: In this article Chesterton uses two humorous stories to illustrate a serious point, that it's the "inviolable law of all civilisations that the thing you attempt to extirpate you will certainly exaggerate." Don't force your way into the home of two elderly ladies, he says, and they won't draw swords. Don't treat a omnibus conductor's beer like a science lesson, and he won't "punch your fat 'd head off." And while his prediction hasn't literally come true — modern bankers don't carry battle-axes — within many societies lawyers and shrill cries about "my rights" have substituted for naked steel as people fuss over victimhood or weak and inadequate replacements for a healthy religion and natural affections.[5]

The potential to become unbalanced is as true of a love for one's nation as it is of the affection these two spinsters have for their home or this conductor for his beer. For Chesterton, love for one's country was healthy when tempered by the beliefs of Christendom and the values of a broader European civilization, derived in part from

4. For Chesterton's contempt for eugenics, see his *Eugenics and Other Evils*. Notice that Chesterton sees determinism as the root cause of many evils. The same deterministic mind-set that said, "Race is destiny" also lies behind today's "Race is diversity." The former said race was so important that it determined whether someone created culture or destroyed it. The latter says beliefs are so heavily determined by race that achieving a numeric diversity of races automatically creates a diversity of views. The two share a racist belief that race determines mind. Much as the Germans accused the English of being traitors to a common Teutonic racial heritage (see September 5, 1914, Ch. 2), those who accept modern racial determinism demand that every one in a given race think much the same or be branded a traitor. Determinism not only denies that people can think in any real sense, it becomes angry and hostile when people dare to think differently.

5. C.S. Lewis discussed a similar idea in the sixth chapter of *The Four Loves* (1960). Our loves, he warns, are half-gods that cannot "take the place of God." Only "'when God arrives (and only then) the half-gods can remain.' Left to themselves they either vanish or become demons."

Greece and Rome. Without solid roots, that love can die, resulting in cosmopolitanism and pacifism. As we see in his after-the-war articles, that results in what might be called the Appeasement Syndrome—an obsession with achieving a transitory peace at any price, a refusal to sympathize with injustices heaped on smaller countries, an indifference to repressive governments elsewhere, and in extreme cases, either an unwillingness to defend one's own country or a zeal to find fault with it. Those unhealed injustices then encourage yet more aggression, sowing the seeds for another war. In this article Chesterton refers to the early currents in that modern mind-set when he describes those who, "teach all men that war and revolution are worse evils than surrender and slavery."

At the other extreme, deprived of balance, love for one's country can become jingoistic, leading to militarism, intense nationalism, and racist ideologies such as the Teutonism he will criticize during World War I and continue to denounce after the rise of Hitler until his death in 1936.[6] (Criticizing Nazi ideology before Nazism existed, Chesterton could be called "Hitler's First Foe.") For Chesterton, both attenuated and exaggerated nationalism share a common root—a willingness to let might triumph over right. They also often work toward the same end, the most terrible of wars.

That's why I open this book about war with Chesterton's delightful tale about sword-waving spinsters. There is a connection. It's classic Chesterton to use ordinary human traits to illustrate larger issues. Although presented with humor, those spinsters really are a "warning" and a "sign in heaven about the apocalypse of London."

Notice too that his ideal, healthy religion has a light-hearted, Italian touch. "The men in happier lands," he writes, "shall live lightly with their faith, and take off their hats to Heaven as to an old companion." He says much the same about how a healthy society handles emotions: "Make your civilisation reasonably romantic, and anyone who is unreasonably romantic will be hooted down the street." Virtue often lies in a relaxed and reasonable midway point between two extremes.

Perhaps the two most important people in our civilisation at present are the two elderly ladies who defended their residence with drawn swords. They are in the true sense a portent, that is, not merely a wonder, but a warning; they are a sign in heaven of the apocalypse of London. At first one feels disposed to deal with their case merely fancifully; to let one's imagination run loose along the line of thought suggested. One thinks of their rallying round them a band of gay and desperate maiden-ladies, living in the saddle and by the sword, making raids from the hills and leaving burning cities in their terrible trail. One imagines them returning to carouse in their caverns amid gold and blood, calling tempestuously for tea as they hurl down their cutlasses and carefully remove their gloves. But I think, upon the whole, I prefer to contemplate the simplicity of the mere fact. I like to think of those amiable and respectable elderly modern ladies standing together in their parlour, the tea-cosy and the muffins on the table, the daguerreotype of Cousin Eustace and the

6. "Jingo" is little used today. The *Oxford English Dictionary* defines it as: "A nickname for those who supported and lauded the policy of Lord Beaconsfield in sending a British fleet into Turkish waters to resist the advance of Russia in 1878; hence, one who brags of his country's preparedness for fight, and generally advocates or favours a bellicose policy in dealing with foreign powers; a blustering or blatant 'patriot'; a Chauvinist." The word comes from the lines "by Jingo" in a music hall song popular at that time.

coloured print of Queen Victoria on the walls, the neat bookshelf containing *Enquire Within, The Lamp-Lighter,*[7] and an album with pink pages—and in their hands two enormous and shining cavalry sabres with which they are conscientiously ready to slaughter their fellow-creatures....

The ladies with the swords are interesting in exactly the same manner that the Agapemone is interesting; of course, in a much more reputable sense, and I apologise to the poor ladies for the comparison.[8] But their similarity consists in this , that they are both evidences of the violent outbreak of elemental things in the suburbs. **It is the inviolable law of all civilisations that the thing you attempt to extirpate you will certainly exaggerate.** Our modern cities, particularly the suburbs of our modern cities, are strictly and carefully designed to be sensible and secular; therefore they will certainly, before long, be on fire with the most senseless kinds of superstition. The men in happier lands shall live lightly with their faith, and take off their hats to Heaven as to an old companion. In Clapton you will have straight roads and straight talks, and a total ignoring of the mysteries. Therefore in Clapton you shall have a man screaming in the sunlight that he is divine, made the stars, turning open sin into a sacrament. You shall teach all men that war and revolution are worse evils than surrender and slavery, that a blow is ungentlemanly, and a crusade caddish. Therefore the weapons that citizens will not take maniacs shall discover and brandish, and when men have left off wearing swords, women shall begin to wave them. **For the truth is that the eternal things are rising against temporary things. The gods are rebelling against men.**

We must be prepared for an increasing number of incidents of this type, Cockney incidents of a violent and ludicrous romance. We must not be unduly surprised at two London females carrying great swords. Before we have done with the matter we shall see bankers carrying battle-axes, curates hurling javelins, governesses girt with great knives, and charwomen settling affairs of honour with rapiers. **The arguments by which the scientific persons attempt to prove that men must become more mechanical or more peaceful always ignore one not unimportant factor—the men themselves.** Civilisation itself is only one of the things that men choose to have. Convince them of its uselessness and they would fling away civilisation as they fling away a cigar. The sociologists always say what will happen in the material world, and never seem to ask themselves what would be happening meanwhile in the moral world. A perfect allegory of this may be found in a passage of Mr. Barry

---

7. *Everybody's Enquire Within* was a popular magazine. *The Lamp-Lighter* may have been a less well-known magazine, a musical score, or Charles Dickens's humorous 1838 tale, *The Lamplighter,* which includes the lines, "lamplighters are a strange and primitive people; that they rigidly adhere to old ceremonies and customs which have been handed down among them from father to son since the first public lamp was lighted out of doors."

8. Agapemonde (Greek for "abode of love') was a religious cult whose beliefs were as Chesterton described. In his day, they were headquartered in London's Upper Clapton, where in 1892 they built a church under the leadership of Henry James Prince (1811–1899). Chesterton describes a sun-worshiping cult similar to them in his Father Brown mystery, "The Eye of Apollo." It believed that, "if a man were really healthy, he could stare at the sun," to which Father Brown replies, "If a man were really healthy, he would not bother to stare at it."

Pain's delightful book, *De Omnibus*.[9] The scientific working-man endeavouring to explain to the others the law of gravity, or some such triviality, asks the omnibus-conductor what would happen if he, the speaker, dropped a penny into his, the conductor's beer. I quote from memory: "'It 'ud drop to the bottom wouldn't it?' says the scientist. 'Yuss,' I says, 'that's one of the things that 'ud lappen. Another thing 'ud be that I should punch your fat 'ed off at the root for takin' a lib with my liquor.'" That is the sacred and immortal voice of mankind replying to the insolence of the specialist. The sociologist tells us that all sorts of things under certain conditions must happen, that the obliteration of nationality must happen, that the command of everything by science and scientific men must happen; and all because some particular economic or material fact must happen. "Yuss," we says. "That's one of the things that'll 'appen. Another thing'll be that we shall punch their fat 'eds off at the root for takin' a lib with the moral traditions of humanity." Their evolution will go on exactly until our revolution chooses to begin.[10]

If we cannot provide the great cities and the great suburbs with some kind of poetry, they will simply go on breeding these broken fanaticisms that make women wave sabres and men found insane religions. If we will not have religion, we are reduced to the even more annoying necessity of having religions. If we will not have romance in dress, in carriage, in mode of thought, the romantic element in mankind will materialise itself in the form of a great clout on the head with a cavalry sabre next time we go to call on a maiden lady of independent means. **For it cannot be too often insisted upon that the way to avoid sentiment becoming too sentimental is to admit the existence of sentiment as a plain, unsentimental fact, a thing as solid and necessary as soap.** Some unhappy Stoics in the modern world are perpetually concealing their emotions for fear of what they call "scenes." And the consequence is that they are always having scenes from morning till night. The sensible Stoical English father goes purple in the face and swears and splutters against the sensible and Stoical English son. The sensible and Stoical English son goes red to the roots of his hair, and curses and gasps and exclaims against the sensible and Stoical English father. And all because they will not simply and sanely confess their emotions. All because they will neither of them merely say, "My dear father (or son) I am horribly fond of you, and at this moment it would give me enormous pleasure to throw a chair at your head." Their reluctance to admit their emotions becomes the most violent of all their emotions. Their shame of sentiment makes them more sentimental than any man need naturally be. Romantic and openly emotional people never make scenes. They never make scenes, because to them emotion is an easy and natural thing, a thing as evident and human as a man's nose, a thing to be

9. Barry Pain (1867–1928) was an English journalist, poet and humorous writer. His *De Omnibus, by the Conductor* was published in 1901. In an article in the *Leader* (July 28, 1945), George Orwell claimed that, "within our own century, England has produced no humorous writing of any value," but he took note of Barry Pain and added, "no English light verse of any value within this century, except Mr. Belloc's, and a poem or two by Chesterton."

10. Chesterton wrote on the possibility of this revolution in "The Secret People," which is Appendix A in the Inkling edition of *G.K. Chesterton: A Criticism* written by his brother Cecil Chesterton.

carried as lightly as a man's walking-stick. **No, we must do what has been done in the South of Europe. Make your civilisation reasonably romantic, and anyone who is unreasonably romantic will be hooted down the street.**

G.K. Chesterton, "Our Note-Book," *Illustrated London News* 129 (October 7, 1905), 490. US edition: October 21, 1905. Published elsewhere as "Fanaticism in the Suburbs."

SCIENTIFIC BARBARISM

August 4, 1906

Civilisation in the best sense merely means the full authority of the human spirit over all externals. Barbarism means the worship of those externals in their crude and unconquered state. Barbarism means the worship of Nature; and in recent poetry, science, and philosophy there has been too much of the worship of Nature.

EDITOR: Understanding what Chesterton believed about war requires a grasp of what he saw as the difference between civilisation and barbarism. The distinction he made isn't the oft-repeated axiom that the civilised have (or should have) outgrown war, while barbarians have not. Rather it lies in *why* and *how* a society fights. Civilised societies enter and practice war differently from barbarians. This 1906 article demonstrates that the arguments he would use against Germany from 1914 on were not wartime propaganda, but ideas he had long held important. Chesterton did not link civilization to cultural or technical sophistication. When they become deterministic, worshiping Nature and "forces outside man" (such as heredity and environment)—advanced societies become barbaric. So the German people, the source of so much beautiful music and useful science, could become the most horrid of barbarians without abandoning their symphonies and operas. In that lies the answer to the oft-asked question, "How could the nation of Bach and Beethoven become the tool of Hitler?"

Keep in mind that for Chesterton a healthy civilization must have a healthy religion. In *Eugenics and Other Evils* (1922), he would link the determinism that he calls here barbarian with a literary style common among atheists, one that sees humanity driven by "forces outside man" and thus not in control of its destiny.

> The mark of the atheistic style is that it instinctively chooses the word which suggests that things are dead things; that things have no souls. Thus they will not speak of waging war, which means willing it; they speak of the "outbreak of war," as if all the guns blew up without the men touching them."[11]

As a result, those who believe in a soulless humanity are drawn to mechanistic solutions for social ills. If wars are caused by guns rather than the choices people make, then disarmament or a World State with a monopoly on weapons should bring peace. Get the "things" right, they think, and you make the world right. Viewed from a grimmer angle, since concepts such as "freedom" have no meaning, there are no limits on the use of force. Everything that is possible is permissible. Totalitarian states, such as those Hitler, Stalin and Mao tried to create, are as easily justified in a deterministic world as an idyllic, utopian world without war. Perhaps that's why those who claim

11. G.K. Chesterton, *Eugenics and Other Evils* (Seattle: Inkling Books, 2000), 40.

to be championing the latter are so often taken in by the blandishments of the former. The two share a common belief that human "things are dead things."

SOMEBODY writes complaining of something I said about progress. I have forgotten what I said, but I am quite certain that it was (like a certain Mr. Douglas in a poem which I have also forgotten) tender and true.[12] In any case, what I say now is this. **Human history is so rich and complicated that you can make out a case for any course of improvement or retrogression.** I could make out that the world has been growing more democratic, for the English franchise has certainly grown more democratic. I could also make out that the world has been growing more aristocratic, for the English Public Schools have certainly grown more aristocratic.[13] I could prove the decline of militarism by the decline of flogging; I could prove the increase of militarism by the increase of standing armies and conscription. But I can prove anything in this way. I can prove that the world has always been growing greener. Only lately men have invented absinthe and the *Westminster Gazette*.[14] I could prove the world has grown less green. There are no more Robin Hood foresters, and fields are being covered with houses. I could show that the world was less red with khaki or more red with the new penny stamps. But in all cases progress means progress only in some particular thing. Have you ever noticed that strange line of Tennyson, in which he confesses, half consciously, how very *conventional* progress is?—

Let the great world spin for ever down the ringing grooves of change.[15]

Even in praising change, he takes for a simile the most unchanging thing. He calls our modern change a groove. And it is a groove; perhaps there was never anything so groovy.

Nothing would induce me in so idle a monologue as this to discuss adequately a great political matter like the question of the military punishments in Egypt.[16] But I may suggest one broad reality to be observed by both sides, and which is, generally speaking, observed by neither. **Whatever else is right, it is utterly wrong to employ the argument that we Europeans must do to savages and Asiatics whatever savages and Asiatics do to us.** I have even seen some controversialists use the metaphor "We must fight them with their own weapons." Very well; let those controversialists

12. The lines "O Dowglass! O Dowglass! Tendir and Trewe" come from an allegorical Scottish poem about Robert the Bruce, "The Buke of the Howlat" (trans. "The Book of the Owl") written about 1450 by Richard Holland. The poet's life illustrates Chesterton's point about just how difficult progress can be to define. Holland remained loyal to the House of Douglas though good times and bad.

13. In Britain "public schools" are exclusive private schools, public only because they train for public service.

14. Herbs added to alcohol give absinthe a beautiful green color, and the *Westminister Gazette* had a green border.

15. From Alfred Lord Tennyson's 1842 poem, "Locksley Hall." Chesterton would regard as dangerously naive its utopian vision: "Till the war-drum throbb'd no longer, and the battle-flags were furl'd/In the Parliament of man, the Federation of the world." See Chesterton's articles on the League of Nations in Chapter 7.

16. This may have been the Denshawai Incident, which took place in an Egyptian village of that name on June 13, 1906. Five British officers wanted to shoot pigeons there, but the villagers protested, considering them domestic fowl much like our chickens. A riot resulted, with villagers being wounded and one officer dying from a sun stroke. Four villagers were hung for the death of the officer, and others were sentenced to hard labor. The British officers, who claimed to have done nothing wrong, were given immunity from prosecution.

take their metaphor, and take it literally. Let us fight the Soudanese with their own weapons. Their own weapons are large, very clumsy knives, with an occasional old-fashioned gun. Their own weapons are also torture and slavery. If we fight them with torture and slavery, we shall be fighting badly, precisely as if we fought them with clumsy knives and old guns. **That is the whole strength of our Christian civilisation, that it does fight with its own weapons and not with other people's.** It is not true that superiority suggests a tit for tat. It is not true that if a small hooligan puts his tongue out at the Lord Chief Justice, the Lord Chief Justice immediately realises that his only chance of maintaining his position is to put his tongue out at the little hooligan. The hooligan may or may not have any respect at all for the Lord Chief Justice: that is a matter which we may contentedly leave as a solemn psychological mystery. But if the hooligan has any respect at all for the Lord Chief Justice, that respect is certainly extended to the Lord Chief Justice entirely because he does not put his tongue out. Exactly in the same way the ruder or more sluggish races regard the civilisation of Christendom. If they have any respect for it, it is precisely because it does not use their own coarse and cruel expedients. According to some modern moralists, whenever Zulus cut off the heads of dead Englishmen, Englishmen must cut off the heads of dead Zulus.[17] Whenever Arabs or Egyptians constantly use the whip to their slaves Englishmen must use the whip to their subjects. And on a similar principle (I suppose), whenever an English Admiral has to fight cannibals the English Admiral ought to eat them. However unattractive a menu consisting entirely of barbaric kings may appear to an English gentleman, he must try to sit down to it with an appetite. He must fight the Sandwich Islanders with their own weapons; and their own weapons are knives and forks. But the truth of the matter is, of course, that to do this kind of thing is to break the whole spell of our supremacy. All the mystery of the white man, all the fearful poetry of the white man, so far as it exists in the eyes of these savages, consists in the fact that we do not do such things. The Zulus point at us and say, "Observe the advent of these inexplicable demi-gods, these magicians, who do not cut off the noses of their enemies." The Soudanese say to each other, "This hardy people never flogs its servants; it is superior to the simplest and most obvious human pleasures." And the cannibals say, "The austere and terrible race, the race that denies itself even boiled missionary, is upon us: let us flee."

Whether or no these details are a little conjectural, the general proposition I suggest is the plainest common-sense. **The elements that make Europe upon the whole the most humanitarian civilisation are precisely the elements that make it upon the whole the strongest. For the power which makes a man able to entertain a good impulse is the same as that which enables him to make a good gun; it is imagination.** It is imagination that makes a man outwit his enemy, and it is imagination that makes him spare his enemy. It is precisely because this picturing of the

17. Chesterton is probably referring to the Anglo-Zulu War of 1879, in which a major British defeat at the Battle of Isandlwana early in the year forced Britain, worried about maintaining control of its empire, to defeat the Zulus quickly, European arms proving more than a match for Zulu speed and mobility. The war is dramatized in the films *Zulu* (1964) and *Zulu Dawn* (1979). *Shaka Zulu*, a 1986 television miniseries, explores earlier Zulu history.

other man's point of view is in the main a thing in which Christians and Europeans specialise that Christians and Europeans, with all their faults, have carried to such perfection both the arts of peace and war.[18]

They alone have invented machine-guns, and they alone have invented ambulances; they have invented ambulances (strange at it may sound) for the same reason for which they have invented machine-guns. Both involve a vivid calculation of remote events. It is precisely because the East, with all its wisdom, is cruel that the East, with all its wisdom, is weak. And it is precisely because savages are pitiless that they are still—merely savages. If they could imagine their enemy's sufferings they could also imagine his tactics. If Zulus did not cut off the Englishman's head they might really borrow it. **For if you do not understand a man you cannot crush him. And if you do understand him, very probably you will not.**

When I was about seven years old I used to think that the chief modern danger was a danger of over-civilisation. I am inclined to think now that the chief modern danger is that of a slow return towards barbarism, just such a return towards barbarism as is indicated in the suggestions of barbaric retaliation of which I have just spoken. **Civilisation in the best sense merely means the full authority of the human spirit over all externals. Barbarism means the worship of those externals in their crude and unconquered state.** Barbarism means the worship of Nature; and in recent poetry, science, and philosophy there has been too much of the worship of Nature. Whenever men begin to talk much and with great solemnity about the forces outside man, the note of it is barbaric.[19] When men talk much about heredity and environment they are almost barbarians. The modern men of science are many of them almost barbarians. Mr. Blatchford is in great danger of becoming a barbarian.[20] For barbarians (especially the truly squalid and unhappy barbarians) are always talking about these scientific subjects from morning till night. That is

18. W.H. Auden said the same about Tolkien's *The Lord of the Rings* in the *New York Times* on January 22, 1956. Evil, that is, has every advantage but one—it is inferior in imagination. Good can imagine the possibility of becoming evil—hence the refusal of Gandalf and Aragorn to use the Ring—but Evil, defiantly chosen, can no longer imagine anything but itself. Sauron cannot imagine any motives except lust for dominion and fear, so that, when he has learned that his enemies have the Ring, the thought that they might try to destroy it never enters his head, and his eye is kept turned towards Gondor and away from Mordor and the Mount of Doom.

19. Hitler: "A stronger race will drive out the weak, for the vital urge in its ultimate form will, time and again, burst all the absurd fetters of the so-called humanity of individuals, in order to replace it by the humanity of Nature which destroys the weak to give his place to the strong." *Mein Kampf* (Boston: Houghton Mifflin, 1943), 132.

20. Robert Blatchford (1851–1943) was editor of the *Clarion* newspaper and (at that time) a socialist and a Fabian, as well as stridently anti-Christian and dogmatically opposed to the idea that people have a free will. His 1904 *Not Guilty: A Defence of the Bottom Dog* excuses all human evil-doing as the result of factors beyond human control and hence no one's responsibility. Chesterton had countered by pointing to a man, both rich and well-bred, who nevertheless "goads poor men for their rent like a threadbare landlady in the Harrow Road." To that Blatchford replied, "Is Mr. Chesterton in a position to inform us that his bold, bad peer is not a degenerate? Is Mr. Chesterton sure that he has not inherited a degenerate nature from diseased or vicious ancestors? No insanity in the family? No gout? No consumption? No drunkenness?" *Not Guilty* (New York City: Albert and Charles Boni, 1913), 83–85. Spreading a net that broad, Blatchford could find a 'reason' for evil in anyone. Unfortunately for his argument, even more reasons for doing evil might exist in the past of a man who is good. How could he make sense of that? At the end of his book, he's driven to the illogic of appealing to our goodness to issue "a verdict of Not Guilty" for crimes and sins (p. 167). But if we can't choose not to do evil, how can we choose to forgive? Chesterton commented on Mr. Blatchford in the July 26, 1913 *Illustrated London News* (Ch. 1). For a fuller discus-

why they remain squalid and unhappy; that is why they remain barbarians. Hottentots are always talking about heredity, like Mr. Blatchford. Sandwich Islanders are always talking about environment, like Mr. Suthers.[21] Savages—those that are truly stunted or depraved—dedicate nearly all their tales and sayings to the subject of physical kinship, of a curse on this or that tribe, of a taint in this or that family, of the invincible law of blood, of the unavoidable evil of places.[22] **The true savage is a slave, and is always talking about what he must do; the true civilised man is a free man, and is always talking about what he may do.** Hence all the Zola heredity and Ibsen heredity that has been written in our time affects me as not merely evil, but as essentially ignorant and retrogressive.[23] This sort of science is almost the only thing that can with strict propriety be called reactionary. **Scientific determinism is simply the primal twilight of all mankind; and some men seem to be returning to it.**

Another savage trait of our time is the disposition to talk about material substances instead of about ideas. The old civilisation talked about the sin of gluttony or excess. We talk about the Problem of Drink—as if drink could be a problem. When people have come to call the problem of human intemperance the Problem of Drink, and to talk about curing it by attacking the drink traffic, they have reached quite a dim stage of barbarism. The thing is an inverted form of fetish-worship; it is no sillier to say that a bottle is a god than to say that a bottle is a devil. The people who talk about the curse of drink will probably progress down that dark hill. In a little while we shall have them calling the practice of wife-beating the Problem of Pokers; the habit of housebreaking will be called the Problem of the Skeleton-Key Trade; and for all I know they may try to prevent forgery by shutting up all the stationers' shops by Act of Parliament.[24]

sion of Chesterton's views about free will and how they "raise the question of the very possibility of any morals," see Chapter VII of *The Autobiography of G.K. Chesterton* (New York: Sheed & Ward, 1936), 180–184.

21. Chesterton mentioned Robert Bentley Suthers in *Orthodoxy* (1908, Ch. 2), where he wrote: "When I was engaged in a controversy with the *Clarion* on the matter of free will, that able writer Mr. R.B. Suthers said that free will was lunacy, because it meant causeless actions, and the actions of a lunatic would be causeless. I do not dwell here upon the disastrous lapse in determinist logic. Obviously if any actions, even a lunatic's, can be causeless, determinism is done for. If the chain of causation can be broken for a madman, it can be broken for a man."

22. Hitler: "Blood sin and desecration of the race are the original sin in this world and the end of a humanity which surrenders to it." *Mein Kampf* (Boston: Houghton Mifflin, 1943), 249.

23. Émile Zola (1840–1902) was a French novelist who wrote a series of 20 novels called Les Rougon-Macquart between 1871 and 1893. The series follows the standard hereditarian pattern, tracing the history of two families, born of the same mother (Adelaide Fouque), but having two different fathers, one a respectable farm laborer named Fougon and the other an alcoholic criminal named Macquart. Henrik Ibsen (1828–1906) was a famous Norwegian playwright whose plays, such as his *A Doll's House* (1879), claim that personal faults are inherited.

24. Alas, these modern 'barbarisms' have grown stronger since Chesterton's day. In today's Europe, scientific determinism means that a vicious serial murder is "not guilty," at least to the extent that he cannot be executed. Seeing the root of problems in "material substances" means that, although murder is not deterred by capital punishment, it can be prevented by controlling a thing—the gun. But notice that this alleged sympathy with the victim isn't extended to other matters. Someone who has taken ten lives isn't expected to pay with his own life, but someone who has cheated the government out of ten million Euros is not allowed to pay for his crime by giving the government a mere tenth of what he stole. The inconsistency is revealing. Murder is regarded as determined by external factors, but tax evaders have an invincible free will against money's powerful temptation. There's also the disturbing inconsistencies of Europe's anti-capital punishment laws, particularly in Germany, where Article 102 bans it. The *Washington Post* drew a Chesterton-like parallel between opposition to capital punishment and barbarism: "But the actual history of the German death penalty ban casts this claim in a different light. Article 102 was in fact the brainchild of a right-wing politician who sympathized with convicted Nazi

I cannot help thinking that there is some shadow of this uncivilised materialism lying at present upon a much more dignified and valuable cause. Everyone is talking just now about the desirability of ingeminating peace and averting war. But even war and peace are physical states rather than moral states, and in talking about them only we have by no means got to the bottom of the matter. **How, for instance, do we as a matter of fact create peace in one single community? We do not do it by vaguely telling everyone to avoid fighting and to submit to anything that is done to him. We do it by definitely defining his rights and then undertaking to avenge his wrongs.**

G.K. Chesterton, "Our Note-Book," *Illustrated London News* 129 (August 4, 1906), 150. US: August 18, 1906. Published elsewhere as "The Indefiniteness of Progress."

MILITARISM AND BOYS

October 6, 1906 (excerpt)

A child's instinct is almost perfect in the matter of fighting; a child always stands for the good militarism as against the bad. The child's hero is always the man or boy who defends himself suddenly and splendidly against aggression.

EDITOR: There's a great difference between someone who opposes a particular war for good reasons, as Chesterton did the Boer War (1899–1902), and a pacifist who opposes all wars without exception. Chesterton deals with the latter here and criticizes their attempts to deprive boys of the chance to play a soldier and a hero.

Because great dangers often demand great physical prowess, society particularly needs boys to grow up into heroic men. In a healthy society, most people learn the difference between a hero and a coward as children. Boys, Chesterton says, often instinctively sense this difference, which is reinforced by the games they play and the books they read. The "rehearsal" of brave deeds in their imagination is good when the deeds are good and only becomes bad when the deeds being imagined are bad.

Chesterton's concern about raising boys to be heros rather than pacifists, explains why he defended 'Penny Dreadful' tales. He liked the thoughts they create in a young boy's mind. Here's an excerpt from a tale by Edward L. Wheeler, *Deadwood Dick's Doom* (*c.* 1899). An unsavory man has caught a pretty young Indian maiden alone in the wilderness far from her father, Chief Red Hatchet.

> "No, no! Siska not kiss pale-face," she answered, struggling to release herself. "Paleface bad man, and Red Hatchet be angry at him."
>
> "That don't matter to me. A kiss I'm going to have before you go, or my name's not Carrol Carner. So pucker up those pretty lips, my beauty, and submit to the inevitable."
>
> "No, no! Help—help!" she screamed, struggling so violently that he found it impossible to accomplish his design.

war criminals—and sought to prevent their execution by British and American occupation authorities. Far from intending to repudiate the barbarism of Hitler, the author of Article 102 wanted to make a statement about the supposed excesses of Allied victors' justice." Killing thousands of innocent civilians was to mean, at most, a life in prison more comfortable than many ordinary people were experiencing in impoverished post-war Europe. [Charles Lane, "The Paradoxes of a Death Penalty Stance," *Washington Post* (June 4, 2005), A17.]

> "Curse you! you are as strong as a young bear," he gritted, savagely.
>
> "Aha! I have you now, though, and now for my kiss!"
>
> "Not by a jugful, stranger!" a stern voice cried, accompanied by rapidly approaching footsteps, and the next instant Carrol Carner found himself lying at full length upon the ground while over him stood a handsome fellow in sportish dress—valiant Deadwood Dick. "Ha! ha!" he laughed, sarcastically—"what a figure you cut now, don't you, my presuming pilgrim? You reckoned you had this little girl dead to rights, didn't you, you infernal skunk, because she was alone and unprotected? But, you see, all signs fail, when the wind blows me down."[25]

Of course, it's also possible to engage boys in what Chesterton calls here the "rehearsal of an essentially evil practice," so their fighting instincts are perverted. The Nazis did that with the Hitler Youth, convincing many boys that Germans were the victims of an evil Jewish conspiracy. There's a chilling example in the Prologue to Erika Mann's 1938 *School for Barbarians*. There she describes a meeting she had with a German woman who'd been rated a "perfect Nordic" by Nazi scientists. Nevertheless, she and her husband desperately wanted to leave Germany to protect their young son from Nazi indoctrination. Meeting in secrecy, she gave Erika an example of just how poisonous Germany had become when she described something that happened to a Jewish surgeon, who was a family friend and the father of a boy named Wolfgang.

> She adds: "Have you any idea what a great man Wolfgang's father was, before the government changed? He was a physician and surgeon—my husband's superior at the hospital. Just after Hitler came in, they had an emergency operation, a little 'Aryan' boy with appendicitis. Peritonitis had begun; it was a matter of life and death, you see, and the Professor, who still held his post, was performing the operation himself. And in the silence of the operating room, deep under the anaesthetic, the child began to scream, suddenly, shouting phrases cut so deep into his soul that they remained even during the death under ether. "Down with the Jews!" he cried out, "Kill the Jews, we have to get rid of them!" My husband tells me that moment gripped him—the calm Jewish professor, going steadily on with the operation, the knife not trembling, everything going ahead to save that screaming child. And, really, on the other side, a thing like that is far worse than any humiliation for a child, far uglier, more hopeless. It drives me mad to think that my son might ever be able to turn to death and murder in his sleep, because he had been taught to do so, and because I had no right to stop that teaching.[26]

As Chesterton would often stress, those deprived of healthy ways to express their instincts, often adopt—or can be made to adopt—unhealthy ones. Erika Mann warned of Nazism's militaristic 'School for Barbarians' and its obsession with killing. In the article that follows, Chesterton warns of a danger at the opposite extreme, something we might call a pacifist "School for Indifference," which leaves children, as they grow up, unable to fight any evil no matter how great, particularly evils that do not affect them personally and especially evils inflicted by the strong on the weak.

Finally, keep in mind that, like any good writer, Chesterton was flexible with words. Here he adopts the language of opponents and applies "militarism" to looking with

25. Quoted from G.K. Chesterton, *Chesterton Day by Day* (Seattle: Inkling Books, 2002), 52–53. Yes, the writing is dreadful, that's why they were called penny dreadfuls. Chesterton praised the sentiments not the style.

26. Erika Mann, *School for Barbarians* (New York: Modern Age Books, 1938), 16–17. Erika (1905–1969), who had a Jewish mother, was the daughter of the Nobel Prize winning novelist Thomas Mann.

favor on soldiers. Later he applies the term negatively to situations where military objectives are too influential and where it leads to the glorification of violence.

In many of the papers that I read, and in some that I commonly agree with, there is a continual stir about an alleged immorality in teaching young boys the use of the rifle. Of this notion of immorality I am unable to make head or tail. I do not say that I am in favour of this form of national defence; I can imagine many objections to it: the objection I can most clearly imagine is simply that it is no use; that it would not do anything towards defending the nation. I can imagine some wild, paradoxical fellow maintaining that the French army or the German might not immediately turn tail at the sight of a cadet corps. Such frenzies my fancy can grasp. But when people tell me that it is wicked to teach boys to shoot with a rifle at a mark, I do not even understand the meaning of the words they use. Their explanations make the matter darker still. **What can they mean when they say that we must not put militarism into boys? Can we by any possibility get militarism out of boys? You might burn it out with red-hot irons; you might eventually scourge it out as if it were a mediaeval devil; but except you employ the most poignant form of actual persecution, you certainly will not prevent little boys thinking about soldiers, talking about soldiers, and pretending that they are soldiers.** You may mortify and macerate this feeling in them if you like, just as you may mortify and macerate their love of comrades, or their love of wandering. You may shut them up in a monastery and never let them see women. You may starve them and never let them touch bread. But I do not think you are justified in saying, when your victim has been fasting for five days, "Shall we put into his mind the complex conception of food? Shall we shock his innocence with the suggestion of a bun? Shall we perplex his pure simplicity with that notion of regular meals which has brought us to so many fits of indigestion?"

This is exactly what is done in the case of shooting. We grown-up people have made a mess of eating, as we have made a mess of everything else. We have made a mess of fighting, as we have made a mess of everything else. We have corrupted with an impure Epicurism the exalted, nay, the austere, joy of eating. The greediness of a schoolboy is something clean and chaste, which is above our heads—an armed and awful virginity. The bun is not a thing which we have passed: the bun is something perfect and terrible to which we cannot attain. We are not innocent enough to share the pure appetite of the schoolboy. We are not good enough to be greedy. And exactly as we have corrupted the original appetite for feasting, so we have corrupted the original appetite for arms. **A child's instinct is almost perfect in the matter of fighting; a child always stands for the good militarism as against the bad. The child's hero is always the man or boy who defends himself suddenly and splendidly against aggression.** The child's hero is never the man or boy who attempts by his mere personal force to extend his mere personal influence. In all boys' books, in all boys' conversation, the hero is one person and the bully the other. That combination of the hero and bully in one, which people now call the Strong Man or the Superman, would be simply unintelligible to any schoolboy. To put the matter shortly, a boy feels an abysmal difference between conquest and victory. Conquest has the sound of something cold and heavy; the automatic operations of a powerful army. Victory has the sound of something sudden and valiant; victory is like a cry out of the living mouth. The child is excited with victory; he is bored with conquest. The child is not an Imperialist; the child is a Jingo—which is excellent. The child is not a militarist in the heavy, mechanical modern sense; the child is a fighter. Only very old and very wicked people can be militarists in the modern sense. Only very old and very wicked people can be peace-at-any-price men. The child's instincts are quite clean and chivalrous, though perhaps a little exaggerated.

But really to talk of this small human creature, who never picks up an umbrella without trying to use it as a sword, who will hardly read a book in which there is no fighting, who out of the Bible itself generally remembers the "bluggy"[27] parts, who never walks down the garden without imagining himself to be stuck all over with swords and daggers—to take this human creature and talk about the wickedness of teaching him to be military, seems rather a wild piece of humour. He has already not only the tradition of fighting, but a far manlier and more genial tradition of fighting than our own. **No; I am not in favour of the child being taught militarism. I am in favour of the child teaching it.**

Of course in the case of those few people who regard all war—that is, every act of physical force—as immoral, I can see that such an instinct in boyhood must appear as a mere evil lust to be suppressed. Of course I agree that the mere fact that the actual exercise is harmless, that the rifles are only aimed at targets, would not excuse it if it were the image or rehearsal of an essentially evil practice. I should not be in favour of a class in which English boys were taught to burn alive a stuffed cat; or American boys to burn alive a stuffed negro. I should not like the Board Schools to establish a thing called Poker Drill, in which the little boys learnt to beat imaginary wives with small wooden pokers. I should not recommend little classes in cannibalism, for the cooking of dummy missionaries.[28] And if I thought that war as such was really as wicked as wife-beating as such or cannibalism as such, I should certainly join with those who resent the rifle class and the cadet corps. Even here, as in so many other questions, the most fanatical position is really the most reasonable. Even the man who thinks war wrong and objects to rifle corps is not so mad as the man who thinks war wrong and does not object to rifle corps. Only to those who disapprove of all war I would add this reminder: Their only conceivable meaning is

27. This is a child-like euphemism for "bloody," a term some in Chesterton's day considered impolite.

28. Chesterton is criticizing play that pretends to do evil, which is justified with a claim that "no one is actually being hurt." His criticism of burning alive "a stuffed cat," applies equally well to some video games. Imagining oneself doing evil is a step along the road to actually doing so or, at the very least, to becoming indifferent to evil done by others. Whether violent games make someone more inclined to violence is hotly debated today. What does not seem to need to be debated is that the addictive nature of those games makes those who play them unwilling to concede even the possibility that imagined violence might lead to actual violence. To that extent, they have become calloused to the victims of violence and less able to become a genuine hero.

that they disapprove of bodily violence. In that case they are bound to disapprove of government as much as of war. Surely there is something quite repulsively mean in saying that force must not be used against a conqueror from abroad, but force may be used against a poor, tired tramp who steals chickens. A Quaker has no right to be a soldier; but neither has he any right to be a magistrate. **It is not only war that is an appeal to violence. Peace is an appeal to violence.** The order and decency of our streets, the ease of exchange, and the fulfilment of contracts all repose ultimately upon the readiness of the community to fight for them, either against something without or against something within. Every city is a city in arms. As you and I and the rest of the respectable Londoners walk down the street we are all clanking with invisible weapons. We have taken the essential responsibility which is involved in war in merely being citizens of a State; we have declared war in favour of certain practices which we approve and against certain practices which we disapprove. It is a dreadful responsibility to declare that burglary is bad for mankind. It is a dreadful responsibility to declare that burglars shall be hurt because we think them harmful. It is a dreadful responsibility; but we have taken it. The decision has all that daring appeal to dogma which is the essence of revolution. Government itself is a revolution. The State itself is a *coup d' état*.

The romantic child, therefore, must expect to be discouraged by the man who disapproves of all coercion. I only hope that the romantic child will not be coerced by the man who disapproves of all coercion. That man must be left on one side. He may be an absolute saint. He must be (as many saints were) an anarchist. But for somewhat saner people who may have some lingering doubts on this matter I think one point should in conclusion be made clear. It is a misunderstanding of the whole nature of boyhood and youth to suppose, merely because a boy or man has a certain weapon, or certain dexterity with that weapon, that he will always be using it to the annoyance or the destruction of his neighbours.[29] There is nothing that boyhood or the romantic spirit enjoys so much as preparing for an entirely remote contingency. Scores of young men buy revolvers; they, never shoot anybody. Scores of young men carry sword-sticks; they do not run anybody through.[30] When I was a boy, I

29. For more on why some people think this way, see his remarks about determinism on August 4, 1906 (Ch. 1).

30. Chesterton was one such young man. His brother wrote: "Both Battersea and Fleet Street are, I believe, adequately policed. But Mr. Chesterton insists on traversing them armed with a sword-stick, and generally carrying a revolver in his pocket." Cecil Chesterton, *G.K. Chesterton: A Criticism* (Seattle: Inkling Books, 2007), 125. Nor was Chesterton's 'just-in-case' behavior unusual. A recent editorial in the *Times* (London) notes the following:

> We are so self-congratulatory about our officially disarmed society, and so dismissive of colonial rednecks, that we have forgotten that within living memory British citizens could buy any gun—rifle, pistol, or machinegun—without any licence. When Dr. Watson walked the streets of London with a revolver in his pocket, he was a perfectly ordinary Victorian or Edwardian. Charlotte Brontë recalled that her curate father fastened his watch and pocketed his pistol every morning when he got dressed; Beatrix Potter remarked on a Yorkshire country hotel where only one of the eight or nine guests was not carrying a revolver; in 1909, policemen in Tottenham borrowed at least four pistols from passers-by (and were joined by other armed citizens) when they set off in pursuit of two anarchists unwise enough to attempt an armed robbery. We now are shocked that so many ordinary people should have been carrying guns in the street; the Edwardians were shocked rather by the idea of an armed robbery.
>
> If armed crime in London in the years before the First World War amounted to less than 2 per cent of that we suffer today, it was not simply because society then was more stable. Edwardian Britain was rocked by a

used to carry chocolate in my pocket; not because I liked it (I didn't), but because I was told that it was a concentrated and sustaining food, and I had always before my mind the extreme probability of being lost in an open boat, lowered down a dry well, snowed up in a hut, or imprisoned in a cellar. I never have been; but I still carry the chocolate, full of an infinite and hungry hope. Indeed, my favourite hero in fiction is the White Knight in *Alice in Wonderland*, who carried a mouse-trap on his horse, for fear a mouse should ever get on to it.[31] And I admit a modern nation with a Navy is very like the White Knight....

G.K. Chesterton, "Our Note-Book," *Illustrated London News* 129 (October 6, 1906), 466.
US: October 20, 1906. Published elsewhere as "Boyhood and Militarism."

Hating Nations Intelligently

October 20, 1906

There are plenty of good people about just now who are telling us that we should not hate foreign nations. I will confine myself to expressing the aspiration that if we do hate foreign nations we may at least hate them intelligently.

Editor: After World War I broke out, Chesterton would remind his readers that, unlike many of his fellow Englishmen, before the invasion of Belgium he had shown no particular dislike or fear of Germans. This article and the next illustrate what he thought of them before the war. Chesterton was a brave and intelligent man. In his writings, reason always triumphs over fear. Although he was a successful journalist, he never behaved like many journalists, who careen from crisis to crisis, never resting or reflecting on what is really important.

Prince Hohenlohe-Schillingsfürst made a fuss about something: the Kaiser made a fuss about Prince Hohenlohe-Schillingsfürst, and we and our newspapers are still making a fuss about the Kaiser.[32] But in all our fussing, there is very little serious meaning, very little allowance for or even comprehension of the spirit and conditions of Germany. **There are plenty of good people about just now who are telling us that we should not hate foreign nations. I will confine myself to expressing the aspiration that if we do hate foreign nations we may at least hate them intelligently.**

---

series of massive strikes in which lives were lost and troops deployed, and suffragette incendiaries, anarchist bombers, Fenians, and the spectre of a revolutionary general strike made Britain then arguably a much more turbulent place than it is today. In that unstable society the impact of the widespread carrying of arms was not inflammatory, it was deterrent of violence. [Richard Munday, "Wouldn't You Feel Safer with a Gun?" *Times Online* (September 8, 2007).]

31. Chesterton is referring to Chapter 8 of Lewis Caroll's 1871 *Through the Looking Glass*: "'I was wondering what the mouse-trap was for,' said Alice. 'It isn't very likely there would be any mice on the horse's back.' 'Not very likely, perhaps,' said the Knight: 'but if they *do* come, I don't choose to have them running all about.' 'You see,' he went on after a pause, 'it's as well to be provided for *everything*.'"

32. Chlodwig Karl Victor, Prince of Hohenlohe-Schillingsfürst stepped down from the German chancellorship in 1900 and died in 1901 after a rather uneventful six years in office. Chesterton's *Collected Works*, vol. XVII, suggests this "fuss" began with a 1899 congratulatory telegram sent to Boer resistance leader Paul Kruger (1825–1904). Notice that Chesterton's point is that Germany is so poorly understood in England that a "fuss" in Germany could still be causing a fuss in the English press long after it had died out in Germany.

By all means hate the French if you want to; but do not hate them because they are careless, romantic, untrustworthy; because they are not. Hate them because they are thrifty, pessimistic, and bitterly practical: because they are. By all means dislike the Irish if you can, but do not dislike them because they are unfit for politics; dislike them on the ground that they are particularly fitted for politics, and screw out of Governments unfair advantages for themselves. Do not hate them for the absurd tag that they do not know what they want. Hate them for the excellent reason that they do know what they want and get it; Land Bills for instance.[33] And the case is exactly the same in this modern journalistic wrangle as to whether we shall or shall not hate Germany. Hate Germany by all means if it gives you any Christian comfort, but look at Germany first. Do not put down to exceptionally dreadful purposes or exceptionally sinister men things that are merely a part of the common colour and routine of another European nation. Do not see a German conspiracy where there is nothing but a German custom. Do not fill your newspapers with panics and furies about "significant utterances" and "sensational disclosures," which, to anyone who knows Germany at all, appear ultimately as absurd as if a German were to say that the British Empire claimed to annex the earth because of the phrase that the sun never sets on it, or that English soldiers were more bloody-minded than other soldiers because they wear red coats.

The German Emperor is a minor poet, and no doubt he does suffer from some of the faults of the artistic temperament. But it would be a vital misunderstanding of Germany to suppose that his superb fiats or solemn rebukes were the outcome merely of his own personal eccentricity or romanticism. He is just as much doing his duty as a German King when he is exalted and theatrical as King Edward VII. is doing his duty as an English King when he is agreeable, accessible, and a man of the world. It is a question of two national traditions. The Germans expect from a King what we call egoism, just as we expect from a King what we call tact.[34] The whole reposes upon an entirely different conception of the proper pose or conduct of a governing class. **The Germans like a King who remembers that he is a King. The English like a King who forgets that he is a King.** The same phenomenon can be observed in the aristocracy of the two countries. The essence and whole virtue of a Prussian aristocrat is that he is stiff. The essence and whole virtue of an English aristocrat is that he is loose. Their typical kind of gentlemen is like a Prussian noble whom I once met—made upon the ground-plan and main principle of a poker. Our typical kind of gentleman is a man like Mr. Balfour, who can be folded up like a foot-rule—a man who "sits" (in the words of Disraeli) "on his shoulders," the man who

33. Some historians claim the second Irish Land Act (1881) was so effective at protecting the rights of tenant farmers that it left little incentive for the Irish to buy land for themselves.

34. Edward VII (1841–1910) had the misfortune to wait 59 years to become king, longer than any other British sovereign. As king he was so unremarkable, when he smoked cigars where his mother Queen Victoria had forbidden smoking, it considered worthy of mention. As Chesterton suggests, the difference between German and English kings comes from royalty adapting to cultural expectations rather than personality traits. Edward's father had been the German Prince Albert of Saxe-Coburg-Gotha.

"rises" (in the words of Mr. Belloc) "as politicians do, by sections of his frame."[35] We like a look of carelessness in the governing class; they do not. You may like or dislike the German way; you may like or dislike the English way; personally and emotionally, of course, I, being English, like the English way, and I think the German way horrid. But realise that in this imperfect world of ours faults go with English merits and merits with German faults. Remember how much idleness, how much anarchy, how much amateurish politics and chaotic law go along with the ease and geniality of the English gentleman; remember that if the German ruler looks responsible; it is very often because he feels responsible; remember that the poor devil is really made to pass examinations; remember that he is made to learn something else besides amiability and cricket.

It is never easy to fix the nameless essential of a nation; but there is one test or dodge by which it may be almost done. The dodge is this: to take the two most divergent figures of that nation that one can possibly imagine, and then to ask oneself what they really have in common. There is something in common, for instance, between Walt Whitman and Artemus Ward: whatever that is, it is America.[36] There is something in common between Rabelais and M. Combes: it is a certain bold banality, a cutting of strong truisms in stone; it is a passion for the ordinary; it is France.[37] There is something in common between a Scotchman like Hume and a Scotchman like Thomas Carlyle: it is the close proximity of very abstract intellect with a kind of coarseness, which Stevenson sketched in *Weir of Hermiston*, and which is the permanent paradox of Scotland.[38] There is something which is Irish and which is common to an Irishman like William Blake and an Irishman like Parnell; to an Irishman like Edmund Burke and an Irishman like W.B. Yeats; to an Irishman like Sheridan and an Irishman like Bernard Shaw: it is fighting; it is Donnybrook Fair.[39] Now if we apply this principle to such a case as that of the English and the German

35. Political cartoonists portrayed the tall, lanky Arthur Balfour (1848–1930) almost lying down when he sat. He was Britain's Conservative Prime Minister from July 1902 to December 1905. C.S. Lewis said Balfour's *Theism and Humanism* (Inkling Books, 2000) was one of the ten books that most influenced his thought.

36. Walt Whitman (1819–1892) wrote free-style poetry more popular in France than America. Artemus Ward, pen name of Charles Browne (1834–1867), wrote humorous tales in a folksy style later taken up by Mark Twain.

37. François Rabelais (1494-1553) was a fun-loving friar who wrote 'eat, drink and be merry' tales. Émile Combes (1835–1921) was an unpleasant French politician best known for his hostility to Catholicism.

38. David Hume (1711–1776) was a Scottish philosopher and historian, as well as a naturalist, rejecting religion altogether in formulating his philosophy. Thomas Carlyle (1795–1881) was a Scottish writer and philosopher, who abandoned the Calvinism of his parents, but remained in some sense religious. *Weir of Hermiston* (1896) is an unfinished novel by Robert Lewis Stevenson (1850–1894), regarded by some as his greatest work. Abstract intellect and coarseness blend in a tale that, if completed, would have a father banish his son to a village, where the son commits a murder out of love for a young woman. The father as judge then tries and sentences his son to death. Shocked by what he has done, the father then dies.

39. William Blake (1757–1827) was an English poet and painter as well as a harsh critic of slavery, and some see an Irish flavor to his writings. (Chesterton would publish a book about him in 1910.) Charles Parnell (1846–1891) was a talented Irish politician and an aggressive champion of Home Rule for Ireland in Parliament. Edmund Burke (1729–1797) championed the rebellious American colonies in Parliament and was a pioneer conservative thinker and critic of the French Revolution. William Yeats (1865–1939) was an Irish poet and playwright. His poems "September 1913" and "Easter 1916" championed the rights of Irish workers. Frances Sheridan (1724–1766) was an Irish novelist and playwright, who defied a harsh father trying to keep her illiterate. Chesterton's friend George Bernard Shaw (1858–1950) loved to write controversial plays. Donnybrook Fair, held in Dublin, was so notorious for its drinking and fighting that it was banned in 1855.

ruler, we can see the matter quite clearly. No two English Kings, I suppose, were ever more different than Charles II and George III. No two Kings were ever in their own way more popular than Charles II and George III. And in both cases you see the same essential of the English popular kinghood — the King who has forgotten his crown. George III was admired because he behaved not like a King, but like a country gentleman. Charles II was admired because he behaved not like a King, but like a — well, let us say, like a town gentleman. The one paraded his domesticity; the other paraded his lack of domesticity.[40] Neither of them paraded his kingship. And the English enjoyed and admired this apparent obliviousness and ease; the less the monarch thought of the monarchy the more the people thought of it. The people liked to be always remembering what the King had forgotten. The people liked to be always picking up his crown when he had dropped it.

Now if we wish to do justice to Germany (and justice to Germany is much more important than peace with Germany, as the soul is more important than the body), we must always remember that there is a German spirit or atmosphere in this matter different from our own; and it might help us to remember it if we took, in the case of Germany also, the types of two very diverse Princes. To the ordinary English mind it would perhaps be difficult to imagine two men more different than the present Emperor William and the late Prince Consort. But if you think of them seriously, and with an attempt at sympathy, you will see that there is a distinct tone or quality common to the clamorous Kaiser, who reviews armies, and the silent consort who encouraged picture galleries and exhibitions.[41] **They both have the fundamental German conception, the idea of the governing class as a grave body which educates the nation, pouring upon it a sort of paternal culture.** Our aristocracy has quite as much power — it has more political power; but there has never been in it this educational notion; to my English instinct it appears priggish. **The rich are as much our masters, but they are not so much our schoolmasters. To my feeling there is something even unchristian about such solemnity in an earthly hierarchy. Christianity has permitted aristocracy, but it has never permitted aristocracy to be taken seriously.** It is Brahminism to take aristocracy seriously. And I do feel myself that it is a great merit in the English aristocracy that it cannot be taken seriously.

Nevertheless, as I have said, we must understand this German thing even in order to dislike it. And we must not regard the Kaiser as a mountebank or an American advertiser merely because he, like other German princes, is resolved to shout culture at his people or to drill them in art and music. He is a dabbler in the arts; but so was

40. Charles II (1630–1685), the "Merry Monarch," lived a hedonistic lifestyle and acknowledged 14 of his illegitimate children, while having no legitimate children. George III (1738–1820) was known at "Farmer George" because of his thrifty lifestyle and interest in agriculture. His madness left him not knowing who he was.

41. Prince Consort was Emperor William's father, Frederick III (1831–1888), who died of cancer of the larynx only 99 days after taking the throne. His personality was so different from that of his son William II, the Kaiser Wilhelm II of WWI infamy, that some historians believe that, had the father lived longer, he would have steered Germany away from militarism and toward a constitutional monarchy.

Frederick the Great.[42] And so in a certain degree are all the typical German Kings, from his own mild and unobtrusive father to the mad King of Bavaria who galloped in armour in the moonlight.[43] My own prejudices are rather on the rebellious side, and I am quite prepared to blame German despots for being despots. But I am not prepared to blame German despots for being German.

The length of this may serve to show how long it takes even to indicate the atmosphere of peoples; yet our contemporary journalist, both bellicose and pacific, always assume that it can be summed up in two or three established phrases. And, indeed, this is the one moral of the matter. There are many leaders (of whom Mr. Stead[44] is typical), there are many newspapers, religious and other, who are always urging the cause of peace and the futile tragedy of war. Unfortunately, it often happens that these writers and journals are the very writers and the very journals who repeat as axioms the immense misrepresentations and misunderstandings which are the real possibility of cruel cleavages in Europe. Only too often it is the friends of peace who talk as if every Roman Catholic were superstitious, every Frenchman immoral, every American corrupt, every Russian oppressed, every German burdened with the caprices of an insane Emperor. Too often it is the friends of peace who say that Spain must be decaying because she is Popish. Too often it is the friends of peace who say that French newspapers must be contemptible because they are violent. **No treaties and no conferences will really secure peace if these enormous bigotries are permitted to remain brooding over vast tracts of our continent.** And if one attempts to lift even a corner of the veil it means writing voluminously and seemingly at random, as I have been doing for the last hour.

G.K. Chesterton, "Our Note-Book," *Illustrated London News* 129 (October 20, 1906), 546. US: November 3, 1906. Later published as "On Hating Germany and Other Nations."

Koepenick's Comic Captain

October 27, 1906

Soldiers have many faults, but they have one redeeming merit: they are never worshippers of force. Soldiers more than any other men are taught severely and systematically that might is not right.

Editor: On October 16, 1906, Wilhelm Voigt, an unemployed Berlin shoemaker wearing a second-hand captain's uniform, took a train to Koepenick, a Berlin

42. Chesterton is more critical of Frederick the Great in these articles: January 26, 1913 (Ch. 1); January 1, May 20, June 24, August 19, 1916 (Ch. 4); December 15, 1917 (Ch. 5); January 18, 1919, and September 13, 1919 (Ch. 7).

43. King Ludwig II of Bavaria (1845–1886) was known to the English as "Mad King Ludwig" and to the Germans as *Märchenkönig*—Fairy-tale King. His Neuschwanstein Castle inspired Disneyland's Sleeping Beauty Castle.

44. Thomas William Stead (1849–1912), a crusading journalist and an avid spiritualist, went down with the *Titanic* while sailing to America for a peace conference. He is best known for the 1885 Eliza Armstrong case, where, in an attempt to dramatize the horrors of prostitution, he "purchased" a thirteen-year-old girl. Despite his intentions—to force passage of a bill to raise the age of consent from 13 to 16 that had been held up in Parliament for several years—he was prosecuted and spent three months in prison. He described why the law was needed in a much-discussed series of articles in the *Pall Mall Gazette* entitled, "The Maiden of Modern Babylon."

suburb, and ordered several soldiers he found there to accompany to the city hall. There he boldly charged the city's major and treasurer with fraud. He confiscated 4000 marks, taking care to sign a receipt, and ordered some of the soldiers to take the two officials to Berlin for questioning. Changing into civilian clothes, he disappeared with the money. Ten days later he was arrested, but popular amusement with his crime would lead the Kaiser to pardon him after serving less than two years of a four-year sentence. In the same issue of the *Illustrated London News* in which this article appeared, the editors would note: "For years the Kaiser has been instilling into his people reverence for the omnipotence of militarism, of which the holiest symbol is the German uniform. Offenses against this fetish have incurred condign punishment. Officers who have not considered themselves saluted in due form have drawn their swords with impunity on offending privates."

A famous and epigrammatic author said that life copied literature; it seems clear that life really caricatures it. I suggested last week that the Germans submitted to, and even admired, a solemn and theatrical assertion of authority. A few hours after I had sent up my "copy," I saw the first announcement of the affair of the comic Captain at Koepenick. The most absurd part of this absurd fraud (at least, to English eyes) is one which, oddly enough, has received comparatively little comment. I mean the point at which the Mayor asked for a warrant, and the Captain pointed to the bayonets of his soldiery and said, "These are my authority." One would have thought anyone would have known that no soldier would talk like that. The dupes were blamed for not knowing that the man wore the wrong cap or the wrong sash, or had his sword buckled on the wrong way; but these are technicalities which they might surely be excused for not knowing. I certainly should not know if a soldier's sash were on inside out or his cap on behind before. But I should know uncommonly well that genuine professional soldiers do not talk like Adelphi villains and utter theatrical epigrams in praise of abstract violence.[45]

We can see this more clearly, perhaps, if we suppose it to be the case of any other dignified and clearly distinguishable profession. Suppose a Bishop called upon me. My great modesty and my rather distant reverence for the higher clergy might lead me certainly to a strong suspicion that any Bishop who called on me was a bogus Bishop. But if I wished to test his genuineness I should not dream of attempting to do so by examining the shape of his apron or the way his gaiters were done up. I have not the remotest idea of the way his gaiters ought to be done up. A very vague approximation to an apron would probably take me in; and if he behaved like an approximately Christian gentleman he would be safe enough from my detection. But suppose the Bishop, the moment he entered the room, fell on his knees on the mat, clasped his hands, and poured out a flood of passionate and somewhat hysterical extempore prayer, I should say at once and without the smallest hesitation, "Whatever else this man is, he is not an elderly and wealthy cleric of the Church of England. They don't do such things." Or suppose a man came to me pretending to be a qualified doctor,

45. The Adelphi is a large theater in London's West End.

and flourished a stethoscope, or what he said was a stethoscope. I am glad to say that I have not even the remotest notion of what a stethoscope looks like; so that if he flourished a musical-box or a coffee-mill it would be all one to me. But I do think that I am not exaggerating my own sagacity if I say that I should begin to suspect the doctor if on entering my room he flung his legs and arms about, crying wildly, "Health! Health! priceless gift of Nature! I possess it! I overflow with it! I yearn to impart it! Oh, the sacred rapture of imparting health!" In that case I should suspect him of being rather in a position to receive than to offer medical superintendence.

Now, it is no exaggeration at all to say that anyone who has ever known any soldiers (I can only answer for English and Irish and Scotch soldiers) would find it just as easy to believe that a real Bishop would grovel on the carpet in a religious ecstasy, or that a real doctor would dance about the drawing-room to show the invigorating effects of his own medicine, as to believe that a soldier, when asked for his authority, would point to a lot of shining weapons and declare symbolically that might was right. Of course, a real soldier would go rather red in the face and huskily repeat the proper formula, whatever it was, as that he came in the King's name.

Soldiers have many faults, but they have one redeeming merit: they are never worshippers of force. Soldiers more than any other men are taught severely and systematically that might is not right. The fact is obvious. The might is in the hundred men who obey. The right (or what is held to be right) is in the one man who commands them. They learn to obey symbols, arbitrary things, stripes on an arm, buttons on a coat, a title, a flag. These may be artificial things; they may be unreasonable things; they may, if you will, be wicked things; but they are weak things. They are not Force, and they do not look like Force. They are parts of an idea: of the idea of discipline; if you will, of the idea of tyranny; but still an idea. No soldier could possibly say that his own bayonets were his authority. No soldier could possibly say that he came in the name of his own bayonets. It would be as absurd as if a postman said that he came inside his bag. I do not, as I have said, underrate the evils that really do arise from militarism and the military ethic. It tends to give people wooden faces and sometimes wooden heads. It tends moreover (both through its specialisation and through its constant obedience) to a certain loss of real independence and strength of character. This has almost always been found when people made the mistake of turning the soldier into a statesman, under the mistaken impression that he was a strong man. The Duke of Wellington, for instance, was a strong soldier and therefore a weak statesman. But the soldier is always, by the nature of things, loyal to something. And as long as one is loyal to something one can never be a worshipper of mere force. For mere force, violence in the abstract, is the enemy of anything we love. To love anything is to see it at once under lowering skies of danger. Loyalty implies loyalty in misfortune; and when a soldier has accepted any nation's uniform he has already accepted its defeat.

Nevertheless, it does appear to be possible in Germany for a man to point to fixed bayonets and say, "These are my authority," and yet to convince ordinarily sane men that he is a soldier. If this is so, it does really seem to point to some habit of high-falutin' in the German nation, such as that of which I spoke last week. It almost looks as if the advisers, and even the officials, of the German army had become infected in some degree with the false and feeble doctrine that might is right. As this doctrine is invariably preached by physical weaklings like Nietzsche[46] it is a very serious thing even to entertain the supposition that it is affecting men who have really to do military work. It would be the end of German soldiers to be affected by German philosophy. Energetic people use energy as a means, but only very tired people ever use energy as a reason. Athletes go in for games, because athletes desire glory. Invalids go in for calisthenics; for invalids (alone of all human beings) desire strength. So long as the German Army points to its heraldic eagle and says, "I come in the name of this fierce but fabulous animal," the German Army will be all right. If ever it says, "I come in the name of bayonets," the bayonets will break like glass, for only the weak exhibit strength without an aim.

At the same time, as I said before, do not let us forget our own faults. Do not let us forget them any the more easily because they are the opposite to the German faults. Modern England is too prone to present the spectacle of a person who is enormously delighted because he has not got the contrary disadvantages to his own. The Englishman is always saying "My house is not damp" at the moment when his house is on fire. The Englishman is always saying, "I have thrown off all traces of anaemia" in the middle of a fit of apoplexy. Let us always remember that if an Englishman wants to swindle English people, he does not dress up in the uniform of a soldier. If an Englishman wants to swindle English people he would as soon think of dressing up in the uniform of a messenger boy. Everything in England is done unofficially, casually, by conversations and cliques. The one Parliament that really does rule England is a secret Parliament; the debates of which must not be published—the Cabinet. The debates of the Commons are sometimes important; but only the debates in the Lobby, never the debates in the House. **Journalists do control public opinion; but it is not controlled by the arguments they publish—it is controlled by the arguments between the editor and sub-editor, which they do not publish.** This casualness is our English vice. It is at once casual and secret. Our public life is conducted privately. Hence it follows that if an English swindler wished to impress us, the last thing he would think of doing would be to put on a uniform. He would put on a polite slouching air and a careless, expensive suit of clothes; he would stroll up to the Mayor, be so awfully sorry to disturb him, find he had forgotten his card-case, mention, as if he were ashamed of it, that he was the Duke of Mercia,[47] and carry the whole thing through with the air of a man who could get two hundred witnesses and two thousand retainers, but who was too tired

46. All his life Friedrich Nietzsche (1844–1900) was troubled by illnesses, including vision problems, migraine headaches, and stomach aliments. In 1889 he went insane and uncommunicative due to syphilis or brain cancer.

47. Mercia was an ancient English kingdom in the Midlands. Since it did not exist in Chesterton's day, any claim to be "the Duke of Mercia" should have been seen as obviously bogus.

to call any of them. And if he did it very well I strongly suspect that he would be as successful as the indefensible Captain at Koepenick.

Our tendency for many centuries past has been, not so much towards creating an aristocracy (which may or may not be a good thing in itself), as towards substituting an aristocracy for everything else. In England we have an aristocracy instead of a religion: The nobility are to the English poor what the saints and the fairies are to the Irish poor, what the large devil with a black face was to the Scotch poor—the poetry of life. In the same way in England we have an aristocracy instead of a Government. We rely on a certain good humour and education in the upper class to interpret to us our contradictory Constitution. No educated man born of woman will be quite so absurd as the system that he has to administer. **In short, we do not get good laws to restrain bad people. We get good people to restrain bad laws.** And last of all we in England have an aristocracy instead of an Army. We have an Army of which the officers are proud of their families and ashamed of their uniforms. If I were a King of any country whatever, and one of my officers were ashamed of my uniform, I should be ashamed of my officer. Beware, then, of the really well-bred and apologetic gentleman whose clothes are at once quiet and fashionable, whose manner is at once diffident and frank. Beware how you admit him into your domestic secrets, for he may be a bogus Earl. Or, worse still, a real one.

G.K. Chesterton, "Our Note-Book," *Illustrated London News* 129 (October 27, 1906), 578. US edition: November 10, 1906. Published elsewhere as "The Captain at Koepnik."

Chesterton's New Masthead

January 5, 1907 (excerpt)

In the foreground (you will observe) I am myself seated, clad in that close and clinging fifteenth-century costume which best sets off my elegant but too ethereal figure.

Editor: Chesterton's success at the *Illustrated London News* became obvious with this issue, when a tiny heading for two-column articles became an elaborate masthead for three-column articles. Except for a single picture in the center, which usually bore no relation to his topic, his words now filled an entire page in the typically 32-page publication. In a mere seven years from when he first became known,

Chesterton had become that important. Although his remarks here have nothing to do with war, they do illustrate that Chesterton did not take himself too seriously.

I PERCEIVE with astonishment, mingled with gratitude (and terror, which is the very soul of gratitude) a beautiful picture erected upon the top of this article. Such decoration is all to the good; and if the Editor chooses to print all my words in different colours I, for one, shall consider them vastly improved. Still, you may dwell for a moment on the composition of this admirable design. In the foreground (you will observe) I am myself seated, clad in that close and clinging fifteenth-century costume which best sets off my elegant but too ethereal figure. I am engaged (somewhat ostentatiously) in dipping a quill pen in ink; and I seem to be wearing (in case of accidents) another quill pen in my hat. A long procession of the most important human types pass behind me, for none of them have the courage to pass in front of me. The two busts or terminal figures which decorate the seat are portraits of the Editor and his trusty lieutenant....

G.K. Chesterton, "Our Note-Book," *Illustrated London News* 130 (January 5, 1907), 4. US edition: January 19, 1907. Published elsewhere as "A New Version of Richard III."

International or Cosmopolitan

June 22, 1907 (excerpt)

It will generally be found, I think, that the more a man really appreciates and admires the soul of another people the less he will attempt to imitate it.

EDITOR: At the heart of Chesterton's world view was a belief that communities and nations have a unique character that should be respected and not homogenized by national or cosmopolitan interests. That's the central point of his 1904 novel, *The Napoleon of Notting Hill*. In this excerpt he summarizes what he believes about national character (followed by a lengthy discussion of the French character not included). He will write more in articles on April 6 and August 10, 1918 (Ch. 6). Here he distinguishes between international and cosmopolitan. Later he treats the terms as equivalent, probably because his foes claimed to be both.

IT is obvious that there is a great deal of difference between being international and being cosmopolitan. All good men are international. Nearly all bad men are cosmopolitan. If we are to be international we must be national. And it is largely because those who call themselves the friends of peace have not dwelt sufficiently on this distinction that they do not impress the bulk of any of the nations to which they belong. International peace means a peace between nations, not a peace after the destruction of nations, like the Buddhist peace after the destruction of personality. The golden age of the good European is like the heaven of the Christian: it is a place where people will love each other; not like the heaven of the Hindu, a place where they will be each other. And in the case of national character this can be seen in a curious way. **It will generally be found, I think, that the more a man really appreciates and admires the soul of another people the less he will attempt to imitate it; he will be conscious that there is something in it too deep and too unmanageable to imitate.** The Englishman who has a fancy for France will try to be French; the Englishman who admires France will remain obstinately English. This is to be particularly noticed in the case of our relations with the French, because it is one of the outstanding peculiarities of the French that their vices are all on the surface, and their extraordinary virtues concealed. One might almost say that their vices are the flower of their virtues....

G.K. Chesterton, "Our Note-Book," *Illustrated London News* 130 (June 22, 1907), 943. US edition: July 6, 1907. Published elsewhere as "Understanding the French."

WEAKEST LINK

July 20, 1907 (excerpt)

The simple reason is that the weaker brethren have everything in their hands. No chain is stronger than its weakest link.

EDITOR: Normally, Chesterton focused his articles on a single theme. Here, he has several themes, the most important being his comments about a nation being no stronger than "its weakest link," along with his warning to be careful not to use weak linking words such as "and or but" to join something serious to something minor, trivializing a serious debate. As we mention later, his 'weakest link" argument applies particularly strongly to those who try to weaken a country's resolve in wartime.

THE plain fact that no chain is stronger than its weakest link is one of the primary facts at the bottom of democracy and equality. Suppose, for instance, our society, or any society, were in serious danger. The fool would look first to the fortunate members of society to see whether they would lead us. The wise man would look first to the unfortunate members of society to see whether they would give us away. Modern Imperialism and hero-worship asks us to look for what it calls the "strongest man." Ancient religion (with much more worldly wisdom) asked us to consider "the weaker brethren." **The simple reason is that the weaker brethren have everything in their hands. No chain is stronger than its weakest link. Therefore, the weakest links are the most important.** The weakest links have the greatest power instantaneously to destroy the chain; the weakest links are the strongest. If some element can really contrive to be wanting, to be absent, to keep out of the way, that element has often altogether its own way. The strongest link of all is the Missing Link.

This is true of all political combinations, of national defence, of commerce and journalism, and a hundred other things. But I wonder whether anyone has noticed how true it is even of the smallest thing—even of mere words and the arrangement of words. It is true of language; it is true even of grammar. For instance, in the chain of a sentence, what we call the weakest links are certainly the conjunctions.

We all despise "and" or "but." Yet though they are humble they are often the most important words in the sentence. Those little conjunctions involve the whole nature and construction of the sentence, and the whole of its effect on the human mind. It would often be better for a public speaker to have his nouns and adjectives altered than to have his conjunctions altered....

That is the worst of the present state of affairs—that before we can point out what is important we have to try and introduce the habit of talking about important things. We have to try and get the important things made the most important not only in every argument but in every sentence. We have to try and teach people not to say "Lord Jinks, though a scoundrel, is a gentleman." We have to try and teach them to say, "Lord Jinks, though a gentleman, is a scoundrel." Until that simple inversion of words is effected, we shall have certainly neither Christianity nor democracy, and almost certainly neither patriotism nor public spirit. England will not be saved until we fight cowardice, not only when it expresses itself in nouns and verbs, but when it hides itself in conjunctions.

We are surely approaching a period of English history when it will have to be settled whether the aristocratic party system in its present form is to continue; whether the evils of its languor, its unreality, its vulgar ambitions and its false issues are greater evils or less evils than the turbulence, the doubt, and the dangerous emotions of a true democracy. Let us approach this problem with all seriousness, and let us take either side as our judgment of men and morals dictates. There is a vast mass of things to be said both for democracy and for aristocracy. But let us at least endeavour, whatever conclusion we come to, to get the words into the right order. It may be that the rule of the masses, democracy, would destroy England. If that is true let us object to it because it would destroy England; but do not let us say, "Whether or no democracy would destroy England, we can all agree that it would be nice to have a she-republic on the coins." It may be, on the other hand (I myself incline to this view) that aristocracy has already destroyed England; and that we must fight for its popular resurrection. If we think that, let us attack the oligarchical system for being cowardly and corrupt. Do not let us say, "Whatever view we may take of the allegation that oligarchy is cowardly and corrupt and has destroyed England, we must admit that it is favourable to the science of heraldry." Let us realise that the whole question is what view we take of oligarchy. Let us realise that the whole question is whether or no democracy would be good for England.

G.K. Chesterton, "Our Note-Book," *Illustrated London News* 131 (July 20, 1907), 80.
US: August 3, 1907. Also published as "Conjunctions in the Sentence and Modern Thought."

Giving Up War

April 25, 1908

There are some things more important than peace, and one of them is the dignity of human nature.

EDITOR: Many those whom Chesterton spent his life debating were intellectuals with flaws typical of their class. Devoted to manipulating words, they developed a utopian belief that anything they could put into words was possible. (Put another way, they believed human nature was as malleable as a magazine article or political pamphlet.) As one historian has observed, in turn of the century Britain, this thinking was particularly common on the political left: "Socialism—broadly, a criticism of the existing economic basis of society—did not, in Britain, originate with the worker. It's beginnings were intellectual, literary, and often utopian."[48]

This focus on society as a thing to be manipulated led to a fascination with something that really can be manipulated—technology. Intellectuals might grudgingly admit that history gave little comfort to their dream of an idealized world, particularly the nasty business of war. But they comforted themselves by believing that the past had been without some new development that might put an end to fighting. For many socialists it was a new economic order that would make life so pleasant the causes of war, thought to be hunger and poverty, would disappear. Others were like H.G. Wells, believing that deadly, long-range new technologies such as bombers would give a tiny clique the power to control an unruly humanity. Finally, there were those who thought that technology would make war so horrible that no one would want to fight.

Chesterton isn't distracted by technology. Although it makes war more horrible, he says, the machinery of war has not altered why wars are fought. And although travel is faster and easier, real differences between people remain. If anything the problem has grown worse as secularized people no longer understand religion.

CAPTAIN Fletcher Vane, it seems, in his article in the *Spectator* on the possible suppression of war, has done one decidedly good thing.[49] He has attacked the theory of M. Bloch.[50] The theory of M. Bloch, the reader will remember, was that war will die of its own terrors; the race of armaments will produce engines so enormous and so anti-human that no one will dare to encounter them. Captain Fletcher Vane denies this on the ground of historical fact; he maintains that the growth through recent centuries of arms of precision has made no difference to the readiness or reluctance of men to fight. A line broke in the Middle Ages at about

48. Alfred F. Havighurst, *Twentieth-century Britain* (New York: Harper & Row, 1962), 26.

49. Francis Fletcher-Vane (1861-1934) was a bundle of contradictions. He was actively anti-war between 1907 and 1912, but served as a British officer for much of his life, which may explain why he understood, better than a banker like Bloch, that soldiers could adapt to the horrors of a WWI battlefield. The remarks Chesterton references appeared in the April 18, 1908 issue of *The Spectator*. They include: "The fact, however, is known that the proportion of killed and wounded to uninjured men is very much the same from Poietiers to Magersfontein, taking Blenheim and Mars la Tour on the way. Roughly speaking, the time when men find it convenient to take up a safer position, or find that they have important business elsewhere, is arrived at when from fifteen to twenty per cent of their comrades have been killed or wounded." In his 1916 book, *The Principles of Military Art,* Fletcher-Vane noted: "It is difficult as we have seen lately, to light a consuming fire of patriotic enthusiasm in the breast of a man who has no real and visible stake in his country, whose home is a crowded arid baby-ridden room hired by the week from a merciless landlord and who realises but too acutely that all the country does for him is to make him work as much as it can for the smallest wage possible. If he be not an absolute fool he will grasp the truth that he only becomes really interesting to his government when it is in some crisis." The title of his 1930 autobiography, *Agin the Governments,* captures Fletcher-Vane's contrary spirit.

50. Ivan Bloch (1836–1902, a.k.a. Johann von Bloch, Jean de Bloch and Ivan Bliokh) was a Polish banker who wrote the six-volume *La Guerre Future* (1898), abridged for the English-speaking world as *Is War Now Impossible?* (1899). He correctly predicted the horrors of trench warfare, but was wrong to believe that wars would then end.

the same chronological and psychological instant at which it breaks now. Captain Vane is probably right in denying the Bloch hypothesis on that ground. But on any ground, it is as well that the Bloch hypothesis should be denied.

There are some things more important than peace, and one of them is the dignity of human nature. It is a humiliation of humanity that humanity should ever give up war solely through fear, especially through fear of the mere machines that humanity itself has made. We all see the absurdity of modern armaments. It is a grotesque end for the great European story that each of us should keep on stuffing pistols into his pockets until he falls down with the weight of them. But it is still worse that we should only be friends because we are too nervous to stand the noise of a pistol. Let the man stop the pistol by all means. But do not let the pistol stop the man. Civilised man has created a cruel machinery which he now, it may be, finds bad for his soul. Then let civilised man save his soul and abandon his machinery. But the Bloch theory does not really abandon the machinery at all. It hangs the machinery *in terrorem* over the head of all humanity to frighten them from going to war for any cause, just or unjust. Man is cowed into submission by his own clockwork. I would sooner be ruled by cats and dogs. They, at any rate, are our fellow-creatures, not merely our creatures. **I would have any war, however long and horrible, sooner than such a horrible peace. I would run any risk rather than submit to such a spiritual indignity as that man dare not, for the most crying justice or the most urgent chivalry, turn one of his own handles. War is an absolute calamity; so be it. Then let man silence his guns; but, in the name of human honour, do not let his guns silence him.**

Captain Vane, having rejected this theory on other and historical grounds, goes on to suggest several ways in which, as he feels, modern war might possibly terminate. One of them is a point often urged in these days. It is what is called the shrinkage of space. I have not Captain Vane's text before me (I am writing these words in Bruges,[51] where his works are less known than they should be), but I quote a good summary of the idea from a daily paper: "No less powerful a factor is the shrinkage of the world, which is bringing about that intimacy and understanding among the peoples which make war less and less thinkable. Paris is nearer in time than Brighton was a century ago, and St. Petersburg and Constantinople are as near as Edinburgh."

But this creed also (common in our time) contains several mistakes. First of all, it is surely a mistake to suppose that wars arise merely from a barbaric ignorance. **A man does not fight another man because he does not know him. Generally he fights him because he knows him uncommonly well.** Many modern peace societies act on the supposition that if they bring a great many Germans to see Englishmen, or a great many Englishmen to travel in Germany, they will never want to fight each other. But this seems to assume that all ordinary Englishmen believe that Germans have tails. It assumes that an average German regards an average Englishman as

51. Probably the beautiful city of that name in Belgium. Chesterton did not normally make this sort of reference, but, given the argument he is about to make, he wants to demonstrate that he understands modern travel.

a monster from the moon. The moment the German has seen the Englishman, counted his arms and legs, ascertained that he has the normal number of eyes or ears, realised, in short, that he is human, he will then drop all dreams of hostility. But this is missing the whole point of the modern antagonism. **It is a morbid and suicidal thing for two great nations to hate each other. But when they do hate each other it is not because their aims are different, but because their aims are alike.** A Prussian would not dislike an American for being an American Indian. On the contrary the Prussian, if he disliked him at all, would dislike him for being too like a Prussian: for rivalling Prussian commerce, or Prussian education, or Prussian Imperialism. **Modern hostility is a base thing, and arises, not out of a generous difference, but out of a sort of bitter and sneering similarity. It is because we are all copying each other that we are all cursing each other.**

And secondly, I deny (in the moral sense) that space has shrunk at all. I deny that Paris is nearer to our imaginations than it was a century ago; I should say without hesitation that it is much farther off. It is much easier to go to America than it was, but it is not any easier to understand it when you have got there. It is rather more difficult. Dickens may have taken nearly a month to reach the great Republic, but he found it a Republic of English republicans, with some ordinary faults. Mr. H.G. Wells can get there in a few days, but he would be the first to admit that, as far as making head or tail of it is concerned, one might almost as well stop at home. He does not find, as Dickens did, an ordinary English democracy with the ordinary exaggeration of democracy and optimism in England. He finds a frightful hotch-potch (I was going to say hell-broth) of new races, of which no man can even guess the end. America is physically nearer, but morally much more distant. When Sir James Douglas sailed from Scotland to Spain with the heart of Bruce, he probably sailed very slowly; but when he got to Spain he found a set of Christian knights just like himself, with whom he shook hands on the spot.[52] Sir Thomas Lipton, in *Shamrock XI*, would, no doubt, get from Scotland to Spain much quicker; but the British millionaire tea-merchant would not find a crowd of millionaire tea-merchants waiting for him eagerly on the shore of Spain. He would only find what he would call a superstitious peasantry. He would find people whom he could understand far less than Sir James Douglas understood the Spaniards of the Middle Ages. It takes a shorter time to reach the place — but a longer time to see it. Spain is physically nearer, but morally more distant.

The real truth of the matter is that there are now all over the world, at regular intervals, places where you can get a Scotch-and-soda. These places have come closer together: but the spaces in between them have not come closer together. You can get a Scotch-and-soda under one particular palm-tree in the desert. There are trains to that palm-tree. You can get a Scotch-and-soda on one particular crag of

52. The Scottish Sir James Douglas (1286–1330) fought in the Scottish Wars of Independence. When Robert the Bruce died in 1329, he asked Douglas to carry his heart to Jerusalem and place it in the Church of the Holy Sepulchre. On the way, Douglas stopped off in Spain to assist in driving out the Moors and died in battle.

the Himalayas. There are lifts up to that crag. There is, in other words, a very swift and smooth system of transit for coarse, rich people between all the places to which coarse, rich people want to go.[53] The article I have quoted speaks significantly of Brighton and Paris. Brighton and Paris are now much nearer to each other. But a decent village in Picardy is not an inch nearer to Paris. And a decent village in Sussex is not an inch nearer to Brighton.

There is no more deadly delusion, none more full of quite practical peril, than this notion that trains and wires have created a real understanding between the nations. Do you think that Chinamen will love you because you can write a Chinese telegram? Chinamen (and very right they are) will not love you until you can write a Chinese love-letter. **The world has not shrunk at all. It is not one iota more easy at this moment to understand the Cannibal Islands. It is only more easy to look at them and misunderstand them. The misunderstanding has actually grown greater, because we ourselves have abandoned many healthy and instinctive things which would have helped us to sympathise with the savages.** On the same page on which I read of these hopes from the coalescing and combining of the planet, I found a Moslem service called dirty or disgusting because it involved the idea of blood. A few hundred years ago we should have realized that our own religion involved the idea of blood. But we have got further away from understanding their religion by ceasing to understand our own.

G.K. Chesterton, "Our Note-Book," *Illustrated London News* 132 (April 25, 1908), 592. US: May 9, 1908. Also published as "On the World Getting Smaller."

THE IMPORTANCE OF WHY

August 15, 1908 (excerpt)

Again and again I have found this a sound tip or test in the justice of any matter: wait until the people who like it have argued in favour of it; if they can once be induced with open hearts and mouths to say what is good in the thing, you are pretty certain to discover whatever is bad in it.

EDITOR: In his 1936 autobiography Chesterton explained why he was among the few Englishmen to oppose the Second Boer War (1899–1902), which was fought against Dutch settlers in South Africa. His explanation gives a glimpse into why the Fabian left—bureaucratic socialists such as Sidney Webb and Bernard Shaw—supported the Boer War but criticized WWI.

I began arguing with Mr. Bernard Shaw in print almost as early as I began doing anything. It was about my Pro-Boer sympathies in the South African War. Those

53. How "coarse, rich people" can confuse this issue, particularly when enamored with technology, is illustrated in a chapter aptly titled "Machinery, The New Messiah" written by Henry Ford: "Machinery is accomplishing in the world what man has failed to do by preaching, propaganda, or the written word. The aeroplane and radio know no boundary. They pass over the dotted lines on the map without heed or hindrance. They are binding the world together in a way no other systems can. The motion picture with its universal language, the aeroplane with its speed, and the radio with its coming international programme—these will soon bring the whole world to a complete understanding. Thus we may vision a United States of the World. Ultimately it will surely come. [Henry Ford, *My Philosophy of Industry* (New York: Coward-McCann, 1929), 18.

who do not understand what the Fabian political philosophy was may not realise that the leading Fabians were nearly all Imperialists.... And even Bernard Shaw, though retaining a certain liberty to chaff everybody, was quite definitely an Imperialist, as compared with myself and my friends the Pro-Boers.... It was the same, for that matter, with Mr. H.G. Wells; then a sort of semi-detached Fabian. He went out of his way to scoff at the indignation of the Pro-Boers against the Concentration Camps. Indeed he still maintains, while holding all wars indefensible, that this is the only sort of war to be defended. He says that great wars between great powers are absurd, but that it might be necessary, in policing the planet, to force backward people to open their resources to cosmopolitan commerce. In other words, he defends the only sort of war I thoroughly despise, the bullying of small states for their oil or gold; and he despises the only sort of war that I really defend, a war of civilizations and religions, to determine the moral destiny of mankind.[54]

In this article, Chesterton explains why he became a critic of the Boer War and the standard he uses to judge major issues, waiting "until the people who like it have argued in favour of it; if they can once be induced with open hearts and mouths to say what is good in the thing, you are pretty certain to discover whatever is bad in it." Keep in mind the "open hearts and mouths." The more evil a cause, the more likely it is to lie. That's why the news media is often a bad source. Those who intend to deceive pay special attention to journalists, manufacturing a story the press likes. As a result, the news media often becomes a tool of others, tailoring what we hear, favoring one point of view over another, restricting our thinking to narrow channels, and even portraying evil as good and the good as evil, as they did during the Boer War. In debates about that war, Chesterton had personal contacts with those he opposed. When we lack that, we need to search, talk, and read more widely to discover the truth.[55]

A writer benefits from taking care about his opinions, even when they are unpopular. Chesterton's opposition to the Boer War put him together with a minority that included pacifists with whom he had little in common. Yet because his opinion was well thought out and well-argued, he earned wide respect. In his book, *Chesterton*, Cyril Clemens notes: "Chesterton was the one British writer, utterly unknown before, who built up a great reputation, and it was gained, not through nationalistic support, but through determined and persistent opposition to British policy."[56]

54. G.K. Chesterton, *The Autobiography of G.K. Chesterton* (New York: Sheed & Ward, 1936), 229–230. For Chesterton's opposition to the war at *The Speaker*, where he began to write in the fall of 1899, see John D. Coates, *G.K. Chesterton as Controversialist, Essayist, Novelist, and Critic* (Lewiston: Edwin Mellen, 2002), 43f. Coates notes that most British supported a war popular in the press: "*The Speaker*'s team felt this shame about their country precisely because they loved their country so much. As [Edward C.] Bentley put it, 'To be a patriot is not in itself a passport to happiness.' He singles out Chesterton as being 'deeply unhappy' about the war: 'He loved the English people with a more deep and understanding love than is within the compass of most of us.'" (p. 56–57).

55. Using a contrived crisis to push through the first stages of a concealed agenda is a common political trick. It was one reason for the "war to end all war" rhetoric at the start of WWI. The war was to be used to get into place internationalist schemes that might otherwise never happen. Attempts to carry out those schemes distracted attention from more practical measures advocated by Chesterton and others to make the next war less likely. Chesterton's technique also works well with the debate over abortion in the U.S. in the late 1960s. Legalization supporters began with a media campaign about a "population bomb." There was no such danger. Birthrates in developed societies so low, they threatened the long-term economic health of those societies. The real agenda was to limit births, particularly among poor minorities. Only later was rhetoric about "choice" adopted.

56. Maisie Ward, *Gilbert Keith Chesterton* (London: Sheed & Ward, 1944), 111. From p. 20 in Clemens' book. To understand Chesterton's perspective, keep in mind that the war pitted some 448,000 British troops, almost all of them transported from distant Britain, against some 80,000 Boers who lived on the land where they fought.

THE actual proposals of the people who call themselves advanced are harmless enough. It is their arguments for the proposals which prove that the proposals are harmful. It can be maintained that Socialism would not upset the family; but it is maintained that Socialism would upset the family, and ought to be thanked for doing so. It is tenable that women having votes would not alter the intercourse of the sexes; but it is distinctly declared that it would alter the intercourse of the sexes, and a good job too. If a man offers me a medicine, it may be good or bad; but if he offers me a medicine along with a pamphlet in favour of suicide, then I am suspicious of the medicine, even if, like many successful medicines, it consists only of some kind of coloured water. If a man tells me that a certain road is safe for cyclists, but at the same time stuffs into my hand a long roll of lint, a bottle of embrocation, and a number of surgical appliances, I cannot very easily disconnect the two ideas. So, if a man proposes a small change, but is full of the language and allusions connected with a large change, it is difficult for us to think of the small change when we have once thought of the large one. Suppose a man says, "There ought to be a tunnel from St. Paul's Station to Farringdon Street," none of us feel any particular disposition to object. But suppose a man says, "There ought to be a tunnel from St. Paul's to Farringdon Street. For, after all, St. Paul's Cathedral is not an edifice in the most elevated style of architecture. It was abruptly erected by the vandal Christopher Wren in the corrupt and filthy reign of Charles II.[57] Its only apparent dignity is due to its elevated and effective site, and that site will be used to even better effect when a nobler building has replaced it. Therefore, it may be said with certainty that a tunnel to Farringdon Street," etc. If this were said, a somewhat moderate degree of subtlety would be required to discover that, if the tunnel were constructed, the Cathedral would fall down.

Again and again I have found this a sound tip or test in the justice of any matter: wait until the people who like it have argued in favour of it; if they can once be induced with open hearts and mouths to say what is good in the thing, you are pretty certain to discover whatever is bad in it. For instance, the negotiations just before the Boer War were really a network of mystery and hypocrisy on both sides; therefore, I waited to make up my mind until I heard the moral arguments. And I decided; because I found that the moral arguments on our side were immoral arguments. Doubtless the Dutch had numberless examples among their individual citizens of rapacity, of double dealing, of secret cruelty or sudden injustice. Still their talk was of the truth of treaties, of the sacredness of national boundary, of the simple pride of Republican institutions, of the colossal courage of the weak. That is the talk of a people who are wronged. Doubtless there were among the English fighting in that field (certainly there were, for I knew them) men who lived and died only for a chivalrous fancy, of redressing wrongs, or even more manly principle of professional honour. Still our talk was of the need of expansion, of the hopelessness of the weak

57. One of the many talents of Christopher Wren, (1632–1723) was architecture. He designed 53 of London's churches, including St. Paul's Cathedral. Even in his own lifetime, his architectural style was hated by some.

resisting the strong, of everything being inevitable, of everything being better in the long run. That is the talk of a people who are doing a wrong. Such a people is condemned not by its crimes; it is condemned by its justification. It was only when I had read the defences of the thing that I saw that it was indefensible.

In other words, the whole trouble is this: that a very small, innocent proposal often has tied on to its tail a whole huge and guilty philosophy. What people do is often not the supreme question, even if they blow up cities or lay waste continents. What people do is often of far less importance than why they do it....

G.K. Chesterton, "Our Note-Book," *Illustrated London News* 133 (August 15, 1908), 219. US: August 29, 1908." Also published as "Listening to Modernist Arguments."

HUMANITARIAN HATE

September 19, 1908

Of these humanitarians it is hard to say otherwise than that they hate humanity.

EDITOR: Chesterton takes on a modern sacred cow, those such as Russian novelist, Leo Tolstoy, who call themselves humanitarians and champion causes such as pacifism and vegetarianism. Such people, he says, don't really love people because they will not accept them as they are: "They are compassionate to it [humanity] doubtless, as one may be compassionate to the most revolting animal. But their dislike of it appears to be general and fundamental." The gifted Polish novelist, Joseph Conrad, agreed with those views, applying them to H.G. Wells.

> Perhaps in a last bid to sustain their friendship, Conrad dedicated his 1907 *The Secret Agent* to Wells, but no correspondence between them after it was published has survived. In early 1918, Conrad would explain to Hugh Walpole, another writer, that his final quarrel with Wells had centered on their differing views about humanity, and that he had told Wells: "The difference between us, Wells, is fundamental. You don't care for humanity but think they are to be improved. I love humanity but know they are not."[58]

Chesterton's insight holds true across a wide spectrum of ideologies. Pacifists hate little boys for playing war games, vegetarians treat meat-eating as if it were cannibalism, feminists criticize women who stay home to raise their children, and environmentalists regard people as mere polluters, showing less regard for a baby in the womb than for a baby whale in that same situation. The abstractions they worship are more important to them than actual people, whose troublesome humanness is often seen as a hindrance and a problem.

FOR some week or two past, all the papers that I like have been talking almost entirely about Tolstoy.[59] This did not make me like them any the less; it is very right that this great European figure should be properly studied and honoured upon the festival of his old age. He has had it in him to win real literary glory; he has it in

58. The remark to Walpole is in Ruper Hart-Davies, *Hugh Walpole* (Macmillan: New York, 1952), 168. See also *The Pivot of Civilization in Historical Perspective* Michael W. Perry, ed. (Seattle: Inkling Books, 2001), 39.

59. The famous Russian novelist Leo Tolstoy's eightieth birthday was celebrated on September 9, 1908.

him now to despise the glory that he has won. He now goes about telling everybody not to read the novels that alone have made his name. There is something magnificent about that. It requires a great man, in the first instance, to write a masterpiece. But it requires a very great man to repent of a masterpiece as though it were a sin. Most of those who have discussed Tolstoy on the occasion of this anniversary have complained of this condemnation; they have lamented the fact that a great novelist should seek to expunge his own great novels in accordance with some pedantic doctrine of his old age. But, upon the whole, I think Tolstoy is, in this matter, not only great, but right. We all owe him much, considered as a great artist; but we all owe him even more as the great opponent of art—of art in the sense of art for art's sake. **Tolstoy is never more admirable than when he is declaring that art ought not to be the mysterious amusement of a clique, but the obvious self-expression of men: art is a language, and not a secret language.** It is a part of his greatness, therefore, to feel that what he has to say is more important than how well he once succeeded in saying it; and I for one quite agree with him that his novels (which are all right) are far less important than his philosophy, which is all wrong. He has this really great quality, that his faith is greater than himself; he shall decrease, but it shall increase. He represents a whole school of thought and a whole tone of feeling in Europe; something that was prophesied by the Quakers and fumbled about by Shelley.[60] He has really achieved something which he is quite magnanimous enough to like; Tolstoyanism is more important than Tolstoy.

The emotion to which Tolstoy has again and again given a really fine expression is an emotion of pity for the plain affairs of men. He pities the masses of men for the things that they really endure—the tedium and the trivial cruelty. But it is just here, unfortunately, that his great mistake comes in; the mistake which renders practically useless the philosophy of Tolstoy and the whole of his humanitarian school. **Tolstoy is not content with pitying humanity for its pains: such as poverty and prisons. He also pities humanity for its pleasures, such as music and patriotism.** He weeps at the thought of hatred; but in "The Kreutzer Sonata" he weeps almost as much at the thought of love. He and all the humanitarians pity the joys of men.[61]

Of these humanitarians it is hard to say otherwise than that they hate humanity. They are compassionate to it doubtless, as one may be compassionate to the most revolting animal. But their dislike of it appears to be general and fundamental. Suppose I happened to be acquainted with a discontented elephant who said, "I pity all my fellow-elephants because they are so big and heavy; I hate this

60. The Quakers were early pacifists. Percy Shelley (1792–1822) was an English poet, a rebel, and one of the first modern artists. His championing of various social causes (including vegetarianism), in keeping with the modern style, is discredited by his intensely selfish personal life. To give but one example, he neglected and then abandoned his pregnant first wife to run off with a sixteen-year-old girl.

61. *The Kreutzer Sonata* is an 1889 Tolstoy novella that argued for sexual abstinence within marriage, something even less likely of becoming common than his pacifism. The following year, Tolstoy defended the idea in *Epilogue To The Kreutzer Sonata*, arguing that, "we must cease thinking that carnal love is something peculiarly exalted; we must come to understand that the aim which is worthy of man is to serve humanity, his country, science, or art (let alone serving God)."

idea of having a long, flexible nose; I feel ashamed of myself for having such large tusks; I think it is a great shame that our children are always elephants too; I wish I had five legs or three, but four is such an awkward number; I think it most unfair that elephants should be worried with large, flapping ears, and large, reflective intellects"—if an elephant went on talking like this, there would come a point when we should say, "My good creature, what you dislike is being an elephant. You do not hate tusks or trunks or fatness or four legs. You hate elephanthood—or elephantishness, or elephantitude, or elephantiasis, or whatever be the abstract name." So if a man says, "I love humanity, and I pity it. I pity it because it is bewitched with the sickening superstitions of poetry and romantic love; I pity it for being burdened with the family and the foolish worries of fatherhood; I hate to think that human affections are chained to certain sites and sacred places; I detest the fantastic notion of a nation and a flag; I weep when I think that so much of mankind is engaged in external ceremonies; I wish men would not sing war-songs; I wish girls would not play with dolls":—in this process, as in the other, there comes a point in which one says to the man who is speaking, "What you dislike is being a man. You are at least next door to hating humanity, for you pity humanity because it is human."

These people are always telling us to make a larger morality and a more universal creed that shall take in all sorts and conditions of men. But the truth is that they themselves are the chief obstacle and exception to such a universal agreement. There really are some things upon which humanity is practically agreed, but unfortunately these are exactly the things with which the humanitarians do not agree. In short, there is sympathy between all men, with the exception of these apostles of sympathy. For instance, all men, savage and civilised, feel that they are in some spiritual way different from the beasts. When Europeans kill a man they do it with a ceremonial which would be absurd in killing a beast. When South Sea Islanders eat a man they do it with a ceremonial quite absent from their ordinary meals. Both peoples feel that the act, however traditional or necessary, is still possibly wicked and certainly dreadful. But the only men who do not feel this special sanctity of humanity are the humanitarians. They are the very people who tell us that it is cannibalism to eat a veal cutlet. So there goes one plank of the platform on which all men might stand together. Again, it is practically common to all men to owe life and death to some special tribe or city; to all men except Tolstoyans. It is practically common to all men to have a special horror of the charge of physical cowardice and to desire to disprove it in action—it is common to all men, that is, except Tolstoyans: It is practically common to all men to express religious or domestic feelings by external formalities, such as war-dances or funeral dirges—to all men except Tolstoyans. All men like music; but Tolstoy doesn't. All men like lovers and love-stories; but Tolstoy doesn't. All men like glory and feats of arms; but Tolstoy doesn't. In the face of this it may still be said, in a sense, that Tolstoy loves humanity. But it can certainly be said, in quite as true a sense, that Tolstoy hates humanity with a deep and sincere hatred.

One is reminded of the same difficulty by the talk about Moral Instruction and the Moral Instruction Congress.[62] We must have a philosophy fit for grown-up people before we can simplify it so as to make it fit for children. Men say indignantly that we ought not to be worrying about creeds: we ought to be worrying about education. They might as well say that we must not worry about cats, because we ought to be worrying about kittens. A kitten only means the first stage of a cat. Education only means the first stage of some creed, some view of life. It has been justly objected against purely Catholic teaching in England that it must be the mere teaching of a sect. It has been justly objected against mere Bible teaching that that is also (properly understood) the mere teaching of a sect. But it may be objected against Moral Instruction that it is really the teaching of the smallest sect of all. The particular sort of professors engaged on Moral Instruction are further off from the atmosphere of the populace than the Salvation Army, and immeasurably further off than the Roman Catholic priests. It is no answer to say that the actual things stated by the Moral Instructionists are mostly in themselves harmless. All the things which cause the strongest religious irritation are in themselves harmless. No Catholic can have an intrinsic objection to the Bible; for it is a part of the Church. No Protestant can have an intrinsic objection to the "Hail Mary," for it is a part of the Bible. Protestants who object to a crucifix do not deny a crucifixion. It is in the emphasis upon things that people differ passionately. And so, while I may agree with twenty truisms running in a Moral Instruction pamphlet, I can still think the whole pamphlet immoral.

G.K. Chesterton, "Our Note-Book," *Illustrated London News* 133 (September 19, 1908), 392. US: October 3, 1908. Also published as "A Uniform Creed for Humanity."

A War of Men Not Ships

March 27, 1909

If you perceive your enemy plunging on blindly in a particular direction, the real thing to do, if you have any spirit and invention, is to calculate the weakness in his course and advance yourself in some other direction.

Editor: Some articles are timeless because they contain a single idea that is forever relevant to our lives. Here Chesterton offers us three marvelous ideas.

- Wars are fought by men rather than machines. On them, victory or defeat ultimately depends.
- No weapon is the ultimate one. For every weapon, there is a counter-weapon.[63]

62. The First International Moral Education Congress would meet in London the following week (from September 23–26, 1908). Chesterton is arguing that, while Moral Instruction wants to focus on vague and general moral principles, most people prefer their morality to come packaged in a specific religious framework as part of a creed that includes Bible study or reciting "Hail Mary." Deprived of that framework, people have no interest in "twenty truisms." Like Tolstoy, these moral educators dislike people as they are.

63. He was right. Battleships would be countered in WWI by submarines and torpedo boats, forcing Germany and Britain to keep their largest warships in well-defended harbors. In WWII, aircraft carriers would end the battleship arms race. Before WWII, a similar misconception, that "the bomber will always get through," led to a defeatism that made war more likely. But radar and fighter planes made it costly for Germany to bomb England.

- The key to peace lies is finding a greater love we hold in common to counter the lesser loves and fears that drive us apart.

EVERYONE is talking just now about machines of death made out of steel or iron. People whisper in a panic-stricken way that Germany is building ironclads of the size of small islands; and one can almost fancy that the sun is darkened at noon with flying ships, like a flight of iron birds. **I have my doubts about both the moral and the military value of this sort of imagination. Machinery is only armour, and armour is only clothes; and a very superficial study of some suburban dandies will suffice to show that it is no good to have clothes if you do not know how to put them on.** We do not offer exquisite trousers to a man who has no legs. Neither do we offer difficult machinery to men who have no heads, nor dangerous machinery to men who have no hearts. An obvious historical parallel suggests itself. Armour-plating is no new thing; ironclads are very old and romantic objects. Only in the old time the individual was an ironclad. They plated the man instead of the ship; but they calculated it carefully, so as to repel the shafts and bullets of the enemy. And this making of helmets and breast-plates was a very subtle and exacting trade; the armourer was both an artist and a man of science. A great deal depended on him; men were often killed, like Dundee at Killiecrankie, only because one hole was found in their harness.[64] No doubt there was a certain amount of international competition, and the advisers of a nation said: "Remember that you have to meet the steel coats of Milan," or "Remember that your enemies have admirable blades from Damascus." Still, these fears were kept within the four corners of dignity. I absolutely refuse to believe that any English gentleman at the time of Crecy ever shrieked at the top of his voice: "Nine more new visors for the Knights of Acquitaine!" or "Seven more Barbary horses seen in Gascony!" or "French Government still buying Florentine gauntlets!" And, if we attempt to analyse the difference, I think we shall simply find it to lie in a sense of honour. Such an English gentleman would have thought it cowardly to attach so much importance as all that to a difference of armaments. He would, as a reasonable person, inform himself about the weapons of his enemy; and if he heard that his enemy had a curtal-axe which was rather a neat thing, he would probably go and buy one. But he would not talk as if he could be conquered by the axe, and not by the enemy. He would not talk as if there were a shower and hail of curtal-axes darkening the sun. He would not say that the German axes were growing larger and larger by a huge, incurable law of the cosmos. In the last resort, his own manhood would count for something; and that would despise an open fear of defeat as much as defeat itself. For, after all, the only possible shame of defeat is that it may have befallen us through fear. But we seem eager to confess the fear before we need confess the defeat.

64. John Graham, the First Viscount Dundee (*circa* 1648–1689) was killed in the Battle of Killiecrankie (July 27, 1689). Numerous legends surround his death and that single bullet hole.

That is the obvious difference between the mediaeval Englishman and the modern. He talked of contending against a German knight, not against a German lance. Nor would he have been scared if you had told him that German lances were growing longer and longer, and that whereas ten years ago a German lance was forty feet long, it was now two hundred and forty feet long, and would soon be a mile long. He would deny that this was any reason for his really being afraid of the German knight—a degree of degradation which he would, indeed, have refused altogether to discuss. He would have denied it for two very forcible reasons, both of which are in their turn well worth consideration at the present time.

He would have denied it, first, because his common-sense would have told him that the mere elongation of lances, at enormous expense and without any reference to the swift accidents of battle, was a piece of clumsiness and stupidity in the mere art of war. It would be much more worth while to teach a large number of healthy men to manage a short lance than to teach a few acrobats to manage partially a long lance that could not really be managed. And while a lengthy spear might be likely to strike an enemy first, it would be much worse than useless if it did not strike him at all; as he would simply sit smiling with a spiked mace in his hand until the monotonous lengths of timber had gone by him. Now, the average citizen is not an expert either upon lances or battle-ships. He cannot know much about the subject; but he can (I think) know a good deal about the expert. The good citizen possesses a sense of smell, given to him by God, like that of the dog; he has, in a mystical way, a nose for nonsense. And he smells something wrong when people go on talking blindly about bigger and bigger ships, though he may know nothing about naval war; just as he would smell something wrong if people went on talking about longer and longer lances, though he might know nothing about the technique of tilting. Common-sense tells a man that indefinite development in one direction must in practice over-reach itself: that wearing ninety overcoats cannot be the way to cure a cold, that drinking ninety pots of beer is by no means a protection against thirst. **If you perceive your enemy plunging on blindly in a particular direction, the real thing to do, if you have any spirit and invention, is to calculate the weakness in his course and advance yourself in some other direction. You ought to take advantage of his infatuation, not to imitate it; you ought to surprise his plan of campaign, not copy it laboriously.** If he is building very big ships, the best thing you could do would probably be to build small ones; ships lighter, quicker, and more capable of navigating rivers. If he has gone quite dotty on long lances, the chances are that you will win the battle with daggers. But there is another reason besides this more flexible experimentalism in war which would, I think, have prevented this fine old English gentleman from going in for a mere blind race in the length of spear-shafts. He would have known that if lances really grew longer and longer past all reason, there would certainly come a point when Europe would step in and stop it. Europe was a great deal too keen on the common sport of chivalry to let it be wiped out by cut-throat competition. They would have had sumptuary laws to cut short a gentleman's lance as they had them to cut short his plumes or his expenditure. But these could only have been enforced by a general agreement of Christendom. And in those old, barbaric, superstitious, dim, dark, and damned ages, there would have been a general agreement of Christendom.[65] It might have been an agreement full of artificial feudalism, it might have been ratified by ecclesiastical mysteries, but it could have been obtained. **It is all nonsense to say that we Europeans could not have an agreement about disarmament. We could have it right enough if we were Europeans. We could have it well enough if we loved our civilisation as much as we hate each other. People cannot love Europe, because Europe is either a map or else a mythical lady who was carried off by a bull.[66] But men could love Christendom, because it was an idea.**

Therefore with all the heartiness proper to one who is wholly ignorant of the subject, I throw down my two private doubts, which are almost strong enough to be called suggestions. First, I gravely doubt whether our hurried emulation in arms is not a great deal too much a mere breathless and crazy copying. If the other schoolboy throws big snowballs, it is the mere instinct of hurry to throw bigger ones; but it might be much better strategy to keep one's head, to throw a smaller snowball and to throw it straight. **In short, I disbelieve in this modern war exactly because it is always talked of as a war of guns and ships, and never as a war of men. And secondly, I doubt whether this competition of longer spears or larger ships need go on at all, if once the nations could find something positive upon which to combine.** Of course they cannot combine on mere peace; peace is a negation, like darkness.[67] Is there any affection or institution or creed on which we can combine?—that is increasingly the question. It is our dreadful condition that we agree too much on all the things in which we ought to vary—arms, methods, and the arts of war. And we differ hopelessly on all the things on which we ought to agree—motives, reasons, and beliefs. In the things of life and love we are separated; in the things of death and blood we imitate each other. In a healthy existence the inmost thing should be secure, but the outer gestures energetic and varied. But with modern Europe it is the limbs that are heavy and the heart that has unrest.

G.K. Chesterton, "Our Note-Book," *Illustrated London News* 134 (March 27, 1909), 444. US: April 10, 1909. Also published as "The Modern Arms Race."

Journalistic Fear Mongering

January 8, 1910

There was always a dim element of irony and doubt mixed with popular poetry and popular religion. But journalism demands blind and prostrate faith.

65. See the May 20, 1916 article (Ch. 4), where he describes "a permanent balance of Christian nationalities."

66. In Greek mythology, Europa was a beautiful Phoenician woman carried off by Zeus disguised as a bull. How her name became that for the European continent is debated.

67. Chesterton explains this in more detail in the December 31, 1910 issue of the *Illustrated London News* (Ch. 1).

Editor: Perhaps because he was a journalist, Chesterton did not trust newspapers. Fed by the press, a *fear of Germany* helped feed the military competition that preceded World War I. A generation later, a press-led *fear of war* with all its horrors fed the equally harmful climate of appeasement that preceded World War II. Because it allows a few to affect so many, any press-induced fear can lead to disaster. Not easily frightened, Chesterton opposed both waves of fear-mongering.

We hear a great deal just now about political interruptions which cause laughter, but I heard one the other day which might well cause tears. The circumstances are not specially relevant. Let it suffice that I was speaking in a small hall in a country town — a hall filled in the strange way that is so common in such cases. I mean that the audience consisted of some elderly people right up in the front, who were prominent but silent, and some very undeveloped people right at the back, who were noisy but shy. Between these two there was a great gulf fixed, and one's voice echoed desolately across it. **I happened to be expressing an opinion on the truth of which I need not linger, but an opinion to which I am firmly wedded, that the military and naval strength of Germany is much exaggerated.** I think the people who see the Kaiser as omnipotent are like the people who saw the Emperor of the French as omnipotent just before 1870. It is not a prediction, but a tradition. Their heads are really full of the last war, not of the next: like the cautious and sensible Irishman in the story, they are prophesying what has happened already. Moreover, I am old enough to remember that, through all the early days of Imperialism and Mr. Kipling, it was Russia that was always represented as this ruthless giant, clad in steel and striding ever nearer and nearer.[68] It seems as if a ruthless giant somewhere must be absolutely necessary to their scheme of the universe. Then other things happened, and our journalists had suddenly to leave off railing at Russia for being strong, and begin railing at Russia for being weak. That is exactly what they had done some fifteen years before about the strength and the weakness of Napoleon III. But I do not desire to dwell on this opinion, true or false, but to lead up to the strange and touching interruption which on this occasion it called forth. When I had remarked that Frenchmen and Germans of my acquaintance, as well as Englishmen specially well informed, took a much more moderate view of the matter, there came from the back of the hall a shrill, boyish voice, uttering these remarkable words: "Yer don't read yer papers."

I could have fallen on his neck and wept. Such innocence as that has something tragic and sublime about it. It had never crossed his mind, you see, even for one wild moment, that a man might read his papers and not implicitly believe them. No suspicion had ever dawned on his mind that there was a slight party bias delicately discernible in the *Evening News* or the *Star*; that there was a slight note of eagerness,

68. Chesterton was referring to Rudyard Kipling's early tales such as his 1886 *Departmental Ditties*. The "nearer and nearer" were Russia's attempts to spread its influence southward as far as British India and not to any scheme to invade England, which would have been difficult geographically. British rule in India depended on agreements with local rulers who could, if the balance of power shifted, easily make an alliance with Russia.

almost amounting to exaggeration, in the *Daily Mail.* **For him every printed word was not only a solemn fact, but was the supreme form of truth, beyond which there was no appeal.** And he could only suppose that some defect in my eyesight, or in my education, prevented me from learning the great truths which the posters of the *Daily Mail* had to tell. My mother had not taught me to read, or I had spent all my halfpennies in chocolate cigars; and so I was shut out from those feasts of infallible information of which the gates stood so wide for him. The growth of this singular spirit is somewhat distressing, especially in country districts. For if there is one fine and rich quality which we do expect in a rustic, it is suspiciousness. I am distressed by this spread of simple faith. I am sure that no yokel ever believed in the ghost as these yokels believe in the newspaper. I am sure no peasants in the Middle Ages gave such smooth and swift and automatic credence to any tales of fairies or legends of saints as these honest lads do to the vast cosmopolitan crazes and partisan travesties of the halfpenny Press. **There was always a dim element of irony and doubt mixed with popular poetry and popular religion. But journalism demands blind and prostrate faith. And journalism seems to get it.**

One of the worst features of this vast illusion consists in this: that, newspapers lying thick as leaves everywhere, so many people grow accustomed to certain images or occurrences in newspapers long before they happen to have seen them in real life. It is obvious that when a fire, a murder, or an interrupted wedding occurs, very few can immediately see it, while millions immediately read about it. But the result is that millions have a conventional picture in their minds which is as different as possible from the real picture, but which nevertheless colours their sentiments and even deflects their philosophy.[69] What notion, let us say, has the average Englishman of what really happens when there is "A Scene in the House," "A Welsh Revival Meeting," "A Freak Dinner," "A Skirmish with the Mad Mullah"? I will take one example from the same fragment of my own experience. All through the present political crisis and all other political crises, I have read in the papers a vast amount about meetings being broken up by "an organised opposition." The words suggest to me what I have no doubt they also suggest to the millions of people who read them. They suggest a cunning strategist who has planted blocks and groups of his boldest and most effective men in various parts of a hostile meeting to open a campaign of question and repartee which shall culminate in the moral defeat of the platform. That is what I always read into the words "organised opposition." This is what really happens. About twenty minutes after the speakers have begun to address a small and sympathetic assembly, chiefly consisting of their friends with their wives and children, the door at the end of the hall abruptly opens and about fifteen boys walk in in a line as stiffly as if they were made of wood. They sit down as far away as possible from the people whom they propose to defy; and no entreaties or taunts will induce them to come an inch nearer. They say abruptly at intervals——"Good old Joe!" or whoever may be their favourite statesman. If the man on the platform

69. Chesterton describes media-created events in the *Illustrated London News* for March 18, 1916 (Ch. 4).

says that bread ought to be cheap, they say—"What about Chinese Labour?" If he is discussing the Navy, they say—"What about the Big Loaf?"[70] In moments of special animation they say—"Who are you?" a very sensible question. Towards the end of the proceedings they get up all at once and all go out together, still looking like wood and making a sort of wooden clatter with their feet. It was only after this dark manoeuvre that it dawned on me that the stiff pantomime that I had just been watching really was this cunning, elaborate, and diabolically diplomatic thing called "an organised opposition."

In such cases surely newspaper phraseology misleads. One does not talk about the mechanism of a poker. One does not talk about the organisation of a row of pokers. In the incident I describe there was no sort of art, and even no sort of deception. Nobody pretended for a moment that these boys were voters, or that they had come to listen, or that they had come separately or by accident. The thing was perfectly defensible on the assumption that politics is a game; but even in that sense one could not call it a game of skill. **The only point, however, that I wish to make here is that round such common newspaper phrases as "an organised opposition" there clings a connotation of drama, tactics, and intellectual excitement which entirely disappears when one sees the real thing—the little boys in their adorable simplicity stumping in and stumping out again.**

Of course, one could give hundreds of other instances. When the newspapers describe "A Scene in the House," one gets an impression of green benches broken up, hats smashed, and the Speaker's wig all crooked on his head. A friend of mine was in the House while one of these "scenes" was going on. Happening at the moment to be thinking about a sonnet or some such thing, he did not know there had been a scene till he read it in the paper next morning. This is where the modern imaginative world called journalism differs from the old imaginative world of peasants and children. In fairy tales the objects were mostly familiar; it was only the power that was mystical. A peasant had never seen a bean-stalk grow up into the sky; but he had seen a bean-stalk and he had seen the sky. A child had never seen a cat in boots; but he had seen boots and a cat. **The trouble with the new world of fancy is that it consists so much of vast things of which plain people can form no picture: financial hoards, scientific machinery, colossal navies, enormous emigrations—images so huge that they do not stir the imagination, but crush it.**

G.K. Chesterton, "Our Note-Book," *Illustrated London News* 136 (January 8, 1910), 40. US: January 22, 1910. Also published as "Political Interruptions."

70. "Chinese labour" referred to importing Chinese workers into South Africa to replace white workers. "Big Loaf" was a slogan used by free trade advocates to emphasize that duty-free imported grain made bread cheaper, a policy that made English farmers unhappy. Both were highly emotional, bitterly debated issues.

RACE AND POLITICS

April 30, 1910

Never once would it flash across the Aryan mind on the heights of Hampstead that all such race theories are rubbish.

EDITOR: At a time with racial theories about culture and personality were fashionable and progressive, and in an era when they were taken seriously in literature and regarded as an especially scientific way of looking at the world, Chesterton poured scorn on them. This 1910 article demonstrates that his contempt for Teutonic race theories existed before German professors used them to criticize Britain for not supporting Germany in the war. Chesterton was well ahead of almost every other writer in attacking the peculiar sort of racism that led to Hitler.[71]

THAT able and ironic journalist who writes the paragraphs called "Table Talk" in the *Daily News* has got into a discussion with some of those wild theorists who think that everything can be explained by "race." They are amazing people. There is nobody to beat them at the great scientific art of first laying down a rule too absurd for anyone to believe and then softening it with exceptions too bewildering for anyone to follow. I remember one man who was a champion of this school. He was an Australian; I forget his name, but I remember his theory; which was that Europe was divided into dark-haired people and fair-haired people, and that all the good had come from the fair-haired people and all the bad from the dark-haired people. Also all the fair-haired people lived in the north of Europe and loved light, liberty, justice, and civilisation; while, on the other hand, all the dark-haired people lived in the south of Europe, and were very fond of darkness, misery, oppression, superstition, and failure. No doubt the doctrine would considerably simplify our social and political relations if it could only be established; but in this latter formality there were hitches, as even the ardent theorist himself began to perceive. For instance, he was a democrat and admired the French Revolution; but certainly that effort had been largely made by dark-haired men, often by very dark-haired men, like the southern French contingent who (as Mr. Belloc writes) "came north and destroyed the monarchy. " This brought the theorist to a pause, but it did not baffle him. After a few minutes' reflection, he cried, with great cunning, "Ah, that was a fair-haired spirit working in the dark-haired people." It was then mildly pointed out to him that not only had the dark-haired people fought for the Revolution, but the fair-haired people had fought against it; the Germans and the Scandinavians had rallied to royalty and aristocracy. "And there you are again!" retorted the logician triumphantly. "You see, that was the temporary manifestation in a fair-haired people

71. For more examples of his contempt for Teutonism, see the articles for September 5 and October 10, 1914 (Ch. 2), as well as June 14 and June 28, 1919 (Ch. 7). Although not included here, in a March 17, 1923 article he ridiculed scholars who wrote about Teutonism, pointing out that "common-sense knows what is covered by the world German; but science never knows what may not sooner or later be made to come under the word Teuton." *The Collected Works of G.K. Chesterton*, XXXIII, 65.

of a dark-hair philosophy." I have often wished I were that man. He must have found the making and defending of theories very easy and jolly work.

My Australian friend has vanished from my existence for ever, but he seems to have left a very good substitute and representative in Mr. Joseph Banister, of Hampstead, the gentleman who has raised the racial question in the *Daily News*. Mr. Banister briefly and lucidly explains that Socialism is only the uprising of the base and slavish pre-Aryan tribes, who live in low places like Edinburgh and Dublin, against the brave and beautiful Aryan people who live in high places—like Hampstead.[72] The people at present in possession of most of the property, the Rothschilds, the Ecksteins, and the rest, owe their purity and chivalry chiefly to the fact of their Aryan origin (so, at least, I understand Mr. Banister's argument), while, on the other hand, if a man is very poor, you may comfort him by telling him that he is also pre-Aryan. The following startling description of a Labour Member will possess interest, not to say entertainment, for those who happen to know any Labour Members—

> The leaders of the various socialistic, pro-foreign, and anti-national movements in England are generally of Scotch, Welsh, or Irish origin; they usually possess the low stature, low foreheads, black hair, high cheek-bones, thick lips, dark complexions, and beady eyes of the pre-Keltic races; and their speeches and writings are characterised by the shallowness, frothiness, ignorance, conceit, boastfulness, abusiveness, untruthfulness, exaggerations and unfairness which distinguish the utterances of the people of non-Aryan origin.

Now, if anyone were mildly to point out to Mr. Banister that this exuberant description does not quite fit the facts, I am sure he would betake himself at once to the simple but ingenious logic of my friend who found the fair-haired notions in the dark-haired heads. If you ventured to remark, for instance, that Mr. Shackleton is scarcely "of low stature," he would say that this was the Aryan vastness swelling out a non-Aryan (Mr. Shackleton) to its own enormous outline. If you were to remark that Mr. Ramsay MacDonald, so far from having a low forehead and all the other apish attributes, is a quite unusually handsome man, Mr. Banister would cry out, "Ah, yes; that is the not uncommon case of Aryan good looks grafted, as it were, upon an essentially ugly pre-Aryan person." If you suggested that Mr. Henderson is quite the reverse of dark, Mr. Banister would say that he is a pre-Aryan accidentally bleached like an Albino. If you were to urge further that he is quite the reverse of short, it would be answered that he is a pre-Aryan pulled out, like a telescope. If you said that you had examined Mr. Keir Hardie in vain, looking for his beady eyes; that you had made a disappointing journey to Mr. Snowden's house, on purpose to see his thick lips; and that you had stared quite hard at Mr. Will Crooks without being able to detect anything alarmingly pre-Aryan about his cheekbones—if you urged all this, the answer would be the same wild and smiling absurdity—*exceptis*

---

72. Chesterton knew his geography. Edinburgh is in Scotland and Dublin in Ireland. Hampstead is one of London's wealthiest and most artistic suburbs. Politically, it's the home of "Hampstead Liberalism."

excipiendis:[73] if the facts do not fit into the theory, then the facts are exceptions, and there is an end of them. The exceptions prove the rule, and prove it all the more if the world contains nothing but exceptions to it, and hardly any examples at all.[74]

If Mr. Banister be supposed to refer to other groups, if by his "anti-national" party he means the Nationalist Party (it sounds like his paradox), we should again have to go patiently and ploddingly to work, pointing out to him that the facts did not fit anywhere: that Daniel O'Connell was not short; that Mr. T.P. O'Connor is not dark; that Mr. Stephen Gwynne's eyes are not in the least beady, nor Mr. Dillon's lips thick—and so on, until Mr. Banister had transferred his crazy theory to some other mixed and ordinary group of men.[75] **Never once would it flash across the Aryan mind on the heights of Hampstead that all such race theories are rubbish; that political, religious, and commercial groups of men come together because they agree about politics, religion, or commerce; and that there is no group which does not contain, within the range of local possibility, all shapes of skull and all shades of complexion.** There is no negro on the front Conservative bench; and there is none in the Irish Party. There is no Eskimo in Mr. Asquith's Government; nor is there in the Socialist Party of Great Britain. But within limits geographically probable there is every sort of person on both sides and in all sections.

The objection to this appeal to prehistoric "race" is much sharper and more final even than the objection that its facts are mostly fancies and its deductions fallacies. **The objection to the race theory is that it is not wanted. It is explaining something that explains itself.** It is, indeed, ludicrous to suppose that, in the chaos of falling Rome, men carefully sorted themselves out according to the shapes of their skulls: they had precious little interest in skulls except to smash them. But the point is that we know more or less how they did sort themselves out, and why. Any man who is a Christian knows why the Christian Celts fought with the heathen Teutons; also why the Christian Teutons fought with the heathen Teutons afterwards. **We do not need to know about the skulls; we know about the brains.** That general resistance to the barbarians, which extends from the half-historic Arthur to the wholly historic Alfred, obviously was not a racial war; for the two kings were of different races.[76] But we not only know what it wasn't, we know what it was. It was a religious war, and the religion it saved survives still. Just so it is idle to say that men become Socialists

73. Latin: "Excepting what is to be excepted."

74. David J. Shackleton (1863–1938), the third Labour Member of Parliament, was known as the Lancashire Giant. Ramsay MacDonald (1866–1937) was a Parliament Labour Party leader. At this time, Arthur Henderson (1863–1935) headed the Labour Party. Keir Hardie (1856–1915) was a Scottish socialist and one of the first two Labour Members of Parliament. Philip Snowden (1864–1937) would later become the first Labour Chancellor of the Exchequer. William Crooks (1852–1921) was a Labour politician and a Fabian.

75. All these men were prominent Irish nationalists. Daniel O'Connell (1775–1847) championed Irish Catholicism through non-violent politics, noting in 1796: "The altar of liberty totters when it is cemented only with blood." Stephen Gwynn (1864–1950) was an Irish journalist and at this time a Member of Parliament. John Dillon (1851–1927) was an Irish nationalist and a leader in the United Ireland League.

76. That is, from King Arthur (perhaps in the late fifth or early sixth century AD) to Alfred the Great (*c.* 849–899). Chesterton tells of the latter in "The Ballad of the White Horse," available in *G.K. Chesterton's Early Poetry*.

because they are short and dark and thick-lipped. I *know* why men become Socialists, for I have been one myself.

G.K. Chesterton, "Our Note-Book," *Illustrated London News* 136 (April 30, 1910), 636. US: May 14, 1910. Also published as "The Racial Question and Politics."

Cultivating His Garden

September 17, 1910

But another kind of international criticism has arisen which is more mischievous than the most ignorant of these denunciations. And that is the habit not of wildly and ignorantly blaming, but wildly and ignorantly praising, another nation.

Editor: Perhaps stimulated by the role he played in opposing the Boer War, Chesterton may have thought more about the good and ill that accompanies nationalism than any other writer of his day. Here he gives practical advice about praising and criticizing one's own country and that of others. Notice that what Chesterton says about cursing one's own country applies to "every good patriot" and not necessarily those embittered that their country isn't following their particular agenda.

The right and proper thing, of course, is that every good patriot should stop at home and curse his own country. So long as that is being done everywhere, we may be sure that things are fairly happy, and being kept up to a reasonably high standard. So long as we are discontented separately we may be well content as a whole. **Each man is cultivating his garden; and you cannot cultivate a garden without digging it up or without stamping it down. And these gardens of the children of men are so strange and so different that each man is probably alone in knowing even which are the flowers and which the weeds.** But so long as grunts, snorts, curses, and cries of despair come over every garden wall we may be pretty certain that things are all right, that the flowers will arise in splendour and the wilderness blossom like the rose. So long as good Americans go on railing at their anarchy and graft, so long as good Englishmen curse our snobbery and squirearchy, so long as there are Germans to murmur at officialism and Scotchmen to make game of theology, so long as Irishmen insist that they are conquered, and Frenchmen are quite sure they are betrayed—so long as this genial and encouraging groan goes up from all Europe, so long we may feel certain that Christendom is going forward with her mighty cohorts triumphant on her eternal way.

But this wholesome habit of grumbling by one's own fireside has been crossed by customs considerably more perilous and responsible. The commonest trick, of course, is to lash one's self into a kind of cold and abstract rage about somebody else's business that one very imperfectly understands, to demand of heaven and the High Court of Parliament how long the poor women of Japan are to black their teeth or the police of Russia to black their newspapers, without in the least knowing how it feels to a Jap or a Russian, or whether the thing, in its own environment, seems as natural as blacking one's boots or as comic as blacking one's face. Nevertheless, these criticisms of foreign countries, although commonly wild and impertinent, are not the worst forms of international interference, and may sometimes even do good. The Russian censor's ink may not be so black as it is painted; still, the general tendency of such officials is towards obscurantism and oppression, and a foreign protest, even if ignorant, may work on the side of the internal freedom of that country. Again, if it be wrong to look a gift horse in the mouth, it is yet more ill-mannered so to examine an Oriental lady who has dressed and painted herself, not for your taste, but for that of Oriental gentlemen. Still, it would be safe to hazard that Oriental ladies are, on the whole, too much controlled by the conventions of the harem rather than too little; so that there again it may be argued that criticism from outside may encourage reform within. I am no admirer of the popular preacher or idealistic publicist on a platform who rises to a whirlwind of seraphic scorn and self-satisfaction because he himself (as it happens) has never cut up an Armenian with a scimitar or boiled a missionary in a pot. But if there is a Turk somewhere who cuts up Armenians in a light, absent-minded kind of way, not seeing any harm in it, I think he might be told that it is "not done." If there are any cannibals who conduct their cuisine in ignorance of the fact that there is a feeling against it in more fastidious tribes, then I think they should be told of this foreign disapproval. And I can imagine that even if the European critic made mistakes (as no doubt he would) about the details of anthropophagy, the criticism might still convey the required rebuke from outside.[77] Even if the critic described as baked a bishop whom every child remembered vividly as boiled, even if he referred to curates when they were not in season, I still think that the sincere horror of the European's tone might shake the Cannibal Islanders in this, their mere insularity of taste.

But another kind of international criticism has arisen which is more mischievous than the most ignorant of these denunciations. And that is the habit not of wildly and ignorantly blaming, but wildly and ignorantly praising, another nation. This, I say, is worse: because it hinders the real patriots of that nation in their attempt to cure its real abuses. No one but a patriot can know the worst about his people. No one but an American citizen can understand the real incubus of Mr. Rockefeller: a gigantesque nightmare. We can catch glimpses of the vision, but it must always be different from our own. No one but an Englishman, again, can understand how helpless and how omnipotent are the English aristocrats: how the English aristocrats have lost faith in everything, even in aristocracy: and how yet they fill all the seats and avenues, a crowd that cannot be cleared by the police. No one but a Frenchman has any right to rebuke French brutality: the other nations are not brutal (or virile) enough to understand it. No one but a German has any business to balance the beautiful dreaminess against the practical obedience of his people, or to guess which will win.

77. Anthropophagy is a sophisticated but little-used term for cannibalism. Chesterton also mentions it in his June 19, 1915 (Ch. 3) and September 2, 1916 (Ch. 4) articles.

And this reminds me that I have before me a flaring instance of the ill-luck of such international admirations. It is a document that takes no account of such obviously perplexing elements as French brutality and German dreaminess; it proceeds on the simple principle of French badness and German goodness. Frenchmen, it says, are feminine. They have a horror of severe methods, which is doubtless why they have to be rebuked for crowding round the guillotine. They are hysterical, which must be the reason of the steady toil and greed and wealth of their peasants. Germans, on the other hand, are masculine. Germans are simple: this can be noted in the German artistic books and book-covers, in the hundred Aubrey Beardsleys to our one that sprawl on every German decorative page. Germans are silent, like the Kaiser.[78]

I am sorry that I have no larger space left to deal with this outburst, an article called "The Psychology of the Conqueror," by an Englishwoman in Germany. It reminds me of "Ouida" at her worst and the penny novelettes at their best.[79] The Englishwoman prostrates herself before the beautiful big boots of the Prussian soldier in a riot of sentimentalism. Like other female writers on the Viking Breed, she gets a little mixed. She says she has noticed a trait which may be called the psychology of the conqueror; which is as if I said that I had noticed a cabbage which was the Botany of the Brussels Sprout. She also calls it the knowledge of the power of force — a very recondite discovery like that of the potency of the energy of the might of violence. Also her perfect German is praised in a somewhat confused manner, being first described as a strenuous conqueror, and then as a very meek dog on a chain who is much too frightened to bark too loudly or to frolic too blithely. The Government, it seems, fills all Germans with awe; and there are (so far as I understand the argument) no robberies or swindles of any sort in Germany. The one most firmly embedded in my memory was the swindle of the bogus Captain Koepenick.[80] That certainly illustrated German submissiveness, but scarcely, I think, German efficiency.

Evidently, however, it has not crossed the lady's mind that Prussian discipline may, perhaps, arise not from the fierceness of the people, but rather from their tameness. As a matter of fact, the Germans have not conquered very much in history as a whole. About fifty years ago they beat the French, and about fifty years before that the French very soundly beat them.[81] We are simply blinded by one accident of chronology if we let the Prussians' capturing Paris make us forget that the Parisians have captured at some time nearly every town in Europe. If we set history as a whole, there is no more doubt that the French people are the more military than

78. The short-lived Aubrey Beardsley (1872–1898) was to British art what his friend Oscar Wilde was to literature — decadent, erotic, controversial, and suspected of being homosexual. The German Kaiser was notorious for making embarrassing remarks that created international incidents.

79. Chesterton kindly left the woman unnamed. "Ouida" is the pen name of Maria Louise Ramé (1839–1908), author of some 40 novels and children's stories. Her style is seen in from *Under Two Flags*, (1867): "Beauty himself, with a characteristic philosophy, had a sort of conviction that the German race would set everything square. He stood either to make a very good thing on it or to be very heavily bit. There could be no medium."

80. For the hilarious tale of Captain Koepenick, see the *Illustrated London News* for October 27, 1906 (Ch. 1).

81. Germany's military ascendency over Europe extended over the seventy-five years from 1870 until 1945. Today the wheels of history have turned again and neither is a major military power, although the French, with economic interests in Africa, are perhaps better equipped to act outside their borders than the Germans.

there is that the German people are the more musical. But if you ask why it is worth while to answer such pro-Teuton servilities, the truth is exactly here: Germany is a great and splendid nation; there are millions of sensible German patriots grappling with the sins and follies which are part of her problem. And just when they are doing their best, this insane idolatry from the foreigner comes in, upsets all the German wise men, and comes to the rescue of the German fool.[82]

G.K. Chesterton, "Our Note-Book," *Illustrated London News* 137 (September 17, 1910), 412. US: October 1, 1910. Also published as "Patriotism and National Self-Criticism."

Wars Out of Love

December 31, 1910

A real soldier does not fight because he has something that he hates in front of him. He fights because he has something that he loves behind his back.

Editor: In this article, Chesterton demonstrates his knack for turning conventional wisdom upside down. Wars, he says, have love rather than hate as their *primary* cause. In article that follows, he clarifies the *secondary* role of hatred. In a January 29, 1916 article (Ch. 4), he comments, "For it is intensely important to grasp that combatants do not commonly disagree about things, but about the value of things." He took up a similar theme just after Christmas of 1923.

> People still go about gravely repeating that Christianity was refuted by the Great War, which is rather like saying that Noah's Ark was refuted by the Flood. The Ark was only built because men were likely to be drowned in a deluge; and the Church was only founded because men are liable to be swept away perpetually by a deluge of dark passions and destructive sins. But the Church certainly never said that there would be no sins and no wars; and some of the more mystical adumbrations about the last days seemed to suggest that there would be more sins and more wars. An enemy is quite free to charge religion with what he would call a hopeless lack of progressive faith; but not free to charge it at the same time with hopelessness and with holding out delusive hopes. As a point of plain fact, it was the rationalistic critics of Christianity who held out the delusive hopes. It was their rationalistic optimism that was refuted by the Great War.... In short, it is simply self-evident, to any fair-minded person who lived through that period, that it was the whole anti-clerical and agnostic world that was busy prophesying the advent of universal peace; and it was that world that was, or should have been, abashed and confounded by the advent of universal war.[83]

Notice the scorn he heaps on well-indoctrinated intellectuals who are unable to love their own countries and, as a result, "can do nothing whatever for the cause of

82. Chesterton correctly links this 'German' idea to non-German sources. Modern belief in German racial superiority began with a Frenchman, Count Arthur de Gobineau (1816–1882). The Count used race-based theories in his (pre-Darwin) 1853 *Essai sur l'Inégalitié des Races Humaines* to justify the rule of French nobles, thought to be of Germanic origin. As rule by nobility became unacceptable, the emphasis shifted to regarding entire peoples as fit or unfit. The idea that the German people were superior was popularized by an Englishman, Houston Stewart Chamberlain (1855–1927), author of *Die Grundlagen des neunzehnten Jahrhunderts* (1899), translated as *The Foundations of the Nineteenth Century*.

83. *The Collected Works of G.K. Chesterton* vol. XXXIII, 258. From *Illustrated London News*, January 29, 1924.

peace, with all their conferences and courts of arbitration, and donations and plutocratic pomposity." Chesterton remains as relevant today as in 1910.

I NEVER can quite understand why it is that when the newspapers mention Christmas and its lessons they begin to talk at once about international disarmament. **It is certainly a Christmas ideal that unjust wars should cease; but not more than unjust Governments, or unjust trades, or unjust law-suits, or any of the numberless other ways in which men torture or betray their kind.** The usual and popular translation of the song of the angels is "Peace on earth: goodwill among men." Apart from the accuracy, it might be worth while to point out that the two are very different things. Peace on earth might mean something quite different from goodwill among men. Peace on earth might mean a still panic, lying flat before a universal tyrant. Peace on earth might mean every man hating his neighbour, but fearing his neighbour just one shade more than he hated him. "They make a solitude and call it peace." So said the old Roman satirist; but the silence of which he spoke was at least a dead silence.[84] How if we make a living silence—a silence of mute millions or slaves? And how if we call that peace?

This, of course, leads me to the case of Mr. Carnegie.[85] **I have put up, as best I might, with millionaires of my time when they decreed war, sudden and sensational war, as everyone admitted; mean and immoral war, as I believed. I have got used to millionaires when they dictate war. But if they begin to dictate peace I positively rebel.**

Mr. Carnegie ought to know as well as anyone else how curious quarrels can arise in this human family of ours. Mr. Carnegie, to say the least of it, is scarcely a Christmas person. If he came down the chimney (carrying a free library) it would hardly console the children for the absence of Santa Claus carrying a bag of toys. I can scarcely conceive any personality, in fact or fiction, who would fit in less with Christmas than this mechanical millionaire, with the head of metal and the theories of clockwork; a cold complication of the Yank and Scot. He typifies machinery, and like most machinery, he goes wrong at times.

84. The Roman historian Cornelius Tacitus (*c.* 56–*c.* 117 AD) ascribes these words to a leader in ancient Briton. To us who dwell on the uttermost confines of the earth and of freedom, this remote sanctuary of Britain's glory has up to this time been a defence. Now, however, the furthest limits of Britain are thrown open, and the unknown always passes for the marvellous. But there are no tribes beyond us, nothing indeed but waves and rocks, and the yet more terrible Romans, from whose oppression escape is vainly sought by obedience and submission. Robbers of the world, having by their universal plunder exhausted the land, they rifle the deep. If the enemy be rich, they are rapacious; if he be poor, they lust for dominion; neither the east nor the west has been able to satisfy them. Alone among men they covet with equal eagerness poverty and riches. To robbery, slaughter, plunder, they give the lying name of empire; they make a solitude and call it peace. [*The Life of Julius Agricola* (98 AD).]

85. Andrew Carnegie (1835–1919) made a vast fortune in steel and spent the last years of his life building libraries and other charitable works. This later champion of peace began accumulating wealth through business contacts and investments made during the U.S. Civil War. Suspicion surrounds his convenient absence in Scotland, while those he employed dealt brutally with the 1892 Homestead Strike, one of the most notorious in U.S. history, and one in which seven workers were killed. As Chesterton suggests in the next paragraph, an industrialist who can't settle disputes with his own workers without violence is unlikely to know how to prevent wars.

One vital mistake is made about this matter by Mr. Carnegie and his kind. They persistently say, and they actually seem to think, that wars arise out of hatred. There may have been wars that arose out of hatred, but at this instant I cannot recollect a single one. In this, as in many other matters, the truest tale in the world is the *Iliad* or Siege of Troy. Wars never begin in hatred; they either arise out of the honourable affection a man has for his own possessions; or else out of the black and furtive affection he has for someone else's possessions. But it is always affection; it is never hate. The Greeks and Trojans did not hate each other in the least: there is scarcely one spark of hatred in the whole of the *Iliad,* save that great flare that comes out of the hero's love for Patroclus. The two armies are strewing the plain with corpses and dyeing the very sea with blood from love and not from detestation. It all arises because Paris has conceived an evil affection for Helen, while Menelaus cannot cease to love her. In other words, both hosts are fighting, not because fighting is not nasty, but because they have something nice to fight about.

That will be found to be the feeling of all real soldiers everywhere. "The distant Trojans never injured me." **A real soldier does not fight because he has something that he hates in front of him. He fights because he has something that he loves behind his back.** Tolstoy and other advocates of an abject submission have often urged this fact of the non-existence of hatred as an argument for the non-existence of war.[86] The little French peasant (says Tolstoy) does not really hate the little German student; why then should they fight? The answer comes with all the most high and disdainful thunders of the human soul. They fight because they love, not because they hate: the Frenchman strikes because France is beautiful, not because a German happens to be ugly. The German strikes because Germany must be loved, not because France cannot be loved. And until the advocates of peace have understood and allowed for this affectional root of military energy, all their words will be wind and waste. A man loves a certain tree; and twenty men propose to cut down that tree. He may kill the twenty men, and that may be very tragic; but he does not hate the twenty men: he loves the tree. If one may love a tree one may love a forest; if a forest, one may love a valley; if a valley, a whole country or a whole character of civilisation. One may love it rightly, like Menelaus, or wrongly, like Paris. But it is always desire and not repugnance. Whatever beautiful affections or base appetites inspired the Boer War, it was not inspired by primary dislike or disgust. I do not suppose that there was one real case of Briton or Boer hating each other in the whole course of the affair. And the peace propagandist has got seriously to face the question of these special attachments. We will remove from the discussion all the ugly affections, all the evil loves that are largely the making of the conflicts of mankind. We will suppose that we are speaking only of the chivalrous or the domestic attachments that make up much of the slender dignity of man. And still the question remains for the peace propagandist to answer. Does he mean that the British soldier ought not to love his colours? Does he mean that the Boer farmer ought not to love his farm?

86. Chesterton discussed Tolstoy in the September 19, 1908 issue of the *Illustrated London News* (Ch. 1).

There seems, indeed, to be a strange forgetfulness among writers and thinkers of the actual sentiments of the mass of men in these matters. They do not understand how positive and virile are men's loves. I saw in the *Nation* the other day an article called "The Grey Novel," which was devoted to praising (doubtlessly most justly) a novel by Mr. Arnold Bennett.[87] But I do not deal here with the novelist, but with the critic. In Mr. Bennett's story, it appears, there is a description of Paris during the siege of 1870; and the reviewer says admiringly that Mr. Arnold Bennett treats the situation economically, as it appeared to the small tradesman, without any glory or tragedy.

Now in the name of the Seven Champions of Christendom,[88] who is this reviewer that he should say that "small tradesmen" felt no glory or tragedy in the defence or desolation of France? If he had said so to the small tradesmen themselves during the siege, they would have torn him to pieces. Surely the reviewer is "realist" enough to appreciate such a reality as that. Surely it is perfectly plain that it is precisely the ordinary man, the little clerk or shopkeeper, who does feel the patriotic sentiment on the verge of Jingoism. **It does not require wealth or culture to love one's country: on the contrary, one has to be in rather an advanced and alarming stage of wealth and culture to avoid loving one's country.** If there were any people in Paris during the siege who felt no glory or tragedy (which I very gravely doubt) they are much more likely to have been polished and ingenious politicians or Rationalist professors at the Sorbonne, than "small tradesmen" or men of the people. And it is exactly because this class has, in the modern world, been so strangely cut off from the collective sympathies and loyalties of the race that they can do nothing whatever for the cause of peace, with all their conferences and courts of arbitration, and donations and plutocratic pomposity. You cannot make men enthusiastic for the mere negative idea of peace; it is not an inspiring thing. You might make them enthusiastic for some positive bond or quality that bound them to others and made their enemies their friends. You may get Tommy to love Jimmy; you cannot get Tommy to love the mere fact that he is not quarrelling with Jimmy. So it would be far easier to make an Englishman love Germany than to make him love peace with Germany. Germany is a lovable thing; peace is not.[89] Germany is a positive thing; one can like its beer, admire its music, love its children, with their charming elf-tales

87. Arnold Bennett (1867–1931), a popular British novelist, described how he got that portion of the novel in his 1908 *The Old Wives' Tale*. Realizing that it was set during the 1870 Siege of Paris and not wanting to take the time to do proper research, he got an elderly Parisian couple to tell him their experiences, noting in his preface: "The Siege of Paris had been only one incident among many in their lives. Of course, they remembered it well, though not vividly, and I gained much information from them. But the most useful thing which I gained from them was the perception, startling at first, that ordinary people went on living very ordinary lives in Paris during the siege, and that to the vast mass of the population the siege was not the dramatic, spectacular, thrilling, ecstatic affair that is described in history." To keep his literary output high and lucrative, Bennett found it convenient to universalize the long-ago recollection of a single couple to that of all "ordinary people." During the Siege of Paris, ordinary people were forced to eat rats, so it's unlikely that Parisians, whatever their patriotism, regarded it as "very ordinary." It's also easy to suspect that he selected his source to fit his prejudices.

88. St. George, the Apostle Andrew, St. Patrick, St. Denis, St. James Boanerges, St. Anthony the Lesser, and St. David, the patron-saints of England, Scotland, Ireland, France, Spain, Italy, and Wales respectively.

89. Chesterton mentioned this idea earlier in the *Illustrated London News*, March 27, 1909 (Ch. 1).

and elf-customs, appreciate the beaming ceremony of its manners, and even (with a brave effort), tolerate the sound of its language. But in the mere image of a still and weaponless Europe there is nothing that men will ever love, either as they can love another country or as they can love their own.

G.K. Chesterton, "Our Note-Book," *Illustrated London News* 137 (December 31, 1910), 1024. US: January 14, 1911. Also published as "Christmas and Disarmament."

More Sacred than Nations

January 14, 1911

But hatred is created by the collision; hatred does not create it. Love creates it—some kind of affection or desire, good or bad, base or noble.

Editor: Even with a topic as grim as war, Chesterton knew how to be humorous and practical. Both this article and the previous one bring to mind Israeli Prime Minister Golda Meir's observation that peace would come to Israel when Arabs learn to love their children more than they hate Jews.

One awkward thing in journalism (such as I am now reluctantly composing) is that the title, the thing that the reader reads first, is generally the thing that the writer writes last. It does not, indeed, apply to this page with its fixed headline; but in journalism as a whole it is really a source of error. The title is taken as a highly symbolic crest, when it is really only a rather sprawling and towering sort of tail-piece. And the words that are good for the top of the column are by no means, as a general rule, good for the beginning of an argument. Hence we have a class of headlines that are not so much the head of the matter as the somewhat serpentine termination of it. Hurriedly glancing across a newspaper yesterday, I saw the following words in large letters on top of a paragraph, "No Donkeys' Bones in Bread." I had not time to see what it meant. But as it stood, I found the assurance satisfactory, but scarcely (to my simplicity) surprising. I had never anticipated the peril that was here dispelled and calmed. If ever it were my duty (through some train of adventures which I have difficulty in thinking out) to disintern the skeleton of a donkey, it would not have occurred to me to look for it in a row of penny loaves. My ingenious opponents will doubtlessly remark that whenever I eat bread I insert into it the jaw-bone of an ass: but my jaw-bone would be astonished and even hurt if it encountered any other parts of a similar animal. Now I have no doubt that this (to me) incomprehensible headline was followed by a quite comprehensible, possibly a lucid and eloquent paragraph. The paragraph doubtless would have explained first why people thought there were donkeys' bones in bread, before it went on to the great glad news that there are none. But it shows very typically how in journalism the first sentence is really the last one, and all the paragraphs are printed upside down.[90]

90. The bones, worthless otherwise, may have been ground up and used in bread as a cheap filler.

I have got into considerable trouble with some correspondents because I tried a week or two ago to point out that, in the matter of war and peace, we suffer from this habit of beginning at the beginning of the paragraph and not at the beginning of the question. That is, we start with a phrase and not with a thought; we talk about "The Peace Propaganda" or "The War Fever," and do not see that all these journalistic phases are quite late products of the real philosophic conflict, which has been going on for thousands of years. To talk thus is not to begin at the beginning, but to begin at the end—merely because the end lies nearest.

What I pointed out was this, that to refer wars to hatred was to be content with a secondary cause instead of a primary one. No doubt, if a British army marched through Berlin, a German would have a certain tendency to hate me; and I am quite certain that, if a German flag were hoisted on the Nelson column, I should have a strong disposition to hate the German. But hatred is created by the collision; hatred does not create it. Love creates it—some kind of affection or desire, good or bad, base or noble. I particularly explained that wars were produced by positive appetites, which are much viler than mere enmity; by lust for money, or by that final stamp of a coward, the lust for power over others. I only say it begins in these affirmative desires, good or bad. War breaks out between two tribes when one tribe finds gold in a mountain which another tribe worships as sacred. The second affection is as soaring as heaven; the first affection is as flat as hell. But they are both affections; they are not repulsions or natural dislikes. The heroes are above hatred, the financiers are below it.

Sometimes, though not very often, for the risk of great wars is too heavy, another positive affection enters—the affection for fighting itself.[91] This, again, has nothing to do with mere hatred; but it is so forgotten in our stagnant cities that when it does appear it cannot be comprehended. I saw in a very well-written weekly paper an article on the armed disturbance in the East End, called "The Fascination of Horror." It explained the presence of great crowds in a crowded district, where men were risking their lives right and left, by some curious psychological theory that there is an attraction in what is ugly and sordid. The simple answer seems to me to be that one man fighting a hundred, even if he be a blackguard, is not ugly and sordid. It was not the fascination of horror—if anyone understands what that is. **It was the fascination of fighting, which every man understands whose back has not been broken in slavery. This positive pleasure in seeing defiance and daring I am willing to add to the list of the positive pleasures that may provoke war.** But this alone provokes it very seldom, as I have said, because this is at bottom a sort of heroic joke; and modern war is neither a joke nor, as a rule, particularly heroic. Broadly speaking, wars do not happen in the modern world except through very strong lawless desires and very strong lawful affections.

91. Confederate General Robert E. Lee (1807–1870) expressed this sentiment in 1862 when he told General James Longstreet (1821–1904) that "It is well that war is so terrible—otherwise we should grow too fond of it."

Now the point I wished to put to the admirable peace propagandist is this—that since these conflicts arise from real desires, good or bad, there are only two ways in which they can be permanently overcome. One is to say that people shall not have these particular attachments to an island or a valley, to a costume or a creed. The other is to say that they shall have them, but shall also have some other very vivid and almost concrete attachment that can cover and control them all, as the worship of a particular god, or the crusade against a common enemy, or the admission of a common code of conscience. I say to the peace propagandist, "Either an Irishman must love Ireland, or you must invent something that he can love more than Ireland. I shall be interested to see you try." But certainly it is utterly useless to talk about peace and the mere absence of hatred. It is useless to introduce German editors to English editors and ask them not to hate each other. They don't hate each other. The life of an editor leaves little place for such powerful emotions. But in some foggy way the English editor does love England; and in his own blinking style the German editor does love Germany. Neither of them knows at what moment all that they like most may be menaced by something that they don't in the least understand. The one remedy is to remove the affections: let the Englishman no longer like heavy breakfasts, rambling roads, irregular villages, personal liberty. Let the German no longer like long serious meals, long glasses of light beer, elaborate birthday formalities, and the habit of sitting quite still with a radiant face. The other method is that they should hold some other definite thing more sacred even than these. I can see no third method.

I have written this article by way of reply to numberless correspondents who seem to imagine that I revel in human carnage and drink hot blood. I wish to point out that, so far from being opposed to peace, I have taken the pains to think out the only two possible ways in which it could be achieved. One is by the Buddhist expedient of the elimination of all desires.[92] The other, I think, is by the Christian expedient of a common religion.

G.K. Chesterton, "Our Note-Book," *Illustrated London News* (January 14, 1911), 44. US: January 28, 1911. Also published as "The Causes of War."

Excuses with Distant Parallels

October 21, 1911

The truth is that since the Roman Empire became Christian, at any rate, if not for a long time before that, the idea that mere success in conquest constituted true authority has been inconceivable to Europeans.

92. An example is John Lennon's song, "Imagine," which was influenced by Buddhist beliefs. It includes the lines: "Imagine there's no Heaven/ It's easy if you try.... Imagine there's no countries/ It isn't hard to do/ Nothing to kill or die for/ And no religion too/ Imagine all the people/ Living life in peace/ Imagine no possessions/ I wonder if you can." Notice the intense double standard. The Beetles, John Lennon included, grew rich from their intellectual property, fiercely protecting their copyrights and trademarks. Why shouldn't ordinary people, on a far more modest scale, be able to keep their property, religion, and native lands?

EDITOR: This article is especially relevant today. In it, Chesterton first debunks a moral equivalence that equates a cruel loan shark with an elderly woman with a modest investment. He then turns to the collapsing Turkish empire with a warning that applies as well to today's militant Islam. The Roman Empire, he said, could learn from a conquered Greece, but an aggressive Islam is "a master who cannot learn from his slave." "[I]n its rigid division between friends and foes, in its refusal to tolerate or to mix," lies an inability to assimilate and become natives in a new land.

THERE are certain people who are always using distant things that we don't understand in order to confuse much closer things that we do understand. Those direct acts of evil which in healthy communities call forth a blow in the face, with us often call forth some elaborate excuse founded on some far and fantastic parallel. If I object to some vulturous old usurer who has grown fat on the toil and panic of the poor, there will always be an academic Socialist who will explain that nothing can be done till we have abolished interest itself; and that therefore any old lady who has a few pounds in a railway company is just the same sort of person as the usurer. If I express regret that a castle from which a continuous family had gone forth to Ascalon, to Flodden, and to Naseby[93] should be bought by the keeper of a rather disreputable fried-fish shop, there is always a historical student who will say that the old family also were upstarts once, and supplanted some other family about eight hundred years ago. If I say that one nation should not use mere force against another nation without cause, there will always be some aged evolutionary ass who will say that "if it comes to that" (as he loves to put it) there was some doubt about the legality of Hengist and Horsa,[94] and that there might be a law-suit about Scotland between the Picts and Scots. **All these remote parallels are fallacious for a perfectly simple reason. We do see the definite harm done by the usurer; we do not see such definite harm done by the old lady, even if it exists.** We do know that the change which drives out the genuine Squire before the false one is a change for the worse; we do not know whether the change that put in the genuine Squire was a change for the worse or not. We do know when a man is thieving before our eyes; we do not know whether Hengist ever really thieved, because we do not know whether he ever really existed.

Perhaps the strongest case of this is in our current discussions about the Turks. I do not mean the Young Turks; they would be a subject for a far gayer and lighter article than this. I mean the Old Turks. I mean the only Turks whom anyone with a historical sense can take seriously: the real Turks, who had the only two things worth having in this world, faith and the fighting spirit. Now just as there are some who will admit an ape to a family party, just as there are some who will raid because Hengist raided, so there are some who will say that Turks have as much right in

93. Chesterton's examples span almost 500 years. The Siege of Ascalon (1153) led to the capture of the greatest Egyptian frontier fortress by Crusaders. In the Battle of Flodden (1513), the English defeated an invading Scottish army. The Battle of Naseby (1645) was the most important battle in the English Civil War.

94. Hengest and Hengist were brothers in legends that claim their victory over the Picts led to a large wave of immigration to England from Germanic Europe, taking over Pict land.

Tripoli as Englishmen in England. The point is perfectly simple. There may have been raids in Essex and Suffolk, but nobody would suppose so from the look of them. A more unpromising place for a massacre could hardly be imagined. But Albania is strangely different from Essex.

The truth is that since the Roman Empire became Christian, at any rate, if not for a long time before that, the idea that mere success in conquest constituted true authority has been inconceivable to Europeans. Whether we call it idealism or hypocrisy, Christian conquest has always found it necessary to profess some reason in general morality. This is true from the rudest phases of the Dark Ages to the subtlest phases of our own. Alfred makes a treaty (or, as the Anglo-Saxons call it, a Pact) with the Danes and cannot drive them further till they have broken the treaty themselves. William the Conqueror does not call himself William the Conqueror: he calls himself William the Inheritor—he claims, that is, through the promise of Edward and the oath of Harold. Edward I does not go to Scotland as a "civiliser," in the immoral modern phrase. He does not go to make Scotland his: he declares it is his already; and supports his claim to suzerainty with legal arguments very nearly as tangled, pedantic, and false as those of a first-class modern barrister. Edward III does not claim France in the name of Crecy: he claims it in the name of the highly modern notion of the political right of Woman to rule. Henry V does not claim France in the name of Agincourt: he claims it in the name of Edward III. Cromwell, though a most unpopular military despot, professes to rule by the people's will; the Whig aristocrats that expelled the Stuarts and warred on the French profess that they "have popular support"; Napoleon I does not rule by Triumph, but by Referendum; Napoleon III does not claim by the *Coup d' Etat*, but by the subsequent elections; the Prussians do not demand Alsace and Lorraine on the ground that they can demand anything, but on the ground of their Germanic origin and of a natural right to the Rhine; Italy does not ask for Tripoli on the bare ground that she wants it, but on the ground of its European origin and of a natural right to the Mediterranean.

Now, many of these pretences were hypocritical, and all may have been mistaken; but they bear witness to a fixed European morality which the greatest conquerors have at no time been able to ignore. But in the case of the Mohammedan civilisation there has been no such ethic about boundaries or just titles. A good Moslem king was one who was strict in religion, valiant in battle, just in giving judgment among his people, but not one who had the slightest objection in international matters to removing his neighbour's landmark. This is what gives a certain evident falsity to the tone of the Young Turks when they talk French rationalism about justice and truth. If Turks had ever cared a straw about justice in these matters, they would never have been in Tripoli, nor yet in Turkey.[95] It may be said that the same would apply to many European Powers that occupy the provinces of some older race. But

95. Believing that Tripoli lay within its zone of influence, on September 29, 1911, Italy had declared war on Turkey and on October 1, it defeated Turkey in a naval battle at Prevesa. By revealing the weakness of the Ottoman Empire, the Italio-Turkish War encouraged Balkan nationalism and contributed to the outbreak of World War I.

here comes in exactly the important difference. Whether the English are or are not the aborigines of England, they behave as if they were. Whether the Tuscans or Lombards are Italians or Goths, they settle down in Italy and serve it; they behave like an ancient people. Whether the wanderings of the Gauls began in France or not, they have ended there: the Gauls are at home. **But Turkish government not only originated in a raid: it is a raid. It is a raid in its ferocity, in its military machinery, in its rigid division between friends and foes, in its refusal to tolerate or to mix.** Century after century, in district after district, this ancient and extraordinary empire still breaks out again and again, behaving as only the wildest soldiers can in the sudden sacking of a town.

It is not wholly fanciful to suppose that this spirit of detached and empty domination has a religious root, and is connected with the Moslem horror of idolatry, with the featureless austerity of its art and the whole of that somewhat inhuman simplicity which prevents them having local images and special shrines. They are not fascinated and held by human landscapes; they do not fall under the spell of the country they conquer. Its moss does not grow on them; they are not taken hold upon by its ivy or its vines. In their triumphs there is never that romantic reversal and revenge of which the Roman poet speaks in the instance of Hellas. Under them, conquered Greece has never led captive her conqueror.[96] **As regards courage and moral strength and stoicism, the Turks might compare themselves with the Romans. But Rome lay upon Greece like a sponge: Turkey lay upon Greece like a stone.** The Turks never thought either of persuading the people or of preserving the monuments. There is no hope in a master who cannot learn from his slave.

It is always an arguable question whether people who have a country need condescend to have an empire.[97] I am one of those who have always tried to persuade England not to condescend to that provincial—nay, suburban—idea of imperial expansion. But upon either view it is evident that there must be great danger in people who possess an empire without ever having possessed a country. The Turkish Empire is the one perfect piece of Imperialism: that is why it is going to pieces. It is as if one saw afar off what looked like a forest: but, on coming nearer, found it was only flocks upon flocks of birds of prey, bold and vigilant and orderly and silent, but hanging in heaven without ever touching the soil.

G.K. Chesterton, "Our Note-Book," *Illustrated London News* 139 (October 21, 1911), 625.
US: November 4, 1911. Also published as "The Turks and European Morality."

96. A reference to the Roman poet Horace (65–8 BC), who wrote: "Captive Greece took captive her rude conqueror and brought the arts to Latium."

97. In *The Napoleon of Notting Hill*, Adam Wayne says: "Notting Hill is a nation. Why should it condescend to be a mere Empire?" (Bk. V, Ch. 1, "The Empire of Notting Hill.")

Doubting Informants

November 18, 1911

For the mere desire to "make a protest," which merely means to enjoy an emotion, I have no respect whatever. The only object of telling a man to do something is to get him to do it.

Editor: Well-known and widely respected, Chesterton was often asked to endorse causes. Here he explains why he rarely does so. Note his opinion of journalism's artificial excitements as seen from the inside. He also explains how to determine when we know the truth well enough to speak out. Keep in mind that, when the situation was clear, Chesterton did join others in speaking out, as he did for Belgium and Serbia during World War I. Finally, notice that his arguments against the Boer War were not based on any "denunciation" of the war taking place on the European continent. The French and Germans were as likely to be misinformed as the English.

You and I are in these days constantly being asked to sign some petition or join in some protest against some alleged scandal, generally a foreign one. I do not wish to make myself a judge for anyone else in such a matter; but in the foreign cases I, for one, always flatly refuse. My first reason for doing so is painfully simple and practical. Speaking as an ordinary European who loves his own country and admires nearly all the rest, I know for a fact that such protests always have, and always must have, exactly the opposite effect to that which they seek. If you want to make evictions sharper for Irishmen or farm-burning hotter for Boers, you could not do it more effectively than by telling the ordinary Englishman that foreigners were in league with Ireland or the Transvaal in the matter. Anyone who really does not understand such international irritation in the crisis of a conflict does not deserve to have a native land, if indeed he has one. I was opposed to the South African War, and I said a great many angry things about it; but I was never such a fool as to use the argument that the Continent was placarded with denunciation of our flag and derision of our army. I was interested, not in agitations, but in Boers. **For the mere desire to "make a protest," which merely means to enjoy an emotion, I have no respect whatever. The only object of telling a man to do something is to get him to do it.** And if you tell him to do it when you know perfectly well that it will make him do the opposite, I will not only call your enthusiasm hysterical, I will take the liberty of calling it insincere.

But there is a deeper and more disquieting reason why I, for one, will not join in these periodical ramps of righteous indignation against Frenchmen or Russians or Belgians or Italians. To put the matter quite curtly, I will not abuse my neighbours till I can trust my informants. I am quite sure that, as far as the masses are concerned, the indignation is a real indignation; and I have no doubt that in many cases the wrong is a real wrong. But I am not sure by any means that the agitation is always begun with a good motive or directed towards a good end. **Unless I know this I may**

be assisting to build up, behind a screen of petitions, some tyranny or robbery much worse than that against which my signature is being used.[98]

I have seen so many of these extraordinary temporary excitements, and I have begun to recognise a process perpetually repeated. Somebody finds a sapphire-mine within a mile or two of Peking. Nothing is said about it: but a month afterwards the profligate habits of the Emperor of China's aunt are causing frightful scandal in Clapham and Streatham. A particular port in Iceland would be highly convenient to the entirely new tactics of the Navy. Our naval experts observe a proper official reticence: but the hideous secrets of the Icelandic walrus-hunting begin for the first time to leak out. Some part of the public begins to display a sympathy with Monteblanco which would be highly inconvenient to our promising anti-Monteblancan policy. Nothing is said about the policy: but the previously placid countenance of the Prince of Monteblanco begins to change before our eyes, and is slowly distorted into the visage of a demon. He is revealed as a traitor to his wife, a tyrant to his children, a curse to his country, and a reproach to mankind. Perhaps he really is all these things — many highly respectable people are. But it seems odd that we hear now only about his crimes, when we heard previously only about his respectability. In short, the process with which I have become familiar is banal enough, and is very little varied in each case. A nigger has a cocoanut, and you want the cocoanut. Well, a cocoanut is a mere trifle; there is no need to talk about a cocoanut. But a human soul, my brethren, is a serious matter; and the state of that nigger's soul is something frightful to think of. Gluttony has been his ruin, and the Simple Life is his only hope.[99] It must again be clearly pointed out that when I say that these excitements are artificial, I am not necessarily saying that they are without foundation. The Transvaal was badly governed; Cuba was badly governed; Leopold of Belgium was an old rascal; Dreyfus was, we all admit, a much wronged man. But these things would never have been urged on us with such utterly disproportionate iteration and extravagance, with such unscrupulous exaggeration, and yet more unscrupulous omission, unless there had been behind them some project or conspiracy or crusade over and above that just and normal intolerance with which we should regard all human evil, and especially our own. **Until I know the aim of that project, until I know the morality of that crusade, I will not move. I will not join the protest of the worms against the tyranny of the birds only to find that I have been made a cat's-paw for the cat.**

98. One telling example would be 'reactionary' and 'feudal' Russia, which in six years would fall into the hands of a communist regime far more repressive and murderous than any Czar.

99. In other words, to take away his cocoanut, he must be forced to live a poor and simple life. In this context, it helps to remember what Chesterton wrote about the Ku Klux Klan in 1924: "It is sufficient to say that one of its brightest ideas is to call a gentleman a Kleagle, thereby (it will be noted) achieving the triumph of assimilating the word "eagle" to the alliterative diction of the Klan. The thought of being terrorized by people on that intellectual level suggests a nightmare of falling into the hands of cheerful chimpanzees. There is something quite subhuman about such stupidity as that." *The Collected Works of G.K. Chesterton*, vol. XXXIII, Lawrence J. Clipper, ed. (San Francisco: Ignatius Press, 1990), 404. From the September 13, 1924 *Illustrated London News*.

To this it will quite honestly be answered, "But can the common citizen, then, have no views on foreign policy?" This is a reasonable objection, and there are two answers to it. First, of course, my objection only holds while we are ridden, saddled, and bridled (or rather, gagged) by a small circle of publicists, who can tell the public all that will excite it, without really telling it why it is being excited. If we could destroy that ring, then we could trust our broad impression of public utterances as we trust our broad impression of local gossip. But there are only one or two passes in the mountain up which news can come now. And I will not make war until I trust the sentinels.

The other answer is this. There is one way in which we can test the sincerity of such revelations. By one sign you can really detect the sham agitation: by the sign of its sudden, silent, and utter disappearance. We exchange compliments and form coalition governments with the Boers: they are the same Boers whose filthy habits and horrid cruelty sent us chivalrously to the relief of the women in the Gold Reef City; the men who broke engagements, betrayed garrisons, and flogged ambassadors. Nobody mentions, or dreams of mentioning, those charges now. We have been in consultation, almost in alliance, with the French military system, ruled by the same French officers, those fiends who, in order to hound one unhappy Jew to shame, put broken glass in Picquart's omelette and pistol-bullets in Labori's back. No one mentioned these things through the whole of the *Entente Cordiale*.[100] That is the test of the mechanical agitation. Like all mechanical things, and unlike all living things, it can stop dead. You cannot pull a horse up as quickly as a motor.

That is why I am still so old-fashioned a Radical as to believe in the old Gladstone tradition against the Turk in Europe: for the tyranny of the Turks, though doubtless exaggerated and misreported like most other things that men have reason to hate, does not end abruptly in this way. It does not end at all. It crops up again and again, when it is not wanted for a crusade, when it is not convenient to a politician. It might be maintained that the Bulgarian Atrocities were convenient to Mr. Gladstone.[101] Nobody will maintain that the Armenian Atrocities were convenient to Lord Rosebery.[102] Nobody will maintain that the recent Albanian Atrocities were convenient

100. Georges Picquart (1854-1914) was the French intelligence officer who discovered that someone else had written the document used to falsely accuse the (Jewish) Captain Alfred Dreyfus of treason. He was falsely prosecuted himself, but eventually exonerated at the same time (1906) as Dreyfus. Fernand Labori (1860-1917) was the attorney who defended Dreyfus. During the second Dreyfus trial he was shot by someone who was never captured. The 1904 *Entente Cordiale* was the first in a series of agreements between England and France. While not a formal mutual defense treaty, those agreements were one reason England entered the WWI on France's side. Chesterton's point is that, when it suits certain powerful interests, ugly matters such as the Dreyfus Affair aren't allow to surface. Scandals and outrages are suppressed or manufactured to suit hidden agendas.

101. In spring of 1876, Bulgarian rebelled against Ottoman rule and the harsh taxes imposed on non-Muslims. The Ottoman response was swift and brutal, but the destruction of some 80 villages and the murder of their inhabitants led to an outcry across Europe and to Bulgarian independence two years later. William Gladstone (1809–1898) had just completed his first period as Prime Minister when they occurred. In 1876, he published a pamphlet, *Bulgarian Horrors and the Questions of the East,* attacking the Disraeli government for doing nothing about what happened. The "convenient" controversy that followed helped him return to power in 1880.

102. Chesterton is referring to the Armenian Massacres of 1894-1897, which preceded the even more murderous ones during World War I. Lord Rosebery (1847–1929) was Prime Minister in 1895–1895 and was so unsuccessful in office, he couldn't have relished yet another problem.

to anybody: except, perhaps, to the friends of Abdul Hamid, a company which must be small and select.[103] That is the only test for us now; correct observation of the things that recur and the things that do not. We must be content with history; we cannot trust current report.[104]

G.K. Chesterton, "Our Note-Book," *Illustrated London News* 139 (November 18, 1911), 812. US: December 2, 1911. Also published as "The Common Citizen and Foreign Policy."

Observing the Military

September 14, 1912

Man is not a fighting animal: otherwise he would not want flags and music and codes of honour to help him to fight. Man must be defined most subtly: he is a running-away animal—who does not run away.

Editor: In the summer of 1912, Chesterton received an invitation to watch military maneuvers on the sparsely populated Salisbury Plain in central-south England, where the British army trained its soldiers. Here's what he observed. Notice his openly professed ignorance of military tactics. During the war, Chesterton recognized that limitation and would write little about Britain's often clumsy (or worse) military tactics. Perhaps one reason Chesterton is so often right is because he refuses to write on topics he knows little about.

I am writing this week not only about a subject I do not understand, but because I do not understand it. It will be vain to bombard me with the corrections of the expert; for I avowedly offer only the corrections of the ignoramus. It is because I am ignorant that I am trustworthy: it is because I am ignorant that I am telling the truth; indeed, one has to be a very ignorant journalist to do that. I have always been haunted with a feeling that riots, festivals, football matches, fires, shipwrecks, would really leave quite a different impression on a fresh mind from that conveyed by the stale reporter of them. I will take as a case the actual glimpse I have just had of the Manoeuvres on Salisbury Plain.

I wish to insist that for my purpose here I should be useless if I were not ignorant. Defile the darkness of my ignorance with so much as one gleam of rational knowledge of the subject, and my description would be useless. For I speak only of the actual impression of soldiers in action as it is felt by an outsider seeing them for the first time. Under such conditions, even a mistake may be a truth; the mistake made by a raw observer may be the same as would be made by a raw recruit. The science of war is not, indeed, in this sense peculiar: the number of things I do not

103. The "Albanian Atrocities" may refer to harsh measures the Young Turks took against a 1910 rebellion in Albania, after they had forced Sultan Abdülhamid II (1842–1918) from power in 1909.

104. Chesterton makes a brilliant point here. Issues that resurface year after year are unlikely to have been manufactured for a covert, transitory agenda. He mentions the Turkish atrocities. Others include the Nazi persecution of Jews, Soviet behavior during the Cold War, and today's war on terrorism, which is the continuation of a long struggle stretching back to seventh-century Arabia. In each, there is a genuine evil to be opposed. Only those who want to *suppress* our awareness of those enduring evils have a hidden and unpleasant agenda.

know would astound the world. Whenever I write to the effect that great masses of people in London look as if they had had no breakfast, I am quite kindly reminded that I have not studied dietetics. If I should say that it is a little illogical to enlarge and enrich Buddhism by totally eliminating Buddha, they tell me that, after all, I have not studied the Higher Criticism.[105] If I should say that miners are of some importance, in so far as they are the only people who can mine, I should be gently but firmly reminded that, after all, geology was never my subject. If I should hint to our leaders of popular education that parents are often necessary to the production of children, they will ask me how long I have been studying the special problems of the slums. I am well used, therefore, to the reproach of ignorance; but in this case it does not really affect the question, or rather, it affects it the other way. I am not here concerned with what experts know or even with what men experience, but solely with the extraordinary difference between a direct vision of something one has never seen before, and all the wild and false impressions created by magazines and newspapers in the minds of outsiders like myself. I have read the Military Expert in most newspapers, and my general impression was that if he was an Expert (which I sometimes doubted) his main object was to prevent anybody else being an Expert too. Instead of trying to explain technical terms in simple terms, he seemed to begin with whatever phrases his reader could not possibly understand. Apart from the Expert, I have read a fair number of articles written by journalists about soldiers. I do not profess to understand the soldiers. But I am afraid I am beginning to understand the journalists.

There is no space to describe what such operations are like; perhaps I may attempt such a description some other time. I will merely point out some of the things that such operations are not like, though more than half our ephemeral literature has taught us to expect them to be so. Some three or four false notions block reality. When you see any of the following things in our light militant literature, I, as an ingenuous infant with my eyes open, implore you not to believe them.

(1) **Do not believe them when they say, as they do perpetually nowadays, that modern war is really uninteresting because the distances are so great; and men cannot even see each other.** You might as well say that chess is dull, because the castles are kept tight in two corners. That indefinite and unknown distance is true at the beginning of the sham battle: but it is the whole object of the battle to prevent its being true at the end. If things really remained like that there would have been no battle at all. When the scientific soldier (who writes in the newspapers) says that modern enemies are always at an infinite distance from each other, I shall henceforth suspect the scientific soldier of having retired from the fight at an ingloriously early stage of it. Modern war is not dull because no soldier ever sees the opposite soldier. Modern war is dull because no civilian is ever, in the ordinary way, allowed to have the faintest inkling of what it is all about. It is dull to the daily reader because it

105. Chesterton is indirectly referring to scholars, chiefly from Germany, who were saying that we know so little about what Jesus said and did, that an ordinary person might conclude they were taking Jesus out of Christianity.

makes no sense: the Military Expert sees to that with unfailing faithfulness and military vigilance. I happened to have the good fortune to see the sham fight on Salisbury Plain in the company of friends who had themselves been soldiers, and who were quite incapable of the mystery necessary to Experts. And I assure you that when some four large facts were laid down, about as simply as the four chalk lines round a tennis court, the distances did precious little to diminish the excitement. When once we knew a battalion was expected, we watched for it on the line of the land, as men clinging to a spar watch for a sail upon the last line of the sea. The dim clump, like a wood moving across the horizon, was quite as exciting then as when its members, staring and sweating in the sun, stumped past us and took the ridge in our rear. For in war, as in all real things, there is an eternal trysting-place; and all things meet at last. Men always wish to meet if they are friends; they wish to meet if they are enemies; they wish to meet even if they are soldiers at play.[106]

(2) Do not take your ideas from Grenadiers in the Park—still less from German Grenadiers in a German Park. **I think a great deal of the honourable irritation against "militarism" among my friends in town whom I know to be human and sincere, must arise from the sight of such stiff red figures marching in step.** The pacifists feel they are looking at men dressed as no sane man would dress himself and walking as no self-respecting man would walk of his own accord; and they fancy such men under a sort of spell or dehumanising hypnotism, and imagine that yet worse nightmares of slavery must be enacted in the great dark plain of Salisbury and round the sacrificial rocks of Stonehenge. Then they read in the papers that some regiment "formed" along the top of a ridge, and then "advanced" on an enemy. The image evoked in a common cockney brain like my own is that an iron phalanx went forward all interlocked, like an armoured train. What you really see is utterly different. What you see (to begin with) is literally nothing. Then you see some grey streaks in the grey-green turn suddenly into very vivacious and excitable boys, who run helter-skelter across a field, and then fall flat on their stomachs. That is the strong primary note upon which the Press never presses: I mean the perpetual impression of running; of little brown men at the double. Long after it was over, my head was full of their little racing legs, like the figures in a zoetrope or a cinematograph.[107]

(3) Do not say a sham fight is dull because there is no "blood-lust," and man is a "fighting animal."[108] **Man is not a fighting animal: otherwise he would not want flags and music and codes of honour to help him to fight. Man must be defined most subtly: he is a running-away animal—who does not run away.** Nor is the sham fight dull because there is no blood-lust or bloodshed. To begin with, the sham fight is not dull. But such dullness as there really is in it arises from the moral fact that no one knows what it is about. It lacks the high moral pleasure of fighting for justice. But it has the high intellectual pleasure of seeing how things happen; the

106. Chesterton is right. In World War I, opposing trenches would sometimes be only a hundred feet apart.

107. The zoetrope is a toy that displayed moving images. The cinematograph is a motion picture projector.

108. Chesterton criticizes pacifists using "blood-lust" in the *Illustrated London News* on October 17, 1914 (Ch. 2.)

crisis of luck or retribution; and it is truly this high intellectual pleasure that sends all those little figures shouting and singing up a hill.

(4) Do not call triumph inevitable or an army a machine. But to show the falsehood of this I should need to tell the whole story; and this is a very hurried article, written upon Salisbury Plain.

G.K. Chesterton, "Our Note-Book," *Illustrated London News* 141 (September 14, 1912), 376. US: September 14, 1912. Also published as "Thoughts on Modern Wars and Armies."

Liberalism's Lost Courage

June 21, 1913

But what Johnson meant was that, if a man can be made to tremble, he can be made to do anything—to steal or lie or kill or commit nameless wrongs.

Editor: Throughout this book, Chesterton repeatedly returns to his belief that the liberals of his day lacked courage. Although the liberalism of 1913 England isn't quite the liberalism of today, it's easy to see the parallels, particularly in his remark: "The man who ties himself to the mere pacific ideal can never be certain of preserving any other. Rather than run the risk of war, he will give up slaves to the slave-driver and peoples to the tyrant." That also describes those 'realists' who were willing to concede Eastern Europe to Soviet tyranny rather than risk nuclear war, and those who want to consign the Middle East to various dictatorships because they fear unstable oil supplies and terrorist attacks. Without courage, all other virtues soon vanish.

In Chesterton's day that loss of courage meant that, in the rising tensions that preceded World War I, some liberals wanted to tilt Britain's foreign policy in favor of the more powerful Germany rather the more democratic France. Fortunately, Germany's brutal invasion of neutral Belgium in August 1914 made that almost impossible. Most liberals did support the war, although their support dramatically weakened toward the end. When it did, Chesterton's criticism was scathing. According to him, there are at least three ways a lack of courage reveals itself.

- **Imagining a moral equivalence.** Unable to understand bravery, cowards accuse those who see a war as necessary of having evil motives. As a result, they often attack their own nation's leaders and soldiers more harshly than a genuinely evil foe. Chesterton deals with these 'blood-lust' arguments in his October 17, 1914 (Ch. 2) and November 11, 1916 (Ch. 4) articles.
- **Lacking perseverance.** Much the same character traits required for bravery against sudden danger are necessary to stick to a difficult task to the end. That failing is concealed behind claims that those who want to fight to win are "never-endians." Chesterton deals with that argument in his January 12, 1918 article (Ch. 6).
- **Unwilling to punish.** A coward's mind is filled with fears, particularly a fear of the ruthless and strong, leading to an indifference about the weak. After the war, Chesterton will repeatedly criticize those who fret about the feelings of Germany while ignoring the sufferings of smaller countries such as Belgium and Poland.

Of course, the chief reason Germany failed to learn not to make war rests with the Germans themselves. But the most important secondary reason was the unwillingness of many outside Germany to make the hard choice to force Germany to change or, after Hitler took power, to restrain German aggression. Chesterton was sensing that serious character failing in this article, written a year *before* the *First* World War.

One of the deepest and most sagacious of the conversational answers of Dr. Johnson ran, I think, something like this: "Why, Sir, strictly speaking, physical courage is not a Christian virtue. Nevertheless, a Christian man should cultivate it; for he who has lost that virtue can never be certain of preserving any other."[109] **But in our own more refined age not only is courage not called Christian, but cowardice is actually called Christianity.** Motives entirely base, selfish, materialistic and timid, are supposed to have some kind of savour of the Gospel about them so long as they lead to peace and not to war. Of course, every Christian man, if he be sane, thinks that peace is better than war; and if his horror of war is a compassion for stricken soldiers or an indignation at trampled rights, it is the sentiment of a Christian and even of a saint. But what I complain of is that this spiritual superiority is claimed by Pacifists whose motive is almost as elevated as Falstaff's when he pretended to be a corpse on the battle-field of Shrewsbury.[110] To keep the peace for money may be as wicked as to make war for money. These rhetoricians may call the merely physical case against war "an advance" in human ethics; but to me it seems not half so like advancing as it is like running away.

---

109. Chesterton's half-remembered quote combines two passages in James Boswell's *The Life of Samuel Johnson.*

> We talked of publick speaking—Johnson. "We must not estimate a man's powers by his being able, or not able to deliver his sentiments in publick. Isaac Hawkins Browne, one of the first wits of this country, got into Parliament, and never opened his mouth. For my own part, I think it is more disgraceful never to try to speak, than to try it and fail; as it is more disgraceful not to fight, than to fight and be beaten." This argument appeared to me fallacious; for if a man has not spoken, it may be said that he would have done very well it he had tried; whereas, if he has tried and failed, there is nothing to be said for him. "Why then, (I asked,) is it thought disgraceful for a man not to fight, and not disgraceful not to speak in publick?" Johnson. "Because there may be other reasons for a man's not speaking in publick than want of resolution: he may have nothing to say, (laughing.) **Whereas, Sir, you know courage is reckoned the greatest of all virtues; because, unless a man has that virtue, he has no security for preserving any other.**" ["1775: aetat.66"]

> Dr. Mayo having asked Johnson's opinion of Soame Jenyns's *View of the Internal Evidence of the Christian Religion;*—Johnson. "I think it a pretty book; not very theological indeed; and there seems to be an affectation of ease and carelessness, as if it were not suitable to his character to be very serious about the matter." Boswell. "He may have intended this to introduce his book the better among genteel people, who might be unwilling to read too grave a treatise. There is a general levity in the age. We have physicians now with bag-wigs; may we not have airy divines, at least somewhat less solemn in their appearance than they used to be?" Johnson. "Jenyns might mean as you say." Boswell. **"You should like his book, Mrs. Knowles, as it maintains, as you [Quaker] Friends do, that courage is not a Christian virtue."** ["1777: aetat.68"]

Notice that Johnson actually wrote that the Quakers and the shallow religiosity of Soam Jenyns (1704–1787), who was someone Johnson loathed, were the ones claiming that courage wasn't a virtue—rather than historic Christianity. There's also this remarkable passage from seven years later.

> We talked of a certain clergyman of extraordinary character, who by exerting his talents in writing on temporary topicks, and displaying uncommon intrepidity, had raised himself to affluence. I maintained that we ought not to be indignant at his success; for merit of every sort was entitled to reward. Johnson. "Sir, I will not allow this man to have merit. No, Sir; what he has is rather the contrary; I will, indeed, allow him courage, and on this account we so far give him credit. We have more respect for a man who robs boldly on the highway, than for a fellow who jumps out of a ditch, and knocks you down behind your back. **Courage is a quality so necessary for maintaining virtue, that it is always respected, even when it is associated with vice.**" ["1784: aetat.75"]

110. In Shakespeare's *Henry IV,* Part 1, Act 4, Scene 1. Falstaff is a comic character who never pretends to be a hero. His remarks include: "The better part of valour is discretion; in the which better part I have saved my life."

I remember that Mr. Norman Angell, though an able writer, tied himself into a most curious knot on this part of the question. He proved—or at least, attempted with no little ingenuity to prove—that war was never in the long run materially profitable, even to the victorious party; that winning a battle, in short, was as much waste of money as losing it.[111] All this part of his argument he set forth in a manner that was lucid and by no means unconvincing. Then, of course, people with a rather more spirited (and spiritual) turn of mind asked him in return: "But what am I to do if I am wronged? Is a nation never to defend its frontiers or a populace its liberty because they may be the poorer at the end of the struggle?" To this Mr. Norman Angell made a most extraordinary answer. He said, in effect, that when poor old Europe had grown pure and sweet enough to believe in his gospel of peace, she would also have risen against such little weaknesses as crushing a mob or humbling an enemy. But, unfortunately, he had just been explaining his gospel of peace; and it did not involve any purity or sweetness at all. He had proved to his own satisfaction that everyone ought to avoid war for purely selfish reasons. It obviously follows that everyone might avoid war and continue to be purely selfish. It follows even more obviously that anyone who had so acted for his own advantage would be quite free, and quite likely, to press his advantage in any other way; as in the bleeding of a defenceless debtor, the policing of an unarmed crowd, or the retention of a rich but reluctant province. He tells us to give up our swords because swords are valueless; in fact, he tells us to sell our swords and have the best of the bargain. He cannot after that talk about how generous we shall be if we give away such valuable things. He advises Tommy Atkins not to take the King's shilling; but not on the ground that it is a shilling, but on the ground that it is a bad shilling.[112] After that it is absurd to say: "To what starry heights will the soul of Atkins have soared when he is too proud and free to accept a coin that is not negotiable? After that he will surely never drink or swear, or flirt with housemaids again." If Mr. Norman Angell has proved anything, he has proved that even the worst man must abandon war. He cannot now argue that it will want the best man to do it.

But where the great sanity and yet subtlety of Dr. Johnson's remark can be found is in the effect of this wrong kind of Pacifism on all the other ideals of the people who hold it. If physical courage is not quite a Christian virtue, surely physical cowardice is not a Christian virtue. Christianity would have been at a considerable disadvantage in the reign of Diocletian if it had been.[113] But what Johnson meant was that, if a man can be made to tremble, he can be made to do anything—to steal or lie or kill or commit nameless wrongs. And, in a milder and more philosophic style, it is the same with the wrong kind of peacemakers. **The man who ties himself to the mere pacific ideal can never be certain of preserving any other. Rather than run the risk of war, he will give up slaves to the slave-driver and peoples to the tyrant.** And

111. Chesterton is referring the Angell's *The Great Illusion: A Study of the Relation of Military Power to National Advantage*, which was republished, revised and enlarged, numerous times. For an excerpt, see Appendix C.

112. Tommy Atkins is the traditional name for an English soldier.

113. The Diocletian Persecution (303–304) was the last and most brutal that Christians would face from Rome.

this is, I am sorry to say, rather conspicuously the case with the organs of that body of political opinion with which I should still, in the matter of general ideal, associate myself. It is a serious thing to say, and I say it very seriously, but I believe that if Byron fought for Greece to-day, English Liberalism would back up Turkey against Byron; that if Garibaldi defied Austria to-day, English Liberalism would back up Austria against Garibaldi; that if Kossuth defied Austria, English Liberalism would back up Austria against Kossuth; that if Kosciuszko defied Russia, English Liberalism would support Russia against Poland; that every one of the heroes of Liberalism would be now regarded simply as an enemy of peace.[114] **In other words, this one appetite for peace (which is, if the motive be right, a holy and sacred appetite) has eaten up all the other appetites of the political idealist—the appetite for liberty, the appetite for nationality, the appetite for self-government, the hunger for justice, the thirst for religion.** All these are to be sacrificed because a few prosperous people choose to invent an entirely new Christian virtue out of the natural human distaste for being spiked with long bits of steel or peppered with small bits of lead. Take the most obvious example. Any man must be a madman, or worse still, a mere journalist, who encourages the chances of a war with Germany. In so far as Liberals seek to avoid such a catastrophe, they are not only Liberals, but patriots. But I have noticed in their papers of late a positive disposition to praise Prussia; and to praise it at the expense of France. Liberal journals urge, not only how nice the Prussians are, but even how nasty the French are. Now I say that any European Liberal who is on the side of the Prussians against Paris is on the side of the armies of Xerxes against Athens.[115] I can respect any enthusiast who is trying to put the peace of God upon Europe; though the peace of God passeth all understanding; and especially his understanding.[116] But this is not the peace of God, but the Peace of Vienna.[117]

It was not astonishing that Montenegro, which was so small and did so much, should be coerced by Austria, which is so large and which did nothing at all.[118] That is the ordinary absurdity of modern Europe, in which the first mark of a great Power is its impotence. But it was remarkable that all that part of the English Press which

114. Lord Byron (1788–1824) championed Greek independence from the Ottoman Empire. Giuseppe Garibaldi (1807–1882) helped to free Italy from Austrian domination. Lajos Kossuth (1802–1894) fought for Hungarian freedom. Tadeusz Kościuszko (1746–1817) led the 1794 Polish and Lithuanian revolt against the Russian Empire.

115. After years of planning, the Persian emperor Xerxes the Great (reigned 485–465 BC) invaded Greece in 480 BC. A series of battles on land and at sea weakened his strength, and he was forced to withdraw. The war is best known for the Battle of Thermopylae, in which 300 Spartan soldiers, assisted by other Greeks, halted a far larger Persian force for seven days, fighting to the death so Greece and Sparta might remain free.

116. Philippians 4:7. The verse before tells believers to "be anxious for nothing," which is an appeal to courage, and the following verse tells them to turn their minds to what is true, honorable and right, an attitude that would not allow evil to be overlooked or tyrants left unopposed. Courage is a Christian virtue closely linked to faith.

117. The Congress of Vienna (1814–1815) placed Europe under five Great Powers (United Kingdom, Austria-Hungary, Prussia, France, and Russia), who crushed desires for self-rule and restricted dissent, buying peace at the price of liberty. That's what Chesterton means by the "appetite for peace" eating up the other human desires. The resulting unfulfilled "appetite for nationality" in the Balkans and Austria's attempt to maintain its Great Power status would be the sparks that ignite WWI. Chesterton writes this a year before the war.

118. In 1912–1913, Montenegro, Greece, Serbia, and Bulgaria rebelled against the Ottoman Empire, fighting the Balkan Wars and winning their independence. Before WWI, the little country was pressured by the much larger Austria-Hungary and during the war it was occupied by Austro-Hungarian troops.

was supposed to stand for liberty and small nations should have been on the side of inactive Austria and against active Montenegro. **But the Liberal philosophy has lost its respect for personal courage; and he who has lost this virtue can never be certain of preserving any other.**

G.K. Chesterton, "Our Note-Book," *Illustrated London News* (June 21, 1913), 920.
US: June 21, 1913. Also published as "Courage and the Liberals."

MILITARISM AND CHILDREN

July 26, 1913

Very young people ought to be grounded in primary and necessary morality. Now it is not a part of primary and necessary morality that it is always wrong to hit a man.

EDITOR: Chesterton appears to be defending "militarism," but he's actually standing up for children whose minds are not developed enough to understand what distinguishes a good soldier from an evil militarist. An army that defends a country from invasion is good. One that seats Caesar on the throne is not. This article builds on what he said about children in his October 6, 1906 article (Ch. 1). Today, it's easy to suspect that some modern educators, like Ferrer before them, don't understand that children should be taught only "primary and necessary morality," leaving more complex topics like war until they are older and better able to understand abstractions. It's also true that some adults never grow beyond the "primary" morality of a child.

What he says about "false universalism" explains why well-meaning people often adopt silly or evil causes. They split the world into "progressive" and "reactionary" camps. A "progressive" about one idea is expected to be "progressive" about others, with harsh policing used to keep all "progressives" thinking alike.

THE crank, to whom I made some references last week, has another characteristic which leads us to another subject — for, indeed, he only has it when he is the nicest sort of crank, and the nicest sort of crank is rare. And the difficulty about him is not that he differs from everybody else, but that he cannot believe that anybody else differs from him. He thinks things are self-evident which are really in the last degree questionable; and he thinks opinions are universal which the mass of mankind has never heard of. He labours under the fixed idea that you and I do not know what our own opinions are, and he kindly explains them to us. He says, "As a Christian, you must admit that all armaments are in theory immoral"; and if I answer that neither Christianity nor my modest self admits anything of the kind, he says it is a paradox. He says, "As a Socialist, of course you would be in favour of divorce reform"; and if I tell him in all simplicity that I am not a Socialist, and if I were I need not be in the least in favour of divorce reform, he entertains some extraordinary notion that I am pulling his leg. Whereas I have no desire of the kind — except, perhaps, a faint desire to pull his nose for being so abominably stupid.

As a rule, however, the particular kind of man I mean can by no means be called stupid, and he is almost always in good faith. The great defect of his mind is, as I say, this false universalism—this perpetual repose upon a unanimity that isn't there. For example, I read in the *Clarion* the other day an article written in an excellent spirit and with evident sincerity about Mr. Belloc and certain schemes of secular education, such as those which were associated with the name of Ferrer.[119] The writer, with a warmth of wonder that was not only genuine but plainly generous, expressed his mystification as to how any man with such sound popular sympathies and such high public ideals as the author of *The Servile State* could fail to sympathise with such just and enlightened schemes of instruction.[120] He then gave some examples of the sort of things that these secular schools teach; and it was perfectly apparent, not only that he thought they were good things, but that he was quite certain that Mr. Belloc, or I, or anybody else, would think so too. He is free to think so, and he does think so; but the fact remains that he is wrong. These things, which honestly seem to him radiant and cosmic truisms, honestly seem to me to be little, low, crabbed, provincial superstitions. For instance, the writer makes a good start by saying that Ferrer taught in his schools that militarism is a crime. He obviously implied the comment: "I suppose nobody has any fault to find with that!" Now, I say it is a crime to tell a child that militarism is a crime. It is giving the child a false conscience at the very time when the conscience is most direct and most realistic. Mr. Robert Blatchford, the Socialist Editor of the Socialist paper in which this protest appeared, happens to be an old soldier. To tell a child that militarism is a crime appears to me to be simply a wicked act, exactly as it would be wicked act to point out Mr. Blatchford to a child in the street and say: "That man has been a criminal."[121] **For a child lives in a kind of fairyland of facts; and anything you tell him will be as simple and as vivid as the man who lights the street lamps, or the man who leaves the little milk-cans, or the horse in the stable, or the cat on the hearth-rug.** If you manage to get the meaning of the word "militarism" into his head at all (which is by no means certain), he will simply take it on trust from you that all soldiers are wicked men; and that, even this anti-militarist critic would probably admit, is not self-evident.

119. Francesc Ferrer i Guàrdia (1859–1909) was a Spanish radical executed in 1909 by the Spanish government. In 1913 his book on education was translated into English as *The Origins and Ideals of the Modern School*.

120. Hillaire Belloc's *The Servile State* (critical of English capitalism) had been published the previous year (1912).

121. Chesterton explained where he agreed and disagreed with Blatchford in his 1936 autobiography. After describing the "lopsided exaggeration of Christian charity" that lay behind Blatchford's zeal to claim that 'Underdogs' could not be held responsible for their evil deeds, Chesterton went on to write: "And I awaken from all these dreams of the past suddenly, and with something like a shout of laughter. For the next episode in my life was one of helping certain friends and reformers to fix the terrible truth called Responsibility, not upon tramps or drunkards, but on the rulers of the State and the richest men in the Empire. I was trying to put a chain and collar of Responsibility, not on the Underdog, but on the Top-dog. And the next thing that I was to hear about Blatchford was that he also, bursting with indignation, was demanding justice, punishment, vengeance almost without pardon, upon other strong tyrants who had trampled on the weak; and was fiercely nailing the arrogant princes of Prussia with Responsibility for the invasion of Belgium. So do paper sophistries go up in a great fire." *The Autobiography of G.K. Chesterton* (New York: Sheed & Ward, 1936), 183–184.

For "militarism," in the sense in which the word can really be of rational use to grown-up people, is a relative word, a word referring to exaggeration and disproportion. It means that sociological state when the engine employed to defend the society against hostile societies preponderates too much in the settlement of the society's internal affairs. People in ancient Sparta suffered from militarism. People under Cromwell and his officers suffered from militarism. People who had emperors imposed on them to suit the fancy of the Pretorian Guard suffered from militarism. Prussia, under Frederick the Great, suffered from militarism; as Prussia has pretty well ever since.[122] But this is a criticism of the misuse and not the use of a power. It does not prove that the Spartans were not within their rights in dying at Thermopylae; or that Germanicus was not glorious when he called on the legions to follow the Roman birds.[123] It does not show that Prussian troops were not doing their duty either at Rosbach, or Leipsic [Leipzig], or Gravelotte.[124] It does not show that Cromwell's soldiers were not fighting for England either at Dunbar or at Dunkirk.[125]

But all these questions of over-concentration or loss of balance in morals and politics are ludicrously unfitted for educational purposes. If Ferrer really did teach that militarism was a crime, Ferrer was an extremely incompetent schoolmaster. **Very young people ought to be grounded in primary and necessary morality. Now it is not a part of primary and necessary morality that it is always wrong to hit a man.** Nor is it a part of primary and necessary morality that it becomes wrong if the hitters all stand in a row, or if they all wear the same kind of buttons. It is quite possible for an intelligent grown-up person, with the subtlety that comes from complex experience, to be very much worried about the hitting, or very much bored with the buttons. Such a person is perfectly justified, when talking to people of similar experience, in using exaggerative and even vituperative language to balance the excess that he denounces; he is perfectly justified in calling a social extravagance a crime.

I should not blame the critic in question for a moment if he were arguing with Mr. Blatchford himself about armaments, and he said: "The truth is, Blatchford, you have been a soldier yourself, and it has warped you. The iron has entered into your

122. In Greek Sparta, military training dominated all life. Oliver Cromwell (1599–1658) was a military commander who used his army to dissolve Parliament and make himself ruler of Britain. Frederick the Great (1712–1786) used his army to enlarge and strengthen Prussia, beginning (some say) the tradition of Prussian militarism.

123. Three hundred Spartan soldiers died at the Battle of Thermopylae, defending all Greece from a Persian invasion. Germanicus (15 BC–AD 19) was a brilliant and popular Roman general. Chesterton is probably referring to AD 14, when Roman legions, unhappy that Tiberius had been made emperor, wanted to march on Rome and make Germanicus their emperor. He refused, insisting they remain loyal to the Roman Eagle (*Aquila*) they bore.

124. In the Battle of Rossbach (1757), Prussia under Frederick the Great defeated France and Austria. The 1813 Battle of Leipzig was the largest in Europe before WWI and Napoleon's greatest defeat in the Napoleonic Wars. The Battle of Gravelotte (August 18, 1870) was the largest battle in the Franco-Prussian War.

125. At the Battle of Dunbar (1650) during the Third English Civil War, Oliver Cromwell's army defeated a Scottish army. In 1658, during the Anglo-Spanish War, 6,000 of Cromwell's troops helped 20,000 French troops take Dunkirk from Spain in the Battle of the Dunes.

soul; you are a militarist; and you make me feel what a crime all this militarism is."[126] That is the way that thinking people of mature years, and of all opinions, do talk to each other about the toppling compromises and terrible reactions of a complicated civilisation. **But to tell a child that militarism is a crime is merely to do one of two things; either to make him dread a shifting and shapeless bogey, or to hate a harmless grenadier.**

G.K. Chesterton, "Our Note-Book," *Illustrated London News* 143 (July 26, 1913), 128. US: July 26, 1913. Also published as "The Cranks of Secular Education."

PRUSSIAN KINGS

December 13, 1913

Now if we heard that an English King had insisted on painting frescoes in St. Paul's Cathedral, or had produced an original patriotic opera at the Savoy, or had started reviewing books for the Morning Post, we should not think that he had added to his dignity.... But the Germans have always expected their Kings to be aesthetes.

EDITOR: Chesterton was not irredeemably hostile toward Germans, as some might claim. In this article he seems to have mistaken the still-fluid situation surrounding the Zabern Affair of the previous month as an indication that Prussian militarism had suffered a secret but nevertheless fatal collapse, thanks to machinations of the Kaiser. After the war began, he would realize that evil spirit was not about to be "cast forth like a devil out of the body of the great Germania." The "old ramrod" of Prussia had not been broken.

It's important the realize that behind Chesterton's mistake lay a principle that is true in the broad sense. Healthy societies are ones that over generations have learned balance and good sense. Owen Chadwick described the process this way:

> *No man is an island*—man is a moral being because he is a social being—man is reasonable as he accompanies and learns from other reasonable beings—his life as a mere individual is solitary poor nasty brutish and short, only in his group can he be free, and thinking and civilized. This group or community is no construction of himself, nor of a moment. It is inherited, painfully built up over generations, carrying a received tradition of law or constitution or convention, a community not composed merely of the persons which then compose it, with a will which is no more than the decision of the majority in number, but with a will of its own, a 'general' will, linking past with present and present with future, the continuity of a civilized city or state.[127]

One of Germany's problems was that it was a new nation, forcibly created a half-century earlier by Prussian armies based on an aggressive ideology Otto von Bismarck called "iron and blood." It was still learning—or more accurately not learning—how to behave. Making matters worse was the bullying nature of Prussians themselves, something Bavarians liked no more the French. Europeans in that era would explain

126. For the irony of Mr. Blatchford being accused of being an evil "militarist" because of his past, see the footnote about him accompanying the Chesterton article in the August 4, 1906 *Illustrated London News* (Ch. 1).

127. Owen Chadwick, *The Secularization of the European Mind in the 19th Century* (Cambridge: Cambridge University Press, 1975), 30–31.

the problem by remarking that Germany was, "too big for Europe, too small for the world." It was big enough to threaten the peace of Europe, but too small to fulfil its global ambitions. After the Zabern Affair, Chesterton hoped Germany would learn from the experience. It did not. He would be more pessimistic after World War I.

The Zabern Affair happened when a German officer used an insulting term (*Wackes* meaning "wacky") to describe the people of Zabern, a town in Alsace that had been occupied by Germany since the Franco-Prussian War (1870–1871). Chesterton, writing here while the dispute was still unresolved, sees the Kaiser as sympathetic to the local population. Those written later tend to be more negative of the Kaiser, which isn't surprising. Germany's leader was notorious for changing policies on whims.

Odd as it may sound, Hitler partially agreed with Chesterton's assessment of how the world viewed Germany. In August of 1941 he said: "The German made himself detested everywhere in the world, because wherever he showed himself he began to play the teacher. It is not a good method of conquest. Every people has its customs, to which it clings, and nobody wants lessons from us."[128] But Hitler's answer was for Germans to continue to conquer and rule, but to remain aloft, preventing events like the Zabern Affair by letting those they ruled over "live as they like," and suppressing revolution by bombing cities.

IT has always struck me that the German Emperor is a person whose real character would repay study. I need hardly say that I shall never see him close enough to study it. But I am sure there is no truth in either of the two ordinary versions of him: the first, which represents him as a crusader permanently in the moonlight; and the second, which represents him as a mountebank permanently in the limelight. The latter version may be seen in English caricatures, the former in German statues—which are funnier than English caricatures. Certainly, he is not a crusader, as Abdul Hamid was very pleased to discover.[129] He is very modern, I should think rather nervous, but decidedly thoughtful. And like most very modern people, he is not in the moonlight, or in the limelight, but in the dark. And it happens that both the theory of the crusader and the theory of the quack have been curiously negatived by what appears to have been his personal action in yielding promptly to the protest of the Alsatian populace. The offending garrison is removed; the young man whose weakness began the trouble seems to have resigned; and when the newspapers hint that the Kaiser was throughout opposed to the extreme militarists in the matter, I, for one, have no difficulty in believing it, though it is in the newspapers. A man is not necessarily unwise because he is fond of changing his clothes; the hundred uniforms may be merely the artistic temperament. And I think the artistic temperament must have the credit of making him sensitive to a certain change that has come over the atmosphere and the destiny of his country. I do not mean that a period will be put to the greatness of Germany. That need not happen; and it would be a bad thing if it

128. Adolf Hitler, *Hitler's Secret Conversations*, (New York: Farrar, Straus and Young, 1953), 20.

129. 'Abdu'l-Hamīd II (1842–1918) was Sultan of the Ottoman Empire (Turkey) from 1876 to 1909. Germany's chief interest in the region lay in building the Bagdad Railroad, begun in 1888. It would transport German military and industrial goods to the Middle East, returning with oil. From 1903 on, the British were concerned that, the railroad would allow Germany to trade with their East African colonies unhindered by the Royal Navy.

did. But I mean that a certain element in Germany can no longer stand for Germany. The Emperor has not given up the gun; but he has broken the old ramrod.

One difficulty we have in understanding his position is that our own monarchy has been for so many centuries a political compromise, and often not a particularly English compromise. It is long since we had a quite indigenous King (and he had one shoulder higher than the other);[130] after that the Tudors were Welsh, the Stuarts were Scotch, the Hanoverians—were Hanoverians. And we do not generally realise exactly what it is that a more monarchical sort of monarch is expected to do. It might be put roughly thus: he is expected to guess right about the real state of public opinion, and not the more or less fictitious account of it which most of us get from counting votes and considering labels and hearing the resolutions of parties and groups. A man who guessed right, for instance, would say in modern England that, although twenty trades unions had passed resolutions for Female Suffrage, it is still the fact that working men do not like Suffragettes.

In this connection the very title of the potentate is in a sense symbolic. He is not called the Emperor of Germany, which might mean a mere invader and conqueror. He is not called the Emperor of the Germans, which might mean a mere elected official or formal representative. He is called the German Emperor, and the first duty of a German Emperor is to be German. And if behaving like a German sometimes strikes our temperament as bordering on behaving like a jester, we must remember that it is only our temperament, and that many of our ways would seem to a German just as wild. For instance, it is not more ridiculous that an officer in society should wear all his uniforms than that he should refuse to wear any of them. If we were not accustomed to it, a wig would make a judge quite ridiculous—except in those unfortunate cases where he is ridiculous already.

Now if we heard that an English King had insisted on painting frescoes in St. Paul's Cathedral, or had produced an original patriotic opera at the Savoy, or had started reviewing books for the *Morning Post*, we should not think that he had added to his dignity. But that is because the English tradition is that he ought to be a good sort and a good sportsman, and for the rest leave us pretty much alone. But the Germans have always expected their Kings to be aesthetes. Even the mad King of Bavaria was not so mad—for Bavaria—as he would have been for Buckingham Palace. Much of the dislike felt in English society for the Prince Consort arose from our feeling something priggish in what his countrymen would think merely princely—the patronage of art and education. It may well be that William III[131] knows better than his British critics; knows that Germans do not really *mind* a monarch being a dilettante, even if they smile at it. And I think his many-sidedness

130. This was the sickly and short-lived Edward VI (1537–1553), the son Henry VIII had so desperately sought.

131. In his reference to William III, Chesterton apparently means William (1882–1951), son of the German Emperor William II, who renounced his right to the throne at the end of World War I, never becoming Emperor.

has perhaps helped him to realise that the time has come when a certain spirit must be cast forth like a devil out of the body of the great Germania.[132]

The whole principle and power of the Prussian Junker has collapsed, just as the Krupp gun, which was its symbol in metal, has collapsed—though not, of course, so obviously or in so many places at once. The gun failed almost simultaneously under a physical test in one part of Europe and a mental test in another. The Servians spiked that gun in the East, and the Socialists spiked it in the West.[133] The collapse of the extreme Prussian theory of militarism is, of course, an inner collapse; and therefore for many a secret collapse. But I do not think it is a secret for those in the inner ring; and among these I fancy that one of the most intelligent is the Emperor himself. He will go on making the flamboyant speeches, as he went on wearing the flamboyant uniforms: it was his duty, and he did it. He may talk again at any moment about his Mailed Fist. But he will not really try to handle the situation with a Mailed Fist. A Mailed Fist makes the human hand very clumsy. **The whole of that particular Prussian fashion has been an attempt to make pride do the work of power: and it has failed.**

There is no unfriendliness to Germany, or even to Prussia, in saying this. It is a historic habit, and presumably a historic necessity, that a particular type should for a certain time stand for a nation. But the nation is always a much more living and a very much more lasting thing than the type. As far as the facts go, we might as well represent John Bull as painted blue like an Ancient Briton as represent him with the extinct agricultural costume in which he figures in all cartoons and caricatures. But even after that costume was extinct there was another type which stood for England, and which has since been shown to be anything but all England. The merchant, the man of the successful middle-classes, the employer of labour, the man who was generally a Radical and nearly always a Protestant, the great triumph of the industrial system, the great artist in scientific machinery, the founder of Free Trade, the foe of Ireland, he was for many decades the central and typical Englishman, not only in his own eyes, but in the eyes of Europe. There can be no doubt that the young Lieutenant who has apparently resigned after the Alsatian tomfoolery was the typical Prussian in his own eyes. Unfortunately, he has been the typical Prussian to Europe also. But uncomfortable things are happening to the two types. England and Germany may discover that their representatives misrepresent them.

G.K. Chesterton, "Our Note-Book," *Illustrated London News* 143 (December 13, 1913), 986. US: December 13, 1913. Also published as "The German Emperor."

132. At the end of his column in the September 12, 1914 issue of the *Illustrated London News* (Ch. 1), Chesterton would concede that spirit had not been cast forth and that Germany still needed, "a casting-out of devils."

133. Two events suggested rule by Germany's old elite, including the Junkers, was ending. "In the East" refers to the Balkan Wars (1912–1913) in which Serbia (Servia) won independence from the Ottoman Empire, Germany's ally in the east. "In the West" refers to the 1912 election, where the Social Democratic Party, popular in the industrialized Rhineland, doubled its representation in the Reichstag, becoming Germany's largest party.

2

Battling Racism

1914

1914

Racial Nonsense—Editor

Earlier we described how the great respect accorded to Europe's royalty and its traditional ruling classes could not survive the horrors of the Great War. Like nature, society abhors a vacuum. For over a century, other ideas had been struggling for supremacy. One of the most successful replaced an old aristocracy centered on the bloodline of a few with a new aristocracy built around an entire nation or, in scientific and historical terms, with the "blood" of a contrived race larger than one nation. Those ideas were particularly popular among Germans and among the well-educated classes in England and the United States. Chesterton usually called this idea "Teutonism," but others referred to this allegedly superior group as "Aryans" or "Germanic tribes." In the summer of 1935, as the menace of Nazism grew in Europe, Chesterton would describe his own early experience with the idea.

> When I was in my first, as distinct from my second childhood, people gave me little brown and green books by Mr. Edward Clodd and even Professor Max Müller; which told me the whole story about how the Aryan race came out of the high plateaux of India, and marched westward, wiping out all the lesser breeds without the law, and spreading all over Europe to be the ancestors of all really respectable European peoples. I was taught, according to the morals and metaphysics of the time, that as they were my ancestors, they must have been just like me; and as they were just like me, they must have been uncommonly fine people. There did not seem to be very much else that anyone knew about them, except that they had long golden hair, and that they said "Papa" and "Mama"; as is the case with various golden-haired dolls to this day.[1]

In the articles that follow, when Chesterton denounces Teutonism, he's attacking a form of racism once particularly popular among the well-educated and well-read—a belief that the Germans and English constitute a single, superior, pan-Germanic or Aryan race to which both should be loyal. We take up the topic again in the introduction to Chapter 5 and show that it wasn't confined to Germany and England.

1. "Our Note-Book," *Illustrated London News* 187: 1 (July 27, 1935), 154. Edward Clodd (1840–1930) was a prolific writer and a popularizer of Darwinism. Although German born and educated, Max Müller (1823–1900) became an Oxford University professor because the resources to study India (a British colony) were better in England than in Germany. He was upset by how others abused his ideas and believed studying the influence India and Vedantic religion may have made on ancient Europe would improve relations between the two peoples. Others used his writings to contrast those supposedly "Aryan" beliefs with later "Semitic" ideas brought in by Christianity and originating with the Jews—setting a nature religion in contrast to belief in a personal God. He is to be distinguished from Friedrich Müller (1834–1898), a German linguist also mentioned in this book.

Closely linked to racial supremacy were two other ideas. The first was that "might makes right," and the second was that, if a nation wants to be successful, it must be ruled by a ruthless Strong Man. Chesterton traces the German incarnation of both back to the eighteenth century and Prussia's Frederick the Great (1712–1786). The first is what he calls in a July 26, 1919 article (Ch. 7), "the cannibal theory of the commonwealth, that it can of its nature eat other commonwealths." In a December 15, 1917 article (Ch. 5), he describes how the second idea entered English thinking, contrasting the Europe of Christendom, where people who did evil knew they were evil, with the radically new point of view.

> A man broke treaties, trampled on enemies, or betrayed friends, because he was ready to be contemned; he did not expect to be respected. The notion of his being actually admired as a strong man, merely because he behaved like a selfish man, is a notion so new that I can myself remember it rising steadily, like a new religion, in the late Victorian time. I can myself recall the transition in literary fashions from the dull but decent morality of Macaulay to the picturesque but barbarous mysticism of Carlyle.

In the first chapter of his multi-volume history of WWI, Winston Churchill commented on that change in European thinking when he described how quickly Germany's atrocious behavior was adopted by their wartime foes.

> The Great War through which we have passed differed from all ancient wars in the immense power of the combatants and their fearful agencies of destruction, and from all modern wars in the utter ruthlessness with which it was fought. All the horrors of all the ages were brought together, and not only armies but whole populations were thrust into the midst of them. The mighty educated States involved conceived with reason that their very existence was at stake. Germany having let Hell loose kept well in the vain of terror; but she was followed step by step by the desperate and ultimately avenging nations she had assailed. Every outrage against humanity or international law was repaid by reprisals often on a greater scale and of longer duration. No truce or parley mitigated the strife of the armies. The wounded died between the lines: the dead mouldered into the soil. Merchant ships and neutral ships and hospital ships were sunk on the seas and all aboard left to their fate, or killed as they swam. Every effort was made to starve whole nations into submission without regard to age or sex. Cities and monuments were smashed by artillery. Bombs from the air were cast down indiscriminately. Poison gas in many forms stifled or seared the soldiers. Liquid fire was projected upon their bodies. Men fell from the air in flames, or were smothered, often slowly, in the dark recesses of the sea. The fighting strength of armies was limited only by the manhood of their countries. Europe and large parts of Asia and Africa became one vast battlefield on which after years of struggle not armies but nations broke and ran. When all was over, Torture and Cannibalism were the only two expedients that the civilised, scientific, Christian States had been able to deny themselves: and these were of doubtful utility.[2]

Chesterton and Churchill were not alone in this somber analysis of modern European history. Writing shortly after the end of WWII and looking back over some forty years and two world wars, Hannah Arendt would explain what had gone wrong with Europe in this series of remarks in her greatest work, *The Origins of Totalitarianism*.

2. Winston S. Churchill, *The World Crisis* (New York: Charles Scribner's Sons, 1923), 2-3.

If race thinking were a German invention, as it has been sometimes asserted, then "German thinking" (whatever than may be) was victorious in many parts of the spiritual world long before the Nazis started their ill-fated attempt at world conquest. Hitlerism exercised its strong international and inter-European appeal during the thirties because racism, although a state doctrine only in Germany, had been a powerful trend in public opinion everywhere....

The historical truth of the matter is that race-thinking, with its roots deep in the eighteenth century, emerged simultaneously in all Western countries during the nineteenth century. Racism has been the powerful ideology of imperialistic policies since the turn of our century....

Until the fateful days of the "scramble for Africa," race-thinking had been one of the many free opinions which, within the general framework of liberalism, argued and fought each other to win the consent of public opinion. Only a few became full-fledged ideologies, that is, systems based upon a single opinion that proved strong enough to attract and persuade a majority of people and broad enough to lead them through the various experiences and situations of the average modern life.... Few ideologies have won enough prominence to survive the hard competitive struggle of persuasion, and only two have come out on top and essentially defeated all others: the ideology which interprets history as an economic struggle of classes, and the other that interprets history as a natural fight of races....

.... As a matter of fact, the doctrine that Might is Right needed several centuries (from the seventeenth to the nineteenth) to conquer natural science and produce the "law" of the survival of the fittest....

.... Darwinism offered two important concepts: the struggle for existence with optimistic assertion of the necessary and automatic "survival of the fittest," and the indefinite possibilities which seemed to lie in the evolution of man out of animal life and which started the new "science" of eugenics.

The doctrine of the necessary survival of the fittest, with its implication that the top layers of society eventually are the "fittest," died as the conquest doctrine had died, namely, at the moment when the ruling classes in England or the English domination in colonial possessions were no longer absolutely secure, and when it became highly doubtful whether those who were the "fittest" today would still be the fittest tomorrow. **The other part of Darwinism, the genealogy of man from animal life, unfortunately survived. Eugenics promised to overcome the troublesome uncertainties of the survival doctrine according to which it was impossible either to predict who would turn out to be the fittest or to provide the means for the nations to develop everlasting fitness....** Finally, the last disciples of Darwinism in Germany decided to leave the field of scientific research altogether, to forget about the search for the missing link between man and ape, and started instead their practical efforts to change man into what the Darwinists thought an ape is....

.... Selected inheritance was believed to result in "hereditary genius," and again aristocracy was held to be the natural outcome, not of politics, but of natural selection, of pure breeding. To transform the whole nation into a natural aristocracy from which choice exemplars would develop into geniuses and supermen, was one of the many

> "ideas" produced by frustrated liberal intellectuals in their dreams of replacing the old governing classes by a new "elite" through nonpolitical means.[3]

Arendt wrote *after* the events she described. By that time, eugenics and fashionable race theories—the mad dreams of "frustrated liberal intellectuals"—had been discredited, at least as overt national policies, by the horrors of Nazism. (As covert policies they remain to this day.) But Chesterton was writing prospectively and even prophetically. He was criticizing ideas that were new as the rising sun and as intellectually fashionable among enlightened elites as legalized abortion is today. In fact, the racial theories and eugenics that he opposed were considered so progressive and scientific, that his criticisms of them earned him the label 'reactionary.' In a review of his *Eugenics and Other Evils* (1922) entitled "A Foe of Progress: G.K. Chesterton, Esq.," Dr. Marie Stopes' magazine, *Birth Control News*, had this to say about him.

> His tendency is reactionary, and as he succeeds in making most people laugh, his influence in the wrong direction is considerable. It would be much less than it is were people grounded on the basis of essential scientific truths which he so often juggles with in order to cheat them into following his arguments into the ditch or gutter.[4]

For those who have yet to study the illuminating history of the birth control movement, Marie Stopes was the British counterpart to America's Margaret Sanger, founder of Planned Parenthood. The two, while they might compete for the media limelight, shared similar views about the necessity for government to control who could have children. The full name of her organization made that clear. It was the Society for Constructive Birth Control and Racial Progress (CBC).

The month after reviewing Chesterton's book, *Birth Control News* published a letter from a C.B.S. Mildmay, calling his remarks "Practical Experience." Mildmay praised their domestic agenda, but went on to stress that race building had international implications. His distinction between "Eastern and Eastern Europe races" probably referred to Jews, considered to be of Middle Eastern origin, in contrast to Slavic 'races' such as the Polish. Keep in mind that at this time a pure racial "stock" was thought to be superior, scientifically, to a mixed or mongrelized stock.

> But one feels that unless at the same time the influx of low-caste foreigners, especially from Eastern Europe, is checked, they will fill up the gaps and mongrelize our English and Scotch stock.

---

3. Hannah Arendt, *The Origins of Totalitarianism*, (New York: Harcourt Brace Jovanovich, 1951–1973), 158–160, 178–180.

4. G. K. Chesterton, *Eugenics and Other Evils* (Seattle: Inkling Books, 2000), 163. Quoted from *Birth Control News*, 1:6 (October, 1922), 3. The following month they published a letter from Chesterton's cousin, Patrick Braybrooke (soon to be the author of *Gilbert Keith Chesterton*) that said the following:

> I do most strongly disagree with his ideas of eugenics. I do not consider he has any good knowledge of the miseries of large families on small purses. I am a member of the C.B.C., and I feel that a great part of the reason of G.K.C.'s attitude is dictated by that arrogant fraudulent Church to which he belongs. He allows his mind to be influenced by a celibate priesthood that is usually immoral, and does not marry because it prefers to be thought not of this world. ["Mr. Chesterton," *Birth Control News*, 1:7 (November, 1922) 2. Also in the Inkling edition of *Eugenics and Other Evils* on page 164.]

With stilted phrases such as "his ideas of eugenics," it's obvious Braybrooke did not share Chesterton's literary talent. Notice also how similar his attack on Chesterton's motives for opposing eugenics in the 1920s were with attacks directed at Catholics for opposing legalized abortion in the 1960s and later. The movement's core agenda and rhetoric altered little as its professed agenda changed from eugenic birth control to family planning.

Like the rats, these low-caste foreigners have large families, and are industrious workers and have strong tribal instincts, but compared with our people they are cunning, bloodthirsty and cowardly....

Very likely the Society has this race question in hand. A few strains of strong races like the French (as the Huguenots) or Scandinavians do good in a pedigrees and blend well with us, but these Eastern and Eastern Europe races are altogether inferior to ours.[5]

Three months after their attack on Chesterton's book, *Birth Control News* reviewed another book far more favorably, gushing with enthusiasm for the race building in Lothrop Stoddard's *The Revolt against Civilization: The Menace of the Underman.*

This book is written in a lively style, which makes it easy to read. Much good sense and knowledge lie behind its author's opinions, and as the problems which interest us are here considered from the point of view which even politicians must recognize as coming into their province, we hope that it will be widely read.

To encourage our readers to get the book, we will let the author speak for himself....

"If, then, society is ever to rid itself of its worse burdens, social reform must be increasingly supplemented by racial reform. Unfit individuals as well as unjust social conditions must be eliminated.

"Even those persons who carry taints which make parenthood inadvisable need not be debarred from marriage. The sole limitation would be that they should have no children. And this will be perfectly feasible because, when public opinion acquires the racial viewpoint, the present silly and vicious attitude toward birth control will be abandoned, and undesirable children will not be conceived."

The author is a whole-hearted Constructive Birth Controller:—

"Our particular job is stopping the prodigious spread of inferiority which is now going on. We may be losing our best-stocks, but we are losing them much more slowly than we are multiplying our worst. Our study of differential birth-rates showed us that if these remain unchanged our most intelligent stocks will diminish from one-third to two-thirds in the next hundred years; it also showed that our least intelligent stocks will increase from six- to ten-fold in the same time. **Obviously, it is this prodigious spawning of inferiors which must at all costs be prevented if society is to be saved from disruption and dissolution. Race cleansing is apparently the only thing that can stop it. Therefore, race cleansing must be our first concern.**"[6]

These groups thought "racial cleansing" would protect civilization from barbarism. Chesterton considered what they were doing as no less than barbarism itself. That's why they called him a 'reactionary.'[7]

---

5. C.B.S. Mildmay, "Practical Experience," *Birth Control News* 1:7 (November, 1922), 2. In G.K. Chesterton, *Eugenics and Other Evils* (Seattle: Inkling Books, 2000), 158.

6. *Birth Control News*, 1:9 (January 1923), 4. In G.K. Chesterton, *Eugenics and Other Evils*, (Seattle: Inkling Books, 2000), 160.

7. In his 1908 biography of his brother, Cecil Chesterton wrote: "Mr. Chesterton diverges sharply from Liberalism in that he repudiates altogether this identification of good and bad with progress and reaction. He has a certain vision of a normal human life, and in his view reforms and revolutions must be undertaken not for the purpose of helping mankind on its march to an unattained ideal, but in helping it back to a sanity and health from which it is constantly tending to fall." *G.K. Chesterton: A Criticism* (Seattle: Inkling Books, 2007), 96.

PRUSSIAN PRIDE

August 22, 1914 (extract)

The vices of the Superman might easily be pardoned. It is his virtues that are unpardonable.

EDITOR: For the British, World War I began on the evening of August 4, 1914. For some it came as a complete surprise. For others, it was an event they had long dreaded. One historian summarized the situation this way.

> The nation had been aware of international tensions, but war itself came abruptly. The Liberals in power were by long tradition the "peace party," isolationist in respect to the Continent and, on the whole, rather more favorably disposed toward Germany than towards France. Neither their parliamentary party nor the Cabinet, generally speaking, had seriously contemplated the prospect of war. It was rather to the Conservatives, or at least some of them, that war with Germany had seemed inevitable.
>
> Foreign policy since 1906 had been the well guarded province of the Foreign Office under Sir Edward Grey. Not until 1912 had a considerable portion of the Cabinet been informed of conversations long in progress with France, conversations which led to a significant division of responsibility on the high seas—Britain to take responsibility for the Atlantic and the Channel, and France for the Mediterranean. Even then the Foreign Office denied any actual commitment to France.[8]

Under a liberal government from 1906 on, Britain had stumbled unwittingly into a most terrible war. Not realizing the great danger Germany posed to peace, one member of the Cabinet, Sir Edward Grey, had committed the nation to a cost-saving naval policy that made the nation a *de facto* ally of France. When the fighting began in August 1914, Britain not only had long established treaty obligations to Belgium to honor, it had much more recent military agreements with France. Preparing for war without really believing war was likely had borne a most bitter fruit.

Despite his zest for debate, Chesterton was typically cautious about taking a position before he had gathered enough facts and impressions. His first mention of the war in the *Illustrated London News* is vague and brief—a single paragraph referring to "tremendous international events"—in an issue dated 18 days after war began and at a time when the military situation remained unsettled. As always, he looks beneath the surface and commends a military writer for tracing the roots of the war to a flawed human nature and particularly to the "sin of pride." Read Romney's remarks in the footnote for hints of Chesterton's thinking at the onset of the war. For more on what Chesterton felt about national pride, see his February 26, 1916 article (Ch. 4).

How tremendous international events have ploughed up the soil, and even the subsoil, of the best English minds is well exhibited in a remark by "Romney,"

By equating what is thought to be progress at any given moment with good, liberalism loses the ability to learn from mistakes. Liberals adopted eugenics as part of their "march" toward an idealized race. Now that eugenics has been discredited, many liberals seem unable to connect eugenics with liberalism. "Eugenics is bad," they think, "therefore it can't be anything liberals would support." But today's liberals do support eugenic abortion, and liberal leaders do claim abortion reduces poverty and crime, particularly among minorities. A liberal English professor once pointed to a young black man nearby and whispered to me in a conspiratorial voice, "That's why we need abortion." Although not as open as it once was, Stoddard's "racial cleansing" remains alive.

8. Alfred F. Havighurst, *Twentieth-century Britain* (New York: Harper & Row, 1962), 119–120.

who writes military criticisms for the *New Age*. He says, with a splendid suddenness and simplicity, that pride is a mortal sin, and there is an end of it. The *New Age* is the able organ of Guild Socialism, but its original roots were rather in Nietzsche than in Francis of Assisi. "Romney" is an excellent military critic; but hitherto his criticism has been mainly military. That he should trace any situation back to the sin of pride is really a revelation of modern realities and a realisation of ancient truths....[9]

Similarly, there are controversies everywhere to-day touching the location of an external barbarism. I should apply the same principle. **It does not matter much who is civilised or savage: both civilisation and savagery have their good points. But if there be something that behaves like savagery and boasts of civilisation, then there is the devil in it.** I suppose a Red Indian could scalp a man almost unconsciously. For all I know, a South Sea Island man could eat a man unconsciously. But if the Red Indian calls scalping the last step in cerebral surgery, I suspect there is something wrong. If the South Sea Islander calls cannibalism "The New Diet: No More Beef and Mutton," I begin to feel a faint distaste for him. And so I think most of us, with ordinary experience and charity, could easily excuse what looks like barbaric betrayal and barbaric vengeance, if it were not connected with any claim of larger culture or loftier destiny. **The vices of the Superman might easily be pardoned. It is his virtues that are unpardonable.** It is this element that makes the position of the merely insolent impossible even for their own purposes. Pride does not go before a fall. Pride is a fall, in the instant understanding of all the intelligent who see it.

G.K. Chesterton, "Our Note-Book," *Illustrated London News* (August 22, 1914), 278.
US: August 22, 1914. Also published as "Pride: The Supreme Evil."

9. Romney wrote: "On the other hand, even before any decisive steps have been taken the skilful fencer can tell his opponent's skill from the first tentative touch on the rapier, so may we be permitted to draw a few general conclusions regarding Prussian methods from what has hitherto been exposed of them. And there is one quality which the acute observer had detected in the Prussians long before the beginning of any war, and in which he had predicted their undoing. I refer to what a French journal has aptly called their 'giddy pride.' The Prussian worships force. He has made a philosophy and a system of this worship—and, be it remembered, the majority of those who shout and howl and deride him in respect of the filthy brutality and injustice which that worship entails, were but a month since extolling and imitating him because of it. Who does not remember—except perhaps the guilty parties themselves—the open admiration of German bad faith and unscrupulousness with which our press was filled? The open proclamation that faith and justice were non-existent? that the use of force was absolute? The kissing and slobbering over the precious mailed fist? Now the main thing about pride is that it is sin, and like all sin, though it be temporarily successful, brings its certain retribution. For forty years the Prussian Government, aided by such half-baked and barbarian cads as Treitschke and Houston Stewart Chamberlain, has been engaged in telling the German people that they and their army are invincible; that they are a chosen and a higher race; destined to rule the earth, and so forth. Chief among the results of such fatuity is an exaggerated contempt for the apparently weak, unworthy and unsoldierly jeers at little nations like the Belgians, which, even if they had possessed a measure of justification, could have had no result but to sting the victims into courage. The Belgians are not cowards. They never were, though they may, until recently, have lacked that national and fighting tradition which the defence of Liége will give them for the future. But even if they had been, Prussian brutality would have made men of them. Readers of these notes will remember the frequent protests which I have made against the undervaluation of little nations by military megalomaniacs. They were wrong in the case of Servia. They were wrong in the case of Greece. They have been shown, thank God, to have been wrong in the case of Belgium also. This war will not be fought in vain if it buries such boobies with the lies which they have told us." [Romney "Military Notes," *The New Age* xv (August 13, 1914), 341.]

Harnack's Racial Nonsense

September 5, 1914

The truth is that when there can be no truce to war, there can at least be a truce to nonsense; and the first nonsense we ought to throw into the sea at such a time as this is the nonsense about race.

Editor: In his first full article on the war for the *Illustrated London News*, Chesterton blasts as "nonsense" scholarly German ideas about race. It's one of the few occasions when Chesterton unleashes a bloodthirsty remark, calling the Teutonic-believing Prussian, "a wild animal, to be hunted until he is slain." Chesterton clearly loathes this scholarly Germanic racism.[10] To understand why German professors were drawn to it, we must step back a century before WWI, to an era when a fragmented Germany felt a deep sense of shame after it was unable to stop Napoleon's invasion. That was when what historian Karl Bracher called "the ultimate cause" of Nazism happened, "the deep schism between German and Western political thought, and the emergence of a special German sense of destiny with anti-Western overtones."

> In this sense—not in the sense of a doubtful "ancestor's gallery" of National Socialism—the genesis of National Socialism does, indeed point back to the beginning of the nineteenth century. The national reaction to the Napoleonic perversion of the French Revolution is embodied in Fichte's famous *Addresses to the German Nation* (1807–08), a widely read book which was to play a vital role. Fichte's basic contention was that Germany was selected for a special mission for mankind, which set it apart from the hitherto much admired and imitated French. A battle against undue Western influence (*Überfremdung*) had to be fought, because the "German spirit" was innately superior and destined to become the guiding light of all Germanic peoples, if not of all mankind. In his Fifth Address, Fichte advanced the notion that the Germans are the only people capable of profound, original thought; other peoples, by contrast, are capable only of a superficial, childish understanding of the classical culture of Antiquity.[11]

Although it's a simplification, if Fredrick the Great marks the point when the Germany's ruling class began to abandon Christianity for militarism, barbarism, and gradual conquest, as Chesterton stresses, then Johann Goettlieb Fichte (1762–1814), a much acclaimed philosophy professor at what is today the University of Berlin (formerly Humbolt University), marks the point when German academia began to regard Germanic culture as superior to all others. In that context, their strange interest in Teutonism makes sense. It was an effort to provide a historical framework for a broader and more mystical belief they had been holding for a half-century and more. That's also why isn't it surprising that an idea born in universities still had its most avid followers there a century later.[12] That scholarly history in turn lends legitimacy to the sneer Chesterton directs at German professors such as this Professor Harnack, who, like Fichte, was a distinguished professor in "the peaceful village of Berlin."

10. For a closer look at the scientific racism of Ernst Haeckel, Germany's most eminent zoologist and its premier champion of Darwinism, see the introduction to Chapter 4.

11. Karl Dietrich Bracher, *The German Dictatorship* (New York: Holt, Rinehart and Winston, 1970), 23.

12. In that same book (p. 20), Bracher notes that at the outbreak of WWI, the Pan-German League had "between 30,000 and 40,000 [members], of whom about one-third were engaged in academic professions."

PROFESSOR Harnack, a Higher Critic, and a very worthy old gentleman no doubt, has been expressing a pained astonishment at England's armed intervention on the side of France and Belgium instead of that of his own country; for Professor Harnack appears to hang out in the peaceful village of Berlin.[13] I have always had my suspicions that the Higher Criticism was a good deal above itself, and that most of its reputation in scholarship was due to the rich and vast field of things it hadn't found out. I have no high opinion of the logical methods by which men prove that Jericho could not have been utterly destroyed, because there is none of it left. I am not enraptured with the reasoning which says that Elijah could not have taken a chariot up to heaven, because there is no trace of it on earth. But these things do not greatly affect such religious convictions as I possess. For all they matter to the central truths of Christianity, they may be as they choose: Elijah may go to heaven, and Jericho may go to Jericho. And I willingly admit that I have not a hundredth part of the scholarship necessary to dispute with men like Professor Harnack about texts and documents, especially about the texts and documents which aren't there. I have not even enough learning to discover that a Higher Critic hasn't got any. I will therefore suppose Professor Harnack to be as deep in detailed knowledge as his admirers say he is. **But I should still decline to accept his conclusions if his judgment on things that happened long ago is anything like his judgment on the things that are happening before his eyes.**

By an extra stretch of that comprehensive breadth of mind which his friends admire, Professor Harnack seems to have said that he could, in a subtle sort of way, understand that a Frenchman would probably fight for France rather than Fiji. And (with another onward stride of thought) he found himself forced to contemplate the possibility of a Russian fighting for Russia. But with England his imaginative universality failed altogether: and he said in effect that it was impossible to imagine any reason or excuse for our interference. This is what we may call not knowing the world; and it is one of the most damning defects a historian can have. Anyone who knew the world instead of the "Universe" (a place where dons live), could have told him that, over and above the promise to France and the crime of the frontiers, the

13. Adolf von Harnack (1851–1930) was a liberal Lutheran theologian, best known for his controversial writings on early church history and the history of theology. His appointment to Humboldt University in Berlin was opposed by orthodox Lutherans and only succeeded when Wilhelm II (the Kaiser of the war) intervened on his behalf. Harnack signed "Manifesto of the Ninety-Three German Intellectuals to the Civilized World" (October, 1914). The reasoning of those intellectuals can be seen by comparing two of its clauses with the actual facts.

Manifesto: "It is not true that we trespassed in neutral Belgium. It has been proved that France and England had resolved on such a trespass, and it has likewise been proved that Belgium had agreed to their doing so. It would have been suicide on our part not to have been beforehand."

Facts: Belgium had agreed that Britain and France could enter its territory only *after* it was invaded by Germany. When Belgium refused to allow German troops to cross its land, Germany invaded. Only then did the British and French enter Belgium to assist in its defense, and that was not trespassing or invading.

Manifesto: "It is not true that our troops treated Louvain brutally. Furious inhabitants having treacherously fallen upon them in their quarters, our troops with aching hearts were obliged to fire a part of the town, as punishment. The greatest part of Louvain has been preserved."

Facts: Notice that they do not contest that much of the city's cultural center was destroyed. Instead, they claim the inhabitants of Louvain had no right to defend themselves against a German invasion and were punished accordingly. This is what Chesterton meant when he referred to "the general sentiment that the Prussian is a bully."

general sentiment that the Prussian is a bully has been common among educated people ever since 1870 and before: not so common of course, as it is among Frenchmen; but more common than it is among Russians. And there is something very queer and laughable, by the way, about the German Emperor reproaching us with supporting a backward and barbarous power like the Tsar's; when he himself strenuously supported the Tsar in all the proceedings that could possibly be called backward or barbarous. I do not think it lies in the mouth of William Hohenzollern to reproach us for alliance with a despotism which he did his best to keep despotic.

But the spirit of which Professor Harnack is typical is, even more than that of any War-Lord or Jingo, the intellectual weakness of Prussia.[14] For whether she succeeds or not in war it is certain that she failed utterly in her diplomacy for safeguarding the war. She failed, that is, in every single guess about the human materials involved. She thought Belgium would not resist: and Belgium did resist. She though she could persuade England not to fight: and her own persuasion was the principal reason why England did fight.[15] She evidently exaggerated both the smallness of Servia and the slowness of Russia. And all this kind of preliminary mistake works back to the same kind of philosophy, mind and well-meaning as it is, that gives so large an intellectual halo to men like Harnack. It is the same sort of miscalculation about how men behave that can be found in the academic cloisters where such men prove in various ways that the Gospel was not so much good news as gossip. It is the same mistake that is at the bottom of innumerable suggestions that St. Peters was founded not upon a rock but a cloud. In the same spirit of non-understanding the more peaceful Prussians prove that a "Platonist" Gospel must be far too late because

---

14. In the fall of 1914, Georg Nicolai (1874–1964) and Albert Einstein (1879–1955) tried to get their fellow German professors to sign their "Manifesto to Europeans," which appealed to Europe's common culture rather than German nationalism. Only four German professors, including Nicolai and Einstein, signed it, and one, the philosopher Otto Buek, had also signed the "Manifesto of the Ninety-three." The manifesto hinted at a scheme to make peace permanent by ending Europe's national borders: "The unstable and fluid situation in Europe, created by the war, must be utilized to weld the continent into an organic whole. Technically and intellectually, conditions are ripe for such a development." Einstein biographer Ronald W. Clark, went on to explain what Einstein meant by referring to a short article Einstein sent the Berlin Goethe Association.

> He went on to plead for the outlawing of war and for the European organization he had outlined in the manifesto. "I am also convinced," he concluded, "that in spite of the unspeakably sad conditions of the present time, there should be a political organization in Europe which should outlaw war in the same way that not so long ago the German Reich outlawed war between Bavaria and Württemberg." [*Einstein: The Life and Times*, (New York: Avon, 1971), 237.]

Einstein was born in Ulm in Wurttemberg and grew up in Munich, the capital of Bavaria. He knew how the "German Reich outlawed war between Bavaria and Württemberg." As independent states they were in little danger of going to war with each another, much less of dragging all Europe into war. But forcibly joined to a Prussia-dominated Reich, they made the new Germany powerful enough to drag Europe and much of the world into two of the bloodiest wars in history. Was that what Einstein wanted his "League of Europeans" to become? Conquest, coercion and concentrated power seem a odd way to establish a more peaceful world.

15. On August 4, 1914, in their final meeting before the war and shortly after German troops had entered Belgium, the German Chancellor von Bethmann-Hollweg attempted to persuade the British ambassador in Berlin, Sir William Edward Goschen, that Britain should stay out of the war, telling him that any promise the British had made to defend Belgian neutrality was just "a scrap of paper." The British ambassador replied that Germany needed, "to understand that it was, so to speak, a matter of 'life and death' for the honor of Great Britain that she should keep her solemn engagement to do her utmost to defend Belgium's neutrality if attacked." Chesterton discusses that meeting in more detail in his next *Illustrated London News* article.

Plato was much too early. In the same spirit they prove that Mithras and Jesus were very much alike, especially Mithras.

That mistake is the habit of depending on something that does not exist. Thus, I see that many of Mr. Harnack's friends are reproaching England in the German Press for having "betrayed the cause of Teutonism."[16] You or I could not betray the cause of Teutonism, any more than we could murder a Snark, or elope with a Boojum. There is no such thing as the cause of Teutonism; there never has been any such thing, even in our own minds. **We have had many reasons for liking Germans and many reasons for disliking them. Many of us could hardly live in a world without their music. Many of us could not live in the same house with their metaphysics.** I know more than one Englishman, Mr. Titterton for instance, who would rather live in Munich than in heaven, but who would rather live in hell than Berlin.[17] I can imagine a Bavarian fighting for Germany against France; I can imagine a Bavarian fighting for Bavaria against Prussia; but I cannot imagine any Bavarian fighting for Teutonism, for the simple reason that there is no such thing. The English, unlike the Prussians, probably have some Teutonic blood. So have hundreds of people in North Italy and Spain, to say nothing of France and Belgium. There may be something in the old semi-scientific business about long heads and round heads; but something more than difference is needed before a man will have bullets in his head like plums in a plum pudding. There are, indeed, racial differences which are realities, at least in the sense that they are realities to the eye. In dealing with definite savages we may be allowed to realize that black is not white; and not to look upon the Indian when he is red.

But these feelings, right or wrong, have nothing to do with any racial theories. They are at least experiences; that is, they are shocks. If a clerk in Surbiton obtains permission from his maiden aunt to bring his friend Johnson to dinner, the aunt will need no ethnological training to be surprised when she sees Mr. Jack Johnson enter the room.[18] The clerk may afterwards take out twelve volumes of the *Encyclopaedia Britannica,* and prove that negroes are the nearest to us by blood of all the peoples of this planet. But he will not succeed—at least, not with the aunt. As there is a curious German work written to prove that St. John was a German, there might easily be a German work, equally curious, written to prove that Jack Johnson is a German. There is nothing to be said against these strong curves of constructive theory; except that they are obviously not true. The Prussian professor will expect the Englishman

16. After the war, Germans continued to regard England as their natural ally. In the 1920s, Hitler would describe a German plan to conquer Eastern Europe, noting that, "For such a policy, there was but one ally in Europe: England. With England alone it was possible, with our rear protected, to begin the new Germanic march." *Mein Kampf* (Boston: Houghton Mifflin, 1943), 140. Hitler assumed that, because England had an empire in India and Africa, it would allow Germany to create one of its own in Eastern Europe.

17. William R. Titterton (1876–1963) was a British journalist and a friend of Chesterton.

18. Chesterton is having fun with this prim maiden aunt's reaction. John A. Johnson (1878–1946) was also known as Jack Johnson and the Galveston Giant. An American and the son of former slaves, he was the first black to become the Heavyweight Champion of the World (1908–1915). Ken Burns, who did a documentary on Johnson entitled *Unforgivable Blackness* said, "For more than thirteen years, Jack Johnson was the most famous, and the most notorious, African-American on Earth."

and the German to embrace each other because they are both Teutons. The English professor will expect the English colonel and his Hindoo cook to embrace each other, because they are both Aryans. Neither incident has as yet taken place. **The truth is that when there can be no truce to war, there can at least be a truce to nonsense; and the first nonsense we ought to throw into the sea at such a time as this is the nonsense about race.** The modern English victories were largely won by Highlanders: the mediaeval English victories were largely won by Welshmen: and nobody knows whether they were Teutons or not, and nobody cares. There are no Teutons; but there are Englishmen. There are no Celts; but there are Irishmen. And it is important to remember this to-day, even about such loose and convenient terms as that of the Slav. People talk about Pan-Slavism and Pan-Germanism, but people do not mean it.[19] Supposing half a hundred Europeans were turned loose in a restaurant: I doubt if even a Pan-Slavist could pick out the Slavs. Supposing a Teutonist saw a crowd of men from Manchester, Brussels, Milan, Barcelona, Brixton, Berlin, Bangor, and Budapest, Do you think he could pick out a Teuton among them, as he could certainly pick out a Chinaman or a nigger? I doubt it. I have seen as dark men in Frankfurt as I have seen fair men in Florence: I do not think there is any such animal as the Teuton. But there is certainly such an animal as the Prussian. And I cannot conceive any system of natural history under which he is anything but a wild animal, to be hunted until he is slain.[20]

G.K. Chesterton, "Our Note-Book," *Illustrated London News* 145 (September 5, 1914), 342. US: September 5, 1914. Also published as "Professor Harnack and Teutonism."

Casting Out Devils

September 12, 1914

So that our work with the Prussians is not so much a pulling-down of thrones as a casting-out of devils; not only out of the land, but out of the enemy.

Editor: In this, his second full article on the war five weeks after the fighting began, Chesterton has found his voice. He knows how he must write about the war and what he must say. This is perhaps as good a point as any to contrast the consistency of Chesterton's view of the war with the changing positions of his personal friend but ideological foe H.G. Wells, mentioned near the end of this article. In his 1936 autobiography Chesterton would write:

> Those who now think too little of the Allied Cause are those who once thought too much of it. A rather unstable genius like Mr. H.G. Wells is typical of the whole contradiction. He began by calling the Allied effort, The War That Will End War. He has ended by saying, through his rather equivocal mask of Mr. Clissold, that it was not better than a forest fire and that it settled nothing. It is hard to say which of the two statements is the more absurd. It settled exactly what it set out to settle.

19. Pan-Slavism and Pan-Germanism were movements in nineteenth century Europe that called for the political union of all Slavs or Germans (respectively). Pan-Germanism was one of Nazism's ideological roots.
20. Chesterton takes on Professor Harnack and Teutonism again in *Illustrated London News*, October 10, 1914.

> But that was something rather more rational and modest than what Mr. Wells had settled that it was to settle. **To tell a soldier defending his country that it is The War That Will End War is exactly like telling a workman, naturally rather reluctant to do his day's work, that it is The Work That Will End Work.** We never promised to put a final end to all war or all work or all worry. We only said that we were bound to endure something very bad because the alternative was something worse.[21]

As you read what Chesterton says about all just wars being "religious wars" in this chapter, keep in mind his June 24, 1916 article, where he makes clear that "religion" is meant in the broad sense of a nation's core beliefs.

> What we are fighting is a new and false religion, much more powerful but much less noble than that against which our civilisation strove in the Crusades. But in the clearest minds it may almost be called a religion of irreligion. It trusts itself utterly to the anarchy of the unknown; and, unless civilisation can sober it with a shock of disappointment, it will be for ever inexhaustible in novelties of perversion and pride. Only one principle will inspire all its changes—and that is that in two senses it is always a religion of blood, for its idol is race and its sacrifice is slaughter.

Unfortunately, that irreligion of blood, race and slaughter was not defeated in WWI. Because Europe did not listen to Chesterton's warnings, it required a still more murderous second war to inflict on Germany a sufficient "shock of disappointment."

MOST of us have read that last page of the British Ambassador's experience at Berlin, a page so vivid that it might be a page from a good historical novel, but for the fact that it is historical. The quarrel is concluded by a bitter message from the Kaiser, "which lost none of its acerbity in the mode of its transmission": that the Kaiser had hitherto been proud of his uniforms as an English General and Admiral, but that he must now discard them. **It is part of the permanent disadvantage of the civilised man in quarrel with the barbarian, that the English guest did not feel so free to insult his host as the host to insult his guest.** Otherwise the British Ambassador might have answered that empty British uniforms are not so difficult to fill. The curious may find in the past, or, perhaps, in the near future, some Generals (or even an Admiral or two) who might console us even for the loss of the Kaiser, that scarred veteran of a hundred campaigns. When the Belgians had been invaded (by no more right or reason than if they had been Bostonians) they fought against that frantic aggression till their clothes would not hold together. Alas! their uniforms were by no means uniform. Men fell dead in the queerest clothes, in their last stand for the freedom of their harmless country; some of them wearing military caps and civilian coats; some of them wearing military coats and civilian pot-hats; some of them wearing fashionable trousers and no boots or shoes; some of them wearing

21. Wells published *The War That Will End War* in 1914 and *The World of William Clissold* in 1926. This quote is from *The Autobiography of G.K. Chesterton* (New York: Sheed & Ward, 1936), 253–254. When Wells' 1926 book came out, Chesterton criticized its utopianism by pointing out that it was unfair to compare a past or a present that undeniably existed with a future that might never exist: "When he attempts to show that our present state, which irritates him so much, will lead to the future state, which intoxicates him so much, he breaks down like a very badly built bridge." He goes on to call that "paying your way with blank cheques on the future." *The Collected Works of G.K. Chesterton*, vol. XXXIV, 202–205. From *Illustrated London News*, September 20, 1926.

anything; some of them almost nothing. In this extremity it is possible that some of them would have accepted the cast clothes of the German Emperor.[22]

Nevertheless, there is a certain pathos that is not wholly false about this reluctant repudiation of two out of three hundred uniforms: this mournful contentment with two hundred and ninety-eight uniforms. No one can read that remarkable statement of the British Ambassador without being finally convinced that there was, for whatever reason, real anger at Potsdam about our entry into the Alliance; and, what is everywhere so natural a root of anger—astonishment. It is hard for people in England to understand how England could conceivably have been expected to do anything else but what she did. Nevertheless, if other people are really astonished, we must try to imagine and explore whatever their astonishment may mean.

Put in the most impersonal manner, there cannot really be any question about what happened during the last negotiations, any more than about checkmate or a cheque dishonoured. **Simplified, without bias or the blinding trick of journalistic suppression, it certainly came to this. Germany came to England and said: "If you will break your promise, in the hope of helping me to break my promise, I will reward you with another of my celebrated promises."**[23] Turn the whole story upside down or inside out; believe to the utmost extent in the good intentions of the German Emperor (and I have never been disposed to disbelieve in them, as the files of this paper could show),[24] believe to the utmost extent in the shuffling and shadiness of some modern statesmen (and there, also, like the devils, I believe and tremble—as the files could also show), suppose the Emperor the best he could be, and the British government the worst that it could be, and still I am stumped. Still, I cannot see what the facts can mean, except exactly what I have written above. I am going to lie; if you will lie, too, we can both be trusted to tell the truth. This, of course, is what we call the "scrap of paper" argument. Of its moral quality I will not speak. This page, even in tragic times, is supposed to represent G.K. Chesterton's rambles through life, and not Dante's journey through hell. I cannot locate in the abyss the exact place where political philosophers live; or say whether anyone is punished by living underneath them. It is enough that the word "honour," constantly used in translations from Prussian political speeches, police cases, etc., must certainly mean something entirely different in the original. I think they have a great fortress called "The Broad Stone of Honour."[25] Their theory of it is certainly broad enough.

---

22. The debate over ill-clad Belgian irregulars, called *francs-tireurs,* would continue after the war. See Chesterton's September 13, 1919 article (Ch. 7).

23. At a libel suit in Munich, Hitler would echo the Kaiser's attitude, testifying: "But foreign policy in itself is merely a means to an end. In questions of foreign policy I shall never admit that I am tied by anything." From Konrad Heiden, "Introduction," in Adolf Hitler, *Mein Kampf* (Boston: Houghton Mifflin, 1943), xx.

24. This refers to Chesterton's initial willingness to look for the best in the Kaiser's often unpredictable behavior, such as in his December 13, 1913 article in the *Illustrated London News* (Ch. 1).

25. This is an indirect reference to Kenelm Henry Digby's *The Broad Stone of Honour, or Rules for the Gentlemen of England* (1822), the "broad stone" being the author's favorite fortress, the never-conquered *Ehrenbreitstein* (meaning "honour-broad-stone") at Koblenz on the German Rhine. The fortress was well-known as the German equivalent of Britain's Gibraltar and is mentioned in Herman Melville's *Moby Dick.* Here Chesterton plays on the name to suggest that Germans see honour in a broad (meaning loose) sense.

But apart from the moral matter altogether, I should not have imagined that a commercial Power improved its position by announcing beforehand that everything in the way of paper is waste paper.

Along this avenue of the actual facts it seems useless to seek the cause of the genuine German surprise. I continue to think, therefore (though many have expressed their disagreement), that what I wrote last week is true: that the sincere political surprise comes from a sincere historical delusion, Whether they put it rightly or wrongly, whether they behave ill or well, the North Germans do, I think, quite certainly have a feeling that we are bound to them in some way—or that we ought to be bound. That feeling must have its root in that Teutonism to which I referred in the last issue. It was one of those ignorant theories that are only propounded by learned men. It will not survive this war.[26]

But what it really does prove, as Mr. H.G. Wells has lately pointed out, is the enormous catastrophes that come out of error; or what used to be called heresy. When I was very young I wrote a novel—Lord, what a bad novel!—in which I made the hero say: "There were never any just wars but the religious wars."[27] It was, perhaps, the only quite sound remark in the whole book. Yet though it was in the mouth of a fictitious character in a fantastic story, it was severely criticised as a reactionary paradox. In a very fine article in the *Nation* recently, Mr. Wells has seen and said that war is sometimes a horrible necessity in order to put true ideas in the place of false ones. I do not say this for any cheap controversial purpose. I do not urge Mr. Wells to apologise to the paladins and persecutors whom he has probably reviled all his life. Yet it is certain that if the Crusades had succeeded, there would have been no Balkan Wars; and if the Southern effort in the Thirty Years' War had succeeded, there would have been no Prussia.[28] I merely welcome the first great truth gathered of thus horrible harvest: the truth that if you think wrong, you go wrong.

26. Unfortunately it did. Rather than examine where Germany went wrong, many Germans enlarged their already exaggerated sense of entitlement—claiming to have suffered a "stab in the back" at the end the war and whining about the Treaty of Versailles even though the Treaty of Brest-Litovsk (1918) they imposed on Russia was far harsher. The result was Nazism and yet another war, with Teutonism renamed Aryanism.

27. The quote is from Chapter 3 of his first novel, *The Napoleon of Notting Hill* (1904): "Oh, you kings, you kings," cried out Adam, in a burst of scorn. "How humane you are, how tender, how considerate. You will make war for a frontier, or the imports of a foreign harbour; you will shed blood for the precise duty on lace, or the salute to an admiral. But for the things that make life itself worthy or miserable... how humane you are. I say here, and I know well what I speak of, there were never any necessary wars but the religious wars. **There were never any just wars but the religious wars. There were never any humane wars but the religious wars. For these men were fighting for something that claimed, at least, to be the happiness of a man, the virtue of a man.** A Crusader thought, at least, that Islam hurt the soul of every man, king or tinker, that it could really capture. I think Buck and Barker and these rich vultures hurt the soul of every man, hurt every inch of the ground, hurt every brick of the houses, that they can really capture. Do you think I have no right to fight for Notting Hill, you whose English Government has so often fought for tomfooleries? If, as your rich friends say, there are no gods, and the skies are dark above us, what should a man fight for, but the place where he had the Eden of childhood and the short heaven of first love? If no temples and no scriptures are sacred, what is sacred if a man's own youth is not sacred?"

28. Chesterton assumes a Crusade so successful, the Ottoman Empire would have been restricted to Asia, with no foothold in Europe and no Muslim presence in the Balkans. The Thirty Years' War (1618–1648) was fought primarily in Germany. Although in its broad outlines it was a conflict between Catholic and Lutheran, the presence of Catholic France on the Protestant side may be why Chesterton refers to the "Southern effort," meaning the Hapsburg empire of Austria. He assumes that, with northern Germany under the Hapsburg dynasty rather than the Hohenzollern dynasty (Frederick the Great), Prussia would have developed in a less militaristic direc-

Mr. Wells thinks, and I think so, too, that in the case of the Prussian we are really warring against a delusion.[29] He is like a lunatic with plenty of pistols and a good aim, but liable to shoot a dog out of hatred of cats. Thus he sees the Russian as a yellow-skinned Oriental. He sees the Briton as a yellow-haired deserter. But "they ain't." **It is one of the innumerable shallow phrases of the modern and mercantile peace, that when people are sincere they should not be attacked. Why, it is exactly because they are sincere that they should be attacked.** If a man pretends to be your wife's previous and lawful husband, you can laugh at him as at any other amusing fraud. It he really believes that he is, you will take prompt action to prevent his acting on his belief. An insincere polygamist is an ornament in any modern house: we use him to carry tea-cups. But a sincere polygamist we will blow to hell, if we can, with horse, foot, and artillery.[30] And if you ask us why, we can only answer—because he is sincere and wrong.

The Prussian is sincere and wrong. He really does think that he could do everything better than everybody; like Bottom the Weaver.[31] I have no doubt he thinks that Prussians could play the bagpipes better than Highlanders; or dive for pearls better than the pearl-fishers. Prussians already say they understand Shakespeare; from which manifest scream of madness it will be but one note higher to say that they understand Burns.[32] They understand everything: there was never a madman who did not. **So that our work with the Prussians is not so much a pulling-down of thrones as a casting-out of devils; not only out of the land, but out of the enemy.**[33]

G.K. Chesterton, "Our Note-Book," *Illustrated London News* 145 (September 12, 1914), 374. US: September 12, 1914. Also published as "England's Tie to the Prussians."

Responsibility for War

September 26, 1914

For surely it cannot be more wicked to keep your word for selfish reasons than it is to break your word for selfish reasons.

tion and been more like Bavaria and Austria. The problem with that is, while Prussia dominated the fighting in WWI, it was Austria's harsh treatment of Serbia that triggered the war. Given the usual temptations of might over right, the (southern) Hapsburgs could behave as badly as the (northern) Hohenzollerns. Finally, keep in mind that Chesterton made these remarks to suggest to those enamored with Wells's prophetic powers that European history might be better if "the paladins and persecutors" Wells "has probably reviled all his life" had succeeded.

29. Chesterton, H.G. Wells, and 32 other prominent writers joined in a letter "To Russian Men of Letters" published in the *Manchester Guardian* on December 23, 1914. After praising Russian literature, it noted: "You, like us, entered upon this war to defend a weak and threatened nation which trusted you against the lawless aggression of a strong military power." H.G. Wells, *The Correspondence of H.G. Wells*, David C. Smith, ed. (London: Pickering & Chatto, 1998), 400–401.

30. That is, all the combat army branches of that day: the calvary, infantry, and artillery. Armor came later.

31. Bottom the Weaver is an arrogant and conceited character in Shakespeare's *The Midsummer Night's Dream*.

32. Robert Burns (1759–1796) was Scotland's national poet and many of his poems are in Scottish.

33. In a December 13, 1913 article, Chesterton expressed the hope that for the Kaiser, "the time has come when a certain spirit must be cast forth like a devil out of the body of the great Germania."

Editor: In this article, Chesterton looks at who was responsible for starting the war, avoiding the morass of motives that can be endlessly debated and looking instead at deeds which cannot be denied. Some might consider his argument unfair. "Yes," they would say, "Germany did technically begin the war when she crossed the Belgium border. But given a slightly different set of circumstances, France or Britain might have done the same thing." That's unlikely. What Chesterton says over and over really is true. Germany did have a different way of looking at war, inspired in part by the writings of their greatest military theorist, Karl von Clausewitz (1870–1831), the author of *Vom Kriege* (*On War*). The problem with Clausewitz is with how he draws the lines when discussing war.

First, Clausewitz claims, "War is thus an act of force to compel our adversary to do our will." When war is defined that way, then the line between a just war and an unjust one disappear. War simply happens because one country wants to impose its will on another, and all talk about right and wrong becomes irrelevant. At the personal level, this resembles arguments about abortion that focus on 'choice,' ignoring the great ethical significance of the choice being made.

Second, Clausewitz fails to draw a fast and hard line between wars and almost everything else nations do. "War," he famously said, "is therefore the continuation of policy by other means. It is not merely a political act but a real political instrument, a continuation of political intercourse, a conduct of political intercourse by other means." Again, notice the lack of a line. For him, a war that kills millions is no different from diplomacy, which may inconvenience a few well-paid diplomats with long meetings in otherwise pleasant locales. Each is merely a point on a long and unbroken line that determines what Country A is doing to impose its will on Country B.

Third, Clausewitz has little patience with those who would place limits on how a war is fought. The fact that nature places no physical limits on what can be done, he says, means that man need place no limits on what he does: "The use of force is theoretically without limits. Philanthropic souls may imagine that there is a way to disarm or overthrow our adversary without much bloodshed, and that this is what the art of war should see to achieve. Agreeable as it may sound, this is a false idea, which must be demolished." Remember, if the sole purpose of the war is to impose on one's will on another, then limitations of how a war is fought—limits Chesterton calls by the old-fashioned term of *chivalry* and that protect non-combatants from harm—have no meaning. They make no more sense than an athlete who wants to win a race competing with weights strapped to his legs.

The first two explain why Germany began the war with the invasion of Belgium, violating a well-established, almost-century-old treaty. The third is why Germany did not hesitate to take reprisals against Belgian civilians and why, despite the outrage and the risk of the U.S. entering the war, it sank unarmed passenger vessels.

Vom Kriege was published in 1832, two years after Clausewitz's death, but the same point of view pervades his much briefer 1812 essay, "I Believe and Profess," which was a protest against the French occupation of Prussia.

> I believe and profess that a people never must value anything higher than the dignity and freedom of its existence; that it must defend these with the last drop of its blood; that it has no duty more sacred and can obey no law that is higher; that the shame of a cowardly submission can never be wiped out, that the poison of

submission in the bloodstream of a people will be transmitted to its children, and paralyze and undermine the strength of later generations.[34]

Clausewitz fails to say anything about *individual* freedoms of citizens or any rights that another people might have and claims that there is "no duty more sacred" and "no law that is higher" than the "freedom" of a nation to do as it wills. He was not alone in such blasphemous thinking, and such attitudes led by a direct path to the atrocities of World War I and the far greater horrors of World War II.

THE reported decision of Mr. Woodrow Wilson to abandon for the present his idea of suggesting a European peace is as clear-headed and credible as was the idea itself. Mr. Wilson, like M. Poincaré, belongs to the small group of honestly strong men who think before they act, for thinking is the hardest work in the world, and the most repugnant to our nature.[35] Therefore the lazier sort of politician takes refuge in activity. The Superman, the Man of Action, acts before he thinks: he has to do his thinking afterwards. It is very typical of the North Germans that they have turned "Hamlet" from a play into a puzzle, and make it merely mean that thought impedes action.[36] Yet there is quite as good thought as Hamlet's, I will not say in Macbeth or Hotspur, but in Falstaff and Bottom the Weaver. Hamlet failed to act not because he thought, but because he thought in a particular way that does destroy the intellectual bases of action. In short, Hamlet failed to act because he had been taught to think at a German university. For him there was nothing save to be Hamlet or else Fortinbras—a mere Force.[37] But both the Frenchman and the American have generally escaped, though by very different avenues, this false and confusing alternative. And by thus really thinking before action and towards action, their action is generally not only more discerning, but actually more decisive.

A good instance can be found in the swiftness with which the American Presidency seems to have discovered the impossibility of such plausible offers in this particular case. First, quite apart from who is right or wrong in the war, there are elements in Europe which the American citizen is happy enough not to have experienced, but which the American citizen is almost certainly shrewd enough to see. There were very many during the North and South War who wanted England, and Europe perhaps, to intervene in America. At that time our sympathies would have been entirely with the South: nor am I, to-day, without any sympathy with those sympathies.[38] Yet I think we are most of us glad, and (so far as one may dogmatise

34. Karl von Clausewitz, *War, Politics and Power,* Edward M. Collins, ed (Washington: Regnery, 1965), 207. The other quotes are from pages 41–42 and 53.

35. As President, Woodrow Wilson did his best to keep the U.S. out of the war. Raymond Poincaré (1860–1934) was President of France during the war (1913–1920). In 1912, as Prime Minister, he pursued a strong anti-German policy, forging close ties with Russia. Without those efforts, France might have lost the war in the first few weeks.

36. See Chesterton's chapter, "Shakespeare and the Germans," in *The Blinded Soldiers and Sailors Gift Book* (1915).

37. Fortinbras, the Norwegian crown prince, speaks the last words in Shakespeare's *Hamlet.* He does nothing in the tale but serve as a "mere force" to command the obvious—that Hamlet be given an honorable burial.

38. Chesterton isn't for slavery. As with the Boer War, he favors small over large and local over distant. That's why he doesn't want the British Empire to assist the Confederacy, as it might have done given the country's need for cotton. Remember that this is 1914. The modern hypocrisy of being loudly against slavery in the distant past, while doing nothing about it where is still exists (particularly Muslim regions of Africa), was not yet fashionable.

of another nation) I think most Americans are glad, that the real claims of Robert Lee or the real claims of Abraham Lincoln were not settled in a town like Hatfield or a town like Huddersfield.[39]

The English aristocrat was not fit to comprehend the Virginian aristocrat, even when he made him out much more aristocratic than he was. The man in Birmingham could not really estimate the man in Boston—even when he over-estimated him. But all this is an understatement of the comparison. The most chivalric champion of States Rights never really felt that Massachusetts or Old Virginia was a sovereign nation in the sense of France or Russia: Bull Run could not leave so deep a cleavage as Jena, nor Gettysburg as Sedan.[40] To put the point it its most practical form, I do not believe there was one poor, gallant, ragged "Reb" or "Yank" in those soul-stirring democratic armies who did not know he was an American. But I have passed my life among hundreds of highly educated Englishmen who did not know they were Europeans. They know it now.

Touching the actual challenge shock of battle, there is nothing to be said but what I said previously in this place. There is no need to answer the German case, for there is no German case. Even if it were true that our defence of Belgium was based on our own interests, it leaves the moral advantage, at the very least, on our side rather than the German. **For surely it cannot be more wicked to keep your word for selfish reasons than it is to break your word for selfish reasons.**[41] Mr. Asquith, I imagine, has never regarded himself as a saint because he did not invade Belgium.[42] But he might still have regarded himself as a scoundrel if he had. All

39. England has several towns named Hatfield and one called Huddersfield, but none are major cities. Chesterton probably means that it was better for America to solve its conflict over slavery without meddling by distant, small-town Englishman. He made a similar point about nations not generally meddling in the internal affairs of other nations in the September 17, 1910 issue of the *Illustrated London News* (Ch. 1).

40. Chesterton balances his examples. The First Battle of Bull Run (July 21, 1861) was the first major battle in the Civil War and a Southern victory, while the Battle of Gettysburg (July 1–3, 1863) was the turning point in the war and a Northern victory. At the Battle of Jena (October 14, 1806), Napoleon's France defeated Prussia, while at the Battle of Sedan (September 1, 1870), France's Napoleon III was defeated by Prussia.

41. Here is how the British Ambassador to Berlin described his final meeting with the German Chancellor:

> I found the Chancellor very agitated. His Excellency at once began a harangue, which lasted for about twenty minutes. He said that the steps taken by His Majesty's Government was terrible to a degree; just for a word—"neutrality," a word which in war time had so often been disregarded—just for a scrap of paper Great Britain was going to make war on a kindred nation who desired nothing better than to be friends with her. All his efforts in that direction had been rendered useless by this last terrible step, and the policy to which, as I knew, he had devoted himself since his accession to office had tumbled down like a house of cards. What we had done was unthinkable; it was like striking a man from behind while he was fighting for his life against two assailants. He held Great Britain responsible for all the terrible events that might happen. I protested strongly against that statement, and said that, in the same way as he and Herr von Jagow wished me to understand that for strategical reasons it was a matter of life and death to Germany to advance through Belgium and violate the latter's neutrality, so I would wish him to understand that it was, so to speak, a matter of "life and death" for the honor of Great Britain that she should keep her solemn engagement to do her utmost to defend Belgium's neutrality if attacked. That solemn compact simply had to be kept, or what confidence could any one have in engagements given by Great Britain in the future? The Chancellor said, "But at what price will that compact have been kept? Has the British Government thought of that?" I hinted; to his Excellency as plainly as I could that fear of consequences could hardly be regarded as an excuse for breaking solemn engagements, but his Excellency was so excited, so evidently overcome by the news of our action, and so little disposed to hear reason that I refrained from adding fuel to the flame by further argument.

42. Herbert H. Asquith (1852–1928) was the British Prime Minister at the start of the war.

the commonest contracts of law and commerce are of interests: but in the coarsest bargain of cash and goods, it is thought good to deliver the goods, and bad merely to secure what Prussian diplomatists would call "the needful."[43] Upon the pure point of logic, therefore, I cannot see, and have never even begun to see, that England keeping her promise can be worse than Germany breaking her promise, even if it were true that Germany acted from the high, sincere motive of forcing all human beings to sit out a play by Sudermann, or that England acted from the low, crafty motive of protecting the English ports.[44]

It is the same with the only other dispute in the history of the War that can be studied in the same dry and logical light: the ultimatum from Austria with which the whole matter began. It is impossible to read it and the incidents surrounding it without feeling certain that Austria made and meant to make aggressive war. She was in the position of that most sinister sort of bully who may be disappointed by getting what he wants.[45] Nay, in a sense Austria is surety for the fairness of Servian resistance, for Austria actually had to formulate a set of claims that no nation could fairly accept. She had to compose a work of art in the intolerable, a torture-engine of insult: and there would have been still less excuse for Austria making such a claim if there had been any excuse for Servia submitting to it. As it was, Austria was merely making war on a peaceable neighbour, a comparatively virtuous act: if she had really expected to keep the *peace* on such terms, she would have been lower than the kidnapper of children or the usurer of the slums. There cannot, therefore, be the least logical doubt that Austria provoked and precipitated war; and all discussions about the moral wildness of the Servians or the moral pathos of the Hapsburgs are irrelevant to that fact. If the Servian King had killed the Archduke with his own hand, Servia could not be more certainly responsible for shedding the blood of a man than Austria is for shedding the blood of a continent. She may have been tempted and used by Prussia; but I am speaking of who is right or wrong in the cold sense of the answer to a sum or the signature to a document, and in that sense the case of Servia, like the case of Belgium, is simply unanswerable. Call England a huckster, a hypocrite, a naval monopolist, a colonial filibuster, a haughtier Venice and a baser Carthage: and the fact remains that England was for keeping the treaty and Germany was for breaking it. Call Servia a desperado, a savage, a plotter, a murderer from the

43. "The needful" is a variation of 'end justifies the means' reasoning. Germany *needed* to win the war, so any *means* of achieving that *need* was justified, even the violation of treaties establishing Belgian neutrality.

44. Hermann Sudermann (1857–1928) was a Prussian dramatist and novelist. Chesterton's dislike may be directed at his four-act play, *Die Heimat* (1893), translated into English as *Magda* (1896), with its fashionable stereotypes: a cruel, reactionary father (Lt. Col. Schwartz) and a talented, rebellious daughter (Magda), who runs away from home, becomes a famous singer, and has a child out of wedlock. After many years, father and daughter meet and exchange these words: Schwartze: "I implore you—Come here, my child—nearer—so—I implore you—let me be happy in my dying hour. Tell me that you have remained pure in body and soul, and then go with my blessing on your way." Magda: "I have remained —true to myself, dear father." Schwartze: "How? In good or in ill?" Magda: "In what—for me—was good." Magda's life, focused only on herself, parallels a nation that acts only in its own interest. The only evil-doers in such a moral universe are those interfere with the self or nation in its self-expression. That's why Germany can see nothing but evil in Britain's defense of Belgium.

45. Chesterton is right. Austria's demands were deliberately outrageous to provoke a war in which the large Austria hoped to punish little Servia for its insolence. Its bullying collapsed when Russia chose to intervene.

beginning; and the fact remains that Servia was for keeping the peace and Austria was for breaking it.

These, the mere facts, would prevent any rally to the cause of the Germanies; but when we come to the subtler thing called the cause of peace we find ourselves in sight of the high-minded error that the neutral countries appear to have considered and avoided. It might plausibly be said, "Granted that Great Britain and Servia were right to fight, surely they would be glad if they could respectably leave off fighting." It is here that we must realise that differences between the historic divisions of Europe and the local varieties of America of which I spoke at the beginning. **The Pacifists often tell Europeans that they should try to imagine a United States of Europe. I should like to tell Americans that they must try to imagine a Disunited States of America.** Suppose Virginia had separated from America as thoroughly as America did from England. Suppose California were not only different, but as different as Spain. Suppose Utah were not only as eccentric, but actually as independent as Turkey. It is then that we come back on the real dangers of the European tradition; and the most dangerous things about it, I need hardly say, are its virtues—or, if you will, its ideals.

For here is the heroic paradox of the thing. England has her interests, as Servia has her faults; but to suppose that these are the springs of action would be exactly to miss the main fact of the European situation. **This is a war of the peoples, and is much too intellectual for diplomatists to understand. The truth is—that mankind resents insult much more than injury.** And the Thing we are fighting has succeeded in insulting all that is best in each of us. This should be noted, for it is spiritually very important. What Prussia affronted in Servia was not the Balkan intrigue, but the just national self-respect. What she affronted in Russia was not the arbitrary police tradition, but the real religion and the real call of the blood. And what she has insulted in us is not the guttersnipe glory of Mafeking Night, but all that remains of that mercantile probity which can alone save a nation of shop-keepers from become a nation of shop-lifters.[46]

G.K. Chesterton, "Our Note-Book," *Illustrated London News* 145 (September 26, 1914), 438. US: September 26, 1914. Previously published as "England's Interests and England's Honour."

BLAMING SERBIA

October 10, 1914

If Professor Harnack can really persuade himself that the English are the same as the Germans, why cannot he persuade himself that the Serbians are the same as the Germans?

EDITOR: The Servia of Chesterton's previous articles becomes Serbia in this article, a change that may have been part of an effort to improve its image and make sure the small country did not get saddled with the blame for starting the Great War. (The

46. Mafeking Night on May 17, 1900 celebrated a British victory in the Boer War and is considered by some to be the high point of British imperialism. For Chesterton, who opposed the war, it was mere "guttersnipe glory."

former name may have suggested Britain was merely *serv*ing the interests of *Serv*ia.) In this article, Chesterton goes beyond arguing that Britain has a responsibility to defend little nations such as Serbia and argues that for some five centuries, Europe has owed a great debt to the Christians of the Balkans. They have kept Europe free of invading Islamic armies, a debt deserving of repayment.

Chesterton usually restricts each article to a single topic, but in this one he closes by supplementing the remarks he made a month earlier (September 5, 1914) about Professor Harnack and Teutonism. Chesterton wasn't the only one to notice how badly Germany's professors were behaving. Shortly after Chesterton's article, *The Nation* published an editorial that included the following remarks.

> It really seems as if some of the professors who have rushed into print to defend Germany's cause are doing it quite as much harm as the enemy. Take, for instance, the appeal "To the Civilized World," published by ninety-three German *savants,* which has just reached us. Some of the most distinguished names in Germany are signed to it.... Yet the appeal itself is discreditable to their intelligence, and is certain to react against their cause. We waive the fact that the English in which it is couched is grotesque, with merely one citation: "The iron mouth of events has proved the untruth of the fictitious German defeats, consequently misrepresentations and calumny are all the more eagerly at work."[47]

Anyone turning over the current papers, of more than one party and more than one continent, will become rather bored with the cant about Serbia. He will grow tired of the criticisms on that country; and still more with the apologies for it. Serbia needs no apology: she is more likely to extort one. She is what everyone knew her to be: a small, strong, painfully patriotic nation, which as done a great work that the Great Powers did not dare to do. The Turk insulted Vienna. Vienna would not avenge the insult: Belgrade did avenge it.[48] Hence these tears, these boiling crocodile tears of jealousy and an imperial shame. It is therefore necessary to urge against the Serbians all the facts that prove them to be of a simpler or even more savage race. It is said that these Slav Princes are killed by their subjects; while the more enlightened German princes can often be trusted to kill themselves. In short, we are asked to forget the whole sudden triumph of the Last Crusade, which expelled the Turk from Europe, because that great chivalric effort was effected by peoples whose record was rude and bloody.

47. "Blundering German Professors," *The Nation* 99 (October 29, 1914), 513. Prof. Harnack was one of the 93 "*savants*" who signed the appeal. Germany had not been defeated in the sense of being thrown out of France, but the primary purpose for its preemptive attack through Belgium had failed. Germany feared encirclement—a war in which France and Britain attacked from the west while Russia attacked from the east. To counter that possibility, it planned to attack first and defeat France quickly, so its forces could move east to stop Russia's huge but slow-to-mobilize army. When it failed to surround Paris and win a quick victory, in part thanks to Britain's small but highly professional army, it lacked sufficient forces to win in either the east or west. That's why Harnack was angry at the British for thwarting those well-laid plans.

48. Like the Turkish-dominated Ottoman Empire, Austria-Hungary ruled over many nationalities. Multiethnic empires tend to be unstable and must squelch rebellions. As a result, Austria-Hungary was willing to overlook insults from Turks that it would not tolerate from Serbs and others who fought against Turkish rule in the Balkan Wars (1912–1913), which Chesterton seems to be calling the "Last Crusade." Serbian success against the Turks might be copied by ethnic groups in the Austria-Hungary empire.

Anyone acquainted with history will smile a little. We ourselves did things equally criminal, in the days when *we* were capable of doing things equally chivalrous. Indeed, we did few things so respectable as the regicide attributed to the Serbian house. An entirely lawful King of England was secretly butchered by the mother of the victor of Crecy.[49] Another lawful King of England was secretly butchered by the father of the victor of Agincourt.[50] I have not observed that this private gore is allowed to bespatter the public glory. I have not noticed that Scotchmen blush slightly at the mention of Bannockburn because poor Comyn's murder certainly paved the way to that victory.[51] I have not noticed that Noncomformist ministers shrink from mentioning the rise of the Puritans, because the dagger of Felton and the death of Buckingham certainly was a signal for the whole Puritan revolt.[52] I am not aware that any old Tory was ever restrained from toasting Trafalgar or Talavera, because of the extreme indelicacy of Marat being murdered in his bath.[53] Great crimes go side by side with great times. Only, strange as it may seem, the Serbians and all the States struggling against the Turks have lived through great times for centuries.

Consider for a moment what the actual character of their history has been. The effort of the Crusades was sufficient to stop the advance of Islam, but not sufficient to exhaust it. A few centuries after, the Moslem attacked once more, with more modern weapons and in a more indifferent age; and, amid the disputes of diplomatists and the dying debates of the Reformation, he succeeded in sailing up the Danube and nearly becoming a central European Power like Poland or Austria.[54] From this position, after prodigious efforts, he was slowly and painfully dislodged. But Austria, though rescued, was exhausted and reluctant to pursue, and the Turk was left in possession

49. At the Battle of Crécy (1346) in northern France during the Hundred Years' War, Edward III of England (1312–1377) used the long bow to defeat Philip VI of France (1293–1350). His mother, Isabella of France (*c.* 1295–1358), played a major role in removing from power and killing his father, Edward II (1284–1327).

50. In the Battle of Agincourt (October 25, 1415) England's Henry V (1387–1422) defeated a much larger French force in a battle in northern France. (The battle is dramatized in Shakespeare's *Henry V.*) His father, Henry IV (1367–1413) removed Richard II (1367–1400) from the throne and probably killed him.

51. In the Wars of Scottish Independence, the Battle of Bannockburn (June 23–24, 1314) was a major victor for the Scots led by Robert Bruce (1274–1329). John III Comyn (*d.* 1306) was a contender for the Scottish throne and his murder eight years earlier by Robert Bruce cleared the way for Bruce to become King Robert I.

52. John Felton (*c.* 1595–1628) stabbed to death George Villiers, the first Duke of Buckingham (1592–1628), an event which became part of Alexandre Dumas' *The Three Musketeers* (1844). English Puritans were angered by the Duke's negotiations with France, in which he tried to trade English assistance in France's war with Huguenots (French Protestants) for French assistance in fighting the Spanish in the Palatinate on the Rhine River.

53. Both battles came during the Napoleonic wars and pitted English against French. The Battle of Trafalgar (October, 21 1805) was an English victory and the most important naval battle in the war. The Battle of Talavera (July 27–28 1809) in Spain was inconclusive, with both English and French withdrawing after the fighting. There is no direct connection between the battles and the killing of Jean-Paul Marat (1743–1793). But Marat was one of the most violent leaders in the French Revolution, and English Tories were no doubt delighted to see him dead.

54. Chesterton would write of people incapable of understanding what was going on and compare Islam with Prussia in a July 20, 1915 letter to E.C. Bentley: "It is a stagnant state of mind created in people who have never been forced by revolution or other public peril to distinguish between the things they are used to and the thoughts for which the things are supposed to stand.... So long as St. Paul's Cathedral stood in the usual place they would not mind if there was a Crescent on top of it instead of a Cross. By the way I see the Germans have actually done what I described as a wild fancy in the *Flying Inn*; combined the Cross and the Crescent in one ornamental symbol." Maisie Ward, *Gilbert Keith Chesterton* (London: Sheed & Ward, 1944), 340.

of the countries he had devoured in his advance.[55] Most human beings do not know what human nature is. They have never seen it on a raft, or in a retreat, or in any kind of wreck, in which men really feel themselves lost or left behind. **Any general of an army, any captain of a ship, will tell you that such things are terrible, even for five days, even for five hours. In this case it lasted for five centuries.** The Christians strove to keep their faith, though they had lost their frontiers; strove to keep their courage even when they had lost their faith. And through all those centuries, that which should have come to their rescue never came. And when the full circle of five hundred years had rolled, it came to the rescue of their oppressors.

Those who talk for or against Austria must remember what Austria is—or, what is even more important as most human beings go, what it is supposed to be. It is customary to say that Austria is an incongruous and patchwork empire; and, while this is true, there is an answer to it. The answer is that Austria is not an empire: it is the Empire. Its original position was that it had as much right to be patchwork as the political system ruled by Tiberius or Hadrian.[56] In theory it is the Holy Roman Empire; that is, the Roman Empire christened. The double-headed eagle on its shield is not (as many suppose) a joke, like the Siamese Twins. It means that Austria claims the Empire of the East and of the West—that one eagle looks towards Constantinople and the other towards Rome. It is, therefore, all the more unfortunate that this bird should have come to be associated with obstructing the revival of Italy and preventing the recovery of Byzantium.

It appears to me impossible to get the perspective of the present war, unless the Balkan War stands up in the landscape as large as that great Black Mountain from which its guns began. I will not, I repeat, pause here upon the pigmy sneers and more pigmy apologies of those whose minds are full of the fact that there was once an assassination in a Serbian palace. Let those who study the multiplication-tables of murder decide for me how many Belgian peasants make one Serbian King. **My own taste in murder has always been rather for the knife of Brutus, which strikes upward, than for the knife of Nero, which strikes down; but I will not urge such particular tastes here.**[57] Of the Serbians and the other Balkans, it is enough for me

55. For Austria, the two major battles in the struggle against Islam were the Siege of Vienna in 1529 and the Battle of Vienna on September 11–12, 1683. The arrival of Polish troops on the outskirts of Vienna on September 11 (not accidentally the same date as the attack on the Twin Towers in New York City) was the high-water mark in the Islam's centuries-long effort to conquer Europe. While most of Europe was saved from death or forced conversion, the Balkans remained under Ottoman rule. Chesterton's five hundred years date roughly from the fall of Constantinople in 1453.

In *The River War* (1899), Winston Churchill wrote something similar about Europe's struggle with Islam.

> No stronger retrograde force exists in the world. Far from being moribund, Mohammedanism is a militant and proselytising faith. It has already spread throughout Central Africa, raising fearless warriors at every step; and were it not that Christianity is sheltered in the strong arms of science, the science against which it had vainly struggled, the civilisation of modern Europe might fall as fell the civilisation of ancient Rome. [Quoted in Martin Gilbert, *Churchill and the Jews: A Lifelong Friendship*, (New York: Henry Holt, 2007), 53–54.]

56. These are two Roman Emperors: Tiberius Caesar (42 BC–AD 37) was Roman emperor from AD 14 until his death in 37. Hadrian (AD 76 –138) ruled from 117–138. Both were well-respected and typified Rome at its height.

57. Brutus was one of those who killed the powerful Julius Caesar in 44 BC. The Emperor Nero brutally persecuted Rome's Christians in 64 AD, attempting, it is said, to blame them for a fire that struck the city.

that they went where we would not go, and led when Europe would not follow: and that because of them the world is changed.

If I may turn to lighter topics, the scholarship of Professor Harnack has, as we have already seen, left on his mind an impression that there is something called Teutonism. You and I, the English, have broken the obligations of Teutonism. In this, surely, we get a glimpse of the solemn depths of the Deutsche Kultur. **A man need not keep a promise he as made: and therefore we need not keep faith with Belgium. But a man must keep a promise he as never made—or, indeed, ever heard of. And therefore we are bound to keep faith with Teutonism, whatever it may turn out to be.** I remember reading years ago a book that must have been inspired, if not written, by some of these strange provincial Professors who have found their first importance during the last few weeks. It was all about Teutonism.[58] Its method was admirably simple. The author took certain ideas which he happened to like, and said they were German ideas. Then he took other ideas which he didn't happen to like, and said they were French ideas. And whenever he was stumped in history, by the French fighting for the right ideas, he said it was the Gothic blood moving in Gaul. And when he was stumped again, by the Germans fighting for the wrong ideas, he said it was the Gaulish blood stirring in Gothland. Thus if Mr. Bernard Shaw and I bet on a horse (an incident almost inconceivable) and he wins, then you see it was a Chestertonian spirit in him that made him win, and a certain Shavian influence on me that made me lose. It seems to be a very good way. I wonder if it is not more adopted; and I specially wonder if it is not adopted by the Germans in dealing with the Balkan War and its great results.

If Professor Harnack can really persuade himself that the English are the same as the Germans, why cannot he persuade himself that the Serbians are the same as the Germans? And the Russians? Why not explain the Russian victories by saying that here again the all-pervading and all-subduing gods of the North have subdued the sullen mortals of the South. The racial point would be just as easy to prove, in the ridiculous way that such racial points are proved. There are a reasonable number of men in Russia whose hair looks like picked oakum, as there are in Prussia—or in Perthshire. There are a reasonable number of men in Austria whose hair looks like black astrachanl, as there are in Spain—or in South Bucks.[59] Let Professor Harnack merely strain his enlarged mind to a further enlargement—to take in some of those "new truths" which some, in their antiquated way, call lies. Let him but enlarge the significance of Teutonism a little, and he should be able to claim all the courageous acts of the last ten years for his country. Instead of regarding the English as racial recreants and traitors, why should he not regard the Russians and the Serbs as racial representatives and allies? The Slavs have done everything that has been done for long past: they drove the Asiatic from his stolen lands, they burst up the peace of the oppressors. When Slavs have done so much as that, it is clearly necessary to

58. Previously, Chesterton discussed Teutonic theories in the *Illustrated London News*, April 30, 1910.

59. Perthshire is a county in central Scotland, and South Bucks is a district in southeast England, thus anyplace.

prove that they are not Slavs, but Teutons. Surely it is a small thing to ask any man of science to prove that!

G.K. Chesterton, "Our Note-Book," *Illustrated London News* 145 (October 10, 1914), 498. US: October 10, 1914. "The Serbs in History: Harnack and Teutonism."

Pacifism's Dead Words

October 17, 1914

It is cold humbug for any people of the European race to pretend that they recognise the Teuton race or the Celtic race, and are delighted with the one or disgusted with the other.

Editor: Chesterton attacks pacifists for using meaningless and dead words such as "blood-lust" and "race-hatred." European wars, he reminds them, are wars between people who know each other well and differ little in their appearance. He blasts as absurd the idea that Europeans differ racially, a foul idea that will bring untold grief in the next generation. It's also revealing that the very people who claim to hold the key to world peace are so quick to slander those who disagree with them, a trait perhaps linked with the vanity of pacifist leaders that Chesterton later discusses.

In one of those small and terrible touches in which the private letters of soldiers abound, there was a phrase about a small side street being so choked with German dead that some of them had not even had room to fall, but remained in various standing or leaning postures, looking as if they were alive. To me there is something beyond the most fiendish fancy in that scene in broad daylight—that lifeless mob, that voiceless struggle, that waxwork erectness, that waxwork immobility. The soldier, however, only mentioned it as explaining the practical difficulties of penetrating a town; and in this aspect also the incident is not devoid of imagination or even of allegory.

Just as that modern military progress was choked with dead men, so our modern mental progress is choked with dead words. I do not mean phrases I think false, as one thinks of a false religion or political remedy: I mean dead—in the sense that they have no life in them, even in the minds of those who use them. They are the trophies of talking nonsense for thirty or forty years; they are stereotypes set up in times of security and thoughtlessness; they flow easily from the pen, and they have no reference to anything good, bad, or indifferent. The Pacifists in particular find their path impeded by odd catchwords, which they have become quite used to repeating, but which obviously do not allude, however distantly, to anything in the world. For instance, there is really a great deal to be said against war, especially modern war, with its huge scientific engines and huge conscript armies. It is merciless, it is mechanical; it uses or destroys man and nature for its own purpose. It is anti-domestic like a press-gang, and often secretive like a conspiracy. It makes things depend on small rings of statesmen and diplomatists, often corrupt and always cynical. It has aspects nobody can be proud of, such as the institution of spies. It necessarily interferes with that fundamental carelessness which is akin to kindness and is the wisest of the customs of mankind. It gives the mere scientific expert a more dangerous power than he has in any other department even of the modern world. Also it kills people. Every one of these objections is a real objection, great or small; but we, objecting to these things as much as other men born of women, repeat that in a certain clear case and just cause we think it right to endure them. We are naturally interested in what our dissentient fellow-citizens have to say about it, and we look at Pacifist pamphlets or papers for a re-emphasis of the evils which we have admitted. We find practically nothing of the sort.

We find a string of dead phrases like a string of stale fish. Phrases which fall to pieces one after another if you take hold of them one after another; phrases which have obviously never been exposed to the climate of criticism. I open a highly superior Peace paper, and I find first the phrase that it is always easy to arouse the blood-lust.[60] Now if the man had said that it is always easy, in the metaphorical sense, to make bad blood—to blacken reputations, to revive grudges, to play on particular vanities or inflame particular hopes—he would have been saying what is true, even if it is not new. As it was, he was saying something simply because it was old—familiar to him, the appropriate words, a rhythm that was almost a lullaby. What is the blood-lust? Have you and I any blood-lust? Do we know anybody who has any? Most of us by this time have kindred and close friends who we have known all our lives and whom we saw a little while ago, perhaps for the last time. Had they any blood-lust? Did they look as if they had? Do we, who for one accident or another can only serve with the pen, demand red ink and wish that it was German blood? If our cause is wrong it is wrong because of the vanities, self-deceptions, and jealousies of civilised human beings; and doubtless the German honestly accuses us, as we accuse him, of a disproportionate self-importance. But a disproportionate self-importance is not a thirst for blood, any more than it is a thirst for beer. **The simple truth is that, somewhere in the mid-Victorian time, philosophers talked about war and tried to explain it away, hoping soon to sweep it away. It was the fashion just then to find all human history in the Zoological Gardens. They had heard something about the tiger tasting blood, so they said that such things as the Crusades and the French Revolution happened because we had not quite sufficiently "let the ape and tiger die."**[61] We still had a stripe of the tiger about us somewhere: and that made us die for our country like Kosciusko, or be burned for our faith like Joan of Arc.[62] Whether tigers do die for their country or consent to be burned for their opinions, I am not naturalist enough to say; but the naturalists seem to think it was all right. So they started this fashion which is now no more than a phrase: of suggesting that General Joffre wants to bite Prussians and General French to follow him on hands

60. Chesterton criticized Shaw for this same empty appeal to an "imaginary malady called blood-lust" on September 18, 1915, during a debate in the letters section of *The Nation*.

61. "Ape and tiger" is an allusion to Tennyson's poem "In Memoriam." For more, see Appendix E.

62. Tadeusz Kościuszko (1746–1817) was a famous Polish general, fighting for its independence. Joan of Arc (1412–1431) played a similar role in the history of France.

and knees licking up the blood.[63] In truth, of course, almost every other bad motive can move men in war except this animal pleasure in its cruelty.

I read on in my Pacifist paper, and I find some such phrase as "encouraging race-hatred." This may have had some meaning in some cases: such extreme cases as white men and black men; for some white men, otherwise honest and humane, do affirm that they feel the physical division. But who can take such a thing seriously touching a war between the intensive and entangled tribes of Europe? The town of Dunkirk, I think, has been taken over or occupied by the French, by the Spaniards, by the English, by the French again, and most probably by the Flemings or the Dutch. In the chances of war even to-day it might be occupied by Bavarians or Austrians. Does anyone really believe that the people of Dunkirk felt a physical loathing of all these varying Europeans in the sense in which men speak of a physical loathing of the negro? When they brought the good news from Ghent to Aix, does anyone really believe that the messenger from Gand was struck all of a heap by the evident ethnological superiority of the inhabitants of Aachen?[64] **There cannot be any such thing as race-hatred in Europe. But in the case of black, red, or yellow men, the colour prejudice may possibly be a real nervous trouble. In the case of white men it is not a nervous trouble: it is a cowardly trick.**[65] **It is cold humbug for any people of the European race to pretend that they recognise the Teuton race or the Celtic race, and are delighted with the one or disgusted with the other.** If there be such almost bodily aversions which I, thank God, have never found, they are certainly not to be found within the small, domestic, disputed square which we call Europe. It is a family down to the fullest details of family quarrels. Its very fields are paved with battlefield above battlefield, but also with treaty above treaty. It is an alternate and eternal trysting-place of friends and foes. And if those who have met each other thus ceaselessly, century after century, so punctually in the same confined space, so frequently in the same unending quarrel—if these do not know each other, no men will ever know each other till the end of the world.

I have taken these two examples as suggesting a sort of dead language which encumbers all our present controversy. There are a great many bad things in war; it may be that there are a great many bad motives for it. But the desire to slay simply is not there; and the racial repugnance simply is not there. To hear some of such talk, one would suppose that Englishmen and foreigners had never met before, in old battle or in modern business. It is ridiculous when the German papers talk as if the German soldier would burst upon Europe as a Superman, obviously different

63. During WWI, Jacques Joffre (1852–1931) was a popular French general, while John French (1852–1925) commanded the British Expeditionary Force.

64. Gand is the French name for Ghent, Belgium, and Aix is Aachen, Germany. "How They Brought the Good News from Ghent to Aix" is an 1845 poem by Robert Browning, who admitted it was not based on any historical event. Only one rider of three completes the epic 100-mile journey, and at the end of the poem, he is concerned only for his horse, who collapsed from the effort to reach the city. Interestingly, there exists a recording of Browning reciting the first stanza of this popular poem, which is one of the first recordings ever made.

65. Notice how Chesterton equates racial hatred with a "cowardly trick."

from everyone else. We have seen him at Waterloo—and at Jena.[66] But it is equally ridiculous when English papers talk as if the British soldier burst upon France as a man more magnificent than that nation of warriors had every seen. Both seem to forget that all three have very often met before. The field over which the war is moving is a mosaic not only of French but of English defeats and victories. It is no more of a novelty for us to be fighting across the Channel than it is for the Germans or the French to be fighting across the Rhine. The truth is that Western Europe had a knock on its head some centuries ago, and its memory is only slowly coming back. But we can at least be done with the dreams and half-delusions that haunted its slow recovery: the false expectations of the past, the crazy pictures of the future. Let the Pacifists tell us about looting and spying and spoiling the dead, for these are the horrors of war. But let them never tell us any more about the blood-lust and race-hatred, about a man being half a tiger or the European being half a cannibal. For these are the horrors of peace, the nightmares which could only have come to us while we slept; and in this hour we are awakened.

G.K. Chesterton, "Our Note-Book," *Illustrated London News* (October 17, 1914), 556. US: October 17, 1914. Also published as "The Dead Words of the Pacifists."

1914

War, Noble but Unnatural

November 21, 1914 (excerpt)

For the highest mark of Christian civilisation is this capacity for feeling that the sword is at once noble and unnatural; and the more unnatural it is, the more noble it is.

Editor: This article, with its broad look at war, is an apt place to put an extraordinary compliment that a fellow journalist, Julius West, made of Chesterton in 1915. While writing of the many changes the war brought to England in the autumn of 1914, he turned to its harmful effects on the news media and the ugliness that resulted.

> Those of us who had not the fortune to escape the Press by service abroad, especially those of us who derived our living from it, came to loathe its misrepresentation of the English people. There seemed no end to the nauseous vomits of undigested facts and dishonorable prejudices that came pouring out in daily streams. **Then we came to realize, as never before, the value of such men as Chesterton.** Christianity and the common decencies fare badly at the hands of the bishops of to-day, and the journalists threw them over as soon as the war began. But, unfortunately for us all, G.K.C. fell seriously ill in the early period of the war, and was in a critical state for many months. But not before he had published a magnificent recantation—for it is no less—of all those bitternesses which, in their sum, had very nearly caused him to hate the British. It is a poem, "Blessed are the Peacemakers."
>
> Of old with a divided heart
> I saw my people's pride expand,
> Since a man's soul is torn apart

66. Chesterton chose his examples well. Napoleon defeated the Prussians at Jena on October 14, 1806. Almost nine years later, the Prussians helped the British defeat Napoleon at Waterloo on June 18, 1815.

By mother earth and fatherland.

I knew, through many a tangled tale,
Glory and truth not one but two:
King, Constable, and Amirail
Took me like trumpets: but I knew

A blacker thing than blood's own dye
Weighed down great Hawkins on the sea;
And Nelson turned his blindest eye
On Naples and on liberty.

Therefore to you my thanks, O throne,
O thousandfold and frozen folk,
For whose cold frenzies all your own
The Battle of the Rivers broke;

Who have no faith a man could mourn,
Nor freedom any man desires;
But in a new clean light of scorn
Close up my quarrel with my sires;

Who bring my English heart to me,
Who mend me like a broken toy;
Till I can see you fight and flee
And laugh as if I were a boy.[67]

When we read this poem, with its proclamation of a faith restored, Chesterton's temporary absence from the field of letters appears even more lamentable.[68]

On November 25, four days after the article that follows was published, Chesterton was defending England's declaration of war against Bernard Shaw in an auditorium filled with Oxford University students, when he became dizzy and had to quit. Returning home obviously sick, he tried to write a letter to Shaw. Before he could finish, he became so sick, he collapsed into bed, breaking it down. A doctor was called in and then specialists, but no one could agree what was wrong. Heart trouble, gout, kidney failure and a throat infection were all blamed. In the end, it may have been several illnesses complicated by extreme exhaustion. On Christmas Eve he fell into a coma that he would drift into and out of for several weeks. In mid-January he began a slow recovery. Only on Easter Eve did his wife become sure that he would recover.[69]

This is the last article Chesterton would write for the *Illustrated London News* until he recovers and is strong enough to write the May 22, 1915 article which opens the

---

67. In Middle English an Amirail was "a Saracen ruler or commander, an emir, an admiral." Admiral Sir John Hawkins (1532–1595) built the English navy that defeated the Spanish Armada. Vice-Admiral Horatio Nelson (1758–1805) is England's most famous naval leader. After fighting at Naples in 1799, he was accused of turning "his blindest eye" to the killing of prisoners by his monarchist allies. Chesterton's "Battle of the Rivers" may refer to the Battle of Charleroi, a key German victory fought along the Sambre and Meuse rivers in late August 1914.

68. Julius West, *G.K. Chesterton: A Critical Study* (London: Martin Secker, 1915), 179–181. Chesterton's friend Bernard Shaw was the target of many of these harsh attacks.

69. For a more complete account of Chesterton's illness, see Joseph Pearce, *Wisdom and Innocence: A Life of G.K. Chesterton* (London: Hodder & Sloughton, 1996), 213–220.

next chapter. In the intervening months, the magazine faithfully kept his column vacant, awaiting his return, a mark of their great respect for him.

ON every sword that is made by man, while the workshops of the world turn out that terrible kind of cutlery, ought to be graven the two mysterious phrases which were on the fairy sword of King Arthur. On one side was written "Take me," and on the other "Cast me away." If no more than this dim fable recalled the doubtful hero of Camelot, we should know that he defended Christendom against the heathen. **For the highest mark of Christian civilisation is this capacity for feeling that the sword is at once noble and unnatural; and the more unnatural it is, the more noble it is.** People talk of drawing the sword and throwing away the scabbard; but when it is drawn really splendidly, one feels always that the swordsman may throw away the sword as well. Perhaps the truest parable of the central and civilised spirit of Europe is that of the Norman knight who rode into battle like a juggler as well as a *jongleur*; [Fr. juggler] not only singing the rhymes of Roland, but throwing his sword into the air and catching it again—expressing, in a profoundly Christian paradox, at once his dexterity with the weapon and his indifference to it. This is very symbolic indeed of the real history of our peaces and our wars. Europe (and especially France) has never thrown up the sponge; but Europe (and especially France) has often thrown up the sword, sending it flying into the seven heavens of abandoned idealism, but always with a sub-conscious conviction that it can be caught again if necessary. Sometimes it is not caught again; and the result is an unexpected catastrophe, and the triumph of inferior things. Sometimes it is caught again, as it has most certainly been caught again by the French during the last few months. But though the French in this campaign had been more victorious than all their fathers under Louis or Napoleon, they would not found an empire—certainly not an empire that would endure. The French never built their European influence upon concrete foundations, for concrete foundations forbid the flowers and grass of the world to grow. Anyone can see, I think, something almost consciously temporary about the tremendous omnipresence of Napoleon: something merely suggestive, as of a resolute man making a rapid sketch, and leaving the rest to his followers—or even his foes. Such great success is abnormal; and the really great men know it is abnormal. Upon the other side of the blade is written "Cast Me Away."

Among the second-rate or semi-savage traits of modern Germany is the absence of this sense. Many of the Prussian writers have obviously come to think war normal. Nay, many of them can bring themselves to think an armed peace normal, which is even more inhuman and extravagant. The Prussian goes to bed in his uniform. His head has become part of his helmet. And, sincere as we are in the wish to destroy German militarism without destroying German culture, we shall really (in all probability) find it a very fine and delicate piece of marksmanship to shoot off his helmet without shooting off his head. **He has come, in some confused way, to regard all cultivation in art or science, all organisation in labour or**

comradeship, as a means to an end. And that end is what most of us, in the abstract, would call the end of the world. The violence which for us is incidental, for him is involved and implied. The trunk of the tree may be the old German tower, the civic and even sleepy sentinel of so many old German towns. The trunk, I say, may be the tower; the flower may be the flag; but the fruit is the cannon-ball. Of this great and prosperous people one may say, in a horrible parody of the old phrase of ascetic devotion, that all life is a learning to die!

That is, the Hun has grown used to the horse; he sticks to the saddle; he has become a quadruped, like the centaur. The parallel is not false. He has fallen in the scale of animals, precisely because he has permitted himself to make militarism neither a pageant nor a plot, but a habit, like the habits of beasts and birds. It might be argued that he *could not* disarm, as it used amiably to be argued that if some of the old misers had been washed there would have been nothing of them left at the bottom of the bath. Now there can be no doubt, to say the least of it, that a complex and sympathetic case can be made out for Frederick in the Seven Years' War, or even the treatment of the Ems despatch, and certainly much more for the resentment against the French after Jena and the Napoleonic occupation. It is, therefore, quite human and conceivable that the Prussians should have appeared on a particularly high horse after Rosbach, after Leipzig, or after Sedan.[70] But it is a bad thing to get on to so high a horse that one cannot get off it; and the Prussian's horse has simply run away with him. **What was, perhaps, originally a series of spirited self-defences has, by this time, linked itself up and lengthened into one long perspective of perpetual offence.**[71] The exception has become the rule, and that is the worst of all possible tyrannies. Now this kind of thing is quite different from any action, however fantastic or however severe, which a State can adopt at a special crisis which it knows to be a crisis. The latter is a sign of strength in the sense that it is a sign of strength to leap aside lightly. The former is only a sign of strength in the sense that it is a sign of strength to sit down heavily....

G.K. Chesterton, "Our Note-Book," *Illustrated London News* 145 (November 21, 1914), 690.
US: November 21, 1914. Also published as "The Current Scene."

70. These were three German victories over the French, coming in 1757, 1813 and 1870 respectively.

71. Living in "perpetual offense" at what has been done to you illustrates the danger of adopting the role of victim with a long list of wrongs to be avenged by victory in war. One of Germany's leading modern historians had this to say of his nation at the outbreak of the war. "Germans of today can look back only with dismay, after having passed through two disastrous wars in a generation, on the abrupt change from the idea of a purely defensive war to that of a war of conquest that then took place in Germany. Not that the entire German nation was implicated in this change, but it did involve a wide strata of the middle class and especially the intelligentsia. It almost seems as though the Germans had suddenly become intoxicated in anticipation of victory, turning a blind eye to their desperate plight." Gerhard Ritter, *The Sword and the Scepter: The Problem of Militarism in Germany* (Coral Gables: University of Miami Press, 1972), 23.

3

Battling Pacifism

1915

1915

Chesterton's Pen—Editor

During Chesterton's prolonged absence, the *Illustrated London News* carried a notice that "owing to the illness of Mr. G.K. Chesterton," it would not publish his column that week. His almost fatal illness lasted longer than expected, but the paper kept his column open. Years later, Chesterton described what happened.

> Immediately after the outbreak of War, I was bowled over by a very bad illness, which lasted for many months and at one time came very near to ending so as to cut me off from all newspaper communication and this wicked world. The last thing I did while I was still on my feet, though already very ill, was to go to Oxford and speak to a huge packed mass of undergraduates in defence of the English Declaration of War. That night is a nightmare to me; and I remember nothing except that I spoke on the right side. Then I went home and went to bed, tried to write a reply to Bernard Shaw, of which about one paragraph may still exist, and was soon incapable of writing anything. The illness left certain results that prevented me, even when I had recovered, from doing anything more useful than writing....
>
> When I first recovered full consciousness, in the final turn of my long sickness, I am told that I asked for *Land and Water*, in which Mr. Belloc had already begun his well-known series of War articles, the last of which I had read, or been able to understand, being the news of the new hope from the Marne. When I woke again to real things, the long battles before Ypres were over and the long trench war had begun.[1] The nurse, knowing that I had long been incapable of really reading anything, gave me a copy of the paper at random, as one gives a doll to a sick child. But I suddenly asserted in a loud and clear voice that this was an old number dealing with the first attempt before Nancy;[2] and that I wanted all the numbers of the paper that had appeared since the Battle of the Marne. My mind, such as it is, had suddenly become perfectly clear; as clear as it is now....
>
> At my clear and reiterated request, they brought me the whole huge file of the weekly paper; and I read it steadily through, understanding all the facts and figures

1. The Battle of the Marne was fought from September 5–12 and halted the Germans before Paris. The First Battle of Ypres was from October 19 to November 22, 1914 and brought an end to the Race to the Sea, during which both sides tried to outflank their enemy by moving northward, only to be met by opposing trenches that eventually covered almost all the disputed land from Switzerland to the North Sea . His illness struck during the last week of November, so he remembered the conclusion to the Marne but not that of Ypres.

2. This was roughly the last week in August, when Germany responded to French attempts to take Alsace-Lorraine by mounting an offensive on Nancy, forcing the French to withdraw and defend the city.

and diagrams and calculations, and studying them so closely that I really felt at the end that I had not lost very much of the general history of the War.[3]

SEIZING THE PEN

May 22, 1915

It is not true, of course, that all Prussians would insult prisoners or slaughter children. But it is true that all Prussians are brought up with a wrong moral attitude towards such things; and are taught to see something of magnificence in the successful tyrant rather than in the spirited slave.

EDITOR: This is Chesterton's first article after his illness. The quote at the end of the first paragraph is of great importance in understanding Chesterton's intentions during the war. It's from a lengthy and once well-known poem, "The Ring and the Book" (1868–1869) by Robert Browning (1812–1889), based on an actual court case in Italy. A Count Guido had been found guilty of murdering his wife and her parents after suspecting her of adultery. In Book X of the poem, the reforming Pope Innocent XII (1615–1700) debates whether to grant clemency, an action that would win the approval of many. After much internal debate, the Pope, recognizing he is old and may die soon, seizes a pen and signs the Count's death warrant with these words: "Enough, for I may die this very night: And how should I dare die, this man let live? Carry this forthwith to the Governor!"

Chesterton understood the relevance of that bold deed. Having recently come close to death, he must make a similar choice. With this article, he chose the boldness of that Pope, rejecting two popular alternatives. He rejects militarism, which would mean hating the Germans while imitating their methods. He also rejects pacifism, which would require him to tolerate "a cancer" he knows has killed Germany and may destroy all Europe. Like "Browning's Pope," he will take up his pen.[4]

This article also illustrates Chesterton's marvelous ability to think independently. While virtually all England was outraged over the sinking of the *Lusitania*, it took a Chesterton to point out that, "our enemies have no more scored off the British Empire by sinking the largest Atlantic boat than they would have conquered the Indian Empire by shooting the largest Indian elephant." His point is that in any conflict it is important to distinguish between events that are important militarily and events that merely stir up emotions. During the American Revolution, Ben Franklin said much the same when he argued: "Britain, at the expense of three millions, has killed 150 Yankies this campaign, which is £20,000 a head; and at Bunker's Hill she gained a mile of ground.... During that same time 60,000 children have been born in America. From these data his mathematical head will easily calculate the time and expense necessary to kill us all, and conquer our whole territory."[5]

3. G.K. Chesterton, *The Autobiography of G.K. Chesterton* (New York: Sheed & Ward, 1936), 255–258.

4. For more on how Chesterton viewed "The Ring and the Book," see *Robert Browning* (1903), where he devotes an entire chapter to explaining why it was the "great epic of the age." He also calls it the "epic of free speech," because Browning allowed every major character in his tale, good or evil, to argue their point of view, much as all Europe was debating who was responsible for the war. In 1903 Chesterton pointed out that, after listening to all sides, we must then decide who is right and act accordingly. Being open minded isn't an excuse for inaction.

5. Stanley Weintraub, *Iron Tears* (New York: Free Press, 2005), 37.

Since I last wrote in this place I have had an entirely new experience called being ill, which, trivial as it was compared to the tragedies surrounding it, was quite close enough to death to make anybody reasonably charitable and modest. Nor I do think it has been otherwise. I have no "bloodlust," whatever that may be. I do not think I even hate the enemy. Mr. William Watson has given his distinguished authority to the culture of such hatred, and says that we should "take a leaf out of the enemy's book."[6] But I do not want the German book, or any leaves out of it. I think it is a book without which any gentleman's library is complete. Nor do I particularly want to write about the war; rather I want to write about everything else. I should like to write an enormous Miltonic epic about the universe, and call it "Paradox Regained."[7] **But oceans of universalism and toleration leave unchanged the simple intellectual certainty which I had and have—that the articulate and effective Prussian is the enemy of the human race; a cancer that has killed Germany and would have killed Europe.** If I were as moribund and as responsible as Browning's Pope, I could still say of the junket, as of Count Guido—

> For I may die to-night,
> And how should I dare die, this man let live?

It should always be remembered that the Germans are right in claiming that they are cultured and that they represent a culture. They do. No white men are such savages by the mere light of Nature. *Nemo repente fit Tirpitzimus.*[8] Whatsoever things are evil in them, whatsoever things are impure, whatsoever things are of bad report—these have truly been cultivated, as poisonous plants can be cultivated; and this explains the paradox of the kindly Germans and the horrible Germany.[9] For it is the nature of a poison to affect different people in different degrees, so that the sanest Prussian has an insane spot in him, the result of his culture. I think I observed somewhere years ago that I could trust the uneducated, but not the badly educated. That is exactly our reason to-day for preferring the fierceness of Serbia to the fierceness of Prussia. **It is not true, of course, that all Prussians would insult prisoners or slaughter children. But it is true that all Prussians are brought up with a wrong moral attitude towards such things; and are taught to see something of magnificence in the successful tyrant rather than in the spirited slave.** It is also true that every Prussian is taught that he could never be the slave, but could

6. Like Chesterton, William Watson (1858–1935) courted unpopularity by opposing the Second Boer War (1899–1903) and supporting Home Rule for Ireland. Chesterton described "The Political Poetry of Mr. William Watson" in *The Fortnightly Review* LXXIV (November 1903), 768. When WWI began, Watson found himself in the unaccustomed position of supporting a popular war and that may have led to the excessive zeal that Chesterton describes. In May 1917 Watson published a collection of poems about the war called *The Man Who Saw*.

7. In the *Illustrated London News* on August 1, 1925 (not in this book), Chesterton wrote: "All my life, or at least the latter part of it, I have been trying to discover the meaning of the word "paradox." It seems to have two meanings—a statement that seems to contain a contradiction or to be intrinsically improbable, and a statement that happens to be different from the catchwords common at a particular moment."

8. Some have observed that this is a pun on a line in one of Juvenal's satires, "Nemo repente fuit turpissimus," or "No one suddenly becomes wicked." Chesterton replaced wicked with a sound-alike, made-up word, *Tirpitzimus*, an allusion to the Admiral Alfred von Tirpitz (1849–1930), head of the German Imperial Navy (1914–1916).

9. Prussianism, Chesterton is suggesting, is the opposite of the biblical command in Philippians 4:8.

always be the tyrant if he chose.[10] This self-satisfaction is the sole spring of all the more showy and sensational evils. And it needs neither malice nor bitterness to see that the only possible cure for it is ruinous military defeat. In short, we are fighting against the Smile that Won't Come Off by any other process. Whatever may happen first in the passes of the Carpathians or the gorges of the Vosges, there is only one valley to which the German host must at last be driven—which is called the Valley of Humiliation.[11]

But there is one aspect of the matter which most of our newspapers insist on far too little, and some of them not at all. Yet it is a character particularly to be kept in view, precisely because it enables us to keep our hearts hot but our heads cool. And logic and patience are things necessary for justice or even for successful revenge. I mean the fact that the Prussian's recent proceedings show beyond question that his head is not cool, whatever his heart may be. There is a danger that in denouncing the vastness of his crime we may exaggerate the vastness of his power. He retains his old pantomimic liking for doing things on a large scale; but the practical results are not equally large.[12] Affairs like the *Lusitania* awaken the maximum of hatred while doing the minimum of harm.[13] It may seem odd to call the *Lusitania* a minimum; but I am talking of military or naval harm, as weighed by the science of war. The Pro-Germans held up their hands in horror at Serbia because its last King was murdered; but at least he was the King, and he was the prop of foreign interference and foreign tyranny. But what good does it do the Germans to assassinate Mr. Charles Frohman?[14] In a military sense, to use Bismarck's phrase, it would not be worth the bones of one Pomeranian grenadier to blow up ten such ships with ten such crowds of travellers.[15] Morally considered, it was a huge crime; but as an act of war it was a huge irrelevance. Humanly considered, we have lost a good ship. But inhumanly considered—that is, Teutonically considered—they have lost two good torpedoes. These great pleasure-boats have only a sort of Barnum celebrity; their size and swiftness give them the interest that attaches to freaks. But our enemies have no more scored off the British Empire by sinking the largest Atlantic boat than they would

---

10. This may allude to Abraham Lincoln's remark: "As I would not be a slave, so I would not be a master. This expresses my idea of democracy. Whatever differs from this, to the extent of the difference, is no democracy."

11. The Carpathians are mountains to Germany's east, while the Vosges are to Germany's west along the Rhine. The only chance of reforming Germany, Chesterton believes, is the severe and humiliating defeat the nation will suffer at the end of WWI. Chesterton will emphasize this in the last year of the war and its aftermath.

12. Chesterton uses an interesting analogy. In the *Oxford English Dictionary*, "pantomimic" is a adjective meaning "That uses gestures, mime, or mimicry." It's hard to imagine a stolid Prussian gesturing like an excitable Italian, but Chesterton means that on the world stage Germany uses "large" gestures that accomplish little, like a speaker waving his arms wildly. Sinking the *Lusitania* aroused strong emotions—it was a grand gesture in a perverse sense—but it did little to harm Britain's ability to make war. Modern terrorism is similarly 'pantomimic.' preferring gestures over substance. See his October 30, 1915 article, where he refers to "sanguinary pantomimes."

13. The *Lusitania* was sank by a German submarine on May 7, 1915, two weeks before this issue was published.

14. The American theatrical producer Charles Frohman (1860–1915) died in the sinking of the *Lusitania*.

15. In the summer of 1875, with the Balkan rivalry between Russia and Austria hinging on which side Germany took, Bismarck, with a family estate in Pomerania, told the Reichstag, there was "no interest on behalf of which it is worth our risking—excuse my plain speaking—the healthy bones of one of our Pomeranian musketeers."

have conquered the Indian Empire by shooting the largest Indian elephant.[16] What they have done is to add enormously to their living enemies without adding to their dead ones. Some people have talked with terror and some with admiration of the German efficiency; but this sort of thing is not efficiency, and those who do it cannot really be efficient in any virile intellectual sense. The thing is murder; but it is also sentimentalism. It is a *crime passionel*, of a kind that is akin to suicide.

This is the truth that we want to tell the Germans—that their acts are horrible, but not terrible. Such hope as Germany has left depends entirely upon this notion that she can spread a sort of nightmare over all our cities and counties.[17] It is our business to show her that she cannot. Among the many shrewd things said by the great Napoleon, one of the shrewdest was "Never do what the enemy wants." The present enemy wants to make our flesh creep even more than to make our blood flow; and it is for us who cannot give our blood in battle to show at least that the flesh of Englishmen is not a creeping thing. And the mass of Englishmen do show it, save when they catch the hysteria of a few irresponsible papers. When the Superman drops about a hundred bombs and kills but one woman at Southend (which is not exactly the brightest jewel in the British crown), we mourn for the one woman, but we laugh at the hundred bombs. We laugh at them because they are funny. And if anyone thinks such cheerfulness reckless or vain, there is a very simple reply: Read the letters or listen to the talk of the poor fellows who have been where the German guns do aim and the German shells do hit, and you will find their letters and their talk full of an incessant jesting, which should make any man ashamed of being solemn about the blundering Zeppelin or the indiscriminate bomb. If they who have seen Prussian victories can still laugh, surely we who have seen nothing but Prussian failures may be permitted to smile. There in the green fields of France, and not on the green benches of Westminster, are the real representatives of the people of England; and in nothing more representative than in mixing all their tragedy with frank and genial farce. **The most unlettered lad in the trenches is more worthy to be the countryman of Shakespeare and Dickens than those who pervert the**

16. Before the war, Germany and Britain were fierce rivals at building the biggest and fastest ocean liners.

17. Horror creates outrage, inspiring action. Terror paralyzes with fear and makes "our flesh creep." Chesterton believes contrary emotions (such as laughter and jesting) are the best response to attempts to terrorize, making an England at war a Merry England. His editor at the *Daily News* described Chesterton doing just that.

> I sometimes think that one moonlight night, when he is tired of Fleet Street, he will scale the walls of the Tower and clothe himself in a suit of giant mail, with shield and sword to match. He will come forth with vizor up and mount the battle-steed that champs its bit outside. And the clatter of his hoofs will ring through the quiet of the city night as he thunders through St. Paul's Churchyard and down Ludgate Hill and out on to the Great North Road. And then once more will be heard the cry of "St. George for Merry England!" and there will be the clash of swords in the greenwood and brave deeds done on the King's highway. [A.G. Gardiner, "Gilbert K. Chesterton," in Cecil Chesterton, *G.K. Chesterton: A Criticism* (Seattle, Inkling Books, 2007), 174.]

With his remarks about horror and terror, Chesterton described to near perfection the great divide that developed in the United States and around the world after the September 11, 1991 attack on the World Trade Center. Some were horrified at the evil they had seen and responded with outrage, action, and humor. Others were so paralyzed with fear, their every action was seen as fraught with danger. For the latter, even their sense of humor vanished and jokes about terrorism or the mere mention of the word in news stories became too much to handle. As Chesterton will note in the next chapter, "Legs can be used for other purposes than that of running away." We can run to a fight as well as run away from it. Note too the merry fighting in *The Napoleon of Notting Hill*.

English language to the praise of an un-English pessimism. The soldiers are still claiming, and we will continue to claim, the right to say, not only "St. George for England," but "St. George for Merry England," when all is done.

G.K. Chesterton, "Our Note-Book," *Illustrated London News* 146 (May 22, 1915), 653. US: May 22, 1915. Also published as "Taking a Proper View of Prussians."

FREE AND SEPARATE

May 29, 1915

One fact has emerged out of all this frenzy and pain as a thing incombustible might come out of a furnace: the sincerity, the reality, the eternity of free, separate, and sovereign peoples.

EDITOR: Chesterton criticizes pacifists for impractical, halfway solutions that would neither keep the peace nor allow people to live free. In 1926 he would deal with a similar proposal for a "international Police Force controlled by the League of Nations." The proposal, Chesterton said, "made my blood run cold." The peace it would impose "appears to me so terrifying that a war of the whole world would seem in comparison to be a sort of soothing platitude." He raises practical problems with such a force, including what language they would speak, but he makes clear where the real danger lay. As "the only armed police of the world," it made sense to ask whether it was not "possible that the League of Nations would be controlled by the armed police."[18] The Praetorian Guard played a similarly dangerous role in later Roman history. In the end, king-makers become more powerful than the king.

IT is customary to talk about the war fever; but in those who still exhibit it, the peace fever is much more feverish. With these people peace is not as much a prejudice as a mania. There is said to be a sort of person in the lunatic asylums who thinks he is a chicken. But even he is only somewhat exaggerating his legitimate claim to know his own business best. He is too modest to commit himself to the proposition that all human beings are chickens. That, however, is very much the proposition to which the extreme Pacifist commits himself, for he really talks of man as if he were talking of some other animal; as if a naturalist were to class men with poultry merely because they have two legs. **Legs can be used for other purposes than that of running away; and man's highest moral and mental powers can be used for other purposes than that of keeping the peace.** Mere Pacifism has in this crisis failed fully to support anything or anybody, even its own best exponents, and that for a perfectly simple reason: that mere Pacifism is morally wrong. Mere peace does not fill the heart; it does not satisfy the conscience or even the affections. I have heard of a person having the highly unpleasant accomplishment of being able to stop his

18. The Joseph M. Kenworthy (1886–1953) article Chesterton describes was published in the *Humanist*, but its content may be reflected in a book, *Peace or War?*, that Kenworthy published in 1927 with a foreword by H.G. Wells). Kenworthy was odd. He claimed, as a junior officer, to have been privy to a high-level Navy conference that deliberately steered the *Lusitania* into danger to create an incident. No evidence supports his charge. The ship was sunk because its captain ignored repeated warnings by the Royal Navy to steer a different course. From the October 9, 1926 *Illustrated London News* in *The Collected Works of G.K. Chesterton* vol. XXXIV, 176–180.

heart from beating; and men of a generous and civilised breed can only reject the case for just anger and battle by an artificial stoppage of the heart.

It is one of the results of this that those Pacifists who are too old to drop their doctrine entirely, but too healthy-minded to apply it entirely, are driven to the most extraordinary compromises.[19] One of the most brilliant and idealistic of our Liberalists, for example, admitted that complete peace could only be imposed on the world as the Roman peace was imposed; that is, by a central armed force superior to any other that could take the field. He seemed to admit that the Hague Conference would have to be equipped with such coercive powers if it was to do any good. But he added that he himself would prefer that it should be naval rather than military power. This seems to me a startling incidence of the utterly meaningless moderation of men who lose their own dogmas but cannot find any other. **A central power to police the whole world into peace may be, as this writer would think it, the dawn of political perfection. It may be, as I should think it, a nightmare of political oppression.** But I cannot conceive why the act of oppression should be any better because you do it in a boat; or why the act of peace and justice should be any worse because you do it in your boots and walking about on dry land. It is hard to see what there is more 'Christian' (I use the word as these people use it) about interfering in other people's business with a naval gun than with a field-gun. It is also obvious, of course, that coercion applied by a cosmopolitan navy alone would not be even cosmopolitan; for it could not be universal. A war might rage between the Hungarians and the Poles and go on for ever; because Warsaw is scarcely a seaside resort. On the other hand, if anybody tried to do anything in particular in the Hebrides or the Channel Islands, the international Tolstoian fleet could give them a devil of a time. I see a dreary vision of the poor peacemaker sailing round and round Europe in a great big ship with a great big gun, bumping into all sorts of capes and islands, but trying in vain to stop a war going on somewhere in the middle of Russia. I give this one instance out of a hundred merely to show the hopeless chaos of compromise into which the minds even of the ablest peace philosophers have fallen. Because they are men, because they are Europeans, because they are inheritors of an older and more manly morality, they simply cannot at this moment enforce the full Quaker doctrine of supporting any peace against any war. But, like all men who have lost their own first principles, they cast about trying to draw the line somewhere and draw it everywhere but in the right place. They will distinguish between land wars and sea wars, between Colonial wars and Continental wars, between wars against cultured peoples and wars against uncultured peoples, between wars that are approached

19. Chesterton often fails to mention names, perhaps to avoid personalizing a debate. One remote possibility is John Scurr's "The Pathway to Peace" in the August 18, 1914 *Daily Herald*. It called for the abolition of conscript armies and the creation of an international navy. As it became obvious the war was not going to end quickly, 1915 saw the creation of peace organizations. The League to Enforce the Peace began on April 9 at Independence Hall in Philadelphia with former President William Howard Taft as its first president. The League of Nations Society was founded in England during May 1915 and supported by Edward Grey and Herbert Asquith, both liberals.

slowly and diplomatically, and wars that are undertaken swiftly and suddenly.[20] But somehow they cannot bring themselves simply to distinguish between wars that are right and wars that are wrong. **I should say, rather, perhaps, attacks or resistances; for the war itself is not one thing at all, but is necessarily the collision of two things. And one half of the war is right simply because the other half of the war is wrong.**

I see that Mr. H.G. Wells, whose immense imagination and sensibility make him feel the personal agonies of war with the vividness necessary to a great novelist, is dreaming once again of his old ideal of a governmental peace for the whole planet. In an interesting article in the *Daily Chronicle*, he insists that the world must submit either to this or to a sort of endless tough-and-tumble of rude and ignorant wars. We have, he says, to choose between the World State and the War Path. He will know that I do not speak scornfully, but quite simply and quite seriously when I say that if I have so to choose, I unhesitatingly choose the War Path. Small wars between small States have gone on with the utmost fury and confusion without preventing those who waged them from doing a great many other things. They managed, somehow or other, to snatch a moment to carve the Elgin Marbles; or the Gothic stone; they took a weekend with Socrates or St. Francis; they snatched a moment to build the Tower of Giotto.[21] **But as the modern world is constituted, a Hague Convention, backed by infantry, cavalry, and artillery, would merely arm prigs with the weapons of cut-throats.** It would, in practice, be almost as unrepresentative as a Parliament. It would probably be particularly subject to the very sort of Imperial wire-pulling with which we are now at war. The whole of that deliverance from a Central European tyranny which now seems possible, and in which Mr. Wells rejoices as much as I do, was begun, not by the large nations coming together, but by the small nations breaking loose. The Concert of Europe was an utterly voiceless concert until its silence was broken by the first shot from the hills of Montenegro.[22] The nations were strong where the empires were weak; and the whole progress of the present struggle has been marked by nation after nation rising from the dead. Belgium is more Belgian than it ever was before: it was never so unconquerable until it was conquered. Poland is more Polish than it ever was before: it had never been so united as it has been since it was divided. One fact has emerged out of all this frenzy and pain as a thing incombustible might come out of a furnace: the sincerity, the reality, the eternity of free, separate, and sovereign peoples. It is a strange time to talk of a World State when the poor little princes of the poor little nationalities are already beginning to show themselves stronger than the Prince of the World.

20. Although Bertrand Russell did not intend to make his ideas "Christian," Chesterton may be poking fun at his "The Ethics of War" in the January 1915 *International Journal of Ethics* (excerpted in Appendix E).

21. The beautiful Bell Tower of Giotto in Florence is a marvelous example of Florentine Gothic. Construction required three architects and a quarter of a century (1334–1359). While it was being constructed the Black Plague, far worse than any war, killed over one third the population of Europe.

22. Between 1815 and 1822, the Great Powers (Austria, Britain, France, Russia, and Prussia) divided Europe among themselves, creating a Concert of Europe and a balance among the larger powers that was intended to keep the peace. As Chesterton points out, it maintained order only by leaving smaller countries "voiceless."

There is one simple little question which I should like to ask of all those who would turn the healthy and human peace we may hope for in Europe into the iron peace of an international militarism. I should like, especially, to ask it of anyone who claims, as I claim, the name of a liberal. If he denies the justice of war, does he deny the justice of revolt? Suppose the World State exists; suppose no flags or frontiers are recognised; suppose no uniform exists save that of the sacred cosmopolitan policeman. Does he deny the right of a part of the World State to rise against the rest, if it considers itself overborn by tyranny; as the French rose in the eighteenth century? If he forbids just revolt, he is forbidding the first principle of liberalism. If he permits revolt, he is permitting war; merely deprived of the songs and emblems that gave it poetry and distinction. The World State would be permitted to shoot its prisoners of war: that is almost the only difference.[23]

G.K. Chesterton, "Our Note-Book," *Illustrated London News* 146 (May 29, 1915), 688.
US: May 29, 1915. Also published as "The Peace Fever."

Spoiled by Words

June 5, 1915

Nor have I any doubt that our war will be the stronger for a vivid sense of what we are fighting for; while an abandonment of its essence would mean the slow drying-up of all the fountains of our courage. For we are not fighting for something before us, but for something behind us: not for Empire, but for home.

Editor: Chesterton's belief that something had gone wrong with Germany wasn't the prejudice of an ill-taught journalist too busy to do proper research. It is an opinion shared by many present-day scholars. In *Roots of German Nationalism*, one historian notes this about the prominent Czech historian, Hans Kohn.

> Koch sees another tragic element in German history in the misconception of *Geist* (spiritual depth) and *Macht* (authoritarian power). In the 18th century the Germans, both intellectuals and others, underrated the importance of power and overrated purity of spirit. This attitude changed in the 19th century from one extreme to the other. Germans remained fundamentally apolitical, animated by a haughty contempt for politics, but still they emerged as a dynamic nation whose will centered on power and the power-state. From a life of spirit, they turned to the pursuit of power.[24]

There's much more than that in this article. Read with care Chesterton's final remarks, quoted above. They explain the spiritual roots of Europe's current malaise, almost a century after he penned them. Without a "vivid sense" of home and nation, many modern Europeans have lost all sense of belonging to a people and a culture whose way of life is worth preserving and defending. So few Italian, French, and German children are being born because there's nothing about being Italian, French, or German that's seen as worthy of being passed on to a new generation. These Euro-

23. Since a World State would recognize no state other than itself, anyone who rebelled against it would be a traitor who could be shot when captured rather than treated as a soldier with a country of his own.
24. Louis L. Snyder, *Roots of German Nationalism* (Bloomington: Indiana University Press, 1978), 241.

peans also lack the will to resist a militant Islam that's intent on destroying their way of life because, although they enjoy that way of life, they do not believe in it in the sense of seeing it or anything else as worth fighting for. In Chestertonian terms the "fountains" of their courage — the sense of belonging to something much bigger than themselves — have dried up. For contrast, recall the close of the classic 1942 film *Casablanca*, staring Humphrey Bogart as Rick and Ingrid Bergman as Ilsa.

ILSA. And I said I would never leave you.

RICK. And you never will — But I've got a job to do, too. Where I'm going you can't follow. What I've got to do, you can't be any part of. Ilsa, I'm no good at being noble. But it doesn't take much to see that the problems of three little people don't amount to a hill o' beans in this crazy world. Some day you'll understand that.[25]

The ancestors of today's Europeans fought and died to defeat invading Muslim armies because they believed in what Chesterton calls Christendom — a complex set of beliefs developed over the centuries from many different sources, including Jews, Christians, Greeks, Romans, and even a greater understanding of courage learned from the paganism of Northern European tribes (as shown in *Beowulf*). Many present-day Europeans, particularly the European elite, believe in little more than getting through this life as comfortably as possible. That's why the European Union rejected attempts to even pay lip-service in its constitution to the continent's Christian heritage. For them, that heritage — —and indeed any historical heritage — is gone. Europe is dying because in Chestertonian terms it lacks a spiritual home to defend. It has no deep-seated source of beliefs, no "fountains," to provide it with courage and conviction.

If I were Grand Inquisitor, I would try to burn out of the world not so much certain beliefs as certain phrases. **I would argue with people about creeds; but I would kill them for catchwords.** Short of this, much might be done by voluntary asceticism and self-denial. Journalists might take a vow not to say "a strong man" for eight months, after which time they might begin to have some faint adumbration of what, if anything, they meant by it. They should fast from the word "slacker." They should not allow themselves to say "doing his bit" upon great feast-days. But other phrases should be extirpated utterly, because they are part of a whole view of life which has been proved to be apish and impertinent. As things stand, they choke the channels of human thinking everywhere. The clear heresies like Fatalism or Antinomianism are bad for conduct; in them action is spoiled by thought.[26] But in these things thought is spoiled by language. Especially by the same language used again and again. I have seen a hundred times, if I have seen it once, the phrase about the present war: "We want not people who talk, but people who do things." There are I know not how many confusions in those few words. To begin with, it is within the humble capacities of human nature to talk sense. Probably the best thing that an enforced civilian can at present do for his country is to talk sense. It is also possible

25. Dialogue from John Gassner & Dudley Nichols, *Best Film Plays of 1943–1945* (New York: Crown, 1945), 692.

26. Fatalism argues that people are unable to change the course of events, and thus offers no reason to do good, since the outcome, for good or ill, is preordained. Antinomianism claims there is no moral law that people (or a certain sect) must obey, removing any guidance about good and evil. Both are "bad for conduct."

to do nonsense, as the Germans do when they "go bang, bang!" (as the children say) over English watering-places, or as some Englishmen do when they try to suppress German music.[27] Then, of course, the phrase involves the division of men into two different kinds—those who can speak and those who can act. This is an idiot simplicity, like dividing men into those who hear and those who smell. There is not, and never has been, the smallest grain of evidence that the two capacities are incompatible; and all the largest historical evidence proves that they generally go together. Danton, "who stamped his foot and armies came out of the earth," Chatham, who sent the English flag round the world, were both of them primarily and supremely men of words.[28] They could talk well and act well; and their chief obstacles were powerful dummies who could do neither. But, in contradiction to the plainest fact, this absurd tag still trails its length along; and a man is often supposed to be able to do everything merely because he cannot tell anybody what he is doing.

Another endless rut into which many of our writers have slid is a phrase about fighting the Germans with their own weapons. Now, first of all, a sensible person does not fight anything with its own weapons. He does not bite a shark, or scratch a tiger. The wise man will not place his principal hopes in the possibility of tossing a bull. He will not be found, in his scientific rambles, endeavouring patiently to sting a hornet. It is sufficiently obvious, one would think, that victory over an opponent can best be obtained not by using the methods with which he is familiar, but the methods with which he is not familiar. But when we come to moral and intellectual differences this self-evident truism seems to fade from the minds of men. If we were at war with the King of the Cannibal Islands, these people would say that our Admirals ought to eat their prisoners. At least, they show no perception of any intellectual principle that could save them from such a conclusion. It does not seem to dawn on them that we do not eat savages for the same reason that we do conquer them: because we are not savage.[29] We do not swallow human gore for the same reason that we do not swallow slavery and humiliation: because they make us sick. I am sorry to see that even so candid and humane a writer as Mr. Blatchford, to whom we all owe so much, slips into the same rut.[30] He says sarcastically that we are not allowed to use certain forms of retaliation because our Government is so kind to the Germans. Now certain special retaliations may be right or wrong; but it is mere slipshod sentimentalism to suggest that those who think them wrong have any particular Teutonic sympathies. Would Mr. Blatchford, for instance, say that we should poison wells because the Germans poisoned them? And, if not, why not?

27. The second refers to efforts, early in the war, to suppress performances of music by German composers. "English watering-places" may refer to German efforts to boycott resorts that had catered to English tourists.

28. Georges Danton (1759–1794) played a major role in the French Revolution. Chatham probably refers to William Pitt, First Earl of Chatham (1708–1778) and British Secretary of State during the Seven Years' War (1754, 1756–1763). Given the wide extent of the fighting, some considered it the first world war.

29. Chesterton argued this point in more detail in the October 6, 1906 issue of *Illustrated London News* (Ch. 1).

30. Robert Blatchford (1851–1943) was editor of the *Clarion* newspaper and (at that time) a socialist and a Fabian.

The real reason, of course, would be the same for him as for me; and we should not refrain out of respect for Germans, but out of respect for ourselves.

This plain principle must be the test in all talk about the morality of methods. For it is the whole challenge that is rending the world. **We are fighting for human self-respect: we cannot possibly lose what we are fighting for, even in order to fight better. The Prussian sticks at nothing in pursuit of triumph because he understands nothing except triumph.**[31] Losing the battle is to him what losing his soul is to a dévot—a thing he hopes normally to avoid, a thing he hopes it may not be too hard to avoid, but a thing which, first and last, he must avoid, and the avoidance which will dwarf everything else that is endured. But we do not and cannot make our salvation consist solely in our success. We do not and cannot think of defeat as the worst thing possible, any more than we can think of war as the worst thing possible. To us a defeated Kosciusko, or a defeated Robert Emmet, is not disgraced by defeat; but a defeated Bismarck would be simply a detected rascal.[32] I am not pronouncing here upon any particular instance, which would require a military and scientific knowledge which I do not possess; but I am pronouncing upon what the test must be, and especially upon what it must not be. It must not be merely the question of whether the enemy is or is not doing some particular thing. They said in the Middle Ages, I think, that the Devil was the ape of God. It must not be said in any ages that we were the apes of the Devil. When I say "we," I mean, first, my own countrymen; further, the totally different nations called Ireland and Scotland; and, finally, all the countries which have kept the chivalry and charity of Christendom for much more than a thousand years. They are now, thank God, practically all embattled in defence of that chivalry and charity, and are doing justice upon the proved enemies of both without a particle of doubt or fear. The only limit they will recognise will be the strictly rational one which I have stated. They cannot strike those who would destroy their chivalry by destroying it themselves. For the fighting spirit as we value it is the flower of a great many other things, and cannot be separated from them. A kind of courage can exist in a merciless and unmagnanimous soldier, as it can exist in a merciless and unmagnanimous wild pig; but it does not happen to be the kind of courage that our brethren have died to keep alive. They have died for a certain spirit not at all easy to define, and not at all necessary to define as long as we have got it. That spirit cannot exist without other virtues besides the virtue of fortitude: it has always in it something that looks before and after, the memory and the promise

31. A prominent German historian reinforces Chesterton's remarks: "Beyond any doubt the extreme militarism that had already struck root in Germany, by virtue of the Prussian tradition, was enhanced to the ultimate degree by the impact of the Great War, with its challenge to survival and its encouragement of victory at any price." Gerhard Ritter, *The Sword and the Scepter: The Problem of Militarism in Germany* (Coral Gables: University of Miami Press, 1972), 23. Ritter, who lived from 1888 to 1967, was 26 years old when the war began and fought in the infantry. Chesterton correctly predicts that Germany will not learn from defeat because its national "soul" is too closely linked to being victorious. Germany will conclude that its defeat was due to a "stab in the back."

32. Andrzej Kościuszko (1746–1817) is a Polish national hero, but his victories in battle were negated by a political settlement. Robert Emmet (1778-1803) led in a failed Irish rebellion, getting captured and executed. Otto von Bismark (1815–1898), the "rascal," altered parts of the Ems Dispatch to start a war between Germany and France.

of peace. The old light Cavalier lyric clangs to-day with a deeper and more dreadful resonance; in many darkened English homes is heard the dead voice which says—

I could not love thee, dear, so much
Loved I not Honour more.[33]

But it is equally true that such healthy and military pride cannot stand alone or grow out of nothing: it must have something to defend, and something that is worth defending. It is equally true that the spirit of Christendom is saying also—

I could not love thee, Honour, so much
Loved I not Goodness more.

Nor have I any doubt that our war will be the stronger for a vivid sense of what we are fighting for; while an abandonment of its essence would mean the slow drying-up of all the fountains of our courage. For we are not fighting for something before us, but for something behind us: not for Empire, but for home.

G.K. Chesterton, "Our Note-Book," *Illustrated London News* 146 (June 5, 1915), 715. US: June 5, 1915. Also published as "What We Are Fighting For."

Conscription Debated

June 12, 1915

It is always best in emergency to rely upon habit. Custom does not make people slow; it makes them quick.

Editor: Today, knowing what we do about the horrors of trench warfare, the early enthusiasm young men on both sides displayed for joining the fighting is difficult to understand. In Britain that early zeal was particularly intense. By the end of the war's first month, almost 500,000 men had volunteered, overwhelming the War Office's ability to process, much less train them. Historically, as an island nation Britain had kept a small professional army of volunteers that, in combination with the powerful Royal Navy, could be thrown into any dispute on the continent to tip the balance in its favor. But World War I was preeminently a land war rather than a naval one, and one in which enormous casualties had to be constantly replaced by new men.

After the initial rush, recruiting fell off, so much so that by the summer of 1915 volunteers were not enlisting in sufficient numbers to satisfy the plans British generals had for major offenses in 1916. As a result, many British leaders began to talk of Conscription (important enough to be capitalized), particularly Lloyd George, then head of the Ministry of Munitions, who wanted a draft so the skilled munitions workers he needed could be prevented from enlisting. These were the people who had practical reasons for Conscription as a temporary measure, believing it necessary to win the war. Chesterton mentions them in the first paragraph and expresses a willingness to go with their judgment.

33. Richard Lovelace's "To Lucasta, Going to the Wars" (1649) reads: "Tell me not, Sweet, I am unkind,/ That from the nunnery/ Of thy chaste breast and quiet mind/ To war and arms I fly./ True, a new mistress now I chase,/ The first foe in the field;/ And with a stronger faith embrace/ A sword, a horse, a shield./ Yet this inconstancy is such/ As thou too shalt adore;/ I could not love thee, Dear, so much,/ Loved I not Honour more."

Chesterton, however, opposes those who have more ideological reasons for supporting Conscription — reasons that have little to do with the current war. Some were copycats, although he doesn't use the term, people who see Conscription as a necessary part of modern life and yet another thing to be copied from the Germans. Conscription was also being supported by the usual suspects — those who use any crisis, manufactured or real, to get into law something most people find intrusive and unnecessary. As Chesterton points out, they see Conscription as a way of making everyone conform to their rules, much like Teetotalism, Compulsory Education and Compulsory Insurance (for injury and old age), all things Chesterton loathes. (Notice how he capitalizes each in this article.) The British, Chesterton is saying, have their own ways of doing things and everything will go better if they stick to those old and familiar ways and don't try to imitate others, particularly the Germans.

In the end, the authorities went with Conscription. The National Registration Act of July 1915 would require all men and women from 16 to 65 to register. The Military Service Act of January 1916 then began Conscription for single men between 18 and 41. Just as Chesterton had warned, changing how things were done resulted in unforeseen complications. The new act contained too many exceptions, particularly for marriage, that could be used to evade a call up, and actually reduced enlistments. Only when a second Military Service Act of May 1916 took affect, extending Conscription to married men, did enlistment numbers rise.

On the same day this article was published, Chesterton wrote to Bernard Shaw, thanking him for kindness shown during his long illness. He stressed two themes that repeat throughout his wartime writing: that this would be a long and difficult war and that there was in Prussia a demonic "evil will" that must be fought and destroyed.

> You probably know that I do not agree with you about the War; I do not think it is going on of its own momentum; I think it is going on in accordance with that logical paradox whereby the thing that is most difficult to do is also the thing that must be done. If it were an easy war to end it would have been a wicked war to begin. If a cat has nine lives one must kill it nine times, saving your humanitarian feelings, and always supposing it is a witch's cat and really draws its powers from Hell. **I have always thought that there was in Prussia an evil will; I would not have made it a ground for going to war; but I was quite sure of it long before there was any war at all.**[34]

A very charming Tory lady happened to say to me the other day, "But we shall never get Conscription if we don't get it now." Personally, I do not doubt, she was as patriotic as anybody else; but what she said was, *par excellence*, the essentially unpatriotic thing. It is as anti-national as the similar sentiment on the other political "side," that Total Prohibition should be enforced now, simply because no sane people would ever dream of enforcing it at any other time. **At this moment a patriot will not wish to get Conscription or to get Teetotalism or to get anything else, except the better of the Germans.** Whether Conscription will help or hinder us in

34. Maisie Ward, *Gilbert Keith Chesterton* (London: Sheed & Ward, 1944), 332. This doesn't contradict Chesterton's relative (to others) lack of concern with German militarism before the war. It's possible to see someone as having an "evil will," but believe that for other reasons they're unlikely to act. (Even the most violent criminal won't attempt to rob a police station.) WWI was a product of both a German "evil will" and major blunders.

that is a matter for the authorities; and a very difficult matter even for them. If they want it we must give it them, not because they are the best conceivable people who could decide, but because they are the only people who can decide. If we are always whining for a man with "a genius for governing," we are simply proving ourselves destitute of an equally noble gift—a genius for being governed. If the doctor whom I have asked to save my life tells me he cannot save my leg, it must be amputated. But if he enters with a smile and a large knife, and says "You will never have any amputation if you don't have it now," my legs will recover their normal capacity either for kicking him downstairs or for running away. After that I will write him a long and friendly letter setting forth my philosophical position; explaining that I like my leg regarded as a case and not merely as an opportunity; and even offering to go without the pleasures of amputation altogether rather than merely exchange a limb for an experience.

When we come to the stage of decision we must do as we are told, as every democracy in the world is doing; and the firmer the democracy the firmer the discipline. But while we are at the stage of taking counsel we cannot do better than consider carefully all the elements of the situation, but especially the less obvious and the less hackneyed ones. In military affairs, as much as in any other affairs, there is such a thing as more haste and less speed, such a thing as too many cooks spoiling the broth, such a thing as asking too much and therefore getting too little—above all, such a thing as a deadly ignorance of the sort of people one is dealing with. Taking hold of a gun by the wrong end and pointing the butt at the enemy is not more mistaken than taking hold of a man by the wrong end and pointing his thoughts towards what repels him in war rather than what inspires him. We see this fatal error in the Prussians themselves, who sat down to deduce the conduct of Irishmen, Belgians, Italians, Americans, as if they were simply units in a calculation; the result of which was a series of the wildest and worst guesses that men ever made about men. Especially and supremely the Germans were ignorant of the English. I hope we shall not have to say that the English were ignorant of the English also.

Now amid all the current talk about Conscription, there is one human and historical fact to be remembered which millionaires of the hustling type do not remember simply because they do not know. **It is always best in emergency to rely upon habit. Custom does not make people slow; it makes them quick.** There may be ninety-nine ingenious and elegant ways of putting on one's boots: but if it is necessary to put on one's boots to catch a train it is better to put them on as one usually puts them on, simply because it will take less time and will avoid any unexpected hitch. People called upon suddenly to fight will fight best in some way that they know, as a man threatened with the blow of a cudgel will ward it off with his arm and not with his leg. The English have done as much fighting as any people in Europe, but they have always done it in a particular way of their own. They have always been represented by a strong but comparatively small body which, acting with allies, has more than once turned the whole fortune in the European field. The position of the officer towards his men has not the inhuman superiority of the German, nor the realistic utilitarianism of the French. It is, in its strength and weakness, the peculiar English relation between the gentleman and the "man." The bond between them is not militarism, but rather sport. To that relation a certain insular sense of freedom is quite essential. There may be snobbishness in it, and not a little sentimentality; but avowed and ticketed slavery is against its very nature. Now the great Continental nations do not feel that there is any slavery in coercion by the State, and that for a very simple reason. The peoples who have great armies for great frontiers have again and again defended those frontiers with a universal valour which could not be enforced, any more than it could be purchased. They have, therefore, heroic memories of conscript armies. A soldier of the Revolution was forced, but he did not *feel* forced—

> Or all the shouting boys in Lombardy
> Behind the young Napoleon charging through[35]

But our military memories have not been of that kind, simply because they have not been on that scale. **In our best fighting there has always been an idea of individual adventure, as there has been in our colonising.** The average English workman understands the idea of his son running away to sea. He obscurely sympathises with the son; he probably expects him to come back an Admiral. He understands the dignity of the village ne'er-do-weel, or even the village idiot, when he goes off with the recruiting sergeant covered with ribbons: he already sees the young man covered all over with Victoria Crosses. But the average English workman would not understand compulsion if it were called compulsion; and if it came from the correct officials of the State he would dislike it all the more. He does not care about the State, though he cares a great deal about the country. It was probably in reference to this rather accidental way of doing things that a somewhat acid Irishman, the great Duke of Wellington, said the English Army was the scum of the earth. But he knew as well as anybody that this extraordinary hotchpotch of amateurs and tramps and jailbirds could hold out with a heroism of their own; and they held out longer than even he expected. And I gravely doubt whether Wellington, in the middle of the war or on the eve of inevitable battles, would have exchanged the scum of the earth for the salt of the earth that filled the armies of France.

To show that the point is purely practical, being concerned with an alteration in armies actually in their full activity, I will take it as affecting an ideal of my own. **I believe that pure Democracy is the manliest government for men.** I think it has proved itself so in the places where it has been rooted already. Mere reactionaries who say that democracies cannot govern or fight must explain as best they can the example of modern France, where practically nobody is talking nonsense, simply because the whole French people does not want any nonsense talked. But if the Brit-

35. From "Ballade of Unsuccessful Men" by Chesterton's friend, Hilaire Belloc (1870–1953). The actual lines are: "And all the lads that marched in Lombardy/ Behind the young Napoleon charging through." It closes with a reminder that our judgments about failure can be wrong: "Prince, may I venture (since it's only you)/ To speak discreetly of The Crucified?/ He was extremely unsuccessful too:/ The Devil didn't like Him, and He died."

ish authorities tried to turn Britain into a pure democracy between the last German cannonade and the next one I should think they had taken leave of their senses. To produce a society with a Citizen Smith-Dorrien and a Citizen Thomas Atkins,[36] to prevent the poor from saying "Sir" to the rich or to make the rich say "Sir" to the poor, to dig out of the mind of a yokel the idea that the best thing on earth is to be a gentleman — is a thing that simply could not be done to or by a nation at war. Taken unawares, with all her vulgarities and generosities, all her living instincts and dead anomalies upon her, this poor old country of ours is fighting with such weapons as she can handle against something whose sins seem scarcely human. **We need all that history and social habit can give to steady us. The English must simply be English until England finds deliverance, merely because they must be sane until this insane period has passed.**

1915

There is one other consideration which I will put in as material for a decision, though this also is on the side least represented in our Press. When the English borrow from foreigners, especially from Germans, some scheme of social discipline, they have an unfortunate habit of turning it into something else, something that is not only unpopular but unpractical. Twice in recent times they thus copied. The first case was Compulsory Education; the second case was Compulsory Insurance. I do not think either of the examples encouraging.

G.K. Chesterton, "Our Note-Book," *Illustrated London News* 146 (June 12, 1915), 749. US: June 12, 1915. Also published as "The Problem of Conscription."

CASTING DOWN IDOLS

June 19, 1915

So we do not wish, of course, to kill all Germans or prevent them from being German, any more than we killed all Turks or prevented them from being Turkish. Rather we would cast down the idols and lift up the men.

EDITOR: In this article Chesterton moves from a German journalist's remark about "a new German spirit" in his nation's religion to explaining why the current war is, at its heart, a religious war and why that is better than a racial war. For Chesterton, a religious war is one about great ideas rather than petty territorial land-grabs, althought it doesn't necessarily involve specifically religious beliefs.[37]

A PROMINENT German journalist, in discussing the future of German religion, especially with reference to German missions, said that it would be impossible

36. The British, Chesterton is saying, are not ready for an almost rankless army. General Horace Smith-Dorrien (1858–1930) commanded the British II Corps in the war. Tommy Atkins ("Tommy") was a name for the typical British soldier. It apparently began as a sample name in military documents and was popularized by poems such as Rudyard Kipling's "Tommy," which includes: For it's Tommy this, an' Tommy that, an' "Chuck him out, the brute!"/ But it's "Saviour of 'is country" when the guns begin to shoot."

37. See what Chesterton wrote on September 12, 1914 (Ch. 2). Notice also the similarity between this journalist's remarks and what another journalist would write eighteen years later in support of Nazi Germany, which is quoted in the introduction to the August 19, 1916 article (Ch. 4).

to associate further with the English Protestant missionaries after the war. This was not only because the English missionaries "would certainly be filled with malice and spite," but because German Christianity (in this writer's opinion) will be "very different from English Christianity." It will be, he says, "a manly Christianity, and permeated with the new German spirit." This, he adds, will make it particularly attractive "to Mohammedans and heathens."[38]

It might be suggested that though "manly Christianity" may be very suitable to Mohammedans, it may not be so suitable to Mohammedans as Mohammedanism. It also might be suggested that if Christianity needs to be "new," it does not need to be Christian. In justice to the Turks, it should also be said that, if they are as rude as the Germans in war, they are much more polite in peace. But the most important point in the parallel is one from which many seem to shrink. Mr. Charles Buxton,[39] the distinguished writer and traveller, who was recently wounded by Turkish assassins on account of his great sympathies and services for the Balkan peoples, has been interviewed by the *Christian Commonwealth*, which gives (I presume correctly) his opinions on a possible settlement with Germany. His views seem to me singular in themselves, and especially singular in him. He seems to rebuke those who hope for a final breaking of the Prussian power, as if indicating that so powerful, widespread, and well armed a combination cannot be reduced to impotence. I should say that it is precisely because it is powerful, widespread, and well armed that it must be reduced to impotence. It is a paradox, but a very practical truth, that what is indispensable is generally nearly impossible. **Unless the enemy were strong enough to hurt us, it would not be necessary, or indeed justifiable, for us to hurt him.** But if the attitude be strange in any case, it is especially strange in one with Mr. Buxton's almost romantic record. Surely he of all people ought not to say that it is impossible ultimately to break the back of a great Empire with great military prestige. If Turkey had been left powerful, if Turkey had been left united, if Turkey had been left as Mr. Buxton would apparently leave Germany, the Turks would have been far too happy shooting Macedonians to trouble about shooting him. What Mr. Buxton thinks it impossible to do is what Mr. Buxton has been largely instrumental in doing. He has seen—and, as I imagine, approved—the cutting-down of one of the great conquering empires of the Continent to the smallest margin of what it has

38. Hitler also preferred militant Islam. Of the Frankish victory over the Moors in the Battle of Tours in 732, he said: "Had Charles Martel not been victorious at Poitiers—already, you see, the world had fallen into the hands of the Jews, so gutless a thing was Christianity!—then we should in all probability have been converted to Mohammedanism, that cult which glorifies heroism and which opens the seventh Heaven to the bold warrior alone. Then the Germanic races would have conquered the world. Christianity alone prevented them from doing so." Adolf Hitler, *Hitler's Secret Conversations* (New York: Farrar, Straus and Young, 1953), 542. Hitler's hatred of Christianity and his idolization of Islam led him to think poorly. If Christianity was so "gutless," how was it able to defeat Muslim invasions in the east and west and drive them out of Spain? And if Islam created such a warrior race, why was it dominated in his day by European powers? Finally, why is Europe's weakness to Islam coming only as it rejects Christianity and secularizes?

39. Charles R. Buxton (1875–1942) and his brother Noel Buxton (1869-1948) wrote *The War and the Balkans*. In it, the Balkan nations are said to need more land, much of it to be taken from the Turkish Empire, which would be reduced to just four provinces. (Today's Turkey has 81 provinces.) See *The War and the Balkans* (London: George Allen and Unwin, 1915), 99–100. During their travels, a Turkish assassin wounded both brothers in October 1914.

conquered. We could not send the Turks back to their own country, because they never had one; we could only in a certain large degree distrain upon stolen goods. But we did take away from them — or, rather, Mr. Buxton's very brave friends in the Balkans did — enough to prevent their being a power in the sense of keeping other people powerless. There cannot be the smallest moral excuse for restricting the Turks to little more than Constantinople which is not also a moral excuse for restricting Prussianism to little more than Berlin. That it is much more difficult to do makes it much more necessary to do it. And if we do not do it, if we do not disarm Prussia as we have disarmed Turkey, then indeed, in the very wise words of a French Socialist uttered the other day, "the greatest effort ever made by the human race will have been made in vain."

I should agree with Mr. Buxton on the general rule that no European nation should be reduced because it is defeated. But I cannot understand why he should see that the Turkish case is an exception, and not see that the Prussian case is an exception also. They are exceptions for this vital reason, that they do not reciprocate a nationalist toleration. They will not place their community inside the European community; they are always outside it, whether as outcasts or as invaders. The Turks put themselves above all national affections upon a supposed supernatural right, now a thousand years old and only now beginning to wear thin. The Prussians put themselves above all national affections upon a supposed natural right, which is now only fifty years old. The natural right is more unnatural than the mystic one.

The profound impossibility of Prussia consists ultimately in this: that she has broken an implied understanding among all Christian men by taking victory too seriously. **Glory is only a good thing when it is a good joke. With all the other peoples success has been a legitimate vanity and not a lawless pride.** The French were naturally proud of having ridden into the gate of almost every European city; but they were equally satisfied with having ridden out again; and they were quite as conscious of their defeats as of their victories, draping the statue of Strasburg [Strasbourg] and probing the wound of Waterloo. The Russians were naturally proud of having in 1812 conquered the unconquerable soldier of the Revolution; but they did not therefore despise France, or generally indicate that nobody could fight or govern unless he was in the habit of consuming large quantities of tallow.[40] The English were naturally proud of having a Navy that was like a book of boys' adventures; but though they had defeated a great foreign Armada in the past they do not talk as if there could never be another great foreign Armada in the future. To the healthier groups of European men victory is not so much, after all; it is an incident, and not a state. The old European view is sublimely expressed in the great war epic about the noble King of France who had ten thousand men, and when they were up they were up and when they were down they were down; an admirable summary of most

40. For Chesterton's remarks on the then-common belief that Russians eat tallow, see his "The English Blunder about Russia" in *The Soul of Russia*.

military proceedings.[41] But the Prussians have broken all this implied balance of battles by building on one victory a domination that is meant to last for ever. They built on the battle field of Sedan not a temporary trophy, but a tower of eternal brass. What happened after or during 1870 was not primarily the union of Germany, but rather the division of Europe: it was divided into Germans and non-Germans. It was made something more even than a racial, it was made a biological division. There was supposed to be a fundamental and physical superiority, as of the German eagle over the Gallic cock. Hence Prussia could not, and cannot, be trusted merely to take her turn from time to time in the leadership of Europe. She is an anarchic power in this essential sense that she has not the rhythm and return upon itself of a living thing. This is the further menace of the extraordinary German mentality; that it is perpetually in a state of transformation, and, upon the whole, of transformation for the worse. Those who follow the dancing dervishes of the Prussian academies have no notion of what will be the next whirlwind of nonsense. The Prussian professors would certainly defend cannibalism if they were allowed to call it Anthropophagy. Only one dogma will always remain sacred, the dogma of the German's superiority. Only one duty will never be lifted off him: the duty of praising himself. He is free to do everything except repent.

This is a religious war. Mr. Buxton reproves Mr. John Buchan[42] for having said that we must cut down the groves and altars of the enemy. But, indeed, there is a symbolic truth in the remark: in the sense that if we could destroy the altars there would be the less need to destroy the men. A religious war is more rational than a racial war; but it can also be more humane. A mere war against niggers would be a war against every nigger. But a war against Voodoo, the negro devil-worship, would be only a war against niggers in so far as they worshipped devils. Black magic could not be a mere heritage like black blood. It would be necessary to respect the freedom and sanctity of the land where the good niggers go. **So we do not wish, of course, to kill all Germans or prevent them from being German, any more than we killed all Turks or prevented them from being Turkish. Rather we would cast down the idols and lift up the men.**[43]

G.K. Chesterton, "Our Note-Book," *Illustrated London News* 146 (June 19, 1915), 783.
US: June 19, 1915. Also published as "On Taking Victory Too Seriously."

PACIFISM AND TREASON

July 3, 1915

But the principal Pacifists or Semi-Pacifists in our politics to-day are about as idealistic as a dishonest army contractor.

41. This may refer to the "Song of Roland." The Roland of legend served Charlemagne and experienced both victory and defeat, dying fighting the Muslims in the Battle of Roncevaus Pass (778).

42. John Buchan (1875–1940) was a Scottish politician and historical novelist. During World War I he wrote for the War Propaganda Bureau and *The Times* (London).

43. See Shaw's clumsy claim that the English want to destroy the Germans as a people in Appendix D.

EDITOR: In England, Chesterton saw a disturbing link between pacifism and cowardice, particularly in their unwillingness to punish evil doers. Although he often criticized Suffragettes, here he praises two of them for their patriotic zeal.

DR. Ethel Smyth, the distinguished musician, has written a very excellent letter to the *Morning Post* upon the palliation of treason. She, like Miss Christabel Pankhurst, was one of those fiery Suffragettes who have found in this war a much more wholesome vent for their zeal than could be found in the sterile idolatry of the Vote.[44] They are very right. What was really wrong with the sexes in the long plutocratic peace was not that women were not men: it was that men were not men. But this healthier enthusiasm is, naturally, more persuasive in an artist and a woman of genius than in so very political a politician as Miss Pankhurst. In one point, indeed, I think that Miss Smyth's artistic temperament leads her to overrate her enemies, that is, the enemies within our gates. She says that they may be idealists; adding that Brutus was an idealist, but this did not prevent Dante damning him for a traitor. Some one or two very hoary Pacificists are idealists in this impossible sense: though even they (while worthy of all respect) are clinging pathetically to a word rather than to an ideal. **But the principal Pacifists or Semi-Pacifists in our politics to-day are about as idealistic as a dishonest army contractor.** One or two middle-class men on the make, very imperfectly disguised as Labour Leaders; the clerks of some ordinary foreign financier; and here and there a prosperous but secretive person who looks uncommonly like an ordinary foreign spy—these seem to me to exhaust the list of those who want peace, save in the sense in which we all want it. Even the best of them are not misled by ideals, but by a mutton-headed materialism which cannot conceive that a poor man can be patriotic. They cannot grasp the subtle truth that a man born in Hoxton is also born in England.[45] It needs no frantic spirit of martyrdom to be in a small minority which mostly consists of millionaires; and in a few such patches of preposterous wealth (and certainly not among the poor) is to be found the real poison of anti-patriotism. All the ideals that really were ideals, Socialism, Syndicalism, and, last but not least in this case, Suffragism, have been swept along by the overwhelming ideal of a death for justice. All the idols that were of real gold have been melted in this furnace. But the gods of the heathen are stone and brass.

It should be strictly seized, for it is enormously important, that in this great trial those who have been really loyal are those who have been really revolutionary. It is the moderate Socialists who are Pacifists; the fighting Socialists are patriots. Mr. Ben Tillett would have been regarded by Mr. Ramsay MacDonald as a mere firebrand;

44. Ethel M. Smyth (1858–1944) was an English composer and women's suffrage leader. Christabel H. Pankhurst (1880–1958) was a prominent women's suffragette. In 1913 she wrote *The Great Scourge and How to End It*, claiming that votes for women would dramatically reduce sexually transmitted diseases.

45. At this time, Hoxton, just north of central London and the financial district, was where many of the poor lived. In the July 24, 1915 *Illustrated London News* (Ch. 3), Chesterton will write sympathetically of, "the broken clerk or craftsman in Hoxton, drifting from lodging to lodging like a stray cat." Elsewhere he noted: "I can understand a teetotaler being horrified, on his principles, at Italian wine-drinking. I simply cannot believe he could be more horrified at it than at Hoxton gin-drinking." *Eugenics and Other Evils* (Seattle: Inkling Books, 2000), 84.

but it is precisely because Mr. Tillet was ready to go on fighting Capitalism that he is ready to go on fighting Krupp.[46] It is precisely because Mr. MacDonald was weak in his opposition to domestic tyrants, that he is weak in his opposition to foreign ones. The wobblers who wanted a one-sided arbitration to end the strikes would to-day accept a one-sided arbitration to end the battles. But the men who wanted strikes want nothing but shells. That great artist, Mr. Will Dyson, laid aside the lethal pencil with which he had caricatured the sweaters and the middlemen, and sharpened a yet deadlier one to draw all the devils in Prussia.[47] The consistent Collectivists, such as Mr. Blatchford or Mr. Hyndman, who were jeered at as "agitators" can now be jeered at as Jingoes.[48] **It is the snobs, the Socialists of the Servile State, the men of intrigue and not of indignation, who are traitors to their country as they were traitors to their class. It is they who plead for the Prussian. It is they who tell us to forget and forgive; that is, to forgive the kidnapper and forget the captive.**

The fruit of this fighting spirit and training can certainly be claimed by Miss Smyth and Miss Pankhurst. I never blamed them for fighting, but for having nothing worth fighting for. Dr. Smyth is concerned with a communication sent to her about some of the proceedings of the Pacifists who went to the Hague.[49] Why they went there, what they did there, or what any of them imagined they could do there, I know no more than the dead. I heard somewhere that some Pacifist was to drag herself round to all the Courts of Europe and tell the Kings that war is an unpleasant business: a fact of which no one could be more vividly aware than they are. I should not like to be the person who intruded even upon poor old William with so fresh a fragment of information. But even the fact that the thing was intellectually idiotic does not alter the fact that it was morally indefensible, and Miss Smyth is quite justified in insisting on the point. But every day is revealing such weak spots, especially in the wealthier circles: and some of them are considerably more menacing than the poor prigs who went toddling to the Hague. Some may understand why the two great Glasgow merchants (who earned solid gold out of solid iron for the killing of Scotch and English soldiers) should have been recommended to leniency by a jury, but I confess I cannot understand it in any way.[50] Either there must have been good

46. Ben Tillet (1860–1943) was a sailor and dock worker who became a trade union leader and organized the London Dock Strike (1889). After working as a clerk, Ramsay MacDonald (1866–1937) became active in Labour Party politics. In 1914 he opposed Britain's entry into WWI. He was Britain's Prime Minister in 1924 and from 1929–1935. As Prime Minister, his blindness to the dangers that Hitler posed led Winston Churchill to remark in 1935: "Occasionally he stumbled over the truth, but hastily picked himself up and hurried on as if nothing had happened." Krupp was Germany's giant steel and armaments manufacturer.

47. Will Dyson (1880–1938) was an Australian illustrator who moved to Britain and supported the war. Chesterton contributed to his 1916 *War Cartoons* and wrote the introduction for his 1917 *Australia at War.*

48. At this time, Robert Blatchford, (1851–1943) was a socialist who wrote for *The Clarion*. Born into wealth, Henry M. Hyndman (1842–1921) became a Marxist in about 1881 and helped to create the British Socialist Party. His support for WWI divided the party and in 1916 the pro-war faction became the (ill-named) National Socialist Party (UK), which later merged back into the Labour Party.

49. From April 28 to May 1, 1915 over a thousand women met in the Hague, Netherlands for the International Congress of Women which would, they thought, come up with a way to end the war. Afterward a small group of the delegates traveled "to all the Courts of Europe." This is apparently what Dr. Smyth was criticizing.

50. According to the June 3, 1915 *New Age,* a leading socialist newspaper, a firm of iron merchants had been charged with supplying iron ore to Germany's Krupp steel works through Amsterdam after the war began.

things in their favour which did not come out in the printed reports, or there must have been very bad things in their favour which cannot come out at all. If the jurymen imagined that the Judge was going to condemn these two mercantile gentlemen to be boiled in oil, I can understand their movement of anticipatory compassion; but surely any decent death would be good enough for a traitor. Whatever these things mean, they mean something serious; such things are done either by an atrocious carelessness or a much more atrocious care. What we have to realise is how very close to our politics is a kind of commerce disloyal to every law that makes a sovereign State. It is serious that men in such a position should commit such a crime; but it is more serious that men who can commit such a crime can get so easily into such a position. It is like finding rats in one's bed. It means that the gutters and the sewers are besieging the house itself; it means not only that the rat is in the wrong place, but that the cat is not in the right one.

The Prussians, I believe, have a hobby of collecting the crimes of this country, many of them of the same historicity as the terrible Mr. Packlemerton of Jarley's Wax-Works.[51] But if we are wise we shall not deny that there are things in our history of which it is impossible to be proud. Thus, we shall concede to the Germans that we were thoroughly disgraced by the friendship and alliance of Frederick the Great, by whose escape from just punishment Europe has ever since been left at the mercy of the thieves of Pomerania and Brandenburg.[52] We shall frankly admit that we are ashamed of the German troops who did our dirty work in Ireland and America. We shall no longer conceal from the inquiring Teuton what we know touching those soldiers of Blücher who at Waterloo and after brought us almost as much infamy as assistance.[53] In truth and sorrow and humility, we confess to the Germans that we have done many German things. We admit our past weaknesses in negative as in positive matters. We ask their pardon for having neglected their education. It repenteth us that we did not teach them better manners when they picked Denmark's pocket and kicked France when she was down. But of all the sins we have to confess in the face of our enemies the worst lay in imitating something of their spiritual pride, in failing in self-criticism, and abounding in self-praise. And this fault will yet bring punishment of a prostrating kind, if we show it by refusing to probe these ugly problems of our recent finance and to face the probable perils of our commercial position. The patch of evil is very small, but very sensitive. The element of treason will save itself if it can. If it is saved we are lost.

We must get rid after this war of that hotch-potch of charity and cheap cynicism which softened any lapse of the luxurious orders, and was ready to treat treason as a

51. Charles Dicken's *The Old Curiosity Shop* (1841) includes a traveling Jarley's Wax-Works where a waxed figure is described this way: "'That, ladies and gentlemen,' said Mrs Jarley, 'is Jasper Packlemerton of atrocious memory, who courted and married fourteen wives, and destroyed them all, by tickling the soles of their feet when they were sleeping in the consciousness of innocence and virtue.'"

52. Chesterton described Britain's failure to deter Prussian expansion in greater detail in his 1915 book, *The Crimes of England*. "Dirty work in Ireland and America" is a reference to Germany mercenaries—the infamous "Hessians" of the American Revolution, who were also used to crush a rebellion in Ireland in 1798.

53. This alludes to the looting that Blücher permitted when Paris was occupied in the summer of 1815.

sort of eccentric theory. It is the only danger there is for us; and therefore, of course, it is the only danger that our Panic Press does not mention. The danger is in a certain heavy English habit of associating riches with respectability, and refusing to believe in conspiracy when it is associated with comfort. **When the time comes for a treaty and a peace there will be considerable wealth and influence to the hand of those who have never heartily shared the anger which is the hope of the world. Among these there will be some whose spirit is worse than alien; and these will say they are being generous to Germany, when they are only being mean to England.**

G.K. Chesterton, "Our Note-Book," *Illustrated London News* 147 (July 3, 1915), 3.
US: July 3, 1915. Also published as "The Materialism of the Pacifists."

Honour and Modesty in War

July 24, 1915

And decent war is not "the best way of settling differences"; it is the only way of preventing their being settled for you.

Editor: Chesterton did not confine his criticism to Germany. In this article he points out the failings of England and what must be done about them. This same year he also publishes a book, *The Crimes of England,* which blames many English faults on his fellow citizens' willingness to imitate Germany.

The central fact of the present situation is that the North German has not yet discovered that the greater part of humanity dislikes *him*. What it dislikes is not militarism, nor Zollvereins, nor naval rivalry; it is not submarines nor Zeppelins.[54] It is not even massacres. It is a certain state of the soul, which can be, and is, expressed by certain movements of the arms, legs, shoulders, and head. Again and again the Prussian says in his simplicity. "When I reflect how good, wise, and strong I am, I cannot imagine why people dislike me." And the answer never flashes even by chance across his mind: "People dislike me because I reflect how good, wise, and strong I am." He is quite honestly bewildered by what seem to him the hostile antics of people utterly different from each other — Boers, Irishmen, Poles, Yankees, and Jews.[55] He cannot see why they rage together, for to see that he would have to look, not outside, but inside. He cannot find the key of the mystery, because he has swallowed the key.

If we are wise we shall constantly consider this fact, and remember that we owe much of our support to this fault in our enemy, and not to our own faultlessness. The Boers and Irish do not support England because England is a model, but because Germany is a bogey; not because the British Constitution is a holy thing,

54. The Zollverein was a customs union between German cities (1828–1871) that led to a wider political union. Zeppelins were dirigibles used to bomb London.

55. Despite the differences between them, all five are groups in which Chesterton detected a national spirit, even though at this time only one (America's Yankees) had won their independence. Today only the Boers lack a country of their own.

but because the Prussian system is a holy terror. We may hope, and there is good ground for hoping, that these allies of ours may learn through the alliance something of what is really generous and beautiful in England. But we shall be merely eclipsing our minds with a cloud of vanity if we pretend that they have not, in the past, seen mostly what is ungenerous and ugly. The deepest and worthiest retort to the German proclamation of virtue would be a confession of sin. The savage says, "I am a good German." And the civilised man answers, "I am a bad Englishman, and altogether unworthy of England." *In hoc signo vincet.*[56]

The Pacifists are, even among modern men, the most ruled by phrases rather than ideas. It is notable that any one of their questions has to be put in a particular form of words. Translate the question into any other form of words, and it can no longer rationally be answered as they wish. Thus they will say, "Can war be the right way of settling differences?" Ask instead, "What shall prevent me from putting forth my whole strength to defend whatever makes life worth living?"—and they have no answer. If your life is made worth living by German sausages, you would certainly be unwise to interfere with the German trade in them; if it is made worth living by the honour and memories of a free people, nothing can prevent you from sacrificing everything else to save them. **And decent war is not "the best way of settling differences"; it is the only way of preventing their being settled for you.**

Among these fixed phrases of the Pacifists there is a maxim about "conquering evil by good." They seem to mean conquering aggression by cowardice, conquering tyranny by slavery, conquering the assertion of wrong by the abandonment of right, and conquering Germany by betraying France. But as some of us, tutored in the cryptic schools of superstition, do not happen to think that cowardice, slavery, betrayal, and the denial of right are "good" things, we answer that to use them would not be to use good against evil, but merely to add one evil to another. But there is one moral matter in which we really can return good for evil without merely strengthening the evils; one weapon from the armoury of the saints is, even in a worldly sense, stronger than the world. That weapon is humility.

We must greatly purify ourselves even to be worthy of this war. This hell, as they call it, is so very much nearer heaven than England has yet been in her hundred years of prosperity and peace that we must be ready for abnegations more trying than any physical ones, for the refusal of all that mental comfort upon which we have lived so long. We must be content to answer to the Prussian: "Yes, I also am evil; perhaps I am as evil as you say—only not quite so vilely evil as to sell the world to you." We are not above our task; we have only, in the noble words of M. Cammaerts' poem

> La fierté de rester honnête
> Quand le lâcheté nous serait si bon.[57]

56. Latin for "In this sign he shall conquer." British humility, Chesterton is saying, will win more friends and thus more victories than German arrogance.

57. Émile Cammaerts (1878–1953) was a Belgian poet and writer who moved to England in 1908. Chesterton's lines resemble two passages in his "Apres Anvers"—"After Antwerp." They are: "Et la joie de rester honnête/

And wherever there remains a trace of the old vulgar and insular condescension, we must stamp on it as if it were literal and legal treason.

It is not wholly stamped out. A capable and very sane lady said to me recently that she was a little nervous about the French. I said I did not see what there was to be nervous of, unless it were of the French skinning all the Germans alive. She admitted that what distressed her was the fact that French soldiers did not play football between the actions, but sat and thought about their homes. In short, what had distressed and (apparently) surprised her was that the French soldiers were not English soldiers. She really could not see that practical courage and endurance no more involve playing football than playing dominoes — a game the French have often found agreeable in the intervals of defying artillery and dying on barricades. But, indeed, the unfortunate expression stirred even deeper things. Every nation has suffered for its sins in this great trial, and England also will suffer by whatever can weaken her in her worship of compromise and wealth. We had begun only barely in time some fruitful repentance about Ireland; and even so have left a small and embittered group which cannot believe our word.[58] But, indeed, the treatment of the Irish by the English is not very much worse than the treatment of the English by the English. **The great curse of this country — a curse which does not lie thus upon France or Russia, or even, in the same universal sense, upon Germany — is the bad distribution of property which leaves millions vagrant or dependent, without status, without rights, without even definite duties.** We must not be too proud to learn from the peasantries of France and Russia and Belgium; we must not let the cant of the clubs cover the very real nakedness of the land. The Russ ploughing with his ancient plough in his ancient commune really has something which we have not given to the broken clerk or craftsman in Hoxton, drifting from lodging to lodging like a stray cat. We must, in short, endure to face the fact that, if the poor Frenchmen sit and think of their homes, it is often because they have homes to think of.

The war has come on Europe like a thief in the night — and naturally, since the men of Prussia who planned it were thieves from the beginning.[59] It has caught every country in some unready and incongruous posture. It has found us not only with our reforms unfinished, but (by a weakness almost special to ourselves) with a positive pride in leaving them unfinished. It is, as I have said before, that crazy

Quand la lâcheté nous serait si bonne." — "And sing the joy of courage/ When cowardice might be sweet." And, "Et la fierté charitable/ Quand la Vengenance nous serait si bonne!" — "Sing the pride of charity,/ When vengeance would be so sweet!" Emile Cammaerts, *Belgian Poems*, Tita Brand-Cammaerts, trans. (London: John Lane, 1915), 14–17. (French and English are on facing pages.) In 1917 Cammaerts published *Through the Iron Bars, Two Years of German Occupation in Belgium*, which closes with: "The whole policy of Germany is determined by her first stroke in the war. That stroke was delivered against a small nation. The whole policy of England and of the Allies is determined by their first efforts in the struggle, and these efforts were made to protect a small nation against Germany's aggression. Never has the choice between right and wrong been made plainer in the whole history of the world." Cammaerts later wrote *The Laughing Prophet: The Seven Virtues and G.K. Chesterton* (London: Methuen, 1937).

58. The Home Rule Act of 1914 giving the Irish self-government did not take effect until after the war (1920).

59. Germany rightly denied that it planned the *specific* war that broke out in August 1914. But with great attention to the military details, it had planned to attack France through Belgium in *any* situation where war seemed likely. Facing the potential of a two-front war, it hoped to defeat France before Russia could attack in the east.

compromise which will have half a loaf, even when it could easily get a whole loaf Dickens discovered long ago that the question for the politician was How Not To Do It.[60] It is yet more complex when the question is how not quite to do it.

If we can keep close to clean and Christian modesty, England at the end of the war will not only be victorious, but (what is not always the same thing) she will be strong. Nobody expects that underbred and overschooled gutter-snipe who is the governing type of Prussia to understand such humility; he can make what he likes of it. It is a question of a spirit, and a spirit in which all powerful work has been done: "Deal not with us after our sins, neither reward us after our iniquities." Thus endured, this catastrophe may really, and without cant, mean some clearance of the fogs of corruption and scepticism; and the very earth and air of our country after the conflict may smell like South England after rain.

G.K. Chesterton, "Our Note-Book," *Illustrated London News* 147 (July 24, 1915), 99. US: July 24, 1915. Also published as "German Evil and English Weakness."

A World of Pigmies

August 7, 1915

We have had from the beginning, and we shall keep to the end, that superiority which the Prussian is only beginning to understand: the power to imagine failure.

Editor: Chesterton, in his first article after the first anniversary of the war's beginning (August 4, 1914), takes a look at how Germany has been changed by the war. He detects in an odd remark by the German Chancellor (Theobald von Bethmann Hollweg), "The Germans are fighting for their lives against a world of pigmies"—a revealing hint that, "The enemy has at least risen from the notion that Germany finds it easy to win to the manlier notion that Germany is hard to beat." Echoing those words, Chesterton tells his readers: "We are fighting against something more than pigmies, and for something more than our lives. We are not only determined to be victorious, we are determined to be vanquished, and vanquished again and again, so long as the only other course is the acceptance of these pirates and their peace."

In *The Lord of the Rings*, J.R.R. Tolkien, who would fight in the Battle of the Somme (July 1–November 18, 1916), used similar words about continuing to fight whatever the odds in his account of the Battle of Pelennor Fields. Borne by a giant prehistoric bird, the Lord of the Nazgûl has attacked the Rohirrim calvary, sending them fleeing in terror. Their king, Théoden, is left behind under his dead horse. As Merry, a small Hobbit, later recounts, only one knight, Derhelm, remains to protect the king.

> Then out of the blackness in his mind he thought that he heard Dernhelm speaking; yet now the voice seemed strange, recalling some other voice that he had known.
>
> "Begone, foul dwimmerlaik, lord of carrion! Leave the dead in peace!"

60. Charles Dicken's *Little Dorrit* (1855–1857) includes these marvelous lines: "The Circumlocution Office was (as everybody knows without being told) the most important Department under Government.... Whatever was required to be done, the Circumlocution Office was beforehand with all the public departments in the art of perceiving—How Not To Do It."

A cold voice answered: "Come not between the Nazgûl and his prey! Or, he will not slay thee in thy turn. He will bear thee away to the houses of lamentation, beyond all darkness, where thy flesh shall be devoured, and thy shrivelled mind be left naked to the Lidless Eye."

A sword rang out as it was drawn. "Do what you will; but I will hinder it, if I may."

"Hinder me? Thou fool. No living man may hinder me!"

Then Merry heard of all sounds in that hour the strangest. It seemed that Dernhelm laughed, and the clear voice was like the ring of steel. "But no living man am I! You look upon a woman. Éowyn I am, Éomund's daughter. You stand between me and my lord and kin. Begone, if you be not deathless! For living or dark undead, I will smite you, if you touch him."[61]

The German Chancellor is reported as having said: "The Germans are fighting for their lives against a world of pigmies." It is recorded chiefly as a curiosity of printing; for in the newspaper he was represented as saying that the Germans were fighting for their liver. Prometheus, perhaps, might be described as fighting for his liver; and so far, the parallel is dignified and cannot offend.[62] Otherwise, the superficial might suppose the Germans were engaged in an activity purely hygienic, like the people who ride for their liver. However, the version I gave first is evidently the correct one; and the responsibility for the mistaken word lies, apparently, with an English newspaper.

But the Chancellor's statement, as conjecturally amended above, is really interesting: for it is an example of a certain quality very common in the German pronouncements even when they are—as, to do him justice, the Chancellor's generally are—among the more rational and respectable. That quality is a fundamental division in the mind between two totally antagonistic points of view. The first is the frame of mind in which the Germans began the war; the second is the frame of mind in which alone they now find it possible to conduct it. The first is the base pride of a brute victory; the second is that nobler pride which can look in the face of defeat. It is true that all Germans are educated; but they are not only not equally educated; they are divided into two very distinct intellectual castes: the professors and middle-class intellectuals who admire and inspire the Germans, and the Prussian oligarchs who despise and who rule them. Anyone reading the biographies of men like Bismarck will notice that Prussian autocracy and reaction are defended upon two precisely opposite grounds, according to whether they are addressing the plain, patriotic bourgeoisie or the governing clique. **Publicly, they justify the despotism because Germans can rule anybody. Privately, they justify the despotism because Germans cannot rule themselves.** This really educated country, then, is divided into two types; those who know and those who know better. Now,

61. For Tolkien's tale viewed chronologically, see Michael W. Perry's *Untangling Tolkien*.

62. In Greek mythology the titan Prometheus brings fire to man, angering Zeus, who punishes him by having an eagle pick at his liver every day. The newspaper that said "liver" for "lives" probably replaced "s" with "r."

at the beginning of the war both these classes were quite confident of victory, even of instant victory. But, of course, they were confident for very different reasons. Those who had the information knew that their country was armed to the teeth for the sole purpose of this war; because they had themselves armed it. Those who only had the "culture" were stuffed with rubbishy fairy-tales about the Teutonic Race being the natural conqueror of all others. The real rulers were not so stupid as to think that one German could beat two Frenchmen. They were confident on the much more sensible ground that they could, in brute fact, bring two Germans against every one Frenchman; or, in other words, that every one Frenchman must try to beat two Germans. It was a vastly inferior force of French and English which the German millions smote last September, and swept down from the Sambre and Meuse.[63] And it was still a vastly inferior force of French and English which rallied under that shock and, rushing again to battle, bore the German millions backwards into the night from which they came. Never in the whole history of the world was there a clearer or fairer test, or a clearer or fairer triumph. Never was one man proved more plainly to be the better and master of another than Joffre was proved the better of von Kluck.[64] Those pallid people who have begun to say that we and our Allies cannot beat the Germans are, in an almost arithmetical sense, talking nonsense. They are saying that we cannot do with our whole army what we did with half of it. The proof is that the Prussians have begun to realise this simple fact themselves; hence the appearance in their utterances of a new tone and temper which does not in the least harmonise with their old instinct of bragging. Hence jarring sentences, jerkily doubling on themselves, such as the one attributed to the Chancellor, which is at least exactly like numberless German sayings of today that could easily be quoted. The speaker cannot make up his mind whether to admire his country for being easily victorious or being heroically vanquished: "The Germans are fighting for their lives against a world of giants." That is obviously what he should in consistency have said; and it would be a rather fine thing to say. But the Prussian Old Adam of brutishly unintelligent superiority awoke even in the middle of a sentence, and he could not bear to admit that Russia was large, even as an ogre.[65] He abruptly substituted the word "pigmies": which will, no doubt, have the effect of making Russia feel how very small she is. The change was all to his own disadvantage in the eyes of any imaginative and chivalric person. "*Il me faut des géants!*" of Cyrano de Bergerac is an outbreak of inward good and greatness; a volcano of virtue.[66] "*Il me faut des nains*"

63. The Sambre and Meuse are two French rivers near where important battles were fought in 1914.

64. Joseph Joffre (1852–1931) was commander-in-chief of the French army at the start of the war. He broke the German offensive at the First Battle of the Marne (September 5–12, 1914). Alexander von Kluck (1846–1934) commanded the German First Army, which was on the right and supposed to encircle Paris in the west. When he moved his army east to assist a cautious General von Bulow, the Germans lost their chance to win quickly.

65. Because neither creates an interest in the truth, arrogance and bigotry result in illogical thinking. In this case, the Allies were seen as a threat to Germany's existence and mere "pigmies," two things that cannot both be truth. For Nazism, the Jews were both rat-like vermin and running a brilliant and sinister plot to rule the world.

66. In Act 1, Scene 1, VII of Edmond Rostand's 1897 play, *Cyrano De Bergerac*, Cyrano cries out: "Oh, for an army to attack!—a host! I've ten hearts in my breast; a score of arms; No dwarfs to cleave in twain!. . . (Wildly): No! Giants now!" The two French phases could be translated: "I need giants" and "I need pigmies."

most decidedly is not. It does not sound so very difficult to fight even a world that is only full of pigmies. It seems a work too low even for Krupp, and worthy rather of an insecticide. It was the regular and appropriate type of talk for Prussians in peace. It is unfit even for Prussians in war.

What has *really* happened in the year of war that has just closed is strictly and correctly marked by this change in the German tone. One might almost call it this break in the German voice. The enemy has at least risen from the notion that Germany finds it easy to win to the manlier notion that Germany is hard to beat. What has happened to the superstition of merely academic Germany, the fancy that Germans were, by nature, better fighters than other men, it is hardly worth our while to inquire. It is of less importance at this moment than the theory that the earth is flat. The legend of the natural military mastery belonging to the Teuton has already received its death-blow. And though the Germans, by their excellent preparation and munitionment[67] were to win the war after all, and were to enter every capital in triumph, that legend would not rise from the dead.[68]

But the saner self-satisfaction of their military specialists has also failed. It has failed for the excellent reason that the grounds on which it was legitimately founded are gone. It was founded on a numerical superiority—which no longer exists: a monopoly of certain forces—which no longer exists: an advantage of ambush and abrupt aggression—which, naturally, no longer exists.[69] But we are still different from the wisest and sanest Germans in this: that though we can be increasingly confident of success, our whole argument does not rest on success. **We have had from the beginning, and we shall keep to the end, that superiority which the Prussian is only beginning to understand: the power to imagine failure.[70] We are fighting against something more than pigmies, and for something more than our lives. We are not only determined to be victorious, we are determined to be vanquished, and vanquished again and again, so long as the only other course is the acceptance of these pirates and their peace.** We answer with that noble alternative of the martyrs in the Scripture: if our God be God, yes, or even if our men be men, they shall deliver us: but *if not,* if our chances were as black as they are in truth brightening; if the omens were as disastrous as they are in fact favourable; if with all we can do we have come to nothing but darkness and the end of the way,

67. *Oxford English Dictionary* gives, as the first to use this term in print, Chesterton's friend, Hilaire Belloc, who used it in an article in *Land & Water* on May 29, 1915. It was used as late at 1935, but the modest difference between armaments (cannons and shells) and munitionments (just the shells), apparently made it of little value.

68. Unfortunately, this prediction proved untrue. The Germans under Nazism became even more enamored with their racial superiority and chose to blame even their lost war on a 'stab in the back.'

69. Germany had a larger population than France, began with more weapons (especially machine guns and heavy artillery), and had the advantage of striking the first blow. The British and its empire negated the first, the French now have more weapons, and after a year of fighting, there are few surprises. The war is a stalemate.

70. This resembles the critical contrast in J.R.R. Tolkien's *The Lord of the Rings*. Sauron fails, in part, due to a lack of imagination. Awed by his immense strength, he cannot imagine defeat. Able to think only in terms of power, he does not imagine, until the very last moment, that his foes would seek to destroy the Ring rather than use it. In contrast, his opponents can imagine themselves corrupted by the power of the Ring and refuse to use it.

know that we will not bow down to the idol these savages have set up for a god, but which they cannot even carve so as to make it look like a man.[71]

G.K. Chesterton, "Our Note-Book," *Illustrated London News* 147 (August 7, 1915), 163. US: August 7, 1915. Also published as "The Changing German Tone."

PACIFIST INCOMPETENCE

August 14, 1915

I should, on the whole, advise the English not to build their safety on the novel and rather unnational logic of persecution, even of justifiable persecution. I should advise them to build on the grand, firm, and enduring foundation of the Pacifist's controversial incompetence.

EDITOR: As the war lengthened, both the anger of those protesting against the war and the insecurity of those supporting it increased, leading some of the latter to demand that pacifists be silenced. Chesterton, confident as always in what he believed, argues that censoring and prosecuting pacifists is not necessary and that it is not the English way to resort to persecution even in wartime.

IT is often a strategic mistake to silence a man, because it leaves the world under the impression that he had something to say. For this reason I would not proceed against the very small organisations which urge the conclusion of peace—or, in other words, the leaving of Prussia in possession of her spoils. Coercion, like conscription, is a legitimate expedient, but not a very native, and therefore not a very easy, one; I **should, on the whole, advise the English not to build their safety on the novel and rather unnational logic of persecution, even of justifiable persecution. I should advise them to build on the grand, firm, and enduring foundation of the Pacifist's controversial incompetence.** After some study of all his works, I have come to feel confidence in him. He can be trusted to fail: and the more publicly he fails the better. I set him on a high tribune; I encircle him with the silence of a crowded amphitheatre; I cry aloud "*Favete linguis!*"[72] Then he opens his mouth wide: and no words come forth. Or, what is the same thing, words like the following: "We believe that the right course is not for us to admonish peace lovers in other countries as to their duty in regard to their Governments, but to show that we are in earnest by demanding that Britain's part in the war shall be brought to an immediate, honourable, and righteous finish." What can we possibly do with a thing like that, unless it were to answer, with equal gravity, that we are in favour of a square, circular, and triangular finish, or that we incline rather to a thin, fat, and middle-sized finish? It is simply self-evident that an *immediate* peace could not be an honourable one, since, apart from all explanations with Germany, we should have to have an explanation

71. Chesterton offers similar advice, to fight on no matter how dark the circumstances, in his marvelous *The Ballad of the White Horse* (1911). There King Alfred, the hero of the tale, is told, "I tell you naught for your comfort,/ Yea, naught for your desire,/ Save that the sky goes darker yet/ And the sea rises higher." For that ballad and other Chesterton poems, see *G.K. Chesterton's Early Poetry* (Seattle, Inkling Books, 2004), 138–139.

72. A quote from the Latin poet Horace (65–8 BC) meaning, "With silence favor me." It was a warning not to use words that carry religious omen.

with our Allies. No; these people can be trusted—to trip. Everything they try to say can be twisted inside out with a turn of the hand. It is far better to treat them so, as they turn up, than to move against them as serious heresiarchs, and provide them with a heresy they have not the wits to invent.[73] The words I quote are from a queer piece of paper circulated by something called "The Stop-the-War Committee." Being deprived by Heaven of the power of speech, it relieves its feelings chiefly by capital letters, one or two words in almost every sentence being thus printed without any particular reference to what the words are. Thus: "The BEST and most HUMANE course would be to negotiate rather than to drive the Germans out." To which, in the same reverent spirit of imitation, I can only answer that it is JUST AS well, as A RULE, to form some NOTION OF WHAT words mean when you use THEM. And what the word "negotiation" must mean, at the very best, is manifest enough. Note that negotiation has nothing to do with moral persuasion, which the finer sort of fanatics would probably put forth as superior to war. If Mr. Scott Duckers (who seems responsible for the piece of paper) could go to the Kaiser and speak to him with such soul-inflaming eloquence that the Kaiser burst into tears and called off the dogs of war, the incident (though improbable) might well be maintained to be more noble than an action in the field.[74] But to negotiate is to exchange; and any influence brought to bear on Prussia in that manner must mean giving something up to Prussia to gain something from her. What is it that we can give up to Prussia? Whatever it is, if it were a patch of African swamp, it would have stuck up over it like a notice-board the proclamation: "Bestowed by the Powers of Europe as a Reward for Invading Belgium."

The level of reasoning reached by these luckless people may be inferred from the following: "If the breach of treaties were to be regarded as affording an excuse for war, international law would not diminish causes of war, but multiply them." **In other words, there will be dignity in a law so long as nobody ever thinks of obeying it; but less dignity in the law if anybody even attempts to get it obeyed.** If the law against assassination by poison were a law never put into force, this bright thinker would, I suppose, congratulate himself on not "multiplying" causes of litigation. There would certainly be fewer poison cases; only there would be more poisoning. Yet, in the very next sentence, the writer flounders from the practical denial that international law can be enforced at all to the implication that it should be enforced with as much precision as private law. "Under private law," he says (I dispense with his absurd capital letters), "breach of contract is no excuse for murder." Study that sentence: it is the picture of a mind. In private law breach of contract is always punished, by penalties which vary from the mildest, which is loss of all the advantages

73. A heresiarch is the founder of a heresy or the leader of a heretical sect.

74. James Scott Duckers, "Stop the War" committee chairman, described his imprisonment for refusing military service in *Handed-over* (London: C.W. Daniel, 1917). The idolization of such behavior is hardly new. In *War and the Future: Italy, France and Britain at War* (1917), H.G. Wells wrote, "while the London *Times* is full of schemes of great state enterprises... the so-called socialist press of Great Britain is chiefly busy about the draughts in the cell of Mr. Fenner Brockway and the refusal of Private Scott Duckers to put on his khaki trousers."

of the contract to the offending party. The reason we can punish it thus temperately and in proportion is, of course, that in private law we have all the parties in our hand; and by the ordinary pressure of police can secure the injured as much as he deserves or restrain the wrongdoer as far as we think fit. But we should inflict death if we could inflict nothing else, and if the only alternative were a universal repudiation of contracts. Put the bargain-breaker in the position he holds as an armed Sovereign, and "murder" becomes the only thing we could do. Suppose each purchaser, after receiving a penny loaf, and refusing to produce a penny, could shut himself up in a turret of steel from which it took military attack to dislodge him. That military attack would be undertaken. If it were not, the country would be conquered and ruled by an aristocracy of thieves. What this pamphleteer calls murder, what we call war, is what happens when the robber has a robber-band and a robber-stronghold. The outside of this piece of paper is much funnier than the inside. On the front is written in enormous scarlet letters "Shall British Blood and Treasure be Sacrificed for Nought?" To which the answer seems to be "No," with the obvious corollary that if there were an "immediate finish" they would have been sacrificed for nought. The back is better. It says, "Are you an Out-and-Outer?" and also, "Either be a Militarist and say, 'On with Carnage,' or do Your Part to STOP THE WAR." It seems quite certain that there is no third course. So I think I will be a Militarist and I will say "On with the Carnage" at intervals during the day. I hope this is being Out-and-Out; and it does not seem very difficult. For the rest, there is the ignorant catchword about our being where we were last year, which is exactly what we are not, upon any argument. One might as well say so of a man who has lost his foot to avoid blood-poisoning. Had there been no amputation he would be a perfect biped. He would also be a corpse. There is only one thing about this pamphlet on which one can possibly be serious; and that is not only serious, but sad. Mr. C.H. Norman, whose name appears along with that of Mr. Duckers, is not a fool.[75] He is a man who has often been right, and who has generally had something of the right spirit even when he was wrong. I will

75. Chesterton referred to pacifists such as C.H. Norman in the December 11, 1915 *Illustrated London News* (Ch. 3) as those who "mean nothing but good." Others shared his high view of Norman's sincerity. After conscription laws were passed, Norman was in legal trouble when the government denied him conscientious objector status. In his defense, letters were published in the May 18, 1916 issue of *New Age*, including Bernard Shaw, who wrote:

> I understand that in cases of conscientious objection to military service the question is always raised whether the objector is suddenly alleging scruples which he had never expressed before for the purpose of evading duty, or whether his objection is a consistent part of opinions which he has been known to hold and express before there was any immediate prospect of war or of compulsion to military service. I can hardly imagine any doubt arising in your case; however, I am quite prepared to testify that you have been to my knowledge, both in public and private, a most determined, uncompromising and indefatigable anti-war propagandist for the last ten years. I will not wound you by calling you a fanatic; but you have been so entirely reckless of your own interests in advocating your view that nothing but your exceptional and indispensable skill in your profession could have saved you from suffering very severely for your repeated defiances of popular opinion. I have not the smallest doubt of your entire disinterestedness and sincerity.
>
> As I do not share your views on the subject of the present emergency, I feel bound to add that you are the last man in the world I should like to see sent into a barrack. I should expect the whole regiment, officers and all, to throw down its arms at the end of about three weeks as a result of your indefatigable propaganda and the very plausible arguments and stores of information which you command. It is, therefore, entirely in the interests of the military authority that I wish you a happy exemption. Any sort of martyrdom would greatly increase your influence; and, to be quite frank with you, I do not want your influence to be increased until the war is over.

believe that he originally attacked tyranny out of real sympathy with the wrongs of the unfortunate; and that he came to attack the patriotic tradition under the impression that it was a form of tyranny. What he calls militarism, I call self-defence; but I think he would have sincerely called it selfishness. But what can we say of this "peace" except that it is almost literally a fatty degeneration of the heart? How can what was once generous end in such ghastly lack of generosity? How does an idealist come at last to things so spiritually squalid as the surrenders and betrayals advocated here? I cannot believe that Mr. Norman would treat two human companions, though they were escaped convicts laden with loathsome crimes, as England is recommended to treat France and Russia in this case. I cannot believe he would leave any human being whom he could save with his own life under such smiling insult and victorious iniquity as this would leave the million human beings of Belgium. **The man who should carry out in practice the recommendations of this pamphlet would not be a Pacifist any more than a Militarist. He would be nothing so loyal as a German spy. He would be a coward; a man surrendering to power because it is powerful; a man deserting friends because they are in danger; a man disappointing the broken-hearted of the deliverance promised to them; a man praising the peace of a shambles and the "negotiations" of a slave-market—**

Who would not laugh if such a man there be?
Who would not weep if Atticus were he?[76]

G.K. Chesterton, "Our Note-Book," *Illustrated London News* 147 (August 14, 1915), 195. US: August 14, 1915. Also published as "The Illogic of the Pacifists."

EDITH CAVELL

October 30, 1915

Apparently only those who pay no respect to treaties are privileged to pay no respect to womanhood.

EDITOR: Edith Cavell (1865–1915) was an English nurse. When the war began, she was matron at a hospital in Brussels, Belgium that was taken over by the Red Cross. While in that position, the Germans accused her of helping hundreds of allied soldiers to escape to neutral Holland. They gave her a quick trial and shot her early on the morning of October 12.

Although perhaps technically legal in wartime, many were outraged at what Chesterton calls the sheer "meanness" of the deed. In one of the few remarks she made in her defense, Cavell said that she helped these men escape because she feared that, if

76. These lines are from "Epistle to Dr Arbuthnot" (1734) by Alexander Pope (1688–1744). The poem is a satire on prominent people of that day. This particular stanza, which describes someone as easily flattered and weak as Chesterton regarded many pacifist leaders, closes with the lines: "Damn with faint praise, assent with civil leer,/ And without sneering, teach the rest to sneer;/ Willing to wound, and yet afraid to strike,/ Just hint a fault, and hesitate dislike;/ Alike reserv'd to blame, or to commend,/ A tim'rous foe, and a suspicious friend;/ Dreading ev'n fools, by flatterers besieg'd,/ And so obliging, that he ne'er oblig'd;/ Like Cato, give his little Senate laws,/ And sit attentive to his own applause;/ While Wits and Templers ev'ry sentence raise,/ And wonder with a foolish face of praise./ Who but must laugh, if such a man there be?/ Who would not weep, if Atticus were he?

caught, the Germans would shoot them.[77] Along with war documents published in 1923, Charles F. Horne explained the public response.

> The height of execration roused by the Cavell case depended, however, on something far other than its legal status. It arose from the victim's sex and high character. No truly "cultured" race could slay a woman for a deed of kindliness, for following the mother instinct to save and to protect. If a man-made law condemns her, real men ignore that law. Nothing showed more sharply the gulf between Germany and the rest of the world than the fact that German officials with one voice insisted on enforcing their law against Miss Cavell.... They knew well how public sentiment would execrate their deed; but being Prussians they thought the "frightfulness" of this example would aid them more than its shamefulness would harm them. Thank God, they underestimated the courage of the human race![78]

The execution further strained Germany's relations with the United States. The First Secretary of the American legation at Brussels, Hugh Gibson, warned that there would be consequences. In a statement issued after she was shot, he noted: "We reminded him (Count Franz von Harrach) of the burning of Louvain and the sinking of the *Lusitania*, and told him that this murder would stir all civilized countries with horror and disgust. Count Harrach broke in at this with the rather irrelevant remark that he would rather see Miss Cavell shot than have harm come to one of the humblest German soldiers, and his only regret was that they had not 'three or four English old women to shoot.'"[79]

The execution of Edith Cavell helps to explain the harshness of Chesterton's *The Crimes of England*, which would come out in November. In that book, he puts a different spin on 'you too' arguments that responded to German atrocities by pointing to England's sins. Some of his nation's crimes, Chesterton argues, resulted from giving Germany an undue influence in England, an influence that extended all the way to a monarchy borrowed from Germany. The book's harsh stance against German *Kultur* drew criticism, even in England, but it should be remembered that both the Cavell execution and the millions of nameless civilian dead in World War II support Chesterton's harsh view of Prussianism. History is clearly on his side.

THERE is not much that can be said, or said easily, about the highest aspects of the murder of Edith Cavell. When we have said, "Dear in the sight of God is the death of his saints," we have said as much as mere literature has ever been able to say in this matter. But there are many lessons in it concerning the living problem with which we are still engaged. And one of the most important was in the sublimely simple and direct demeanour of the victim herself: especially her candour and con-

77. Cavell's fears were justified by Germany's behavior. See Chesterton's September 1, 1919 article (Ch. 7).

78. *Source Records of the Great War*, Charles F. Horne, ed. (New York: National Alumni, 1923), 369. Notice that he credits this outrage to *chivalry* and *courage*—a chivalry that protects woman and children in wartime, and a courage that stands up to those who do not. In our modern and less cultured world, even when the helpless victims run into the thousands, many find the "frightfulness" of terrorist deeds a reason for meek surrender rather than bold action. That indicates that both chivalry and courage are lacking. Note too the lack of dissent among high German officials about this execution. That is why Chesterton considers Germany's problems to be deeply ingrained in its culture and why they require stern medicine.

79. Count Franz von Harrach was a member of staff of Baron von der Lancken, German military governor. The previous year he had been Archduke Franz Ferdinand's bodyguard. Riding on the sideboard of the Archduke's car, he was present when the Archduke was assassinated on June 28, 1914—the spark that ignited WWI.

tempt of legalism. She was especially the representative of a full and ripe civilization, as against that powerful half-civilization which is attempting to destroy it, in the fact that she hungered and thirsted after the whole truth: that she was impatient of anything less than what the French, who are its great champions, call the *vraie vérité* [true truth]. That spirit refuses to be defended by fallacies: it tears its way through sophistries like shrapnel through barbed wire, even when the barbed wire is erected as a defence for it. Like a far-seeing chess-player, it scorns to spin out a game that is already decided. In this, as in so many things, it is in marked contrast with that pedantry which has become a poison in the Prussian brain. In the trial of the English nurse, the culprit summed up like a judge. And it was the judges who have shuffled like culprits.

Modern Germany is great in wealth and long preparation; it is not great in anything else; it is not even really great in tyranny. On every occasion it has hidden itself in that hasty network of excuses which its greatest victim especially despised. The quality of *meanness* curiously marks all its merely intellectual activities. It was the same, for instance, in the case of Belgium. In answer to that ancient and awful question: "Hast thou slain and also taken possession?" the Prussian is obliged to answer "Yes; and I have libelled also." He stooped to declaring that he had at last found an excuse for a crime—which in any case, he had committed without excuse. He had nothing to say in defence of having murdered his neighbour except that he had also robbed him; and that robbing him of his papers had been the means of robbing him of his reputation. If everything he said against his unhappy victim had been as true as it was false, he would still have been much the more abject figure of the two. And exactly the same note of pettiness and posthumous malice marks all his attempts to excuse himself over the Cavell case. In one of his monkey tricks of vanity, he has even attempted to twist this tragedy into a very unsoldierly sneer about the accidents of the military campaign. He says that the Allies have not yet had occasion to murder any hospital nurses in hostile countries, because they do not hold so much conquered territory. This would appear to mean, by the operations of normal logic, that if we had violently annexed Denmark in order to seize the Kiel Canal and all the ships in it, we should by that deed of chivalry have earned the right to butcher good women for behaving as such. But as our record is devoid of any such acts of virtue, we cannot hope to partake of the purer pleasure of the Prussian paradise.[80] **Apparently only those who pay no respect to treaties are privileged to pay no respect to womanhood.** Even more mentally inept, if possible, is the excuse attempted by the most responsible Prussian official involved: the suggestion that the shot was as inevitable as one which should kill a Russian woman fighting in the Russian lines as a man. The parallel is not only a pedantry; but it is, like most pedantries, obviously unphilosophical. Nobody would blame the Prussian soldier whose bullet pierced a woman in a Russian uniform; first, because he is only expected to see the uniform; and, second, because killing her is very probably the only way of preventing her kill-

80. This is probably an allusion to Islam, where wars of conquest allegedly win a soldier maidens in Paradise.

ing him. But Nurse Cavell was not wearing any uniform of war, but the universally recognized uniform of peace; and she was not trying to kill German soldiers, but, on the contrary, trying to cure them. That the same human compassion which led her to help Germans to health led her also to help Englishmen to home, was certainly a technical offence; and among any people who could be regarded as sane, would have received some technical punishment. Indeed, it might have received a fairly heavy punishment, and one answering all possible purposes of German self-protection, and still not come within a thousand miles of this extravagant act of vengeance. I need only allude here to that other network of small evasions which entangled the efforts of the American and Spanish intercessors: it is all of a piece. It is that smallness of Germany which has been so much more startling to us than the bigness of Germany. But what I have just said of the more obvious course of imprisonment, if the thing was done to protect the Prussian power, brings me to the last fact which is vital to us in this war.

The thing was not done to protect the Prussian power. It was done to satisfy a Prussian appetite. The mad disproportion between the possible need of restraining their enemy and the frantic needlessness of killing her, is simply the measure of the distance by which the distorted Prussian psychology has departed from the moral instincts of mankind. **The key to the Prussian is in this extraordinary fact: that he does truly and in his heart believe that he is *admired* whenever he can manage to be dreaded.** An indefensible act of public violence is to him what a poem is to a poet or a song to a bird. It at once relieves and expresses him; he feels more himself while he is doing it. His whole conception of the State is a series of *coups d' état*. In Poland, in Alsace, in Lorraine, in the Danish provinces, he has wholly failed to govern; indeed, he has never really attempted to govern. For governing means making people at home. Wherever he goes, and whatever success he gains, he will always make it an occasion for sanguinary pantomimes of this kind.[81] And awful as is the individual loss, it is well that now, at the very moment when men, wily or weak, are beginning to talk of conciliatory possibilities in this incurable criminal, he should himself have provided us with this appalling reply.

G.K. Chesterton, "Edith Cavell," *Illustrated London News* 147 (October 30, 1915), 546. This article was published separately from his regular "Our Note-Book" column. That may have been to make clear that the opinion expressed was not that just of Chesterton, but of the paper itself.

Henry Ford's Pacifism

December 11, 1915

There are other Pacifists, many of them men who necessarily command respect, who may attempt to create the reconciliation without understanding the quarrel. Such men will mean nothing but good and do nothing but harm.

81. For more on Prussian "pantomimes," see the May 22, 1915 article (Ch. 3).

Editor: Perhaps only Chesterton would be clever enough to introduce the somber and hard-working industrialist Henry Ford as a "celebrated American comedian" and compare him to the owner of a circus. That was in keeping with his belief that the best way to deal the grim seriousness of many pacifists was light humor. Notice too how in this case pacifism has been seduced by a conspiracy theory. Those who can't intelligently explain the world often resort to nonsense.

Keep in mind that Henry Ford as a political activist has not aged well. Perhaps because his politics—a naive pacifism and conspiracy theories blended with a virulent anti-Semitism—is so embarrassing, today he is remembered almost exclusively as a maker of cars for the masses. Bringing up Ford the pacifist will, as Chesterton suggests, "queer the pitch" of more appealing spokesmen. But at least as late as Aldous Huxley's 1932 *Brave New World*, Ford was regarded as a significant enough agent of social change that Huxley's twenty-sixth century consumption-obsessed utopia dates itself to "A.F. 632" where the "A.F." stands for "After Ford." Ford also has the dubious distinction of being the only American mentioned in Hitler's conspiracy-riddled *Mein Kampf*: "It is the Jews who govern the stock exchange forces of the American Union. Every year makes them more and more the controlling masters of the producers in a nation of one hundred and twenty millions; only a single great man, Ford, to their fury, still maintains full independence."[82]

Ford illustrates several of pacifism's least pleasant characteristics. In its effort to square the moral circle, portraying war as always and under every circumstance wrong, pacifism often behaves strangely. Sir Walter Scott's poem, "Marmion" (1808) described their difficulty perfectly: "O, what a tangled web we weave, When first we practise to deceive!"

If war is always wrong, then *all* those making war must be shown to be wrong without exception. That requires pacifism to deny even the most obvious evidence about how a war began and is what Chesterton means when he refers to those who "attempt to create the reconciliation without understanding the quarrel." It must blur the often clear line between a powerful aggressor (Germany) and his helpless victim (Belgium), as well as those helping the victim (Britain and France). That's why Chesterton devoted himself to refuting those arguments in 1914 and 1915. Along with that denial, must come other explanations for why the war began, including conspiracy theories as bizarre as Ford's claim that "financiers" started WWI. There is an inner logic to pacifist lies. Limiting a war's causes to the narrowest of reasons by the smallest of groups makes their goal of world peace seem more achievable.

But the tangled web does not end there. To keep a war from being seen as moral, the suffering of the victims of aggression must be minimized or even denied. During WWI, that was difficult. Britain was flooded with Belgian refugees, many of them very articulate. But those refugees would return home after the war, and, in the years between the wars, pacifists labored long and hard to spread the idea that German atrocities in Belgium were little more than wartime propaganda, and that the war wasn't the result of German aggression, but of greedy armaments industries in all the

82. Adolf Hitler, *Mein Kampf*, Ralph Manheim, transl. (Boston: Houghton Mifflin, 1943), 639. In the second German edition, "a single great man, Ford" became "only a very few." Earlier in the book, Hitler complained that, while German "Protestantism will always stand up for the advancement of all Germanism," it also "combats with the greatest hostility any attempt to rescue the nation from the embrace of its most mortal enemy, since its attitude toward the Jews just happens to be more or less dogmatically established." *Mein Kampf*, 113.

belligerents.[83] One of life's unfortunate realities is that those who know the truth are often less inclined to make sure it triumphs than those whose entire world view will collapse if the lies they believe are discredited.

The result is history—a Europe unprepared for the next wave of German aggression and violence on a far greater scale than the Belgian atrocities. In 1945, when evidence for those atrocities became undeniable, the press in Allied countries had to explain why they had said so little about them during the war. Their explanation was that they thought this was a repeat of the atrocity propaganda of the First World War. A crime concealed behind pacifist lies had led to an even greater crime taking place virtually unhindered. That's what Chesterton means in this article when he says that pacifists often "mean nothing but good and do nothing but harm."

In the end, while the fighting is going on, the more radical pacifists often make their own sort of war—an ugly one of lies and distortions directed at their own nation. They become a nation's "weakest link," as Chesterton had written in a July 20, 1907 article (Ch. 1). Note too that because aggressor nations almost always silence their pacifists, a democracy waging a just war will be more hobbled by its pacifists than a repressive dictatorship waging an unjust war. Even when they don't hand victory to the evil side, pacifists can make a war longer and bloodier. Pacifists are an aggressor's best friend.

Pacifism is driven by an inevitably destructive logic. In its efforts to distort the moral scales, confirming its belief that war itself is always evil, pacifism can't permit anyone engaged in a war to appear good, least of all its victims and heroes. They *must* attack those who are courageously doing good on the battlefield or intelligently leading the war at home. As a result, the "war crimes" of the good, whether real or manufactured, get more attention than the far greater crimes of those doing evil. This means that the very logic of pacifism drives it to serve evil rather than good. As Chesterton will put it at the close of an August 3, 1918 article (Ch. 6): "Pacifism and Prussianism are always in alliance, by a fatal logic far beyond any conscious conspiracy."

Finally, notice Chesterton's stress on the fact that it will take "a long time and a terrible agony" to rid the continent of "the whole European evil, from which we have increasingly suffered for two hundred years." He understood that the German problem had no easy solution. He calls it the "European evil," in part because Europe as a whole had done little to hinder its development since the time of Frederick the Great, and in part because other European countries, Britain included, had engaged in many of those same practices in countries such as Ireland.

MR. FORD, the celebrated American comedian, is now on tour with his company; and the type of advertisement, as well as the troupe itself, are much in the manner of Mr. Barnum.[84] How, happily, the humourist manages to keep his inventions remote from any too painful reality may be judged from the following remark, which he is reported as having made to an interviewer—

83. This isn't to deny that some atrocity propaganda was spread. Chesterton knew better than to trust his colleagues in the press. He based his arguments on atrocities for which the evidence was undeniable and, in most cases, on those the Germany government itself defended as justified. He knew that a German submarine sank the *Lusitania*, because the German government awarded the U-boat captain with a medal for the deed.

84. P.T. Barnum (1810–1891)was one of the founders of the Ringling Brothers and Barnum and Bailey Circus.

> I believe that the sinking of the *Lusitania* was deliberately planned to get this country into war. It was not planned by any one nation. It was planned by the financiers of war.

I think that is quite sufficient as regards Mr. Ford in relation to the probabilities of politics. There seems no limit to such a line of thought, and I am surprised that he has not carried it further. **I have often denounced the internationalism of finance myself. I believe that banks are often really the fortresses of a silent invasion. But I have some difficulty in believing that bankers swim under the sea to cut holes in the bottoms of ships;** I presume Mr. Ford thinks that several millions of bank clerks, disguised as German soldiers, crossed the frontier and laid waste Belgium, while the peaceable German Army remained at home. It may be that by "financiers" Mr. Ford means munition-manufacturers, for his style is by no means clear; and I myself have often pointed out that the German firm is Krupp and Kaiser, and not Kaiser and Krupp.[85] But the attempt to explain the collision of all human ambitions and interests by the mere materials through which they work is a thing fit for a lunatic asylum. I could not make Mr. Ford commit a murder by giving him a revolver as a Christmas present; even if, in the warmth of my affection, I had made it for him myself. Nor could anybody make thousands of ordinary men march and starve and die happy, merely by providing them with pieces of metal for the purpose. Nobody could make them carry heavy rifles by making heavy rifles for them to carry. The whole thing is windy nonsense born of wealth and security, and a gaping and ghastly ignorance of all that makes men behave like men. **That pride and ambition and avarice often lead to wars is true, and another matter; but that has nothing to do with the mindless materialism which would explain things by their tools.**[86] Torture, for instance, is a horrible thing; and real religious enthusiasts have often tortured each other. But if any man were to tell me that they tortured each other because the manufacturers of instruments of torture wanted to sell them, I should take the liberty of calling him a fool. I do not believe that the Reformation came because shopkeepers wished to do a brisk business in racks. Nor do I believe that the epidemic of witch-burning in the seventeenth century was due to a conspiracy of timber-merchants. People wanted to fight under such insult and wrong as the ultimatums to Serbia and Belgium long before there were any modern armaments or modern armament firms. I have sometimes even fancied that people wished to travel before the invention of the Ford Car.

There is one way in which Mr. Ford and his tour will probably do good. It will queer the pitch of much more plausible and presentable individuals if they attempt to prevent the thorough purgation of Christendom. **There are other Pacifists, many of them men who necessarily command respect, who may attempt to create the reconciliation without understanding the quarrel. Such men will mean nothing**

85. Krupp was Germany's giant steel and armaments manufacturer. Today it's a part of ThyssenKrupp AG. For a detailed history of the firm, see William Manchester's *The Arms of Krupp: 1587–1968*.

86. Elsewhere Chesterton referred to this as the "atheistic style." See his October 6, 1906 article (Ch. 1).

but good and do nothing but harm; but they will certainly do less harm if they find, wherever they go, the torn and faded posters of Mr. Ford's unsuccessful circus. I have been told (I do not know whether there is any truth in it) that during American elections the opponents of some politician will send round a sort of living caricature of him; another man dressed up in undignified imitation of him, and carrying on (I need hardly say) in a manner little to his credit. These artistic wire-pullers send their walking-cartoon not *after* the hated politician to parody him, but *before* him, to take the words out of his mouth. So that astonished statesman finds his most sober remarks hailed with happy laughter. I do not suggest that we should apply this method to the Pacifists ourselves; or attempt to forestall Mr. Morel or Mr. Philip Snowden by sending some funnier person in front of them.[87] For one thing, I do not see how there could be any funnier person than Mr. Morel or Mr. Philip Snowden. And for another, such jokes in the grand style require the champagne-like air which seems to serve that nation (symbolically called Carrie Nation) as a substitute for champagne.[88] But if it is difficult for us to do it ourselves, we ought to be all the more grateful to Mr. Ford if he will do it for us. And I cannot imagine anything more likely to turn a premature peace into a permanent joke than a man who begins his persuasion of the world by telling us a story about the sinking of the *Lusitania*, by which the Prussian Government defended what it did not do.

For the responsible Pacifists in America, the matter which I would ask them to consider is this. **They must not be surprised if it takes a long time and a terrible agony to tear up from the earth what we are trying to tear up; for it is the whole European evil, from which we have increasingly suffered for two hundred years.** The American democracy is to be congratulated on having been founded far away from us, and when the evil was only beginning to grow.[89] But for the very reason that America is to be congratulated on escaping it, America is not specially qualified to understand it. It is a natural temptation for Americans to tell us how to solve the problem of militarism; just as it was a natural temptation for us to tell them how to solve the problem of negro slavery. But the greater part of what we talked about negro slavery was nonsense. It was full of that frailty in the mind by which men

87. The pacifism of journalist Edward D. Morel (1873–1924) was clearly pro-German. Before the war he wrote *Morocco in Diplomacy* (1912), taking the side of Germany's 'gunboat diplomacy' in the Agadir Crisis (1911). After the war began, he helped found the Union of Democratic Control, the largest of the anti-war groups, whose approach to ending the war, including no change in borders, favored Germany. When Chesterton criticized pacifist groups who did not want aggressors punished, he primarily meant the Union of Democratic Control. Philip Snowden (1864–1937) was a Labour Party politician whose pacifism led him to support conscientious objectors.

88. This refers to the U.S., home of Carrie Nation, the famous prohibitionist, and "grand" jokes like Mr. Ford.

89. In *The Crimes of England*, Chesterton described how Germany turned to autocratic rule and militarism two centuries before with Frederick the Great (1712–1786). Edward Collins, a modern military historian, described what happened in a similar fashion: "It [Prussia] had been raised to the first rank by the intrigues, wars and autocratic control of Frederick the Great, who had in turn capitalized upon the success of his predecessor in developing the Prussian army. The army had, in fact, become the pivotal element in the Prussian state, and all economic, social, and political institutions had been subordinated to maintaining the size and efficiency of the army. Prussia was a poor state and the size of the army could be maintained only by practice of the most rigid economies in all other state functions. To accomplish this, the state was rigidly organized and disciplined." Edward Collins, "Introduction" in Karl von Clausewitz, *War, Politics and Power* (Washington: Regnery, 1965), 3.

can always be most emphatic about what is furthest off. Emancipation would have seemed a very easy matter to Dickens or Thackeray; but it seemed a very difficult matter both to Lincoln and to Lee. And I think it will call a smile to the lips of the most earnest American Pacifist if he reflects on what welcome either Lincoln or Lee would have given to an English proprietor of hansom-cabs who should suddenly have commanded both sides to embrace, immediately after the Battle of Chancellorsville. And it is equally unnecessary for any American to go outside his own national history if he wishes for some image of the mind of the decent European who, desiring peace as much as any American, is yet at this moment absolutely adamant for war. No American was more Pacifist, as none was more Puritan, than James Russell Lowell.[90] He was much too Pacifist, as he was much too Puritan, for my own private fancy; and his lecturing voice was easily drowned for me in the great wind of Walt Whitman. In his earlier poems he preached a literal peace-at-any-price, in its most precise and even most priggish form. He said that all war was murder, and that he had no need to go any further than his Testament for the fact. He thought it the most scorching satire to suggest that civilisation could get forward on a powder-cart. But he did not talk like that when he stood in the furnace of reality in which we stand to-day. And when other people began to talk like that to him, when the Fords of that day wanted a premature peace between North and South, he said something rather different, which I think, I can roughly remember —

Come, Peace, not as a mourner bowed
For honour lost and dear ones wasted,
But proud to meet a people proud
With eyes that tell of triumph tasted ...
Come, such as mothers prayed for when
They kissed their Cross with lips that quivered,
And bring fair wages for brave men,
A nation saved, a race delivered.[91]

G.K. Chesterton, "Our Note-Book," *Illustrated London News* 147 (December 11, 1915), 756. US: December 11, 1915. Also published as "Mr. Ford's Peace Plan."

90. James R. Lowell (1819–1891) was an American poet and abolitionist.

91. These are the closing lines to James R. Lowell's poem, "Mr. Hosea Biglow to the Editor of *The Atlantic Monthly*," written during the Civil War and published in *The Biglow Papers* (Second Series, No. 10). Here is the passage that Chesterton was "roughly" remembering: "Come, Peace! not like a mourner bowed/ For honor lost an' dear ones wasted,/ But proud, to meet a people proud,/ With eyes thet tell o' triumph tasted!/ Come, with han' grippin' on the hilt,/ An' step thet proves ye Victory's daughter!/ Longin' for you, our sperits wilt/ Like shipwrecked men's on raf's for water./ Come, while our country feels the lift/ Of a gret instinct shoutin' 'Forwards!'/ An' knows thet freedom ain't a gift/ Thet tarries long in han's o' cowards!/ Come, sech ez mothers prayed for, when/ They kissed their cross with lips thet quivered,/ An' bring fair wages for brave men,/ A nation saved, a race delivered!"

4

Battling Militarism

1916

1916

Ernst Haeckel—Editor

In 1922, Chesterton introduced *Eugenics and Other Evils* with a short section entitled "To the Reader," which described how his original draft for the book had almost been discarded after the war began.

> And then the hour came when I felt, not without relief, that I might well fling all my notes into the fire. The fire was a big one, and was burning up bigger things than such pedantic quackeries. And, anyhow, the issue itself was being settled in a very different style. Scientific officialism and organisation in the State which had specialised in them, had gone to war with the older culture of Christendom. Either Prussianism would win and the protest would be hopeless, or Prussianism would lose and the protest would be needless. As the war advanced from poison gas to piracy against neutrals, it grew more and more plain that the scientifically organised State was not increasing in popularity. Whatever happened, no Englishmen would ever again go nosing around the stinks of that low laboratory. So I thought all I had written irrelevant and put it out of my mind.
>
> I am greatly grieved to say that it is not irrelevant. It has gradually grown apparent, to my astonished gaze, that the ruling classes in England are still proceeding on the assumption that Prussia is a pattern for the whole world. If parts of my book are nearly nine years old, most of their principles and proceedings are a great deal older. They can offer us nothing but the same stuffy science, the same bullying bureaucracy and the same terrorism by tenth-rate professors that have led the German Empire to its recent conspicuous triumph. For that reason, three years after the war with Prussia, I collect and publish these papers.[1]

Don't take his sarcastic remark about "tenth-rate professors" literally. He intended it as a insult and not a description of their professional ranking. One German professor who drew Chesterton's ire was Ernst Haeckel (1834–1919), an eminent zoologist and the foremost advocate of Darwinian evolution in Germany. In the second chapter of *Orthodoxy* (1908), he described how Haeckel's materialism resembled madness.

> It must be understood that I am not now discussing the relation of these creeds to truth; but, for the present, solely their relation to health. Later in the argument I hope to attack the question of objective verity; here I speak only of a phenomenon of psychology. I do not for the present attempt to prove to Haeckel that materialism is untrue, any more than I attempted to prove to the man who thought he was Christ that he was labouring under an error. I merely remark here on the fact that both cases

1. G.K. Chesterton, *Eugenics and Other Evils* (Seattle: Inkling Books, 2000), 11.

> have the same kind of completeness and the same kind of incompleteness. You can explain a man's detention at Hanwell by an indifferent public by saying that it is the crucifixion of a god of whom the world is not worthy. The explanation does explain. Similarly you may explain the order in the universe by saying that all things, even the souls of men, are leaves inevitably unfolding on an utterly unconscious tree—the blind destiny of matter. The explanation does explain, though not, of course, so completely as the madman's. But the point here is that the normal human mind not only objects to both, but feels to both the same objection. **Its approximate statement is that if the man in Hanwell is the real God, he is not much of a god. And, similarly, if the cosmos of the materialist is the real cosmos, it is not much of a cosmos.** The thing has shrunk. The deity is less divine than many men; and (according to Haeckel) the whole of life is something much more grey, narrow, and trivial than many separate aspects of it. The parts seem greater than the whole.[2]

Eager for influence, Haeckel wrote books for the general public. As Chesterton notes, behind Haeckel's marvelous descriptions of natural wonders lay a grey, narrow and unappealing world view called Monism. We find that larger view in his oft-reprinted *The History of Creation* (1876). We will focus an edition from Chesterton's day (1914) and the most important chapter—Chapter 27 of Volume II, titled the "History and Pedigree of Man." Haeckel's target was the Judeo-Christian view of man, a view he dismisses by claiming the "anthropocentric conception of the universe—the vain delusion that Man is the centre of terrestrial nature, and that its whole aim is merely to serve him—is overthrown by the application (attempted long since by Lamarck) of the theory of the descent of Man.[3] As Copernicus' theory of the universe was mechanically established by Newton's theory of gravitation, we see Lamarck's theory of descent attain its causal establishment by Darwin's theory of selection."[4]

Haeckel's ideas had major problems, including the logical inconsistency of attacking Christianity for placing *all* the races of men at "the centre of terrestrial nature," while championing a system that divided humanity into many races, ranking them according to an elaborate scheme and placing one race at the apogee of the biological world. If ranking man, a clearly defined biological species, above all other animals was unscientific, what sense does in make to rank one ill-defined race of men above the others? Yet that is precisely what Haeckel did. Even more disturbing, by giving scientific approval to racial ranking he fed the already exaggerated sense of self-importance felt by many Germans. That justified wars of aggression as a natural Darwinian struggle between races and provided useful Haeckel quotes for later Nazi propaganda.

Like many zoologists, Haeckel enjoyed classifying, so he divided humanity into 12 large species and 36 smaller ones. Odd as it may sound today, his first great distinction between higher and lower rested on the shape of hair follicles. A distinction that might have made sense in a small way between two closely related varieties of dogs was extended to people and made a matter of immense importance.

2. G.K. Chesterton, *Orthodoxy* (Garden City: Doubleday, 1959), 23–24. At that time, Hanwell, which is located in west London, was called the London County Asylum and took in the insane poor.

3. Jean-Baptiste Lamarck (1744–1829) was a French naturalist who advocated a pre-Darwinian theory of evolution based on the inheritance of acquired characteristics. Nicolaus Copernicus (1473–1543) was a Polish priest who developed the scientific theory that the earth revolves around the sun. Isaac Newton (1643–1727) was an English physicist who developed a theory of gravitation that explained the astronomy of Copernicus.

4. Ernest Haeckel, *The History of Creation* (New York: D. Appleton & Co., 1914), II, 364.

> Of the twelve species of men distinguished on the following table (p. 416), the four lower species are characterized by the woolly nature of the hair of their heads; every hair is flattened like a tape, and thus its section is oval.... All *Ulotrichi*, or woolly-haired men, have slanting teeth and long heads, and the colour of their skin, hair, and eyes is always very dark. All are inhabitants of the Southern Hemisphere; it is only in Africa that they come north of the equator. **They are on the whole at a much lower stage of development, and more like apes, than most of the *Lissotrichi*, or straight-haired men.** The *Ulotrichi* are incapable of a true inner culture and of a higher mental development, even under the favourable conditions of adaptation now offered to them in the United States of North America. No woolly-haired nations has ever had an important "history."[5]

As we might expect, within the broader and higher race of "straight-haired men," Haeckel found that one stood above the rest.

> **The Caucasian, or Mediterranean man (*Homo Mediterraneus*), has from time immemorial been placed at the head of all the races of men, as the most highly developed and perfect.** It is generally called the Caucasian race, but as, among all the varieties of the species, the Caucasian branch is the least important, we prefer the much more suitable appellation proposed by Friedrich Müller, namely, that of *Mediterranese*.[6] For the most important varieties of this species, which are moreover the most eminent actors in what is called "Universal History," first rose to a flourishing condition on the shores of the Mediterranean.... This species alone (with the exception of the Mongolian) has had an actual history; it alone has attained to that degree of civilization which seems to raise men above the rest of nature.[7]

During World War I, we don't find Chesterton criticizing "Teutonism" for being anti-Semitic, not because he was tolerant of the attitude (as his response to Nazism would show), but because at that time European anti-Semitism was in a quiet period between the ugly sentiments of the late 1800s and the far viler ones of the 1930s. But there is within Haeckel's racial ordering more than enough justification for scientific anti-Semitism. According to Haeckel, although both Germans and Jews were in the same broad racial classification, the Mediterranean Man, they were quite far apart.

> Even the languages of the two principal races of the Mediterranean species—the Semitic and Indo-Germani—cannot be traced to a common origin, and consequently these two races must have separated at a very early period. Hamo-Semites and Indo-Germanic are, at most, only connected far down at the root.[8]

Nazism would find that 'far down the root' claim useful. It can be used to place Jews further down the evolutionary tree much like those inferior "woolly-haired men." But instead of hair being the distinguishing feature, the Nazis would talk of another trivial physical trait—noses.

Finally, there is Haeckel's most dangerous idea—the supremacy of one race and the eventual succumbing of all the others to it "in the struggle for existence."

5. Ernst Haeckel, *The History of Creation* (New York: D. Appleton & Co., 1914), II, 414–415. The United States reference is to former black slaves as among the "four lower species." He claims they lack "true inner culture" as well as "higher mental development."

6. Friedrich Müller (1834–1898) was a German linguist. He is to be distinguished from Max Müller (1823–1900), also mentioned in this book, who studied comparative religions, particularly that of India.

7. Ernst Haeckel, *The History of Creation* (New York: D. Appleton & Co., 1914), II, 429. In comparison to Babylonians, Jews, and Greeks, Germany's history was recent, although Haeckel does not mention that.

8. Ernst Haeckel, *The History of Creation* (New York: D. Appleton & Co., 1914), II, 430.

> The total number of human individuals at present amounts to between 1,300 and 1,400 millions.... Of course the relative number of the twelve species fluctuates every year, and that too according to the law developed by Darwin, that in the struggle for life the more highly developed, the more favoured and larger groups of forms, possess the more positive inclination and the certain tendency to spread more and more at the expense of the lower, more backward, and smaller groups. **Thus the Mediterranean species, and within it the Indo-Germanic, have by means of the higher development of their brain surpassed all the other races and species in the struggle for life, and have already spread the net of their dominion over the whole globe.** It is only the Mongolian species which can at all successfully, at least in certain respects, compete with the Mediterranean. Within the tropical regions, Negroes (Sudanians and Kaffres), Nubians, and Malays are in some measure protected against the encroachments of the Indo-Germanti tribes by their being better adapted for a hot climate; in the case of the arctic tribes of the polar regions is similar. **But the other races, which as it is are very much diminished in number, will sooner or later completely succumb in the struggle for existence to the superiority of the Mediterranean races.** They are already for the most part becoming exterminated by the so-called "blessings of civilization;" also by direct conflicts and by sexual intercourse. The American and Australian tribes are even now fast approaching their complete extinction, and the same may be said of the Dravidas, Papuans, and Hottentots.[9]

On an impeccable scientific foundation established by Haeckel and other eminent German professors, the Germans would build their ever-growing sense of superiority and their ambitious plans for conquest. Against that biologically inspired militarism, the new pacifism would prove particularly weak and impotent.

CRIMES UNPUNISHED

January 1, 1916

It is one of the paradoxes of the war that the Pacifists who insist on its enormity do not seem to realise how enormous it is. They call it a crime; and yet they want to cure it with a compromise.

EDITOR: Chesterton points to a serious inconsistency in pacifist rhetoric. They claim war is evil, and yet they seem indifferent to assigning blame for the evil being done in this exceptionally bloody war. In modern terms, their belief that all war is wrong has led quite logically to a strange moral equivalence that regards everyone involved in the fighting as equally wrong: the powerful aggressor (Germany), his helpless victim (Belgium), and those defending the victim (Britain and France). It seems that, in their zeal against war as an abstract evil, they have become indifferent to genuine war crimes committed against real people.

9. Ernst Haeckel, *The History of Creation* (New York: D. Appleton & Co., 1914), II, 432–433. Although in this passage Haeckel described a future populated with the somewhat broader "Mediterranean races," note his use of the plural. The Darwinian struggle never ends. Once the world is peopled with Mediterranean people, a new struggle for supremacy would begin within that group, one in which Haeckel believed the "higher" Indo-Germanic race was favored. Haeckel was patient and willing to wait for slow natural processes. Nazism was Darwinism in a hurry, unwilling to wait. Like eugenics, it wanted to take evolution into its own hands and force a particular result. Bertrand Russell used similar arguments in support of genocidal colonial wars in Appendix E.

It is one of the paradoxes of the war that the Pacifists who insist on its enormity do not seem to realise how enormous it is. They call it a crime; and yet they want to cure it with a compromise. They dilate on the universality of the horror like men talking of the rent seals and falling stars of the Apocalypse, the portents of plagues and persecutions leading up to the Day of Judgment. And then they do not want it to lead up to a Day of Judgment, or even of logical human justice. They want it to lead up to a mere splitting of the difference, as if it were about the bill of a dressmaker or the nuisance of a dust-bin. I think it strange that men of a sensitive and artistic sort do not see the imaginative inappropriateness of this. The war of the world is much too great an evil to be stopped by a small good. There are a great many entirely practical objections to a premature peace, a peace such as people like Dr. Horton and Mr. J.A. Hobson have suggested.[10] There is the most practical objection of all—which is that the Germans want it. There is the objection that it would leave them with their navy and many other resources intact, and ready for a special war against their special enemy, England, then probably isolated from all her Allies. There is the objection that it would leave them with their prestige intact, at a time when the theatricals of Prussian omnipotence can still be taken seriously by neutrals and civilians. There is the objection that it would constitute a surrender to the least independent and least national elements in Europe, to all that cosmopolitan wealth which is prepared to lend money, but very reluctant indeed to give it. There is (for those who care for such things) the objection that it is wrong. But over and above all these direct considerations, there is a primal and colossal incongruity, about which our mere instincts ought to guide us. A compromise with Prussia (and any possible peace to-day must be a compromise with Prussia) would be a great many things—it would be the suppression of a truth and the falling into a trap; it would be the reprieve of a murderer and the restoration of a tyrant; it would be an illogicality and an injustice and a howling blunder. But it would also be an anti-climax. It would be a bathos; and imagination will not tolerate such an epic ending in a bathos. Everything that is great in the mind of man asks for some greatness in the settlement. Whatever else we have, we must have a peace that shall be worthy of the war.

Pacifists even, or rather Pacifists especially, will agree that whoever really went about to create this universal carnage committed a stupendous crime. If there be any man among calm neutrals, as there are many among angry Germans, who can and does truly believe that Germany was caught in a net of aggressive conspiracy, let him look for a real German triumph. It will take some looking for; but I will never think less of a man for hoping to the last for historic justice. It will mean the end of England and all we are; it will mean the end of France and all we owe to her; but these things are better than the end of all reason and right in the story of the

10. Dr. Horton may be Dr. Lydiard Heneage Horton (1879–1945), a psychologist who studied shell shock and trench nightmares during and after WWI. John A. Hobson (1858–1940) was an English economist and socialist who opposed WWI and joined the Union of Democratic Control. In 1914 he published *Toward International Government*, advocating an international body to keep peace. However, he opposed the League of Nations and, shortly before he died, wanted the U.S. to join the war against Nazism.

world. If Prussia was a lamb among wolves, let the blood of the lamb cry to heaven for vengeance. I cannot myself understand how anybody who has ever read a Prussian proclamation, or even seen a Prussian officer, can think that Prussia played the part of such an innocent animal. But "there is no lack of beasts on God's earth," as it says in *Esto Perpetua*,[11] and it may be that she is a new and deceptive combination. It can arguably be said that the Englishman is a wolf in sheep's clothing; so I suppose it can be said that the Prussian is a sheep in wolf's clothing. Anyhow, it is said that Germany was a victim, if it is said by nobody except Germans. If anyone who says this really thinks this, let him carry his thought through to its right and triumphant conclusion. Let him hope for the justification of every German boast, for the realisation of every German illusion. Let him trust that Hindenburg, though he has failed to conquer the Russians six times, may succeed the seventh time, because seven is a lucky number. Let him hope that Von Kluck may again go on throwing large armies at Paris until he hits it.[12] Let him pray that the German Emperor may not die of hope deferred, with Calais written on his heart.[13] Let him hope to see the British Navy battered by disaster after disaster which shall culminate, as with a crescendo and a crash, in several German ships coming out of their canal.[14] Such toppling triumphs are not too great as compensations for a people wantonly dragged out unwilling into a world of war. Assuredly, if we are not right we are very wrong. If we sowed this planet with such a pestilence and then disclaimed our responsibility, then we are indeed a league of blasphemous hypocrites; and we deserve the last horrors that the universe can hold—yes, even a German peace.

But if it was not we, it was they; and if it was they. It was not a misunderstanding. Of that there is a perfectly plain test. No man can complain of a misunderstanding when he has publicly and positively refused to understand. When people are merely puzzled with each other's conduct, they ask to have it explained; they do not, like the Germanies, refuse to have it explained. Serbia asked for delay, and Austria refused it. Sir Edward Grey asked for a consultation of the Powers, and Germany refused it.[15] These facts might possibly be reconciled somehow with the idea that the German Powers wanted a necessity or even a right. They cannot be reconciled anyhow

11. Latin: "May it be forever," The quote is from a book by Chesterton's friend, Hilaire Belloc, *Esto Perpetua: Algerian Studies and Impressions* (London: Duckworth, 1906, republished in 1911, 1925 and 1969), 160. In that travelogue, Belloc is taking a meal with an old man who has offered a meat he says is sheep. Belloc is doubtful, "'Good Lord!' I said, 'it might be anything. There is no lack of beasts on God's earth. I took another bite and found it horrible." For Belloc, that sheep turned out to be a camel. For Chesterton, a Prussia claiming to be an innocent lamb is actually a wolf. At the close of Belloc's book, *Esto perpetua!* is used on parting to mean "You shall not die."

12. Paul von Hindenburg (1847–1934) was a German field marshal on the Russian front. Commanding the First Army, General Alexander von Kluck (1846–1934) lost the war for Germany when he abandoned the original plan calling for him to encircle Paris to the west, and came to the aid of von Bulow's Second Army east of Paris.

13. When English rule over the French port of Calais ended in January 1558, Queen Mary I of England is supposed to have said: "When I am dead and opened, you shall find 'Calais' lying in my heart."

14. During the war, both Britain and Germany maintained what was called a 'fleet in being,' preferring to keep their important ships in Scapa Flow (British) or near the Kiel Canal (Germany), where each could threaten the other without being in much danger. A weapon unused is better than one used and destroyed.

15. Edward Grey (1862–1933) was Britain's Foreign Secretary in 1914. On the eve of the war, Germany refused his call for a consultation between the great powers because its mobilization had already begun. He is said to have told a friend, "The lamps are going out all over Europe; we shall not see them lit again in our lifetime."

with the idea that they wanted an explanation. Whatever was in their minds, their minds were made up. They may have had some hope of peace in the sense of a hope of panic and impotence among their rivals. The more serious among them hardly pretend that they wanted to keep Serbia out of war; but they may have wanted to keep Russia out of war. But even if so, they hoped to keep her out of it by daring her to come into it. If I knock a man over and take his watch, I do not want a fight. I want a watch. But Russia was much more morally bound to fight for Serbia than any private citizen to fight for his private timepiece; and the broad facts remain as I have stated them. We conceivably might make some sense of the story by supposing that the Central Powers were demanding what seemed to them a legitimate or inevitable fight. We can make no sense of it at all on the theory that they were not demanding a fight. And this Inferno is the fight they demanded.

In a sense it is due to the very height and pride of the Prussian challenge that we should answer it as decisively as it is offered. Those who do not understand how decisive it is do not know anything of Prussian history. **It would have been an almost incredible coincidence if this war had not been rooted in the ambition of Prussia. All the similar conflicts immediately before it were rooted in the ambition of Prussia.** She never dreamed of disavowing that ambition until a month or two ago, when its chances for the first time began to look dark. That Prussia desires to dominate is as much a mere fact of history as that the Catholic Church desires to convert, or that modern physical science desires to discover. Those who, faced with the testament of Frederick the Great and the tradition transmitted by Bismarck, can suppose that everybody alike blundered into this war may just as well believe that Captain Peary blundered towards the North Pole, or that the Crusaders happened to stroll absent-mindedly in an easterly direction. **To those who know the story, a premature and partial settlement is almost more comic than it is tragic. This thing is rushing upon us with all the force behind it of three hundred years of a fixed idea; and in order to be checked it must be shattered.**

G.K. Chesterton, "Our Note-Book," *Illustrated London News* 148 (January 1, 1916), 3. US: January 1, 1916. Also published as "A Peace Worthy of the War."

1916

INSIDE THE GERMAN MIND

January 15, 1916

It is one of the peculiarities of this deep-hearted German way of writing that it is either impossible to see the point at all or it is possible to see the point a long time before the explanatory writer gets to it.

EDITOR: Mark Twain made fun of the German language, noting the troubles it created in his *A Tramp Abroad* (1880): "Surely there is not another language that is so slipshod and systemless, and so slippery and elusive to the grasp. One is washed about in it, hither and thither, in the most helpless way; and when at last he thinks he has captured a rule which offers firm ground to take a rest on amid the general rage and turmoil of the ten parts of speech, he turns over the page and reads, 'Let the pupil make careful note of the following exceptions.' He runs his eye down and finds that there are more exceptions to the rule than instances of it."

In this article Chesterton pokes fun at two examples of the "most weird weaknesses" of the German language. This first was the *War-Chronicle,* a series of booklets in five languages intended by a M. Berg to spread Germany's view of the war. The second was a newsletter called the *Protestant Weekly Newsletter* edited by a well-known German scholar and writer, Professor Adolf Deissmann. Chesterton pokes fun at how the professor's defense of his nation sounds after it has been translated into English, blaming the problem, in part, on German education, culture and language.

Professor Deissmann mentioned the newsletter that Chesterton received in the fourth edition of his *Light from the Ancient East*. Writing four years after the end of the war, he remained the same "deep-hearted" scholar intensely concerned about the solidarity of "oecumentical Christiandom," that Chesterton had described six years before. Reading what he wrote, his sincerity and commitment is obvious. He genuinely enjoyed the relationships that had been divided by war. Since neither men was the sort to let politics stand in the way of friendship, it is easy to suspect that, had the two met, they would have become friends. On the other had, there is also a sense in which Deissmann's strong feelings have overridden his reason. Germany had serious ills that could not be cured by well-meaning scholarship and friendly international correspondence, so Chesterton's anger is not without justification. Good people who do nothing to set their country right must bear part of the blame for the evil it does. Here is how Deissmann addressed his German and English-language readers in his most popular book in its first new edition to be published after the war.

> The cruel fate that overtook mankind in 1914 made deep inroads even on the studies to which this book is devoted. It carried off on the battlefield, or by starvation, privation and sorrow of heart, many of the scholars, middle-aged as well as young, who are named in the following pages, some of them tried and trusted friends of my own; and of the survivors it also demanded its tribute. Me it kept (to say nought of other things) for full seven years almost completely cut off from my old field of study. From 1914 to 1921, in such hours as were not claimed by the University, I devoted myself almost exclusively to fostering the solidarity which should prevail amongst all Protestants and throughout oecumenical Christendom, and which was most seriously endangered by the struggle of the nations. This I attempted by means of my *Evangelischer Wochenbrief* (circulated from Advent 1914 to the beginning of 1917 also in English, under the title *Protestant Weekly Letter*), by an extensive daily correspondence with individuals in connexion therewith, by organising, and by a considerable amount of attendance at conferences at home and abroad.[16]

Not listed among those burdens, but mentioned by his translator, R.M. Strachan is the time Prof. Deissman, "spent in tedious journeys half-way around Berlin to visit his English translator in internment either at Plötzensee Prison or at Ruhleben." Deissman may have lacked Chesterton's mental toughness and clarity of thought, but he was a good and kind man none the less. In his June 24, 1916 column in *Illustrated London News* (Ch. 4), Chesterton describes him as a "a very amiable old gentleman."

16. Adolf Deissman, *Light from the Ancient East,* Lionel R.M. Strachan, transl. (New York: Harper & Brothers, 1927), ix. The quote from the translator is on page xix.

It is the work of German education to fill up insufficiency with self-sufficiency. In a sense, it is true that the Prussian Government knows how to make its subjects contented: it knows how to make them contented with inferior things. Perhaps the most ignominiously inferior thing is superiority. If making a population of important pigmies is the greatest good of the greatest number, there is really a sense in which Germanic culture and control achieve it. Their sense of perfection makes them permanently imperfect. In the calm absence of all self-criticism there is made possible a fine flower of fatuity not to be found in any less protected land. This enormous ineptitude must be touched on with humility, not to say fear. England and America have been tempted to such Pharisaic fooleries; but the English and American sense of humour (though the two are very different) have kept such things within bounds. But if Prussia really conquered us, we might all be like that.

It is a fatuity that finds expression in the very style and grammar. I have received a whole sheaf of German-English pamphlets, including a booklet called *War-Chronicle*; and on reading them I am chiefly arrested by the most weird weaknesses in the mere diction, long before I come to the universal weakness of the case.[17] I will give only one or two instances of a sort of ill-luck in language. Thus, we must expect recriminations about destruction of buildings on one side or the other. But whichever side manages things worse, there can surely be no doubt about which explains them worse. The first thing I find is a sentence like this: "The church of Langemarck has been completely destroyed owing to French and English shells and shrapnels, as is proved by the many holes in the walls."[18] I can see what the man means; but in the mere logic of language it is hard to see how you make a hole in what is entirely destroyed. We must expect different versions of the responsibility for the death of noncombatants on a battlefield. According to the report of the Russians, "The German troops admit that they were reluctantly obliged in the course of these attacks to shoot thousands of Russians, including many women and children." The Germans apparently say, or attempt to say, that this was because the Russians put women and children in the place of peril. But what the Germans actually succeed in saying is this: "Our guns were reluctantly obliged to demand toll of many of their lives."[19] Have any of my readers ever had the happiness to see a reluctant gun? I like to think of the cannon coyly shrinking from being handled by human beings, but forced by the masterful Germans to come forward and do itself justice. **In my Prussian pamphlet the two sentences are put in parallel columns, somewhat innocently purporting to show that the Germans speak the truth and the Russians falsehood. All that the two sentences really prove is that the Russians at least say what they mean to say, and**

17. A bound copy of *War-Chronicle* with issues from August 1915 to February 1916 contains contain no indication of a source other than a tiny note on the last page: "Printed and Published by M. Berg." The Library of Congress gives the city as Berlin. The British Library says it was published in German, English, French, Dutch, and Spanish and has copies of 18 issues between December 1914 and October 1917.

18. This is from *War-Chronicle* (September 1915), p. 29 in a section titled "German Soldiers' Letters."

19. This table is in *War-Chronicle* (September 1915), p. 11, under the heading "Russian Falsification." The remark about reluctant guns is from an official German General Staff report. The Russian remarks are from a newspaper. Notice it follows the "atheistic style" of writing described in the introduction to the October 6, 1906 article

that the Germans cannot even do that. Yet again, we must expect a rather entangled use of the *tu quoque*[20] touching the negotiations before the war. But there are some statements which the Germans really need not ask us to accept, and this is one of them: "Graf Metternich's reports in the winter of 1912 clearly show that the British Ministers then frankly admitted their solicitude for Great Britain's relations with England and France."[21] Surely not. I feel sure there is some mistake. Great Britain's relations with England, as they say in the King's Speech, continue to be favourable. Other remarks on the same diplomatic topic are simply impossible to understand. What does this mean, for instance? "Of course, the present war is shown as an example for German slyness. We do not want to disturb these illusions, but must draw attention to the remarkable fact that the English proclamation as supporting the statement that the war is one of German aggression refers to faithless Italy." Why should we show an example for German slyness? What does he mean by saying that we refer to faithless Italy? Surely he cannot mean that we refer to her as faithless. "Faithless" appears to be of the nature of a short sharp cry, breaking involuntarily out of him in the course of the sentence. But why, then, is it a remarkable fact that we should refer to Italy? I cannot tell. As the German says in Mr. Belloc's book, "It is in the dear secret of the all-wise Nature-Mother preserved."

Now I am not picking holes, or pointing to them, in a merely supercilious and superficial spirit. I do not suggest that the German case is like the church at Langemarck, and is entirely destroyed by having a few holes in it. But I do think one can look through such holes and see something of the interior of the German mind. These flounderings in phraseology do correspond to certain flounderings in philosophy. For instance, the German does reach the point of describing a gun as being reluctant to kill a woman, through a mistake in his mechanical creed. The mistake is that he does instinctively think it is the gun that kills the woman; he is drilled to forget that it is really a man who kills her. Then his sentimentalism begins to soak through his systematising; and the bashful piece of artillery is the remarkable result. And a brief study of the sentence about the wall with holes in it will afford the young student an excellent model of the dangers of saying a thing first and attempting to prove it afterwards.

Some letters from Professor Deissmann of Berlin which accompany the little book are marked also by this curious collapsible style.[22] They are further marked by a reeking cant of humanitarianism used in palliation of inhumanity, with which I will not pretend to patience. **If it is really part of the Prussian's duty to butcher my brothers (and sisters), I should be very much obliged to him if he would not**

20. Latin for "You too." Responding to criticism by accusing critics of doing the same thing.

21. *War-Chronicles* (September 1915), 5. This is in a section titled, "German Reply to British Foreign Office Statement" regarding Anglo-German negotiations in 1912.

22. Prof. Adolf Deissman (1866–1937) was one of intellectuals and theologians (including Adolf von Harnack) who signed the pro-German "Manifesto to the Civilized World" of October 1914. In the text that follows, "Evangelical" is used in the German sense to mean Protestant, especially Lutheran and Reformed. It bears no relationship to the post-WWII American use of the term for theologically conservative Protestants.

weep over them. He assures me that there is no hatred in his heart, the state of which organ does not interest me, because it is quite clear that, whatever may be in his heart, there is nothing in his head to stop him from going on as he does; and nothing short of a bullet in his head seems likely to have that effect. I will give one case of the curious confusion of words which in so many of these cases covers an, equally curious confusion of conscience. Speaking of some Lutheran assembly or other, he says, "The Synod expresses its grateful satisfaction that synods, congregations, and individual Christians of America have courageously and vigorously protested against the American export of ammunition for the enemies of Germany and its allies, as contradicting Christianity, and therewith connects the expression of hope that our fellow-believers across the ocean will continue to maintain this standpoint. At the same time, the Synod requests the High Administrative Body of the Church to make efforts toward the Committee of the German Evangelical Churches for a similar publication in the name of Evangelical Christianity in Germany."[23]

I fear we must not find, in the haziness of the style, a hope that the Synod is asking the Evangelical Christians in Germany not to manufacture munitions. Yet it is difficult to see how the Synod can, with any consistency, mean anything except this. What is the sense of saying that an American is not a Christian if he makes a gun to be fired off, and then saying that a German is a Christian when he makes a gun and fires it off himself? Alone among the nations, the Yankees are to be the only Quakers, solely in order that the Germans may be the only militarists. America is to be superior to armaments, that Prussia may be superior in armaments. But whether the Professor and his Synod mean this or mean the opposite or mean anything at all, the quality of the diction makes it difficult to determine.

There are other passages which are not particularly obscure, but are extremely laborious, and have something indescribably amusing about them, if you read only a little of them at a time. **It is one of the peculiarities of this deep-hearted German way of writing that it is either impossible to see the point at all or it is possible to see the point a long time before the explanatory writer gets to it.** Much of it is concerned with the Higher Criticism of the Bible, a sport held dear in their dark forests, and of what Professor Deissmann calls "the blessed reciprocal effect of international Biblical research."[24]

G.K. Chesterton, "Our Note-Book," *Illustrated London News* 148 (January 15, 1916), 67. US: January 15, 1916. Also published as "The Haziness of Current German Rhetoric."

Why War?

January 29, 1916

There is no disputing about tastes—that is why there is fighting about them.

23. *Evangelischer Wochenbrief* was circulated in English as the *Protestant Weekly Letter.*

24. Just after the war began, Chesterton gave his opinion of theologians who studied higher criticism (especially Prof. Harnack) in the *Illustrated London News* on September 5 and October 10, 1914 (Ch. 2).

Editor: Chesterton continues an argument about the causes of war that he raised a little over five years earlier in the December 31, 1910 issue of the *Illustrated London News* (Ch. 1), when he wrote that wars arise from our loves rather than our hates. By 1916, with both sides exhausted by the fighting and replacement soldiers getting harder to find, the entry of the United States into the war would mean an Allied victory, so Chesterton turns his attention to arguments being used by those who wanted to keep the U.S. out of the war. (See also the article that follows this one.)

War, or the possibility of war, is the price we pay for the liberty of the mind. It can be rendered improbable by conversion—that is, by a common creed touching what things are sacred. It cannot be rendered impossible anyhow, except by denying our right to hold anything sacred.[25] **For it is intensely important to grasp that combatants do not commonly disagree about things, but about the value of things.** It is idle to say you are only fining a man a farthing, if he chooses to say it is his lucky farthing. It is waste of breath to call a thing a rag when he calls it a flag. This is the fallacy of those who, like Mr. Gerald Stanley Lee, the able American critic, imagine that a war must be a misunderstanding, which social intercourse and explanation would have set right.[26] Such explanations can only settle matters of material fact. It would undoubtedly be a good thing if we could always get these facts right; and it is one of the damning points in the Prussian and Austrian record that those countries refused any delay and debate concerning them. It would have been a good thing if the English people had known in time that the tale about James II and the warming-pan was false.[27] It would have been a good thing if the American people had known in time that the tale about the *Maine* outrage was false.[28] But unless we know what *value* was attached by James II to his religion, or by the Protestants to theirs, we could not correctly have predicted any avoidance of the quarrel which has turned to wormwood the waters of the Boyne. And the Spanish-American War similarly depended on the importance attached by Spain to her American colonies and the United States to their American hegemony. Where both sides admit the same facts, there can still be a quarrel about the values. Mr. Stanley Lee, in an entertaining article in *Everybody's Magazine*, says that the armed forces of Europe are only trying to express themselves in a clumsy way; and suggests that they might as well do it by using all their efforts to move a mountain, and then move it back again.[29]

25. That's what John Lennon's song "Imagine" demanded. See the footnote in the January 14, 1911 article (Ch. 1).

26. Gerald Stanley Lee (1862–1944) was the author of *Crowds*, the bestselling nonfiction book in the U.S. for 1913, and the less-known *We: A Confession of Faith for the American People During and After the War* (1916).

27. Mary of Modena (1658–1718) was Catholic and the queen consort of King James II of England. Protestants fearer that if she had a son, the English throne would again become Catholic. When she did have a son in 1688, rumors circulated that a baby had been smuggled into her bedroom in a warming pan. Two meetings of the Privy Council were necessary to put down the rumors. A few months later, the Glorious Revolution removed James II from the throne, and the struggle over his removal included the Battle of the Boyne in 1860 Ireland.

28. The cause of the explosion that sank the *U.S.S. Maine* in Havana harbor on February 15, 1898 is still debated, but it is unlikely Spain would have done anything to start a war it was almost certain to lose.

29. Stanley Lee's article was in the January, 1916 issue of *Everybody's Magazine*, a popular American magazine that supported U.S. entry into the war. That same issue featured articles on "America's Neutrality as England Sees It," that included contributions by H.G. Wells, Bernard Shaw, and G.K. Chesterton.

Accepting the figure, I would suggest that a mountain is very often a sacred object, like the chief mountain of Japan, or like Ararat and Sinai. I would also suggest that it often contains diamonds or valuable minerals. Suppose such a hill to be dedicated to monks and inaccessible to miners, and you have a working model of the origin of most wars. Suppose some ruler quite convinced that the consecrated isolation merely keeps legitimate wealth from the world, and he will probably fight—he almost invariably does. If he does, you cannot prevent the mountaineers defending their mountain, except by proving to them that their diamonds are more precious than their deities, which is generally an impossibility, and seldom, in my humble opinion, an improvement.[30] The only other way is for the ruler to be converted to the mountain religion, for which he may feel a distaste. It is simply sterile to say that a mountain is only a lump of stone. So is a diamond. It is ultimately only a matter of opinion whether a stone is a precious stone; and men have as much right to think a pebble is a talisman as to think it is a jewel.

Mr. Stanley Lee's article is about some American millionaires and their views of peace, and does not here otherwise concern me. I have no opinion of the idealism of such persons. It does not interest me that men who first become gold-bags afterwards become gas-bags.[31] But I should think Mr. Lee was right in saying that poor Ford is rather an unusually honest little man, as such men go.[32] When, however, Mr. Lee innocently cries, "Who will want to fight us?" because Ford cars might be made cheap enough for the working classes, I respectfully inform him that he has not the faintest idea of what fighting is all about. There is not, thank God! the remotest probability of England and America fighting each other. But I will tell Mr. Stanley Lee, with the sincerity of an admirer, that rather than accept a cheap Ford car along with the cheap Ford philosophy and the cheap and chippy[33] Ford ideals of life, not only I, but nearly every man who earns his living in Europe, would see the whole story of the white man wiped off the world in blood. Yet I am sure Mr. Ford feels certain that we should lose nothing in a society organised according to his convictions—to say this is, indeed, merely to say that they are his convictions. And it is a conviction of the same kind which has forced the world into war: but in this case the conviction, which was a German conviction, was not only narrow, but had an intensity akin to insanity.

Mr. Stanley Lee, stepping out of his front door one fine day, may find two men wrestling for their lives, and perhaps trying to prevent each other getting at the

30. Chesterton's "religion" could include the love for a home and homeland as displayed by the Boers in the Second Boer War, which pitted farms against diamonds. See the introduction to his August 15, 1908 article (Ch. 1).

31. Chesterton is mocking the fact that, at that time, wealthy industrialists such as Henry Ford and Andrew Carnegie thought that their success in one narrow area (making cars or steel) meant they had a special expertise to solve the world's ills, including war. Today's entertainment celebrities often share that same delusion.

32. See Chesterton's opinion of Henry Ford and his peace ship in the December 11, 1915 issue (Ch. 3).

33. *Oxford English Dictionary* definitions for "chippy" include the contradictory: "cross, irritable" and "lively, brisk." Chesterton may mean Ford's ideals are as irritating as someone feeling cross finds someone who is overly cheerful. He's also objects to a philosophy that happiness lies in consumerism—in owning "a cheap Ford car." Aldous Huxley made this same link between Henry Ford and consumerism as religion in *Brave New World* (1932).

hip-pocket for the traditional Transatlantic purpose. He may afterwards discover that one of these persons firmly believes himself to be Azrael, the Angel of Death, while his opponent believes him to be an unfortunate gentleman escaped from medical care in a strictly guarded building in the neighbourhood. Now, it is useless for Mr. Lee merely to blame both of them for fighting, or even to pity both of them for fighting. *They* are not engaged in any common activity at all. *They* do not exist, in any collective sense. They are in different universes. In one universe the Angel of Death is doing his duty and exercising his legitimate discretion, and a blasphemous Anarchist is disputing his qualifications. In another universe a perspiring private citizen is trying to master a bloody-minded maniac. **That is why there is war in Europe at this moment: simply because the Germans are as certain that they are the natural masters of mankind as we are certain that they aren't.** But it must be insistently noted that the quarrel is one about spirit and quality, and cannot be dissipated by any discoveries about facts. The kind of madman who thinks he is an angel does not necessarily, or generally, think he has wings. Similarly, Germans do not actually think that Frenchmen have tails. But they do think that Frenchmen have the small vivacity and malice of monkeys; that they are a breed inferior to the German, in the same aboriginal sense as in the case of monkeys. And to this there is no answer except that Frenchmen do not think so; that persons conventionally considered sane and acquainted with Frenchmen do not think so; that, in fact, nobody in the world does think so, except the German who says so. But since, by his own hypothesis, he is the only person who is qualified to judge, of course he goes on saying it. He also goes on acting on it; and he had no more scruple about breaking a treaty to stab the French in the back than about setting a trap to catch a monkey by the tail. It is not I who say this of the Prussian moralist, but he. Again and again he has asserted that only Germans can judge of German morality, just as we should say that men must be the judges of justice or mercy to monkeys. But the fact to be emphasised is that this sense of the superiority of German civilisation is a purely spiritual obsession, and cannot be proved or disproved. The barbarians of Berlin do not actually think that their wooden Hindenburg is made of gold.[34] They only think he is as good as gold, while everybody else thinks he is lumber. **There is no disputing about tastes—that is why there is fighting about them.** The modern moral philosophy of Germany includes, among other things, an infinite faith in the force of wishing, and the denial of doubt. They hold that the wish is not only father to the thought, but father to the fact. They have a more than supernatural belief in belief. This explains the repetition of ritual phrases about power and punishment on the smallest occasions, as in the private letters to Von Papen.[35] The modern Ger-

34. During the war, wooden statues of Hindenberg were used to raise money for the war. After contributing a certain amount of money, a German could hammer a nail into the statue.

35. As a military attache at Germany embassy in the U.S. between 1913 and 1915, Franz von Papen (1879–1969) developed a ring of spies and saboteurs to disrupt aid to Britain and draw Mexico into the war against the U.S. When his plans to blow up the Welland Canal between Lake Erie and Lake Ontario were discovered, he was forced to leave the country. Ever the schemer, he played a key role in Hitler becoming German Chancellor.

man shuts his eyes and tries to feel like a blind fate. He blows his own trumpet in order to deafen himself.

We must therefore expect the glitter of his brutality, the illusion of his omnipotence, to last much longer than it would with a people who had any modesty in the face of objective creation. On the mere facts, it might be said, the Prussian superman must already be doubting such an extraordinary superiority in himself. The answer is that the more he doubts the more he denies his doubt; that he is drilled to dismiss humility like a whisper of devils. He has to repeat "I cannot fail" like a creed—or rather, like an incantation.[36] It is here more than anywhere else that he is at issue with the whole tradition of truth. It is childish to deny his physical courage; but he has no real moral courage. "I cannot fail" means in reality "I dare not fail."

G.K. Chesterton, "Our Note-Book," *Illustrated London News* 148 (January 29, 1916), 131. US: January 29, 1916. Also published as "Is the War Just a Misunderstanding."

PRIDE AS SIN

February 26, 1916

Modern Germany offers a large number of other characteristics, good and bad; but what distinguishes that country is its committing itself wholly and seriously to a belief in the practical value of pride.

EDITOR: Pride, Chesterton suggests, makes it difficult for Germans to see where they are wrong, while the English, for all their faults, are more willing to accept criticism. Given our modern 'pride in being proud,' notice what he says about the addition of pride transforming "any other sin" into "the unpardonable sin." Pride may not be the root of all sin, but it is the sin that prevents all the other sins from being corrected. It keeps us from seeing our need for forgiveness and change.

ALL great wars are wars of religion; and most of them are waged to settle some point of doctrine. This war, it may be well to repeat, is fundamentally concerned with whether pride is a sin. The modern treatment of the question is typical of the cross-purposes in which we live. Stated as I have stated it, it would strike most modern people as a piece of high and dry pietism, or what undergraduates, I believe, used to call "pi." Yet nearly everybody feels it as a fact when they consider sin objectively—that is, as they mostly do consider it, in other people. **What pride is can be practically tested in this fact—that the addition of it to any other sin makes it the unpardonable sin.** The evidence of this is quite everyday evidence. The inflammable fellow who is always led a dance by women can keep the affection of men, even of the best men. Such a squire of dames may be a disreputable squire, and by no means deserve to be knighted. But the lady-killer deserves to be killed,

36. After WWI, Hitler would write: "Let the German people be raised from childhood up with that exclusive recognition of the rights of their own nationality, and let not the hearts of the children be contaminated with the curse of our 'objectivity,' even in matters regarding the preservation of their own ego." *Mein Kampf* (Boston: Houghton Mifflin, 1943), 113-114. For more on German pride see Chesterton's August 22, 1914 article (Ch. 2).

as the unmistakable ogre in a fairy-tale, who is also a lady-killer, is killed. And what makes the difference between the two types is solely the presence and absence of pride. For the same reason there is more that is laughable, and therefore lovable, in the old miser than in the new millionaire—the kind of millionaire who prides himself on only nibbling a bean instead of gnawing a bone. The squalid life is more decent than the simple life, because it is more modest. The miser only paraded his poverty in order to hide his wealth; but the other parades both. There is the same savour in the sayings of some of those who are most anxious to-day to prove that it is conscience that has made cowards of them all. **The fear of arms may at least be the instinct of an untrained but healthy animal. But the hatred of arms is a sheer perversion, a morbid reversal, like a mad dog's hatred of water.** I count myself among the admirers of President Wilson, and I think it unintelligent to test him by an ordinary public speaker's tag like "too proud to fight." There is the same idealess parroting about the Prime Minister's perfectly trivial and fugitive phrase, "Wait and see."[37] I do not believe for a moment that Mr. Wilson would be too proud to fight if he saw an advantage in fighting. But if we were to take the phrase as representing a complete philosophy, it would certainly be a philosophy of a curiously concentrated badness. We could only tell such a philosopher that there is no sin in fighting, but a great sin in being proud. Everywhere, in short, the highest charity will choose upon this principle. It can have indulgence for self-indulgence, but not for self-satisfaction; and least of all for what was called self-help.

Modern Germany offers a large number of other characteristics, good and bad; but what distinguishes that country is its committing itself wholly and seriously to a belief in the practical value of pride. It is this, of course, that renders particularly repulsive many of its excesses which are also self-indulgences. Murder itself is more amiable as a weakness than as a strength. But in order to seize the substance of this, I should not take any of the obvious excrescences of crime as my example. I should take an average extract from current German criticism and controversy. The spirit of which I speak is as present in the mildest and most rationalistic defence of Germany as in the wildest rhetoric of its cultus of hatred. And I could not take a better example than the very plan of a book that has recently appeared in Germany. It is especially directed against England; and so long as the Germans go on producing such books they will go on proving again and again, and much more clearly than I can, all that I am saying here. The work in question is called "Right or Wrong, My Country!" which I presume to be a learned German reconstruction of "My Country, Right or Wrong."[38] It is very typical of them that they should get a popular phrase so nearly right and so entirely wrong. But the title is by no means the only thing that

37. Herbert Asquith (1852–1928), Britain's Prime Minister from 1908–1916, had a reputation for avoiding controversial issues by adopting a "wait and see" attitude. Chesterton is correctly suggesting that Woodrow Wilson isn't opposed to entering the war under any circumstances but has a cautious 'wait and see' attitude.

38. I could not locate a WWI edition of this book, but it's apparently the same book published under that title in Nazi Germany: Albert Herrmann, *Right or Wrong, My Country! or The Immorality of English Policy Confessed by English Authors* (Bielefeld: Velhagen & Klasing, 1941 and other years). Harvard's library lists as a second author Heinrich Gade, no doubt the same "Professor Gade" mentioned by Chesterton.

they have succeeded in their simplicity in reading backwards. The work is further described as "The Immorality of English Policy Confessed by English Authors," and apparently consists of such criticisms as our writers have brought from time to time against our Governments: such as the eloquent invectives against Warren Hastings, the denunciations by Gladstone and others of the Chinese War, the satires of Swift about the treatment of Ireland, the established English repudiation of the treatment of America, and so on.[39] It is compiled by Professor Herrmann and Professor Gade, it is published in Leipzig, and I sincerely hope that it will be circulated all over the earth.

It is amazing to me that even professors should not see that such a book is a compliment and not an insult. So far from objecting to such a record being printed, an Englishman may well desire that it should be written in gold or carved in marble: that the laborious Germans should chip out every word of it on some of their elephantine stone buildings, to remain for a thousand years. **By all means let the latest generations of this earth be made aware that there never was an English wrong without an English protest.** Let our own enemies tell the world that our mistakes have been corrected mistakes and our conspiracies exploded conspiracies. It will be fortunate for us if our foes can confirm that noble compliment which Newman paid us—perhaps the highest compliment that can be paid—"They are as generous as they are hasty and burly; and their repentance for their injustice is greater than their sin."[40]

What do the professors imagine they are proving except that English debate is often free and that English history is often fair? It is in the best tradition of England that such protests should remain as English monuments. And it is in the worst tradition of Germany that they should be regarded as English defeats. There is, perhaps, no ground in the world on which a wise Englishman would more willingly accept battle as between the two intellectual systems. For, whatever advantages German culture has created, it does not even permit of this inward criticism and control. No man in his five wits will maintain that it is self-evident that German policy has been spotless. Even a professor cannot really believe that there was no case against the invasion of Silesia or the partition of Poland.[41] He must know, to say the least of it,

39. Warren Hastings (1732–1818), the first governor-general of British India, spent many years defending himself against charges of corruption. William E. Gladstone (1809–1898) was British Prime Minister four times and a strong critic of the First Anglo-Chinese War (1839–1842), which was also called the First Opium War since it purpose was to force China to accept imported British opium. Jonathan Swift (1667–1745) was a gifted Irish writer who authored satires criticizing English policies in Ireland, including "A Modest Proposal," which appeared to recommend that the English add properly cooked Irish babies to their diet. America's rebellion against British rule was justified and supported by English leaders such as Edmund Burke (1729–1797).

40. In a 1864 defense of his Catholic beliefs, *Apologia Pro Vita Sua*, Pt. 2, John Henry Newman (1801–1890) wrote: "Still more confident am I of such eventual acquittal, seeing that my judges are my own countrymen. I think, indeed, Englishmen the most suspicious and touchy of mankind; I think them unreasonable and unjust in their seasons of excitement; but I had rather be an Englishman, (as in fact I am,) than belong to any other race under heaven. They are as generous, as they are hasty and burly; and their repentance for their injustice is greater than their sin."

41. Silesia, now a part of Poland (with a small portion in the Czech Republic), was seized by Prussia's Frederick the Great in 1742 during the War of Austrian Succession. It remained a part of Germany until 1945. Three parti-

that there was an ugly side to the story of the Ems message.[42] Whether or no such a thing can be defended, it can certainly be attacked. It seems to me mysterious that anyone approves of it; it is manifestly preposterous to say that everyone approves of it. Therefore, if among such professors and their pupils no one disapproves of it, we can only infer that their vanity is too weak or their fear is too strong. Either they are not frank or they are not free. And it is the sober and quite unrhetorical truth that, as the great nations go, they are not frank and not free: that such a chorus of national condemnation for national acts as they have collected in our case would not be possible in their case. What they lack is not the thing blamable, but only the blame.

But it would be a mistake to suggest that in this matter the Prussian is merely respecting the policeman. The Prussian is respecting the Prussian; the image he worships is not even a picture, but only a looking-glass. And the great question being now tried in Europe, which can be suggested by many symbols or figures of speech, can be expressed, perhaps, best of all by saying that it is the philosophy of the mirror against the philosophy of the window. For humility means making the subjective objective—realising that to the universe oneself is not I, but only he.

G.K. Chesterton, "Our Note-Book," *Illustrated London News* 148 (February 26, 1916), 259. US: February 26, 1916. Also published as "My Country, Right or Wrong."

Zeppelins and the Press

March 18, 1916

War, among other things, is work; and very hard work. Now, hard work is one of the two or three things which, of their nature, cannot be conveyed in literature, far less in journalism.

Editor: Although Chesterton was a journalist, he did not hesitate to take on his profession it did more harm than good. He criticized it before the war on October 6, 1906, January 8, 1910, January 14, 1911, and September 14, 1912 (Ch. 1), as well as afterwards on May 6, 1922 (Ch. 7). During the war, he targeted for criticism particular points of view expressed in the press, especially alarmism, defeatism and pacifism.

In this article, he dismisses Zeppelins inaccurately dropping a few bombs as being of no more threat to the British war effort than turnip ghosts. He points out that if no fuss is made about them, the Germans will conclude that they're ineffective and "write off his Zeppelin raids as a bad debt"—a solution that would be much more effective and less costly than pulling much-needed aircraft from the front to attack them. He also criticizes the current state of government-press relations, where "the government is perpetually adjured to do something," when the result merely prevents more important things from being done—a problem that remains with us today.

tions of Poland (1772, 1793 and 1795) divided the rest of Poland between Prussia, Russia, and Austria.

42. In July 1870, Otto von Bismarck, the German chancellor, edited a telegram the Prussian King Wilhelm I had sent him describing a meeting with the French ambassador. As a result, the meeting seemed harsher than it was, angering Germans and provoking France to start the Franco-Prussian War, which they lost.

The average patriotic citizen has by this time, I am glad to say, a fairly settled attitude towards the political scandals and panics created by the more pessimistic Press. It is very much the attitude of the man who said he did not believe in ghosts because he had seen too many of them. Such disturbing revelations are unconvincing, not so much in their details as in their design, and, above all, their repetition. The real excitement of war has quite a different rhythm from the excitement of news; it recurs at different and much longer intervals; and we can no more expect a continuous supply of it than expect Christmas every day or harvests all the year round. I am ready to believe, indeed, I am rather predisposed to believe, that politicians frequently fail; but I do not believe that the failures of politicians are timed to suit the successes of journalists. The soldier does not die daily for the purposes of the daily Press; and the most ill-armed or badly handled battalion does not report at the instant of peril in the style of a serial, or go to pieces to fit the moment fixed for going to press.

It is common enough to associate gloom with dullness; but, in truth, our gloomy journalism is not dull enough to be true. **War, among other things, is work; and very hard work. Now, hard work is one of the two or three things which, of their nature, cannot be conveyed in literature, far less in journalism.** That is why literature, especially modern literature, unfortunately tends to busy itself with the bewilderments of the small minority who are in possession of money. The private divorces and private re-marriages that occupy the long drawing-room scenes in so many modern plays resolve themselves very largely into the matter of private means. There is no such thing possible in drama as a scene in a workshop; at least, in a workshop where anybody does any work. A dramatist has to do something which some say no gentleman should do—he has to make a scene. If we happen to know the truth about what the newspapers call "a scene in the House of Commons," we know that the scene is very often made by the journalists, and is quite unknown to the House of Commons that is supposed to have indulged in it.[43] The politicians learn in their papers at breakfast next morning of the world-shaking crisis in which they have taken part. Even legislators do a little more work than is compatible with a series of incessant scenes. But because what was once the free English Parliament has unfortunately fallen to be a rather artificial and unrepresentative affair, such falsification of something already false does not do so very much harm. But when this daily appetite for dramatic display is applied to war, the drama of which moves upon different pivots of moon and sun, of months and even of years, it becomes a weak and evil appetite; for it is falsifying something that is really important, really representative, and really popular. And if we are to appreciate wherein war is really momentous we must emphatically realise, first, that it is largely monotonous.

We can realise this quite well if we take the case of any other strenuous and largely materialistic enterprise, that is more or less akin to war. If we told a man to dig a tunnel a hundred miles long, we should not expect him to be always finding

43. Chesterton described these contrived scenes in the *Illustrated London News* for January 8, 1910 (Ch. 1).

buried treasure to make a flutter in the evening papers. If the Government fitted out a ship to find the South Pole, we might very well expect, in the light of what we know of Governments, that many things would be found wrong with the ship's equipment and many perils overlooked in the calculation of her course. But suppose somebody brought out every day something that professed to be the log of the ship; and suppose it consisted entirely of stowaways found in every corner and maroons left on every island, like a boy's adventure-book. We might think the captain an ordinary, or even an insufficient person; but suppose, by this account, he had a shipwreck the first day, a mutiny the second' day, a defeat by pirates the third day; suppose the next day's issue denounced him for his unpardonable failure to catch the Great Sea Serpent, and the next contained a detailed and horrible description of the interior of Davy Jones's Locker. In that case, I venture to say, we should not believe that this stimulating diary was really the ship's log at all. We should not disbelieve it because we believed that the ship's captain possessed all the qualities of Nelson and Columbus. We should disbelieve it because we happen to know that a sea-voyage consists mostly of sea. Whether the work is successful or unsuccessful, it is generally slow work. When we have reflected on the fact that the chief occupation of a sailor is sailing, we may have prepared our minds for the paradox that the chief occupation of a soldier is soldiering: that it is an occupation which is frequently dull for him, and is generally quite unintelligible to us. But this preference of news to facts has produced one effect which poisons what might well be quite legitimate criticism. I mean the confusion by which practicality is conceived as the same as activity. **There is a disposition to ask for a sham "man of action" who is merely a man who is always acting; whereas the only valuable man of action is the man who knows when to act.** The Government is perpetually adjured to do something; when, as a matter of fact, the something would merely have the effect of preventing other things being done.

I know no better working example than the case of the Zeppelins. I would not factiously infringe a scheme laid down by legitimate authority: I will pull down the blinds when I light a lamp; and I would, if necessary, put my head in a bag when I light a cigar. But when the pessimist Press calls on all our rulers and administrators to concentrate on a campaign against Zeppelins, I take my head out of the bag, so to speak, and am disposed to express myself with some violence. If I am to abuse the Government at all, I shall certainly abuse it for making too much fuss about Zeppelins, not for making too little. I grudge to the Germans the pleasure of putting out a single candle; I should not think the burning of a German city the smallest compensation for it. Surely, the ideal to be aimed at is that the enemy should merely write off his Zeppelin raids as a bad debt; an expenditure showing as little return in a moral sense as it admittedly shows in a military sense. We want to make the thing a mere waste of ammunition. Suppose that Germany's stock of vegetable provisions is running low; and suppose she nevertheless thinks it worth while to set aside a certain number of turnips to make turnip ghosts. I suggest that in such a case we decline to believe in turnip ghosts. I more particularly suggest that we do not make the Lord High Exorcist of Turnip Ghosts more important than all our admirable captains fighting by land and sea.

Men working with the invisible and monotonous industry which, as I have said above, is the soul of military science, have brought English aviation to a very high point of efficiency, especially for those purposes of military observation which are by far its most important purposes. Yet it has actually been proposed that all forms of aviation should be united in a separate service: or, in other words, that air-craft should be taken away from those who use it to outmanoeuvre mighty armies, and given to those whose business it is to protect you and me from a few dangerous fireworks. **Surely it would be far saner to say we would have no protection against Zeppelins at all than to say that our local trouble should be allowed to entangle the tremendous plans which can alone save the world.** It may be reasonable to adopt some scientific precautions against Zeppelins, as we already adopt some scientific precautions against lightning, especially in connection with particular and important buildings. But we cannot conduct life with lightning-conductors, or war with any similar apparatus. And I would as soon regard the whole thing as a thunderstorm, and guard against it with nothing more than an umbrella, if the only alternative is to halve and hamper the authority of those unadvertised leaders who are saving our country, not with umbrellas, but with guns.

G.K. Chesterton, "Our Note-Book," *Illustrated London News* 148 (March 18, 1916), 355. US: March 18, 1916. Also published as "Press Interference in the Conduct of the War."

War Between Races

April 8, 1916

I think it probable that the Germans really did think the rest of Europe rotten; and, therefore, did expect to smash up the other States like sticks.

Editor: Chesterton criticizes noted Germans for believing in their nation's superiority. Notice his remark that German intellectuals were taught to regard this conflict in Darwinian terms, "as a war between one race which is always growing stronger and other races which are always growing weaker." At least among their intellectuals, no other country seems to have taken evolution as seriously as the Germans. For Chesterton that illustrates all too well the folly of those who can only learn from books. Their books taught them that Germany should be the victor in any struggle and that made it difficult for them to learn from defeat in battle or war. He was right. It would take another and far bloodier war to teach Germany its lesson.

An article in *Der Tag*, by Hermann von Rath, contains among other things a denial of the alleged German food-deficiency—a denial which may be correct for all I know, or for all I very much care. But it contains also the following rather fascinating comment: "The unexpectedly long duration of the war has failed to affect either the iron discipline of our troops or their chivalrous war-methods. But our enemies must not deceive themselves as to what will happen if there is real scarcity. Then the *furor teutonicus* would reveal itself in all its violence.[44] A desperate rage would take the place of the fight for existence. All scruples would be abandoned in the passionate impulse to achieve an end of the war by terrifying horrors." So now, it will be generally agreed, we know what to expect. We must be careful to keep Germany supplied with sufficient food for the conduct of her campaign against us, or she may be tempted to conduct that campaign in an improper manner. In some transport of rage, for instance, she may yet find herself violating the neutrality of some small neighbouring State. She may yet be driven to some new and dreadful expedient, such as sinking a liner. Under the insupportable provocation of the remissness of our supplies, fiends may whisper to her suggestions which would now seem to her unthinkable, such as corrupting the politics of America or poisoning the springs of Africa. She might bombard a watering-place when it was entirely unfortified. She might even shoot a hospital nurse for being a humanitarian.[45] It may seem morbid thus to imagine the details of so distant and hypothetical a nightmare; but it is only by seeing them in a vision, almost as if they had really happened, that we can make vivid the value of that necessity for the German commissariat which is among the first of our national duties. To tell the truth, I do not know very well what to say about Hermann von Rath and his remark. I fear I only weaken it by comment.

But there is embedded amid its wilder beauties a phrase which can more or less be taken seriously, and which is not without its interest. Von Rath remarks, "The unexpectedly long duration of the war has failed to affect either the iron discipline of our troops or their chivalrous war-methods." With the last observation, of course, it is easy enough to agree. From the first moment when the German invaders poured, looting, raping, and torturing, past the ruins of Liège, their chivalrous war-methods have certainly remained unchanged.[46] But the earlier part of the sentence deserves a little more logical analysis. It would be very interesting to know exactly what von Rath realises and intends when he speaks of "the unexpected length of the war." It is the official German theory that Germany, so far from expecting anything touching the end of the war, did not expect the war at all. Germany, according to this theory, did not look forward to being attacked suddenly; and it would be much more absurd to suppose that she looked forward to being defeated suddenly. The destruction of the German Empire may have been an unscrupulous task, but no one can imagine a German admitting that it could ever have been an easy one. We shall be safe in

44. This term was first used by the Roman poet Lucan (39–65 AD) in his *Pharsalia* (or *Bellum civile*) to describe the fierceness of German tribes fighting Rome. In the Middle Age it came to describe German aggression. More recently, the "desperate rage" is that of the "Arab street." In each case, the threat of violence replaces reason.

45. These were things that Germany had already done. Africa may refer fighting in East Africa under German General Emil von Lettow-Vorbeck (1870–1964). A brilliant guerilla fighter, he harassed the British, tying down a much larger force without suffering a major defeat. Later he opposed Hitler and was so well-respected that his former foe, South Africa, paid him a small pension. For the execution of Edith Cavell, an English nurse, see the *Illustrated London News* for October 30, 1915 (Ch. 3).

46. The heroic defense of Liège by Belgian troops in obsolete fortresses delayed the Germans just long enough the French were later able mount an effective defense before Paris, ending Germany's chance for a short war.

assuming, therefore, that it was not the prolonged German resistance that was unexpected. What has surprised the German writer, therefore, is the prolonged resistance of the Allies. And when we have grasped this fact we shall have grasped the key to the whole story of Prussia and the world to-day.

I confess that for me personally there was never anything unexpected about the prolongation of the war. I never thought Hell an easy city to take. The only legitimate effect that prolongation can have is a ratification. As it reveals link after link of the chain of enslavement these men have wound round the world, it adds reason upon reason for unwinding it to its last coil. Her bad conduct was only a reason for fighting Prussia; but her good Organisation is a reason for destroying her. It is true that the unnatural and temporary power of Prussia is not really so much due to its Organisation of itself as to its disorganisation of the recognised system of Christendom. She would have had little pleasure or profit even out of being a tyrant to her people if she had not been an anarch among her neighbours. Nevertheless, the majority of her critics, including myself, would be content to tolerate a certain exaggeration in the praise of her discipline, if it meant a redoubling of the efforts against her power. But she herself had no such belief in the danger of underrating an enemy. **She has, in fact, reduced under-rating the enemy to a philosophy. All her intellectuals were deliberately taught to regard a European war not as what it obviously is—the collision of great and incalculable powers, at a frightful risk to all of them; but as a war between one race which is always growing stronger and other races which are always growing weaker.** "After the war," says the Privy Councillor Muthesius, "there will be two worlds—the sinking Latin world and the rising Germanic world. No one is any longer in doubt as to which of these worlds the future belongs. Victory by the Germanic world was decreed long before the war. Italy had long been eliminated; and as for France, her power for a long time had been only a matter of tradition."[47] The Germans found traces of this tradition on the road to Paris, especially in the town of Guise, with its picturesque historic memory; and so strong was the local influence of the legend that the Germans recoiled for a considerable distance before an army of half their size.[48] Later, and a little further south, the tradition was so strong that they themselves fell into the quaint old custom of turning sharply to the left and retreating very precipitately across the River Marne and the River Ourcq. A mere tradition has held them ever since behind the line of the Aisne; but a revival of interest in the remote past drove them back yet further

47. This may refer to Hermann Muthesius (1861–1927), a talented architect and the author of *Der Deutsche nach dem Kriege* (1916). The book apparently has not been translated into English, but its title means "Germany after the war," which fits perfectly with the remark Chesterton quotes. Muthesius's praise for the English arts and crafts movement in *Das englische Haus* (1904, translated as *The English House*) led to the Muthesius Affair in 1907, with accusations of insufficient loyalty to Germany. The quote above criticizes the "Latin world," while England was considered part of the "Germanic world." That's why Germany saw racial treason in Britain fighting alongside France. "Privy Concillor" may refer to his 1904 appointment as *Regierungs und Gewerbeschulrat*.

48. A French attack in Battle of St. Quentin (August 29–30, 1914) led to a German retreat at Guise and played a role in General von Kluck's decision to turn left rather than encircle Paris to the west, as Chesterton notes.

over a great space of Champagne. And to-day the Tradition stands astride of the Meuse, like some fabulous Colossus: and the Tradition will not move.

"No one is any longer in doubt as to which of these worlds the future belongs." I should hesitate to put it so strongly as that. I entertain an opinion on the matter; but it is not even yet so positive as the Privy Councillor's was—and, perhaps, still is. But what interests me is the confirmation of the more responsible hint given by the other German, von Rath—the passage in which he speaks of the unexpected length of the war. **I think it probable that the Germans really did think the rest of Europe rotten; and, therefore, did expect to smash up the other States like sticks.** What the Germans mean by their culture is that for them the world is a museum. They have labelled it all; and generally speaking, they have labelled it all wrong. They paste an inscription "Glass, with Care," on something which happens to be made of iron; and then they try patiently to break it, as they are trying to break Verdun.[49] They write "Gold" on something that is only brass; and then they try to negotiate with it as they are trying to negotiate with their educational culture in Turkey. They are sure that a Greek is a sort of fossil; and they will not alter their mind although the fossil moves. They are sure that an Italian is a kind of mummy; and they would not disbelieve, though one rose from the dead. They were certain they knew the drugs that would soothe Belgium and silence England; and, like some pig-headed physician in Molière, they did not care if they accorded with the case so long as they accorded with the Pharmacopoeia.[50] They still insist that the British Army is at this moment very small, and entirely mercenary and plebeian, though it lies in front of their noses for miles and miles. It was so in the books from which alone they can learn. There is one true phrase in the article of Muthesius from which I have quoted—I mean the fact that, while he dismisses France as merely a Tradition, he speaks of the necessity of preaching and preserving "The German legend." For a legend, in that sense, is a tradition that is not true.

G.K. Chesterton, "Our Note-Book," *Illustrated London News* 148 (April 8, 1916), 456. US: April 8, 1916. Also published as "The Unexpected Length of the War."

Polish Patriotism

May 20, 1916

If there is one thing that the war has proved past the imprudence of the last pedant to deny, it is that the European is to the point of death a patriot: Any attempt to build on any basis but nationality is not only desperate but dead.

49. The Germans began the Battle of Verdun as a war of attrition. They intended to create a situation where French had to defend Verdun at all cost to protect Paris. When Chesterton's article came out, the battle was six weeks old. It would continue for over eight months more, making it one of the longest and most costly battles in human history. In the end, Germany's losses were almost as great as France's and it had fewer men to replace those losses. Germany had intended to break France at Verdun, but as Chesterton suggests, the battle demonstrated that, at least in this war, the French could not be broken. World War II would be a different matter.

50. In his plays, Molière (1622–1673) ridiculed physicians who used Latin but knew nothing about medicine.

Editor: Again, Chesterton blasts the Prussian sense of superiority and its insensitivity to the national aspirations of countries such as Poland. He will continue this discussion in the next (June 24, 1916) article. Notice also his spirited defense of Polish nationalism after the war in Chapter 7.

The attitude that only German patriotism was legitimate wasn't confined to Prussians. Historians such as Heinrich von Treitschke influenced that most Prussian of Austrians, Adolf Hitler. This is seen in remarks Dr. Werner Best, Nazi Germany's Reich Commissioner for occupied Denmark (November 1942 to May 1945) made to Frank Brandenburg, a German teenager who set out in the late 1970s to understand his nation's past by interviewing those who had played a major role in Nazi Germany.

After the war, Dr. Best spent six years in prison for his role in Nazi atrocities. It gave him, he told the young Brandenburg, ample time to understand "what had gone wrong in the years between our glorious emergence in 1939 and our ignominious defeat in 1945." Asked to explain Germany's failure, he replied this way:

> "Primarily one single flaw, Herr Brandenburg. One serious, fundamental flaw in the Führer's psyche. Of course, there were many flaws and errors that contributed to the catastrophe, but without that basic flaw of the Führer's, all of them together would have meant nothing." He stroked his pate, "Six years gave me ample time to arrive at my conclusion, you may be assured.
>
> "One flaw? You refer to the Führer's anti-Semitism?"
>
> Best shook his head irritably. "No, no," he said. "Not at all." he paused, as if organizing his thoughts. Frank was about to prod him when he continued.
>
> "The flaw to which I refer," Best went on, "is one of concept, and the resulting relationship between the Reich and any given territory annexed by the Reich. The Führer was not able to think in terms of the population of such a territory, or country, as a whole, but only as individuals or special groups of individuals. He had no realization of the importance, the power of the spirit of the national commonalty. Except in Germany. He did not realize that it was equally strong among the 'inferior' people of the nations he conquered. That power is not centered in short-lived individuals, but in the timeless common people. I call it the 'populace principle' of command. The Führer did not realize that individuals, or small groups of individuals, do not act or react in the same manner as the populace as a whole."
>
> He leaned forward in his chair, intent on explaining his theory.
>
> "So. While eliminating individual opponents or threats to his authority the Führer at the same time—uh, helotized the country, he made serfs or slaves of the *populace*, Herr Brandenburg, the populace as a whole.
>
> "Let me give you some concrete examples. The Führer's flaw, his inability to recognize the populace principle, was first manifested in 1939, with the subjugation of Czechoslovakia. By creating a menial, a lackey nation, helotizing and degrading the populace—he insured affront, discontent, and resistance, instead of laying a foundation on which to build a growing positive relationship. Disregard of the populace principle, not so?
>
> "After the blitz victory in Poland it was the same. And in France—where up to one hundred and fifty of the populace were executed in retaliation for each German killed by the resistance. A violation of the populace principle, which led to

greater resistance and a vastly diminished opportunity for positive interaction with the people.

"And in the Ukraine, Herr Brandenburg. I had been in contact with anti-Communist leaders since 1939. If the Führer had assured them a national state of their own they would have mustered in excess of two million soldiers to fight on the side of the Reich, soldiers who knew how to fight in the vastness of Russia. It would have meant victory for Germany. But instead, the Führer chose to subjugate, to helotize the Ukranian people, thereby creating an army of populace partisans that fought to the death against him, ensuring defeat.

He spread his hands and fixed his eyes on Frank.

"So you see, Herr Brandenburg, the Führer's disregard for the populace principle cost him the war—and the Reich."[51]

TREITSCHKE, the prince of Professors, has a passage about certain difficulties experienced by Frederick the Great in his highly original settlement of the question of Poland.[52] Certain aristocrats of that country, he says, behaved with the utmost ferocity and showed what the Professor calls "that indifference to the feelings of other nations which is so characteristic of the Poles." That, so far as I remember, is the only excuse which he offers for the partition of Poland, beyond a phrase about the necessity of protecting "faithful East Prussia" against Polish insensitivity to altruistic considerations. It occurs to me that if the Professor were to meet on a lonely road three men who professed their intention of cutting him into three pieces with a large knife, he might himself show a certain indifference to their feelings in the struggle which ensued.[53] He might, perhaps, go so far as to maintain that their insensibility to his feelings was even greater that his to theirs. But the phase has always stuck in my mind as a curious example of the hopelessly lop-sided sentimentalism which assists the mere savagery of the Prussian. Poland ought to have consideration for the feelings of other nations, though other nations have no consideration even for the existence of Poland. If East Prussians are faithful to Prussia, they must be rewarded; but if Polish aristocrats are faithful to Poland, they are ferocious and highly inconsiderate. Yet this mere insanity of injustice is the nearest approach to a mild and philosophic consideration of the Polish question that the Prussians have ever given. Compared with their other publicists who have considered the case, Treitschke might be called liberal-minded. **The normal attitude**

51. Ib Melchoir and Frank Brandenburg, *Quest: Searching for Germany's Nazi Past, A Young Man's Story* (Novato, CA: Presido Press, 1990), 194–195. Despite what Dr. Best said about anti-Semitism being irrelevant, a blindness to the rights of Jews—at that time a nation without a land—is an example of denying the 'populace principle.' Notice that many of the internationalists, cosmopolitans and pacifists Chesterton criticizes also share a similar blindness to or a disdain for deeply held national identities. All display the tendency, mentioned here by Dr. Best, to see people as no more than isolated individuals or as groups with narrow special interests.

52. Heinrich von Treitschke (1834–1896) is perhaps Germany's best known historian. Chesterton's quotation probably comes from a five-volume work that one noted historian described this way: "In his *History of Germany in the Nineteenth Century*... Treitschke preached the supremacy of the State whose instrument of policy was war and whose right to make war for honor or the national interest cannot be infringed upon." Barbara Tuchman, *The Proud Tower* (New York: Ballantine, 1966), 243.

53. The "three men" were Prussia, Russia and Austria, who partitioned Poland between 1772 and 1795.

of the rulers of the German Empire was concisely and correctly summed up by another Professor who said, "The only privileges granted to the Poles should be to pay taxes, to serve in the army, and to shut their mouths."[54] For the three hundred years of its historical existence, that is the authentic and unvarying voice of the Power which to-day is reaching out its arms to the East and to the West for the sympathy of the lesser nations.

It is quite a mistake to imagine that when we say such things we are merely throwing something or anything at a sort of Aunt Sally.[55] We are drawing a portrait, the picture of something which we happen to dislike, but which would be there whether we liked it or not. The solid proof of this is that features which would be called favourable are just as much parts of the portrait as those that are unfavourable. Thus, when the Kaiser says that he has kept the peace for forty years, I do not deny it: nor am I at all surprised at it. It is one of the features in the portrait of the historical Prussian that he does remain in repose for long periods, and cannot be provoked from that repose either for vengeance or idealism. It is true that Prussia is often concerned to maintain the peace. It is also true that whenever she ends the peace, it is always with some extremely sudden act of violence or treachery. Thus old Frederick William avoided war as carefully as he collected warriors.[56] In the next generation his son made war—without even the decency of declaring war. Thus Frederick the Great carefully kept the peace when he had gained all the advantages of the war. In his last days, like an enormous boa-constrictor, he digested the dead fragments of Poland and Silesia in an ancient and an evil sleep. Prussia was never even faintly excited either by the religious or the republican enthusiasms which wrestled like two giants in the Revolutionary Wars. Her part in them was small and private, either as a mercenary or a neutral. For her full revenge against the French Revolution she waited until 1870; and her first stroke was a forged telegram. As Professor Cramb truly says, in his somewhat pro-German criticism of Germany, "Prussia never stuck until her hour struck"—that is, until she saw a special chance of striking, comparatively without risk and entirely without warning.[57] In 1740 it was invasion without declaration; in 1870 it was interception and forgery; in 1914 it was violation of a neutralised State.[58]

I have thought it worth while to repeat these realistic matters here, because this policy of Prussia at the moment resolves itself into one idea: the Prussian hopes to hide himself in the dust that he has raised. He would hide his familiar features as

54. This must be the remark: "The theologian Lezius, in addressing a gathering of Protestant professors and students of theology, indicated very forcibly just what pan-Germanism meant for the non-Germans in Germany. He said that the Prussian Poles should have but three privileges:—'To pay taxes, serve in the army and shut their mouths.'" [From Theodore Dehon Jervey, *The Great War: The Causes and Waging of It* (Columbia, SC: The State Co., 1917), 16–17.] The reference seems to be Friedrich Lezius (1859–1939), Professor of Church History at the University of Köningsberg and author of the 1918 *Deutschland und der Osten* (Germany and the East).

55. The original Aunt Sally game was played in English pubs by throwing a stick at a figure of a woman's head.

56. This refers to Frederick William I (father of Frederick the Great), who was known as the "Soldier-King."

57. Probably John Adam Cramb (1862–1913), author of *Germany and England* (New York: E.P. Dutton, 1914).

58. These were the First Selesian War, the Franco-Prussian War, and World War I.

behind a sanguine cloud of slaughter. But his red mask of war is even more misleading than his white mask of peace. What he was at the end of the long peace before 1870, what he was at the end of the long peace after 1870, that he will be at the end of any peace he may make to-morrow if we are such fools as to leave him strong enough to break it at his leisure. And if we want to know what he will then do to Europe, if he can, we shall be safe in asking ourselves in the light of such phases as I have quoted, what he has done to Poland. If he is successful, he will simply tell us to shut our mouths. But if he is unsuccessful, he will almost certainly tell us that we are wounding the feelings of the faithful Germans.

It is ours to resist both tendencies, not only in our enemies, but in ourselves. We cannot too often tell ourselves that what divides us from them is our view of Europe, which they regard as a loose and uncompleted Roman Empire, with its Rome in Berlin; but we as a permanent balance of Christian nationalities. The Partition of Poland was the worst insult to that European equality; but it was not the only one. We ourselves have been tempted in Ireland to such Prussian egomania and perversion; but we have conquered it in ourselves and have already laid, if only in Land Acts and local government, the foundations of a more far seeing and statesmanlike solution. If we are wise, we shall permit no morbid return upon ourselves to disturb the saner prospect. Before the dust of the Dublin disturbance settles, some of us may be tempted to say, with more justice than Treitschke, that our feelings have been disregarded.[59] But if we are wise, we shall not allow any such personal and temporary feelings to have much effect on our policy at all. Such unaltered composure will be a strength, not only because of the real smallness of the interruption, but because of the real largeness of the original design. The great foundations of a new Ireland are already laid. They have been laid by men of varied but converging types of insight, especially of the most English type of insight; and the new Ireland will be Irish. I happen myself to be a wholly convinced Home Ruler: but Parliamentary labels like Home Rule rather confuse than convey the impersonal and impartial truths of which I speak. Some of the strongest part of the work has been done by men whose label was Unionist, especially by the great and generous George Wyndham, whose glory increases with the years that pass.[60] There will be no return to-day or to-morrow to that idiot idea, which inspires the Prussian permanently, and once inspired us spasmodically, that patriotic white men anywhere can be considered as a sort of impossible aborigines. **If there is one thing that the war has proved past the imprudence of the last pedant to deny, it is that the European is to the point of**

59. This refers to the Easter Rising in Dublin from April 24–30, 1916. It called for Irish independence.

60. George Wyndham (1863–1913), Chief Secretary for Ireland (1900–1905), helped pass the 1903 Irish Land Act (see the next article). Maise Ward wrote of him in *Gilbert Keith Chesterton* (London: Sheed & Ward, 1944), 234.

> Gilbert met many politicians in other ways, but only with one of them did he feel a really close harmony. Of George Wyndham's opinions he said in the *Autobiography* that they were "of the same general colour as my own," and he went on to stress the word "colour" as significant of the whole man. To depict him in political cartoons as "St. George" had not in it the sort of absurdity of the pictures of the more frigid and philosophical Balfour as "Prince Arthur." George really did suggest the ages of chivalry. "He had huge sympathy with gypsies and tramps." There was about him "an inward generosity that gave a gusto or relish to all he did."

death a patriot: Any attempt to build on any basis but nationality is not only desperate but dead. Any attempt to build either on cosmopolitanism or cosmopolitan imperialism will be like building upon the quicksands which be between the solid lands.[61] The Prussian will probably continue his see-saw of opportunist bragging and whining. He will continue to shed blood when his neighbours are conquered, and to shed tears when they refuse to be conquered. He may plunge into swamps yet deeper than the swamps of Poland. But we have come out upon the high road of Christendom, and we shall not lose it again.[62]

G.K. Chesterton, "Our Note-Book," *Illustrated London News* 146 (May 20, 1916), 642.
US: May 20, 1916. Previously published as "The Cases of Ireland and Poland."

GERMANY'S INHUMANE HOPE

June 24, 1916

The real case against them is to be found in the phrase which they perpetually employ; that they have a future.

EDITOR: Much of the debate about WWI and a U.S. entry into the war hinged on arguments about who was worse, the English or the Germans, with some engaging in precisely what we see today— moral equivalence arguments that try to equate democracies, especially the United States, with brutal dictatorships. Chesterton isn't one to argue that England was without fault—throughout his life he would condemn its failings. But he did argue that the difference between the two nations was one that, as he says here, "is not one of degree. It is a radical and, perhaps, incurable difference in kind." Put another way, England can be reformed, but Germany must be transformed, with its essential character changed into something quite different.

While Chesterton is willing to admit that a part of Germany's problems lay in the worship of a barbaric past (the Huns of European folklore), he also believes that much of it lay in a progressive idea, in the idealization of a future in which German ideas and German technology ruled the world. He will continue this discussion in the next article (August 19, 1916).

IT was legitimate to hope that before these lines appeared in print we might have some news of the possibility of some Irish Government for Ireland. Only a very few people now resent it; and they are of the sort who prefer a fight even to the things they fight for. In this paper I deal with Irish questions with some deliberate restraint; partly because it cannot be an arena for retort and rejoinder; but more because I know that it circulates in foreign places, and has long had a sort of cosmopolitan

61. Cosmopolitanism focused on weakening patriotism, while cosmopolitan imperialism wanted a World State.

62. In the introduction to his 1922 *Eugenics and Other Evils* (quoted at the start of this chapter), Chesterton points out that during the war he felt that "scientific officialism" exemplified by Prussia was being discredited by the war. His remark that Europe had returned to "the high road of Christendom, and we shall not lose it again," reflects that same mid-war optimism, which, as he notes in *Eugenics*, proved untrue. Europe had not learned to strike a proper balance among the competing interests of the individual, family, community, religion, nation, the European continent, and humanity. It would continue to stress one or two at the expense of the others.

position like the *Times*, responsibly sustained.[63] Under these circumstances, I am in no way ashamed of saying much less than I should say if I were only addressing my own countrymen. But by the most moderate statement the chapter of English history which closes here has been almost to the very last an exceedingly black one. I regard things like the excellent Wyndham Land Act[64] rather with the relief of one paying off a debt than the rollicking self-righteousness of one conferring a present; and when an eloquent religious leader describes the Irish as "petted and coddled," I think such language not only monstrously false, but mortally dangerous. But if anyone attempts, as some in America have attempted, to use the English sins in Ireland as a sort of set-off against the Prussian sins in Europe, they fall into a blunder of the simplest and most enormous sort. If anyone thinks that there is any sort of comparison between this evil, with which a member of the Alliance has been hampered in the past, and that great evil with which the whole Alliance is at war in the present, then that person does not understand the time in which he was born or the sights that are before his eyes.

Calmly and clearly seen, the difference is not one of degree. It is a radical and, perhaps, incurable difference in kind. The English misrule in Ireland might have been a million times worse than it was, or a million times worse than the wildest American Fenian[65] has ever alleged it to be, and the two diseases would still be as different in their whole cause and cure as a slight tendency to anaemia is different from a thundering apoplexy. It would, perhaps, be a truer simile to say that England, in its function towards the Irish, has suffered that cardiac defect which is called fatty degeneration, which greater exercise can avert. But Prussia has had a disease of the heart which its very exercise increases.

The difference is this: that Prussian progress is even more oppressive than Prussian reaction. It was not the Prussia of the old black gunpowder, but the Prussia of the new asphyxiating gas that was a menace to men and nations. **It was not the antiquated Lutheranism of Frederick William, but the modern atheism of Frederick the Great that was and is the military religion of Berlin.** It is not in the least that Germans believe in being retrograde; it is, on the contrary, that Germans believe above all things in being "advanced"; and they advance with chemical bombs in their hands. The real case against them is to be found in the phrase which they perpetually employ; that they have a future. They believe in the future; they worship the future; and, to a person of Christian or chivalric instincts, their future is more

63. Notice Chesterton's sense of fair play. The *Illustrated London News* published his column, but did not have a place where his critics could respond. The paper specialized in heavily illustrated news rather than opinion.

64. This was the same 1903 Land Act mentioned previously. It solved the problem of English landlordism over poor Irish tenant farmers by loaning farmers the difference between what they could afford to pay and what their landlord wanted for the land. (A 1909 act required that they purchase the land.) By 1914 some 75% of Ireland's tenant farmers were buying their land. Chesterton claimed this subsidy is more like "paying off a debt" the English owe the Irish for mistreating them than "conferring a present" on them. A similar solution was used to end slavery in the British Empire. The Slave Abolition Act of 1833 freed slaves over a period of four years and paid slave owners in the Caribbean 20 million British pounds, a cost much less than that of the American Civil War.

65. A Fenian was an Irish nationalist. The term arose in the 1850s with the Fenian Brotherhood.

fearful and inhuman than anybody else's past. German hopefulness is the most horrible thing in the world; worse than the worst hopelessness of the most hopeless obscurantists. When they say that theirs is the young nation, they mean it; and they mean that our nations are old and about to die. "And good shall die first, said the prophet." "And people shall help them to do so," said *their* prophet, Nietzsche, when he spoke of the weak perishing off the earth.[66] When they say, in their innocent anthropologies, that the Teutons are the true warriors of the world, they mean it; and they mean that they will always regard the possession of blue eyes as a natural reason for giving black eyes. But they regard this idea as fulfilling itself even more perfectly in Zeppelins or lachrymatory shells than it was ever fulfilled in firebrands or battle-axes. Professor Deissmann, evidently, as Prussians go, a very amiable old gentleman, replied in effect to the remonstrances against the tools of mere torment which Germany is using for weapons, by saying that they seem to him only further steps in scientific progress.[67] He suggested that similar sentimental protests were probably made against the change from stone hatchets to steel swords. When they say that a submarine (or submarine mine) assassination, such as the assassination of Lord Kitchener, is obviously and entirely innocent, they mean it; and they mean to be still more innocent if they can manage it. **That is the unique note of the Prusso-German peril. Its inspiration is neither Protestantism nor Catholicism, neither Royalism nor Republicanism; it is Futurism.**[68] What the German Hegel said of the whole cosmos is really true of the German's own private cosmos. The German is not a being, but a becoming.[69] In other words, whatever it is that we dislike in him, and however much or however little we dislike it, he is going to give Us a great deal more of it. He does not believe in proportion, like an artist. He believes in growth, like an animal—or a vegetable.

Now, there is nothing whatever to be named in the same world with all this in the stale and local grievances, like that of Ireland, which afflict or defile the other civilised Governments. For instance, the old feeling against the religion of the Irish

66. The first quote is from "Dolores" (1866), in *Poems and Ballads, First Series* by Algernon Swinburne (1837–1909). Swinburne was one of the decadent poets, anti-Christian and often writing on sadomasochistic themes. In selecting him, Chesterton was choosing a poet many would consider among the least moral of English poets. Chesterton then contrasts him *favorably* with Germany's celebrated Friedrich Nietzsche (1844–1900), who in Chapter 8 of *Beyond Good and Evil* glorified the triumph of the strong over the weak, naming as "more complete men," the "barbarians" who "threw themselves upon weaker, more moral, more peaceful races" and claiming that "life itself is *essentially* appropriation, injury, conquest of the strange and weak, suppression, severity, obtrusion of peculiar forms, incorporation, and at the least, putting it mildest, exploitation."

67. Chesterton also wrote on Prof. Deissmann on January 15, 1916 (Ch. 4), where he is described in more detail. Here Chesterton points out that "Zeppelins or lachrymatory shells" (lachrymatory referring to causing tears or gas warfare) are more effective as "tools of mere torment" than as means to win a war. Lord Kitchener was killed when his ship struck a modern weapon, a German mine.

68. Chesterton is adapting "Futurism," a term normally used for an art form more popular in Italy and Russia than Germany, and applying it to the world view of some Germans. It's easy to see why he might do that. The 1909 "Futurist Manifesto" by Filippo Marinetti (1876–1944) proclaimed "We want to glorify war—the only cure for the world—militarism, patriotism, the destructive gesture of the anarchists, the beautiful ideas which kill, and contempt for woman." In 1919, his Futurist Political Party was absorbed into Mussolini's fascist party.

69. The German philosopher Georg W.F. Hegel (1770–1831) is noted for exceptionally obscure remarks such as: "The true is its own becoming, the circle that presupposes its end as its aim and thus has it for its beginning—that which is actual only through its execution and end."

may have been right or wrong; but no sane man will deny that it is less bitter than it was. It has weakened under the influence of a spirit specifically modern, whether we praise that spirit as toleration, or lament it as indifference. A man who objects to Home Rule because it is Rome Rule is certainly old-fashioned, even if he is right. Belfast, much more than Oxford, is the home of lost causes. I do not condemn it on that account; I commend it for adhering to lost causes if it really thinks they are just causes. By a process more recent, but equally decisive, the habit of despising such peoples as the Irish for not being "of Germanic race," while still teeming with possibilities for Germans, will be received with a singular silence by Englishmen. The Germans themselves have seen to that. Indeed, it is amusing to note that, after all their plans to corrupt Irish soldiers or equip Irish expeditions, the one and only piece of help the Germans have given to the Sinn Feiners is to have made the Teuton much more unpopular than the Celt. A witty Irishman, best known to us in England as Norreys Connell, has put the new situation with considerable point in a poem, in which he says that he and his countrymen are still the enemies of Old England, but the friends and allies of Young England.[70] With Germany, it will be noted, the precise opposite is the case. It is precisely the New Germany which we feel as the deadliest foe of the free peoples; and if we retain any affection in the matter it is certainly for Old Germany. **The English instruments of torture are to be found in their museums; but the German instruments of torture are to be found in their chemical factories.** Nothing resembling the German energy of science and innovation in the art of tyranny can be found in the areas once oppressed by England, or even the areas oppressed by Russia—or, for the matter of that, the areas oppressed by Turkey. These are the ends of old religious quarrels, not the beginnings of new rationalist experiments. There still exist English prejudices and Russian prejudices; but the answer is in the very fact that they are prejudices. Caste insolence, imperial rapacity, racial contempt—these are a part of European prejudice; but they are a part of Teutonic progress. These things are our obscurantism, but Germany's enlightenment. It is true to say that almost every modern German is enlightened; and the light in his body is darkness.[71]

What we are fighting is a new and false religion, much more powerful but much less noble than that against which our civilisation strove in the Crusades. But in the clearest minds it may almost be called a religion of irreligion. It trusts itself utterly to the anarchy of the unknown; and, unless civilisation can sober it with a shock of disappointment, it will be for ever inexhaustible in novelties of perversion and pride. Only one principle will inspire all its changes—and that is that in two senses it is always a religion of blood, for its idol is race and its sacrifice is slaughter.

G.K. Chesterton, "Our Note-Book," *Illustrated London News* 146 (June 24, 1916), 782.
US: June 24, 1916. Previously published as "English Misrule in Ireland—and the Prussians."

70. Norreys Connell was the pen name of Conal H. O'Riordan (1874 - 1948), an Irish playwright and novelist.
71. An allusion to Matthew 6:23 in Jesus' Sermon on the Mount.

GERMANY AS GOD

August 19, 1916

So precisely in the phrase about "our German God" the word "God" is a flourish. But the word "German" is a God.

EDITOR: In 1933 a German journalist published a book explaining why he supported Hitler's new Germany. In the first chapter he described meeting a soldier who had been his friend during the war. Their meeting, the first in twelve years, ended in a heated argument. Notice the religious significance he attaches to Germany.

> Gradually, too, I realized that my companion had already ceased to understand the spiritual language of the people and therefore could not grasp the fluctuating significance of events. We went on talking for a while, M. expounding the humanitarian ideals which had driven him away from Germany, while I tried to explain the specific essence of Germany which had estranged me from general ideas—and, as had often happened before, we suddenly both shouted the same question simultaneously, "Then, what is it you really believe in?"
>
> "In eternal truth!" exclaimed M., which I declared, almost in the same breath, "In eternal Germany!"
>
> And perhaps because he fancied I had not heard him, M. shouted once more, "In infinite goodness." And no less loudly I cried out, "In Germany!"[72]

Chesterton's warning in the article that follows could not be more prophetic. Long before Hitler rose to power, many Germans had made a god of their nation. That development lay at the heart of the nation's ills. Hitler himself noted that the development came before his time and praised it: "The Germanic race created the notion of the State. It incarnated this notion in reality, by compelling the individual to be part of a whole. It's our duty continually to arouse the forces that slumber in our people's blood."[73]

Chesterton's loathing for Frederick the Great was matched by Hitler's admiration for him. Hitler had a portrait of Frederick in his Berlin bunker at the end of the war. In early 1942, he told Luftwaffe Field Marshall Erhard Milch: "When one reflects that Frederick the Great held out against forces twelve times greater than his, one gets the impression: 'What a grand fellow he must have been!' This time, it's we who have the supremacy."[74]

SOME little time ago I made a remark in this place to the effect that "the atheism of Frederick the Great was and is the military religion of Berlin."[75] The statement has been disputed in the *New Age* by Dr. Oscar Levy, a neutral living, I believe, in Switzerland, but a close and very able critic of English letters, and one very generous in his appreciation of this page.[76] I have already found it necessary to discuss

72. Friedrich Sieburg, *Germany: My Country*, Winifred Ray, trans. (London: Jonathan Cape, 1933), 41–42.

73. Adolf Hitler, *Hitler's Secret Conversations* (New York: Farrar, Straus and Young, 1953), 29

74. Adolf Hitler, *Hitler's Secret Conversations* (New York: Farrar, Straus and Young, 1953), 213.

75. The full quote is in his June 24, 1916 article (Ch. 4): "It was not the antiquated Lutheranism of Frederick William, but the modern atheism of Frederick the Great that was and is the military religion of Berlin."

76. The article Chesterton refers to is: Oscar Levy, "An Open Letter to British Intellectuals," *The New Age* XIX:12 (July 20, 1916), 273–274. Oscar Levy (1867–1946) was German born, but lived in England, France and Switzer-

the point in another place and in connection with another argument. But, as Dr. Levy says that he sees this paper regularly, I feel it is a habit which calls for every encouragement, and perhaps for some acknowledgment here. It will be enough to say, touching the occasion of the matter, that Dr. Levy takes the Christian religion in North Germany much more seriously than I do—partly, I cannot but think, because it is not his own religion, and he knows the less about the difference between the real and the sham.[77] He begins by telling me that the Prussian soldiers have some Lutheran motto about God actually engraved on their helmets; but (as he himself seems partly to anticipate) I am much less interested in their helmets than in their heads. He proceeds to tell me about an incident in the German Army in which a sergeant, having divided his company into Jews, Protestants, and Catholics according to regulations, was infuriated by the presence of an unclassified individual who said he had no religion. The sergeant told him with great ferocity that if he did not find a religion by next Sunday he would be visited every other Sunday with what we should call detention in barracks. As most English readers will notice, there is a funnier and more irreverent English parallel to this anecdote, about an Oxford undergraduate with "doubts," who was told by the head of his college that he would have to provide himself with "a God of some kind" by next week. But the irreverence of Oxford is the reverence of Berlin. The sort of incident which we tell as an indication of religious indifference is actually the best that Dr. Levy can find by way of a German example of religious enthusiasm. In England we should call such a don a Sadducee; but in atheist Prussia he appears by comparison to be a Zealot.[78]

---

land. He oversaw an eight-volume translation, *The Complete Works of Friedrich Neitzsche* (1909–1913). Although Jewish, his writings are said to criticize the Jewish religion, and that may be why his defense of German religiosity seems so odd. He saw all religions from the outside and purely by their external behavior.

77. Christopher Duffy on Frederick's religion: "In religious matters he moved from a Calvinistic determinism (which he probably adopted just to annoy his father) to a deism which he was prepared to uphold in the face of the outright atheism which became fashionable in some intellectual circles in the 1770s. He believed that Christianity in its various forms, of which Protestantism represented the least objectionable, served a useful social purpose, but Frederick's God remained a distant one, who could have no conceivable interest in the outcome of wars, let alone the welfare of the individual." *Frederick the Great: A Military Life* (London: Routledge, 1985), 289.

78. Levy's concluding remarks in that July 20, 1916 *New Age* article illustrate Chesterton's point that in Prussia even irreligion is enforced with authoritarian zeal. Earlier, Levy had explained that *Flick und Putzstunden* meant the niggling little tasks a soldier could be given to deprive him of any free time.

> And G.K.C. calls such a God-fearing system, a system which enforces the fear of God by the fear of *Flick und Putzstunden*, 'the modern atheism of Frederick the Great'—of Frederick the Great, the sceptic, the freethinker, the Voltairian, the Royal Philosopher, who once gave out the memorable words: '*In meinem Lande kann jeder nach seiner Fasson selig werden*'—('In my country everybody can live and go to heaven in his own fashion').

Like Frederick the Great, Hitler believed religion must support the State, which was above God:

> In these years and particularly at the first flare [of war], there really existed in both [Catholic and Protestant] camps but a single holy German Reich, for whose existence and future each man turned to his own heaven." *Mein Kampf* (Boston: Houghton Mifflin, 1943), 114. In 1941, Hitler went further. In the future Nazi State, he wanted religion privatized, church and state separated, and education secularized: "I envisage the future, therefore, as follows: First of all, to each man his private creed. Superstition shall not lose its rights. The Party is sheltered from the danger of competing with the religions. These latter must simply be forbidden from interfering in future with temporal matters. From the tenderest age, education will be imparted in such a way that each child will know all that is important to the maintenance of the State.... We'll see to it that the Churches cannot spread abroad teachings in conflict with the interests of the State. We shall continue to preach the doctrine of National Socialism, and the young will be no longer be taught anything but the truth. [Adolf Hitler, *Hitler's Secret Conversations* (New York: Farrar, Straus and Young, 1953), 51–52.]

Thus the very example Dr. Levy gives of German religion would alone convince me of German irreligion. It is apparent from the tale itself that the German sergeant was quite careless about the widest divisions of cosmic belief, but very careful about the narrowest and strictest unity of military discipline. He had been told to divide his company into Catholics, Protestants, and Jews; and he would have obeyed with equal indifference if he had been told to divide it into Fire-Worshippers, Fetish-Worshipers, Thugs, Assassins, Satanists, and Communicants of the Black Mass. If the man with no religion could have come back with a sufficient following to make it officially convenient to turn them into a fourth group of worshippers of nothing, or worshippers of a blue baboon, the official would have been perfectly content. But there is another way in which Dr. Levy's argument proves too much. A conscript army is supposed to contain men of all kinds. Now nobody who has ever visited Germany in the most casual fashion can pretend to believe that men of all kinds in Germany can be classified as orthodox members of the Protestant, Catholic, or Jewish Churches. The sharpest impression produced on a visitor to modern Germany was well expressed in my own experience by a little girl who said, "The boys in the street are saying there is no God." Long before war or rumours of war, I can remember the sort of atmospheric change produced on my own mind by passing from Besançon through the Gap of Belfort to Frankfort. **It was the change of passing from a country in which a considerable (though diminishing) number of people were trying to kill Christianity to a country where everybody of any intellectual pretensions assumed that Christianity had been killed long ago.** And it *was* killed long ago so far as Prussia could kill it. It has been absent from Prussian policy and philosophy in a sense utterly distinct from that in which any ordinary wrong-doing is inconsistent with the Christian ideal. Spanish torture or Muscovite terrorism have been appeals to precedent, the belated citation of some sanctity needing defence. Prussian torture and terrorism do not quote precedents; they create precedents. They are based fundamentally on the idea that the past falls into a bottomless pit of forgetfulness. They believe neither in angel nor spirit; but least of all in the Recording Angel. Dr. Levy will at least admit that this philosophy is common, though not universal. And the admission that it exists at all is sufficient evidence that the military divisions he describes do not express Germany. In other words, we cannot read what is in the German heads upon the German helmets.

But if I am asked more generally where I get the impression that modern Germany is irreligious, I get it first of all from its religious utterances. While the German Emperor is talking about himself I can leave his mind as much of a mystery as the minds of most other modern men; I can be agnostic about his agnosticism. But when he invokes God I am absolutely certain he is an atheist. Nor is this any idle paradox; it is a very common experience about the serious and frivolous use of words. Suppose somebody said that a line in some old English nautical song which contained a reference to Father Neptune proved that the English sailors in the days of Dibdin or Marryat were pagans who literally worshipped Poseidon with altars and sacrifices.[79] We should answer, I imagine, that the very tone of the reference of Neptune, as compared with other references to "Providence" or Heaven" in the same songs, was enough to prove that they did nothing of the sort. It would be obvious that the English ballad-writer was only referring in an ornamental way to the sea. It is equally obvious that the German rhetorician is only referring in an ornamental way to the earth—to the elemental laws of nature and the physical hierarchy of evolution. He simply personifies Nature; only he calls it "he" instead of "she." This, and this alone, gives at least a sort of nonsensical sense to the talk of the Germans about their "German God." Or, to take another example, a man acquainted with religion—at least in the Christian sense—could probably guess that we do not pay supreme worship to the god Eros, and guess it merely from the little Cupids on the valentines. The difference may be too delicate to describe; but he would feel that it is not precisely their most serious deities that men treat precisely in that fashion. Well, the modern Germans do treat the Holy Child precisely in that fashion. A Christmas card actually appeared in Germany depicting the Infant Christ as knocking a nail into the wooden statue of poor old Hindenburg.[80] Note that this point is not to be confused for a moment with a certain grotesque gaiety in the details of the divine story. There would be nothing heathen about depicting the Christ child as playing with St. Joseph's tools, and knocking a nail into a nursery toy. In other words, there would be nothing heathen about showing a divinity as taking light things lightly. The point in the German picture is that the Christian divinity is taken lightly while something else is taken seriously; and that something else is the heathen divinity. The Christ Child is a mere ornamental Cupid attending upon Hindenburg. The graceful and charitable image is merely added like a ribbon or a favour on the uniform of the service of force and pride. So precisely the names of the pagan deities—Neptune or Venus, Apollo or Jupiter—are used by modern poets merely as florid figures of speech. **So precisely in the phrase about "our German God" the word "God" is a flourish. But the word "German" is a God.**

When I say that the militarism of Prussia is founded on the atheism of Frederick the Great, it is not a cant of polemics or an appeal to prejudice. It is a historical fact without which a historical phenomenon cannot be understood. Russia has a religion—one may say that Russia is a religion—and has done wrong for its sake. England has neglected her religion for other things, and has done wrong for those other things. France has a standing quarrel about religion; and has done wrong both for religion and against it. But the unique point and power of Prussia have been rooted in her scepticism. Every step in her success has been due to what Frederick would have called her superiority to superstitions. It was always upon her atheism that she acted; and she is only in this stupendous hour beginning to be proved wrong.

79. Charles Dibdin (1745–1814) was British musician, dramatist, novelist, actor, and the composer of some 1400 songs, including nautical songs such as 'Twas in the good ship 'Rover.'" Captain Frederick Marryat (1792–1848) was an English novelist and one of the first to write tales of the sea including *Mr. Midshipman Easy* (1836).

80. To encourage giving, those who made contributions to the German war effort were allowed to drive a nail into a wooden statue of General Paul von Hindenburg.

G.K. Chesterton, "Our Note-Book," *Illustrated London News* 149 (August 19, 1916), 210. US: August 19, 1916. Also published as "The Irreligion of Germany."

Cowardice and Revenge

September 2, 1916

This is not Pacifism, nor even idealism of the crankiest kind; it is a particularly crude and cowardly kind of snobbishness; and there would be infinitely more of the sense of human brotherhood in the most brutal human revenge.

Editor: Chesterton sometimes quotes two opposing views, each different from his own, that, taken together, demonstrate the good sense in what he is saying. Here he quotes one of England's leading pacifists and an Englishman who is a German apologist—two people many would regard as having radically different beliefs—to illustrate why Germany must be punished for starting the war. A "crude and cowardly kind of snobbishness," he says with contempt, often makes people unwilling to confront a powerful evildoer. His remark also explains the inability of many present-day liberals to criticize radical Islam, today's counterpart to Prussia.

Some of the passion Chesterton shows in this article may be because this very month his younger brother Cecil joins the British army as a private. He would be wounded three times and die of an trench-caught illness after the end of the war.

If there is one modern fact for which I must confess an undiluted contempt, it is the fact that the infliction of pain or death is called punishment as long as it is inflicted on the poor and ignorant, and is only blamed as revenge when anyone wishes to inflict it on the wealthy and the strong. It is legal to strangle some miserable creature who has consented to a murder; but it is "vindictive" to shoot a great captain who has commanded a massacre. Pity I can understand, and punishment I can understand; but what are we to say of the servile topsy-turvydom which will punish the most pitiable object and pity a person on the ground that he has hitherto only been envied? Mrs. Swanwick, the Suffragist who has reappeared as a Pacifist, has recently declared that there must be no punishment for the responsible Prussian.[81] She puts it specifically on the ground that they were promised, or promised themselves, the conquest of the whole world; and they have not got it. This, she says, will be punishment enough. If I were to propose, to the group which is supposed to inspire the Pacifist propaganda, that a man who burgled their strong boxes or pilfered their petty cash should suffer no punishment beyond failing to get the money, they would very logically ask me if I was an Anarchist. If I proposed that anybody trying to knife or pistol another person should walk away and resume his daily amusements if the knife broke or the pistol missed fire, they would certainly ask me if I had contemplated the possibility of encouraging the employment of knives and pistols. Crime can be only insufficiently restrained when the alterna-

81. Helena M. Swanwick (1864–1939) quit the National Union of Women's Suffrage Societies after the war began and became active in the pacifist Union of Democratic Control.

tive is between success and punishment. It could hardly be restrained at all if the alternative were only between success and failure; that is, between success and freedom—including freedom to try again. On these grounds I rather reluctantly accept the necessity of punishing the smaller sort of criminal; though I wish it were done in a less callous and insolent style. **But if I am asked to punish every kind of robber except the robber baron, and every kind of cannibal except the King of the Cannibal Islands, I should immeasurably prefer, for my own spiritual good, to be an Anarchist altogether.**

Now, the Prussian Junkers have never been anything else but robber barons; and the King of Prussia is to mere international murder exactly what the King of the Cannibal Islands would be to anthropophagy. The fact has long been recognised in the older civilisations of Europe; it only happens to be the first time that the fact has touched ourselves. We are asked to deal tenderly with the robber barons, apparently upon the old ground of hesitating before damning a gentleman of such distinction; and with the King of the Cannibal Islands, apparently upon the old ground of the divinity that doth hedge a king—a remark originally put, appropriately enough in this connection, into the mouth of a usurper and an assassin.[82] **This is not Pacifism, nor even idealism of the crankiest kind; it is a particularly crude and cowardly kind of snobbishness; and there would be infinitely more of the sense of human brotherhood in the most brutal human revenge.**

But the theory that Germany (or the power that directs Germany) has been sufficiently humiliated by the failure of her attempt upon the civilised world can be tested in another and a very simple style, by asking whether even those who realise that they have lost this war have any sort of objection in principle to another war. The truth is that even the Prussian who surrenders surrenders more arrogantly, and even more menacingly, then anybody else triumphs. Thus Mr. Houston Chamberlain, the remarkable runaway Englishman who has had the privilege of proving in his own person that Germanism is a poison which can work on men of other blood, has written a new pamphlet called "Germany's War Aims," which notably illustrates these two parallel facts and their contrast.[83] Chamberlain is quite sufficiently intelligent and well informed to know that, by this time, it is impossible for the Germans to crush altogether what they call (very absurdly) "the world-dominion of England." He therefore carefully insists that "even if Germany were armed for such undertakings, they would be neither in her practical interests nor in accord with her ideals."

82. As a murderer, King Caludius arrogantly makes this claim in Act 4, Scene 5 of Shakespeare's *Hamlet*: "What is the cause, Laertes,/ That thy rebellion looks so giant-like?/ Let him go, Gertrude; do not fear our person:/ There's such divinity doth hedge a king,/ That treason can but peep to what it would,/ Acts little of his will."

83. Houston Stewart Chamberlain (1855–1927) was a pro-German English writer whose championing of Aryan supremacy in his 1899 *Die Grundlagen des neunzehnten Jahrhunderts* (*The Foundations of the Nineteenth Century*) had a major influence on Nazi ideology. In 1916 he became a Germany citizen and wrote in support of the German war effort. His earlier war essays were published in England as *The Ravings of a Renegade, Being the War Essays of Houston Stewart Chamberlain*, Charles H. Clarke, trans. (London: Jarrold & Sons, 1915). In the *Illustrated London News* for January 24, 1925, Chesterton wrote that Houston Chamberlain going to Germany was like, "Judas Iscariot going to his own place." *The Collected Works of G.K. Chesterton*, xxxiii, 487.

In other words, he sees that the largest and simplest of the ambitions of *Der Tag* is already hopeless.

What is his general view of German rights and duties in the universe and in the future? It is stated clearly enough: "If Germany is not conscious of having taken over from God a world-mission.... if it does not trust itself to accomplish more and other things than the little world-dominating island people... then there is nothing to wish for, nothing to hope for; and it was criminal folly to begin war instead of obediently submitting at the very outset to the 'world-powers,' England and Russia." It will be noted that Houston Chamberlain cheerfully confesses that the Germans did "begin war," and only admits it to be criminal on the supposition that it is folly; that is, that the Germans were not prepared to play their domineering part to its last extreme. Again, he says, in his queer metaphysical dialect, "But in reality Germany has the means to say 'I,' and to enforce 'I': that is her war aim. " Then, after the disclaimer I have already quoted, he adds: "But what must happen is the victorious maintenance of Germany's will against England's will; England's arrogance must be broken, humiliated; England must recognise that Germany is superior to her." And this, we are to remember, is not the pride but the moderation of Germany. This is how she will consent to compromise, not how she would prefer to triumph. This is not the formula in which she would assert her natural claim to destroy and remake mankind; these are the chastened terms in which she renounces it, at least for the time being. I add the last clause, for it is the most practical part of the matter. The extravagance of the passages I have quoted soars beyond the reach of satire; and the mildest thing that can be said about them is also the most important. And that is the fact that in all Chamberlain's words, moderate or immoderate, there is no suggestion that Germany should not strike again at the first opportunity; but the plainest possible intimation that it will be her duty to do so.

Now, I by no means sneer at the sentiment which would spare to a sinner any penalty beyond his own sorrow. I think it the worst and widest gap in the historical imagination of the moderns that they cannot realise the revolution wrought in this matter even by the official Christianity at which they are always jeering. I think it a colossal fact that the Church created a machinery of pardon, where the State could only work by a machinery of punishment. I think even the State might safely pardon a vast number of those it punishes; and if I were myself in contact with a burglar who was sorry for his burglary, I think it highly probable that the burglar would escape. He cries aloud in despair that there is "nothing to wish for, nothing to hope for," not because Germany was ready "to begin war," but because she was not ready to end it by ending a good many other things as well. It is still the first clause in his simple Christian creed "to say 'I' and to enforce 'I.'" He only appeals for our sympathy because he has found it possible to say "I" (which does not seem so very difficult) but has found that "to enforce 'I'" is, comparatively speaking, the devil of a business. If such a philosopher despairs and gives himself up to the police, it is not in the least because he has failed as a moralist, but solely because he has failed as a burglar. So far from regarding his failure even as a sufficient punishment for his crime, he does not admit that there has been any crime, and therefore, very naturally and logically, will not admit that there has been any punishment. **If in the face of such brazen insolence and impenitence, we permit the German Empire to escape and to strike again, I shall for once appear among the apologists of the Germans; for I really do not think that the Germans will be to blame.**

G.K. Chesterton, "Our Note-Book," *Illustrated London News* 149 (September 2, 1916), 764. US: September 2, 1916. Also published as "On Pardoning the Prussians."

AVERTING THE PERIL

September 16, 1916

Our chances of averting that peril do not depend on petty reprisals for his brutalities, or on playing the monkey to any of his monkey tricks.... They depend upon keeping open the gulf that separates common good and evil from this sinister and even insane exception in the chronicles of Christian men. And if we do not do it, our danger is that we shall waste the wealth of our wrath in breaking tools and toys, and the evil itself will escape us.

EDITOR: Chesterton issues one of his strongest warnings that the English must not become indifferent the long-term significance of the horrors that Germany is committing. Germany's problem, he says, do not lie in armament factories or fleets of ships, those are mere "tools and toys." Its evil is moral and spiritual. He also warns against a moral equivalence he describes as claiming, "Attila waging war to destroy civilisation were pretty much the same as Charlemagne waging war to save it."

Evil has its own moral equivalence. Many Germans saw their destructive behavior in war as necessary firmness. Hitler expressed that view in September of 1941, when he linked the Nazi atrocities then happening in Eastern Europe with those in Belgium during World War I: "The old Reich knew already how to act with firmness in the occupied areas. That's how attempts at sabotage to the railways in Belgium were punished by Count von der Goltz.[84] He had all the villages burnt within a radius of several kilometres, after having had all the mayors shot, the men imprisoned and the women and children evacuated."[85]

WHEN the last great Zeppelin raid swept upon London, two scenes were enacted by which an Englishman would be very willing that his country should be judged. The first, of course, was that extraordinary scene—one might almost say vision—in which a man mounted to assail and destroy that winged fortress, enormous as the flying island of Laputa, with an equipment which was by comparison like that of a witch riding on a broomstick.[86] The other was the scene in which the mangled remains of the enemies fallen out of the sky were honourably buried in a

84. As the German military governor of occupied Belgium at the start of the war, Colmar Freiherr von der Goltz (1843–1916) dealt harshly with civilians, shooting hostages when nearby rail lines were destroyed.

85. Adolf Hitler, *Hitler's Secret Conversations* (New York: Farrar, Straus and Young, 1953), 25.

86. Chesterton picked a marvelous literary allusion. In Jonathan Swift's 1726 *Gulliver's Travels*, the enormous flying island of Laputa destroys rebellious cities by darkening their skies or descending down and crushing them.

soldiers' grave with the salutes and the farewell of soldiers.[87] When on a previous occasion some members of a Zeppelin crew were taken alive, a few voices were heard suggesting that they should be denied the privileges of prisoners of war; but these few voices almost instantly died away, and were silenced by a universal silence. Such small revenges are in any case unworthy of the dignity of indignation. They are also futile and inconsequent, for these men are merely tools by the very definition of their trade. We might as well revenge ourselves on the Zeppelin as on the crew of the Zeppelin. To break the furniture may be a pardonable expression of a passing anger; but the only kind of anger we have, or have any right to have, is not of the passing sort. It is a great and responsible anger against men who are in great and responsible stations. Touching the work and destiny of such men, I have always repeated the view that the highest human tradition has taken of such extreme examples: that the only good to be made out of them is to make them examples. There are cases where execution is expiation, and where death is in a true sense the only pardon. I believe we have the right to wage war until we can do justice upon princes and captains as we do it upon thieves and assassins. But when this intellectual conviction is confused with a notion of copying the enemy's methods, it is not fulfilled, but actually frustrated.

A little clear thinking is very much needed in this matter, in which both sides go by association rather than ideas. **On the one side, the Pacifist congratulates himself on avoiding "militarism" when he turns the whole world over to be trampled on by the Prussian Guard. On the other side, the Jingo congratulates himself on avoiding "sentimentalism" so long as he is allowed to butcher and blunder out of pure sentiment.[88] Neither really asks himself what object he is trying to achieve, and what means are the most practical for achieving it.** Now, our object, or at least (if I may in modesty so express it) my object, is to isolate and punish the Prussian power. And when this aim is vividly envisaged, it becomes plain that the real reason for refusing (as far as is reasonably possible) to copy the Prussian malpractices is the same as the reason for refusing all peace or parley with the Prussian monarchy. The more we insist that the terms must be our terms, the more do we weaken ourselves if the methods are their methods. To see the reason for this is a matter not of sentiment, but intelligence. Our whole controversial case against Prussianism is to prove it exceptional. It is obviously a part of that case, if possible, to leave it exceptional. Our whole hope of getting a monster killed and not scotched depends upon our keeping fresh the original human horror at its monstrosity. It may be illogical, but it will certainly be natural, if that horror is somewhat dulled if, by the end of the war, everybody seems to be fighting with pretty much the same weapons. It may be unjust, but it is certainly not unlikely, that men will forget who it was who

87. This was the raid of September 2, 1916, the first in which a night fighter downed a Zeppelin. Sixteen Zeppelins attacked London and one was attacked from below and shot down by William Leefe Robinson (1895–1918), who received a Victoria Cross three days later in the midst of widespread public celebration over his victory.

88. This "butcher and blunder" comment is one of the few occasions when Chesterton allowed himself to criticize how English and French generals were fighting the war, particularly their obsession with a "sentiment" called *élan*—a fighting spirit that expected soldiers to charge at machine guns across open fields in suicidal folly.

used them first. If a European State, at war with other States, suddenly began to eat its prisoners, the other States would be justified in breaking off all intercourse and international discussion, and destroying it without further speech. But if the other States began, however reluctantly, to eat a prisoner here and there, they might still maintain much of their logical case, and even something of a rather relative moral superiority. But obviously there is one thing they could not possibly maintain, and that is the innocent and instantaneous disgust at the mere sight of a cannibal.[89] Yet it would be precisely upon that innocent disgust that they would base their whole claim to crush a mere nest of cannibals. Even if they only on rare occasions took a bite at a man, even if they were only found cautiously and considerately nibbling at a man, they would be biting holes in their own case: they would be nibbling away the natural instincts which were their chief allies in the whole war. They would be making the crime of their enemy a less exceptional thing, and therefore the crushing of their enemy a more exceptional thing. If at the end of the war it seemed less horrible to eat a man, it would seem more horrible to shoot a man-eater.

Now, the gross neglect of history in modern England makes it essential to emphasise again and again the fact that the Prussian policy has really been something as exceptional in Christian history as cannibalism. That ignorance makes us constantly lump together the crimes and the conventions of the past. It makes men talk as if a Pope who poisoned people were pretty much the same as a Pope who excommunicated them; as if a Caesar making his horse a consul were pretty much the same as a Caesar making his slave a freed man; as if Attila waging war to destroy civilisation were pretty much the same as Charlemagne waging war to save it. It is exactly as if we were to draw Jack the Ripper as the recognised picture of John Bull. It is as if we were to say that Mme. Sarah Bernhardt kept a tiger because it is considered a domestic habit to keep a cat;[90] it is as if we said that a City man waiting for an omnibus found it much the same thing to wait for a Zeppelin.

The social order of the past differed in some details from our own; but there was the same sense, or an even greater sense, of the distance between the ordinary and extraordinary. Because a mediaeval knight rode on a horse he would not have been the less surprised to meet a Centaur; and when our fathers came across a monster they recorded it as a monster. And the Prussian monarchy was regarded as a monster. That it had brought a new and naked anarchy into international relations was a commonplace of Christendom like the statement that England specialised in sea-power or that the Grand Turk was pressing upon the frontiers of Eastern Europe. It was indeed known that Prussia systematically relapsed into long periods of peace; but it was also known that the name of that peace was preparation for war. The period

89. This is precisely what happened with two German "innovations," unrestricted submarine warfare and bombing cities, which were used by both sides in World War II. Only poison gas was not used again against soldiers, and that was, in part, because it was ineffective on the rapidly changing front lines of that war.

90. Sarah Bernhardt (1844–1923) was a gifted French actress who liked wild animals and once had a tiger cub as a pet. Mark Twain said of her: "There are five kinds of actresses: bad actresses, fair actresses, good actresses, great actresses, and Sarah Bernhardt." Later actresses imitated her eccentricities, wrongly assuming that would demonstrate they had her enormous talent.

of rest—or rather, of militant immobility—between the forgery of Ems[91] and the violation of Belgium was neither more nor less significant than the period of rest between the Partition of Poland and the treacheries of the Napoleonic Wars, or the period of rest between the Napoleonic Wars and the forgery of Ems—to say nothing of the pillage of Denmark or the swindling of Austria. If we had peace to-morrow, and the peace lasted for another fifty years, we should be no more safe than in the cavern of a dragon asleep. The truth that wants telling, the truth upon which our practical future hangs, is that the dragon is a dragon—that the word is not, as his friends would suggest, a misprint for dragoon. **In other words, what is the matter with him is not "militarism," but tyranny and treachery and a thirst for the things of death.**

We have admittedly reached a state in the campaign in which the peace may be more menacing than the war. The enemy of Christendom cannot now escape by merely piling up his tyrannies, and if he piles them up it is rather because ruin is his consolation as well as his prize—because unkindness is a sort of comfort to him, as kindness is to happier men. But he may escape by some treaty that shall be a treason, and a parent of future treasons. Our chances of averting that peril do not depend on petty reprisals for his brutalities, or on playing the monkey to any of his monkey tricks. They depend on the contrast between the brute and monkey and the dignity of man which he has insulted. **They depend upon keeping open the gulf that separates common good and evil from this sinister and even insane exception in the chronicles of Christian men. And if we do not do it, our danger is that we shall waste the wealth of our wrath in breaking tools and toys, and the evil itself will escape us.**[92]

G.K. Chesterton, "Our Note-Book," *Illustrated London News* 149 (September 16, 1916), 322.
US: September 16, 1916. Also published as "Our Real Case Against Prussianism."

1916

DEFECTIVE NATIONAL FEELING

October 7, 1916

Christendom, with whatever corruptions, was a community of nations recognised as nations, as a city of citizens recognised as citizens. It was because North Germany was outside this national idea, not because she was inside it, that all barriers have been broken and all crimes eclipsed.

EDITOR: Chesterton begins by examining H.G. Wells' latest book, the once popular but now largely forgotten *Mr. Britling Sees It Through*. (He'll be more critical in an October 28 article.) In the latter half of this article, Chesterton uses paradox to suggest Germany's problem isn't an excess of nationalism, as many were saying, but a nationalism so new and immature, it has yet to recognize that a nation can only exist within

91. Chesterton often mentions the Ems telegram that Bismarck altered to provoke the 1870 Franco-Prussian War. The other events are situations over the past century and a half when Prussia had demonstrated a desire to conquer and crush. Chesterton wants to drive home the point that Prussian aggression is not new.

92. This is exactly what happened. Those who made the treaty ending the war focused on forcing Germany to destroy their "tools and toys" of war and limiting (they thought), its ability to make more. The real evil escaped.

a "community of nations." He equates trans-national cosmopolitanism—considered (then and now) as the height of modern, fashionable thinking—with a barbarism in which "all barriers have been broken" down, moral and territorial. Chesterton believed humans live best within boundaries such as nations, communities and families.

Wells refers to Chesterton briefly in the other 1916 Wells book mentioned in this article, *What is Coming?* In Chapter IV of that book, "Braintree, Bocking, and the Future of the World," Wells attempted to draw a practical, Chesterton-like parallel to the problems his anticipated World State (or a nation-hostile League of Nations) would face. He found that parallel on "a certain stretch of road between Dunmow and Coggeshall." In Wells' eyes, that road—like a national border—committed the unpardonable crime of dividing the more urban town of Braintree from the more rural town of Bocking. The result was to his mind a shocking blow to national efficiency, "a Bocking water main supplying the houses on the north side and a Braintree water main supplying the south." The road, he feared, demonstrated that "the British are quite unfit to control their own affairs, let alone those of an empire." And who was responsible for defending that dreadful state of inefficiency—none other than G.K. Chesterton and his co-conspirator Hilaire Belloc. Of them, Wells had this to say.

> It may of course appeal perhaps to the humorous outlook of the followers of Mr. G.K. Chesterton and Mr. Belloc, who believe that this war is really a war in the interests of the Athanasian Creed, fatness, and unrestricted drink against science, discipline, and priggishly keeping fit enough to join the army, as very good fun indeed, good matter for some jolly reeling ballad about Roundabout and Roundabout, the jolly town of Roundabout; but to any one else the question of how it is that this wasteful Bocking-Braintree muddle, with its two boards, its two clerks, its two series of jobs and contracts, manages to keep on, was even before the war a sufficiently discouraging one. It becomes now a quite crucial problem.[93]

If asked, Chesterton might reply that people are different, that this split between the two towns, with their different classes and cultures, allowed them to get along and avoid the civic equivalent of war. Fences, highways and borders make for good neighbors. If they were joined, whose policies would dominate, those of Braintree or Brocking? The urbanized Wells probably assumes those of Braintree would. He makes the classic mistake utopians often make, thinking their vision of the World To Come is the right one. And because they want to impose their vision on the world, they assume their foes have the same agenda. But Chesterton wanted a world that was not only varied and different, but that would remain so safe behind national borders. The very poem about Roundabout that Wells references is a defense of a world of fun and inefficiency, one where the roads wander simply because they've always wandered.

Five days after the article below was published, Chesterton's brother Cecil resigned as editor of the *New Witness* to train and join the fighting in France. Chesterton would take over for him in addition to his many other responsibilities.

93. H.G. Wells, *What is Coming? A European Forecast* (New York: Macmillan, 1916), 80–81. Interestingly, Wells goes on to criticize the lack of centralized government control for the same sorts of "muddle and waste" that many today blame on *having* a centralized government dictating from afar what can and cannot be done. Wells' remark about "the jolly town of Roundabout" refers to a poem in *The Flying Inn* (1914) that includes a series of humorous reasons why England's roads twist and turn so much: "And I should say they wound about/ To find the town of Roundabout/ The merry town of Roundabout/ That makes the world go round."

Mr. H.G. Wells has written a book, with the title of *Mr. Britling Sees It Through*, which is almost avowedly a diary of the war, but a singularly beautiful diary. Indeed, as might be expected, not only Mr. Wells's characteristic perceptions, but even his characteristic doubts, give him an almost divine inspiration in a diary—much more than in a prophecy. It is the virtue of a diary that it is vivid; but it is also in a sense its virtue that it is short-sighted. There was a foolish fashion of classing Mr. Wells, on account of his scientific hobbies, as if he were some metallic and unfeeling instrument, like a forceps or a scalpel. Assuredly, if Mr. Wells is any sort of scientific instrument, he is a barometer. If a barometer could walk about like a human being, we should probably find it a rather touchy human being. But the barometer is excellent evidence that science has a use for sensibility, and, in a sense (with apologies to the barometer), for fickleness. This any lover of Mr. Wells's work could guess; but there is much more than this in *Mr. Britling Sees It Through*.[94] There is that profoundly inspiring thing called tragedy. The tragic poet is not trying to break the limitations of time and space like an Anarchist (or an amateur prophet); he is grandly conscious of the limitations, like an artist. There is surely in this book something like an unconscious satire by the Wells who is wide awake to-day on the Wells who had a topsy-turvy dream in which he tried to remember to-morrow. There is surely a noble irony in the superiority of this human document to the book which he published before it, *What is Coming?*—in which he went back to his old trade of prediction. **It is almost startling to note how vague and even weak he is when he is settling the next few centuries on scientific principles, and how virile and vivid he is when he knows not what a day may bring forth.** Familiar as he was with the next few decades, he found he knew precious little about the next few days. Personally, I cannot say how much more I admire him when he plunges into the future than when he peers into it. I think much more of Mr. Britling when he sees it through than when he fancies he sees through it. I agree with the realistic Irishman who said he preferred to prophesy after the event. The saying might really be a very good symbol of how politically practical are the Irish as compared with the English. It may be a great bore that the truisms are true; but they are. And, when all is said or prophesied, to ask *What Is Coming?* is to put on eye-glasses to stare into a mill-stone, a mill-stone of which the very thickness and hardness may be in some manner necessary to the grinding of the mills of God. I think Mr. Britling offers the better moral. Whatever is coming, we will see it through.

---

94. Wells published some 15 books during the war, beginning with *The War That Will End War* in 1914 and ending with *In the Fourth Year: Anticipations of a World Peace* in 1918. Here Chesterton discusses two of his 1916 books, *What is Coming? A Forecast of Things After the War* and *Mr. Britling Sees It Through*. The latter describes the life of a mildly distinguished Englishman (a writer not that different from Wells himself) trying to cope with the war. The book became popular in war-weary Britain, and also marked the beginning of a brief period during which Wells would examine religion for answers to life's questions. These remarks come near the end of the book.

> Religion is the first thing and the last thing, and until a man has found God and been found by God, he begins at no beginning, he works to no end. He may have his friendships, his partial loyalties, his scraps of honour. But all these things fall into place and life falls into place only with God. Only with God.

In the following three years, Wells would write three books with religious themes: *God the Invisible King* (1917), *The Soul of a Bishop* (1917), and *The Undying Fire* (1919).

I make no claim here, however, to review this very vital and very human story. I only mention it or the name of its author in order to mark down what I conceive to be a somewhat momentous error about the ethics of the international situation. Its appearances in the book about Mr. Britling are comparatively few and far between, and are entangled in quite a forest of other fascinating or provocative ideas. But, as Mr. Wells has since amplified and reiterated it elsewhere, it is to be presumed that he means it for one of his more permanent and responsible criticisms upon the war. And it seems to me not only erroneous, but perilous. It is not only founded on a false diagnosis of the past, but I think it is likely to prove very deleterious to the health of Mr. Wells's young friend the future. Indeed, it is a good case of the mistake of being in such a flutter about what is coming as to forget altogether what has come already—and come to stay. And that crystallisation of Christendom which we call nationality is one of the things that have come to stay.

The suggestion under discussion is broadly this: that Germany suffers chiefly from an overdose and debauch of national feeling, and that therefore Nationalism, which has thus destroyed our enemies, must be watched with a wary eye even in our friends and in ourselves, as if it were a highly dubious explosive. Mr. Wells, who has explained this view in many places of late, must not be regarded as one of the dull extremists on the other side. He says he agrees with Home Rule; and I cannot suppose him such a lunatic as not to agree with the national reconstruction of Poland, for upon that essential hang all our hopes of the just peace of Europe or (which is much the same thing) of the adequate restraint of Germany. But the point is not whether he admits that Poland and Ireland have been allowed too little national independence. The point is that he thinks that Germany has been allowed too much national independence. He thinks her nationalism is her narrowness. It is this view that I think false in logic, false in history, and highly perilous in practical politics.

It is false in logic, because Nationalism is a generalisation, as is the nature of any "ism." An Individualist, if there ever was such an animal, does not think that he is the only person who can be an individual. A Collectivist does not think that his cows and acres ought to be collected by an official, and everyone else's left as they are. Nor does a Royalist mean a madman who thinks he is the King of England; nor a Pantheist the other kind of madman who thinks he is all the God there is. All such positions imply an appeal to a general rule; and the Nationalist is only a Nationalist if he appeals to a general rule of Nationalism. Nations, like marriages, or like properties, are a class of things accorded a certain recognition by the conscience of our civilisation. One of them cannot logically plead its own rights without pleading the rights of the class. And to say that a nation which disregards frontiers and annexes or destroys neighbours is suffering from an excess of Nationalism is intrinsically nonsensical. We might as well say that a man who runs away with his neighbour's wife is suffering from an excess of reverence for the institution of marriage. We might as consistently maintain that a man who runs away with his neighbour's watch is too arrogant and implacable a protector of the rights of property. Mr. Wells suggests, in an article in the *Daily Chronicle*, that the German disposition to ram sauerkraut down everybody's throat with a bayonet is an extravagance of national feeling. But it is not; it is a deficiency of national feeling—if only in the matter of wasting sauerkraut on people who do not appreciate it. **What is the matter with the Germans is not that they think German culture is German culture—a platitude after their own hearts which they might have peacefully enjoyed to the end of the world. It is that they think German culture is culture—that it is the highest product of evolution, and is on a higher platform above an ignorant world. In other words, they think something culture which is only custom.**[95]

And as it is false in theory, it is certainly false in fact. In history the Germans have been the least national of all Europeans. The typical nations, first France, then England, Spain, Scotland, Poland, etc., arose like islands in a sea of barbarism for which Germany was rather a loose allusion than a name. The word Allemagne is said to be derived from what practically means Anybody.[96] If civilised men gave the race any title, it was not so much a definition as an expression of ignorance. We find Germans spoken of in this fashion long after France or England had become nations in the sense in which they are nations now. Often Germans were talked of as if they were German measles—merely one of the perils of life, merely something that happened. And so they were; and they have happened again.

Christendom, with whatever corruptions, was a community of nations recognised as nations, as a city of citizens recognised as citizens. It was because North Germany was outside this national idea, not because she was inside it, that all barriers have been broken and all crimes eclipsed. It was because beyond the sacred frontiers lay chaos—which some call cosmopolitanism.[97]

---

95. Chesterton is commenting on a German (Prussian) claim that their *Kultur*, with its strong, authoritarian rule and stress on military prowess and idealistic values, made it superior to the individualistic and materialistic self-seeking of a *Zivilisation* like that of the French. Chesterton disagreed, seeing much of modern German *Kultur* as barbarism. He was willing to tolerate it (in the prewar years) as long as it remained within its own borders, imposing itself on no one else. Only when it revealed itself as incurably aggressive was it to be forced to change. Hitler would echo the German view of *Kultur* when he wrote: "Everything we admire on this earth today—science and art, technology and inventions—is only the creative product of a few peoples and originally perhaps of *one* race. On them depends the existence of this whole culture. If they perish, the beauty of this earth will sink into the grave with them." *Mein Kampf* (Boston: Houghton Mifflin, 1943), 288. The reality was otherwise. In this period, German Jews—not regarded as racially German and a mere one per cent of the population—won a quarter of the nation's Nobel Prizes and were overrepresented in the arts.

96. The French name for Germany, *Allemagne*, either comes from a word meaning "land of all the men" or from a Southern Germanic tribe called the *Alamanni*, whose name may derive from that same word. In this article Chesterton is alluding to what historians later call the *Sonderweg* ("special way") debate. Did the German disaster flow from its late development as a nation—a development in which Germany's economic and military power grew faster than its political and social skills to cope with that change responsibly? For an analogy, think of a teenager who grows up too fast, becoming physically powerful before he becomes emotionally mature. Chesterton was ahead of his time in diagnosing Germany's ills and pointing to their possible cause.

97. Equating cosmopolitanism with chaos makes sense. National borders provide order, placing a dividing line between what is French and what is German, enabling them to get along. By denying the need for borders, cosmopolitans create cultural and political chaos. Much the same can be said for multiculturalism. Of course, for the shrewder and more ruthless cosmopolitans and multiculturalists, the result is an opportunity rather than a problem. Borderless and cultural-less nations require authoritative and bureaucratic central governments to impose order. That's why destroying borders and cultures creates chaos and destroys freedom.

G.K. Chesterton, "Our Note-Book," *Illustrated London News* 149 (October 7, 1916), 406. US: October 7, 1916. Also published as "Mr. Wells and Nationalism."

Lawlessness as Law

October 28, 1916

To come to the core of the matter, it is possible for something to grow strong in human society which is sufficiently widely hated to be called a crime, and yet is sufficiently widely obeyed to be called a tyranny. What is lawless can really become law.

Editor: Chesterton describes the inconsistencies and internal contradictions of pacifism, explaining how its methods make its goal of a world without war less likely. Peace, he says, will not be maintained by pacifist tribunals. It can only be kept by a willingness to wage war and punish aggressors. He describes with near perfection those afraid to take on a rogue nation: "We have dropped into the despicable habit of thinking of the foe of society as a fugitive. We have forgotten that the criminal class can sometimes be as powerful as the police. When this happens, we too often discover the simple solution of never calling it the criminal class." That's precisely how England and France would respond to "Herr Hitler" in the 1930s. They tried to legitimize him, hoping that would make him less criminal.

1916

On October 27, 1916, the day before this article was published, J.R.R. Tolkien, a British signal battalion signals officer in the Battle of the Somme, came down with trench fever. Various relapses kept him from returning to the war. While recuperating, he wrote early drafts of *The Silmarilion* (1977). In a 1960 letter, Tolkien would write of *The Lord of the Rings* that, "The Death Marshes and the approaches to the Morannon owe something to Northern France after the Battle of the Somme."[98]

Those in an extreme revolt against war seem to have a war in their own minds; a war between two quite contrary ideas. One is the urgent necessity of international justice; and the other is the complete impossibility of it. **Pacifists and Semi-Pacifists are perpetually telling us that Europe must have an international tribunal, which, if it be a tribunal at all, must be able to judge and presumably able to punish. Yet the same people are perpetually telling us that it is impossible to punish Germany, and apparently impossible to judge anybody or anything.** They say it is in the power of negotiation to trace the tangles of the most elaborate knot. But when the Prussian in broad daylight cuts the Gordian knot with his sabre, they can only treat the incident as a new, delicate, and more or less hopeless entanglement.[99] What would be a plain provocation, if the ultimatum to Serbia and the invasion of Belgium were not plain? According to this Pacifist theory, a criminal can be read like an open book while he is merely meditating his crime. He only becomes a sacred

98. J.R.R. Tolkien, *The Letters of J.R.R. Tolkien* (Boston: Houghton Mifflin, 1981), 303. He added: "They owe more to William Morris and his Huns and Romans, as in *The House of the Wolfings* or *The Roots of the Mountains*. Both books have been published in *More to William Morris* (Seattle: Inkling, 2003).

99. A legend says that the Gordian knot tied a chariot or ox-cart to a post in Telmissus, that the person who untied that knot would rule Asia Minor, and that Alexander the Great untied it by cutting it with his sword. In a similar fashion, Chesterton says that Prussia wants to rule Europe by striking suddenly and violently.

mystery when he has committed it. The advocate of negotiation offers himself to the world as a Sherlock Holmes who can deduce and balance the most elaborate legal niceties; and then sits down with a knitted brow to the inexhaustible problem of whether Serbia is in Austria or Belgium in Germany.

But not all who specialise in the sentiment of peace are so silly as this. There are a number of genuine idealists who escape this contradiction by concentrating consistently on the ideal of an international tribunal. The other and more muddle-headed Pacifists are now eagerly and openly at work, calling for that premature and patchwork peace which is a flat contradiction to their own theory of the future. **We are more and more loudly assured that the malefactor cannot be punished for what he has done; by the very same people who tell us, equally loudly, that he will never do it again for fear of punishment.** We are more and more openly told that the enemy must be treated on a basis of give and take; which means that the enemy cannot give anything except what he has himself taken. These things, whatever they are consistent with—and they are not always consistent with each other or themselves—are at least quite inconsistent with the ideal of an international tribunal, and a justice of Europe bearing not the sword in vain. And the time, as I have said, is most emphatically come to call on all those who honestly entertain that international ideal to accept the conclusion of their principles. The only possible conclusion of their principles is the punishment of Prussia.

Some members of this school, of which Mr. H.G. Wells may be considered the most brilliant doctor, seem to hold this international ideal in a more absolute sense than I can. Some of them accept literally the definition of "The War That Will End War," or, as Mr. Britling expressed it, "And Now War Ends. " **I cannot see how we can literally end War unless we can end Will. Vegetables are very commonly Pacifists; but becoming a vegetable is not a price that I am ready—or, indeed, able—to pay.** I cannot think that war will ever be utterly impossible; and I say so not because I am what these people call a militarist, but rather because I am a revolutionist. Absolutely to forbid fighting is to forbid what our fathers called "the sacred right of insurrection."[100] Against some decisions no self-respecting men can be prevented from appealing to fortune and to death.[101] **To call the world "a World-State" is simply to call the war a civil war, which is hardly even calling it a bad name.** But whether or no the peace this school desires can be as perfect as it expects, this is certainly the peace it does desire—a peace imposed by international law. And we have a right to ask those who honestly desire it to separate themselves definitely from the other Pacifists, who desire the precise opposite. For the other sort of Pacifism will render this peace not imperfect, but impossible.

100. Chesterton takes up this argument in more detail in the *Illustrated London New* for September 27, 1924. See *The Collected Works of G.K. Chesterton*, XXXIII, 412–416.

101. Chesterton may be alluding to the last words of the *Declaration of Independence*: "And for the support of this Declaration, with a firm reliance on the protection of Divine Providence, we mutually pledge to each other our Lives, our Fortunes, and our sacred Honor."

In so far as this simple dilemma is dealt with at all, it is answered that the Allies are only parties to the suit; that the decision should be general—that is, that it should be partly German. It is argued that the prosecutors ought not to sit upon the bench. But surely it is much more outrageous that the prisoner should sit upon the bench. As another escape from the dilemma, it is suggested that it is rather the neutral opinion of Europe that should speak. But what sort of "opinion of Europe" is it that speaks when France, Germany, Russia, Austria, Italy, and Britain are silent? It is sometimes proposed that the whole matter should be referred to the opinion of America, which is not the opinion of Europe at all. But, speaking as one who has always protested against the current sneers at America, I may surely say that no single nation, however great, can be put in this almost cosmic position. The whole destiny of mankind cannot be settled by the United States, any more than the whole destiny of the United States could be settled by South Carolina.[102]

Now, what we really reach, by all this inevitable elimination, is precisely the truth in the revolutionary idea. It is sometimes necessary to have a civil war, if it be the civil war of civilisation. It is sometimes necessary to set up a revolutionary tribunal, when it is the only way of setting up any tribunal. **To come to the core of the matter, it is possible for something to grow strong in human society which is sufficiently widely hated to be called a crime, and yet is sufficiently widely obeyed to be called a tyranny. What is lawless can really become law.** The Internationalist complains that great and powerful provinces of Europe like Germany and Austria should [not] be judged without their own consent. But, if they were not great and powerful, they would not need to be judged at all. It can only be a considerable section of Christendom that can make a mutiny in Christendom. If Christendom cannot condemn so large a secession, Christendom can never survive any really large peril. What will be the good of an international tribunal that can only save us from the worldwide ambitions of the Republic of Andorra, or the sombre militarism of the Prince of Monaco?

We have dropped into the despicable habit of thinking of the foe of society as a fugitive. We have forgotten that the criminal class can sometimes be as powerful as the police. When this happens, we too often discover the simple solution of never calling it the criminal class. In that paralysis of the commonwealth which is called plutocracy, we allow powers intrinsically anti-social not to attack society, but rather to control it. This truth is seen in commerce in the shocking irony of the very word Trust.[103] It is exactly when the lawless *parvenu* is, in this sense, trusted that he ought to be most distrusted. That many work with him is not a point in the defence, but rather a part of the indictment. The Prussian, the *parvenu* of our history, has created not a nation, or even an empire, but an Armament Trust. What

102. In 1861 South Carolina led the movement to succeed from the union and form the Confederacy, a choice that was not permitted to determine the destiny of the United States.

103. Trusts are agreements in an industry (such as oil, steel, or rail) to keep prices high and wages low. Since such agreements are often not legally enforceable, they require the parties to 'trust' one another. As Chesterton points out, the more powerful a trust is, the greater the crime and the more difficult punishment becomes.

he holds to-day is in a moral as well as a military sense a ring. Like the anti-social commercial combine, the thing is a drilled anarchy. When the upstart hostile to society thus copies for his own ends the discipline and instruction of society, we cannot trust everything to those he has himself disciplined and instructed. We cannot count the votes of his lackeys, or let him be acquitted by the verdict of his slaves. We ought never to have let it reach this point; but when it has reached this point it is war, war in some shape or form, between those who will not accept the *parvenu* power and those who have already accepted it. This is the only sane root of revolution, which is the last shape of law and punishment. For high and human revolution has never been a mere innovation; it has much more often been a resistance to innovation. We have allowed a situation to arise in which, unless punishment is possible, nothing is possible. We have allowed a type to rise from squire to king, and from king to emperor; and with every rise in rank he has grown more of a cad. Now that his horseplay has filled the heavens and the seven seas, and his infamous practical jokes are as plain as the sun and moon—now, if he really cannot be punished, the dreams of international justice have become a part of his own jest, and the laws he has broken will never be mended by men.

G.K. Chesterton, "Our Note-Book," *Illustrated London News* 149 (October 28, 1916), 498. US: October 28, 1916. Also published as "An Extreme Revolt against War."

CHIVALRY IN WAR

November 11, 1916

A war is in its nature a thing with two wills, as a bird is a thing with two legs. We cannot talk of the thing as something with a good or a bad purpose, for the thing we are talking of would not exist at all if it did not consist of two quite opposite purposes.

EDITOR: World War I will end precisely two years after this date. At this point, a war of just over four years duration was some six weeks past its midpoint. Unlike many of his colleagues, Chesterton is not discouraged. He finds much to praise about war in general and this war in particular. He explains why pacifism is flawed and hints at why many in the "aristocracy of intellectuals" are pacifists. Winston Churchill succinctly captured what the war felt like at this point in *The World Crisis* (1923).

> Before the war it had seemed incredible that such terrors and slaughters, even if they began, could last more than a few months. After the first two years it was difficult to believe that they would ever end. We seemed separated from the old life by a measureless gulf.[104]

IN an interesting article in the *Nation* called "On Chivalry in War," I find the following sentences: "In the eighteenth century Swift and Voltaire were singular in thinking that war is fundamentally criminal. To-day we all think so."[105] In that case, it would be truer to say that to-day we all flatly refuse to think. War, like weather,

104. These are the opening sentences to *The World Crisis*, Ch. LIV, "The Teutonic Collapse."
105. "On Chivalry in War" *The Nation* XX:4 (October 28, 1916), 138–140.

cannot in itself be either criminal or saintly; and war as an action undertaken by certain persons may be either one or the other. Only in a state of fallen intelligence akin to fetish-worship could people ever have dropped into the habit of talking about the wickedness of war. It is, indeed, precisely like the action alleged of the savage, who tries a tomahawk for murder and burns it to teach it better manners. One can never praise or blame a quarrel, as if it were one thing—simply because it takes two to make a quarrel. **A war is in its nature a thing with two wills, as a bird is a thing with two legs. We cannot talk of the thing as something with a good or a bad purpose, for the thing we are talking of would not exist at all if it did not consist of two quite opposite purposes. It is like pointing at a railway collision and asking if it is the right train to Brighton.**

In all the long centuries before Voltaire or Swift were born, I imagine the majority of people realised that aggressive war was wrong. And in all the long centuries after the *Nation* is dead (not that I wish it to die) I imagine the majority of people will continue to realise that defensive war is right. **That all war is physically frightful is obvious; but if that were a moral verdict there would be no difference between a torturer and a surgeon.** All this is but an alphabet of ethics; but it is sometimes necessary to return to it for an instant, for so many clever modern writers arrive at random conclusions by short cuts of truancy, and seem never to have been to school. Nevertheless, when all this mere muddle is swept away, there remains a real difference of philosophy about war; and the present war has brought it to a head. It is strictly, perhaps, rather a difference of sentiment than a difference of philosophy; but there is nothing so practical and, in the only useful sense, nothing so business-like as sentiment. I think the two sentiments about war work back to a difference so ultimate that, if I were a German lunatic, I should say it was "beyond good and evil"; and even as it is, I think it is often beyond pleasure and pain.[106] It is concerned with pride and humiliation—that is, with pride in the good sense and humiliation in the bad sense.

It is a notable point for our national cause that very many who honestly believed that no war is necessary admit that this war is necessary. Many Pacifists have been guilty of a noble and chivalrous apostasy. They have turned their coats, and turned forth a khaki lining on the night; but the change in itself is no discredit either to their old uniform or their new one, or to any except the bloodstained uniform of Prussia. But among those who thus regard the war as necessary there are some, I think, who regard it not only as a necessary evil, but as a necessary ignominy. They feel as if they were going on all fours like beasts; they dislike the mud more than the blood. There is no part of the process whatever of which they can think with pleasure except the end of it. The whole of their particular conception of human dignity is broken, and, as it were, bent double as by a degradation. They are few, for they are the minority of a minority. But they are perfectly patriotic, and even painfully sincere.

106. "Beyond good and evil" alludes to Germany philosopher Friedrich Nietzsche, who wrote a book by that name and spent his last years insane, hence Chesterton's "if I were a German lunatic."

In this matter, as in many others, I am on the side of the vulgar majority. But I realise that there is an aristocracy of intellectuals who are quite spontaneous and sincere in the disgust which I describe; and who, while they are too intelligent to be content with merely praising peace, are infuriated by anybody praising war. I remember talking about the matter to one of the two or three most brilliant men of our time—a man whose attitude on the war has been somewhat misunderstood, for it is not so much opposed to our policy as simply opposed to its popularity.[107] I believe he could tolerate the Army; but he cannot endure the mob. But, in the very act of urging that the war should be waged until Prussia was taught a lesson, he spoke of the war itself as if it were some colossal cosmic jest at the expense of humanity. He really felt about soldiers fighting as most men feel about soldiers running away. He could conceive of some vengeance of Nature falling upon us for having despicably dropped below our part. "If we can't do better than this," he said, with involuntary mysticism, "something will come out of a bush." Then he added, with the full effect of such words when they come instinctively from a free-thinker, "God is not mocked."[108]

1916

This feeling, as a feeling, was in him quite unquestionably unselfish and sincere; but it is exactly this feeling, as a feeling, which I hold to be false, futile, and inhuman. That is the spiritual difference, the deepest spiritual difference of the hour. Pile up all the personal infamies of fighting, and the final result for me is still an impersonal pride. I do not, of course, mean pride about myself: say by all means, if you will, that I should not support the test, but I am proud that others can support it. I do not even mean merely that I am proud of my country, though this is the proudest moment of her history. I am proud of being alive on two legs; I am proud of *genus homo* in the books of biology; I am proud of my fellow creatures, of whom so many hundreds of thousands have shown themselves able to support the test of war. There are people who talk, even now, of mutual understanding and peace; in practical psychology there is something much nearer to a mutual understanding in war. But the ground of our pride in man is precisely in all that such intellectuals

107. This free-thinker may be Bertrand Russell (1872–1970), a pacifist of sorts during WWI. He helped to found the No-Conscription Fellowship and the Union of Democratic Control. In lectures given in early 1915 and published as a book the next year, Russell expressed contempt for most people: "Besides the conscious and deliberate forces leading to war, there are the inarticulate feelings of common men, which, in most civilized countries, are always ready to burst into war fever at the bidding of statesmen." [Bertrand Russell, *Why Men Fight?* (New York: Garland, 1971), 91–92.] In a revealing passage reprinted here in Appendix E, Russell describes the sort of wars meeting with his approval—genocidal wars in which a superior race destroys an inferior one and takes over its land. Chesterton mentions Russell in an April 14, 1917 article (Ch. 5).

108. Russell illustrates why Chesterton wrote of an "aristocracy of intellectuals" who distrust what is popular, particularly commonly held beliefs about courage. For this self-appointed elite, courage does not mean "hundreds of thousands" showing themselves "able to support the test of war" in combat. It means a select few who defy public opinion, suffering minor harassments such as short prison sentences (or in Russell's case a fine of 100 pounds). Although their total suffering is less than an ordinary soldier experiences being marched to the front on a quiet day, they regard it as a mark of moral superiority. Chesterton explains two results of this moral arrogance. First, war itself has to be made pointless or evil, lest it give value to the courage of soldiers, as is illustrated by pacifist attacks on soldiers during the Vietnam and Iraqi wars. Second, they want chivalry removed from warfare, again because it attaches importance and even goodness to what soldiers do. Courtesy and restraint under fire can be as impressive as courage. In short, to justify pacifism every aspect of war must be demonized, particularly those demonstrating goodness, bravery and nobility.

regard as his retrogression and collapse. We are exalted because man's will is still untouched by the oldest instruments of torture; because all the engines of terrorism are brought against him in vain; because the question by fire and the question by burning iron are questions which he can still answer, or disdain to answer. He has still the wild sanity of the saints and martyrs; he has not too much horror of horrors. Logically, it may not seem impossible to reconcile this view with the fastidious view of the reluctant fighter; but spiritually there is a prodigious difference in proportion. It will be a matter of great import to future generations whether this mountain of dead is mainly a monument or merely an eyesore; and whether this one entry in our chronicles appears as a blazon or a blot.

But the distinction has a practical point also. It is the purpose of the article "On Chivalry in War" to suggest that courtesy and common rules in warfare were part of a sort of pageant of aristocracy; and that democracies must be expected to fight more brutally, for the very reason that they fight more reluctantly.[109] In experience, this seems totally untenable and untrue. The writer in the *Nation* will hardly maintain that the Prussians are more chivalrous in war than the French. He certainly will not maintain that the Prussians are more democratic in peace than the French. As a fact, some of the most beautiful instances of modern military courtesy occurred in a war in which both sides were citizens of the same great democracy. They occurred in the American Civil War; several of them redeemed the rather cynical politics of Grant, and give a glamour like that of Galahad to the greatness of Robert Lee.[110] But, in any case, the *Nation*'s doctrine is only tolerable upon some assumption of its own that wars will soon entirely disappear—unless the *Nation* prefers the supposition that democracies will entirely disappear.[111] Those who, like myself, doubt whether

109. *The Nation* had written: "For aristocracy, war is a form of sport. No one pretends to regret it or to apologize for it. It means glory, promotion, adventure, excitement. When two aristocracies fight, they will take care to observe the rules of the sport, for any failure to observe them would interfere with the pleasure of both.... In the eighteenth century no one required a reason for killing, and therefore it was still assumed that in spite of the declaration of war, the enemy remained a gentlemen. A democratic army does not want to leave its fireside and its fields, and it commonly loathes the thought of killing, that is why it must be taught to sing a hymn of hate. In the eighteenth century Swift and Voltaire were singular in thinking that war is fundamentally criminal. Today we all think so. If the enemy began a war, and committed an aggression in those days, a spirited aristocracy inclined to thank him for the opportunity. It no more blamed him or hated him than the hunter blamed the fox when he breaks cover." ["On Chivalry in War," *The Nation* xx:4 (October 28, 1916), 138–140.]

110. In the midst of battle, General Lee offered a cease-fire to Grant, so he could retrieve his wounded. At the war's end, General Grant allowed Lee's men to retain their horses and sidearms when they returned home. One reason for the latter may be because Grant knew that when Lee told his men to stop fighting they would do so.

111. *The Nation* and Chesterton saw war fundamentally differently. *The Nation* argued that aristocracies could enjoy wars as sport, while democracies, where the average citizen has more practical concerns than the pursuit of glory, can't enjoy wars and require a false "hymn of hate" be drummed up. Unable to see any reason for war other than the pursuit of honor and glory, *The Nation* believed that every war as so "fundamentally criminal," that it could only be justified by hate and lies. In the 1920s, that sort of anti-war propaganda succeeded. Many came to believe WWI had no justification and that claims of German atrocities were merely propaganda, leading to surprise when Germany, unrepentant and unchanged, behaved even more barbarously in WWII. Chesterton points out that wars can often be justified on reasonable grounds and that, when a war seems right to ordinary people, it can be fought, however bloodily, with civility. (His example is the American Civil War, which the North saw as necessary to restore the union and the South as required to defend a way of life that included slavery.) Chesterton is right when he points out that *The Nation* has set up a dangerous dichotomy. By its logic, we must choose either an aristocracy with chivalrous wars or democracy with ever worsening wars of hate. Assuming democracy isn't to be eliminated, the only way out is "that wars will soon entirely disappear." In his

war can ever be impossible unless liberty is impossible, will not easily accept the prospect of battle becoming more bestial every time it is renewed. They will think this view as dangerous as it is false; and count it a curious instance of how all intellectual perceptions, including that of peace, work out in practice to the wickedest of modern tasks—the whitewashing of Prussia.

G.K. Chesterton, "Our Note-Book," *Illustrated London News* 149 (November 11, 1916), 564. US: November 11, 1916. Also published as "Being Proud about This War."

War's Big Picture

December 16, 1916

To be elated when a village is captured in the morning, and cast down again in the afternoon—this is not to follow the course of a war. It is simply to be ignorant of the very nature of a war.

Editor: The year's end is often when people look back and judge their situation. At the end of 1916, after more than two years of costly war and with many people loosing heart. Chesterton encourages them to turn from "small things" to a larger picture of the war. His article is well-timed. On December 5 Herbert Asquith had resigned and two days later Lloyd George became Prime Minister. The war effort, most agreed, needed the latter's administrative skills.

1916

It is one of the paradoxes of man that a small thing seems so much larger than a large thing. We notice a sky-sign when we do not notice the sky; we realise a landmark when we scarcely realise the land; and we look up with awe at the whirling stars above us, without once becoming conscious of the whirling star on which we stand. A small thing is an object; and a large thing is merely a background. The truth has, of course, very deep roots, lying close to what religion has always said of the dependence and the ingratitude of man. It may not be tactful for the philosopher, meeting a man with a pebble in his shoe, to remind him that he is very lucky to have any legs. It may be incautious for the mystic, when the housewife complains of a cobweb on the ceiling, to tell her that the ceiling might fall on her any minute. But the philosopher and the mystic are quite right, for all that; and the truth of what they say is often disinterred in the earthquake of wartime, when limbs are really carried away by cannon-balls or roofs come rushing down under the shock of shells. In this, war is very like an earthquake, for an earthquake is a thing in which the largest thing we know begins to move, and to remind us for the first time of how long it has been lying still.

last two sentences, Chesterton mentions two ways to have a world without war: 1. By crushing all liberty, including the freedom to fight for one's beliefs and rights (H.G. Wells' World State). 2. On a more practical scale, by concealing from the public reasons that would justify a war (a reverse of those hymns of hate). For Chesterton, that meant the pacifist "whitewashing of Prussia" and its crimes. In a more recent context, it means concealing from the public the horrid crimes of Saddam Hussein in Iraq. So, in the end, the idea that all wars are "fundamentally criminal" is itself criminal because it must be based on either crushing liberty or spreading the most horrible of lies. The latter may explain why pacifists so often support bloody tyrants while they are in power and deny or minimize their crimes afterward. If war is always evil, then no one can be so evil that they require a war to defeat them. For this all-too-common sort of pacifism to be true to its dogma, there can be no good wars.

We have reached a particular point in the present war at which it is supremely necessary to stretch our minds, so as to take in the large things and not merely the small. **For it is not too much to say that the large things are going right and the small things are going wrong. Pessimism or even panic can be created by a simple trick of mental contraction.** It is an optical illusion which can see Roumania and cannot see Russia. It could see the capture of Kut, for the very reason that Kut was a small and isolated outpost, a little dot upon a large plain.[112] It has never grasped the gigantic haul of captures which Brussiloff made in Galicia, for the very reason that it ran into long figures—and with the imagination noughts go for nought.[113] To be told that among a multitude of adventures in aviation such-and-such a proportion of successes shows the English aviators to have the mastery of the German, leaves on the mind only a confused impression, as of a cloud of flies in the air. It cannot compare in conspicuousness and intensity with the excitement of watching one speck in the sky above London and knowing it is a Zeppelin, though the Zeppelin has most probably lost its way, wasted its bombs, and is wavering towards a flaming fall. In this sense it is not even the largeness of the Zeppelin that is impressive, but rather its smallness. It is compact and clear in shape; it is an object, and not a vista or a vast design. The same thing that makes it too small to carry any serious military force, too small to do any wide military damage, too small to attack an army or attempt an invasion—the same thing that makes it too small for these things gives it also the most final and effective advantage of smallness. It is too small to be ignored.[114]

Stretching our imagination to the scale of the war ought undoubtedly to sober us as against any merely vainglorious confidence or any merely negligent satisfaction. But quite as undoubtedly it ought to stiffen us as against the quite fantastic blue devils that have been dancing on a hundred wires during the last few weeks.[115] If there is no instant cause for exultation, there is even less cause for any kind of depression; and there seem to be many people who have no notion of the existence of anything normal between these two extremes. Anything seems sufficient to upset the seat of judgment; the seat of judgment has become a swing or a see-saw. Such an onlooker has often been satirised as an arm-chair critic; but I cannot see that he is any nearer to being on the spot by making his arm-chair a rocking-chair. **To be elated when a village is captured in the morning, and cast down again in the afternoon—this**

112. The Siege of Kut-al-Amara (in today's Iraq) and its fall to Ottoman forces on April 29, 1916 was one of the most humiliating moments in British military history. Britain and its allies suffered some 23,000 casualties defending a small town on the Tigris river that Chesterton aptly calls "a little dot." The British recaptured the town in the Second Battle of Kut (February 23, 1917) as a small part of a much larger campaign.

113. General Alexis A. Brusilov led a large Russian army into Galicia in the summer of 1916. Using an aggressive swarm attack, he overcame superior German weapons, capturing some 330,000 Austrians and Germans.

114. Chesterton discussed Zeppelins in more detail in his March 18, 1916 article (Ch. 4).

115. Chesterton may be alluding to a famous French unit, the *Chasseurs Alpins*, who were nicknamed "*les Diables Bleus*" or "Blue Devils." In 1915, many had hoped their mountain fighting skills would break the stalemate of trench warfare. That "elation" led only to being "cast down again," and the fighting continued. When some of them came to the U.S to promote war bonds, Irving Berlin put them in a song: "I've seen many diff'rent pictures/ Of the devil down below/ And he doesn't stand a show/ With a certain devil I know/ Let me introduce you to him/ You'll be happy when I do/ He's a devil dressed in blue/ And a soldier through and through."

is not to follow the course of a war. It is simply to be ignorant of the very nature of a war. A certain amount of this levity of lamentation, for instance, is unconsciousness of the striking scientific fact that winter comes after summer. This is surely a somewhat dangerous and unworthy way of being affected by the weather. There is only one way of correcting anything so chaotic as this blend of temperament and temperature. It is to look at the large facts, the largest facts that we can find. It is to look beyond the landmarks, which may deceive and alter, and see the landscape which will endure.

Now, the large fact is that the large designs of Germany have not only failed but ceased; and that her comparatively small designs are having a certain success. She first made a large effort upon the West; she was pinned upon the West, and she is now increasingly pressed upon the West. She has since made one last effort to reverse this situation in the Verdun sector; and (to put the matter at its very mildest) she is immeasurably worse off than if she had never made it at all.[116] She made her other large effort in the East, having good hopes of breaking altogether an army beggared of munitions.[117] She was so far from succeeding that the beggared army was able to return re-armed, and not only to roll back but to capture unexpectedly enormous fragments of her armies. After these two large efforts to the West and East she has made no similarly large efforts at all; but she pursued the retreating Serbians, and she is now pursuing the retreating Roumanians. All these are very stale facts; but they are still overwhelmingly the most important facts. We may tire of them, as we may tire of a landscape; but we need not relieve our feelings by falsely asserting that the landscape is a landslide. The truth is, I take it, that it is not a doubt about beating the enemy, but a disappointment because he will take a little longer to beat. This is human enough, heaven knows, considering the incessance of the sacrifice. For that matter, it is very human to wave a white flag or to run away. But people are not called strenuous patriots because they encourage that part of their humanity. A man is not supposed to be saving the Empire when he waves a white rag; but apparently he is when he waves a printed rag. He is not complimented for "realising the seriousness of the war" when he lets his legs run away with him. But apparently he is when he lets his words and his feelings run away with him. Yet it is surely far less pardonable in us, who see so little of the horror, that we should so easily get the horrors. If a man can conquer his twitches when he has to wait in a trench and fix a bayonet, he might surely conquer them when he has only to wait in a club and read a newspaper. No; if our feeling is simply disappointment, we should sharply tell ourselves that such disappointment is very disappointing. When we went to war with the evil so deeply entrenched in Central Europe, we ought to have discounted a hundred delays and

116. The Battle of Verdun (February 21–December 19, 1916) was the longest and the second bloodiest battle of WWI. Because the city held great symbolic and strategic importance to the French, the Germans hoped their attack would draw France into a brutal war of attrition under circumstances favoring the Germans. That failed, and the French, by rotating some 70% of their army into and out of the front, maintained their will to fight.

117. In 1916, Germany came to the assistance of Austria in the east and Bucharest fell on December 6, 1916. On the Eastern Front the struggle was between Russia, who had a huge but ill-equipped army, and the better equipped but smaller forces of Germany and Austria.

expected a hundred disappointments. **When we sent men to be blown about by deathly explosives, we ought at least to have been secure against being blown about by every wind of doctrine; we ought to have known that the sign in which we conquer is the cross and not the weathercock.**

A nurse who had done noble and obscure service in a wild district at the beginning of the war recounted how for weeks and months together she and her little colony were cut off from any news whatever. She said that after a certain number of days they were all gripped with an unmeaning conviction of calamity; and went about their work as if the final defeat of the Allies had been publicly announced in the hospital. Still no news came of any kind; and some days later they were all glowing with an equally mysterious faith, hope, and security about the fate of the world. There was no external cause for their hopelessness; and there was no external cause for their hope. Whether it was a mood or a more mystical sort of trial, the whole transformation scene took place within the walls of their hospital, and even within the walls of their brains. If a state of consciousness were a thing subject to analysis or resolution into its parts, it would be interesting to discover how much of the hilarity or the rather hysterical depression of our cities would still take place if no war news were to reach them at all. **Certainly their psychological condition often seems to have little or nothing to do with the war news that does reach them. And even when that news is whipped up into a froth by journalistic fallacies, even when a panic is deliberately spread, the mystery may still attach to those who spread it, and may vary with the society in which it spreads.** I only recall one fact; whether by an accident or a more divine irony, the days when the little hospital was at its lowest deeps of melancholia were most probably the days in which Manoury wheeled round the western end of the battle-line along the Marne, and Foch rode in triumph through the battle-breach of the Prussian Guard.[118]

G.K. Chesterton, "Our Note-Book," *Illustrated London News* 149 (December 16, 1916), 724.
US: December 16, 1916. Also published as "Seeing the Large Picture."

1916

118. The First Battle of the Marne (September 5–12, 1914) kept Germany from winning a quick victory. On September 6, the troops of French General Michel-Joseph Maunoury (1847–1923) were rushed (some in Parisian taxi cabs) into position to attack the western flank of German General Alexander von Kluck's First Army, thereby saving Paris. During that same period French General Ferdinand Foch (1851–1929) halted the French retreat by ordering his men to attack and uttering words that made him famous: "I am hard pressed on my right; my centre is giving way; situation excellent; I am attacking." Unfortunately those same aggressive tactics, referred to as *élan* in then-fashionable French military theory, worked poorly once the war settled down to unending trench warfare, where all the advantages lay with the defender.

Half a century earlier, during the U.S. Civil War, advances in weapons, particularly artillery and repeating rifles, created the potential for a WWI-like situation to develop. But the borders between North and South were too long in relation to the population for a continuous line of trenches to develop, and the generals on both sides preferred to fight wars of maneuver. Two armies would meet for a climatic battle that would determine who would control a region. Knowing how much fire power the defenders could concentrate at one location, the generals also did their best to outflank their opponents, winning by skill rather than *élan*. Pickett's Charge, on the third day of the Battle of Gettysburg (July 3, 1864), was an exception. As in WWI, that engagement began with an extended artillery barrage followed by over 12,000 Confederate soldiers marching across an open field at the center of the entrenched Union lines. Their casualty rate of over 50 percent warned of what future wars would be like as long as defense retained such an enormous advantage over offense.

5

Battling Teutonism

1917

Henry Cabot Lodge—Editor

Seven of the fifteen articles from 1917 published here deal with some aspect of the Teutonism that Chesterton will call in his April 21 article the "German heresy."[1] In his 1905 classic, *Heretics*, Chesterton explained why understanding a person's basic beliefs was so important and what it meant to be a heretic.

> But there are some people, nevertheless—and I am one of them—who think that the most practical and important thing about a man is still his view of the universe. We think that for a landlady considering a lodger, it is important to know his income, but still more important to know his philosophy. We think that for a general about to fight an enemy, it is important to know the enemy's numbers, but still more important to know the enemy's philosophy. We think the question is not whether the theory of the cosmos affects matters, but whether, in the long run, anything else affects them....
>
> For these reasons, and for many more, I for one have come to believe in going back to fundamentals. Such is the general idea of this book. I wish to deal with my most distinguished contemporaries, not personally or in a merely literary manner, but in relation to the real body of doctrine which they teach. I am not concerned with Mr. Rudyard Kipling as a vivid artist or a vigorous personality; I am concerned with him as a Heretic—that is to say, a man whose view of things has the hardihood to differ from mine. I am not concerned with Mr. Bernard Shaw as one of the most brilliant and one of the most honest men alive; I am concerned with him as a Heretic—that is to say, a man whose philosophy is quite solid, quite coherent, and quite wrong.[2]

Chesterton knew that focusing on beliefs and branding some as heresies was going against spirit of his day. In the first sentence of *Heretics*, he calls this the "enormous and silent evil of modern society." Even some historians have succumbed to that "silent evil" and failed to recognize the importance of a nation's core beliefs, focusing on superficialities such as the prewar competition between Britain and Germany in building battleships. The unpleasant things Chesterton and others said about Germans *during* the war were regarded by many *after* the war (particularly pacifists) as mere wartime fanaticism, and not as an indication that Germany was in some fundamental way flawed. Those people were proved wrong—tragically wrong. When Hitler wanted to draw poison from the German soul, he had deep wells from which to draw.

1. These are the articles for April 21, July 14, September 29, October 20 & 27, November 10 and December 15.
2. Gilbert K. Chesterton, *Heretics* (New York: John Lane Co., 1905), 15–16, 22.

Because heresies are ideas, they can cross borders and infect other nations. Chesterton did not deny that Britain had been influenced by the German heresy. In 1915, he published a book, *The Crimes of England*, detailing those influences. In what follows, we show that those same heresies crossed the Atlantic, affecting one of the best-educated and most distinguished American statesman of the era. My purpose is not to brand him an evil proto-Nazi. He was not. It is to demonstrate that Chesterton was right. By the end of the nineteenth century, a particular heresy, the belief in the cultural superiority of the Germanic race, had spread widely.

On March 16, 1896, Senator Henry Cabot Lodge (1850–1924) spoke to the U.S. Senate in support of restrictive immigration laws then being promoted by his fellow Bostonian blue-bloods in the Immigration Restriction League.[3] He wanted to limit immigration from Eastern and Southern Europe, while doing nothing to hinder those coming from North and Western Europe, particularly the "English-speaking people, the French or the Germans." His reasoning meshes with near perfection to Chesterton's own description of what he saw happening in England as he grew up in the 1880s and 1890s.[4] Lodge even brought the very person Chesterton blamed for spreading those ideas—Thomas Carlyle—into his argument. Keep in mind that Lodge was exceptionally well-educated, having earned the first doctorate Harvard ever granted in political science. What Lodge believed was what many well-educated Englishmen and Americans of his day believed.[5]

Lodge's argument was also a classic illustration of applied Darwinism. To the three major racial divisions of mankind, the senator added what he called the more recent "artificial races... who have been developed as races by the operation during a long period of time of climatic changes, wars, migrations, conquests, and industrial development." "To the scientific modern historian," he claimed, those "sharply marked race divisions which have been gradually developed by the conditions and events of the last thousand years are absolutely vital." What he was talking about is what Chesterton often calls Teutonism, what others have referred to as Aryanism, and what Lodge described it as the spreading influence of "North Germanic tribes."

And yes, this is an early stage in the same madness about racial supremacy that would culminate in the horrors of Nazism, the idea that a superior race, perhaps led by Carlyle's Strong Man (not that different from the Fuhrer Principle), has the right to

3. In the September 7, 1918 issue of *Illustrated London News* Chesterton would commend a recent speech by Lodge (Ch. 6). For the broad historical background to Lodge's remarks, see John Higham's *Strangers in the Land*.

4. See Chesterton's December 15, 1917 article, where he writes: "I can myself remember it rising steadily, like a new religion, in the late Victorian time."

5. In the Foreword to a 1936 booklet about Alfred Rosenberg, chief Nazi theorist, Charles Beard, one of the most respected of American historians, gave a short history of Teutonism.

> Belief in the superiority of the Teutonic race and its mission to civilise the backward races of the earth is not new. Nor has it been confined to Germany. Its origins are old. The creed was first formulated systematically during the struggle of the German states to emancipate themselves from the Napoleonic yoke. In England it was taken up by Kemble, Green, Stubbs, Freeman and Kingsley and made the basis of great historical interpretations. It was carried to the heights of ecstasy by Kipling and Rhodes in the flaming doctrines of British imperialism. In the United States it was sedulously propagated by John Fiske, John W. Burgess, and Madison Grant in the guise of history and science. Although it smelled of the scholar's lamp, it was carried into American naval and foreign policy by Alfred Thayer Mahan, Theodore Roosevelt, and Henry Cabot Lodge, in that "new" age when "America had grown up" and assumed a place as "a world power" in the imperialistic competitions of the earth. Now this creed appears again in all its stark, crude, brutal ignorance in the writings of the German Nazis, especially the work of Alfred Rosenberg. [Charles A. Beard, "Foreword," Alfred Rosenberg, *Mythus I. The Worship of Race* (London: Friends of Europe, 1936), 3. See also Fritz Nova's *Alfred Rosenberg*.]

conquer and rule over other races. Like later Nazis ideologues, Lodge faced a problem. Historically, these North Germanic tribes were not impressive. Other than to note their suicidal fierceness in battle, the Romans had little good to say about them. To justify his belief in their racial superiority, Lodge must engage in historical sleigh-of-hand. He must redirect those Roman comments onto the Celts, abandoning the home-defending Celtic good guys of traditional English history,[6] and making the Saxon invaders into the good guys. We turn back Lodge's 1896 Senate speech.

> How, then, has the English-speaking race, which to-day controls so large a part of the earth's surface, been formed? Great Britain and Ireland at the time of the Roman conquest were populated by Celtic tribes. After the downfall of the Roman Empire these tribes remained in possession of the islands with probably but a slight infusion of Latin blood. Then came what is commonly known as the Saxon invasion. Certain North German tribes, own brothers to those other tribes which swept southward and westward over the whole Roman Empire, crossed the English Channel and landed in the corner of England known as the Isle of Thanet.[7] They swept over the whole of England and the Lowlands of Scotland and to the edge of the seat in Cornwall and Wales, while all the rest of the land became Saxon.
>
> The conquerors established themselves in their new country, were converted to Christianity, and began to advance in civilization. Then came a fresh wave from the Germanic tribes. This time it was the Danes. They were of the same blood as the Saxons, and the two kindred races fought hard for the possession of England until the last comers prevailed and their chiefs reached the throne. Then in 1066 there was another invasion, this time from the shores of France. But the new invaders and conquerors were not Frenchmen. As Carlyle says, they were only Saxons who spoke French. A hundred years before these Normans, or Northmen, northmost of all the Germanic tribes, had descended from their land of snow and ice upon Europe. They were the most remarkable of all the people who poured out of the Germanic forests. They came upon Europe in their long, low ships, a set of fighting pirates and buccaneers, and yet these same pirates brought with them out of the darkness and cold of the north a remarkable literature and a strange and poetic mythology. Wherever they went they conquered, and wherever they stopped they set up for themselves dukedoms, principalities and kingdoms. to them we own the marvels of Gothic architecture, for it was they who were the great builders and architects of mediaeval Europe. They were the great military engineers as well and revived the art of fortified defense, which had been lost to the world. They were great statesmen and great generals, and they had only been in Normandy about a hundred years when they crossed the English Channel, conquered the country, and gave to England for many generations to come her kings and nobles. But the Normans in their turn were absorbed or blended with the great mass of the Danes and the still earlier Saxons. In reality they were all one people. They had different names and spoke differing dialects, but their blood and their characteristics were the same. And so this Germanic people of one blood, coming through various channels, dwelt in England, assimilating more or less and absorbing to a greater or lesser extent their neighbors of the northern and western Celtic fringe, with an occasional fresh infu-

6. Chesterton's "The Ballad of the White Horse" gives the traditional view of King Alfred and English history.

7. No longer an island, the Isle of Thanet is a part of Kent in SE England. In Roman times, it was separated from the mainline by a now-silted-up channel up to a mile wide in places. Historically, it has been a way point for invaders, including the Romans in 55 BC, the Jutes in 449 AD, and Viking raiders in the ninth century.

sion from their own brethren who dwelt in the low sea-girth lands at the mouths of the Scheldt and Rhine. In the course of the centuries these people were welded together and had made a new speech and a new race, with strong and well-defined qualities, both mental and moral.[8]

Notice the importance Senator Lodge attached to tenuous racial links—groups that have little more in common than coming in centuries past from the same region, coupled with what seems to be a perverse enjoyment in conquering other people. Note too the strong sense of superiority he attaches to being Germanic. To justify his German-tilted history, Lodge turns to "brilliant sentences" from the very person Chesterton fingers as the source of Britain's infatuation with Germanic tribes: "one of the greatest of modern English writers"—Thomas Carlyle in his 1839 pamphlet, *Chartism*. No doubt aware of the Roman slander of German tribes, Carlyle claims that, "Hardly an Englishman to be met with but could do something—some cunning thing than break his fellow-creature's head with battle-axes."

As the waves of Germanic invasions ended, he said, "the making of the English peoples was complete." But the spread of now English-speaking Germanic tribes did not stop there. Having conquered England, they then entered "upon their career of world conquest." Central to Lodge's argument for restrictive immigration was a claim that the next Germanic wave had crossed "the great ocean to the North American continent," leading to yet another quote from Carlyle, who gushed with enthusiasm about this new "transatlantic Saxon nation." Excepting the Celtic Irish, who were partly redeemed by having "to some extent intermarried" with their Germanic betters, almost all the immigration to the United States up to that day, at least in Lodge's eyes, came from the same "kindred or allied races." It was because that immigration had waned, that he wanted to keep out "other races of totally different race origin." The migration here, he said, raised, he said, "the possibility of a great and perilous change in the very fabric of our race." He went on to claim that, "If a lower race mixes with a higher in sufficient numbers, history teaches us that lower race will prevail."

In short, the madness about racial supremacy and wars of conquest in which a superior race must conquer and do away with lower races did not begin with Hitler in dimly lit Bavarian beer halls. It was a once respectable ideology with roots that predated Charles Darwin but were strongly reinforced by the scientific aura that surrounded Darwinian thinking. That was Chesterton's German heresy in a nutshell.

Milk and Water Pacifism

January 27, 1917

The note of interrogation is more dangerous than any dogmatic Pacifism or decisive treason, because it is closer to humanity, and yet none the less close to hell.

Editor: Chesterton blasts those who would end the war without the "superlative victory" needed to cleanse "European ethics and politics," simply because that task

8. Lodge's speech is in the *Congressional Record* for March 16, 1896, vol. xxviii, p. 2817–2820. Note the similarity with what Chesterton wrote about these tall tales in the *Illustrated London News* on September 21, 1918 (Ch. 6): "It is their whole case that the ancient world, or the Dark Ages, were periodically refreshed and reformed solely by such barbaric invasions. Such tribal aggressions are to a Teutonist what Crusades were to a mediaeval Christian, or proletarian revolutions to a modern Bolshevik; they are aggressions to the advantage of the world."

would be long, costly, and difficult. He also demonstrates a good understanding of the realities of trench warfare. Deep penetrations were so difficult that a defeat at Verdun would have meant little more than that "the French line would afterwards have run a little way behind the clump of dilapidated houses instead of a little way in front."

It has long been self-evident that the stormy petrels of Pessimism have come home to roost and to feather the nests of Pacifism. Every bit of bad news which the "ginger" school professed to produce in order to arouse us to fighting has now been annexed by the milk-and-water school as a reason for fighting no longer.[9] **Perhaps the strangest fact in this strange war has been the fact that the extreme jingo journalist and the extreme Quaker journalist have told much the same tale—a tale in both cases equally false in fact, and equally contrary to the common spirit and resolution of the English people.** It is probable, indeed, that from Prussia and other distant places the two manifestations seem to be simply identical; and that in a world vivid with colours so much stronger, red with blood or black with mourning, many could not even see the shade of difference between the yellow flag of sensationalism and the white flag of surrender.

The consequence has been the creation of a curious and clumsy fable, which is now far more of a practical obstacle than any fact. There is a vague and very general impression that our experience in the war has been one of unrelieved though not final disaster; whereas in truth it has been one of strictly logical though not rapid success. The Battle of Jutland might well stand as a parable and working model of the Great War.[10] It is something like a new thing in history that a nation should win a victory and then mourn for a defeat. But it is no less comic and no less tragic that even the defeated Prussian should be able to brag and bargain on the basis of a prestige which we have created for him. The whole effect has been produced by idle and irresponsible talking, both of the pacifist and the pessimist sort. And the whole is enough to make one wish that war, like whist, were a game which good manners decreed to be played in silence.

Evidence of the weakness I mean is scattered everywhere through the Press in a way difficult to arrest and define. Here, however, is a phrase I find in the *Nation*, an organ of opinion seemingly open to the approaches of a compromise-peace—

> Yet, in facing this problem, the enemy can, at any rate for the moment, count on a nation ready for the greatest sacrifices. In the main, all military operations come to be a question of price. If troops can be persuaded to risk themselves in sufficient numbers, no position has yet been revealed by this war which cannot be taken. Ver-

9. "Ginger" refers to a spicy, fighting spirit seen in excess in a Jingoist. "Milk and water" in the *Oxford English Dictionary* means: "Consisting of or like milk diluted with water. Hence: insipid, feeble, wishy-washy, mawkish, weakly amiable; (of a person) lacking the will or ability to act effectively." The latter is no small insult.

10. The Battle of Jutland, the largest naval battle of WWI, was fought off the coast of Denmark on May 31–June 1, 1916. It was a tactical defeat for the British navy, because their losses were greater, but it was a strategic victory for Britain, because never again did the German navy mount a major challenge to the British navy. Instead, early in 1917 they returned to unrestricted submarine warfare, soon drawing the U.S. into the war.

dun without the relief of the Somme would have scarcely outlasted a month.[11] And, if Verdun could not hold any longer with all that instinctive and trained fighting skill of the French, how can we imagine any position which is beyond capture if Germany will pay the price? She is not faced with a Verdun. Her present plan is to turn the entrenched positions which have been held against her so long.

It is not necessary to have any special military knowledge in order to see that this passage swarms with military fallacies. What is "a Verdun"? And what is it to be faced with one? A Verdun is a débris of empty houses covering one very small space in the North of France—a ruin which only a very stupid German can have been trying to attack, and certainly no intelligent Frenchman especially trying to defend. Yet the writer talks of a Verdun as if it were some new and enormous and irresistible engine of war. And what precisely is meant by saying that this thing called Verdun would not have outlasted a month?[12] Does it mean that the Germans would really have succeeded in breaking and rolling up the French line in the sector of Verdun? Or does it mean that the French line would afterwards have run a little way behind the clump of dilapidated houses instead of a little way in front of it? The former seems, to say the least of it, highly improbable; and the latter, to say the least of it, not very terrible. The truth is that no war can be a war of positions in the sense in which the word seems to be used here. Campaigns are determined, not by the positive position of towns, but by the relative positions of armies. This, as I have said, is a truth manifest to the very minimum of military information; and this involves another and yet plainer application in the present case. If it be true, as the writer suggests, that any position can be taken by a sufficient sacrifice of men, it must plainly be true that the advantage lies with those who have sufficient men to sacrifice. Expenditure is a matter of reserves; and even the Allies in the East, if they suffer in reserves of ammunition, are vastly superior in reserves of men. In the West they are apparently superior in both. If, therefore, sacrifice can take any positions,

11. The British launched the Battle of the Somme (July 1–November 18, 1916), in part, to relieve pressure on the French fighting the Battle of Verdun (February 21–December 19, 1916). That proved a tragic mistake, because the Somme, with over a million casualties, became one of the bloodiest battles in human history, On the first day of fighting, almost 20,000 British troops died. *The Battle of the Somme,* a British propaganda film with footage shot during the battle, exposed the public for the first time to the horrors of trench warfare. Modern military historians take a point of view similar to that Chesterton paints here. Although the British and Commonwealth losses were roughly 100,000 greater, Germany lost well-trained, seasoned soldiers, while the fighting, as terrible as it was, transformed Britain's raw recruits (88 of 158 British battalions had never been in combat before) into experienced soldiers. The British, backed by the Commonwealth, had more men to put into uniform. Of course, if the British generals had been more capable, they might have achieved the same results with fewer losses. For a detailed account of the battle, see Martin Gilbert's *The Somme: Heroism and Horror in the First World War.* (He discusses the decision to aid the French on page 34.) When the battle began, the British fired 250,000 shells in just over an hour. The sound was so loud, it was heard in north London, nearly 200 miles away.

12. Chesterton is right. The *Nation* was clueless. The French at Verdun not only could hold out for longer than a month, they did. Verdun began on February 21, 1916, while the British offensive at Somme was not launched until July 1, over four months later. The major lesson of trench warfare wasn't that any position could be captured if one side was willing to "pay the price," but that, as Chesterton notes, even the mostly costly offensive barely altered the battle lines, determining only who was in possession of a "clump of dilapidated houses." Machine guns and artillery had made defense far more powerful than offense, making in-depth penetration almost impossible, and rail lines parallel to the front made it possible to quickly transfer fresh troops to halt a breakthrough. In WWII, tanks and aircraft would shift the balance of power to the offense—the infamous German *Blitzkrieg.*

we can certainly take the German positions. That seems the only deduction possible from the writer's doctrine. But it seems to have been the very opposite deduction from the one he wished to draw, so he is obliged to end somewhat lamely by saying: "Germany has made almost incredible sacrifices, and is prepared for far more. Are the Allies prepared to go so far for that superlative victory which alone appeals to certain minds?"

As being myself one of the obscure and unprepossessing minds referred to, I would venture very modestly to answer him. May I ask whether we also have not already made sacrifices, and by what right he supposes that we also are not prepared for more? I can hardly suppose him to suggest that dying for one's country is a discovery exclusively made in Germany. His argument, however, certainly means, if it means anything, that we may grow tired of such tragic effort before the German does. Why this should be so I cannot conceive; but, if it were so, I should count it the most horrible of all possible endings for the war. To abandon our effort because it was vindictive and aggressive, as the Germans say it is, would be one thing. To abandon it because all war is barbaric and sinful, as the Pacifists say it is, would be another and equally logical thing. But to abandon it because we cannot find as much energy for the right as they can find for the wrong would be at once a blasphemy and a bathos. If "a superlative victory" be spiritually essential to the cleansing of European ethics and politics (as "some minds" continue to think, including the mind engaged in spoiling this piece of paper), then surely to fail at the last moment from sheer boredom or loss of nerve is a conclusion not only bankrupt of any national but of any humanitarian meaning. **It is an insult to the abstract dignity of virtue that its enemy should be left to develop all the virtues in defence of his vices. It is a sin against the very soul of things that he should be left to love what is hateful more than better men can love what is lovable.** Fortunately, as a fact, all this nightmare amounts to no more than a piece of verbal inconsequence. There is not and never has been one rag of reason for doubting that civilisation is capable of as much self-sacrifice as savagery; and, for whatever other cause our "superlative" victory may fail, it will not fail for lack of superlative lives and deaths.

I have taken this one instance of a current observation, almost certainly harmless enough in intention, but unconsciously corrupted by a bad tradition of unreality and rumour. Such passages have no purpose except to insinuate a chill of doubt—a chill which the writer himself has caught he knows not where. They will generally be found to end with a note of interrogation. It does not say "We cannot win," but "Can we win?" **The note of interrogation is more dangerous than any dogmatic Pacifism or decisive treason, because it is closer to humanity, and yet none the less close to hell.** For it was in this fashion of false inquiry that human nature itself was betrayed; and I could fancy that men drew the Tempter with the curves of a serpent because they can be twisted into the shape of a question mark.

G.K. Chesterton, "Our Note-Book," *Illustrated London News* 150 (January 27, 1917), 96.
US: January 27, 1917. Also published as "The Dangers of a Doubting Pacifism."

Peace Without Victory

February 3, 1917

If he can see no difference between the attacker and the attacked in the present case, why should he see any difference in any possible future case?

Editor: Chesterton ridicules the reasoning behind Woodrow Wilson's belief that World War I should end with neither side being victorious. He moderates his opinion of Wilson in an April 14, 1917 article written after the U.S. enters the war.

I cannot make out what it was that happened to President Wilson. I rather think he has been murdered. I would suggest, in the Stevenson style, that his corpse has been concealed in a Saratoga trunk and carried off on a Ford car—only that, by the current American opinion, it would be easier to carry off a Ford car in a Saratoga trunk.[13] Or perhaps he was kidnapped alive, and the Ford car took him to the Ford Peace Ship, which marooned him on a desert island to meditate on the freedom of the seas.[14] Anyhow, I believe he is gone, and that an entirely new and entirely fatuous young German, impenetrably disguised behind the President's eye-glasses, sits in his seat at the White House and sends messages to the Senate and to the world. I have never joined in the cheap journalistic jeering at Mr. Wilson for not taking particular forms of action; but, whatever his actions might be, there used always to be a certain detached intellectual distinction about his ideas. In his last message to the Senate it was his ideas that seemed suddenly to have stopped working.[15] Really, if he has not been murdered, one might almost fancy that he has had a knock on the head.

1917

For instance, what can be said of his idea, generally considered as an idea, of peace without victory? **Peace without victory is war without excuse.** And, if he believes in the idea, would he apply the idea to the quarrels after the peace as well as to the quarrels before it? He wishes to establish a league of peace to prevent wars; obviously it could only prevent them by waging war, or threatening to wage war, with any Power that broke the peace. Then he says it can only be founded on

13. In Robert Lewis Stevenson's "The Story of the Physician and the Saratoga Trunk" (1878), the large Saratoga trunk's popularity with Americans and its ability to conceal a body is part of the plot: "Since I came into your room," said he, "although my ears and my tongue have been so busy, I have not suffered my eyes to remain idle. I noted a little while ago that you have there, in the corner, one of those monstrous constructions which your fellow-countrymen carry with them into all quarters of the globe—in a word, a Saratoga trunk. Until this moment I have never been able to conceive the utility of these erections; but then I began to have a glimmer. Whether it was for convenience in the slave trade, or to obviate the results of too ready an employment of the bowie-knife, I cannot bring myself to decide. But one thing I see plainly—the object of such a box is to contain a human body."

14. Woodrow Wilson had just won a narrow election on a platform of "He Kept Us Out of the War," but Germany's return to unrestricted submarine warfare was pushing him toward war. "Freedom of the seas" was a conflict between the U.S. and Britain over the British blockade. The U.S., a major food exporting nation, wanted to profit from shipping food to both sides in time of war. With the world's most powerful navy, the British wanted to blockade its enemies any time it chose, including the shipment of food. For Chesterton's view of Henry Ford's attempts to end the war, see *Illustrated London News*, December 11, 1915 (Ch. 3).

15. On January 22, 1917, Wilson spoke to the Senate: "It must be a peace without victory.... Victory would mean peace forced upon the loser, a victor's terms imposed upon the vanquished. It would be accepted in humiliation, under duress, at an intolerable sacrifice, and would leave a sting, a resentment, a bitter memory upon which terms of peace would rest, not permanently, but only as upon quicksand. Only a peace between equals can last."

an inconclusive settlement of this war, because any other would leave bitterness. But does he intend all its future interventions to be inconclusive? And if they were conclusive, would they not leave bitterness? If an ambitious Power dislikes being beaten by an enemy, would it not also dislike being bullied by a peace league? Are we to act on the principle that every future outrage is to be followed by amnesty and equality, and letting bygones be bygones? If we do not, why should we do it for this particular outrage, which we happen to think particularly outrageous? If we do, is there any sane man who will pretend that such perpetual flattening out of everything, fair and unfair, will not leave bitterness? Will men endure a court of justice which never does anything except tell all the advocates to throw up their briefs? Will they be content with an international magistrate who has no function whatever except to write off debts, to let off malefactors, and to give certificates of bankruptcy to the most fraudulent bankrupts? Is it not obvious that such amnesty would soon become the worst tyranny in the world?

If Mr. Wilson is so much interested in the avoidance of bitterness, there is one very ancient and simple truth that should be brought to his notice, as the chief magistrate of a great commonwealth. There is no bitterness in the heart of man like the bitterness that follows the denial of right. There is not so deep a fury in the thief when he is punished as there is in the innocent man when he is let out on the ticket-of-leave of a thief. That, and that alone, is the precise moral position to which the President's scheme invites us. We are to be freely forgiven for the crime that somebody else has committed—and committed against us. The world is told to bear no malice against us for having been swindled and stabbed, but to regard us with the same equal and serene clemency which is given to the stabbers and swindlers. Belgium must not be harshly criticised for having been harshly treated; she also may share the renewed peace and hope of those who plunged her in slaughter and despair when the fancy took them. France may have a decent veil drawn over the fact that she presumed to defend her frontiers, and even to impede the occupation of her northern provinces. She was even so impetuous as to win a victory over the invaders at the Marne; but the story can, perhaps, be hushed up. Serbia starts afresh with a clean sheet; her enemies are not to throw it in her teeth that they sent her an ultimatum which was the disgrace and the derision of all diplomacy; they are not to reproach her with the fact that she asked for arbitration in vain. The quality of mercy is not strained; it overflows to the relations of Captain Fryatt[16] or the friends of Miss Cavell[17]—a wise moderation will hold them all blameless. They shall be as respectfully treated as the proudest Prussian officer who toasted a prisoner in champagne and then shot him dead, or the most fastidious Prussian doctor who smiled from a safe distance at

16. Charles A. Fryatt was the captain of the *Brussels*, a ship carrying passengers between neutral Rotterdam and England. Twice in March 1915 German U-boats tried to sink his ship, The second time, as the U-boat was lining up to fire a torpedo, he turned and tried to ram it, becoming a national hero. In June 1916. his ship was surrounded by patrol boats, and he was captured, tried and executed over British protests on July 27. Germany claimed that, since he was not in the military, he had no right to attack their submarine, even in self-defense.

17. Edith Cavell was an English nurse who was executed by the Germans on October 12, 1915 for helping British and Belgian soldiers escape. For more details, see the October 30, 1915 *Illustrated London News* (Ch. 3).

the despair of the sick and the deserted. Does it strike Mr. Wilson as barely possible, in the complexities of human nature, that *this* sort of equality of treatment may also produce bitterness? I think we can promise him that it will not stop at bitterness. If any attempt were really made to cover the black-and-white of this human story with such leprous whitewash, those who attempted it would find out a number of fundamental things of which they are apparently ignorant. One of the minor facts would be the fact that an honest man can be much more angry than a knave.

There is some very vile nonsense talked nowadays about this sentiment being merely "vindictive." It is not vindictive, if vindictiveness means merely the desire to hurt somebody who has hurt us. It is an abstract, virgin, and wholly virtuous intolerance of a tale ending wrong. It is the refusal of the intellect to accept the prospect of everything being for ever upside down.

A peace without victory is a violation of that very practical thing which is called poetical justice. Victory is the only meaning of war. It is to war what the light is to a lighthouse, or what the brain is to a man. Men will not toil for a century to build a lighthouse a mile high, and then put no lamp in it and say it will do no harm. A woman will not travail to bear a man child, and then dash his brains out because the body will lie more quiet. Nor will the tribes of men labour to lift to the stars this Babel-Tower of battle, and then put in it no lamp of reason to make a sign to the sea traffic and to mark a difference on the chart. Nor will the earth endure these gigantic birth-pangs to bring forth a dead thing. **Peace without victory is a dead thing; it is only level as the grave is level; it is only equal as we are all equal in the dust.** It is not even like the peace before the beginning of the war, but more like the peace before the beginning of the world and of all living things. Its impartiality is like the impartiality of an ice-age, in which there is no complaint—not because anything is freed, but because everything is frozen. So it would be, at least, if it could exist and endure; but it will not exist, because men's minds have been too awfully awakened; and it would not endure because men would not endure it. There is something in it that is worse than hopelessness; it is not that there is no hope in it, but rather that there is no sense in it.

What would really happen, of course, is exceedingly simple. At the first chance Prussia, at the head of all her slaves, would return to the charge. There is no conceivable reason for supposing that any compromise could cure her of so fixed an idea. It would be impossible then to prove to her that she could not. It would be certainly quite impossible to prove to her victims that she would not. We should all pass our last days in desperate and incessant armament, in desperate and incessant discipline. And if it be said that this would be prevented by the guarantee of a peace league, then we come back to President Wilson and the weakness of his whole position. **If he can see no difference between the attacker and the attacked in the present case, why should he see any difference in any possible future case? To say that a peace league must be founded on an equal treatment is simply to say that a court of**

arbitration must be founded on its own incapacity to arbitrate. It is very simple; and there is no answer to it.

G.K. Chesterton, "Our Note-Book," *Illustrated London News* 150 (February 3, 1917), 126. US: February 3, 1917. Also published as "The Weakness of Mr. Wilson's Ideas."

America Enters the War

April 14, 1917

Anybody who ever supposed that Americans as such were "too proud to fight," in the ironical sense of being too timid to fight, was a fool whose impudence was simply ignorance, and especially ignorance of history.

Editor: Chesterton had criticized President Wilson's waffling two months earlier. He now praises Wilson for bringing the United States into the war, noting, "God Himself will not help us to ignore evil, but only to defy and to defeat it."

The American declaration of war was practically the verdict of history. It is no flattery to say that this great and democratic yet distant population stands somewhat in the position of posterity. It is only upon the largest and plainest matters that it is even a compliment. Posterity may make mistakes; and probably will make many mistakes in matters of detail. We had better be Chinamen and worship our ancestors than be like some modern evolutionists and worship our descendants. Our descendants (if they preserve the family likeness) will muddle a great many things and misunderstand us in a great many ways; but they will see certain historic facts simply as facts, as we see the Norman Conquest or the discovery of America. One of the broad facts they will thus see in bulk is the fact that the Prussian appeared in history as an enemy, exactly as we see that the Hun appeared in history as an enemy. We know very little about the followers of Attila; and that little, like so much that modern learning has deduced from the Dark Ages, is very probably wrong. But that the glory of Attila was a calamity to society, that the power of Attila was the impotence of society, is the verdict; and it will not be reversed.[18]

The first fact which makes the American decision conclusive is plain enough. Yet it needs careful statement in order to avoid, as I have always tried to avoid, the tone of cheap superiority about the long neutrality of a vigorous and valiant nation. **Anybody who ever supposed that Americans as such were "too proud to fight," in the ironical sense of being too timid to fight, was a fool whose impudence was simply ignorance, and especially ignorance of history.** Within living memory America was full of fighting, in a literal sense even yet unknown to England, although England is full of fighters. It was even less likely that they had changed in military quality since Bull Run and Gettysburg than that we had changed in military quality since Plassy

18. Atilla the Hun (405–453 AD) led nomadic tribes from Central Asia on wars of conquest into central Europe that were remember long after as violent and barbarous. Using "Huns" for Germans was intended as an insult.

or Waterloo.[19] Moreover, much that strikes an Englishman in America, like much that strikes him in Ireland, as being mere anarchy is only a different manifestation of mere courage. But when we have guarded against this irritating error, we can safely propound the purely intellectual truth. And the truth is that America had been largely converted, in the manner of a rather mild religious conversion, to the modern ideal of peace, both in its sane and its insane formulae. **The difference might be stated thus: Pacifism really was in America something which it never is anywhere else, though it always pretends to be. It was democratic.** The people, or great tracts of the people, really wanted peace; and were not (as in Europe) merely told by horribly unpopular Socialists that they really wanted peace. It was the poor, plain man of the Middle West who could truly be described as disliking all war. It was not merely the International Proletarian, who can safely be described as disliking or liking anything, since he does not even exist to answer. The most startling proof of this is the fact that there could be in America such a thing as a pacifist popular song—a music-hall ditty that is not patriotic, and is almost anti-patriotic. Try to imagine that "Keep the Home Fires Burning"[20] could be sung enthusiastically with the intention of keeping all males of military age at home by the fireside. Imagine a song about the British Conscientious Objectors in the style of the British Grenadiers. That will suggest the position in which it was possible for a very virile people to applaud the mother's song which ran "I Didn't Raise My Boy to be a Soldier."[21] That mother has already discovered that you always run the risk of doing so, if you raise him to be a man. Now, to have stung all this solid and sincere neutralism into war is a fact which history will count as final. No arguments about whether the pacifist had cause to be exasperated can count for an instant against the fact that he was a pacifist and that he was exasperated. If the Germans did something which made Mr. Bertrand Russell plunge into a suit of khaki and rush out of Cambridge breathing fire and slaughter, it would be quite useless to say that what they did was not provocative.[22] If some German action awoke M. Romain Rolland in his Swiss mountains and made him rush down the slope and die in the carnage of Lorraine, it would be quite clear that his comment on the act was an answer to all possible defence of it.[23] Americans

1917

19. The First Battle Bull Run (June 21, 1861) was the first major clash in the U.S. Civil War and Gettysburg (July 1–3, 1864) marked the turning point in the war. Though brief, the Battle of Plassey (June 23, 1757) is the traditional date for when British rule over India began. At the Battle of Waterloo (June 18, 1915), Napoleon was defeated by British and German armies.

20. The chorus of this popular (1914) British war song goes: "Keep the Home Fires Burning,/ While your hearts are yearning,/ Though your lads are far away/ They dream of home./ There's a silver lining/ Through the dark clouds shining,/ Turn the dark cloud inside out/ 'Til the boys come home."

21. The chorus of that 1915 American hit: "I didn't raise my boy to be a soldier,/ I brought him up to be my pride and joy,/ Who dares to put a musket on his shoulder,/ To shoot some other mother's darling boy?/ Let nations arbitrate their future troubles,/ It's time to lay the sword and gun away,/ There'd be no war today,/ If mothers all would say,/ I didn't raise my boy to be a soldier." Notice that "arbitrate," a legal term, sounds odd in a folk song.

22. The long-lived Bertrand Russell (1872–1970) was a British philosopher and mathematician, as well as an odd sort of pacifist. He supported colonial wars of aggression in his 1915 "The Ethics of War," (see Appendix E), because he felt Europeans would make better use of the lands they conquered, but he was also a vocal critic of Britain's role in WWI. Chesterton seems to allude to him in a November 11, 1916 article (Ch. 4).

23. Romain Rolland (1866–1944) was a French writer who won the 1915 Nobel Prize for Literature. In his *Au-dessus de la Mêlée* (1915, English: *Above the Battle*, 1916) he opposed WWI.

had a right to be neutral, which in the case of Mr. Russell and M. Rolland is perhaps more difficult to expound; but they certainly desired to be neutral, and it is the final criticism on Germany that they could not be neutral, even when they desired it. **The question is yet further clarified by the last provocation actually offered to America—the proposal to treat the self-defence of merchantmen as piracy.** This theory is so plainly an insanity that it is not even a sophistry.[24] It has nothing to do with any international understandings, but with the elementary ethics of cause and effect, of responsibility and reason. **It is precisely as if a magistrate were to pay a band of official highwaymen to stab and rob all pedestrians, and then hang the pedestrians for rioting if they resisted. With this enormous idiocy modern Germany loses her last link not merely with civilisation, but with the human mind itself, and merely barricades herself in a mad-house.** And the moment of that loss is the moment of the entry of America, which may truly be described as the entry of mankind. It is even, as I say, like the entry of unborn mankind. We have talked too much of America as "a daughter nation"; and have tried too often to patronise a daughter when we ought rather to have respected a very distant and very independent cousin. But in this sense there is truth in the tag—the Western democracy speaks for our daughters and our sons even more than for ourselves. The youth of the world has found Pacifism impossible because it has found Prussianism intolerable; it is the rising generation that is knocking at the door of Potsdam, and knocking with a battle-axe; it is the babe unborn that stirs and cries against the Herod who has slain so many babes.

President Wilson, in his great speech, was truly and worthily what somebody was once called fancifully—the orator of the human race. There was a powerful impersonality in his very eloquence which was all the more human because it was not individual, but rather like the mighty voice of a distant but approaching multitude. The simple words with which he ended were among the sort of historic sayings that can be graven on stone.[25] There is a moment when man's moral nature, apparently so wayward, finds its path with a fatality like that of doom. "God helping her, she can no other." That is the answer of humanity to all possible preaching about the inhumanity of war, to libraries of loathsome realism, to furnaces of ghastly experience, to the worst that can be said, to the worst that can be endured. There comes a moment in which self-defence is so certainly the only course that it is almost superfluous

24. This refers to Captain Charles Fryatt, mentioned in the February 3, 1917 *Illustrated London News* (Ch. 5).

25. Wilson closed his April 2, 1917 speech asking Congress for a Declaration of War with these words: "It is a distressing and oppressive duty, gentlemen of the Congress, which I have performed in thus addressing you. There are, it may be, many months of fiery trial and sacrifice ahead of us. It is a fearful thing to lead this great peaceful people into war, into the most terrible and disastrous of all wars, civilization itself seeming to be in the balance. But the right is more precious than peace, and we shall fight for the things which we have always carried nearest our hearts—for democracy, for the right of those who submit to authority to have a voice in their own governments, for the rights and liberties of small nations, for a universal dominion of right by such a concert of free peoples as shall bring peace and safety to all nations and make the world itself at last free. To such a task we can dedicate our lives and our fortunes, everything that we are and everything that we have, with the pride of those who know that the day has come when America is privileged to spend her blood and her might for the principles that gave her birth and happiness and the peace which she has treasured. God helping her, she can do no other."

to say it is the right one. There is nothing else, except to commit suicide; and even to commit suicide is to connive at murder. **Unless a man becomes the enemy of such an evil, he will not even become its slave, but rather its champion. In such an extremity there enters at last an awful simplicity; and we share something of that profound spiritual peace which always possesses the armies fighting in the field. God helping us, we can no other; for God Himself will not help us to ignore evil, but only to defy and to defeat it.**

G.K. Chesterton, "Our Note-Book," *Illustrated London News* 150 (April 14, 1917), 424. US: April 14, 1917. Also published as "The American Declaration of War."

GREAT GERMAN HERESY

April 21, 1917

One moral of our great German heresy is that we should take things as we find them; and we generally find them a long time before the men of science have discovered them.

EDITOR: Chesterton often made fun of people who could read before they could see, meaning those whose theories (heresies) about life kept them from seeing things as they are. In this article he ridicules the Germans and some English for viewing the world through absurd historical and scientific theories about struggles between Teutons and Celts.

1917

IT can hardly be too often repeated that the spell which modern Germany cast over Europe—or at least over important parts of Europe—was mainly an abuse of science. Science feeds upon details; and Germany set out to defeat our inherent ideals by means of details. For instance, derivations are details; and it was the Teutonic trick to set derivations to destroy traditions. We were told in a hundred ways to alter our philosophy to suit their philology. Now one can argue almost anything by philology. One can argue that black is white, and support it very plausibly with derivations. One has only to assert that "black" is probably "blank," while "blank" is obviously "*blanc*."[26] One could prove that courage is cowardice by a sufficiently careful study of the word. It is only necessary to say that "courage" has obviously the same root as "courier," and means running—and then say it means running away. It is the same, of course, with manners as with morals—or, indeed, with anything else. It could similarly be suggested that rudeness is the same as politeness, by a sufficiently learned person—nay, by an utterly unlearned person like myself. It is not disputed that "*chevalier*" and "cavalier" are practically the same word. I need only deduce from this that, if I treat a lady in a cavalier manner, I shall also be treating her in a chivalrous manner. The test of my organ for truth would come when I found that the lady did not like it. It would be tested by whether I then discovered that derivations are often pedantic, or whether I only discovered that women are always illogical.

26. *Blanc* is the French word for white, and in the following *chevalier* is French for knight.

Now the really dangerous part of the Teutonic trick is the latter part—the habit of cutting oneself off from all cure or correction by a reserve of superiority. The examples I have given are intentionally silly; but things quite as vitally silly, but more superficially subtle, may quite easily lead quite clever people astray. A man is not a fool because he has believed some pedantic but plausible derivation to be the fact. He is only a fool if he finds the fact and still prefers the derivation. The lady is a fact; and the treatment she expects is that very solid fact which is called a tradition. The really evil element is a certain spirit which can at once retire before facts and rise above them, by the erection of a tower of pride and disdain. As I have said, it was a habit which hung about Europe in many places, before it was blown away by that very explosive fact which we call the great war. It is still clinging in corners of our own journalism; and there is no more urgent patriotic duty than to clear it out.

For instance, there are many Englishmen who are now ready to admit that they have believed a pack of rubbish in favour of Teutons. But they are not yet ready to admit that they have believed a precisely similar pack of rubbish against Celts. Nobody in his senses wants them merely to substitute a Celtic Theory for the Teutonic Theory, for all such extreme simplifications are only neat because they are narrow. But I do wish them to see, to begin with, that one of these thin theories is as good as the other. It is possible to talk as if all Englishmen were really Angles. It would be equally possible to talk as if all Britons were really Bretons. In folk-lore and the first narratives, certainly, it would be much easier to find a link between Brittany and Britain than between Saxony and what we call the Saxons. But I am not arguing about the precise extent to which the modern Britons are really the Ancient Britons, or to what extent they are really the Ancient Germans—different (it is fondly hoped) from the modern Germans. I am pointing out that our dramatic disillusionment about Germany ought to cure us of all those historic—or rather, pre-historic—generalisations which claim to be racial and are often only remote. And, if such anthropological antics have brought us bad luck in our love, they will bring us worse luck in our hate, and worst of all in our disdain. If it was unwise to worship a German merely because he was called a Teuton, it will be found still more unwise to contemn an Irishman merely because he was called a Celt. Modern Germany is the great example of a certain condition to which culture can undoubtedly come. Roughly speaking, it is the condition in which a professor has to take off his spectacles in order to see. The whole apparatus of formal thinking actually forbids a man to think.[27] He always sees the label or ticket before he sees the thing to which it is attached. If, when he opens the door, a German is standing on the doorstep, he sees a Teuton before he sees the German. If a Jew puts his head in at the window, he sees a Semite before he sees a Jew. And if an Irishman knocks him on the head in a street fight, the head is dimly conscious of having suffered because the man was a Celt, but is too stunned to make the conjecture that it may have happened because

27. In Chapter v of *William Cobbett* Chesterton wrote: "He could see before he could read. Most modern people can read before they can see. They have read about a hundred things long before they have seen one of them."

the man was an Irishman. The ethnologist who takes his ethics in this fashion has to be behind the times in a sense impossible to the most hopeless reactionary. He has to be behind time itself, pottering about in a primeval world before all recorded ages, and peering so persistently into the dark that he has always to shut his eyes in the daylight.

One moral of our great German heresy is that we should take things as we find them; and we generally find them a long time before the men of science have discovered them. Unfortunately, for instance, historic reasons for the Irishman fighting us do exist; but we need not make matters worse by prehistoric reasons which do not exist. **If we had simply looked at Prussians, instead of reading about Teutons, we should never have thought the North German our nearest and dearest friend. And if we simply look at Irishmen, instead of reading about Celts, we shall no longer think they are necessarily our darkest and most hopeless foes.** They are really very different from us in many ways; but they are not ways which need interfere with each other, as the North German megalomania was bound to interfere with everything. The English type of casualness, for instance, is different from the Irish type of carelessness; but neither differs from the other so much as both differ from the carefulness of Prussia. One of them has a vague and the other a vivid religion; but neither of them has a religion of irreligion. Neither is capable of taking lawlessness quite seriously, or of making a mysticism out of materialism. There is a great deal of difference between shooting a pheasant and shooting a landlord; but it is precisely in the recognition of this difference that the two respective marksmen, both of them being Christians, would certainly agree. Precisely what neither of them could do would be to shoot a man as if he were a pheasant, and that is the state of mind ultimately aimed at both by Prussian discipline and by Prussian science. **It is the whole upshot of Teutonic militarism to consider more who commands you to kill than what you are killing; and it is the whole upshot of Teutonic evolutionism to suggest that a Teuton is to a man pretty much what a man is to a pheasant.** It may have needed some such alien extravagance to bring our own differing types together; but I think they will be brought together. I have no belief in what is called the Union; but I have a belief in the unity under the picturesque varieties of the British Isles. That unity rests on history. At the back of all modern history is that war with the barbarians which filled the Dark Ages and has returned in our own; and it was against the same enemy that was struck the blow of King Brian at Clontarf and the stroke of King Alfred at Ethandun.[28]

G.K. Chesterton, "Our Note-Book," *Illustrated London News* 150 (April 21, 1917), 450.
US: April 21, 1917. Also published as "German Philology and Race Theory."

28. Brian Boru was High King of Ireland from 1012–1014. Trying to unite Ireland under his rule, he was killed in the Battle of Clontarf (April 23, 1014) against an army that included Viking mercenaries. King Alfred the Great (*c.* 849–899) defended his Wessex kingdom from a Danish Viking invasion. At the Battle of Edington (Ethandun) in May of 878, he defeated invaders under Guthrum the Old. In 1911, Chesterton wrote of King Alfred and that battle in "The Ballad of the White Horse," available in *G.K. Chesterton's Early Poetry.*

Pacifist Nightmares

June 2, 1917

If a particular man's opinion is not the voice of God, is not common-sense, is not what men call morality, then his conscience is no more necessarily sacred than his nightmares.

Editor: Chesterton wants conscientious objectors free to "talk at large," meaning not be censored or placed in prison. But he objects to their insistence that their beliefs must be respected by everyone else. If a conscientious objector's opinion is so personal that it cannot be understood by others, "then his conscience is no more necessarily sacred than his nightmares."

Short of the disruption of definitely military discipline, I am all in favour of allowing the Conscientious Objector to talk at large. I cling to the hope that, if he talks long enough and large enough, he may at last tell us something intelligible about his conscience. At present the attempt to discover what he means brings us no further than a doubt as to whether he can possibly mean what he says. What he says, so far as I can follow the philosophy of it, is substantially this. There exists in every man a more or less fantastic faculty, in which no two men need be the least alike, which may vary more vitally than a taste in cookery or a trick of the nerves, but which is covered by the term "conscience" because it is so far moral that it concerns the social relations. Or, to put it less delicately, it is so far moral that it may be immoral. From this he takes the first logical step, and says that, if a man has this movement or instinct, he must obey it. This, to begin with, is quite disputable; it involves the question of its authority and origin, of which I will say a word in a moment. But let us grant, in a general sense, that if a man really has such a social (or anti-social) prompting, he ought himself to follow it. If he thinks a harem necessary to his salvation, he ought to have one; if he thinks human sacrifices due to God, he ought to offer them. There have been many conscientious sects preaching and practising such things; and their action is defensible on this subjective principle, that if a man has an ideal he must respect his ideal. But then he takes the second logical step, and says that *we* must respect his ideal. It is here, I fancy, that many of his friends and fellow-creatures will rather abruptly part company with him. If, in any mystical and unthinkable sense, it is possible for Thuggery to be good, they will confine themselves to the more cautious admission that it may be good for the Thug.[29] If sacrificial murder is good at all, they will entertain the more modest idea that it is good for the murderer. In their old-world narrowness, they will probably deny that it can be good for the man who is murdered, or for all the other men who might be murdered. And they will therefore deny that they are bound to run the risk of being murdered by recognising it as good in any sense whatever. And it is

29. Thuggee was a secret religious cult in India that befriended travelers and then, at some lonely spot, ritualistically robbed and murdered them. It existed as early as the thirteenth century and was stamped out by the British in the 1830s. Because India's native rulers had done nothing about the sect (other than tax its ill-gotten income), its elimination made Britain's rule of India more popular. The English word "thug" comes from their name.

quite irrelevant to answer that even the most fanatical non-resistance is not so horrible as human sacrifice. **First of all, it is by no means certainly true; for many of us there is not much difference between the Thug who murders a child and the man who allows the child to be murdered, when he could prevent it with a blow.** But the vital point in logic is not merely this. The point is that the Conscientious Objector bases his whole case on what his conscience says to him, and distinctly and deliberately *not* upon what our conscience says about him. It is his whole case that his moral sense is different from ours, and he cannot logically be surprised at any degree of immorality we may find in it. Our conscience has no concern with his conscience—except to respect it. Why?

The truth is that these scruples are the dregs of an old doctrine, and not the seeds of a new one. The old doctrine is true, as the old dogmatist stated it; but it is almost unmeaning as the new humanitarians state it. The sanctity of conscience consisted in its being the voice of God, which must be universal, or at the least in a *communis sententia* or moral sense of mankind, of which the whole point is that it is universal.[30] **If a particular man's opinion is not the voice of God, is not common-sense, is not what men call morality, then his conscience is no more necessarily sacred than his nightmares.** The old oppressors were pilloried because they did, or made other men do, what the common conscience refuses. Now some may think it idle to straighten out this tangle of false intellectualism; but I, for one, am far from agreeing with them. Evil ideas are at the root of all this enormous evil which plagues the earth at present; and there is no idea more fundamental in it than the false ethic which is in question here. I mean the idea of a conscience which is wholly detached, and therefore wholly demented.

For the Prussian is the supreme and typical Conscientious Objector. His whole position is poised on the idea of a new conscience, incomprehensible to the common conscience of men. He has a conscientious objection to the Red Cross, a conscientious objection to the white flag, a conscientious objection to the tyranny of a scrap of paper. He has a conscientious objection to all the old religion implied in the old international standards; to the prejudice which protects women in war; to the formalities which allow neutrality to nations. He has made his conscience independent of Christendom, and therefore independent of chivalry. If you tell him he is immoral, he will tell you, as the Pacifist does, that he has a higher morality. If you tell him you cannot imagine what morality he can believe in, he will tell you that men cannot imagine his morality until they believe in it. He will say in so many words that you must have a German mind to judge of German actions. If (as is probable) you do not possess a German mind, if (as is also quite possible) you do not even desire to possess one, he will tell you that you must bow down and worship

30. Chesterton mentions *communis sententia* in *The Well and the Shallows* (1935): "It might have taken the world a long time to understand that what it had been taught to dismiss as mediaeval theology was often mere common sense; although the very term common sense, or *communis sententia*, was a mediaeval conception. But it took the world very little time to understand that the talk on the other side was most uncommon nonsense. It was nonsense that could not be made the basis of any common system, such as has been founded upon common sense."

it even if you do not understand it. But when he lays waste provinces and asks for your applause, when he defiles sanctuaries and demands your reverence, when he crowns himself with authority merely because he covers the earth with anarchy, and asks to be accepted as a god because he is behaving like a brute—through all this he is only doing the same thing, in strict logical analysis, as is done by the mildest Conscientious Objector who claims to be exempt from the law. He is asking you to respect his morality, even when you think it immorality.

On another occasion I deprecated cheap talk about democracy, talk implying that this great and (to my mind) true dogma is something self-evident and easy. But in this sense a democratic truism does underlie all the varied symbols and systems of the Alliance. In that sense we are fighting against aristocracy, especially the aristocracy of anarchists. In that sense we are fighting against despotism—against the despotism of moral detachment. We are fighting against the most personal of all rulers, who desires his personal exception to disprove the rule. **Here, indeed, we are fighting not for the last deductions, but the first axioms, of democracy—not for its institutions so much as its ideas. We fight for the right of normal people to define normality.** We will not have the world governed from its lunatic asylums, whether they are called the palaces of ancient empires or the temples of new religions. If this be republicanism, then indeed the most reactionary among us is republican; and democracy is a thing that all of us can accept like daylight. There are few who will not prefer the demagogue—who at least appeals to something presumably common like the light—to the mystagogue who merely prides himself on calling darkness light and light darkness. And we at least mean something when we call conscience the voice of God and a thing venerable among all men.

G.K. Chesterton, "Our Note-Book," *Illustrated London News* 150 (June 2, 1917), 635.
US: June 2, 1917. Also published as "Conscience and the Conscientious Objector."

GERMANS WITHOUT FLAWS

July 14, 1917

The chief case against them is that they do not know there is any religion in the world more real than the dead religion they repeat, as part of a deadly military drill.

EDITOR: Chesterton has quite a bit of fun with *Continental Times*, a pro-German newspaper published in neutral Switzerland. He mentions it again on October 20 and 27, 1917. In a May 11, 1918 article critical of a particular sort of pacifist whose, "hatred of patriotism is very much plainer than his love of peace," he would use the paper as a foil in the ultimate insult, the writing of some ignorant but cocksure pacifists, he said, are "worthy of the waste-paper basket of the *Continental Times*." Even it wouldn't publish them, Chesterton was suggesting. When he felt criticism was called for, Chesterton could also be unsparing of English publications such as the liberal *Nation* (January 12, 1918, Ch. 6).

Having sometimes introduced upon this page the distinguished name of Mr. H.G. Wells in order to differ from him, I may perhaps do so in a sense in order to defend him, though from an attack so absurd that he might hardly think it worth while to defend himself. But somebody has sent me a copy of the Pro-German *Continental Times,* containing a denunciation of his position, and incidentally of my own. It contradicts some of the many truths he has put into the mouth of Mr. Britling;[31] but the most concrete item is his very just and fundamental remark: "This is not a war of races, but of ideas." The answer to this is most extraordinary, for the German writer denies the first clause by a clamorous assertion that England has brought "black, yellow, brown, and red" men into the field. How this can prove it is a race war I cannot imagine. That England has used races remote from her own may be right or wrong; but it must rather prove that England is indifferent to race than that she is concerned about it. If she desires the victory of a race, it must be a striped or spotted race, which is white, black, yellow, brown, and red all at once.

But the contribution to the *Continental Times* has other aspects. Anyone reading this interesting article will soon realise that the difficulty about the Germans is that they are perfect. All nations think themselves better than they are; but all others are so far conscious of their defects as to soften them with sophistry or euphemism. But Germans have no defects to soften: mention any merit whatever, and they will be found to be notably eminent in that merit. Here, for instance, is a perfect passage: "One might reaffirm for the hundred-thousandth time the evidence of all honest observers that the Germans are, of all belligerents, the calmest, most self-critical, and objective-minded." The German criticises himself quite calmly as an object—and that is his criticism! Now if it be said that all patriots are of a piece in such things, I say they are not. I should never dream of saying that the English were the calmest, most self-critical, and objective-minded of the nations; in the middle term especially I think them dangerously defective. I should say the calmest of all belligerent peoples were the Turks; the most self-critical, probably the Russians; the most objective-minded, beyond all question, the French. But let us see a little of what the writer means by German calmness and self-criticism. Take, for instance, what must be for a German critic, who believes in the German cause, the most curious and interesting question about the war. Why was America, which wished to be pacifist, unable to be neutral? Apart from the old quarrel, what about the new quarrels, especially with the new countries? The German critic attributes the situation to certain activities of England, which he describes as follows: "With the thumb-screws of her ruthless despotism and the venom of her lies and corruption she has bullied, driven, or bribed nation after nation, race after race, into an unnatural and cowardly antagonism to the heroic enemy whom she and all her countless allies, dupes, accomplices, and victims cannot overcome—Italy, Roumania, China, Brazil—the United States, betrayed by its Tory traitors and its plutocrats into a 'declaration' of war as heinous as it is pusillanimous and idiotic." Now this language may seem to some to be lacking in

31. Mr. Britling is the central character in H.G. Wells' *Mr. Britling Sees It Through* (1916).

calm. And, though it is certainly not lacking in criticism, it can scarcely be described as self-criticism. It might even be held that the vision is not wholly objective, in so far as the object seen is a thumb-screw attached to the thumbs of President Wilson. And if this is the calmest criticism in the world, the world must indeed be in a state of some unrest. If this is the nearest approach to self-criticism that any European can effect, the chances of international understanding seem slightly dim. Of course, raving nonsense of this sort is not peculiar to the Germans; far from it. What is peculiar to the Germans is the attitude of a man who writes the raving nonsense, and writes on the same page that he can calmly criticise the nonsense, and that he finds it to be the calmest criticism.

In the same way the writer inquires, about Mr. Wells: "Would he be mentally stoic enough to endure a *real* comparison between *Kultur* and culture?[32] Let him contrast the tone, theme, and spirit of the war literature of France and England with that of their enemy." Well, "self-criticism" is a harder matter than he may, perhaps, imagine. But I fancy I am mentally stoic enough to realise, without any temptation to suicide, that there is a great deal of rotten and ridiculous war literature in England, as there probably is in France. But how can we accept the writer's challenge to a comparison more fairly than by comparing it not only with the German propaganda, but with his own German propaganda? For instance, I find another topic—the fame of the soldier—treated with the same inconsistency. "It is true," he says loftily, "that the Germans, unlike the French, have little taste for martial *gloire*." There seems to be something deadly in this word being in French, for the same writer has no objection to saying on the same page that "the glory of German superiority… maintains its almost superhuman ascendancy." Now I should say that practically all men, including Germans and including Englishmen, have some sensibility to "martial *gloire*." Dr. Johnson was hardly a Frenchified person, and he made a similar remark.[33] In so far as the French are peculiar, it is only because, being more "objective-minded," they recognise it more clearly as a separate thing, described by a single word, not to be confused with things higher or lower than itself. And if a man has to express this sentiment, I would much rather he described it as *gloire*, still more that he described it as glory, than that he should describe it as "military achievements so stupendous that the battle-glories of all history pale and shrink into insignificance… not only prodigies but miracles of valour, audacity, strength, enterprise, and sublime heroism." That is what this particular German writer calls it, by way of showing his German indifference to "martial *gloire*," and it takes rather longer to write it all down. Indeed,

32. In this era Germans made much of their *Kultur*, so the contrast is between it and English culture.

33. Samuel Johnson's *Journey to the Western Islands of Scotland* (1775) includes these marvelous words about the meaning of manhood, the importance of community, and the right of self-defense:

> It affords a generous and manly pleasure to conceive a little nation gathering its fruits and tending its herds with fearless confidence, though it lies open on every side to invasion, where, in contempt of walls and trenches, every man sleeps securely with his sword beside him; where all on the first approach of hostility come together at the call to battle, as at a summons to a festal show; and committing their cattle to the care of those whom age or nature has disabled, engage the enemy with that competition for hazard and for glory, which operate in men that fight under the eye of those, whose dislike or kindness they have always considered as the greatest evil or the greatest good.

I have only quoted a part of it, and I confess that I am not mentally stoic enough to copy out all the rest.

Now there is a truth to be extracted from all this trash, which is our real answer to the Germans to-day. What we complain of is precisely what this writer explains: that they do feel confident of their reason and rectitude—and this is what they mean by reason and rectitude. The writer mentions my own name, and says I accuse Prussian aristocrats of Atheism, when their class is "conspicuously one of the most pious and God-fearing in the world." Precisely; Prussian aristocrats are conspicuously God-fearing about as much as Prussian critics are conspicuously self-critical. It is the whole point that such people can fill five columns with ranting self-glorification, and then offer it as a conspicuous example of self-criticism. It is the whole point that they carry language to the point of lunacy to celebrate the triumphs of their soldiers and the terror of their flag, and then turn round and thank God they are not as other men are—vainglorious, romantic, even as this Frenchman.[34] It is the whole point that they roar and rage day and night to call attention to their monumental calm. And similarly it is the whole point that they do think a Prussian Junker pious—and that they think *that* is piety. The chief case against them is that they do not know there is any religion in the world more real than the dead religion they repeat, as part of a deadly military drill. The charge we bring is that the very word "God-fearing" means so little to them that they apply it to men who have reason, in the darkest sense, to fear God—to men who do not fear Him only because they do not believe in Him. This is indeed the piety of Prussia; and it is the atheism of the world.[35]

G.K. Chesterton, "Our Note-Book," *Illustrated London News* 151 (July 14, 1917), 36. US: July 14, 1917. Also published as "German Calmness and Self-Criticism."

1917

War Weariness

August 25, 1917

The new promptings towards a compromise peace are things to be considered with all our wits about us, and therefore with as little war-weariness as may be

Editor: Writing shortly after the anniversary of third year of the war Chesterton criticizes those who are growing weary and want the fighting to end soon. Weariness, he points out, is never a reason not to do something that ought to be done.

The arguments of the small but increasingly active Pacifist party, at the present moment, all really resolve themselves into one—that the world is weary of the war. And, like most of their arguments, it is really an argument against themselves. **For, whatever spirit ought to settle the war of the world, plainly such a problem ought not to be settled by the spirit of weariness. Weariness is not a principle of**

34. Chesterton alludes to Luke 18: 11, where Jesus says: "The Pharisee stood and was praying thus to himself, 'God, I thank Thee that I am not like other people: swindlers, unjust, adulterers, or even like this tax-gatherer."

35. Chesterton described German religiosity as "a new and false religion" on June 24, 1916 (Ch. 4).

action at all. It is merely the inaction of one who fails to act as he would otherwise like to act. If a man is carving a colossal statue of some saint or prophet, he would, of course, expect a Moslem to disapprove of its being carved at all—for the Moslem disapproves of all statues, as the Pacifist disapproves of all soldiers. But even a Moslem might well admit something lamentably illogical in a man who thought it a sacred and splendid task to carve the saint finally failing to do so, merely because of the colossal size of the statue. A man who had walked forty miles, in an agony of endurance, to bring wine to a sick person would probably know that a teetotaler would have ordered some other medicine—for a teetotaler forbids all wine, as the Pacifist forbids all war. But even a teetotaler, if he had any care for the honour of human nature, would hardly expect a man who firmly believed that the wine was life to throw it away merely because the walk was long. Indeed, the case is much stronger than this—for the sculptor would probably believe in sculpture and the wine-bearer would probably believe in wine, for reasons rooted in their past existence and experience; while the war has produced some problems which many people are forced to consider for the first time. **They are, in a sense, fresh questions—and certainly questions which we should try to look at in a fresh way. It is hard to have patience with the fool who actually tells us to try to look at them in a fatigued way.**

Other elements are, of course, invoked; but they are all illogical, for they are all inconsistent with this recurrent assertion of war weariness. Thus the Pacifist sometimes poses as St. Francis of Assisi, with a heart flaming with Christian charity; but the whole point of St. Francis is that he was not weary, and could not be made weary even by extremes of discipline and pain.[36] Sometimes the peace-maker appears rather as a sort of Walt Whitman, opening his arms to a more pagan comradeship with all men. But Walt Whitman, whatever his faults, was not tired; and he positively and passionately repeated that no agony and ugliness of this earth had succeeded in making him tired. Above all he devoted about a third of his poetry to proclaiming that he was not war weary—that he absolutely refused to be weary of a just and necessary war. Such Whitmanites have evidently bowdlerised *Leaves of Grass* of the fine section called *Drum-Taps*.[37] The matter is but a parenthesis; but it is a rather important one, for it cuts away the moral ground of half the appeals for an early peace. We shall, at the start, refuse to accept a war-weary charity as being charity at all, for it is a charity that does not suffer long and does not endure all things.[38]

The new promptings towards a compromise peace are things to be considered with all our wits about us, and therefore with as little war-weariness as may be. We cannot help accepting such fatigue as an accident; we must not on any account accept it as an argument, simply because it is not an argument. Let the international idealists themselves plan any perfect scheme of social reconstruction they choose;

36. St. Francis of Assisi (1182–1226), founder of Franciscan Order, is one of the best known and most beloved of Catholic saints. Chesterton would publish a biography of him, *Saint Francis of Assisi*, in 1923.

37. Walt Whitman (1819–1892) was an abolitionist who supported the Civil War. About a third of the poems in his *Leaves of Grass* are about the Civil War and have been published separated as *Drum-Taps*.

38. This is a reference to 1 Corinthians 13:3–8.

and that scheme also easily might, and probably would, be endangered in process of realisation by exactly the same negative tendencies of tedium and nervous reaction. If we wish to see things as they are, we must try to consider the war now ending as if it had just begun. What we knew, when it had just begun, now needs only a word. Anybody who doubts that the Central Powers cynically and wantonly provoked war must believe two other things instead. First, that the Emperor of Austria (or whoever acted for him) interrupted universal peace by sending an admittedly monstrous ultimatum to Serbia, seriously believing that Russia could not possibly even have anything to say, far less to do, in such a wreck of all her historic plans. Second, that the Emperor of Austria did this without asking whether the German Emperor agreed with him. Anybody who can believe either of these things could believe that the Emperor of Austria stood on his head to be crowned, or that he dressed up as a charwoman and cleaned out the palace every morning. Very well; the Central Powers forced war on the world, and the first thing they did was a violation of neutrality—that is, an annihilation of international law. The German Emperor told Mr. Gerard that there was no more international law.[39] And unless that act of war (which history will simply see as the war itself) is visited at least with definite defeat, to say nothing of definite punishment, there most certainly *will* be no more international law. There will also be no more respect for women in war, no more respect for prisoners of war, no more scruples about torture or slavery—in short, no more European civilisation, which they will have done everything to deny and we shall have done nothing to reaffirm. History will simply say that the barbarians conquered, if history says anything at all. But the subsequent history would not be worth writing; and very probably would not be written.

1917

Those who do not see this as still the head and front of the matter are like men who cannot see the shape of a live animal because it has a long tail. The tail of the war drags along slowly, but it would not drag at all if it were not originally attached to this hoary old atheistic ape. These being the original facts, what are the recent facts? They are far less important, but all their importance points precisely the same way. A compromise peace is not only impossible, but grows daily more impossible. It is precisely the freshest facts, the phrases of the new Chancellor, the acts of the new marine war, the insolent defiances about Alsace, the veto on the Socialist agenda at Stockholm, which prove that Prussia is growing more Prussian than ever.[40] So far

39. James W. Gerard (1867–1951) was U.S. Ambassador to Germany from 1913–1917. In his *My Four Years in Germany* (1917), Chapter XVII, he described a meeting with the Kaiser about U-boats sinking ships with American passengers: "We then had a long discussion in detail of the whole submarine question, in the course of which the Emperor said that the submarine had come to stay, that it was a weapon recognised by all countries, and that he had seen a picture of a proposed giant submarine in an American paper, the *Scientific American*. He stated that, anyway, there was no longer any international law. To this last statement the Chancellor agreed."

40. Events of 1917: The new German Chancellor was Georg Michaelis (1857–1936), who took office on July 14 and would be forced to resign on October 31, because he was seen as too obedient to the German General Staff. He was replaced the next day by Count Georg von Hertling. On January 31, 1917 Germany announced a return to unrestricted submarine warfare that included a denouncement of the "destructive designs of our opponents" to deprive Germany of Alsace-Lorraine. Delegates at the Stockholm Conference held by socialists in July and August could not agree on a peace resolution.

from using the Russian Revolution as a model, she is going to use it as a scarecrow—as an example of the anarchy of the "illiterate" Slav. So far from the doubtful situation having softened her, it has clearly stiffened her. The Germany that escapes will be more uproariously arrogant than if she had won the Battle of the Marne. Needless to say, the talk about evacuating Belgium and Serbia does not even touch this truth.[41] As a fact, it has not even been promised—and, if it were promised, might not be done; but if it were done, it would make no difference. If an army were defeated because it marched out of territory at the end of a war, both sides would be defeated at the end of every war. Not only would it not mean Prussia defeated; it would be an exact replica of Prussia victorious. There was "evacuation" after 1870; the Kaiser did not make Versailles his palace instead of Potsdam.[42] If Alsace does not revert of right to France, the new evacuation will mean exactly the same thing as the old one.

This new fact of the final hardening of Prussia is having visible effects everywhere else if not here. It has clearly acted as a tonic to revolutionary Russia. It brings us language like that of a republican crusade from republican America. If we weaken while all our Allies are strengthening, we shall be exhibited everywhere as the dupes of Prussianism for the second time, and without the first excuse. We shall not have fallen through any of the old myths about the magnanimity of the Teuton, for all those myths are exploded anyhow. Nor shall we have fallen through any wild vision of Russian philanthropy, for such visions were never native to us. We shall have fallen by sheer brainless fatigue. It will be something, perhaps, as pardonable—certainly as pitiful—as a sentry sleeping at his post or a martyr surrendering to stripes. It will be the humiliation of man.

G.K. Chesterton, "Our Note-Book," *Illustrated London News* 151 (August 25, 1917), 208.
US: August 25, 1917. Also published as "On War Weariness."

1917

Lordly Peace-Mongers

September 1, 1917

If we have not the courage to stick to our duty, at least let us have the courage to say so. Let us say frankly that evil has been too strong for us, for it is at least better to call evil strong than to call evil good.

Editor: Chesterton criticizes the blue-blooded pacifists of the Peace Negotiating Committee for lacking the will to continue a difficult war. Notice their aristocratic assumption that whatever they write must be published. Notice also that, to his credit, the editor of the *Illustrated London News* was not intimidated by their social rank.

41. Chesterton is disagreeing with those who thought that Germany's carefully planned withdrawal to a shorter and more defensible Hindenberg Line (still well within France) between February 23 and April 5, meant that the nation might also be willing to pull out of other occupied territories, especially Alsace-Lorraine.

42. After the 1870 Franco-Prussian war, a new (second) German Reich was proclaimed in the French palace of Versailles near Paris. Germany accepted a war indemnity from France and withdrew its troops except for Alsace-Lorraine, which it annexed. Chesterton points out that if WWI ends with Germany withdrawing from France but not Alsace, the result of Germany of losing a war will be little different from one they won in 1870.

SOMETHING called the Peace Negotiations Committee has sent to *The Illustrated London News* a note concerning some memorial it is presenting to the Government. It concludes with a sentence written in large letters and underlined: "Kindly insert in your first issue." The editor, always ready to oblige, has committed it to my care; and I will now kindly insert it, and consider it as kindly as may be. Nor is there much cause for anything but a somewhat weary kindness, so far as we are concerned with the first passage, which presumably establishes the first principle. The memorial urges the Government to take the first chance of securing "A Just and Lasting Peace." Here, by all human analogy, there is no difference or difficulty. In every other conceivable public or private quarrel, we know well enough what we mean by a just settlement. We always mean a settlement by which the wrong-doer is punished, and his victims are recompensed at his expense. We also know what we mean by a lasting peace, such as we look forward to in a well-governed community. It means that few are likely to break the peace, because all know that the breach of it has been, and will be, followed by punishment. In this case there will be a just peace because the Prussian aggressor will be punished; and a lasting peace because his would-be imitators will be warned by his punishment. That is all very elementary, but it may be worth repeating; and I willingly repeat it. I should certainly like this just and lasting peace as soon as possible; and it is, so far, gratifying to know that Lord Peckover, Mrs. Pethick Lawrence, Mr. Ponsonby, Lady Toulmin, and all sorts of important people agree with me.[43]

They proceed to say that the memorial is signed by large numbers of people, and endorsed by organised Labour Bodies representing large numbers of people; but as I know something of how those "Labour Bodies" are "organised," and the way in which they generally "represent" the real labourers, this will hardly detain me. **That sort of Organisation will bring out the remarkable result that most British workmen believe in Teetotalism; and before long will probably prove, in the same way, that most of them believe in Vegetarianism.** The writers also complain of great difficulty in collecting the signatures "owing to the interference of the Police and Military Authorities," which also need not detain us. It is enough to say that anything they suffered from the Military Authorities was certainly very mild compared with what they would have suffered from the nearest mob of ordinary citizens; and that in the presence of the latter they would probably have been much reassured by "the interference of the Police."

It is with the next paragraph, however, that we come to business; and, I regret to say, most of our hopes of agreeing with Lord Peckover and Mr. Ponsonby begin to fade away. They "draw attention to the new international situation created by the Russian Revolution, the entry of America into the war, and the passing by the

43. Alexander Peckover (1830–1919) was Baron Peckover. Emmeline Pethick-Lawrence (1867-1954) was the wife of Labour Party leader Baron Frederick W. Pethick-Lawrence (1871–1961). Arthur A.W.H. Ponsonby, Baron Ponsonby (1871–1946) formed the pacifist Union of Democratic Control. His 1928 book, *Falsehood in Wartime: Propaganda Lies of the First World War*, contains the well-known remark, "When war is declared, truth is the first casualty." Lady Toulmin may be Mary Toulmin (Baroness Carbery, 1867–1949), who wrote as Mary Carbery.

German Parliament of a Resolution rejecting all 'territorial expansions,' and all 'political, economic, and financial oppressions.'" I am not sure what they mean by the particular effect of the Russian Revolution. But at least, I presume, they do not argue that because the Russian Emperor was bad the German Emperor is good, especially as the chief charge against the former was a weak sympathy with the latter. What "the entrance of America into the war" can possibly be supposed to prove, except that war will always be forced by Prussia even on the most peaceable people, I cannot imagine. And the third point—about the resolution passed in the German Parliament—is superficially an example of almost equal simplicity.[44] **I shall begin to be impressed by a Parliament which solemnly renounces oppressions, whenever I come across a Parliament which announces in a loud voice that it is now going to indulge in oppressions.** And though "territorial expansions" be a less questionable term, it is admittedly one which is being questioned on all sides. I may say I do not intend to expand my back garden; but I may add one or two comments which make a considerable difference. One is that what my neighbour imagines to be his garden is really a part of my garden, which is therefore a large and handsome property, and needs no expanding. Another is that I propose to sit on the garden wall with a gun, and shoot him unless he manages what is theoretically his garden precisely as if it were my garden. The former is exactly the attitude of Germany towards Alsace and Posen; the latter is precisely her attitude towards Belgium and Luxembourg. Finally, anybody who happens to know anything about Germany, including the German political writers themselves, will agree that a resolution in the Reichstag commits the German Empire to Anti-Imperialism just about as much as the resolution once passed at the Oxford Union in favour of Socialism has made England a Socialist State.

In truth, these peacemakers have here hit the very note which audibly rings false, like a cracked bell. They themselves feel that they ought, if possible, to produce a new truth—a change in the right and wrong of the war; and they cannot possibly produce it. They themselves realise that there is hardly an Englishman alive who regrets the first rush to the rescue of Belgium; they have to seek for something that has happened since—a change in the moral issue. And they cannot find it, because it is not there. This is precisely the most prominent feature of this war; that there have been no moral changes in the matter in dispute, as compared with the colossal material changes in the condition of many of the disputants. Nobody expected England to have a conscript army or America to wage a European war. But the moral ground on which America came in at the end was of exactly the same sort as the moral ground on which England came in at the beginning. It was that Germany does intolerably treacherous and cruel things; and the things have become more

44. The relevant paragraph from the Reichstag's July 19 resolution gives little reason for hope: "Germany took up arms in defence of her freedom, her independence, and the integrity of her soil. The Reichstag strives for a peace of understanding and a lasting reconciliation of peoples. Any violations of territory, and political, economic, and financial persecutions are incompatible with such a peace." The last sentence can easily be seen as a rejection of any demand that Germany give up Alsace-Lorraine or pay reparations for the war.

treacherous and more cruel. If England was right to defend neutral territory, America was right to defend neutral shipping; Germany has done nothing, except become even more anti-neutral. For anyone who can see a plain moral question in black and white, the question of the war is quite unchanged—except that the black is a little blacker. **The poor peace-mongers cannot find any alternation in the fundamentals of the story at all; and they have to fall back on vague phrases about Russia and America making a difference, without even venturing to say what difference they make.** In other words, they can only insinuate the extraordinary idea that a Russian in a red cap somehow disproves the existence of a Prussian with a red sabre; or the still more extraordinary idea that the time has come for us to be friends with the Germans merely because they have forced many millions of harmless people on the other side of the Atlantic to be their enemies.

Let us talk no more of this trash. If we have not the courage to stick to our duty, at least let us have the courage to say so. Let us say frankly that evil has been too strong for us, for it is at least better to call evil strong than to call evil good. There is more dignity in a man who surrenders to a brigand, or even to a blackmailer, than there is in a liar who covers the brigandage by calling it brotherhood; or in a hypocrite who pompously pretends that the blackmailer is a beggar, that he may be seen of men to give alms. It may be a good thing that Russia has achieved liberty, or a bad thing that she has achieved anarchy;[45] but neither can have any conceivable effect upon the plain fact that Prussia has never achieved anything but tyranny, that we set out with the avowed object of breaking that tyranny, and that it remains unbroken. Let us call our surrender by its own name; and then let us brace ourselves to bear the last and most avenging irony. Let us wait till we discover, as we certainly should discover, that Germany was herself exhausted, that we have fled from a foe who was himself on the point of flight, that we have been bled by a blackmailer with no secret, and been captured by a brigand with an empty gun.

G.K. Chesterton, "Our Note-Book," *Illustrated London News* 151 (September 1, 1917), 234. US: September 1, 1917. Also published as "The False Note of the Peacemakers."

PEACE THAT WILL END PEACE

September 8, 1917

These foolish people trace all the chances of war to the very thing which will always be the best chance of peace—men's habit of dwelling in their own boundaries and minding their own business.

EDITOR: Chesterton explains why he disagrees with creating the powerful international bodies that H.G. Wells and others think will bring world peace.

NEARLY three years ago Mr. H.G. Wells published a series of articles called "The War that Will End War." About three weeks ago he published an article

45. At this point the Russian Revolution had not been transformed into a communist dictatorship under Lenin.

in the *Daily News* called "A Reasonable Man's Peace." Perhaps the chief truth to note about his last scheme was that it will not fulfil any one of the ideals suggested in his first scheme. Whatever else the reasonable man may expect to achieve by his peace, it most certainly will not be a peace that will end war. If he retains any hope of its doing anything of the kind, the reasonable man is a very unreasonable man indeed. Without claiming that Mr. Wells is divinely exalted above all temperamental temptations to being unreasonable, we may postulate that he is a man of penetrating and far-sighted intelligence; and it is therefore more respectful to assume that he sees this as well as we do. He is, perhaps, among those who have only come to think that the first war aims need not be carried out, under the pressure of a notion that they cannot be carried out. Of such critics I have only to say, as I said last week, that if this is what they mean, the world would be saved some waste of words if it were also what they say. I would rather confess that our resources were insufficient at the end than that our intentions were wrong from the beginning. I could still at least maintain that we were morally justified in designing what we were not materially equipped for doing. The destruction of the Prussian power was a more pure, a more chivalrous, and a more humane ideal than the English people has ever set before itself since Alfred raised the West Country against the Danes. We should not need to renounce it as an ideal, even if we were thus compelled to renounce it as a reality. But it is a perfectly plain fact that we are not compelled to renounce it as a reality. We know it is attainable as a reality, by precisely the same knowledge of military and historic facts by which we know it is desirable as an ideal. Anyone who knows what Prussianised Germany was, and is, knows that nothing but the alternative of certain military disaster would ever have set her intriguing for peace at all. Every argument she uses in the Council Chamber is an argument for her defeat in the field.

With Mr. Wells's particular proposals I am not much concerned; nor is it fair to class so clear-headed a man with common advocates of a compromise. A great part of his article is concerned with proposals for "internationalising" certain problems of the Turkish empire and the African continent.[46] Of this I have at the moment only one thing to say—and that is that such disputants, right or wrong, seem to suffer from a strange oblivion of the very crux of the business and the very beginning of the war. This war did not begin because international arrangements were not made, but because they were not kept. If there ever was a thing about which the Great Powers were solemnly and publicly *agreed*, the name of it was Belgium. It was the agreement which produced the disagreement. I cannot for the life of me see why partners should not quarrel at least as much about a country they are all supposed to share as about a country they are all supposed to protect. The experience of human nature suggests that they would probably quarrel more. **But a queer and almost mad notion seems to have got into the modern head that, if you mix up everybody and everything more or less anyhow, the mixture may be called unity, and the unity may be called peace.** It is supposed that, if you break down

46. This would be the breakup of the Ottoman Empire after the war and disputes over colonies in Africa.

all doors and walls so that there is no domesticity, there will then be nothing but friendship. Surely somebody must have noticed by this time that the men living in a hotel quarrel at least as often as the men living in a street. This is a digression, but a relevant one, for the whole discussion is haunted with this hazy idea that mere international intercourse can prevent international irritation. **These foolish people trace all the chances of war to the very thing which will always be the best chance of peace—men's habit of dwelling in their own boundaries and minding their own business.** The only hope of attaining amity lies, not in ignoring boundaries, but, on the contrary, in respecting them. And the only chance of attaining that is to punish the Power that does not respect them. When every sophist has twisted and tangled the matter to the utmost, we always come back to that simple truth. It is not a question of what arrangements we make or do not make. It is a question of what example we make, in the case of those who are ready to disarrange any arrangement. The special point here is, however, that we are not only asked to abandon our ideals, but specially asked to abandon our peaceful ideals. What is offered to us now is not the war that will end war, but the peace that will end all our previous hopes of peace. Those who fancy that the matter can be met by founding a League of Nations, or anything of that kind, are men who fancy that a failure can be covered by naming it as if it were a novelty. They assume that a man who will not respect a treaty will be certain to respect a title. There is already a league of nations as large as any that could have to deal with any formidable secession—that is, any secession that was really worth dealing with. Thus, for instance, such papers as that which is rather ironically called the *Nation* used to tell us that America would, if necessary, join the next war to resist attack on the new settlement. Now America has actually joined the present war; and now they tell us that even America cannot help us to a true settlement. They still talk their unmilitary and unscientific stuff about "stalemate." But what is the good of saying that America would join a League of Nations to threaten any aggressor, if she could only threaten him with stalemate? The chance might at any time be worth his trying. No; whether a group of Great Powers protecting international law is called a League of Nations, or whether it is simply called the Allies, is a mere matter of words. And there is no reason to suppose that a Power which cares nothing for its own word will care for a mere grammatical combination of our words. The ideal of a group of Powers strong enough to control any aggressor is simply one of the ideals we should abandon to obtain an early peace. We shall move towards it only if we show that *this* combination is strong enough to control *this* aggressor; otherwise, we simply move away from it. **Another pacific ideal from which we obviously move away is that of disarmament. Every man who retains his sanity must know that if this war ends equally, or even dubiously, England must become much more military rather than less.** It is self-evident to me that a renewed pressure of Prussian ambitions is a certainty; but for this purpose it is more than enough that it should be an uncertainty. The colossal war preparations of Europe were made because war was uncertain, not because it was certain. So long as it is even possible that Prussia may draw the sword, Europe will certainly wear the shield; and here again we come back to the same simplicity. There is no such peace as was promised us till it is impossible for Prussia to draw the sword—till her sword is broken like the sword of Attila.[47]

I do not, therefore, accuse the Pacifists of violating my visions, but of violating their own. It is they who promised us a peace which may or may not be too perfect for mankind; it is they who refuse the obvious and only way of realising it even imperfectly.

G.K. Chesterton, "Our Note-Book," *Illustrated London News* 151 (September 8, 1917), 266. US: September 8, 1917. Also published as "The Peace That Ends Peace."

Wars More Horrible

September 29, 1917

We hear this conflict called, not unreasonably, the most horrible war of history. But the most horrible part of it is that it would not be the most horrible war. Wars more and more horrible would follow the failure to vindicate and restore Christian equity and chivalry in this one.

Editor: Chesterton continues to address war weariness, pointing out it is emotional rather than rational and that a quick and easy end to the war would not deal with one of Germany's basic problems, an exaggerated self-esteem that refuses to admit wrong-doing. Chesterton is correct when he predicts that, unless Germany's defeat is obvious, Germans will not accept it as such and will find an excuse to go to war again. That's precisely what happened. This is also one of the few places where he deals with a serious flaw in his 'punish Germany until they change' argument. What if the German people as a whole are too arrogant to admit their problem? Then the only answer is exactly what will happen: "Wars more and more horrible would follow," perhaps the most chillingly accurate prediction in all Chesterton's writings.

October saw the publication of what was at that time one of his most widely read books, *A Short History of England*. In a later edition, he explained his intention: "The neglected side of English history does not consist of little things which the learned obscurely conceal, but rather of large things which the learned frequently ignore."[48]

Our present condition is the precise contrary of that which was a commonplace of the philosophy of peace. Long before the war a very modern moral theory of Pacifism had disseminated certain assumptions; and they are to-day the exact opposite of the actual facts. We were told that our brute passions or desires might drive us towards blood and destruction; that our more fanciful feelings of vanity or vengeance might inflame us for war; but that reason and right thinking, if they

47. Chesterton may be confusing a bow with a sword. Edward Gibbon's *The History of the Decline and Fall of The Roman Empire* (Ch. 35, Pt. 3) says that when Attila died in his bed of a ruptured artery: "It was reported at Constantinople, that on the fortunate night on which he expired, Marcian beheld in a dream the bow of Attila broken asunder: and the report may be allowed to prove, how seldom the image of that formidable Barbarian was absent from the mind of a Roman emperor."

48. Joseph Pearce, *Wisdom and Innocence* (London: Hodder & Stoughton), 236. Chesterton was a genius at seeing the "larger things" in history, culture, and the world of ideas that others were ignoring.

prevailed, would always prevail for peace. Turn this position entirely topsy-turvy, and you have something like the truth to-day. **Our brute desires are now all for repose, and almost for sleep; our mere passions would flow in the direction of peace. It is exactly our reason, and it is almost exclusively our reason, which tells us to finish the work of war.** It is exactly right thinking, and it is right thinking almost alone, which tells us that fighting is still right. It has come to a war in the very body of man—as to whether the head shall still be the head of him. It is truly a conflict between the law in the members and the law of the spirit; and the members are semi-pacifist, like so many Parliamentary Members.[49] **Man is not a fighting animal; he is fighting because he is not an animal; he is fighting long after any animal would have fled.** But that which upholds him is not an intoxication or an illusion; it is not something internal—on the contrary, it is the eye by which he can see what is external. He fights, quite literally, because he has not taken leave of his senses. He fights because his five wits are still the five windows which let daylight into the dwelling-house of his reason; he fights because he reasons. So a man reeling in real battle might have his ears dulled or his eyes darkened by wounds and weakness. But so long as he could hear at all, he would hear guns; and so long as he could see anything, he would see nothing but a foe. We also can see nothing but a foe; it is our reason, or all we have of it, that tells us that the foe is a fact—that the foe is a foe. Those who say they have seen his face turned to that of a friend have passed through weakness to delirium.

I have here drawn the truth as darkly as possible, because objective truth can be most clearly seen in the transparent air of tragedy. As a fact, we shall not reel or fall; but the point is that, if we did, the fact would remain the same. And the chief fact is the foe, who would remain with a smile upon his face, whatever we might fancy in delirium or the dreams of death. Even if we were likely to lose heart (which is, thank God, exceedingly improbable), it would be well to keep our head sufficiently to see what else we were losing. And so stupendously is the whole historic order which produced us staked upon this conflict that it would, perhaps, be easier to ask what we are not losing. **We hear this conflict called, not unreasonably, the most horrible war of history. But the most horrible part of it is that it would not be the most horrible war. Wars more and more horrible would follow the failure to vindicate and restore Christian equity and chivalry in this one.**[50] This does not make the fight less ghastly to the feelings; but it *does* make it more inevitable to the mind. It is, even in its most intense agony, still a problem of the reason, and even of the senses—of the sense of external things. And especially of the sense that recognises the posture of the enemy.

Now the posture of the enemy is one in which he is not strictly unique, but is certainly pre-eminent. Other peoples have incidentally fallen into the same fault;

49. This is an allusion to Romans 7:23, where Paul writes, "but I see a different law in the members of my body, waging war against the law of my mind."

50. Christian equity would ensure that wrongdoers are punished and victims compensated. Chivalry would protect the weak from the strong. See the May 10 and September 13, 1919 articles (Ch. 7).

and we ourselves have been perilously prone to it—chiefly, I think, because the very power which is now our enemy was for so long our ally. But this is one of the cases in which we can rejoice that the English were not quite stupid enough to learn all that the Germans were stupid enough to teach. When we regret that our populace has not been thoroughly educated, we should remember that for a long time, at least, it would have meant its being thoroughly Teutonised. **The distinction in question may be defined as the habit of manufacturing self-satisfaction out of any materials whatever. The deadly danger of this process consists in the very fact that it is facile, and therefore infinite; whatever I happen to be doing, I can always praise myself for doing it. If I walk, it shows my energy; if I sit down, it shows my composure; if I fall down, it shows my fearless acceptation of the risk.** This infantile idea is developed with elephantine and laborious thoroughness in the schools of German thought.[51] If the German is loved, it is because he is lovable; if he is hated, it is because he is enviable. If he contentedly merges himself in a foreign country, it shows he is a perfect colonist and citizen of the world; if he is conspicuously discontented and conspicuously detested in a foreign county, it proves he is too truthful and too nobly proud for the delicacies of more decadent societies. If he takes a town in a day, no other man could storm a place with such promptitude; if he cannot take it for ten years, no other man could sustain a siege with such patience. All this is pretty well known; but its practical bearing on the question of reason in war, and the right appreciation of external things, may well be worth noting. **The reason why there must be an unmistakable victory over the German Empire is that anything short of it will be instantly turned, by the Germans, into an unmistakable victory for the German Empire.** They are said to be very rapid and efficient in their manufactures; and they are certainly amazingly rapid and efficient in this sort of manufacture. Slow as they are sometimes called, they are swift enough in turning an accident into a compliment. We have seen this in each of the successive catastrophes or transformations which have been the huge by-products of this huge business. The accession of America to the cause of justice was even more of a controversial blow to the German case than a practical blow to the German policy. It demonstrated to heaven and earth that the Prussian position was indefensible; yet this extraordinary people does not consider it as making their defence more questionable, but merely as making their defiance more admirable. But while the strength of America is to increase their glory in the West, the weakness of Russia must not in the smallest degree diminish their glory in the East. To fail to take Paris, when there are quite inferior forces to defend it, is to be a hero borne down by the brute masses of this world. To succeed in taking Riga,[52] when there is nobody to defend it, is to be the same hero eventually triumphant against odds, and dealing with the masses of mere men as if they were mice. One of the chief arguments of the German

51. Teutonism isn't the only 'ism' with this fault. Look around and you will see many present-day examples.

52. Riga, the capital of Latvia, is the cultural center of the Baltics. German troops entered the city, then annexed to Russia, in early September, 1917, meeting little resistance because of the Russian Revolution. The Treaty of Brest-Litovsk (March 3, 1918) gave the region to Germany. Germany's defeat gave Latvia its independence.

or the Pro-German was the neutrality of America; another was the autocracy of Russia. Both have been turned upside down as facts without ever being withdrawn or even corrected as arguments. This devouring self-approval, far out of proportion to that which is the general weakness of mankind, is the most solid of the external facts which we have to face. **The peace of the world will depend not merely on the facts, but on the German version of the facts; and the facts must be made such that they cannot be perverted, at least past a certain point. It is vain to say that the foe must be merely curbed; if he is not conquered he certainly will not feel curbed—he will merely feel unconquerable.**

It is evident to the senses, for those who have not lost their senses with mere natural fatigue or exasperation, that this familiar fact is the meaning of all the most recent incidents. It is the meaning of the crazy story about a secret message from England begging for peace, which is not at all the sort of way in which our politicians would make peace, even if they were weak enough to make it. Indeed, they would not need now to make peace, but only to allow Germany to make it. It is the meaning of the parade of haughty hesitation over the Pope's proposals,[53] combined with abrupt and airy remarks about the probable evacuation of Belgium. Having tried to make a virtue out of committing a crime, they are now trying to make another virtue out of having failed to commit it. What they want can be put in very plain and popular words; they want to swagger out of Belgium exactly as they swaggered in. What their apologists call the better feeling in Germany is a belated attempt to manufacture a magnanimous act out of the frustration of a mean act. Even if we were forced to abandon the task, there would be no need for us to abandon the truth; and even if our human appetites necessitated (as they do not) our acceptance of something which is not a sleep but a dream, our reason could still salute reality.

G.K. Chesterton, "Our Note-Book," *Illustrated London News* 151 (September 29, 1917), 360. US: September 29, 1917. Also published as "Why We Fight."

PRAISE WITH FAINT DAMNS

October 13, 1917

But this modern school, and till lately this modern world, is not sincere enough to be rhetorical. It is too frightened of tyrants to denounce them as tyrants, and too slavish to say much about slavery.

EDITOR: Chesterton criticizes pacifists for failing to condemn evil in clear and strong language. Instead they "praise with faint damns" and are "too frightened of tyrants to denounce them as tyrants." What he describes has been repeated over and over again, often with tragic results. Recall the furor that erupted when President Reagan denounced the Soviet Union as an "Evil Empire" in a March 1983 speech to the National Association of Evangelicals. Reagan had chosen what Chesterton calls

53. Pope Benedict XV's peace proposal (August 1, 1917) received little attention. Its appeal to the "general good of the great human society" offered no specific answers for territorial disputes and reparations.

a "great... clear and vivid word" that was "suitable to a great transgressor." His critics, more mice than men, preferred words as small and colorless as themselves. Here's the relevant portion of that historic speech.

> Yes, let us pray for the salvation of all of those who live in that totalitarian darkness—pray they will discover the joy of knowing God. But until they do, let us be aware that while they preach the supremacy of the state, declare its omnipotence over individual man, and predict its eventual domination of all peoples on the earth, they are the focus of evil in the modern world.
>
> It was C.S. Lewis who, in his unforgettable *Screwtape Letters*, wrote: "The greatest evil is not done now in those sordid 'dens of 'rime' that Dickens loved to paint. It is not even done in concentration camps and labor camps. In those we see its final result. But it is conceived and ordered (moved, seconded, carried and minuted) in clean, carpeted, warmed, and well-lighted offices, by quiet men with white collars and cut fingernails and smooth-shaven cheeks who do not need to raise their voice."
>
> Well, because these "quiet men" do not "raise their voices," because they sometimes speak in soothing tones of brotherhood and peace, because, like other dictators before them, they're always making "their final territorial demand," some would have us accept them as their word and accommodate ourselves to their aggressive impulses. But if history teaches anything, it teaches that simpleminded appeasement or wishful thinking about our adversaries is folly. It means the betrayal of our past, the squandering of our freedom.
>
> So, I urge you to speak our against those who would place the United States in a position of military and moral inferiority. You know, I've always believed that old Screwtape reserved his best efforts for those of you in the church. So, in your discussions of the nuclear freeze proposals, I urge you to beware the temptation of pride—the temptation of blithely declaring yourselves above it all and label both sides equally at fault, to ignore the facts of history and the aggressive impulses of an evil empire, to simply call the arms race a giant misunderstanding and thereby remove yourself from the struggle between right and wrong and good and evil.

This all-too-common weakness did not end with the collapse of Soviet communism. More recently we see the same behavior in those who seem afraid to call terrorism by its name, encouraging yet more terror and, on their part, yet more covert fear and "weedy words." In great conflicts, as Chesterton points out, words do matter. Words can make the difference between peace and war, between success and defeat, and between freedom and slavery. Called by their true name, evil empires can fall.

Chesterton's closing words draw a parallel between wars, which cause wounds, and pacifism, whose rhetoric causes weakness and weariness. The latter, he says, is an "all-destroying plague" which "is the enemy of all noble things." The words of pacifists can kill what is human in us as effectively as the bullets of militarists.

WE are all familiar with a certain tone in the talk about Germany among those who hanker after a premature, and therefore a German, settlement. **There is a fine phrase about the critics who damn with faint praise; and these critics may be said to praise with faint damns.** When applied to Prussianism, their damns are so exceedingly faint as to be more feeble than the "dems" of Mr. Mantalini.[54] It would seem almost as if they thought that the duty of economising in war included a duty of economising in words—so careful are they to substitute a small word for the great word suitable to a great transgressor, or a colourless word for the clear and vivid word which must have occurred first to anybody. But there is really no economic need for these people to substitute such weedy words for the flowers of rhetoric with which their talents could doubtless have delighted us. A patriotic thrift has, indeed, led some thoughtful citizens to substitute leaves and roots for blossoms in bouquets and garlands; but I have not heard that even they think it extravagant to indulge in the mere names of flowers. They would not think it their duty to christen a daughter Rhubarb instead of Rose, or Asparagus instead of Lily. They do not, I imagine, observe a vegetarian fastidiousness in their literary quotations; they do not observe casually—

> "A pumpkin by the river's brim
> A yellow pumpkin was to him,"[55]

or cite the celebrated remark of Juliet that an onion by any other name would smell as sweet. In short (to quit this somewhat fascinating speculation), there is no reason to suppose that they deprive themselves in daily life of the pleasures of natural eloquence and emphasis, or that their talk upon other topics is such a tissue of unintelligible euphemisms and petty palliations as their talk about the most tremendous issue of the age. And if, in spite of Juliet, they call a rose a rose, they might be expected to call a thorn a thorn, and even admit that it pricks; they might call a poison a poison, and even admit that it kills. They might even bring themselves to refer to deadly nightshade without stopping to describe it as deleterious nightshade. Similarly, if they admit—as most of them do—that Belgium or Serbia suffered a wrong, they might also realise what everybody has always regarded as the right way to speak of a wrong. If Prussia did strike a blow at the peace of the world, we surely shall not be blamed if (looking around us at this moment) we venture to call it a heavy blow. We shall hardly be content with calling it a good hard knock.

But what are called flowers of rhetoric, as a matter of fact, are by no means so much out of season as some suppose. There is a fashion of talking of the orator as merely an actor, and of his fame as though it were as fleeting as that of an actor. Brougham may come to be remembered by a carriage, and Gladstone by a bag.[56] But the view is historically superficial, for it was precisely in the last great practical crisis of European

54. Mr. Mantalini is a weak, whining, complaining, and unimpressive character in Charles Dicken's *Nicholas Nickleby* (1838–1839). This remark is typical of him: "'What a demnition long time you have kept me ringing at this confounded old cracked tea-kettle of a bell, every tinkle of which is enough to throw a strong man into blue convulsions, upon my life and soul, oh demmit,'—said Mr. Mantalini to Newman Noggs."

55. These words play on William Wordsworth's "Peter Bell" (composed 1798, published 1819). "In vain, through every changeful year,/ Did Nature lead him as before;/ A primrose by a river's brim/ A yellow primrose was to him,/ And it was nothing more." The reference to the onion that follows is from Shakespeare's *Romeo and Juliet*.

56. As Lord Chancellor , Henry Brougham (1778–1868) was responsible for Slavery Abolition Act of 1833 and the design of the Brougham carriage. William E. Gladstone (1809–1898) was one of Britain's greatest Prime Ministers. The bag, actually a small suitcase, seems to have been named after Gladstone rather than invented by him.

politics that rhetoric was at its greatest. The orator was an actor in another sense, for he was a man of action. This was true even of lesser things; Brougham left a lasting mark on our educational and Gladstone on our fiscal affairs; but I am referring here to the great words and deeds which were felt to be worthy of great revolutions. And, if these are fairly studied, it will be found that the old eloquence is now avoided—not so much because it was artificial as because it was real. Men (or at least these rather mean men) do not dislike it because its style was ornate, but because its sentiment was simple. It happened to have a picturesque way of putting very plain truths; but these sophists hate them because they are plain, and hate them more because they are truths. That the citizen must die to save the city, that the traitor must die if he sells the city, that the invader is a usurper and the usurper is a tyrant, that the sword is necessary to the ploughshare and the ploughshare to the sword, that the foe threatens to defile the hearths and desecrate the altars, that fighting is freedom, that defeat is slavery—these things to-day are not tropes, but very terrific truisms; and we need a great orator to say them with sufficient simplicity.

But this modern school, and till lately this modern world, is not sincere enough to be rhetorical. It is too frightened of tyrants to denounce them as tyrants, and too slavish to say much about slavery. If I turn from the great words about great things, uttered by the republican rhetoricians of the eighteenth century, to the talk of many humanitarians who call themselves republicans at the present time, I am astounded, not so much at their heresies as at the half-hearted way they hold them and the stammering way they state them. The internationalists are not only unworthy of their country, but utterly unworthy of their subject. They do not merely cover Germany with defences that are false, but with excuses that would be trivial even if they were true. A great empire, responsible for such an apocalypse and judgment of the earth as this war, might just conceivably be right. It could not conceivably be rather wrong.

1917

But all the earnest efforts of the peacemongers at present seem to be devoted to proving that the creation of such an inferno was rather wrong. They are concerned to show clearly that tyranny and perjury are rather wrong; that massacre and enslavement are also rather wrong. They draw the most delicate and elaborate distinctions between this sort of thing and something else, which would be very wrong. I have recently been reading a communication to the *Nation* from a well-known exponent of the case for a compromise with Prussia, and therefore with Prussianism.[57] The

57. This was H.N. Brailsford's lengthy letter to *The Nation*, "Communications: The Russian War Party" in the September 15, 1917 issue (XXI:24), 610–611. In his letter, Brailsford conceded:

> Austria (with some German participation) slowly and secretly concocted an excessive ultimatum to Serbia, refused to delay its execution, or consider Serbia's surprising concessions, or to discuss her proceedings with Russia. On this she was adamant: it was the whole point. Her real contention was that Serbia was her vassal, not Russia's." But he went on to argue that: "In this case [Russian] mobilization was more than buckling on the sword: it was drawing the sword.... It was known, it was frankly advertized [advertised], that if Russia mobilized on the German front Germany would mobilize too, and her mobilization was equivalent to war." He closes with a claim that waters down Germany's guilt by sifting part of the blame to Russia: "In 1914 there were two war-parties in Europe, and between them they made the war.... Our current popular view, Mr. Wilson's view, that one evil will, the will of the rulers of Germany, deliberately made the world war, planned it,

whole upshot of his argument seems to be that Germany may perhaps be called "criminal," but must not be called "Satanic."[58] So far as I can understand the argument, it is admitted that the Central Powers not only made an indefensible attack on Serbia, but offered an almost intolerable provocation to Russia; but it is maintained that this was done in the hope that it would be followed by European peace; or, in other words, by Russian surrender. According to some moral principle which I cannot follow, the writer offers this as making the German case better; but even the writer is really obliged to admit that it does not make it much better. Even as he puts it, it is very weak; and it is worse if it is put more explicitly. Germany may have been criminal because she tried to impose an unjust settlement; but she was not Satanic, because that unjust settlement might really have come into force. In other words, she was rather wrong, because she wanted her neighbour's goods; but she was not very wrong, because she might have got them.

Why in the world should a man grope in such a maze of guess-work, and drudge amid such detailed irrelevancies, not even to prove that black is white, but merely to prove that black is not blacker? I can only suppose that sophistry, being the silliest sort of intellectual pride, is in itself a sort of intellectual pleasure; and that it

---

> dated it, and marched into it with conscious determination—that is a misreading of history which is driving civilization through darkness to suicide.

The letter drew heavy criticism. The next week (September 22, 1917) *The Nation*, pp. 636–637, published "Communication: The Responsibility for this War" by J.W. Hedlam [Morley], who had written *The History of Twelve Days, July 24th to August 4th, 1914; Being an Account of the Negotiations Preceding the Outbreak of War Based on the Official Publications* (1915). He claims Brailsford gives a "very incorrect account" of events, particularly the fact that Germany's warning to Russia had been that "mobilization *against Austria* would lead to war," not mobilization against Germany. It was Austria, with half its army poised to invade Serbia, that could not afford a two-front war, rather than Germany. Germany could have defended itself in the *east* without attacking in the *west*.

As usual, Chesterton gets to the heart of the debate, rightly charging Brailsford with compromising with Prussianism by refusing to admit that, after seeing its Serbian ally bullied, Russia had a right to mobilize its huge but clumsy army. And Brailsford implies that, faced with the mere possibility of an invasion from the *east*—an invasion that would never have happened if Serbia were treated better—Germany had a right (which he calls "perfectly rational") to attack Belgium and France in the *west*, merely because to do otherwise would make it more difficult for Germany to win. That is Prussianism, a belief that in any conflict of interests, the interests of Prussia must always prevail, however much evil that may entail. Chesterton criticizes Brailsford by name in a May 11, 1918 article (Ch. 6), calling his writings, "stilted, supercilious" and claiming that he seems, "more and more interested in small facts—which are too often small false-hoods."

58. The distinction is subtle but important. A criminal knows his deeds are evil, that others rightly disapprove of them, and that if caught his punishment is just. He develops no elaborate system to justify himself. He commits crime because he benefits and thinks he can get away it. In contrast, those who have become 'Satanic' are so wholly given over to evil that they regard wrong as right. They develop sophisticated, scientific, philosophical, economic, literary or religious justifications to justify their behavior. They disregard criticism and see any punishment as unjust. In the twentieth century, the two greatest evils would build on respectable scientific foundations laid down in the nineteenth century by Charles Darwin and Karl Marx. But Chesterton focuses on those who practiced the evil before the rationale developed (Frederick the Great's "cannibal state"), and those who popularized it (Caryle's "Strong Man"). Chesterton mentions both when he elaborates on the criminal versus Satanic distinction two months later in a December 15, 1917 article (Ch. 5).

> Now what the new movement did was to bring mysticism to the help of immoralism. It did not, of course, bring the immoralism—or rather, to speak more strictly, it did not bring the immorality. That, of course, did not come from Carlyle or from Frederick, but from Adam or from Satan. Men did wicked things in all parts of the world, including the most Christian parts of the world. But they seldom thought they were behaving like Christians. A man broke treaties, trampled on enemies, or betrayed friends, because he was ready to be contemned; he did not expect to be respected. The notion of his being actually admired as a strong man, merely because he behaved like a selfish man, is a notion so new that I can myself remember it rising steadily, like a new religion, in the late Victorian time.

instinctively labours to do even the lowliest services for Germany, as the paradise of all sophists.[59] But this is what I mean by the depressing pettiness of the great part of the Pacifist propaganda. In this respect the Pacifists fight upon the most ignoble model of all the models provided for them by their friends (or at least their *protégés*) the Prussians. **This is very like putting pins or pieces of metal in an enemy's food, or dropping germs and small seeds of pestilence in an enemy's water.** The great war is surely too great a thing even to be brought to an end by means so miserably microscopic. And in truth the germ is very typical of this policy in another way, for it is none the more humane because its cruelty cannot inflict wounds, but can only inflict weakness. This sort of sophist is sowing everywhere the germ of one all-destroying plague, which might well be called the sleeping sickness. The name of it is weariness; and it is the enemy of all noble things. But so full are they of the spirit that urges us to yield to mere tedium that the very books and papers in which they urge it are tedious.

G.K. Chesterton, "Our Note-Book," *Illustrated London News* 151 (October 13, 1917), 418. US: October 13, 1917. Also published as "The Rhetoric of the Peacemongers."

Playing the Race Card

October 20, 1917

Personally, I should say that the modern monstrosity among Germans was not a result of race, but a result of culture—like Nero.

Editor: Chesterton returns to the *Continental Times* writer that he had so much fun with earlier in the July 14, 1917 issue of the *Illustrated London News* (Ch. 5).

1917

An article I wrote in this journal upon the preposterous Pro-German sheet called the *Continental Times* has produced an answer in that periodical, which has been sent to me in a conspiratorial fashion wrapped up in an innocent-looking Swiss journal. A writer calling himself "Sagittarius" writes a reply to my "attack," he (whoever he may be) being apparently the author of the amazing argument I analysed. There are several curiosities worthy of passing comment in his new explanation, but before I touch upon them there is one plain and personal question of fact which ought certainly to be cleared up. One thing of which he complains is that I supposed him to be a German, whereas he describes himself somewhat mysteriously as being

59. Chesterton hints that many intellectuals engage in sophistries, defending evil out of "the silliest sort of intellectual pride" Believing themselves wiser than those around them, they labor and strain to make their beliefs different, fearing that if they don't, they will become a part of a 'mob' they despise. They strain against reason and against human experience, against good sense and the most obvious of facts, so they can tell themselves, "I am not as this butcher or this plumber, war-mongering and driven by blood-lust. I am intelligent, sophisticated, peace-loving, and able to engage in nuanced reasoning." In the end they demonstrate the opposite and must engage in extensive historical revisionism to cover their tracks—in this case concealing just how similar Prussianism, which they excused, was to Nazism, against which they feign a loathing they never felt for Stalin's murderous regime. No, says Chesterton, they're not free and independent minds. They're laboring "to do even the lowliest services" for evil-doers such as Prussia. Proudly striving to be seen on the 'right' side of history, they're often in the wrong and bear the responsibility for much human suffering.

"an alien." Now it is perfectly true that, finding an unnamed person writing a very desperate defence of German injustice in a paper published in Germany, I did him the honour of supposing that he had the excuse of patriotism. I am now left without any conjecture about what excuse he has. If he is an Englishman, he is a traitor; if he is an American, he is a traitor. It therefore gives me no pleasure to suppose that he is either; and it seems hardly likely that he is a Turk. But, in any case, it is surely relevant to ask what fatherland it is that he is possibly assisting—or possibly betraying. He writes of me in a highly personal fashion, and even professes to have made my personal acquaintance; but, before there is any more of such talk upon such terms, I think it would be reasonable that I should know his nation and his name.

Another thing of which he complains is that I "suppressed" a series of complicated statements in illustration of his peculiarly contradictory argument to the effect that England is waging a mere war of race. I cannot see in any of them anything but repetition of the same singular inconsistency I noted—the attempt to urge the British use of coloured races to prove that the British cause is racial; whereas, of course, it quite obviously proves the opposite. It is as if he proved that we waged a religious war from the fact that we were in alliance with the deniers of our religion. But, since I am far from wishing to "suppress" such examples of Pro-German muddle-headedness, I will set out in full, and criticise in turn, the points which he complains of my suppressing. The following are the items which he takes as showing that the English cause is racial:—

"(1) English attempts to stigmatise Germans as a race apart, not as human beings, but as monsters." I cannot make head or tail of this. From internal evidence, it may be inferred that the writer, like ourselves, supposes there to be some such people as the Germans, who can be collectively described as something. I cannot see why it should be more "racial" to describe them as monsters than to describe them as heroes, as they so frequently describe themselves. **Personally, I should say that the modern monstrosity among Germans was not a result of race, but a result of culture—like Nero.**

"(2) The ethnological term 'Hun' brought into general use to brand an entire race." This is, to begin with, another example of the truth stated above. Why is "Hun" any more of an ethnological term than any other historical term? When foreign critics have not unfrequently called the English "Carthaginians," did they mean that the English race is Semite? Do Englishmen now mean that the German race is Tartar? What they mean is that the German behaviour is beastly—that is, it is not an ethnological but an ethical term. But in this particular case the question can be completely simplified by a single fact—the historic source of the phrase itself. The person who first made the Hun the prototype and model of the German was the Emperor.[60] When the writer complains of our

60. Kaiser Wilhelm II's infamous reference to Huns came in a July 27, 1900 speech to German soldiers leaving to help quell the Boxer Rebellion (November 1899–September 1901) in China: ""Should you encounter the enemy, he will be defeated! No quarter will be given! Prisoners will not be taken! Whoever falls into your hands

bringing it "into general use," does he mean that such language should only be permitted to Emperors?

"(3) Mongolian, race-conscious Japan incited to filch a white man's colony, an outpost of Caucasian civilisation in the East." Again, the only sense I can make of this, as a part of the contention, is that the English are so proud of their ancient Mongolian race that they desire to destroy all traces of the Caucasian race. The same passion can, no doubt, be noted in the Mongols of Italy and the Mongols of France.

The next two remarks may conveniently be quoted together.

"(4) The aforesaid multi-coloured savages of different races introduced upon European battlefields to slaughter and torture white men. (5) Refined German men and German women given over by the English to outrage at the hands of negroes in Africa, thus breaking down the barriers which all white men had until then united in maintaining against the blacks." The second passage presents the contradiction in a most complicated and acute form. Incidentally, of course, I do not suppose that the English have given Germans over to Africans to be outraged; nor do I think the authority of "Sagittarius" sufficient to establish it: that bold archer, I suspect, makes use of rather a long bow. **That negroes have inflicted cruelties on Germans is very possible, though they must be very black to be blacker than the cruelties which Germans have inflicted on negroes.** But this is a parenthesis apart from the present question, which is whether the English wage a racial war. And on this he actually abuses the English for not doing what he is trying to prove that they do. Apparently his position amounts to this: If the English had united all white men against all black men, that would not be a race war. Because the English attacked some white men, with whom they happened to have a fair quarrel, with the assistance of some black men with whom they had no quarrel, that is what "Sagittarius" calls a race war. I do not know what more there is to be said.

Finally, the last two items may also be taken as one. "(6) The racial pleas of Mr. Wells, addressed to a supposedly 'Anglo-Saxon' America. (7) The psychological roots of England's conception of this war as a racial one—her knowledge that the myth of the superiority of the Anglo-Saxon race had been exploded by the German race." I do not know what Mr. Wells may have said about America; but I do not believe that so acute a critic ever suggested that all Americans were descended from Angles and Saxons. Anyhow, I do not say this about the Americans—nor, for that matter, about the English. Long before the war, I had myself called the Anglo-Saxon race a myth, and I should say pretty much the same about the German race, of which it was always supposed to be a branch. **The simple truth is that the one race which**

is forfeited. Just as a thousand years ago the Huns under their King Attila made a name for themselves, one that even today makes them seem mighty in history and legend, may the name German be affirmed by you in such a way in China that no Chinese will ever again dare to look cross-eyed at a German." (The official text removed the reference to Huns.)

has really been extravagantly exalted, merely as a race, is the German race. And the real root of all the modern exaltations of races, as distinct from nations and creeds, is simply Germany.

So much for the valuable considerations which I so cunningly suppressed. For the rest, I do not know whether "Sagittarius" is an alien who knows how to flatter the Germans while he lives in Germany, or an alien so much flattered by the Germans that he has imbibed the spirit of Germany. But there is something at once astonishing and amusing about his suggestion that I am wholly indebted to him and his article for my impressions of the German sin of self-praise. He may be a Chinaman or a Hottentot, for all I know; it is not from him that I gained my conception of the modern German. I gained it from nearly every single proclamation or public utterance that has come out of modern Germany. I gained it from private as well as public utterances. It is not only true that I have known several Germans; it is also true that I have liked several Germans. And the one weakness I have always liked least, in the Germans I liked most, was always this silly and pompous assumption of some superiority inherent in themselves and their social system. The writer says, with an admirable gravity, "The Germans, unlike the French, British, or Americans, have always been poor hands at national boastfulness." The Germans, as a matter of fact, boast incessantly of every mortal thing in their moral and material circumstances; but they invariably wind up the proceeding by boasting that they never boast.

G.K. Chesterton, "Our Note-Book," *Illustrated London News* 151 (October 20, 1917), 454. US: October 20, 1917. Also published as "Racial Arguments in the War."

1917

GERMANY'S HORRIBLE HOLIDAY

October 27, 1917

It was an insanity of success, a mere intoxication of triumph over the weak, a horrible holiday like the sins committed in a dream.

EDITOR: Chesterton continues his debate with the *Continental Times* and enlarges on his blunt description of the faults of Prussia and Bavaria.

THE primary fact to-day is that the friends of Prussia, who have spent their lives in explaining her triumphant militarism, are now explaining it away! I said something last week about the Pro-German *Continental Times,* in which a writer denounced my work upon this page; and this week I have left over some loose ends of his very loose argument. But most of it is at once stated and answered in the above summary of the new Pro-German policy. The writer was generally concerned to show that the Germans really have a great dislike of military arrogance; and, if it happened to serve the new plan for a German peace, he would doubtless try to show that the Germans have a great dislike of music. The evidence he offers is mostly too trivial to detain us here. He calmly affirms, for instance, that the Germans never boast like the other great nations, and adds, "They have a popular motto: '*Selbstlob stinkt*'—self-praise stinks!" I might mildly remark that even the benighted English have a proverb: "Self-praise is no recommendation"; but I should hesitate to offer this as a proof that the English never praise themselves. Nor will I discuss with him whether certain details on which he dwells, to show that the word "English" is still to be found in Germany, unaccompanied by the word "*Strafe*" (as in the names of hotels, etc.), prove anything more than the fact that we still play Beethoven or have not pulled down the Albert Memorial.[61] I may say something later on about his amusing and yet pathetic misconception of the French character, for his subjects are more suggestive than his remarks. Indeed, there is a certain richness and value in a statement of which every sentence is a mistake, because every sentence would make an essay. Here, however, I will pass on to a more essential matter.

Although the writer in the *Continental Times* is astonished that his style should be mistaken for a German's, it is, as a fact, very much Germanised, and especially so in the trick of perpetually using emphasis, not so as to make things clear, but so as to make them incomprehensible. Nevertheless, it is possible to pick out of a most confusing mass of verbiage one or two coherent assertions which at least mean something, and may therefore be discussed. Thus, in a verbal portrait of myself, in the course of which he compares me to an attorney, a whale, a juggler, a devil-worshipper, a mediaevalist, a conjurer, a burbler (whatever that may be),[62] and a balloon, I can find one clear and rather curious remark about me. He says: "The Chestertonian formula is still further complicated by a private system of morals, ethics, and religion, which he exalts into the one incomparable standard." And he goes on to suggest that this produces my sense of the Prussian indifference to right and wrong. I have devised an esoteric and inner doctrine by which the violation of treaties, which is generally regarded as blameless or desirable, is in some subtle way open to objection. The shooting of non-combatants, the ship-wrecking of neutrals—amusements which would naturally pass amid general indifference or approval—appear to my diseased and secretive mind to savour in some way of offence. This part of the subject, however, I will leave on one side for the moment, for the writer passes on from the personal matter, which is trivial, to an impersonal matter which is important. "I ridiculed the infantile obsession which he and his friend Belloc entertain of the 'atheism' of the Prussian aristocracy and army, and his unearthly logic, ballooning lightly beyond all realities, cries out: 'it is the whole point that they do think a Prussian Junker pious—and that they think *that* is piety'—'that' being the legend of the Prussian which English policy has found it convenient to invent."

61. *Gott strafe England*—"May God punish England" was a war slogan coined by the Berlin-born Ernst Lissauer (1882–1937), best known for his poem, "Hassgesang gegen England" ("Hate Song Against England" often called the "Hymn of Hate"). Its words include: "We love as one; we hate as one;/ We have one foe, and one alone—England!" Ludwig van Beethoven (1770–1871) was a brilliant German composer. At the start of the war, there was talk in England of banning performances by German composers, but fortunately it came to nothing. The Albert Memorial was built by Queen Victoria in memory of her husband, the German Prince Albert of Saxe-Coburg-Gotha (1819–1861).

62. Judging by the *Oxford English Dictionary*, it's someone who speaks "murmurously or in a rambling manner."

Now it is largely on the exceedingly simple untruth in the last phrase that the whole European question turns. The legend of the Prussian, as an insolent and rapacious militarist, is not a thing which English policy found it useful to invent. On the contrary, it was a thing which English policy, for a long time, unfortunately found it useful to disguise. The English were almost the only people in Europe who were not allowed to realise that the Prussian was both a prig and a brute. Originally it was not only the general opinion of Europe, it was also the general opinion of Germany, that he was a prig and a brute. In the year 1800, let us say, such talk of Prussian brutality would have been much better understood in Bavaria than in Britain. Germany has never been kept in ignorance of the idea that Prussia is brutal. Nor has she now been converted to the idea that Prussia is not brutal. She has simply been converted to brutality. The other Germans have again and again called the Prussian callous and offensive; and they have now called for his help because he is callous and offensive, because they have been persuaded that it is a fine thing to be. The Pro-German writer takes a fact, which was not only a proverb in Europe but a proverb even in Germany, and represents it as a fiction fiendishly invented by the only people from whom it was at all successfully concealed.

This is, it may be said in passing, the very simple answer to the reproaches he levels against me for my insensibility to the realisation of many of my own more romantic dreams in Bavaria. They are not, I imagine, any more realised there than in the parts of France or Italy where I have myself found them. But in so far as Bavarians did stand for this spirit, it is the worse for them that they did not stand up for it. If that was the soul of Bavaria, then Bavaria has sold her soul. She has sold it for safety behind the iron shield of a power which nobody in the world, least of all the Bavarians themselves, ever regarded as anything but the mortal enemy of such a soul. And the sin of South Germany has been especially this: that it has humbled itself before the heathen from the north, not although, but because, he was heathen. It has accepted the creed that cruel and cold-blooded methods are the only business methods. The writer observes: "Houston Stewart Chamberlain has become a Bavarian—Gilbert Keith Chesterton, though he knew it not, has always been one—before the war." Houston Stewart Chamberlain has not become a Bavarian; for it was only in his power to become a renegade and a runaway.[63] But if I had been born a Bavarian, I can only hope that I might have distinguished myself by saying a word in favour of Bavaria, when her influence in the world was vanishing into that spiritual void called Prussia. As it is, Bavaria is simply a conquered country like Belgium, with the great superiority, on the side of the Belgians, that they fought before they were conquered. I should no more think of discussing the European situation with the Bavarian than of discussing it with the Kaiser's horse or the Crown Prince's dog. Very likely the Bavarian was a romantic figure, when he was anything; when he cut any figure at all in European politics. To-day we do not talk to him, but to his master.

63. Houston Chamberlain (1855-1927), the son of an English rear admiral, acquired Germany citizenship in 1916.

To explain to the poor Germanised gentleman the nature of the very dangerous thing called France would open vistas of difficulty. He seems much distressed because the French call glory, "*gloire*"; and, indeed, in a sense, this is the whole point. The French call glory glory; they recognise realistically that such an ambition exists in men, and they call it by its name. In calling it by its name they put it in its place; which is higher than greed and lower than religion. The French call glory glory; and the Germans call it "the real miracle of German resistance to the whole world," "the simply marvellous nature of their achievements," "German superiority and all its superhuman ascendancy," the higher culture, the coming race, the new religion, and all the rest of the rubbish. **It is the whole point that they brag without even knowing they are bragging, because they cannot think that the tallest talk can come up to the height of their merits.** It is the whole point that, when offered to them, a compliment is only a commonplace. A Frenchman never makes this mistake. He writes rhetoric rhetorically and romance romantically, because he likes doing each separate thing with logical thoroughness; but he knows quite well that it is rhetoric or romance. When Danton said, "We fling to the kings as a gage of battle the head of a king," he did not think he was making an ordinary remark.[64] He was talking for effect—for a definite effect. But when the German Emperor, talking of some two-penny intrigues about Morocco, said, "I flung down the glove to France," he was saying a thing pompously that might just as well have been said prosaically.[65] And he was saying it because pomposity was a mere habit, and part of his view of himself. The same French tendency to clear differentiation, and the deliberate pursuit of distinct aims, can be seen in some of the French disciplinary measures of which the Pro-German writer complains. I should not care to rely on his facts; but I should think it very probable that the French Government did apply a censorship in war-time more strictly than either the Germans or the English. It would be quite in the national character; but it is a character which I despair of describing to anybody so much soaked in the sulky sentimentalism of modern Germany. I will merely remark that the French use oratory with an object; they impose silence with an object; and when they have torn people in pieces, it has been with an object, if only the object of revenge. **But when a blast of bestial things broke on the world the instant after the Belgian line was crossed, we knew the presence of something which is not in the same world with the most wicked revenge. It was an insanity of success, a mere intoxication of triumph over the weak, a horrible holiday like the sins committed in a dream.** It was well for the world that Prussia failed; but almost as well for it that, for those few weeks, she thought she had succeeded. For since then

64. Georges Jacques Danton (1759–1794) was guillotined by the French Revolution he helped to start. Defying Europe's rapidly arming monarchies, he called for King Louis XVI's execution: "The coalesced kings threaten us; we hurl at their feet, as gage of battle, the head of a king." In contrast, the Kaiser rhetorically tossed down a glove.

65. German hostility toward French influence over Morocco and its desire for "a place in the sun" (meaning a foreign empire like Britain and France) brought the Kaiser to Tangiers in March 1905, where he made a saber-rattling speech that triggered the First Moroccan Crisis (1905–1906). That and a Second Moroccan Crisis in 1911, involving the German gunboat *Panther*, contributed to the climate of distrust before the war.

the world has known what it had need to know, and the nature of something with which Christendom cannot live.

G.K. Chesterton, "Our Note-Book," *Illustrated London News* 151 (October 27, 1917), 486. US: October 27, 1917. Also published as "The Insolence of the Prussian."

Discrediting Despotism

November 10, 1917

But the point at present is still more emphatically this—that if the war now leaves Prussia in any posture of success, she will now, most of all, be the mortal enemy of any sort of democracy whatever.

Editor: With the United States in the war, the ability of the Allies to win was no longer in doubt. What was in doubt, Chesterton says, is whether the Allies have the will to win the victory that is needed, one in which despotism and militarism become discredited in the eyes of Germans. If that fails, he warns, "if the war now leaves Prussia in any posture of success, she will now, most of all, be the mortal enemy of any sort of democracy whatever." That's precisely what happened in the 1930s, when Germany turned to Hitler as a Fuhrer and a modern replacement for the old fashioned despotism of the Kaiser. For more on Chesterton's opening remarks about the harm a "small minority" can do in a democracy, see his July 20, 1907 article (Ch. 1).

1917

There is to-day one enemy of the Alliance, and therefore of the world. He is not the German: he is the traitor. There was certainly treason in the turn of events which involved the Italian retreat; isolated and individual treason, no doubt, but, in the very nature of an army, one traitor can do the work of twenty.[66] There was certainly treason in the rapid and quite irrational rot that corrupted the Russian Revolution—the treason of a small minority doubtless, but it is the very definition of such modern and sham democracy that the small minority always rules.[67] What is most needed now is a living impatience, and even a sort of savage laughter, against the thought of all our mountainous labours being undone by a rat or a worm.

At the beginning of the war our enemies had all the materials of success, and we had only the moral elements with which to defy them. To-day the Allies have all the materials of success, and it is only the moral elements that can be doubtful or divided. It seems a strange thing to say of a man, in a mortal fight, that he can win and that the only question is whether he wants to. But this is really the position of the average doubtful man throughout the Alliance. The masses of America, when they arrive on the scene, the masses of Russia, if they return to it—to say nothing of the great armies already gathered in the other Allied countries—could defeat the Central Powers with a certainty like that of a sum in simple addition. All that can be called

66. In the summer of 1917, the Italian army was troubled by mutinies and low morale. In the Battle of Caporetto (October 24–November 9, 1917), Austrian armies, assisted by the Germans, drove back the Italian army, which suffered heavy losses. Ernst Hemingway described the battle in *A Farewell to Arms* (1929).

67. Aided by Germans eager to get Russia out of the war, in October–November 1917 the Russian Revolution was taken over by the Bolshevik party led by Trotsky and Lenin, ending any hope for a Russian democracy.

doubtful is their purpose, not their power. In so far as they can be persuaded to use their power, there is no doubt that they can effect their purpose. I take it, therefore, that the one thing to be done just now is to take every determining type of man among those who make up the Alliance, and prove to him as plainly as possible that nearly all he loves is lost for ever if he does not decide to do what he is unquestionably able to do. I will address myself first to the man who holds, as I hold, a certain political doctrine which is the oldest ideal of America, and is the greater part of the newest idealism of Russia. I mean, I will address myself to the democrat.

It must first be said that a solid and unanswerable fact has here been rather clouded by fictitious ways of stating it. We are not fighting to give Prussia a Parliament, even if democracy is held to mean no more than a Parliament. The point is rather that, however much or little democracy means, Prussia will always be the enemy both of its form and its substance. **But the point at present is still more emphatically this—that if the war now leaves Prussia in any posture of success, she will now, most of all, be the mortal enemy of any sort of democracy whatever.** She will not now leave to anyone she can influence even that form and façade of self-government which the modern world has established nearly everywhere else. She will not leave so much democracy as would fill the most battered ballot-box or the most old-fashioned despatch-box. She would not, in such a mood, spare the most corrupt Parliament, or show any respect even to the most unrepresentative representatives. She would be more aristocratic than the most exclusive Socialist club. She would be more despotic than the most successful modern Parliamentarian. Real republics and sham republics would for her be equally ridiculous—as ridiculous as they were when she rode over the French Frontiers in the first chaos of the French Revolution, crying out that Jacobins would run like poultry.[68] Put yourself for one second in the shoes of an ordinary man under the North German monarchy, and you will find yourself looking down an avenue of history adorned throughout with the trophies, true and false, of the supposed superiority of such monarchy. This one would be the end of a familiar series. The last act of the great European drama opened by the French Revolution will be concluded. Democracy will no longer be, for its critics, doubtful or chaotic or corrupt or wavering or disappointing; it will be dead. Consider a few plain facts. **First, it is a fact that Prussianised Germany is the one Power left that is totally unrepentant about tyranny. Not a word has ever fallen from the real masters of Germany to suggest that any oppressive Prussian act has at any time needed excuse, or may not at any time need repetition.** There may be other German elements which might eventually come to the surface; I am not discussing that here. I say that if the enemy succeeds now, or apparently succeeds now, it is pure Prussian militarism that succeeds now. If the Army attains any object, nobody will pretend that the Reichstag attained that object. A German success will be a success for Germans, not a success for German Socialists. If there is a victory for Hindenburg, no one will offer congratulations to Haase. If any real advantage remains with

68. The Jacobins were the radicals of the French Revolution and responsible for the murderous Great Terror.

the Germans while they are under their historic Government, the glory of it will go to that Government; and anyone who does not see it must be something very like an idiot.[69]

Second, it is a fact that there has been no German Revolution, and that there is less and less likelihood of any German Revolution. There is least likelihood of all if Germany has anything that could be called a success. It may be that real German failure, if forced home, might awaken some such thing. Again, I am not discussing that here—I am discussing German triumph, or the sort of thing the Germans would certainly call a triumph, though it were really only a triumphant escape. By this, I say, it is self-evident not only that Prussia would score, but that the Prussian type of government would score. It is blazingly obvious that the security of Prussian despotism would be contrasted with the collapse of Russian democracy. That is already the Prussian's lesson from the Russian Revolution; and the only lesson he will ever learn from it.[70] Where in the wild world of unreality did some of our Socialists get the notion that a Russian rebel would be an *example* to a Prussian subject? Putting aside the fact that the Prussian thinks he is himself an example to everybody, what in the world was the Russian example supposed to exemplify? If Berlin was to be an imitation of Petrograd, what was it to imitate? Do we need to be told at this time of day that the Prussian does not specially admire disorder and military failure and fantastic private liberty or licence? The more individuals or groups in the Alliance rebel, the more proud the ordinary German will be of the fact that he can obey. The more our various types of government are divided, the more glad he will be that his type of government is one, and the more certain he will be that it is the only one.

Our own English cosmopolitans are also guilty of a gross exaggeration of English conceit. Nothing can get it out of their heads that Germany and all humanity are pining to possess the British Constitution. They think that anybody in a difficulty must dream day and night of a Parliament—must desire and envy our Speaker's Mace, and possibly our Speaker's wig. That is at the back of the blind delusion that Germany must be longing for what are called "liberal institutions." Even what is good about them the North Germans are not wise enough to want. What is bad about them they are not fools enough to want. If they succeed without them, they will obviously want them even less. One State in Europe, and one alone, will emerge with the old type of military monarchy quite intact. If it also emerge with its military power and prestige quite intact, riding high above a chaos of crude experiments and stale corruptions of every other kind, I should have thought a baby could guess what the world would say.

Lastly, it is a fact that all this moral victory and vainglory is not merely what the Germans are logically bound to declare, it is what they are every day declaring.

69. Paul von Hindenburg (1847–1934) was a famous field marshal during the war and would be President of Germany from 1925–1934. Hugo Haase (1863–1919) was a socialist leader and an advocate of peace negotiations.

70. Chesterton argues that most Prussians prefer despotic security to the uncertainties of democracy. That's precisely the choice they make when they voted in increasing numbers for the Nazi party in the early 1930s.

Even when driven to all the disguises of Pacifism, they cannot disguise this sort of Prussianism. There runs through every official German speech and every inspired German article this profound conviction that their despotism will survive all our democracies. And unless our democracies learn how to combine against it, it most unquestionably will.

G.K. Chesterton, "Our Note-Book," *Illustrated London News* 151 (November 10, 1917), 554
US: November 10, 1917. Also published as "Despotism and the Democracies."

WHITEWASHING BARBARIANS

December 15, 1917

But the point is that the whole heritage of scholarship and civilisation, descending to Macaulay from Milton, and to Milton from the Arthurian romances, still steadily assumes that the barbarians were the enemies of Christendom, that we are the inheritors of Christendom, and that the Germans are the inheritors of the barbarians.

EDITOR: Chesterton explains how England came under the spell of the Strong Man. In the "old proverb about the frying-pan and the fire," Germany is the frying pan producing the ideological heat about the Strong Man and superior races, while England is the frying pan receiving that heat from Germany's flame.

THE old proverb about the frying-pan and the fire has a logical point not always noticed—a point which distinguishes it from similar sayings, like that about the devil and the deep sea, or that which compared the wild dogs of Scylla with the whirlpool of Charybdis.[71] We do not say of the devil, I trust, that the sea is his and he made it. The most fantastic mythologist has not, to my knowledge, narrated that Charybdis was a dog-fancier who provided Scylla with her dogs. But it is the whole point of the homelier phrase that the fire is worse than the frying-pan, because it is the cause of the frying-pan; because it is only the fire that makes it fry. The act of sitting in a frying-pan, if there were no fire, would be an eccentric, but not necessarily a painful habit. And the principle thus grotesquely embodied bulks very large in human history, and must especially be grasped at the tremendous turning-point of history at which we now stand.

I lately promised a correspondent, who had challenged some of my conclusions in these columns, to go a little more fully into the comparison of Britain and Germany, especially touching those evils in imperialism and capitalism which both he and I hold to be very real evils indeed. And the first thing I have to say is to draw attention

71. The sayings: "Out of the frying pan, into the fire." "Between the Devil and the deep sea." ("Between the Devil and the deep blue sea" was popularize by a 1931 song with that name.) "Caught Between Scylla and Charybdis" or "Between the rock and the whirlpool" (Referring to Scylla, a sea monster with six heads, a dog's legs, and a fish's tail that lived on a rock accompanied by wild dogs, and Charybdis, a monster who devours so much water, she creates a giant whirlpool. The two are separated by a sea channel so narrow, avoiding one increases the danger from the other.) Not mentioned is "Between a rock and a hard place." As Chesterton notes, while the basic meanings are the same, the details vary. Scylla and Charybdis were different dangers, a rock and a hard place are virtually the same. Note too that the danger of a hot frying pan exists only because of the fire.

to the intrinsic logic about the frying-pan and the fire. There is a possible relation between two evils in which one is not merely worse than the other—in which it is something very much worse than worse. It is the cause of the evil in the other; and it would still remain ultimately worse even if it happened to be apparently better. To take another parable from the kitchen, it is not so much a case of the pot calling the kettle black, as the coal calling the kettle black—of the soot and smuts and smoke calling the kettle black. And, to realise it in the present case, we must return to those primeval elements—not a little in the nature of fire or of smoke—which have conditioned all the recurrent crises of the history of Europe. If we do not debate first of these fundamentals, we are indeed only quarrelling over pots and pans, over vessels and implements—we are trying to cook with a cold fire and an empty pot. In this case the smoke and fire stand for the elements which we call broadly barbarism.

What altered the whole mind of England in the time of our fathers and grandfathers was a certain historical idea; it was a change in our whole view of the Barbarians and the Roman Empire. **The consistent tradition of all culture, for much more than a thousand years, was the view which we still express when we use the word "vandalism." It is the view that the barbaric invasion was a destruction, which fortunately did not succeed.[72] It was hardly before the time of our more elderly uncles that we began to hear everywhere the new view—that the barbaric invasion was a renovation, which fortunately did succeed.[73]** The new view came from North Germany, and before it came the opposite view was the view everywhere else in Europe, and nowhere more than in England. I will give one small instance out of a thousand, merely because I came upon it casually an hour or two ago. It was a quotation by so strictly nineteenth-century a man as Macaulay from so strictly seventeenth-century a man as Milton.[74] Macaulay, in one of his letters, quotes from Milton, in one of his Latin poems, a line which I find in the original to refer to the wars of King Arthur against the heathen. It may be translated as "To shatter the Saxon ranks with British battle." A man as late as Milton uses the word "Saxon" as directly hostile to the word "British"; but that is not the point. It is that a man as late as Macaulay uses the word "Saxon" as representing the word "German," and he also uses it as hostile to the word "British." He uses it, or quotes it, to express his intention, as an Englishman, "to make fun of certain Germans." I wish he had lived to do it; and, at the present time, he would certainly find a good deal to make game of. **But the point is that the whole heritage of scholarship and civilisation, descending to Macaulay from Milton, and to Milton from the Arthurian romances, still steadily assumes that the barbarians were the enemies of Christendom, that we are the inheritors of Christendom, and that the Germans are the inheritors**

72. The Vandals were an East Germanic tribe that attacked the Roman Empire in the fifth century, plundering Rome in 455 A.D. Pope Leo the Great is said to have persuaded their leader, Geiseric, not to do worse harm.

73. This was the point Henry Cabot Lodge was making in remarks quoted at the start of this chapter.

74. John Milton (1608–1674) was one of the greatest of England's epic poets. Thomas B. Macaulay (1800–1859) was a noted nineteenth-century poet, essayist, historian and politician. He first attracted public attention with an essay on Milton in the *Edinburgh Review* in 1825.

of the barbarians. Macaulay, whatever his limitations, was speaking here simply as an educated European; and in this capacity he was perhaps the last Englishman who told the truth about the monkey tricks of Frederick the Great.[75] But the next great name in his department is that of Carlyle, and with Carlyle the ancient tide has turned, the new flood has come; and it is a flood of flattery for barbarians, flattery for Germans, and especially of flattery for Frederick the Great. Men have begun to worship the sacred monkey.[76]

Now what the new movement did was to bring mysticism to the help of immoralism. It did not, of course, bring the immoralism—or rather, to speak more strictly, it did not bring the immorality. That, of course, did not come from Carlyle or from Frederick, but from Adam or from Satan. Men did wicked things in all parts of the world, including the most Christian parts of the world. But they seldom thought they were behaving like Christians. A man broke treaties, trampled on enemies, or betrayed friends, because he was ready to be contemned; he did not expect to be respected. **The notion of his being actually admired as a strong man, merely because he behaved like a selfish man, is a notion so new that I can myself remember it rising steadily, like a new religion, in the late Victorian time. I can myself recall the transition in literary fashions from the dull but decent morality of Macaulay to the picturesque but barbarous mysticism of Carlyle.** The school of Macaulay would balance the virtues and vices of William Rufus or Warren Hastings;[77] but for the school of Carlyle his vices were his virtues.[78] These great men of letters had long

75. One historian notes, "Frederick's vanity, his contempt for mankind, and his confidence in his own army made him the worst of allies. He abandoned the French in 1742 and again in 1745." He goes on to note: "In a famous passage the historian Macaulay condemned the conquest of Silesia: 'The evils produced by his wickedness were felt in lands where the name of Prussia was unknown; and in order that he might rob a neighbor whom he had promised to defend, black men fought on the coast of Coromandel, and red men scalped each other by the Great Lakes of North America.'" Christopher Duffy, *Frederick the Great: A Military Life* (London: Routledge, 1985), 298. The Macaulay quotation is from the second volume of his 1864 *Critical and Historical Essays*, page 253.

76. Chesterton may be using "sacred monkey" here as he does in the "Conclusion" to *The Everlasting Man* (1925), where it's a characteristic of primitive religions with tales of "a god who entered the body of a sacred monkey." But it's far more likely that he's simply looking back a single sentence. The "sacred monkey" refers to treating with almost religious seriousness this return to barbarism that Chesterton links to the "monkey tricks" of Frederick the Great." That glorification of power began, Chesterton says, in Northern Germany (Frederick's Prussia), and entered British thinking between Macaulay (1800–1859) and Thomas Carlyle (1795–1881), At the core of Chesterton's argument is the fact that Carlyle's last major work was an immense 7 volume *History of Friedrich II of Prussia, called Frederick the Great*, linking the very person Chesterton blames most for originating these ills as a philosophy of government with the person he sees bringing those ills into fashionable English thinking.

77. William II (called "Rufus," *c.* 1056–1100), the King of England from 1087 to 1100, was a ruthless ruler who, according to the *Anglo-Saxon Chronicle*, was "hated by almost all his people." Warren Hastings (1732–1818), the first governor-general of British India, was impeached in 1787 for corruption, but the trial, which began the next year, lasted until he was acquitted in 1795. Many of the difficulties with British rule in India trace back to him.

78. Thomas Carlyle's views are illustrated in "Rights and Mights," Chapter V of his 1840 *Chartism*, where he writes about the Norman invasion which brought "a new class of strong Norman Nobles, entering with a strong man.... strong Teutonic men; who on the whole proved effective men, and drilled this wild Teutonic people into unity and peaceful co-operation better than others could have done! How *can-do*, if we will well interpret it, unites itself with *shall-do* among mortals; how strength acts ever as the right-arm of justice; how might and right, so frightfully discrepant at first, are ever in the long-run one and the same,—is a cheering consideration." With such attitudes he was, of course, no fan of democracy (run by the many rather than the strong) and, faced with the success of democracy in America, he could only rant in 1850: "What great human soul, what great thought, what great noble thing that one could worship, or loyally admire, has yet been produced there?" Thomas Carlyle, *Latter-Day Pamphlets* (New York: Charles Scribner's Sons, 1903), 21.

been dead when the process began to penetrate everywhere; but the forms it took everywhere were the more clearly the fashion because they were both variegated and vulgar. We had the praise of the colonial and commercial expansionist, of the imaginative imperial financier—a kind of pawnbroker who not only received stolen goods, but bribed the policeman to steal them.[79] We had plays and novels about the strong-minded employer of labour, who seemed to think himself astonishingly virile because he could manage to starve a man in a siege, when he would never venture to hit him in a fight.

In point of time, and in point of fact, all this whitewashing of the bully was the result of the whitewashing of the barbarian. It was the result of the new notion that some anarchic strength from the North was the force that had renewed the world. Before that time history had been full of strong men; but nobody had ever heard of the Strong Man.[80] The evils in question were realities, but they were not ideals. In that sense there were always empires, but without imperialism; just as there must be capital, but without capitalism. The "ism" comes from the land of "isms," from the land of the metaphysics of immorality. Therefore any man who allows his anger against the evident evils of England to make him more tolerant to Germany is actually appealing to barbarism itself to cure the thing that it has barbarised. To vary the metaphor of the frying-pan in the direction of greater dignity, he is trying to quench fire-brands in the fire. The whole of the evil romance which has given a soul to our race for wealth and our worship of success has come from the false history which pretends that Christendom was rebuilt by law-breakers and not by law-givers, by robbery and not by chivalry, by pirates and not by priests. It is as if we pretended to find the origin of the word "vandalism" in the fact that the Vandals did not burn our churches, but only built them. Their descendants to-day do indeed build as well as burn; but eye-witnesses are doubtful which of the two acts strikes the eye as the more appalling catastrophe.

G.K. Chesterton, "Our Note-Book," *Illustrated London News* 151 (December 15, 1917), 746. US: December 15, 1917. Also published as "The Whitewashing of the Barbarian."

1917

79. Typical of colonial literature are the stories of Rudyard Kipling. For the "financier," there are tales such as Arnold Bennett's series in *Windsor Magazine*, "The Loot of Cities: The Adventures of a Millionaire in Search of Joy." Historically, John Rockefeller and Andrew Carnegie illustrate ruthless financiers. The giant foundations they established often promote global, anti-national policies that Chesterton sees as at least as bad as colonialism. Chesterton's point is not that human behavior has changed, but that the deeds that made William Rufus hated and resulted in Warren Hastings being prosecuted had, by the 1890s, been put into systematic heresies and many regarded such behavior as good and socially beneficial. The barbarian and bully had become heroes. Germany's heresy was that it carried those ideologies further than anyone else, not that it alone held them.

80. "Among the special factors of the early days of National Socialism was the tremendously important part played by the spectacular rise and near-religious veneration of a Führer. The organizational structure and activities of this new type of movement were based completely on the leader principle. In the center stood the figure of Adolf Hitler." Karl Dietrich Bracher, *The German Dictatorship* (New York: Holt, Rinehart and Winston, 1970), 47.

6

Battling Defeatism

1918

Courage in Decline—Editor

In a speech given at Harvard University on June 8, 1978, the Russian dissident and Noble Prize winner Alexander Solzhenitsyn warned that the West was becoming fatigued by the Cold War, then in its thirty-second year.

> A decline in courage may be the most striking feature which an outside observer notices in the West in our days. The Western world has lost its civil courage, both as a whole and separately, in each country, each government, each political party and of course in the United Nations. Such a decline in courage is particularly noticeable among the ruling groups and the intellectual elite, causing an impression of loss of courage by the entire society. Of course there are many courageous individuals, but they have no determining influence on public life. Political and intellectual bureaucrats show depression, passivity and perplexity in their actions and in their statements and even more so in theoretical reflections to explain how realistic, reasonable as well as intellectually and even morally warranted it is to base state policies on weakness and cowardice. And decline in courage is ironically emphasized by occasional explosions of anger and inflexibility on the part of the same bureaucrats when dealing with weak governments and weak countries, not supported by anyone, or with currents which cannot offer any resistance. **But they get tongue-tied and paralyzed when they deal with powerful governments and threatening forces, with aggressors and international terrorists.**

Fortunately, history did not end there. The "weakness and cowardice" Solzhenitsyn saw in high places did lead to the Soviet invasion of Afghanistan on Christmas day the following year. But in the 1980s, new leaders stepped forward who were not "tongue-tied and paralyzed" by might in the service of evil. Although it infuriated many among the "intellectual elite" where that decline was the greatest, President Ronald Reagan, Prime Minister Margaret Thatcher, and Pope John Paul II, together with the brave captive peoples of Eastern Europe turned history around, bringing about the downfall of Soviet tyranny and an end to the Cold War. Unfortunately, the other great evil that Solzhenitsyn mentioned, "international terrorists," remains, along that same loss of courage and the accompanying "depression, passivity and perplexity."

Sixty years earlier, Chesterton had seen Western democracies facing many of the same problems as Solzhenitsyn saw and spoke out against them with a similar eloquence. After the United States entered the World War I on April 6, 1917, the outcome of the war appeared certain. The resources of Britain, France, the sprawling British Empire, and now the United States were too great for the exhausted Central Powers.

Germany's only hope lay in a desperate gamble. When Russia was taken out of the war by an armistice signed in late December 1917 and the Treaty of Brest-Litovsk on March 3, 1918, Germany could shift its Eastern troops to the Western Front, hoping for a quick victory before the U.S. could train enough soldiers and ship them to Europe to make a difference. Germany's other hope was political, the possibility that her foes would grow tired and loose their will to fight, that they would make an early peace settlement that would leave the German people feeling undefeated, giving future German leaders a free hand to launch yet another war.

During 1918, Chesterton would oppose that growing loss of courage in English intellectual life, particularly among liberals and socialists, with all the skills at his command. He would fight the obsession many of his colleagues had with was later called "peace at any price." As he points out in the first article, these people "do not really care who imposes the peace, so long as they can accept it; nor even how long it lasts, so long as it lasts their time." That, he says, constitutes a "license to tyrants." Over the next two decades, events in Europe would demonstrate just how right he was.

A Peace Too Soon

January 12, 1918

No; what the Nation's whole argument does is simply to proclaim moral anarchy for the whole world, and a licence to tyrants for all time. What it really means, if it means anything, is that collective humanity cannot grapple with any aggression organised on a moderately large scale.

Editor: Chesterton criticizes *The Nation*, a prominent liberal magazine, for lacking the courage and conviction to see that Prussia must be punished for the war she began. He warns that, if the League of Nations adopts their attitude, it will be ineffective at keeping the peace. Evil left unpunished grows worse.

1918

We are still confronted with the crucial question, which can be stated simply enough. It is whether Prussia, if she fails to conquer by a service of brave men, will be able to conquer by a service of cowards? Having always preached terrorism, she is now simply preaching terror; and the title given to it is that of an early peace. Some are so waggish as to add the description of a just and lasting peace. But they appear to be perfectly indifferent, when their views are analysed, to the equity of the peace; and not particularly concerned even about its permanence. Their feeling, being a mere effect of fatigue, is necessarily irrational. **They do not really care who imposes the peace, so long as they can accept it; nor even how long it lasts, so long as it lasts their time.** To provide this brute reaction with exquisitely packed phrases and verbal adumbrations is now the special function of the *Nation*, once famous as a fine organ of Liberal ideals, but now made the instrument of a mere craving and crying for truce. Yet even in this melancholy deliquescence of certain Liberal groups, it is interesting to note the fragments that float here and there, as a witness to what was once a solid concern for international justice and liberty. There is a singular instance in a very recent issue of the paper, which is worthy of some study by those who would understand the chief fallacy and peril of these days. The first part of the passage concerns itself with the incompetent concept of a war of stalemate—one that will be prolonged indefinitely and indecisively. "We can go on bloodily assailing and weakening the foe, and he us"; but there is "no special likelihood" that a victory like Waterloo or Jena will ever be attained.[1] The *Nation* propounds this curious idea of the inconclusiveness of war; and then takes a mysterious pleasure in calling people "Never-Endians" because they wish to win the war and not lose it.[2] The epithet is to me a complete enigma. I should have thought that if anybody deserves to be called a Never-Endian, it is the man who holds this singular doctrine that wars never end. I cannot see how it can be Never-Endian to say, as we say, that the war can end, and shall end, and shall end in the right way. Only the true Never-Endian theory, the theory of the *Nation*, happens to be nonsense. It is not true that any war tends of its nature to go on for ever; if it were, all the wars of history would be going on still. The French in Flanders would find the Nervii still in arms against Julius Caesar; our naval manoeuvres in the Mediterranean would be embarrassed by the ships of Carthage operating in the first Punic War; and our advance on Jerusalem would be through a country torn by the struggles between the Amalekites and the Children of Israel. This, however, is not the fact. What is the fact is that all these wars, and all other wars, came to an end, and came to a decision by defeat and victory; though it is also a fact (and not an unimportant one) that most of these wars went on very much longer than the length of the war of which we complain. But the most important fact of all—the fact by which everything stands or falls—emerges yet more plainly. It is the simple and terrible fact that this war will certainly end in victory, if it is only a Prussian victory.

The writer in the *Nation* suggests that Germany has now something resembling a general offer of peace from the Allies. He appeals solemnly to those softer feelings for which the Prussians are famous in history, seeking to impress them with

1. This quote is from "A Straight Road to Peace," an editorial in *The Nation* XXII:13 (December 29, 1917), 428–429. The magazine had patched together a peace treaty from various speeches by high British officials. Its one objection was to an insistence by Prime Minister Lloyd George that it summarized as: "There must be a destruction of the Prussian military power—*i.e.* a crushing defeat by land." To that the magazine replied:

> No one can say when that point will arrive, nor how many more millions of precious lives, and thousand of millions of treasure, must be spent in order to attain it. Nor is there any special likelihood that an idealized melodramatic 'victory'—a victory of Waterloo, or Jena—will ever be attained. The mass of the soldiers, we imagine, do not believe in it. Both sides have secured considerable successes, and we can fairly claim that we have brought the whole scheme of German aggression absolutely to nought. Each party has gone near exhausting the other. But with neither has the will or the capacity of endurance failed, nor is it likely to fail. We can go on bloodily assailing and weakening the foe, and he us. But if the object of war, as Grotius said, is to attain peace, and if the world is in sight of a peace which is likely to endure on its own merits, why go blindly on?

Notice that this argument places on the Allies, rather than the Germans, responsibility for Germany's post-war attitudes. The aggressor need not change, everyone else must change to please him. That's appeasement in 1917.

2. *The Nation* did not use "Never-Endians" in its December 29 editorial, but it did three weeks earlier:

> Even if the wildest dreams of our Never-Endians were realized to-morrow and Germany's military machine were utterly and finally broken, the mere output of her cradles, the automatic increase of her population, would soon put all such calculations out of account. One thing and one thing only our Never-Endians can accomplish. They can feed Germany with a fresh supply of the moral force she lacks, by transmuting *our* sense of a just cause against her into *her* sense of a just cause against us." ["A Straight Road to Peace," *The Nation* XXII:10 (December 8, 1917), 320–321.]

the opportunity for realising their historic dream of universal love and tenderness. And then he says that if Germany does not respond to it "her guilt will be immeasurable and her punishment sure."[3] If, on the other hand, she accepts it (whatever "it" may be), then "the war is at an end," and that is all that matters. I, for one, had ventured to fancy that the war would never have had a beginning, let alone an end, if Germany's guilt had not already been immeasurable and worthy of some sure punishment. But that is not the point to which I desire to draw attention here. It is to the curious incidental admission almost to be described as a slip, by which the *Nation* here destroys the whole of its present case.

I should very much like to ask the editor of the *Nation*, who is still at least a man of the most striking intelligence, what on earth he means by saying that Germany's punishment will be sure. Why does he say this, having just that moment exhausted himself with proving that no such punishment can possibly be sure? I suppose we may dismiss the idea that he has had a supernatural vision, and seen the souls of Hindenburg and Harden already in the flames of an Inferno.[4] I think it scarcely more likely (supposing him to be still in a medical sense sane) that he thinks such German gentlemen will torment themselves, whipping themselves with briers or clothing themselves in hair-shirts, to expiate the sin of victory. And, if punishment does not come from above or from within, it must obviously come from outside—from other people. But it is the whole point of the *Nation*'s previous argument that such a punishment cannot come from outside or from other people—or, at the very least, that it cannot be "sure" to come. It is its whole point that perhaps, after all, we cannot punish the Germans, or even fully conquer the Germans—that nearly all the other civilised nations, including the millions of the American democracy, cannot really conquer the Germans. He must mean something by his dark and mysterious menace. What is it exactly that somebody will do to a recalcitrant Germany—something which France, Italy, the Slavs, the British Empire, and the American continent cannot do to her? How could there be a larger League of Nations to punish any "guilt" that was "immeasurable" enough to be worth punishing? What other forces are needed to prove to the *Nation* the presence of the moral unity of civilised mankind? Is Iceland to turn the scale? Is Spitzbergen to dictate peace to the world? Is the Island of Rumti Foo roused at last?[5]

3. Chesterton has returned to quoting from the December 29, 1917 editorial. He mocks those who realize that Germany was already guilty for the war, but who keep laying down new conditions and saying, if you don't do this, your "guilt will be immeasurable." But failing each test, only brings up yet another test and another empty, 'if you don't do this, we will really punish you.' That is international politics done like weak, ineffective parenting.

4. Field Marshal Paul von Hindenburg (1847–1934) was idolized throughout Germany for his victories over the Russians in 1914–1916 and regarded as the personification of Prussian virtues. Maximilian Harden (1861–1927) was a German journalist popular for his support of the war. He is best known for the Harden-Eulenburg affair (1907–1909), in which he accused people close to Kaiser Wilhelm II of homosexuality.

5. "The Bishop of Rum-ti-Foo" (1867) was among the satirical and funny "Bab Ballads" written by W.S. Gilbert. It opens: "From east and south the holy clan/ Of Bishops gathered to a man;/ To Synod, called Pan-Anglican,/ In flocking crowds they came./ Among them was a Bishop, who/ Had lately been appointed to/ The balmy isle of Rum-ti-Foo,/ And Peter was his name." Chesterton's point is that those who seek support in the vagaries of "international opinion" are unlikely to find any point sufficient to inspire them to stand against an aggressor.

No; what the *Nation*'s whole argument does is simply to proclaim moral anarchy for the whole world, and a licence to tyrants for all time. What it really means, if it means anything, is that collective humanity cannot grapple with any aggression organised on a moderately large scale. Let anyone attempt such an aggression, and the worst that can conceivably befall him will be a lingering war. This is the most pulverising pessimism; but at least it has a meaning. Coming on top of it, the remark about Germany's sure punishment is absolutely meaningless. If we cannot punish Germany for beginning the war, we cannot punish her for refusing to end it. If we cannot make the Prussian repent of attacking, we most certainly cannot make him repent of conquering; nor can we put any limit to any abuse he may make of such a conquest. If he cannot be brought to book for having enslaved Belgians, then he could not be brought to book if he skinned Belgians or boiled Belgians. He may do so before we have done with him; he may possibly be doing so even as I write. But my point is not even that he does such things; but that, on the *Nation*'s argument, there would be nothing to be done even if he did. The *Nation* is deserting—or rather, destroying—its own argument when it suggests that a certain degree of final insolence and impenitence in the Prussian would really call down punishment upon him. This is, of course, simply because the writer is better than his creed, as the Early Victorian Agnostics used to say about the vicar. He cannot help having been a Christian in his childhood and a Liberal in his youth; and, as a Christian, he still dimly believes in the Crusade; as a Liberal, he still dimly believes in the revolutionary wars. In other words, he cannot but believe, however hazily, that mankind has somewhere the moral resources for resisting and reversing a toppling triumph of iniquity. He may be reassured. His instinct is right—much more right than his reason seems to teach him; and, if the last expenditure of endurance and violence avail anything, he shall see his dream realised and his argument ruined.

G.K. Chesterton, "Our Note-Book," *Illustrated London News* 152 (January 12, 1918), 36. US: January 12, 1918. Also published as "Germany's 'Sure' Punishment."

1918

PACIFIST ILLOGIC

January 19, 1918

For the Pacifist tries to prove that the German example is too bad for us to follow, at the very time when he is also trying to prove that the German ethics are not so bad after all.

EDITOR: Chesterton points to the illogical rhetoric of many pacifists. War is so evil, they say, that it must be ended immediately and forever. But they also insist that this war is not so evil that there is any need to punish Germany for making war.

THERE are some curious contradictions, which I have never seen noticed, in the current Pacifist argument. They serve to recall us to the one point to which we now need most to be recalled. It was that stated long ago by Mr. Asquith, when he spoke of putting a term to the Prussian *power*: not to the shape of the Prussian map or the titles of the Prussian King—not, in other words, to the frontiers which Prussia will always be ready to cross, or the treaties she will always be ready to break.[6] It is perfectly pointless, for instance, to say that the enemy renounces annexations; we might as well say that he renounces the Roman triumph or the mediaeval tourney. Prussia did apply the pagan barbarism of brute annexation, as in Poland and Alsace, later than the civilised Powers; but even for Prussia annexation is no more the modern instrument than arquebus or arbelast.[7] Germany does not annex Turkey; she merely rules it. Germany has not annexed the Austrian Empire; but she has incorporated it, for all that. In short, if the Prussian power, apart from the Prussian legal territory, is left exactly as it is at present, she will achieve a moral suzerainty which will make what were once free States her dependants. We shall not be her conquered and annexed provinces. God forbid! We shall only be driven under the lash to be her allies. We shall not be her captive foes—a most impolite way of putting it; we shall only be her very unwilling friends. We also shall have to acquiesce in silence when new necessities involve her in new crimes—as an Austrian Catholic has to acquiesce in the sacrilege against Christian cathedrals; as an independent Bulgarian has to acquiesce in the massacre of Christian subjects of the Turk. Whenever the Prussian has the fancy for treating Spain or Scandinavia or the South American Republics in the precise way he has treated Belgium or Serbia, we shall be allowed to protest to the precise extent to which Hungary or Bavaria has protested. And all this will follow because the central military power has not been destroyed, as we once vowed that it should be destroyed. **So long as it survives as the one successful organisation of Europe, its philosophy and ethics will permeate Europe. An evil spirit, which once astounded the world, will ultimately have absorbed the world.**[8]

One of the contradictions of which I have spoken concerns itself with the much disputed question of the cruelty of reprisals. Were I discussing it as a matter of general morality, I should say it all depended on whether the moral veto were a matter of contract or of conscience. If we refrain from something because we have agreed with somebody not to do it, it is obvious that if he liberates himself he liberates us.

6. On August 6, 1914, two days after the war began, Prime Minister Herbert H. Asquith (1852–1928) told the House of Commons : "If I am asked what we are fighting for, I reply in two sentences. In the first place, to fulfil a solemn international obligation which , if it had been entered into between private persons, in the ordinary concerns of life, would have been regarded as an obligation not only of law but of honor which no self-respecting man could possibly have repudiated. I say, secondly, we are fighting to vindicate the principle which in these days when force, material force, sometimes seems to be the dominant influence and factor in the development of mankind, we are fighting to vindicate the principle that smaller nationalities are not to be crushed in defiance of international good faith, by the arbitrary will of a strong and over-mastering Power."

7. An arquebus was one of the earliest firearms. Armor would be tested by firing an arquebus against it and improvements in the arquebus eventually doomed armor. The arbalest was a powerful late-medieval crossbow whose bow was made of steel tensioned with a windlass. In skilled hands, it could kill out to 500 yards.

8. Fear of German power was one reason Britain and France turned to appeasement during the 1930s in a futile attempt to avert war. During the Cold War, a similar subjugation without actual occupation was called Finlandization, after Finland, which was allowed to remain democratic only because it did nothing to disturb its powerful neighbor. When I visited Finland in the late 1970s, an engineering student jokingly pointed to the antennas on the roof of a government building that, he said, were pointed eastward so his government could get its orders from the Soviets. More recently, some have accused European governments of tilting their foreign and domestic policies out of fear of radical Islam. There seems to be no evil those filled with fear aren't willing to excuse.

If we refrain from deeper spiritual reasons, this is not necessarily so. I will break a treaty made with the German Emperor if the German Emperor breaks it first, which will probably be the case. But I will not make a treaty with the devil, signed in my own blood and giving him my own soul, merely because the course of German culture and progress leads me to the conviction that the German Emperor has done the same.[9] There, I think, other questions come in, in which I should not allow the German Emperor to influence me in any way. But I do not propose here to debate the general problem of reprisals, because the position I criticise is inconsistent with both solutions. The Pacifist tries to have it both ways; and he is wrong both ways. A study of the statements in papers of the school of the *Nation* or the *Labour Leader* will show two different strands of humanitarian sentiment on the subject, which eventually get entangled in a totally hopeless knot.

For the Pacifist tries to prove that the German example is too bad for us to follow, at the very time when he is also trying to prove that the German ethics are not so bad after all. He thinks it a piece of international reconciliation to say that the enemy's action is a military necessity that may be excused in him. And the next moment he is saying that the same action is a moral degradation that is forbidden to us. I have seen a paragraph in the *Nation* recently rebuking most bitterly an air-raid on a German town, and calling it the worst news of the war. I have constantly seen in the same paper, and in similar papers, the suggestion that there must, after all, be more good in those whom Mr. Ramsay MacDonald calls "our German friends" than is implied by those of us who still labour under the impression that they are our German enemies. I can sympathise with the first sentiment, and I can understand the second; but I can make no sense whatever of a combination of the two. I can at least follow the argument which says, "These men are men and not devils; there must, therefore, be a case for their conduct." I can also follow, and with far more fellow-feeling, the argument which says "Why should we be devils merely because they are devils?" But I draw the line at being asked to differ from them because they are devils, and then to agree with them because they are not. **If an act is so extraordinarily brutal that we must not do it, even in self-defence, they must certainly be very extraordinary brutes if they do it in brute aggression. It cannot at once be too vile to be imitated and too venial to be punished.**

But it is precisely in that one word "punished" that we find the whole point, and the motive of this immoral and muddle-headed inconsistency. **Consciously or unconsciously, the Pacifist is a Pro-German. Consciously or unconsciously, he wishes to save the Germans from being either fought with their own weapons or judged for their own crimes.** But one or other of the two anti-German acts must be right. If these military acts are lawless, why should we not punish them? If they are lawful, why should we not do them? It is quite true that if a criminal has made

9. Chesterton is saying that a contract or treaty can be broken if the other side violates its provisions, perhaps by invading Belgium. But we should never do something inherently wrong, such as killing civilian hostages, because our foe has done so. This is similar to the idea in J.R.R. Tolkien's *The Lord of the Rings* that the power of the Ring should not be used to fight Sauron, but that Sauron must be fought nevertheless.

patterns on his wife with a red-hot poker, the magistrate does not immediately proceed to make patterns on him with a red-hot poker. But the magistrate does immediately proceed to do something; and something which is based on the theory that magistrates have the right to act as magistrates, and criminals have not the right to act as criminals. And the Prussian is in the same position; if he and his methods cannot be accepted by civilisation as methods, they can be punished by civilisation as misdeeds. So that we come back to the point of punishing the oppressor of Europe—which is exactly the point that these people wish to avoid. And they are all the more in anxiety, not to say agony, to avoid it because it can be deduced with more deadly certainty from their own doctrines than from anybody else's.

For, if anybody ought logically to believe in a war of victory, it is precisely the man who was a special champion of peace until he accepted the special case for this war. There were thousands of pacifists who woke up as patriots in 1914, because they thought the crushing of Belgium, with all its peculiar cruelties, was something just too bad to be borne. If these people would consent to think, instead of merely feeling tired, they would instantly see that they themselves are exactly the people who ought now to be hardening, and not weakening, in their war-aims. That which was bad enough to be fought, even by men who hated fighting, is obviously bad enough to be beaten, even if it is hard to beat. I know many whose philosophy had always been far more anti-military than my own who yet most courageously condemned themselves to the danger and drudgery of military service, simply because they could see the fact that Prussianism is something far worse than mere militarism. I would most earnestly and respectfully appeal to these brave men to be as courageous in their thinking as they have been in their fighting. Can they seriously believe that Prussianism is spontaneously ceasing or has at present any particular motive to cease? Can they, above all, pretend for a moment that Prussian cruelties are ceasing, when they are quite vividly and violently increasing and multiplying by land and sea? **This abnormal thing we set out to slay is still abnormal and still alive; it has eaten yet more living things and believes itself yet more alive. There is no escape from the dilemma of either crushing the abnormal or letting it become the normal.** We must either make a model of it or make an example of it; and the example must be an execution.

1918

G.K. Chesterton, "Our Note-Book," *Illustrated London News* 152 (January 19, 1918), 68.
US: January 19, 1918. Also published as "Are the Pacifists Pro-German?."

Pacifist Weakness

January 26, 1918

It is the attitude of the man who chooses the very time at which he ought to stiffen as the time at which to weaken. He only fails at the last moment; and it is always the most important moment.

EDITOR: Chesterton criticizes both pacifists and H.G. Wells, warning of disaster if the war does not end with a clear German defeat. He also criticizes idealists who, rather than stand up for their ideas, intrigue for them behind the scenes, taking advantage of the public's weariness with war to advance a hidden agenda. For more on that, see the August 10, 1918 article, where Chesterton writes, "And the real case against a League of Nations, as preached by some of its prophets, is precisely that the name does not represent their real ideal—but, at the best, a step towards their real ideal; and, at the worst, a mere disguise for their real ideal."

THERE is one particular attitude to which most human beings, including myself, have a very strong objection. It has created all the popular tales about traitors, though it is sometimes more subtle than treason; but it has all the effects, if not the motives, of treason. **It is the attitude of the man who chooses the very time at which he ought to stiffen as the time at which to weaken. He only fails at the last moment; and it is always the most important moment.** Especially he always remembers the reasons that ought to have prevented him from beginning a thing when they only serve to prevent him from finishing it. Sometimes those reasons are rather thin modern theories, which instantly gave way when he found an action desirable, and which now only return to him because he finds it difficult.

Such a man always appears to the popular instinct merely to have played it false; but very often it is his position from the first that has been false. I always feel this about some of the wealthy Quakers, and other theoretic opponents of all war, in their attitude towards this war: They had a right to forbid a war; but they had no right to help it so as to hinder it. And they did, indefinably and perhaps unconsciously, help it so as to hinder it. Pacifists are called fanatics; but I, for one, wish that those among them who are most influential had been far more fanatical. A Pacifist's peace is at least a much better thing than a Pacifist's war. I should feel in the same way about any other extreme or extravagant doctrine, however strongly I disagreed with it. **I think a vegetarian is something like a lunatic when he calls me a cannibal for eating a mutton chop. But I should prefer to find him denouncing my cannibalism to a large crowd, rather than find him conspiring obscurely everywhere to upset butchers' carts and nail up the doors of butchers' shops.** I should think he had a right to do the first, his convictions being what they were; I deny that he has a right to do the second, whatever his convictions might be. I think it both crazy and cruel for a follower of Mrs. Eddy to seek to deprive the sick of the help of any science except Christian Science.[10] But I should think it much worse if the Christian Scientist were only caught stealing the medicine from an invalid's cupboard or the petrol from a doctor's garage. **Idealism is an excuse for insurrection; it is not an excuse for intrigue, which is against its very nature; and with those that were, and are, merely intriguing for peace I pretend to no patience or respect. The horrors of war are a perfectly logical reason for not going to war. They are not a reason for trying to do a thing when you happen to feel excited, and dropping it**

10. Mary Baker Eddy (1821–1910) founded Christian Science, which believes illness is an illusion.

when you happen to feel tired. If you have any intellectual self-respect whatever, you must ask yourself three questions which are as obvious as the alphabet: What you originally decided to fight for; whether you have got it; or whether you can get it by continuing to fight? That it is a ghastly thing to fight, and a still more ghastly thing to be obliged to allow others to fight, is a most vivid and painful truth. But it is a truth, I will venture to suggest, which ought to have crossed a powerful mind some little time ago.

There never was a moment in this mortal trial when it was more necessary to be ruled by the actuality and not the atmosphere. The atmosphere is naturally and necessarily one of weariness, and a reaction towards escape; but it is still the truth that we ought not to escape, even if we could escape, from actuality. I see that some new suggestions have recently been made in this direction by a man of genius who is always suggestive, Mr. H.G. Wells. Mr. Wells is, above all things, a great artist in atmospheres; and he is, as such artists often are, far too much the victim of atmospheres. He is also the victim, I think, of the weakness already described—the lack of something which may be loosely described by the theological term of final perseverance. Even his most successful novels fail only at the last moment. They end, but they do not conclude; the writer seems resolved to escape from a conclusion. They do not end in mere negation or despair, but only in an oblivion of their original object—as if the writer had just caught sight of something else that had nothing to do with it. Hence he is not desperate; but he is, in a definite and double sense, distracted. In much the same way he seems to have side-tracked himself on the subject of the war, running clean off the rails of reality.[11] He has been caught by considerations quite remote not merely from our reasons, but from his own reasons, for having supported the war at all. He has fallen in love at first sight—or rather, at first hearing—with the mere name of Mr. Trotsky and the Revolutionists at Petrograd.[12] He offers them to us as a more democratic type of diplomatist, who are more plain and simple than our own diplomatists. As to that, I am content to answer that we could most of us ask very plainly and simply for things, if we only asked for them and did not get them. The Bolshevik diplomatist demanded that the peace negotiations should be removed to the West; and they were not removed. He demanded that the military forces should not be removed to the West; and they were removed. I believe I have been consistently not only much more of a democrat but much more of a revolutionist than Mr. Wells; I have even been rebuked by him for my extreme and extravagant denunciation of the existing social system. And I should have been ready on many occasions to ask simply and plainly for what I wanted—to say in a commanding voice, "Give property to all the families in the State," or "Punish all Trusts as criminal conspiracies immediately." There would only have been two limitations attaching to these plain and simple things which

11. For Wells' views, see *In The Fourth Year: Anticipations of a World Peace* (1918) and Appendix G in this book.

12. Leon Trotsky (1879–1940) was one of the leaders in Russia's communist revolution. At this time he was leading the peace negotiations with Germany at Brest-Litovsk. The treaty, signed in March 1918, was harsh on Russia, demonstrating Chesterton's point that the enthusiasm Wells has for Soviet negotiating skills is misplaced.

I should have demanded. One is that I should not have got what I demanded—or, perhaps, expected to get it. The other is that I should not have thought it practical to do it while I was admittedly trying very desperately to do something else which we all agree ought to be done.

I would, therefore, draw attention to the detail that there exists in the world at this moment a war; and a German Empire which has been so far successful in that war that it has disarmed Russia, Roumania, Serbia, and Montenegro, and has already so far erected a Middle Europe which overshadows Eastern Europe. To say in face of such a fact that you rather like Mr. Trotsky's tone is as flighty and foolish as to say that you rather like the colour of his eyes. To say that there may be a revolution in successful Germany, because there has been a revolution in unsuccessful Russia, is to throw out wild guesses into the air. There may be; but we can only build with any security upon what is. To say that a republic will certainly be set up in Berlin because it has been set up in Petrograd is about as businesslike as to say that a wooden statue will certainly be set up in Petrograd because it has been set up in Berlin. Personally, I should always have said that the Russian would always have been more democratic than the Prussian; that he had more natural taste for what is revolutionary, as the man of Berlin had more natural taste for what is wooden. But even if we think the Russian example may be followed, it is madness to say it must be followed.[13] We are concerned with calculable facts; and cannot risk all England and all Europe upon possibilities that are quite incalculable. If we have any rights in the quarrel, we cannot conceivably gamble them on a faint hope that Germany may eventually cease to worship the statue of Hindenburg and begin to worship a statue of Haase.[14] I therefore humbly suggest to Mr. Wells that he should return for a moment to the contemplation of real things, and especially of the most real thing remaining in front of us: the fact that we have lost the war, and with it the faith of England and the freedom of Europe, unless we can still force the Prussian to do certain things which he has a prodigious objection to doing. Of these the very least, as Mr. Wilson and Mr. Lloyd George and all our political leaders have said, include a French Alsace-Lorraine and a free and united Poland spreading to Posen and the sea. As for sympathising with revolutionists, I have sympathised with many in many places, even including a place called England; and my sympathy did not suddenly begin yesterday. My prejudices are of older date, and may possibly be of longer duration.

G.K. Chesterton, "Our Note-Book," *Illustrated London News* 152 (January 26, 1918), 100.
US: January 26, 1918. Also published as "The Rails of Reality."

13. Knowing these sentiments, Germany would contrive a change of government just before the war ended to improve its bargaining position. Unfortunately, in the minds of many Germans that saddled the new democracy with blame for the Versailles Peace treaty. Chesterton is right. Germans will not accept the blame for starting the war unless they are given no alternative, as happened with World War II. Even then many Germans were hostile toward the war crimes trials of their leaders, not recognizing any higher authority than their nation.

14. In several articles, Chesterton has fun with the wooden statues of Field Marshal Hindenberg that were used to raise money for the war. Hugo Haase (1863–1919) was an anti-war socialist leader. Chesterton contrasts the two Germans in a November 10, 1917 article (Ch. 5).

Pacifist Defeat

April 6, 1918

It is the peculiarity of the Prussian in history that he has always been allowed to do things which everybody, almost instantly afterwards, saw ought never to have been allowed.

Editor: Chesterton exposes the strange twists of illogical behind many pacifist arguments. Similar illogic existed during the Cold War. The Soviet Union, it was said, posed no treat to the United States, so any fear we might express about them was "inordinate," as then-President Jimmy Carter put it.[15] Yet we must not provoke them, many of the same people told us, because they might unleash a global nuclear war. Both can't be true, and it's difficult to imagine how anyone could fail to see something inherently evil in a government that had killed tens of million of its own citizens.

Constructive fear is objective and reasonable, basing itself on both the power of a foe and his hostile intent which, in the case of Germany in Chesterton's day and the Soviet Union more recently, was considerable. Since it is based on larger facts, it's not easily swayed by moods or passing events. In a December 16, 1916 article (Ch. 4), Chesterton condemned those who lack perspective: "To be elated when a village is captured in the morning, and cast down again in the afternoon—this is not to follow the course of a war. It is simply to be ignorant of the very nature of a war."

Psychology sheds light on this situation. People typically respond to danger in two ways. One takes into account the danger a foe poses and responds with either "fight or flight." The other appears to deny that danger and is called "tend and befriend." With the latter, someone who intends harm is treated as if he were a friend.[16] That's why Chesterton calls these pacifists "Pro-German." They're showing a solicitude for a powerful Germany that they're not showing for weak Belgium. In some situations, the fear that leads to this befriending response can be so strong that those who talk realistically are attacked. A perverted fight response is directed at people who intend no harm—either those in one's own country who want to stand up to the evil or those

15. Carter's single term as President saw him elated over a few minor victories for democracy in June of 1977 and "cast down" in a July 15, 1979 address to the nation in which he said: "The erosion of our confidence in the future is threatening to destroy the social and the political fabric of America." Carter's earlier elation was expressed in a June 1977 speech on "Human Rights and Foreign Policy" at the University of Notre Dame.

> Democracy's great recent successes—in India, Portugal, Spain, Greece—show that our confidence in this system is not misplaced. Being confident of our own future, we are now free of that inordinate fear of communism which once led us to embrace any dictator who joined us in that fear. I'm glad that that's being changed. For too many years, we've been willing to adopt the flawed and erroneous principles and tactics of our adversaries, sometimes abandoning our own values for theirs. We've fought fire with fire, never thinking that fire is better quenched with water. This approach failed, with Vietnam the best example of its intellectual and moral poverty. But through failure we have now found our way back to our own principles and values, and we have regained our lost confidence.

The ease with which a few countries (three of four in Europe) maintained democratic rule no more demonstrated that communism was not to be feared than the Soviet invasion of Afghanistan that followed demonstrated the opposite. In the years since, Carter has shown he will "embrace any dictator" in the oil-rich Middle East while attacking Israel, a tiny democracy. As Chesterton stresses, weakness in positions of power leads to inconsistent policies—bullying innocent little countries and pandering to large evil ones. The result is disaster.

16. In extreme situations, this is called the Stockholm Syndrome, after a 1973 kidnapping in Sweden. In less extreme situations, it leads to a world view filled with phobias and conspiracies. Unable to discipline their own fears, they can't understand those who respond to danger with courage, intelligence, and resolution, as President Reagan did in the 1980s. Conspiracy theorists show a similar fear of fear. They often pick a group who can do them no harm (typically Jews or quiet religious people) for their target. A real foe terrifies them into silence, as Chesterton notes when he points out pacifism's inability to criticize Germany.

in smaller countries who are willing to fight. That explains Neville Chamberlain's curt dismissal of Czechoslovakia as "a faraway country of which we know little," at the time of the 1938 Munich Agreement giving the Czechoslovakian Sudetenland to Hitler. With that blunder, Churchill warned, Britain had "suffered a total and unmitigated defeat." It was "only the first sip, the first foretaste of a bitter cup which will be proffered to us year by year unless by a supreme recovery of moral health and martial vigour, we arise again and take our stand for freedom as in the olden time."

The present struggle against terrorism is generating similar responses. Politicized Islam poses no treat to civilized society, we are told, so we must not become "Islamophobic." Yet we also must tread gently, making no effort to promote democracy or advance human rights in the Middle East, lest we provoke them to kill us. Such muddled thinking can only come from those paralysed with fear. Shakespeare got it in right in *Julius Caesar.* Cowards do die many times before their death, and the first thing that dies is their ability to think clearly, as Chesterton stresses in this article.

Now for an aside. On April 15, 1918, a little over a week after this article was published, C.S. Lewis was wounded by a British shell that fell short of the Germany lines. In his autobiography, he described what happened in the winter of 1918 as he recovered from trench fever in a Le Tréport hospital.

> It was here that I first read a volume of Chesterton's essays. I had never heard of him and had no idea what he stood for; nor can I quite understand why he made such an immediate conquest of me. It might have been expected that my pessimism, my atheism, and my hatred of sentiment would have made him to me the least congenial of all authors....
>
> In reading Chesterton, as in reading Macdonald, I did not know what I was letting myself in for. A young man who wishes to remain a sound Atheist cannot be too careful of his reading.[17]

C.S. Lewis would credit Chesterton's *Everlasting Man* (1925) with persuading him to abandon atheism and become a Christian. Only George Macdonald had more individual books in Lewis' personal library than Chesterton. And it was the good sense that Chesterton demonstrated in articles such as these that changed Lewis' mind.

At the time of writing, the armies of the Entente are in orderly retreat, and the critics of the Entente are in disorderly rout. There has been, so far, no decisive Prussian victory; but there has already been a decisive Pacifist defeat. In that intellectual war in the air, like the war in heaven in the epic, which is waged over the heads of the bodily combatants, the cloudy hosts of compromise or cowardice are clearly divided and scattered. The internationalists are all contradicting each other; and more than one internationalist is excitedly contradicting himself.[18] One philosopher is saying that the Bolsheviks were blameless, and ought therefore to be left to their fate; that we ought to have obeyed them when they told us to abandon everything, and that therefore we could not listen to them when they asked us not to abandon

17. C.S. Lewis, *Surprised by Joy* (London: Collins, 1955), 153–154. At that time, some nine collections of Chesterton's essays had been published: *The Defendant* (1901), *Twelve Types* (1902, enlarged to *Varied Types* in 1908), *All Things Considered* (1908), *Tremendous Trifles* (1909), *Alarms and Discursions* (1910), *A Miscellany of Men* (1912), *The Appetite of Tyranny* (1915), and *Utopia of Usurers* (1917).

18. In a June 22, 1907 article Chesterton distinguished between cosmopolitan and international. Here he doesn't.

them. Another philosopher is explaining that it is unreasonable to expect the German Socialists to mutiny against the German flag, and that therefore we ought to stake all our hopes on the certainty of their doing so. One says that it was our first duty to follow the Russian Revolution to its last extremes, but not in the least our duty to save it in its last extremity. Another says that the German Socialists must first be pardoned because they are Germans and not Socialists; and must then be trusted because they are Socialists and not Germans. But these are only two random examples, out of all the random inconsistencies to which these inhuman sophists have now been driven. We are to establish a universal League of Nations as our chief and most compelling concern; but the whole of the East of Europe is no concern of ours. It is an instant and practical necessity to disarm everybody; but it is an insane and Utopian vision to think of disarming Prussia. The war will be a vain slaughter if it does not create a new heaven and a new earth; and the war was waged solely and strictly in order to secure a technical retirement from Belgium. It is not the fault of the German people, but only of the German royal family; and it is therefore hopeless and useless to think of ridding them of that family. These, and a hundred more illogicalities, were always potentially present in this confused mass of opinion; but the more practical point has now been reached in which mere confusion has become real division. It is not now merely the philosopher who is saying two opposite things at once. It is not only within the same mind, or on the same mouth, that we find the remarkable word which is compounded of yes and no. Some are finding consistency in conflict; are dividing into groups representing the divergent policies; and may even come to criticising each other, almost as freely as they have criticised the right of free nations to defend themselves against aggression. There is visibly forming, for instance, a rather dismal diplomatic group round aristocrats and antiquated Conservatives like Lord Lansdowne,[19] from which intellectuals like the editor of the *Nation*, loth to lose his whole Tolstoyan dream, would want very little to make them break away. It is intellectually impossible, as the examples I have given will show, to compose any intelligible formula that will cover both conceptions; and they cannot for ever take refuge in being unintelligible. Their division is both real and deep. In short, what has not happened to the army that is fighting in the field is exactly what has happened to this army that has been fighting in the air. The Pacifist line is pierced. There has been a real breakthrough, rolling up two separate sections like separate armies; and a stream of new public opinion, which they cannot stop, is pouring through the gap. The one thing to be done now is to see that we do not suffer from the brutal irony of a bad synchrony—that we do not find we have won our moral victory too late to avert our military defeat.

I, for one, do not for a moment believe that such will be our disaster. But it may help to avert it to realize that such has, in the past, been our danger. **It is the peculiarity of the Prussian in history that he has always been allowed to do things which everybody, almost instantly afterwards, saw ought never to have been**

19. This may be Henry Petty-FitzMaurice (1872–1936), 6th Marquess of Lansdowne and a member of Parliament.

allowed.[20] He was suffered to split up Poland with his sword on the supposition that the Pole would soon forget his flag. The Pole has never forgotten it; but the Prussian had been suffered to steal it. He was allowed to attack the Danish crown and take away the Danish provinces, on the assumption that he was the mere representative of the German States and the Austrian Empire. He trampled on the German States and attacked the Austrian Empire; but he had been allowed to take the Danish provinces, and he was allowed to keep them. He was permitted to take the French provinces on a pedantic plea that they were German provinces, that they would be at rest under German rule, and that it was natural that he should rule them. He has shown himself conspicuously unable to rule them, or to rule anything like them; but he had been allowed to take them.[21] It only became plain that he had not the power to govern when he had finally gained the power to misgovern. In all these cases, and many others, the same tragic farce was enacted; the truth was always discovered too late. And we have, of course, seen that same tragic farce enacted in the last few months before our own eyes. The Russian opened his arms to embrace the penitent and peaceful Prussian; and it was only afterwards that he discovered which of the two animals it is that really embraces like a bear.[22] The Prussian is well known to be a methodical and orderly person; and he shows his ticket-of-leave to the policeman every time he plans a new murder. Precisely why his passport or permit has always hitherto been accepted is what the late Mr. Andrew Lang might call a historical mystery.[23] Anyhow, it is certain that the passport is always found to be an accomplished fake, just after its use is an accomplished fact. But the longest run of the most successful criminal comes to an end. I believe the career of this criminal will now come to an end; and I think by this time everybody believes that it ought to come to an end.

Now, in the light of these familiar facts, we shall not find it hard to choose the peacemaker's path for him, since he is now too bewildered to choose for himself. We shall not find it hard to settle whether he ought to narrow his mind to Belgium, as he thinks on Monday, or widen his mind to the whole world, as he inclines to think on Tuesday. He must emphatically widen his mind, difficult as the task may be. In other words, every sane man must know enough of the Prussian game by this time to know that, if he does not save everything, he cannot save anything. Without insanity and suicide, we cannot say that Russia is no business of ours, or that Poland is no business of ours, as we said that Denmark was no business of ours; or that France was no business of ours. **To do so is to give special permission for a process going**

20. This marvelous principle begs to be extended. The most dangerous evil in an era is the one that doesn't get its due share of the blame for what it does wrong. Prussia in Chesterton's day, the Soviet Union throughout much of its existence, and more recently Islamic terrorism—all found eager apologists.

21. The unfortunate events Chesterton describes span almost exactly a century, from the partition of Poland in the late eighteenth century (1772, 1793 and 1795) to the annexation of Alsace-Lorraine in 1871.

22. Russia under the Soviets had sought peace with Germany, only to receive the harsh Treaty of Brest-Litovsky.

23. Andrew Lang, a prolific Scottish writer, is best known for his collection of fairy tales. In 1904 he published a series of "Historical Mysteries" about strange but true stories. Chesterton may be alluding to "Queen Oglethorpe," where the lack of a passport figures in a tale set in the late 1600s.

further, when it has already gone much too far—the process by which Prussia has weakened her rivals separately, and destroyed her victims one by one. I see that Lord Courtney of Penwith has been asking whether we should have gone to war with Germany if she had done no more than conquer and oppress Russia.[24] I think it only too probable that we should not have done so; but surely no man in his wits can now doubt that we ought to have done so. I think it only too probable that we should have stood aside while our enemy seized all the resources of the East for his future wars, just as we stood aside while he gained the grip on Poland that gave him the gates of Warsaw, or gained the minerals of Lorraine with which he now menaces Paris. In short, I think it quite likely that England might have played the fool then, pretty much as Lord Courtney wants her to play the fool now. But I do not believe she will play the fool now. England is now in the heart of Europe, heroically bearing the heaviest shock of the European war. And I think that even the internationalist will have to begin to admit that Europe exists. **It is a severe strain for the cosmopolitan to concede the existence of other countries, or for the humanitarian to embrace the interests of humanity. But, perhaps, with an effort of imagination, it might be done.**

G.K. Chesterton, "Our Note-Book," *Illustrated London News* 152 (April 6, 1918), 402.
US: April 6, 1918. Also published as "Illogicalities in the Air."

PACIFIST PRIGS

May 11, 1918

It indicates the survival of a certain sort of young man who is a Pacifist not because he is a Quaker, or because he is a Tolstoyan, or even because he is an Anarchist—but because he is a prig, and nothing else.

1918

EDITOR: While expressing light-hearted respect for the "dying sect" of post-Christian Puritan pacifists such as the Quakers, Chesterton blasts a new and typically younger sort of pacifist appearing in his day—those whose "hatred of patriotism is very much plainer than his love for peace." He notes that such people are "marked by an imaginative insufficiency which can be compared to nothing except to finding a Commander, in the thick of battle, looking into a pocket-mirror instead of a field-glass."

In his 1952 autobiography, *After All*, Norman Angell, the pacifist writer Chesterton mentions in this article, agreed that a new pacifism had indeed risen at this time, and—perhaps with a glance in his pocket-mirror—credits himself with founding it. To make his point, he quotes a 1913 magazine article.

> It is only four years since Mr. Angell's pamphlet, *Europe's Optical Illusion*, was published, a work as unimposing in form as it was daring in expression. For a time

24. Leonard H. Courtney was the 1st Baron Courtney of Penwith (1832–1918). Hitler saw that many in England were like Courtney, willing to let Germany do as it wanted in the East as long as it left Britain and France alone. In *Mein Kampf*, he stressed that Germany should look for its "living space" in the East. But as Chesterton notes, after the German had occupied Eastern Europe, one nation at a time, he would have "all the resources of the East for his future wars." That failure to make "an effort of imagination"—seeing in advance the importance of Czechoslovakia and Poland to the peace of Europe—would have tragic results.

> nothing was heard of it in public, but many of us will remember the curious way in which reports of its contents and of the effect it was having upon eminent people filtered through from all kinds of odd quarters. The whispers grew gradually in strength until they had swelled into something like a roar; *The Great Illusion* was issued, and 'Norman Angelism' suddenly became one of the principle topics of discussion amongst politicians and journalists all over Europe. Naturally at first it was the apparently extravagant and paradoxical elements in the new Pacifist gospel that were fastened upon most. Here was a man—a man with a pseudonym coming out of nowhere—who was convincing crowned heads and ministers that the whole theory of the commercial basis of war was wrong, that no modern war could make a profit for the victors.... People who had been brought up in the acceptance of the idea that a war between nations was analogous to the struggle of two errand boys for an apple, and that victory must inevitably mean economic gain, were amazed into curiosity. Man who had never examined a Pacifist argument before read Mr. Angell's book... and now, after only four years, organisations responding to his stimulus are springing up all over the country.[25]

But if war doesn't pay, humanity would have learned that long ago, much as it has learned not to sleep naked in the cold or eat dirt. History knows many profitable wars, the most obvious being those of Rome, a city that grew wealthy through conquest. War are profitable for the simplest of reasons—wealth can be moved from one country to another. In ancient wars only a few items were worth the cost of transporting over primitive roads. Modern technology, better transportation, industrial economies, and more sophisticated banking systems make it easier than ever to benefit from war. Today, almost anything can be transported quickly and cheaply. Even more important, the economic domination that results when one country is unwilling or unable to fight and must make unfavorable agreements to avoid war can make militarism extremely profitable for a nation that can merely threaten war without incurring its costs.

Of course, it is true that some aggressions don't pay. Germany didn't benefit from WWI, but that was because Britain and France fought back. A modern war against a nation that refused to fight because it believed that, won or lost, 'war doesn't pay' would almost certainly be profitable. An aggressor could simply march in, take everything valuable, and leave. It wouldn't even be burdened with the hassles of occupation, since it could reconquer this foolish and helpless victim anytime it chose.

Most disturbing of all, Angell's claim that war isn't profitable may have had the opposite effect. Rather than persuade aggressors not to go to war, he may have persuaded them that they needed to be even more ruthless to get what they felt was their due. That explains the harshness that Germany and Japan display in World War II.

Unfortunately, this unwillingness to fight evil because it doesn't pay—to do the adult equivalent of refusing to protect other kids from the playground bully—does not mean an unwillingness to 'fight' in a less brave sense. For some pacifists, aggressiveness in the sense of insulting those who are too disciplined and well-mannered to harm them isn't curtailed in the slightest. Against such people they can be mean-spirited, nasty, and slanderous. It's difficult to understand why people so driven by a hatred of their fellow citizens think they understand the secret to ending wars.

25. Norman Angell, *After All* (New York: Farrar, Straus and Young, 1952), 166–167. From "The New Pacifism" in the October 11, 1913 issue of *The New Statesman*. For an excerpt from *The Great Illusion*, see Appendix C.

What's absent from the new pacifist mind set are two character traits that, combined in one person, are so useful that no society can survive without them. Those traits are a desire to help those in trouble and the courage to do so even in dangerous situations. Every society needs police who risk their lives to stop criminals, fire fighters with the courage to enter a burning school house, and soldiers who fight and risk their lives in combat. That's why Chesterton praised literature for boys that encourages bravery and protecting others.

To explain how this works, some point to shepherding. All too many people, they say, are like sheep. They're easily frightened and not good at protecting themselves. They live in a world that, whether they admit it or not, has wolves who intend to harm them. In the biblical analogy, these sheep need a shepherd. In a modern analogy, they need a sheepdog whose personality makes him want to protect sheep. As Chesterton wrote at the close of the last article, these sheepdog-like people have the moral "imagination" to "embrace the interests of humanity."[26]

But there's a problem with sheepdogs—they resemble their close kin the wolves. Both have sharp teeth and growl. Both are aggressive and willing to fight. Neither acts like a sheep, so some foolish sheep confuse the two. Since both carry guns, a British soldier protecting France from occupation looks like a German soldier burning a Belgian village. That confusion lies at the heart of much of the pacifist rhetoric Chesterton encountered, particularly the claim that Britain's soldiers were driven by "blood lust" (wolves) rather than patriotism and duty (sheepdogs). There are no sheepdogs, these pacifists were claiming, just wolves.

You see this frightened, confused sheep-like attitude in *From Chaos to Control*, a book Angell will publish just after Hitler takes power in early 1933. In it, he finds little in Nazism that disturbs him. "The tremendous success," he writes of the Nazi movement, "has been achieved by a party that not only offers no arguments, properly speaking, but no program. No one knew what the Nazis would really do on coming to power.... Hitlerism is of course merely an acute sense of grievance directed against whatever object the potential adherent of the party may dislike."[27] Lest his readers miss his claim that Germany has no evil agenda, later in the book he makes clear what he and "every serious student" of WWI thought.

1918

> Practically every statesman of eminence connected with the beginnings of the war, every serious student of its genesis, has testified to the fact that the war was the outcome, the inevitable outcome, of the old diplomatic and political system of Europe.... No one pretends now—as the papers above quoted used to pretend—that war was due to the special wickedness of Germans, the sudden swoop of the satanic wolf in a peaceful world lusting to eat such harmless lambs as France and Russia, and to take on at one and the same time a dozen other States. The war arose because the existence of the old system was that the defense of each nation was its own affair, and that the community of nations had no concern in seeing justice done to any member whose rights might be violated by a stronger.[28]

26. An excellent dramatization of this is E.M. Forester's *The Good Shepherd,* an account of a destroyer captain tasked with escorting a convoy across an Atlantic infested with U-boat 'wolf-packs.'

27. Normal Angell, *From Chaos to Control* (New York: Century, 1933), 111–112. The book is based on his 1932 Halley Stewart Lecture, revised to include Hitler's rise to power. Rare among authors, Angell includes his honorary title on the title page. Looking in the mirror, he sees a "Sir Norman Angell."

28. Normal Angell, *From Chaos to Control* (New York: Century, 1933), 179–180. Angell's history is strangely flawed. The war began because most of the world's powerful nations had bound themselves to fight in defense of

Later, Angell demonstrates yet another failing common among pacifists who are internationalists, an inability to recognize that nations have collective personalities that make them to act as one for good or ill. He also forgets that, unlike a democracy, a dictatorship can make a nation march to one drummer's beat and argues instead for what has more recently been called a more "nuanced" view of foreign policy.

> I find it suggestive, by the way, that I am so often accused of oversimplification, of making our problems more simple than in fact they are, by critics who insist upon treating nations as persons. What over-simplification would be grosser, more misleading, more mischievous than that which causes us habitually to talk about nations as a single entity; which led us at the Peace to divide the world into "good" nations and "bad" nations; which leads men of letters like Mr. Kipling to tell us, in this year of grace 1933, that "the" Boche is as evil as ever and has learned nothing since the war?
>
> I am suggesting to you that it is the failure to grasp points as simple as that there is no such thing as "the" Boche, but sixty-five million separate and distinct Boches; that Germany is not one person—things as elementary as this which make us miss the road in public policy, miss the way of escape.[29]

Where do the pacifist intellectuals, if that is the right word, fit into this sheepdog–sheep–wolf continuum? Without generalizing too much, the doctrinaire pacifist is a strange sheep-wolf hybrid. He has the wolf's indifference to the plight of sheep. That's seen in Angell's inability to see evil in German deeds and, later in this book, when Chesterton criticizes pacifist indifference to Belgian suffering under the Germans during the war and to Soviet and German attacks on Poland after the war. For every pacifist pointing out how terrible the war was for Belgians, there seemed to have been a hundred complaining about how 'harsh' the Treaty of Versailles was for poor, unfortunate, misunderstood Germany. They rarely seem to feel the pain of anyone except the wolves whose evil they often deny. In fact, their "imaginative insufficiency" is so great, Chesterton says, they do little in wartime but admire themselves.

In other ways, this pacifist is most a unwolf-like beast. The wolf is not a coward. Risking the sheepdog to get at the sheep requires courage. In that sense, soldiers who served Hitler were as brave as those who fought for Churchill. Both courted death for a cause they believed in. In contrast, pacifists seem unwilling to take real risks. You see that in their zeal for criticizing free societies and their near-silence about murderous tyrannies. Fear is the reason. The sanctions free societies place on dissent are trivial compared to those of dictatorships. There's also the strange sense of the "heroic" they find in their modest fines and short, comfortable prison sentences. Real heros are typically modest and self-effacing. Pacifist 'heros' talk constantly about themselves and their petty sufferings. It's easy to suspect that much of their hostility toward soldiers is that of a pretentious fake hero for a real one.

1918

---

other nations. Russia would fight for Serbia, German for Austria, France and Russia for each other, and Britain for Belgium and France. What Angell sneers at with his "dozen other States" remark was true. German aggression really was wicked enough to be undeterred by the combined might of France, Russia and the British Empire. Angell must distort history because his peace agenda depends on aggressors being deterred by a League of Nations that's only a tiny bit more powerful than the alliance Germany willingly faced in WWI, and that League would be much less likely to act decisively, as events in the 1930s would demonstrate.

29. Normal Angell, *From Chaos to Control* (New York: Century, 1933), 194. The "road in public policy" refers to Angell's desire to see his point of view taught in public schools, leaving children (future adults and voters) unaware of just how poor he is at predicting, much less preventing, aggression.

In short, what this new breed of pacifism shares with militarism is precisely what makes militarism so evil—an indifference to the sufferings of the weak. That indifference can be so great, it leads pacifists to oppose good and just wars and gloat over wars lost to a tyranny that result in millions of refugees (such as Vietnam).

This introduction is long and strongly worded because article that follows is one of Chesterton's strongest condemnations of pacifism.

There still lingers—or rather, lounges—about the world a special type of Conscientious Objector who is luckily in a minority, even in the small minority of Conscientious Objectors. He might more properly be described as an Unconscientious Objector—for he does not so much believe in his own conscience as disbelieve in the common conscience which is the soul of any possible society. **His hatred of patriotism is very much plainer than his love for peace.**[30] **But, just as the instantaneous touch of ice has been mistaken for hot iron, so the unnatural chilliness of his personality is sometimes mistaken for fanaticism.** The most horribly unholy and unhappy thing about him is his youth. Most of the more representative Pacifists are old men and indeed, saving their presence, old noodles. But they are kindly old noodles, and their pacifism is mostly a prejudice left by the last sectarian eccentricities of people who could not wholly cease to be Christians even by being Puritans. These people had always disapproved of what they rather vaguely called militarism, regarding it in some mysterious manner as a form of dissipation. As they had been taught not to look on the wine when it was red, so they were taught not to look on the uniform when it was red. They disapproved of bullets rather as they did of billiards, from a hazy association of ideas that connected it with having a high old time. Whether the experience of war is really a giddy round of gaieties, there are probably many to-day who could testify. The point here is that this sort of conscientiousness was a most comical perversion of the Christian tradition; but was still Christian, in the sense that it was a perversion of that and of nothing else. Some sincerity, some simplicity, some sorrow for others, dignified the dying sect.

1918

But no such lingering grace clings to the remarkable young man I have in my mind. He is cold, he is caddish, he is an intellectual bully, and his intellect is itself vapid and thin. He is marked by an imaginative insufficiency which can be compared to nothing except to finding a Commander, in the thick of battle, looking into a pocket-mirror instead of a field-glass. I remember a debate nearly four years ago in which some followers of Mr. Norman Angell tried to persuade

30. This may allude to Norman Angell's first book, *Patriotism Under Three Flags: A Plea for Rationalism in Politics* (1903). In his autobiography (*After All*, p. 105.), Angell wrote that the book: "describes a phenomenon which was to disturb, perplex, and frighten me during the whole of my life, and to run like a red thread through everything that I was to write during the next half-century. The phenomenon in question was the tendency of human judgment in social and political matters to be utterly distorted, warped, and twisted... by emotional forces within ourselves.... The thing had taken various forms throughout the ages, and men had given it various names: nationalism, herd instinct, patriotism, partisanship, fanaticism, *esprit de corps*." Notice how he equates patriotism with fanaticism and a "herd instinct." Others are "warped and twisted," but not him.

me that, by our moral progress, we had outgrown the very notion of war.[31] When I pointed out that even to abandon war, merely to make money, indicated no moral progress at all, a young Cambridge man put his head on one side and said, "My ethics are not at all ascetic." I can see him still, with his eye cocked up at a corner of the ceiling, and the white light from a high window falling on his funny little head. It happened to be the very day when the Austrian ultimatum went to Serbia.[32]

And, what is worse, the spirit of this cheerless impudence has sometimes spread and chilled the blood of better men. I have noticed it lately in the last stiff pose of people who still try the stale game of blaming everybody for the war, long after the Lichnowsky revelations and the peace imposed on Russia have quite finally fixed the blame.[33] Men like Mr. J.A. Hobson and Mr. Brailsford, in the face of these public facts and popular revulsions, merely become more stilted, supercilious, and limited to a dusty detail.[34] As the big facts, one after another, go against them, they seem more and more interested in small facts—which are too often small falsehoods. Thus Mr. Brailsford attempts to answer an exceedingly able criticism in the *New Age* by suggesting that, while admittedly the Kaiser's Government was chiefly to blame, some individuals in the Tsar's Government may have been partly to blame.[35] What is one

---

31. Norman Angell (Ralph Norman Angell Lane) won the Nobel Peace Prize in 1933, the year Hitler took power. According to the Nobel Foundation: "In 1909 he had published a small book, *Europe's Optical Illusion*, using for the first time the name Norman Angell which he later legalized. In 1910 he expanded this work considerably, retitling it *The Great Illusion*. This book was translated into twenty-five languages, sold over two million copies, and gave rise to a theory popularly called Norman Angellism. This theory, as stated in the book's Preface, holds that 'military and political power give a nation no commercial advantage, that it is an economic impossibility for one nation to seize or destroy the wealth of another, or for one nation to enrich itself by subjugating another.'"

32. That was July 23, 1914, the day that war became almost inevitable. The Austrian ultimatum was so harsh, Russia felt compelled to stand up for Serbia. When Germany chose to support Austria, its war plans required it to prepare for war with Russia by first attacking and defeating France through Belgium to avoid a two-front war. The German invasion of Belgium (to reach France by the easiest path) then pushed Britain into the war.

33. Karl Max, Fürst von Lichnowsky was German ambassador to Britain from 1912 to 1914. In 1916 he privately published a pamphlet accusing the German government of failing to support his efforts to advert war. In 1917 his "Lichnowsky memorandum" became available in the U.S., and in 1918 it was published in *The Disclosures from Germany*. See his: *My Mission to London, 1912-1914* (New York: George H. Doran Co., 1918) and *Heading for the Abyss: Reminiscences* (New York: Payson and Clarke, 1928). In *My Mission*, he laments on page 37: "Such was the end of my London mission. It was wrecked, not by the perfidy of the British, but by the perfidy of our policy."

34. In its January 3, 1918 issue (p. 196), *The New Age* ridiculed what might be called the pacifist's idea of revolution in a new book by John A. Hobson (1858-1940) called *Democracy after the War*, noting that: "Apparently all the reactionaries will be marshalled in one body, and democracy will be marshalled in another body confronting it. Democracy will not then advance at the charge; that would imply militarism and the 'will to power'; it will remain confronting the reactionaries with enthusiasm and considered policy. Whether the democracy will express its enthusiasm by cheering, or passing a good resounding resolution, we are not sure; we suggest a brass band, or, at the very least, a bugler, should be employed to sound the enthusiasm of democracy."

35. On March 14, 1918, *The New Age* criticized Henry N. Brailsford (1873–1958), a socialist journalist active in the pacifist Union of Democratic Control for promoting what is today called a "moral equivalence" between the "Imperialism" of the Allies (Britain, France and formerly Tsarist Russia) and that of Germany. *The New Age* argued that the two could not be equivalent because: "German Imperialism is alone in a position to threaten the whole world.... by reason of the special circumstances of Germany's geographical and economic situation." (This refers to Germany's central location in Europe, its large land army and its great industrial power.) Brailsford replied with a letter in the April 25, 1918 issue of *The New Age* (p. 507), claiming to have never blamed Britain for the war, arguing instead that Russia and Germany share blame: "To sum up, I am not and never was pro-German or anti-English; I was, and in retrospect am, anti-Tsarist. My thesis is that Russia (not England) was to blame as well (I will not say 'as much') as Prussia." Chesterton then replies to Brailsford's letter, arguing that his pacifism makes no sense. If he's glad to see the Tsar, who was "partly to blame" for the war go down, why isn't he eager to see the Kaiser who is "chiefly to blame" defeated? Brailsford had partly cloaked his pacifism

to say to people who balance that tremendous admission with that trivial doubt? Perhaps it will be a practical simplification to say to Mr. Brailsford, "Very well; will you fight till the Kaiser has gone the way of the Tsar?" But ere the Kaiser's crown goes down there are crowns to be broke, and certainly not merely hairs to be split.

But even in its grosser and more aggressive form the thing remains. I remember reading a novel, which appeared some little while ago, which precisely conveyed the particular spirit I mean. It was called *The Fortune*, and it was by Douglas Goldring.[36] In its sub-title and substance it professed to be a sort of romance of intellectual friendship; but it was really rather a romance of intellectual slavery. It described the influence on a young man's life of a friend whose unconventionality ultimately took the form of Pacifism—and whose Pacifism ultimately took, as it always does take, the form of Pro-Germanism. But in this story the relations of the two are in no sense those of friend and friend, or even merely of master and pupil, but rather those of master and servant. **The master exhibits in his anti-militarism the only thing that can ever be really evil in militarism—the beatification of the bully.** In parts it suggests the writing of a rather morbid woman, for such worship of superiority is almost worthy of "Ouida."[37] It makes very little difference to the moral atmosphere, to my mind, that it is not idolatry of a supercilious soldier, but only idolatry of a man too supercilious to consent to be a soldier. And a certain interest lies in the fact that the author, like "Ouida," really writes rather well, so far as the moral atmosphere does not weaken his work. The Pacifist intellectual is effectively and truly described; only he is meant to be magnificent and attractive, and he is made repulsive and even pitiable.

For there is present something I for one have invariably found wherever there is the mere worship of the intellect—I mean the decay of the intellect. The Pacifist—or rather, Pro-German—utterances of the superior young man become more and more inferior; they end by being worthy of the waste-paper basket of the *Continental Times.*[38]

1918

I take an instance at random, as representing the ignorant and essentially commonplace cocksureness of the type I describe. There are countless others, even in this particular novel—which is a very realistic record concerning that type. Here, for instance, is a passage which one who has lingered lovingly over his *Continental Times* will recognise with a sigh—not to say a yawn: "The Germans, with all their faults, are a magnificent race, full of vigour, of imagination, and character. But the

behind a claim that the war wasn't about Britain's obvious interest in keeping Belgium out of German hands, but a "Russo-German" war that Britain should have never joined. The fall of the Czar and the exit from the war of Russia (now communist) had removed his most vocal reason for opposing the war, leaving his arguments, "stilted, supercilious, and limited to a dusty detail."

36. Douglas Goldring (1887–1960) *The Fortune: A Romance of Friendship* (Maunsel: Dublin, 1917).

37. "Ouida" was the pen name of Maria Louise Ramé (1839–1908), author of some 40 novels and children's stories. Chesterton commented on her in the September 17, 1910 issue of *Illustrated London News* (Ch. 1).

38. Chesterton had fun mocking the *Continental Times*. See his *Illustrated London News* articles for July 14, October 20, and October 27, 1917 (Ch. 5). In "Italy and the German Professors," written for *The Book of Italy* edited by Raffaello Piccoli, Chesterton described, "a highly helpless publication called *The Continental Times*, written by Germans for Americans, or rather (to speak more strictly) written by idiots for idiots."

French are dying. They are the Greeks of the modern world; Paris is a reincarnation, if you like, of Athens. The French will be like a corpse round the neck of this country in the future." France is behaving like a fairly lively corpse at present; but, if anything could overpower that almost brutally energetic nation with fatigue, it might be having to read this sort of Teutonist trash for the ten-thousandth time. It were vain, I suppose, to hope for a change; to hint that other historic powers have ultimately declined besides Athens, and without doing so much for the world.

I only refer to the remark, or to the book in which it occurs, because it happens to strike exactly the note of the nonsense I have been describing. **It indicates the survival of a certain sort of young man who is a Pacifist not because he is a Quaker, or because he is a Tolstoyan, or even because he is an Anarchist—but because he is a prig, and nothing else.**[39] Nor is he even a prig through too much conscientiousness, or a pedant through too much learning. He has nothing but ideas which are not only second-rate, but second-hand. He has borrowed from articles on Tolstoy the impossibilism without the idealism; and from articles on Nietzsche the way to be a Superman who will not fight.

G.K. Chesterton, "Our Note-Book," *Illustrated London News* 152 (May 11, 1918), 546. US: May 11, 1918. Also published as "The Unconscientious Objector."

Two Different Leagues

July 13, 1918

A League of Nations really stands or falls with the truth of its title. If it is really a League of Nations it may really be a noble thing; but, as presented by some people, it is rather a League for the Abolition of Nations.

Editor: Chesterton contrasts two visions of a League of Nations under consideration as the war drew to a close. One puts the emphasis on *Nations* and would be a "league of all the men who love their own lands [enough] to respect each other." The other puts the emphasis on *League* and would be a "clique of the very few who forget their own lands to interfere with each other's." Today, the North Atlantic Treaty Organization (NATO) is an example of the former, while the European Union and the United Nations are attempts at the latter. The richness of building the world around independent nations rather than one centralized bureaucracy fits well with Chesterton's world-view. In her biography, Maisie Ward explained that Chesterton believed having a complex set of truths (ideals) was good, but "thinking there is only one truth" was a mistake.

> In an interview, given shortly after its publication [*Orthodoxy*], Gilbert told of a temptation that had once been his and which he had overcome almost before he realized he had been tempted. **That temptation was to become a prophet like all the men in *Heretics*, by emphasizing one aspect of the truth and ignoring the**

39. A prig in the *Oxford English Dictionary* is: "A person who is offensively punctilious and precise in speech or behaviour; a person who cultivates or affects supposedly correct views on culture, learning, or morals, which offend or bore others; a conceited or self-important and didactic person." George Elliot's 1871 *Middlemarch* says, "A prig is a fellow who is always making you a present of his opinions."

others. To do this would, he knew, bring him a great crowd of disciples. He had a vision—which constantly grew wider and deeper—of the many-sided unity of Truth, but he saw that all the prophets of the age, from Walt Whitman and Schopenhauer[40] to Wells and Shaw, had become so by taking one side of truth and making it all of truth. It is so much easier to see and magnify a part than laboriously to strive to embrace the whole:

> ... a sage feels too small for life,
> And a fool too large for it.[41]

Two men, admired and admirable in very different ways, have lately written on the scheme of a League of Nations—Lord Grey and Mr. H.G. Wells.[42] One thing they have in common: it is the thing for which they are the most blamed, and for which they ought to be most praised—their idealism. Whether we accept their ideal or no, we ought to thank them for making it clear as an ideal. To dismiss idealism as impossibilism is not even practical; it is like blaming an archer for aiming at the white, and telling him that pure white is unknown in nature, and that the centre of a circle is an imaginary point without parts or magnitude. The answer is that if you are not aiming you are not even shooting, but only shedding arrows as a fowl sheds feathers. To have an ideal is simply to have an aim; and there is nothing practical in being aimless. But the real mistake arises from supposing that white is the only colour, that we all take as an ideal object anything that happens to be white—as, for instance, whitewash, or whited sepulchres, or the white flag. In other words, the real mistake consists in thinking there is only one ideal, which is at once obvious and colourless. This is no more true of national and international ideals than of any other. It is not admitted, as some seem to suppose, that the ideal that is vaster and vaguer is necessarily higher. Humanity is larger and more varied than a nation; so is a harem larger and more varied than a wife.

A League of Nations really stands or falls with the truth of its title. If it is really a League of Nations it may really be a noble thing; but, as presented by some people, it is rather a League for the Abolition of Nations. It is not a scheme to guarantee the independence of States, but at best to guarantee their safety

40. Arthur Schopenhauer (1788–1860) was a German philosopher best known for his *The World as Will and Representation* (1819). This "World as One Thing" was what Chesterton rejected.

41. Maisie Ward, *Gilbert Keith Chesterton* (London: Sheed & Ward, 1944), 181. In a June 16, 1928 article in the *Illustrated London News* Chesterton compared systems built around one "definite idea" with that of H.G. Wells who, in *The Open Conspiracy* (1928), was advancing a system built around "one indefinite idea," claiming to see in history "a general tendency towards establishing a world control [government]." Chesterton warned: "But it seems to me that a good many things might happen, if there is nothing to control the movement towards control. Ideas can be perverted only too easily even when they are strict ideas; I cannot see how we preserve them from perversion merely by making them loose ideas. A thing like the Catholic system is a system; that is, one idea balances and corrects another. A man like Mahomet or Marx, or, in his own way, Calvin, find that system too complex, and simplifies everything to a single idea. But it is a definite idea. He naturally builds a rather unbalanced system with his one definite idea. But I cannot see why there should be a better chance for a man trying to build up a balanced system with one indefinite idea." *The Collected Works of G.K. Chesterton*, xxxiv, 543.

42. Lord Grey is Sir Edward Grey (1862–1933), British Foreign Secretary from 1905–1916. During the war he supported the idea for a League of Nations and published *The League of Nations* (London, 1918) After the war he became president of the League of Nations Union. H.G. Wells views on the League are in his *In The Fourth Year: Anticipations of a World Peace* (1918), whose Preface is republished here as Appendix G.

if they will sacrifice their independence. There is surely, however, a much more human and more hopeful interpretation of the idea than this. What is wanted, and what might well be provided, is a league for the defence of nationality. Now this primary distinction, in the ideal or the aim, is a good example of how practical it is to discuss aims and ideals. For this brings us at once to the simplest answer to the most serious question: Shall the League consist of the Allies, at any rate to begin with; or are we to wait for the conversion of Germany, or are we to accept an unconverted Germany?

The answer is that the Allies have a right to call themselves a League of Nations, in a sense in which Germany has, in plain fact, no part. It is not a boast; it is not a piece of partisan , or even patriotic sentiment; it is a piece of past history. The Allies may end as a League of Nations because they began as a League of Nations, in the strict sense of a scheme for preserving nationality—or rather, nationalities. It was not only a union of different things, but of things that wished to remain different. They not only helped each other while remaining unlike each other—they helped each other because they wished to remain unlike each other. It was not a desire of the French to be Anglicised, or the English to be Frenchified, that created the Anglo-French Entente: it was the desire of the French to remain French and the English to remain English. The Serbians had a dread of being drawn into the system of Austria; the Belgians had a dread of being drawn into the system of Germany; but nobody ever thought the Belgians were in danger of being drawn into the system of Serbia.

Whatever else the Central Empires may say against their enemies, they cannot say their enemies are all alike, that one description will cover them all—or even that one insult will hit them all. They have to be abused one at a time, and it is necessary to compose a separate slander against each. The one thing which they have had in common is that each nation was in a special and literal sense defending itself—that is, its right to be itself. The Allies have this particular ideal—not in pedantic plans drawn up on paper at the end of the war, but in the real and original pressure of the popular passions at the beginning of the war. They have at least one rudimentary convenience not altogether useless in the formation of a League of Nations—they have the nations.

We hear a great deal in these days about democratic diplomacy. But one thing is quite certain—that, if diplomacy ever is democratic, it will not be cosmopolitan; it will not be, in the sense intended by the intellectuals, even international. If it is in the least popular, it will be very national. Does anybody believe that when an agricultural labourer from Hampshire or Berkshire enlists and fights and dies, he does it for any political combination except England, or appeals to any international tribunal except God? While the labourer's outlook may need to be widened, there is one way in which it could and should be widened, and another in which the change is neither possible nor desirable. I do not think he ever will be, or ever ought to be, taught to forget his county and his country in favour of some piece of world-politics worked by wire-pullers at the Hague. But I do think he could be, and ought to be, taught to remember that other men love other counties and other countries; I think he would be much more in touch with such a truism than many more cultivated and perverted people.

The value of the Alliance, and the great emotions in which it originated, is precisely that it was an imaginative movement of this kind. The poor and plain Englishman did really begin to feel something much more human than a solidarity with the Belgian International—a sympathy with the Belgian nationality. He felt not only for their poverty and their pain, but for their patriotism—for the flag which Intellectuals call a rag and the nation which they call a name. That is the only line along which we could ever really develop a democratic diplomacy. **That is the real hope in the ideal of a League of Nations. If it is genuine, it will be a league of all the men who love their own lands to respect each other. If it is anything else, it will merely be a clique of the very few who forget their own lands to interfere with each other's. Between these two opposites the modern world must choose; and it is typical of modern lucidity that the two opposites are known by the same name.**

G.K. Chesterton, "Our Note-Book," *Illustrated London News* 153 (July 13, 1918), 36. US: July 13, 1918. Also published as "The Ideal of the League of Nations (1)."

Bloodless Pacifism

August 3, 1918

To drop the metaphor, the real point against the cause of Pacifism is that it is not a cause at all, but only a weakening of all causes. It does not announce any aim; it only announces that it will never use certain means in pursuing any aim. It does not define its goal; it only defines a stopping-place, beyond which nobody must go in the search for any goal.

1918

Editor: Chesterton explains why "Pacifism and Prussianism are always in alliance, by a fatal logic far beyond any conscious conspiracy." With no shadowy meetings or secret discussions, two radically different sets of logic can drive two outwardly different groups to advance the same cause toward the same end. In this case, both refuse to allow a people to defend themselves or win their freedom: Prussian militarism because resisting Germanic superiority is futile, and pacifism because armed resistance is evil. In his July 13 article Chesterton attacked a new sort of pacifism then growing in prominence. In this article he criticizes pacifism in general. He also mentions the World State of H.G. Wells and others that was often championed by pacifists as a way to get beyond war, pointing out that it "would have to be guarded with swords and staves like any other State." The same is true of any "universal settlement," such as global disarmament, which could only be enforced with armies and armaments.

I have never pretended to reverence for the ideal modern peacemaker, wearing the white feather of a blameless life—or rather, of a bloodless life. For there are two ways of being bloodless—by the avoidance of blood without, and by the absence of blood within. Nor do I conceal a doubt of whether we can ever, with literal certainty, make mankind bloodless in the first sense except by making it bloodless in the second. Our chief reason for wishing the Allies to secure the prize, for which they have already paid in blood, is the certainty that far more blood would be shed after losing it than after winning it. There is, however, another truth involved in the image which is hardly anywhere adequately noticed. The old truism says that blood is thicker than water; and in any case no good is done by the mere thinning of blood. No good is done by the mere dilution of a deluge. And the particular pacific idealism of which I speak merely dilutes the blood of humanity, and does not either quicken or cleanse it.

To drop the metaphor, the real point against the cause of Pacifism is that it is not a cause at all, but only a weakening of all causes. It does not announce any aim; it only announces that it will never use certain means in pursuing any aim. It does not define its goal; it only defines a stopping-place, beyond which nobody must go in the search for any goal. Now you do not get the good out of any cause by saying, from any motive, that you will never fight for it. A Buddhist is not a better Buddhist, but a worse Buddhist, if he refuses to draw the sword even to avert the extinction of Buddhism—or, if he is not so far the worse Buddhist, Buddhism is so far the worse religion. A Quaker may be obeying Quakerism, but he is not serving Quakerism, in so far as he would refuse to defend it; always supposing that Quakerism has other and more central doctrines to defend, as I believe to be the case. Indeed, I understand that many Quakers really are fighting with effect and distinction in the present war, on the specific ground that spiritual ideals are in peril, which are more precious to them than their ideal of non-resistance. Anyhow, the point is that Pacifism is not a cause, in the sense that Pan-slavism or Puritanism, or even Prussianism, is a cause. It is merely a restriction on the Puritan in his work for Puritanism, on the Prussian in his work for Prussianism, or on the Slav enthusiast in his work for the Slav race. In this highly practical sense, it would merely make the Socialist less Socialistic, the Secularist less secular, and even the Internationalist less international. **For a World State would have to be guarded with swords and staves like any other State; and a universal settlement would want fighting for as much as any other—or rather, more than any other.**

This has a practical application now, as is clear from some current controversies about the old foreign policy of the Liberal Party, to which I conceived myself to belong. Indeed, I should belong to it still, if it were there to belong to. But the Party System, which used the honest Radical and the honest Tory, worked with the names of both and the principles of neither. It has, I hope, perished; but those principles, which it alternately applauded and never applied, are far from having perished. Now in the lingering party quarrel which underlies our patriotic unity, it is too much the custom to rebuke the new Pacifist foreign policy as a belated and benighted fidelity to the old Liberal foreign policy. But this is far too great a condemnation of the liberals; and what is worse, it is far too great a compliment to the Pacifists. Whatever else the Pacifists are doing, the Pacifists most certainly are not following out the old foreign policy either of Fox or of Gladstone. They differ from it at a thousand decisive points—indeed, at practically all points.

The biography of Byron will reveal the surprising detail that he did not die in Greece organising a Quaker meeting. He died organising a military attack.[43] He had, indeed, attempted to found a paper called the *Liberal*, which failed; but his Liberalism ultimately led him to lend his aid to a policy of armament, which did not fail. When Fox and his friends had doubts about the war with France, it was not because they suspected that all fighting was wrong, but because they suspected that the French fighting was right.[44] The primary point of such Liberalism was to sympathise with a nation "struggling to be free." The only possible point of Pacifism would be to tell it not to struggle. And that is precisely the position which most of the Pacifists who call themselves Liberals do adopt to-day in the urgent contemporary cases of Bohemia or Posen or Alsace.[45] These singular Liberals do tell these smaller peoples not to struggle to be free; and, for all practical purposes, not to hope to be free. And the contrast between the Liberal tradition and their own proposals becomes even more acute as that tradition comes nearer to their own period. They are more acutely antagonistic to Gladstone even than they are to Fox or to Byron. Gladstone declared that the thousand battles of Montenegro were more glorious than the battle of Marathon. But the New Liberals do not seem to approve of the battles of Montenegro—indeed, I suppose the New Liberals do not approve of the battle of Marathon.[46] After all, the battle of Marathon involved the death of a number of unfortunate persons, especially (of course) of unfortunate Persians. Miltiades ought, no doubt, to have delayed any military movements, in the hope that there might some day be a Socialist revolution and reconstruction somewhere in the interior of the Empire of Darius.[47] The Athenians ought, no doubt, to have thrown away their shields and spears, and trusted everything to that enlightenment and enthusiasm for international peace for which barbarians are everywhere renowned.

I desire only to point out that, if these truths were hidden from the earliest of the great Greeks, they were equally hidden from the very latest of the great Liberals. I merely note that this view of Marathon would have seemed quite as mad to Gladstone as it would to Miltiades.

The fact is that all this peace business is not the fulfilment, but the frustration, of the old revolutionary plan. It must in its very nature be the frustration of any plan. When the tyrant is in possession of power, and the tribune is striving for freedom,

43. The poet Lord Bryon (1788–1824) died of fever while helping Greece win its independence from Turkey.

44. Charles Fox (1749–1806) was Britain's first Foreign Secretary and skeptical of its role in the Napoleonic wars. William Gladstone (1809–1898), a Liberal, was British Prime Minister four times.

45. Czechs in Bohemia wanted to be free, as did the Poles of Posen and the French in Alsace.

46. Montenegro refers to a series of battles in the mid-1870s, as various Balkan groups, including the Montenegrins, fought to free themselves from Turkish rule. In 1877, Tennyson published a poem in praise of that rebellion called "Montenegro" in *Nineteenth Century*. It was accompanied by an long article by William Gladstone, who encouraged Tennyson to play the same role in their struggle as Lord Bryon had played for the Greeks.

47. Miltiades was the Greek commander at the Battle of Marathon (490 BC), when the much larger Persian invasion force under Darius I was halted on the plains of Marathon.

the appearance of a third philosopher who is striving primarily for peace must of necessity be in favour of the man in possession. **Pacifism and Prussianism are always in alliance, by a fatal logic far beyond any conscious conspiracy.**[48]

G.K. Chesterton, "Our Note-Book," *Illustrated London News* 153 (August 3, 1918), 120. US: August 3, 1918. Also published as "Pacifism: The Weakening of All Causes."

A League to Defend Nations

August 10, 1918

A League of Nations, I repeat, will be an admirable idea if it means a league to defend the nationality of nations.

Editor: Being misquoted in the *Observer* convinced Chesterton that he needed to be clearer about doubts he had expressed about the League of Nations in the *Illustrated London News* on July 13. In doing so, he draws a distinction between two groups seeking world peace. One is clear about its aim, achieving peace by using a League of Nations to abolish nations. One is dishonest, hoping to abolish nations slowly by stealth and deception. Chesterton disagrees with both, but commends the first for giving its opponents "the fairest warning" of what they intend. This article can perhaps be taken as Chesterton's commentary on the European Union.

In *Irish Impressions* (1919) Chesterton described in concrete terms how strongly he believed a nation should be ruled by one of its own. Someone asked him to choose between an Ireland ruled by Johann Goethe (1749–1832), the brilliant German humanist, and Walter Long (1854–1924), a Unionist champion of continued British domination of Ireland who replaced Chesterton's friend George Wyndham (1863–1913) as Chief Secretary for Ireland.

> A brilliant writer... once propounded to me his highly personal and even perverse type of internationalism by saying, as a sort of unanswerable challenge, "Wouldn't you rather be ruled by Goethe than by Walter Long?" I replied that words could not express the wild love and loyalty I should feel for Mr. Walter Long, if the only alternative were Goethe. I could not have put my own national cause in a clearer or more compact form. I might occasionally feel inclined to kill Mr. Long; but under the approaching shadow of Goethe, I should feel more inclined to kill myself. That is the deathly element in denationalisation; that it poisons life itself, the most real of all realities.[49]

A writer in the *Observer*[50] has recently quoted, with far too generous a compliment, something that I wrote in this column to the effect that the idealists who are planning a League of Nations should not at least be blamed for their idealism, since to have an ideal merely means to have an aim, and "there is nothing practical in being aimless." I do not complain of his quoting what I said, since, however strange it

48. To state Chesterton's remark more broadly, replace Prussianism with militarism.

49. Quoted in Maisie Ward, *Gilbert Keith Chesterton* (London: Sheed & Ward, 1944), 343.

50. The *Observer*, founded in 1791, has the distinction of being the world's first Sunday newspaper. At this time it was owned by the wealthy Astor family and was considered a Tory newspaper.

may seem, I happen to agree with what I said. And, since he honoured me to excess in quoting so much, I naturally cannot complain of his not quoting more. Nevertheless, the passage by itself might be taken as part of a very different philosophy. And it is the paradox of quotation that, while the part can never be greater than the whole, it can sometimes cover and hide the whole. I know the *Observer* would be the first to agree that a man should leave as little ambiguity as possible about his opinions on the Great War and the great peace that will follow it.

Briefly and broadly, then, what I meant to maintain about the League of Nations was this: that, whatever we may find to blame in the idealists who write about it, we ought not to blame them for stating their ideal in its most extreme idealistic form. This is the thing for which they are chiefly blamed, and this form of blame is wrong. Such extreme statement is not only more honest, but more practical. It is more practical whether the ideal is right or wrong—indeed, it is specially practical if the ideal is specially wrong. For those who agree with the ideal, it is the finest inspiration. For those who disagree, it is the fairest warning. What is really dreamy and dangerous and anarchic is precisely that sham "practicality" of beginning to do something, without clearly knowing what we are really doing or why we are really doing it. **And the real case against a League of Nations, as preached by some of its prophets, is precisely that the name does not represent their real ideal—but, at the best, a step towards their real ideal; and, at the worst, a mere disguise for their real ideal.** It is that what they really mean is not what Mr. Wilson calls a League of Nations, but what Mr. Wells calls a World State.

It would be easy to make the point clear by parallels that would be at once more familiar and more fantastic. For instance, a man might hold that we should reach a broader brotherhood if men no longer lived in private houses, but all lived in one vast public house, or (since that noble name may shock the sensitive—or rather, the snobbish) in one vast hotel.[51] If he sincerely held this view, it would be much better that he should say so—that he should draw up the plans and define the conditions of the hotel as an hotel. That the initial expense might be rather great, that the ground-plan would be rather large, that it would be difficult to get hold of all the land and still more difficult to get the people to live on it—all this would be no argument against a man who wanted this saying clearly what it was he wanted. On the contrary, those who disliked the idea would have as much reason to thank the theorist as those who liked it; he would be defining for them the thing they disliked. What they would really resent, what we should all resent, would be his beginning to abolish private houses bit by bit.[52] We should probably feel a little vexed if the neighbour next door

1918

51. Public houses usually sold liquor and did not always provide overnight lodging.

52. The Fabians, named after Fabius, a Roman general who moved slowly but deliberately, had just such a covert agenda and imparted it to Britain's Labour Party. In 1894 Sidney Webb would write: "What we Fabians aim at is not the sub-division of property, whether capital or land, but the control and administration of it by the representatives of the community. It has no desire to see the Duke of Bedford replaced by five hundred little Dukes of Bedford under the guise of enfranchised leaseholders.... It has no vain dream of converting the agricultural labourer into a freeholder farming his own land, but looks to the creation of parish councils, empowered to acquire land for communal ownership, and to build cottages for the labourers to rent." Sidney Webb, "Socialism:

began to make holes in the wall, with the object of opening up closer communications with his fellow-creatures. We should be annoyed to discover that he had quietly and tactfully removed the wall itself, leaving us in a large and commodious apartment partly occupied by somebody else's family. We should generally resent the claims of other families to overflow into our family without warning. And all these things would be unpleasant precisely because they would be what some people call compromises, in the sense of immediate and workable applications. They would be well within the sphere of practical politics—that is why they would be an abominable nuisance. Communist housekeeping as an ideal is tolerable, because we know whither it leads and whether we want it or not. As a tendency it is intolerable, for nobody knows where a tendency will lead. And it is these early moderate steps that men rightly dislike—like the first step across the threshold of the uninvited guest. It merely means establishing burglary as a compromise with communism.

It would be easy to give scores of similar cases. A man may say seriously, as Plato or Bernard Shaw might say (though I hardly think seriously) that all babies should be mixed or changed at birth, like the babies in "The Bab Ballads."[53] He might say that all children should be brought up as children of the State, like the children of a Foundling Hospital. This would be intolerable to everything that most of us mean by Christian common-sense. But even this would be better than the same thing done bit by bit—or rather, baby by baby. It would be better than philanthropists behaving in reality as gipsies do in romance, and kidnapping a child according to their mere taste and fancy. It would be better than a state of things in which a father of a family had to count his children every evening, to see that none of them had been snatched away by a stray policeman. In these matters men can endure the idealist, but not the idealistic opportunist. They cannot endure the mere progressive, especially the practical progressive. And along with these things, like the home and the family, goes the thing called the nation. They will not have the freedom of free States gradually filched away, by any sort of cosmopolitan conspiracy, on any ethical excuse. If a man says he has no patriotism, they may give him the respect due to a high-minded lunatic and (more fitly) the respect due to an unhappy man.

A League of Nations, I repeat, will be an admirable idea if it means a league to defend the nationality of nations. Such a thing might well exist—an agreement for the special punishment of a disregard of national frontiers, as in Belgium; or for the recovery of national provinces, as in Alsace. But a League of Nations, in the sense of something to internationalize nations, is not an ideal at all. It is a mere stop-gap. **In short, I am in favour of an alliance of States to fight for the independence of each;**

True or False" (January 1894). in Beatrice Webb *Our Partnership* (New York, 1948), 106. Quoted in Michael W. Perry, *The Pivot of Civilization in Historical Perspective* (Seattle: Inkling Books, 2001), 42.

53. "The Bab Ballads" were light verses written by W.S. Gilbert (1836–1911) before he became famous writing operettas with Arthur Sullivan (1842–1900). Originally published in newspapers, they were so popular they were republished in books. Chesterton may be referring to the 1869 "The Baby's Vengence," in which a poor mother, forced to serve as a wet nurse for wealthy parents, neglects her own baby. That child, jealous of the attention the other gets, exchanges places with him: "We grew up in the usual way—my friend,/ My foster-brother, daily growing thinner,/ While gradually I began to mend,/ And thrived amazingly on double dinner."

I am not at all in favour of a new State expressing merely the interdependence of all. And I think this explanation sufficient to distinguish my own view from much that is to-day trumpeted under the name of a League of Nations.

G.K. Chesterton, "Our Note-Book," *Illustrated London News* 153 (August 10, 1918), 148. US: August 10, 1918. Also published as "The Ideal of the League of Nations (2)."

America Free to Strike

September 7, 1918

America has its own faults; democracy has its own faults; but it means a state where every man is on his hind legs. And it is a posture which leaves the hands free to strike.

Editor: Chesterton praises Senator Henry Cabot Lodge for demanding a peace dictated by the Allies. German professors, he says, "were not wrong in supposing that a thin theoretic pacifism was one of the layers of the spiritual soil in America. But they ought to have suspected it instead of trusting it, because it was the top layer."

The American, once regarded as the most pacifist of the Allies, is revealing himself as the most militant or even militarist of the Allies. That is perhaps the chief fact of the present phase, and it is naturally alarming both the pacifists in England and the militarists in Germany. The editor of the *Nation* (so-called because it is international or anti-nation or anything but national) is shocked not merely into a revulsion, but a reversal of feeling. Having long looked to the impartiality of America to check the fury of France, he is now actually and absurdly driven to appealing to the impartiality of France to check the fury of America. "France," he says, "alone of the European allies is tactically in a position to moderate the American tendency towards a long war and extreme terms." Since Mr. Wilson declines to pour cold water on M. Clemenceau's patriotism it follows as some way I do not quite understand that M. Clemenceau ought to pour cold water on Mr. Wilson's patriotism.[54] I will not speak of the soaring impudence of asking the French, of all people, to thwart the Americans merely to save the Germans. It is enough that men are not very likely to frustrate those who have lately given them help out of pure love for those who have literally given them hell. For the latter phrase, though attributed to a prominent politician, weakens and understates the justice of our own cause. Prussia does give men hell; it is all she has to give, even to Prussians. But our guns are not giving hell, but rather the judgment of heaven.

But a speech like that of Senator Lodge is, as has been said, equally ominous to the war party of Germany and to its partner, the peace party of England.[55] The Germans

54. Georges Clemenceau (1841–1929) was France's Prime Minister from 1906–1908 and 1917–1920.

55. Henry Cabot Lodge (1850–1924) was a senator from Massachusetts (1893–1924). After the war, he worked to keep the U.S. out of the League of Nations, arguing it would entangle the nation in European wars. Chesterton refers to a August 23 speech the *New York Times* headlined the next day on its front page as "Lodge Demands a Dictated Peace Won by Victory." In that speech Lodge said: "No peace that satisfies Germany in any degree can ever satisfy us. It cannot be a negotiated peace. It must be a dictated peace, and we and our Allies must dictate it."

hear a new voice across the Atlantic, which says to them something substantially like this: "Now that your imperialistic war has failed, you are talking about the Peace Congress, about the League of Nations, about the international settlement and the policy of give and take. Under your favour we will believe your acts and not your words. There shall be exactly as large as free and as equal a Peace Congress as that which discussed, with such delicacy and deliberation, whether France was or was not beaten in 1871. You shall appeal to a League of Nations with the same radiant success as France appealed when you pillaged her of her provinces and drained her of her gold. We will allow the same beneficent international intervention which you yourself so generously invited from all the other nations of the earth. We will accept your principle of give and take; and we will give what you gave, and take as you took. It must surely flatter you that your moral practice should be taken as a model; and that we should so far strive to be like you. **We will be like you in all except on little thing; that what you simply did, we have a right to do. You did it without provocation to your personal enemy. We do it with provocation to the enemy of mankind.** Yes; we compliment you when we copy you, as the hangman compliments the murdered whom he has to kill. That is the tone, very unmistakable of more than one message that has come across the Atlantic. It is sounded in Senator Lodge's speech, and in many other speeches and articles. That is the voice that comes out of America; and, assuredly, it is as fierce as the voice that comes out of France. It is something indubitably strange and terrible, something men do not understand in Germany; something men have not always understood in England; something that has its own dangers and terrors as well as its just desires. But if anyone is curious to know what it is, it is democracy.

To begin with, of course, it means that the European mind is beginning to understand another side of the American character. Germans especially and other Europeans too frequently have formed an opinion of American psychology which was bound to be superficial because it was supercilious. There really is an element in America of a strong sort of deracinated Puritanism, a crude and creedless fanaticism. It is something that made a friend of mind, a very able Englishman who lives in America, say to me on one occasion: "There is something about the American business man that always reminds me of the old-fashioned gentleman who fought duels." It is something from which the sensitive can smell danger, a potential rapidity like the swiftness of a word and a blow. It suggests that the carrying of a revolver in the hip pocket has had something of the effect on the figure of the old sword hilt at the hip.

The Germans have left out this little detail altogether in the detailed catalogue of all the characteristics of Americans which their professors have doubtless compiled. **They were not wrong in supposing that a thin theoretic pacifism was one of the layers of the spiritual soil in America. But they ought to have suspected it instead of trusting it, because it was the top layer. Anyhow, the rest of the stratification contains much more volcanic rock.** Most of our Parliamentary Pacifists are about as like a volcano as Primrose Hill: indeed, Primrose Hill would be, for them, a very appropriate mountain of vision, whether they connect the word "Primrose" with the Liberal Lord Rosebery, or the conservative Lord Beaconsfield.[56] Men of this kind cannot have the remotest conception of what American is all about. If one of them went to America at this moment, he would feel like a Christopher Columbus; and think he was looking at red men performing a war dance. Nor have they ever dreamed of how ancient are such dances nor of what red clay man was made.

It seems a pity, when so much is talked about democracy, that so little is thought about democracy. As a fact, one of the virtues of this type of government is that very fierceness and fighting spirit which these critics take for a vice. **If we like to put it in a paradox, the case for a democracy is that it consists entirely of aristocrats.** When reactionaries praise an oligarchy for its dignity, its spirit, and its sense of honour, they fall into a simple fallacy. They forget that oligarchy does not mean the extension of these things: on the contrary, it means the restriction of them. It is like admiring the uprightness of a tribe in which only two or three men are allowed to walk upright. All the other men, walking on all fours, might be happy, but would hardly be dignified. **America has its own faults; democracy has its own faults; but it means a state where every man is on his hind legs. And it is a posture which leaves the hands free to strike.**[57]

G.K. Chesterton, "Our Note-Book," *Illustrated London News* (September 7, 1918), 258.
US: September 7, 1918. Also published as "The Fury of America."

REFRESHED BY INVASION

September 21, 1918

The creed really common to the whole country is the belief that the Teuton is a type having a natural superiority—or, as he would probably put it, an evolutionary superiority.

1918

EDITOR: Chesterton criticizes Germans for not recognizing that the war they began was wrong rather than ill-timed. While nations such as France think well of themselves, Germans concentrate on their "natural superiority" as a race.

WHEN Hindenburg published his complaint about the propaganda of the Allies, there was one feature of the affair which I did not see noticed anywhere.[58] It

56. Primrose Hill is an expensive, fashionable London neighborhood with a marvelous view of central London. Archibald Philip Primrose, 5th Earl of Rosebery (1847–1929), was a (Liberal) Prime Minister from 1894–1895. Benjamin Disraeli, First Earl of Beaconsfield (1804–1881), was twice (Conservative) Prime Minister.

57. Contrast this with the goal of Fabian socialism, footnoted in the previous article, which wants to keep most men dependent and "has no desire to see the Duke of Bedford replaced by five hundred little Dukes of Bedford under the guise of enfranchised leaseholders." Bureaucratic socialism has labored in Western Europe to replace the old aristocracy of blood with a new one based on proper bureaucrat and ideological credentials. Much of the hostility of European elites toward America rests in the fact that it is "a state where every man is on his hind legs," or at least can choose to do so. In Chestertonian terms, what they call American militarism is actually the posture of a free nation that has left its "hands free to strike." Men on their feet fight well, men on their knees do not.

58. On September 6, 1918, with the war going badly for Germany, the German Army's Chief of Staff, Paul von Hindenberg (1847–1934) issued an official address that warned: "The enemy also endeavours to sow dissension

was the fact that he referred only to the material and not at all to moral defence of Germany. He gave a catalogue consisting of about half-a-dozen of the Allies' allegations which he declared to be dangerously disseminated in Germany; but they were all without exception allegations of German weakness and not of German wickedness. In the submarine problem, for instance, he did not complain of our saying that he had committed a crime, but rather of our saying that he had failed to commit one. He did not resent the suggestion that Germany had invaded France, but rather, if anything, the suggestion that France could retaliate by invading Germany. He did not trouble to deny that Germans had crossed the Atlantic to insult America with conspiracy and treason; he desired only to deny, by implication, that a sufficient number of Americans could cross the Atlantic to avenge the insult. To use the language he professed to quote, he was concerned with the idea that America would cook the goose—not with any idea that America would defend itself from the bird of prey. That the German eagle really is a bird of prey is at least a view held or professed by a considerable section of humanity. But, in counting up the causes of German disaffection, the German General regarded it either as a falsehood too absurd to be feared or as a truth too plain to be palliated.

Germans believe in Germans rather than in Germany, as Frenchmen believe in France rather than in Frenchmen.[59] The creed really common to the whole country is the belief that the Teuton is a type having a natural superiority—or, as he would probably put it, an evolutionary superiority. All education is organised to impose it; all history is chopped and expurgated to fit it. It is believed by all good Germans—even when, by a divine mystery and mercy, they manage to combine being good Germans with being good men. There are, of course, better and worse people in Germany; and there are saner and wilder versions of this theory in Germany. By the saner version the Teuton stands towards the other human tribes somewhat as the white man stands towards the black and brown tribes. By the wilder version he stands towards them rather as man stands towards the other animals. Now obviously there is room, even within this extraordinary theory, for many varieties of application and even of abstention. One particular Prussian may doubt the wisdom of one particular Prussian war, as one colonist may doubt the wisdom of one colonial

1918

in our ranks by means of leaflets dropped from aeroplanes above our lines. Ten thousand of these are sometimes gathered up in a day. The enemy knows what strength resides in our State and Empire; hence he seeks by his leaflets and false rumours to arouse distrust among us." Notice that remark contains the same internal contradiction Chesterton noted in his August 7, 1915 article (Ch. 3): "The Germans are fighting for their lives against a world of pigmies." In both claims of German strength are contradicted by their *own* description of their reaction. If their foes are "pigmies," why was Germany fighting for its life in 1915? If the Germans are so confident in September of 1918, why is Hindenberg so upset about these leaflets that he gathers them up as soon as they fall?

59. Today's America is divided, with one group resembling Chesterton's France and one Germany. The former believes in America's ideals, even when those ideals were not practiced. They want their nation to be a "city set on a hill," displaying those ideals to the world. The other disbeliefs in both the ideals and in demonstrating them to the world. They spare no effort to use failures to measure up to those ideals to slander the ideals themselves. Like the Germans, they believe only in themselves. They may no longer openly talk about the "evolutionary superiority" of their race and class, as the Harvard-educated Henry Cabot Lodge once did, but that same German-like arrogance and blindness remains. As Chesterton notes, "All education is organised to impose it; all history is chopped and expurgated to fit it."

adventure. In such a colonial adventure, one colonist may be more humane to the aborigines than another. Some Germans probably did believe it was unnecessary to wage this war, since the same supremacy might be won by what some call peaceful penetration and others commercial conspiracy. So some hunters might think a wild beast could be caught more humanely in a net, while others were catching him more cruelly in a trap of steel. But practically no hunters doubt that man has, in the last resort, the right to catch and kill wild beasts; and practically no Germans doubt that German culture has, in the last resort, the right to impose itself by force beyond its legally established frontiers.

It is their whole case that the ancient world, or the Dark Ages, were periodically refreshed and reformed solely by such barbaric invasions. Such tribal aggressions are to a Teutonist what Crusades were to a mediaeval Christian, or proletarian revolutions to a modern Bolshevik; they are aggressions to the advantage of the world. All this was preached quite plainly by the Germans before the war—or rather, before the first Battle of the Marne. After that first breakdown of the barbaric invasion, Germans have doubtless differed in varying degrees about the success of that invasion. They did not differ about invasion, but about this invasion; they have not altered their minds about war, but about this war. They doubt whether the best time was chosen, whether the best methods were employed—perhaps whether these were the best men to employ them. This is the very simple explanation of Hindenburg's proclamation—of all the points he mentioned, and all the points he omitted. As one of the ruling and responsible group, he wishes to prove to the German people that the time chosen was the best time, that the methods chosen were the best methods, and that he, Marshall von Hindenburg, is still very much the best man.

He does not defend himself from the charge of waging unjust war in a merciless manner, because it is not of that that his fellow-countrymen accuse him. The point he is parrying is something much more practical and personal. It is that he and his sort have mismanaged the campaign; not that they have involved the world in war, but that they have involved the Empire in defeat. It is that the submarines "are no good"—that is, that they are useless, especially in keeping American help from the Allies. It is that "America will cook your goose"—that is, that they are worse than useless, since they have ultimately helped to bring American help to the Allies. In a word, it is that Hindenburg is the goose; and that the goose has cooked himself.

The Prussian power has again and again been most applauded in Germany at the moment when it was most execrated in Europe. When it had crushed everything in Eastern Europe, and seemed about to crush everything in Western Europe, no real voice was raised by the Reichstag against its *right* to crush them. By the confession of the Pacifist papers themselves, the Reichstag majority now threatens to go into opposition—merely to avert the punishment, when it did not attempt to avert the crime. By the confession of the German Socialists themselves, the brutality to Russia made it harder and not easier to denounce the power effecting that brutality. In plain words, such acts have a positive popularity among a people that has heard of nothing but "hammer-blows" in its history. And Hindenburg knows exactly what will decide whether the hammer knocks the nail in his statue or in his coffin.

G.K. Chesterton, "Our Note-Book," *Illustrated London News* 153 (September 21, 1918), 326. US: September 21, 1918. Also published as "The 'Superiority' of the Teuton."

Cursing Germany

September 28, 1918

The only possible way of discouraging war is to curse the man who makes it.

Editor: Chesterton attacks the claim some were making that everyone involved in a war, aggressor as well as victim, is responsible. He insists that the nation actually responsible for the war, Germany, should pay for the harm done, particularly to Belgium and Serbia. He warns that if that is not done, there will be even more wars.

Chesterton often points out that Christendom had built close ties between chivalry and Christianity—chivalry being how Christians had learned, through many failures, how they ought to make war. In contrast, other ideologies have beliefs that lead to more terrible ways of making war. Teutonism, Nazism, Marxism, and militant Islam have displayed on an enormous scale a lack of chivalry and a willingness to demonize and kill all those who do not accept their ideology or are not thought to be worthy of it.

Terrorism is a particularly twisted sort of warfare that targets helpless civilians instead of soldiers, doing almost exclusively what Germany in WWI did occasionally. But keep in mind that it is *chivalry* that these terrorists lack rather than *courage*. In ordinary wars, soldiers who shoot women and children face little risk of being killed and are cowards. Terrorism is different. Killing one's self by crashing into a skyscraper requires a perverted sort of courage. What they lack is the chivalry and decency to distinguish between combatants and noncombatants. Political leaders who accuse terrorists of cowardice are mistaken, probably because our secularized culture has so little understanding of chivalry, that it lacks even a modern word for the concept.

Finally, just as the evil that Chesterton called Teutonism had its pacifist apologists who were attempting to blame everyone for the war except Germany, their modern counterparts often want blame everyone except the terrorists. Their "cursing War" remains remarkably callous to its real victims, either displaying indifference (Belgium in Chesterton's day) or outright hostility (Israel today). Finally, keep in mind that, extending Chesterton's argument, he is saying that those who engage in terrorism, as well as those who support it, openly or covertly, should pay a heavy cost.

So long as we go on cursing War, we shall go on encouraging War. It is a perfectly simple and even self-evident truth, though some would still treat it as a paradox. The only possible way of discouraging war is to curse the man who makes it. The fact would be quite obvious even where the case is less clear—as in calamities that can sometimes be accidents. It would be obvious if men confined themselves to denouncing fire, when they ought to be denouncing arson. If one man burned down another man's house in broad daylight, it would be a plain and positive advantage to the incendiary that we should confine ourselves to abusing the conflagration. He would be delighted if the neighbours would only stand in a ring round the burning house, and bellow and wail in a sort of chorus, "O Fire, atrocious Fire, cruel and devouring element, what graceful architecture and valuable furniture are you not ruthlessly consuming; how many harmless human lives have you not destroyed; how many women have been burnt in you as witches; how many saints and philosophers have been slain by you as heretics; how ruinous you are when you race over a prairie, and how fatal and indiscriminate when you attack the crowds in a theatre! Diabolical and abominable Fire, we curse the name of Prometheus, who brought thee not from heaven but rather from hell![60] Let us pass a unanimous resolution abolishing Fire." That is precisely the way in which some people think about War; but it is obvious that if they talked like that about fire, there would be more fires and not fewer. While the chorus was being chanted and the resolution passed, the practical professor of arson would make his escape and begin to set fire to another house. There would be nothing to stop him from reducing all civilisation to a field of ashes.

The modern suggestion, which takes many forms, to the effect that the great war was vaguely begun by everybody, and should vaguely be ended by everybody, fits this parallel precisely. It is a proposal that we should think about the inhuman fire and not think about the human firebrand. And the rest of the comparison is correct; it not only does not restrain him, but it does definitely encourage him. If we say that this war was everyone's fault, everybody will know that any war he makes will be called everybody's fault—that is nobody's fault. Every man will know that he can at any moment commit a crime which will be called an accident. Every ruler will know that he can, whenever he pleases, perform an act of aggression which will be called an act of God. Or rather, it will not even be called anything so mystical and disputable as the act of God—it will actually be called the act of humanity. **We shall be solemnly told that "all nations are equally to blame" for something which one nation does, whenever that nation may choose to do it. These, stated with strict fairness, are the philosophical and political principles on which we are now again being asked to base what is called a permanent peace. The wilder of these wags also describe it as a reasonable peace.**

The practical form of this problem is the question of compensation for the ravages of the war. Upon that the two parties stand clearly opposed—those who blame fate, which is like blaming fire, and those who are so fantastic as to blame the men who set fire to the other men's houses without the faintest provocation. The case to which this applies most clearly, of course, is the case of Belgium, which nobody even pretends was guilty of any provocation. It is a fact that Belgium was invaded by Prussia and not Persia; it is a fact that Prussia invaded Belgium and not Baluchistan; and it is a fact in the same sense that she did it without cause or quarrel. The German Chancellor confessed that he was committing a wrong; and the German Chancellor

60. In Greek mythology Prometheus favors men over the gods. When he tricks Zeus to benefit mankind, Zeus withhold fire from them. When he gives men fire, Zeus gives them Pandora, a woman who brings untold grief.

himself actually promised to pay compensation for that wrong. He said plainly in the Reichstag, at the very beginning of the war, that he admitted the duty of Germans repairing damage "when their military objective was achieved."[61] It would indeed be an irony if they could not be made to do it when our military objective has been achieved. It would indeed be extraordinary if they could not be forced by common justice to perform, when they are conquered, what they were forced for very shame to promise even when they were conquerors. Yet in this country there are still Pacifists who are more Prussianists than the Prussian Minister. There are still idiots posing as idealists who talk about an international fund to repair the wastage of the Flemish and French fields and cities—a subscription collected from all the States whether innocent or guilty. According to them, Germany must be excused even from what Germany expected, or else pretended very hypocritically to expect. **There is nothing to be said about such people, except that the mere word international seems to mesmerise and stun them; and if somebody were to propose an international pair of trousers to be circulated in rotation among the Presidents of all the Republics, they would not have the moral courage to laugh.**

But, of course, Belgium is only the working model, and by no means even the main example. The ruin of Serbia has been even more complete; and the aggression against Serbia was quite equally unquestionable. If Austria did not wantonly force war on Serbia, no State in all history ever did or ever will force war on another. These cases are far clearer and simpler than the majority of common criminal cases in which men are jailed and flogged and hanged. **But they will serve very well as a simple example of the absurdity of relieving our feelings by raving against the abstract idea of War. War is not an institution, like a post-office, which we are proposing to erect or preserve. War is a consequence of some men being tyrants.** Some man or men read a request for arbitration: some man or men tear it up, and take the full responsibility for tearing it up. In doing so they take the full responsibility of every pang that torments the Pacifist imagination, of every ruin that is lamented by the Pacifist rhetoric. And one thing is absolutely certain—that if such men are not held answerable for doing such things, such men will do them again; and myriads of such men will do myriads of such things again and again until the crack of doom. They can be punished and made to pay after the war; but if they only pay as we pay after the war, just as they have been punished only as we have been punished during the war, then from such evil equality will spring up again every element of pride and peril. These things are obvious—sane men have said them since the war began; but there is a good reason for saying them once again before the war ends. For the

61. Dr. von Bethmann-Hollweg, Imperial Chancellor, said: "We knew France was ready for an invasion. France was able to wait; we were not. A French aggression into our flank in the lower Rhine would have been disastrous, and we therefore were compelled to overrule the legitimate protests of the Luxemburg and Belgian governments. We shall repair the wrong we are doing as soon as our military aims have been reached." From "Kaiser William's War Speech" *New York Times* (August 5, 1914), 2. Of course, Germany had intended to pay for its damages to Belgium with money extracted from a defeated France. The Kaiser's August 4 speech in that same article was even more absurd, claiming that Germany had gone to war to support the emperor of Austria-Hungary, who was "compelled to take up arms for the protection of his empire" from tiny Serbia.

war is already ending, and the hour will soon strike when we shall have not to say this; but to do it.

G.K. Chesterton, "Our Note-Book," *Illustrated London News* (September 28, 1918), 354. US: September 28, 1918. Also published as "On War Reparations."

Nations as Ideals

October 5, 1918

The internationalist and the imperialist are not only similar men, but even the same men. There is no country which the Imperialist may not claim to conquer in order to convert. There is no country which the Internationalist may not claim to convert in order to conquer.

Editor: In the previous article, Chesterton criticized those who wanted the war to end with the injustice of a Germany unpunished. In this article he criticizes many of those same defenders of injustice by demanding that two of Europe's oldest injustices be ended by giving Poles and Czechs their own nations. This article is like one two months earlier (August 3). There he pointed out that pacifism and militarism were linked "by a fatal logic far beyond any conscious conspiracy." Here he notes that the internationalist and imperialist have in common an obsession with conquest.

The prospect of the Allies is not only brighter in its hopes, but broader in its ideals. We have a clearer assurance not only that we shall be able to do our work, but that it will be a great work—greater than seemed probable to most people at most stages of the struggle. We shall not be forced to follow those who bade us be content with barely saving Belgium, or sometimes even bade us be content with barely saving Britain. And the best proof of it is in what they themselves are now saying. The very men who said our aims were merely militarist and materialist have begun to cry about the very contrary in their despair.

Those who lamented our selfishness are now lamenting our unselfishness. They reproach us with idealism, they accuse us of altruism, they positively taunt us with a tenderness for abstract principles and remote peoples. They have no argument left but an abject cry to us to save our skins, to save our money, to save every base interest we have ever been abused for saving, from the devouring idealism of a desire to set the nations free. Here is a passage about the liberation of the Czechs from the ablest and most authoritative organ of the party of compromise, and the reader can judge for himself whether my description is exaggerated: "There are British interests in this war—what British interest does this large and cloudy idealism serve? Our straitened finance? Our impoverished shipping? Our dwindling youth?"[62] Needless to say, the writer goes on to say something about the interests of humanity; but about these he is much vaguer than the vagueness which he claims to criticise. He says we are guilty of idealism. We bow our acknowledgments. He

62. Although I was unable to find it, this quote is probably from the liberal *Nation*, which Chesterton criticizes elsewhere. See his *Illustrated London News* articles for November 11, 1916 (Ch. 4) and January 12, 1918 (Ch. 6).

says it is a large idealism. We accept the compliment. But when he says it is a cloudy idealism we submit that it cannot possibly be so cloudy as his own idealism, even by his own argument. Only a moment before he had said, in a shocked voice, "But Czecho-Slovakia is pure nationalism." We can again accept without grave humiliation the accusation of purity. **It is indeed pure nationalism—that is, unmixed and uncorrupted nationalism, a perfectly clear policy, founded on a perfectly clear principle. It proposes that there should be marked out and recognised a definite domain of a definite shape, with definite frontiers, and definite forms of self-government.** This is certainly in one sense idealism, since such patriotic independence and dignity is a permanent human ideal. But it most certainly is not cloudy idealism, upon any conceivable view of its merits. It may be a fantastic, a frantic, a Utopian and Quixotic supposition that Bohemia might belong to the Bohemians, as Poland might belong to the Poles. But it certainly is not an indefinite or incomprehensible proposition. It certainly is not so indefinite as the very plan, if it can be called a plan, which this writer has just been praising, and of which he can only say that it is "a plan which aims ultimately at unity through internationalism." This is not really an objection that any rational man can bring against Czecho-Slovakia, and it is not really the objection that this writer does bring against it. His real objections to fighting for a free Bohemia are expressed, with brutal sincerity, in much shorter and plainer sentences. It will not serve any British interest. It will not enlarge our finances—that is, give us any financial advantage. It will not increase the number of our ships, or increase the mass and value of our mercantile shipping. And it will not console, with any such solid advantages, the mourners of those dead men who were moved by so cloudy an idealism as to dream that they died for liberty.

I am glad of the contradiction, because it is a compliment. It is not, as I have often pointed out, by any means the only contradiction in which the apostles of compromise are involved. They have a very noticeable habit of saying two contrary things at once against the war, so as to suggest that they would say anything against the war. But all their inconsistencies, with which I have dealt more in detail on other occasions, centre round the great inconsistency involved on this occasion. **It is the gross inconsistency—or rather, the gross injustice—of first saying that England had only selfish aims arranged by secret diplomacy, and then forbidding England to pursue great and generous aims, with no reward but honour and the applause of men set free.**

As has been already said, the reconstruction of Europe by the building of real nations like Bohemia and Poland is a high ideal, and may well, therefore, be a hard ideal; it most certainly is not a hazy ideal. The truly noble quality of nationalism, as distinct both from internationalism and imperialism, is precisely that it does carve out clear shapes, like those made by an artist in architecture or sculpture. **The internationalist and the imperialist are not only similar men, but even the same men. There is no country which the Imperialist may not claim to conquer in order to convert. There is no country which the Internationalist may not claim to convert**

in order to conquer. Whether it is called international law or imperial law, it is the very soul and essence of all lawlessness. Against all such amorphous anarchy stands that great and positive creation of Christendom, the nation, with its standards of liberty and loyalty, with its limits of reason and proportion. More than a hundred years ago, a great crime was committed against this sacred substance and identity by the imperial anarch of Prussia.[63] It was done to Poland; but it might as justly or reasonably have been done to England. We might have been forced, generation after generation, to remain Englishmen without England. But we should have remained Englishmen, as the Poles have remained Poles without Poland. Yorkshire and East Anglia might be given to Germany, Wessex and Sussex to France, Lancashire and the Midlands to America—but England would have been more intense for being invisible, and none would ever have persuaded us that a nation is a name. And if, at the other side of Europe, a united Poland or a united Bohemia had come charging to our rescue with all their chivalry, it is possible that we should not have rebuked them for their large and cloudy idealism.

G.K. Chesterton, "Our Note-Book," *Illustrated London News* 153 (October 5, 1918), 392. US: October 5, 1918. Also published as "The Apostles of Compromise."

Germany's Illusion

November 2, 1918

The only hope for Germany, as well as for Europe, lies in exploding this illusion of the ultimate superiority of the Prussian for the practical purposes of war.

1918

Editor: By late October it was becoming clear that the war would end with a negotiated settlement rather than a major German defeat. Since much of the Allied anger was directed against Kaiser Wilhem II, one popular condition for a peace settlement was the end of the monarchy and the establishment of a democracy. Chesterton, who believed that Germany's problems ran far deeper than her vain and pretentious little king, was skeptical of German efforts to win favorable terms with a mere change of government. Here's a portion of the German telegram to Wilson that he comments on in this article.

> The German Government protests against the reproach of illegal and inhumane actions made against the German land and sea forces and thereby against the German people.... As a fundamental condition for peace the President prescribes the destruction of every arbitrary power that can separately, secretly, and of its own single choice disturb the peace of the world. To this the German Government replies: Hitherto the representation of the people in the German empire has not been endowed with an influence on the formation of the Government. The Constitution did not provide for the concurrence of representation of the people in decisions of peace and war. These conditions have now undergone a fundamental change. A

63. The partitioning of the Polish-Lithuanian Commonwealth between Prussia, Russia and Hapsburg Austria took place in stages in the late 1700s. In 1792, Prussia, which had been allied with Poland, broke off that alliance, allowing Russia to overrun the nation. In 1795 Warsaw became New East Prussia's capital. Then Prussia attempted to Germanize the Poles, unsuccessfully attempting to force its culture and language on them.

new Government has been formed in complete accordance with the wishes of the representation of the people, based on equal, universal, secret, direct franchise.[64]

The statement also announced that German submarines had orders "precluding the torpedoing of passenger ships," but only "to avoid anything that might hamper the work of peace." Germany wants to end the war with the contending armies still on French soil and without any clear admission of German wrong-doing.

This is Chesterton's last article before the war ends on November 11. Because the *Illustrated London News* had lavishly illustrated Armistice issues, it did not publish his column on November 9, 16, and 30, 1918.

THERE is one aspect of the international situation which has hardly been sufficiently emphasised, and that is the connection between the strange German statement about a defensive war and the subsequent German statement about an armistice. It may be remarked, to begin with, that the last official message from the enemy pretended that German rule had wholly changed, but contained also the best possible proof that it has not changed. For it defended German rule, even in the past, when most of us agree that it was misrule. It denied the crimes of the old régime, which might well have been admitted by a really new régime. Men have been talking about a revolution in Germany ever since the beginning of the war with Germany; and many of them would now maintain that the revolution has really come. But, if it had really come, all responsibility for previous orders would have really gone. A revolutionary Government would seem to have no very obvious reason for white-washing the crimes of the reactionary Government it had just managed to overthrow. The Government of Kerensky or Trotsky did not issue a proclamation denying the despotism of the Tsar, protesting against the slanders about Siberian prisons, and refuting the old stories of the knout.[65] It is a proof of the practical continuity of Prussian government that it accepts responsibility for the acts which we regard as crimes—for even in denying the crimes it admits the acts.

And indeed, as I have often pointed out, the pivot of the whole question is in acts which must be admitted—which, even when they are defended, cannot be denied. The German authorities propose that certain committees of neutrals should investigate our case against Germany; but this involves a certain oblivion of what really is our case against Germany. **The case stands as it always did—that our objection is to the plain and public part, even more than the sly and secretive part, of the Prussian policy. It is not that we denounce what they deny; but that we denounce what they defend.** What is clear at present is that the new German Government defends it as the old German Government defended it. When the new representatives of Germany say they protest against the charge of inhumanity, they can only mean, in the case of such evident and enormous type of action, that they do not think it

1918

64. "Text of Germany's Reply to President Wilson," *New York Times* (October 22, 1918), 1.

65. Alexander Kerensky (1881–1970) led the revolution that overthrew the Russian Tsar in February 1917 and was in turn overthrown by Lenin in October of that year. Leon Trotsky (1879–1940) supported Lenin's revolution. The Tsar's repression, including the use of a whip (knout), pales in comparison to that of the Soviets.

was inhumane. But at least there can be no doubt that it was evident and enormous. When, for instance, they specially announced a new submarine war as unrestricted, they exposed it as unprecedented. When they themselves were obliged to speak of the invasion of Belgium as an anomaly, it is something of an under-statement for us to say that it was an innovation. In other words, they have the responsibility of having, upon any argument, introduced certain exceptional and extraordinary things. One of the things we want to know is whether a new German Government still thinks those things necessary or defensible, or whether it is as free to denounce them as Lenin is free to denounce Stolypin.[66] If the latter is true, there may indeed have been a German Revolution, as real as the Russian revolution. If it is not true, then there is something else very different from a German Revolution, even if it is also different in some respects from the original German rule.

Now it is, I fancy, necessary to connect what its words meant in the matter of a defensive war with what its words mean about the proposed armistice. The former was by itself very much of a mystery; and yet it was in itself the solution of the latter mystery. Taken together, they make up a policy that might well be the policy of the original military authorities of Prussia. Those military authorities, if only because they were military authorities, know quite well that there is no such military conception as a defensive war that goes on till the crack of doom. But they may well have the military conception of a defensive war that goes on until the armistice is conveniently concluded, and even goes on with a considerable air of steadiness and success. It is that conception of a triumphant defence up to the very day of peace which probably dominates their minds, and ought in the sense to dominate ours. If they had proposed an armistice first, and failed to get it, they might have had to fall back on proclaiming a permanent defence, and then failed to make it permanent. But their object was to secure an end of war, after having just announced their readiness for a war without end. Thus, the last stages of their old defence might appear as the first start of a new defence. And thus the legend of the unique unconquerable character of Prussianised Germany might be renewed after all. It would still be possible to say that we had not broken the great militarist machine, and that we should never have been able to break it. But victory upon this point is exactly the victory that is really of value, since it is victory not only in the world of institutions, but in the world of ideas. **The only hope for Germany, as well as for Europe, lies in exploding this illusion of the ultimate superiority of the Prussian for the practical purposes of war.**[67]

66. Pyotr Stolypin (1862-1911) was Russian Prime Minister from 1906 to 1911. He dealt harshly with revolutionary groups, instituted agrarian reform, and tried to modernize Russian agriculture.

67. Chesterton correctly suspects that German leaders intend to deny they lost the war, and to do that they must avoid a decisive loss in battle and especially "the actual presence of invaders on German soil." In August of 1942, Hitler would claim: "In 1918 victory was as nearly in our grasp as it was in that of our adversaries. It was a battle of nerves." Adolf Hitler, *Hitler's Secret Conversations* (New York: Farrar, Straus and Young, 1953), 536.

It might be another matter, in many aspects at least, if we really were confronted with an endless defensive war, or even with a long defensive war. But every consideration of common-sense suggests that the war is already rapidly reaching its end, and none the less rapidly because it happens to be the right end. The very fact that the enemy is so anxious to finish it in his way, or the nearest he can get to his way, is itself evidence that we are near to finishing it in our way. What the enemy still wishes to avoid is a real reversal of the relations between himself and us. He would avoid the reversal of Sedan even more than the restoration of Alsace. He does not wish the great war of the world to end with one of the decisive battles of the world. He knows how those great decisions dominate history; and how much is remembered as historic because it is dramatic. The same instinct warns him against the bodily presence of invaders on German soil, which will reverse the more recent tradition that Germany is always invading and France being invaded, and return to the older European tradition that it was the Gauls even more than the Teutons who could, if necessary, cross the Rhine. **Germany in recent times has built up a legend that she cannot be invaded, which would have been a worthier legend if it had not always gone along with the legend that she can always invade other people.** All the accidents of this war have so far supported this legend, and it is because the legend is just on the very point of being falsified that everything else is surrendered in order that the legend may be saved. If the legend is saved, nothing else can be saved. For that legend is the lie that has forced them into their false position in modern Europe.

G.K. Chesterton, "Our Note-Book," *Illustrated London News* 153 (November 2, 1918), 526. US: November 2, 1918. Also published as "The Continuing German Lies."

Looking Back

November 23, 1918

I have tried to think of the great war as it would have appeared to our remote ancestors if they had known it was coming, as it will appear to our remote descendants when they consider how it came.

1918

Editor: In Chesterton's first article after the war, he summarizes some of the major points he has been making for the past four years. First, wars are not the result of impersonal forces as "materialists" claim. They are begun and ended by the "spirit of man," which can be either wicked or virtuous. Second, the pacifists are wrong when they claim that wars make no difference because, no matter who wins, the results will be the "same a hundred years hence." No, says Chesterton, "We should not be here at all to moralise about the ivy on castles and the corn on battlefields, if some of the great conflicts of history had gone the other way." Finally, near the end he explains the philosophy that has guided all he has written in the *Illustrated London News* over the past four years. Chesterton places the Great War just ending among history's great wars between barbarism and civilization. The failure to end it with a clear victory for civilization would result in another and far more barbaric war two decades later.

SINCE I last wrote in this place the end of the war has come as suddenly as an explosion. One of the chief remaining perils is that it should be regarded as an explosion, that is, as something that has simply happened. **It is the curse of all our culture that it abounds in mechanical and materialistic terms, so that things do not seem to have been done by men, because so many men have done them.** We talk of wars breaking out, like fires; of alliances breaking up, like ice; of negotiations breaking down, like bridges.[68] In this case peace came, just as war came, like a bolt from the blue, and the danger is that it should stun rather than startle.[69] It may seem dramatically sudden: but it is possible for a thing to be too sudden to be dramatic. Anyone can realise it who will imagine Hamlet killing Polonius in the middle of the chat with the Players, or Macbeth fighting Macduff when he first comes knocking at the front door after the murder. It would not even be sensational, because the audience would have no sensation of what it meant. In the present case, the danger is that the audience may have such an insufficient sensation of what it means. It may even be possible for some singularly senseless people to regard the end of the war as such people regarded the beginning of the war—as an enormous accident. **Such moonstruck materialists were quite content to say that war "broke out" in 1914. But war did not "break out" in 1914. We might as well say a man had "broken down," when we found him stabbed and bleeding to death on our door-step. This war has been one of the most human of all human events. Men began it; men ended it; but, fortunately, those who ended it were not those who began it.** The whole has been as singly and clearly conducted by the human will as any single combat in an old drama or any duel in private life. And the last phase of it was not only the most strenuous but the most simple phase. The fight of Macbeth and Macduff in fiction was not a more elemental conflict of man against man.[70] The fight of Bruce and Bohun in history was not a more purely personal encounter.[71] Foch parried something as personal and deadly as a sword-thrust, and thrust back with the force of a single sword.[72] It was not the result of accidents or even of circumstances—for accidents or even circumstances cannot create a design, still less a work of art. A statue cannot be carved by a neighbouring earthquake, or even by a neighbouring landscape. Environment does not grow these things: they are made and made by the spirit of man. The war was not an effect of evolution or even of revolution—in

68. Chesterton uses a similar argument in 1922 at the start of the fifth chapter of *Eugenics and Other Evils*, writing: "The mark of the atheistic style is that it instinctively chooses the word which suggests that things are dead things; that things have no souls. Thus they will not speak of waging war, which means willing it; they will speak of the 'outbreak of war,' as if all the guns blew up without men touching them."

69. "Stun" and "startle" illustrate Chesterton's remarkable skill with words. Although they sound alike and happen in the same context, their meanings are radically different. Both are effects that come suddenly, but something that stuns keeps us from thinking, while something that startles wakes us up and stimulates thinking.

70. This is Shakespeare's play *Macbeth*, based very loosely on King Macbeth of Scotland (*c.* 1005–1057).

71. At the Battle of Bannockburn (June 23–24, 1314), Humphrey de Bohun (1276–1322), 4th Earl of Hereford, charged at Robert the Bruce (1274–1329), King of Scotland, only to be felled by Robert and held for ransom.

72. French General Ferdinand Foch (1851–1929) was the supreme Allied commander from March 26, 1918 until the end of the war. After the war, he wanted a peace so harsh, Germany could never attack France again. After the less harsh Treaty of Versailles, he correctly warned, "This is not a peace. It is an armistice for 20 years."

the blind sense of reaction. It was the clear and intellectual answer of human virtue to human wickedness: a story of sin, of sacrifice, and of expiation as purely spiritual as an allegory. The anarchic numbers, the alien names, the vast mazes of military strategy and economic machinery are mere irrelevant complications of the staging; they have never for a moment affected the story. The war did not begin; it was begun, because there is in the heart of man the anarchic art that can begin such things. The war did not end; it was ended, because there is in the heart of man that cleaner creative hope that can endure and can end them.

There is another form of the same materialist fallacy which fools have sown broadcast for the last four years. Its most fashionable form may be summed up in the phrase, "It will be all the same a hundred years hence." I have read pacifist poems and essays in which the old rhetorical flourish to the effect that the corn will grow on the battlefield or the ivy on the ruined fortress, is seriously used to suggest that it makes no difference whether the battle was fought or whether the fortress fell. **We should not be here at all to moralise about the ivy on castles and the corn on battlefields, if some of the great conflicts of history had gone the other way.** If certain barbarian invasions had finally swept certain civilised districts, men would very probably have forgotten how to grow corn, and would have certainly have forgotten how to write poems about ivy.

Of some such Eastern Imperialist it was said, as a sort of proverb, that the grass would not grow where he had set his foot.[73] Europe has been saved from turning gradually into such a desert by a series of heroic and historic wars of defence, such as that of the Greeks against the Persians, of the Romans against the Carthaginians, of the Gauls against the Huns, of Alfred against the Danes, or Charles Martel against the Moors.[74] In each one of these cases the importance of the result does not decrease, but does definitely increase with time. It increases with every new generation that is saved from that destruction, with every new civilised work that is built on that security, with every baby that might never have been baptised or reared, with every blade of grass that might never have grown where it grows to-day.

Of course, the phrase about "a hundred years hence" was originally used in a loose but legitimate sense about petty dynastic and diplomatic wars, which may be all the same a hundred years hence. More often it was used about petty Parliamentary and

73. Attila the Hun (405–453) is said to have claimed, "Where my horse has trodden, no grass grows." In 451, he crossed the Rhine River, sacking cities and slaughtering their inhabitants until forced to retreat after meeting the Romans and Visigoths (Gauls) in the Battle of Chalons some 100 miles east of Paris. It was the last major military engagement of the Western Roman Empire. Attila never mounted another major offensive in the west.

74. These wars protected a civilization against invaders and, in the case of Rome, expanded that civilization. The Greco-Persian Wars were fought between 500 and 448 BC, when Greeks defeated much larger invading forces, with the best known battles being Marathon (490 BC) and Thermopylae (480 BC). Rome and Carthage fought each other in the Pyrrhic War (280–275 BC) and three Punic Wars (264–241, 218–202, and 149–146 BC). The best known struggle was Hannibal's invasion of Italy through the Alps in the second war. The wars ended with the destruction of Carthage and Roman dominance of the Mediterranean. King Alfred the Great (*c.* 849–899) defended England from an invasion of Danish Vikings—history Chesterton rendered as epic poetry in "The Ballad of the White Horse" (1911, republished in *G.K. Chesterton's Early Poetry*). Charles Martel (686–741), known as "Charles the Hammer, defeated the Islamic invaders of Europe at the Battle of Tours in 732—the turning point in Islamic invasions from the west that allowed Europe to remain Christian rather than be forcibly Islamized.

party quarrels within the State, of which it would be truer to say that they are all the same now. **I have my own opinions about those internal political quarrels, but I have deliberately kept them out of the notes it has been my business to jot down on this page for the last four years. Though the form of them has been in the crudest sense journalistic, I have tried to keep the philosophy of them in some sense historic. I have tried to think of the great war as it would have appeared to our remote ancestors if they had known it was coming, as it will appear to our remote descendants when they consider how it came.** It has seemed well to insist on the cause of the war, which has remained unaltered throughout, more even than on the course of the war, which has been differentiated by great desertions and great reinforcements; and immeasurably more than on the course of the political criticism of the war, which has been defaced with the usual varieties of cant and claptrap and ephemeral egotism. **The war will be some thing greater than the greatest men who have fought in it, and therefore infinitely greater than the smallest men who have quarrelled about it.** And it is at least due to all those who have died, and all those who have suffered in their dying, to vindicate their work against a weak-minded cynicism; and to say plainly that very little of the pacific politics of our time, which calls itself civic or constructive, has been half so permanent or so practical or so fruitful for God or man as these four years of destruction.

G.K. Chesterton, "Our Note-Book," *Illustrated London News* (November 23, 1918), 652. US: November 23, 1918. Also published as "The Explosion of Peace."

Victory Will Efface All

December 7, 1918

This is the profound sense in which it was always true to say that Prussia was atheistic; it held that the cosmos has no conscience because it has no memory.

1918

Editor: Chesterton takes on several opponents. He criticizes Prussia for having "no memory" and believing any deed, however foul, will be forgotten. He criticizes cosmopolitans for not recognizing, "Men care more for the rag that is called a flag than for the rag that is called a newspaper." He criticizes H.G. Wells for believing that putting all foreign policy in a League of Nations would eliminate backstairs deals.

At this time, the cost of the war became personal. On December 6, the day before this article was published, Chesterton's only brother Cecil, who had been fighting at the front, died of pneumonia in a French hospital. Of his death, Chesterton would write, "He lived long enough to march to the victory which was for him a supreme vision of liberty and the light."[75]

75. Quoted in Maisie Ward, *Gilbert Keith Chesterton* (London: Sheed & Ward, 1944), 358. A longer remembrance of Cecil by Gilbert is in a new edition of Cecil's *G.K. Chesterton: A Criticism* (Seattle, Inkling Books, 2007).

A Prussian General proclaimed the very Prussian maxim, in the middle of the sack of Belgium: "Victory will efface all."[76] The maxim seems to be changed today to "Defeat will efface all." The two statements really involve the same idea, and have the same motive. It is the idea of irresponsibility through a change of identity. Teutonic Imperialism, even in its triumphs, had always the fundamental idea of forgetfulness. It was always commanding the Pole to forget Poland; the Bohemian to forget Bohemia; the men of Lorraine to forget that they were French; the men of Schleswig to forget that they were Danish.[77] It always held that history was fluid, and had taken new forms; that all landmarks and lines of distinction would be washed out by the wave of the world. Upon this question the two sides in the Great War stood opposed more clearly than on any other. It was the whole claim of Rome and Gaul and Britain that there was something imperishable and, indeed, irrevocable about their creations, and even their crimes. **It was the whole claim of the Teutonic tribal empires that the last success would efface everything. This is the profound sense in which it was always true to say that Prussia was atheistic; it held that the cosmos has no conscience because it has no memory.**[78] It is always looking for what it would call a new world; as some primeval vision of the ancient slime might be called a new world.

But the Allies stand for an opposite and better principle, not only for Europe, but for Germany. And it is clear that not only in Europe, but even in Germany, the more historic idea for which they stand is again beginning to raise its head. It is not so much the revolt of a New Germany, as the return of an Old Germany—or, rather (and that is the point) of the Old Germanies. What we call the modern world is a more ancient world than we thought; and its simplicities will survive its complexities. Men care more for the rag that is called a flag than for the rag that is called a newspaper. Men care more for Rome, Paris, Prague, Warsaw, than for the international railways connecting these towns; or for the international relations that are often as cold, as mechanical, and as dead as the rails. Nobody has any such ecstatic regard for the mere relations of different peoples to each other, as one would gather from the rhetoric of idealistic internationalism. It is, indeed, desirable that the peoples should remain at peace with each other; it would be desirable that the men should love each other; but always with the recognition of the identity of other peoples and other men. **Now, too much of cosmopolitan culture is a mere praise of machinery.**

76. Chesterton mentions a similar quote, "Glory will efface all," in "Peace Reigns at Didant" in Louis Raemaker's *Kultur in Cartoons* (1917). He credits it to the aged Wilhelm von der Goltz, the German military governor of Belgium, also known by the jaw-breaking name of Wilhelm Leopold Colmar Freiherr von der Goltz (1843–1916). The attitude that victors write history, erasing the evil they did, would also be part of German thinking after WWII. Many Germans regarded the Nuremberg Trials as no more than "victor's justice." Victors, Germans thought, not only cover up their own crimes, they manufacture bogus crimes for those they defeated. That illustrates how people often project their own moral failings on to others.

77. Each of these were regions annexed by an expansionist Prussia between 1772 and 1871.

78. This has echoes in the German philosopher Georg F. Hegel (1770–1831). With Hegel, it's easy to suspect that many Germans confuse the fact that he is hard to understand with a belief that he is profound. The mention of "ancient slime" may be an allusion to Darwinian evolution, with its struggle and extinction. In this case national identities are seen as disappearing like unfit species, to be replaced by the Teuton.

It turns ultimately upon the point that a telegram can be sent from one end of the earth to the other, irrespective of what is in the telegram; that a man can talk on the telephone from China to Peru, irrespective of whether he talks Chinese metaphysics or Chinese morals.

Mr. H.G. Wells recently delivered another of his thoughtful and suggestive lectures about the League of Nations. I hesitate to discuss it in detail, because what I saw was obviously only a hasty report which might do him injustice, and lead me to do him injustice also. As I have often explained here, I am quite willing to accept the ideal of a League of Nations if it is really a League of Nations; that is, a league of free nations. I accept it if it means that states should be leagued as England is now leagued with France; but not if it means they are to be leagued as Saxony was leagued with Würtenberg, or as Bohemia was leagued with Austrian Poland until that day of deliverance that we have lived to see. Which of these two ideas is Mr. Wells' idea, I have never been quite certain; but in the remarks which I have seen reported, he seems to have used two phrases which have a very interesting connection, however he himself connected them. One was the statement that a Foreign Office tended too much to the use of the backstairs; with which I quite agree. The other was the statement that we ought to "pool" all our Foreign Offices. With this I not only do not agree, but I do not quite see why he should agree. Secret diplomacy really has been too secret; roughly, because the diplomatists have been too few and too far off. I cannot see how this is mended by making the diplomatists even fewer, and even farther off. And that must surely be the result of concentrating all offices in one great cosmopolitan office. I cannot see why that central office should not have a complete labyrinth of backstairs. And anybody who knows anything of cosmopolitan types and tendencies will feel tolerably certain that it would. Our experience of international intrigues during the war will surely be enough to show us that the most secret of all secret diplomacy is that which is not even officially diplomatic.[79] The relations of Kühlmann and Trotsky were much more obscure and elusive than the relations of Hollweg and Sazonoff. There is more mystification and controversy about the career of Mr. Morel than about the career of Mr. Gerard.[80]

I cannot see why we should have a sharper popular check on such private diplomacy because it was removed far from all our popular tests and traditions. If we

79. At that time, secret negotiations and treaties were seen as one of the war's causes, so Chesterton points out that an international body powerful enough to crush national sovereignty would be powerful enough to engage in even more international intrigue within its bureaucracy, particularly since national elections would offer no check on scheming officials. He is championing the true diversity of "an army with [many national] banners."

80. Chesterton is dealing with historical events that were vivid in his day, but known only to diplomatic historians today. Negotiations for the Treaty of Brest-Litovsk (December 22, 1917 to March 3, 1918) were between Leon Trotsky, representing the new Soviet Union, and Richard von Kühlmann (1873–1948), the German foreign minister. Chesterton contrasts them with earlier relations between Sergei Sazonov (Sergey Sazonoff) (1866-1927), the Czar's Minister of Foreign Affairs (1910 to 1916) and Theobald von Bethmann Hollweg (1856–1921), the German Chancellor (1909–1917). In his third example, Chesterton may be anticipating the behind-the-scenes impact that NGOs (Non-Government Organizations) will have on international bodies such as the League of Nations and the United Nations, when he contrasts the "mystification" surrounding E.D. Morel (1873–1924), head of the pacifist Union of Democratic Control, with a diplomat as well known as James W. Gerard (1867–1951), U.S. ambassador to Germany and author of *My Four Years in Germany* (1917) and *Face to Face with Kaiserism* (1918).

cannot collar the conspirator when he comes down the backstairs in Downing Street, why are we certain to trip him up if he transacts all his business on some neutral spot like the North Pole? **The truth is, of course, that Government always becomes less popular in proportion as it becomes less local.** The perfect democracy is a parish democracy; and though there are, doubtless, defects in this type of community, there are far greater dangers in departing from it too far. The intermediary type which for Europeans seems to be normal, is the type that is national. It is clear, at any rate that the Europeans do return to it when much larger schemes have been laid in ruins. That is why we have seen the triumph of the real Bohemian of the fields and forests over the sham Bohemian of the clubs and cliques. That is why, in comparing the pro-Ally Pole who is a Pole with the pro-German Pole who is a Jew, we can say, without unpardonable levity, that they are as far asunder as the Poles.[81] It is the day of the return of real things. It is Christendom of the nations that returns, and may truly be said to be terrible as an army with banners; for every banner has its separate blazonry.[82]

G.K. Chesterton, "Our Note-Book," *Illustrated London News* 153 (December 7, 1918), 740. US: December 7, 1918. Also published as "On Diplomacy and Nationalities."

Denying Racial Equality

December 21, 1918

It is, indeed, a denial of democratic equality; but what it denies is rather the equality of races than the equality of men.

Editor: Chesterton opens with the question of German reparations, particularly for damages inflicted on Belgium and northeastern France. Some argued that, since Germany wasn't a democracy in 1914, it was unfair to hold it responsible for the decisions of a few. Chesterton's reply is brilliant. He admits that, "No German would have favoured the war if they had known that Germany would lose the war in the fourth year." But he points out that the real issue is, "how many Germans would have repudiated the war if Germany had won the war in the first week." A nation whose people would have enjoyed a victory is a nation that has willed itself responsible in defeat.

Chesterton stresses that Germany's problem is, "a denial of democratic equality; but what it denies is rather the equality of races than the equality of men." Germany's racism did not begin with Hitler in a dimly lit beer hall during the war's troubled aftermath. It has respectable roots in Germany's decades of prosperity and scientific prowess before the war. Wealth and success are more likely to produce arrogance than impoverished and troubled times. The noted historian Charles Beard said precisely that about the "Teutonic myth" in his 1936 introduction to a book exposing Nazism.

81. In 1918, Chesterton already believed what history has amply demonstrated since 1948, that some Jews (here Polish Jews) are different enough culturally and politically from the countries in which they live ("as far asunder as the Poles"), that they constituted a separate nation that, by all rights, should have a nation of its own. Chesterton supported Zionism for the same reason he supported Boers in the Boer War, home rule for Ireland, and an independent Poland. See Chesterton's remarks about nationalism on January 4, 11, & 18, 1919 (Ch. 7).

82. An army with banners alludes to the biblical Song of Solomon 6:4 and 6:10.

> Certainly the creed is not the product, as sometimes alleged, of a mere "inferiority complex." It was never more ardently celebrated than during the closing years of the nineteenth century when the British were conquering the Boers and the Americans were stripping "degenerate Latins" of their empire in the Caribbean and the Far Pacific. Then it was the faith of people beset by a "superiority complex." About all that can be said for it is that it belongs in the same intellectual and emotional class as witchcraft, astrology, and demonology. We can never hope to get rid of it entirely. Perhaps we may reduce its virulence. Yet as a form of blind fanaticism it presents menaces which the nations of the earth must watch with increasing anxiety, especially now that it is armed with all the diabolical weapons of destruction provided by science and invention "in the age of progress."[83]

Chesterton believes ideologies promoting race-based inequality are absurd, but he recognizes that pragmatically they have a "defensible sophistry." Regarding a nation as a superior race *unites* that nation, while the class-based inequalities more popular in Britain and the United States as eugenics *divide* a nation into "fit" and "unfit." The former inspires wars of conquest, which in the case of Germany meant two wars in the twentieth century. In contrast, class-based racism creates internal conflicts in which an affluent, progressive elite (often anti-war) targets socially troublesome groups with various methods intended to reduce their birth rates, usually through the encouragement of sterilization, birth control and abortion.[84] History made Germany particularly susceptible to the former ideology. Unlike Britain and France, modern Germany was divided, only uniting after 1870. It required a racism that united all Germans.

Finally, notice Chesterton's remark, "that race superiority is not inconsistent with a republic. We all know that negro slavery was not inconsistent with a republic." By "negro slavery," he means the American Confederacy, which easily combined democracy with race-based slavery. Pacifists and others were putting their hope in a Germany that transformed itself from a monarchy to a republic in the closing days of the war. Chesterton warns that a republic will not keep Germany from retaining, "The very theory that was the ethical excuse of all their crimes in the past." Fourteen years after Chesterton wrote this article, Germany would place Hitler, history's most infamous champion of Teutonism, into the Weimar Republic's highest political office.

1918

THOSE who have never understood either the war or the peace are now everywhere telling us to forgive, in the sense of forget. But they miss the fact that there is really no question of forgetfulness. Nobody is going to forget that Verdun is battered or Belgium laid waste. No peasant returning to his village fails to notice that it happens to be a heap of stones. No peasant knocks at the front door that isn't there or tries to sit on an invisible chair at an invisible table. The most absent-minded scholar does not look for a book in the library of Louvain.[85] The most innocent inland rustic does

83. Charles A. Beard, "Foreword," Alfred Rosenberg, *"Mythus I" The Worship of Race* (London: Friends of Europe, 1936), 4.

84. See Chesterton's *Eugenics and Other Evils* (Seattle: Inkling, 2000) and *The Pivot of Civilization in Historical Perspective*, (Seattle: Inkling, 2001), edited by Michael W. Perry.

85. Starting on August 25, 1914 and continuing for roughly a week, the German army shot about 100 hostages and destroyed a fifth of the Belgian city of Louvain, including a university library. A judicial report issued by Prof. Leon van der Essen concluded that: "Many of the soldiers and officers may have believed, at the beginning, for a few moments, that they were being attacked by the enemy entering the town or that a civilian attack was taking place. But this mistake cannot have lasted long. It remains established that, in cold blood and without

not book a passage on the *Lusitania*. People, I hope, are not going to forget to rebuild their houses or re-till their fields in France or Flanders: architecture and agriculture are not lost arts. **The question about reparation is therefore perfectly simple. It is not whether these things shall be remembered or forgotten; it is whether they shall be remembered only by the innocent and forgotten only by the guilty. It is not a question of reparation or no reparation; it is a question of imposing the labour of it on those who sinned or on those who suffered.** Somebody will pay to rebuild the house that was burnt; if we do not punish the incendiary, we shall punish the householder. This moral point is childishly plain; but when it is urged the answer is, of course, to draw a distinction between the Prussian Government and the German people. But this contention also depends on a somewhat similar fallacy, which it will be well even now to note.

There is a very simple question to ask about how far most Germans had any responsibility for fighting. It is to ask how many Germans had any delicacy about winning. Many doubtless had an increasing dislike of losing, and have now a very full and final dislike of having lost. But all would agree that, whether or no the game was worth playing, it was certainly not worth losing. No German would have favoured the war if they had known that Germany would lose the war in the fourth year. The question is, how many Germans would have repudiated the war if Germany had won the war in the first week. If the sweep upon Paris had been successful, if the English enlistment had come too late, if Tannenberg had really disarmed Russia in the first few days of battle—in short if Bernhardi's big plan had worked, and left Prussia mistress of the world, how many Germans would have reproached their rulers with their own triumph.[86] Possibly one; conceivably two; almost certainly not three. The victorious Prussian government would have been popular if ever a government was popular.

Common sense will take it for a fact, I think, that Germans would have unanimously welcomed a full German mastery of Europe.[87] The great query of the future

any idea of a serious inquiry, the military authorities persisted in the error and subjected Louvain to eight days' martyrdom, without raising a finger to stop the orgy." When the resulting international outcry reached the U.S., German Foreign Minister Gottlieb von Jagow issued a statement denouncing the *Belgian* government, "which, in spite of reiterated warnings by the German authorities, did nothing, after the capture of Liege, to induce the people to take a pacific attitude." (Exactly what the Belgian government could do in areas under German control was not explained.) The Kaiser's statement, issued on September 7, 1914, was even more outrageous, admitting the deeds, but blaming the victim and feigning concern for them: "Some villages and even the old town of Loewen [Louvain], excepting the fine hotel de ville, had to be destroyed in self-defence and for the protection of my troops. My heart bleeds when I see that such measures have become unavoidable and when I think of the numerous innocent people who lose their home and property as a consequence of the barbarous behaviour of those criminals." After the war, aid from the U.S. and reparations by Germany rebuilt the library. See Alan Kramer, *Dynamics of Destruction: Culture and Mass Killing in the First World War* (Oxford: Oxford University Press, 2007).

86. The Germany victory at Tannenberg in late August 1914 halted the Russian invasion of East Prussia and was their greatest success in the war, making Generals Paul von Hindenberg and Erich Ludendorf national heroes. General Friedrich von Bernhardi (1849-1930) wrote the best-selling 1912 *Deutschland und der Nächste Krieg* (English transl.: *Germany and the Next War*, 1912), which used Darwinian arguments about 'expansion or death' to urge Germany to wage aggressive war.

87. For what Germany's political leaders intended to do had they won the war, see David Stevenson, *Cataclysm: The First World War as Political Tragedy* (New York: Basic, 2004), 104f. According to war aims approved in September 1914, "Belgium would become a 'vassal state', under military occupation and 'economically a Germany

is whether they still desire what they so lately demanded, and whether they will again demand it. **It is here that it is so vital to emphasise, as I have always tried to emphasise, the more fundamental nature of the Teutonic claim. It is not, and it never was, mere despotism or mere militarism. It is a much more deep, and in a sense a much more defensible sophistry. It is, indeed, a denial of democratic equality; but what it denies is rather the equality of races than the equality of men.**[88] It was never so much the right of Hohenzollerns to rule Germans as the right of Germans to rule non-Germans. Now we can all see that race superiority is not inconsistent with a republic. We all know that negro slavery was not inconsistent with a republic. It is not inconsistent with State Socialism as professed by the leaders of Prussian thought. It is certainly not so inconsistent with the Socialism they now profess as with the Christianity they used to profess. In some ways the new disguise would suit them much better than the old. It is no more difficult for a German President to invoke Humanity than for a German Emperor to invoke God. The king claimed God for the work of the most atheistic of kings, Frederick the Great. The professor may claim humanity for the work of the most inhuman of professors, Karl Marx. But the one kind of idealistic imposture is quite as easy as the other. In the cult of the Iron Cross, it was not difficult to remember the material and forget the shape. In the worship of the red cap of liberty, it would not be any harder to forget the shape and remember only the colour. By such a process the principle of blood and iron would remain unchanged through all changes.[89] It would be as easy for the most inhuman of States to organise processions of human fraternity as it was for the most unchivalrous of States to parade a pageant of all its orders of chivalry. If the savage has assumed the garb of mediaeval Europe, he can assume the garb of modern Europe; he can do so much more easily, for his real power is a growth of modern times and not of mediaeval times. And we must always remember, I repeat, that the thing that threatens us is not his mediaevalism, but his modernism.

The economic and political ideal in which the North Germans are now supposed to find their future is not very alien to their past. Many mistakes may arise in this connection by talking, in a hearty but hazy fashion, about Bolshevism.[90] Bolshevism

province', while a 'central European customs association', including France and Scandinavia would 'stabilize Germany's economic dominance' over its members." This customs association "never enjoyed great support from business," which felt it made little sense. See Fritz Fischer's *Germany's Aim in the First World War* (1961).

88. When race is defined by nationality, race-based inequality becomes a more "defensible sophistry" than "mere despotism or mere militarism," because it is has greater depth, uniting a nation around something more emotionally satisfying than mere authority and power. It's still a "sophistry" and hence a lie, but it's a powerful and thus dangerous one. Chesterton warns that it's not narrow, as some might claim. It can blend with other powerful ideas, particularly socialism. Within a few years, precisely that will happen. Nazism will arise, combining race-based nationalism with a "heathen socialism" said to be rooted in pre-Christian Germanic traditions.

89. This alludes an 1862 speech by Otto von Bismarck in which he said: "Not by speeches and votes of the majority, are the great questions of the time decided—that was the error of 1848 and 1849—but by iron and blood" His unabashed defense of might makes right was later modified to a more alliterative "blood and iron."

90. Later Chesterton would write: "What I dislike in Bolshevism is not its disorder but its order; not its wildness but its tameness; its tameness in accepting all that impersonal herding and hardening of the modern mechanical state.... In the worst Capitalist state an honest man may conceivably become independent by accident. In the Bolshevist State he is doomed to be dependent by law." *GK's: A Miscellany* (London: Rich & Cowan, 1934), 298.

may be made to mean a great many things, including an honest human hatred of the oppression of the poor more remote from Berlin than from Babylon. In that sense we have all felt something that can truly be called Christian Socialism. But the thing involved here has a strict and special claim to be called heathen Socialism. It is not true that the peril threatened by the Prussian is Bolshevism. It is still true that the peril threatened by the Prussian is Prussianism. Nor does any social scheme contain more promise of Prussianism than the Marxian and materialistic type of Collectivism. The Prussian Socialism is a strict State Socialism: in other words, the Prussians still believe in the divine right or diabolic right, of the State. **The theory remains that the State is the only absolute in morals, that is, that there is no appeal from it to God or man, to Christendom or conscience, to the individual or the family or the fellowship of all mankind.** The very theory that was the ethical excuse of all their crimes in the past is the first principle of their political philosophy for the future. The fact is surely very relevant to the problem of any remaining menace from the Germans. In practice they cannot at present equip themselves with the power to attack Europe. But they have at least equipped themselves with a theory which is suitable for any such purpose. With their intellectual theories we are still at intellectual war, though we can all hope that it will remain an intellectual war. **The conversion of Germany would doubtless be a greater thing than the conquest of Germany; but Germany must be converted to something more common to mankind than to one of the cold fancies of one of her own fantastic professors.**

G.K. Chesterton, "Our Note-Book," *Illustrated London News* (December 21, 1918), 824.
US: December 21, 1918. Also published as "The Future of Germany."

Christmas versus Yule

December 28, 1918

Nevertheless, a very vital distinction arises between the time when Christendom tried to civilise Germany and the more recent time when Germany tried to barbarise Christendom.

Editor: Chesterton sees Europe embroiled in a war of ideas between historic Christianity and a new scientific paganism of progressives and professors that's similar to barbaric paganism. He warns that we face, "the vast problem of the cultivation and conversion of the German tribes.... The principle must be that of the first missionaries in Germany; that Christianity must decide how much of heathenism may be retained. It must emphatically not be the principle of the latest professors in Germany; that heathenism must decide how much of Christianity may be retained."

Although on opposite sides in this struggle, both Chesterton and Hitler agreed on its essence. In October of 1941, while discussing how "War has returned to its primitive form," a Darwinian struggle for resources, Hitler said: "The law of selection justifies this incessant struggle, by allowing the survival of the fittest. Christianity is a rebellion against natural law, a protest against nature. Taken to its logical extreme,

Christianity would mean the systematic cultivation of the human failure."[91] That is precisely what Chesterton means by "a fight between Christmas and Yule."

WITH the approach of Christmas we are at last able to celebrate, if not in a literal sense the conclusion of peace, at least in another sense the conclusion of war. Those who understand Christmas best will not find a mere incongruity between the great Christian feast and the crusade which it terminates; but even those to whom peace of any kind is a relief may rightly be allowed that relief. And even those to whom Christmas can hardly be an occasion for merrymaking, will assuredly find it an occasion for thanksgiving. Of the deepest grounds of such gratitude it would not be appropriate to write here; but I have noticed that modern reverence often permits the consideration of irreligion where it forbids that of religion. And in some of the negations with which we have been at war, there are still some curious lessons at this season.

The fight of the last four years might be called, among other things, a fight between Christmas and Yule. I do not mean that I wish to divide that historic house against itself, or turn the issue into a duel between a Christian Santa Claus and a heathen Father Christmas. My taste for the fantastic does not go so far as to make the whole festival a battle of holly and mistletoe, in the style of a battle of flowers; or a siege of the home in which the Yule log can be used as a battering-ram, or the Christmas crackers as a form of fairy artillery.[92] Christmas may at least be left at peace with itself, if it cannot be at peace with all men; or rather, if all men will not include it in their peace. **One of the first reforms of Lenin and Trotsky was, I believe, to abolish Christmas. It is not the only point on which the prejudices of the most emancipated Progressives are an exact copy of the prejudices of the most antiquated Puritans.**[93]

1918

But I fancy that Christmas will manage to survive Trotsky at least as long as it has survived Cromwell. Nevertheless, it is true, as I have suggested, that the recent crusade corresponded to a very real difference between the Christian and pagan potentialities of such an institution. As it stands, an idea like that of Christmas is an indivisible unity; but it would in due time have been divided. Its barbarian elements

91. Adolf Hitler, *Hitler's Secret Conversations* (New York: Farrar, Straus and Young, 1953), 43. Unlike Heinrich Himmler (1900–1945), head of the SS and Gestapo, Hitler had no interest in restoring German's pagan past. He said, "nothing could be more foolish than to re-establish the worship of Wotan," and wanted a science-inspired nature mysticism: "The man who lives in communion with nature necessarily finds himself in opposition to the Churches. And that's why they're headed for ruin—for science is bound to win." p. 51.

92. The Jersey Battle of Flowers is a festival held on the island of Jersey (in the English Channel) since 1902. In a happier era, at the end the parade floats were dismantled and a mock battle conducted with their flowers.

93. Hostility to Christmas has a long history. Disliking the merry-making, by an Act of Parliament under Oliver Cromwell, the Puritans banned Christmas in England between 1644 and 1660. (The unpopular law was ignored.) With more brutality and to advance atheism, the Soviet Union banned the celebration of Christmas just after its October 1917 revolution and the ban was not completely removed until 1992. Nazism, as part of its efforts to "barbarise Christendom," tried to replace Christmas celebrations with pagan celebrations of the winter solstice, much as Chesterton suggests might happen. Finally, contemporary liberalism, while regarding with great favor artists who slander religion and offend Jews and Christians (but not Muslims), claims that any public recognition of Christmas must be banned, lest it offend some more pampered group.

would have destroyed its civilised domestication, or rather, dedication. Christmas would have elapsed into Yule; and the living and branching Christmas-tree would, indeed, have been left as a log.

Nobody with any Christian common sense ever dreamed of denying that Christmas contains many elements of heathenism. It is but another way of saying that it contains many elements of humanity.[94] **Nevertheless, a very vital distinction arises between the time when Christendom tried to civilise Germany and the more recent time when Germany tried to barbarise Christendom.** The nature of the combination depends on the nature of the selection; and, therefore, on the authority that selects. It is not a bad thing, but a good thing, that civilisation should borrow from the wild fancies of the Northern forests, so long as it is really civilisation that borrows. But such good things from Germany are like other goods from Germany; they should be demanded, but not dumped. And there has been no duller impudence than the dumping of the pedantry of Prussia upon the piety of Europe. **The modern Teutons were always trying to include a faith in a system of folk-lore; instead of trying, like their far more philosophic fathers, to include folk-lore in a system of faith. They stretched the myth to cover many religions; instead of allowing one religion to cover many myths.** It is in this relation that it is well for us to realise where we stand to-day.

We stand very much where the men of the later Roman Empire and the early Middle Ages stood, when they saw before them the vast problem of the cultivation and conversion of the German tribes. It is in this matter that the relations, as they existed before the war, must be most drastically and decisively reversed. Christmas and other Christian institutions are examples of something that must develop in our direction and not in theirs. The principle must be that of the first missionaries in Germany; that Christianity must decide how much of heathenism may be retained. It must emphatically not be the principle of the latest professors in Germany; that heathenism must decide how much of Christianity may be retained.

For on the whole the old religious selection was a good selection and the new irreligious selection was a very bad one. **Some of us may well prefer the old paganism to the new paganism; some of us would, in any case, prefer a more or less masculine mythology to an emasculated religion.** But suppose the first Christian preachers found, let us say, that the Teutonic tribes at Yule varied their human sociability with a little human sacrifice: we shall hardly, on a large historic retrospect, blame the Christians for deciding to dispense with this formality. **But if we turn to the more**

94. Chesterton is right. With a few exceptions, Christianity has been remarkably tolerant of many "elements of heathenism." The Christian calendar includes days of the week based on Nordic gods (Thursday is Thor's Day), and months based on deified Roman emperors (August after Augustus Caesar). That's quite remarkable. In contrast, modern secularism in various garbs has tried to purge Christian elements from our calendar. Christmas, it says, can't be a publicly recognized holiday. Even stranger, calendar years are to be captioned B.C.E. and C.E., where "C.E." refers to a "Common Era," a term devoid of all meaning. It is as if Christians, unable to change the name of our months, had attempted to claim that, in defiance of all facts, that the month of August was named for Saint Augustine. And don't forget that any effort to efface a person or a group from history is one of the uglier forms of bigotry, an attempt to deny that they ever existed or ever accomplished anything. Similar bigotry—but racial rather than religious—drives those hostile to celebrating the Rev. Martin Luther King's birthday.

modern reformers of Yule, we shall find that what they wish to dispense with is not so much human sacrifice as human nature. The prigs of the progressive schools would sweep away not so much the unkind as the kind elements of a festivity, not the fighting but the feasting. They would debar the poor Teutonic thane not so much from blood as from ale; not so much from the fires of burning homesteads as from the fireside fairy-tales of the home. It was this extraordinary compound of frigidity and ferocity, of scientific prudence and savage lawlessness, that the modern intellect, mostly made in Germany, produced as the proper compromise between the old and new. And the selection is seen to be every bit as bad when we turn from the harmless humours of the old religious festivals to their higher and more moving religious meaning. This is no place for anything more than a suggestion of this mystical case against modernism; but it will be at once apparent that here also the Prussian professor and his foreign pupils removed what was important because it was insignificant. It is obvious that what they removed from Christmas was simply Christ. **The reformers of Yule may have rejected the human sacrifice; the reformers of Christmas rejected the sacrifice for humanity.**

It need hardly be added that on this ground, as on so many others, our policy should point as directly as possible towards the separation of Southern Germany, and especially Bavaria, from the barren cynicism of Prussia. South Germany, for all its enslavement, kept many of the humane traditions which North Germany tried to kill with sneers and speculations. It is altogether to the advantage of Christendom to support the Germany which talked about the Christmas-tree against the Germany that talked about the *Christus Mythus*.[95] It seems to me a somewhat secondary matter whether philosophies are labelled with one long word or another. **It matters little, in the living matter of the mood, whether they profess a Prussian State militarism or a Prussian State Socialism; both of which involve putting the State upon the throne of God.**[96]

1918

G.K. Chesterton, "Our Note-Book," *Illustrated London News* 153 (December 28, 1918), 858. US: December 28, 1918. Also published as "A Christmas of Peace."

95. Chesterton makes delightful fun of scholarly fads such as the *Christus Mythus* (the Gospels treated as myth by German scholars) in the introduction to Chapter 19 of his *The Flying Inn*.

Dr. Moses Meadows, whether that was his name or an Anglicised version of it, had certainly come in the first instance from a little town in Germany and his first two books were written in German. His first two books were his best, for he began with a genuine enthusiasm for physical science, and this was adulterated with nothing worse than a hatred of what he thought was superstition, and what many of us think is the soul of the state.... In his second book he came more to grips with delusions, and for some time he was held to have proved (to everyone who agreed with him already) that the Time Ghost had been walking particularly "rapidly, lately; and that the *Christus Mythus* was by the alcoholic mind's trouble explained." Then, unfortunately, he came across the institution called Death, and began to argue with it. Not seeing any rational explanation of this custom of dying, so prevalent among his fellow-citizens, he concluded that it was merely traditional (which he thought meant "effete"), and began to think of nothing but ways of evading or delaying it. This had a rather narrowing effect on him, and he lost much of that acrid ardour which had humanised the atheism of his youth, when he would almost have committed suicide for the pleasure of taunting God with not being there.

96. Nazism would combine both of Chesterton's false gods into one, calling themselves National Socialists.

7
Battling Internationalism
1919–1922

Grand Schemes—Editor

As was pointed out in the first chapter, the Great War brought an end to a Europe divided between, "a small select aristocracy born booted and spurred to ride and a large dim mass born saddled and bridled to be ridden." With varying degrees of speed and permanence, power moved into other hands. New aristocracies driven by ideologies such as nationalism and socialism grappled for power.

In Britain, victory in the war and a worldwide empire would maintain a semblance of the old order for another generation. The *Illustrated London News* would still publish fold-out pictures of the king, but for the more cynical, his stiff pose, clad in oversized ermine robes and glittering with unearned medals, made him little more than a doll to be dressed up for special occasions. After the war, even more than before, real power lay in the Cabinet, Parliament, and with those educated in the proper schools.

In France, already a republic, little seemed to change. During the war, the nation paid an enormous price in lives and wealth, but after the war it seemed incapable of finding answers to its problems, including the critical one of dealing with German aggression. A French officer, Charles DeGaulle (1890–1970), would write a 1934 book, *Vers l'Armée de Métier,* warning that future wars would be mechanized and mobile, but France would place its hope in an immovable Maginot Line, built between 1930 and 1939, that failed to extend far enough north to cover the invasion route Germany used in World War I. In May of 1940, a highly mobile German army would bypass it.

Russia changed the most. In 1917, it was transformed from one of Europe's most backward and repressive monarchies into a communist state many regarded as the hope of the future. With his usual care, whatever his suspicions, Chesterton would withhold judgment about the new state until its repressive nature became clear. In this chapter you'll find him in touch with what was happening in the Soviet Union and praising Poland for preventing the Russian Revolution from spreading westward. Unappreciative of the sacrifices of others, Western Europe would pay little attention to the price the Polish people paid to keep the rest of Europe free of communist tyranny, much as earlier they had failed to recognized the sacrifices the people of Southeastern Europe had made to protect the rest of Europe from Islamic invasions.[1]

But it was in Germany and Italy where changes took place that would lead directly to World War II. Many of today's sentiments in favor of democracy were not widely held after World War I. A fashionable belief in top-down rule was deeply imbedded

1. Chesterton points to the latter sacrifice in his October 10, 1914 article (Ch. 2).

in the European psyche. The ideas about a "Strong Man" that Chesterton blasted in his December 15, 1917 article were widespread, and a powerful, ruthless ruler was believed to be the only way to deal with military threats and social unrest. In addition, from the late 1920s on, a strong central government was seen as the only way to deal with economic depression. Even among people who preferred democracy, many doubted it had the strength and will to solve its problems. In Italy and Germany that led to dictatorships. In Europe's democracies it led to weak and vacillating leaders who would lack the courage to restrain Nazi Germany.[2] In the midst of all this unrest, Europeans searched for a grand scheme that would bring peace and security. In 1929, Chesterton would mention three mistaken "lessons of the Great War."

> Some said that we must prevent anybody fighting by instantly fighting anybody who attempted to do anything. Some said we must express our hatred of Imperialism by turning the whole world into one huge Empire, more centralized, more organised, and probably more destructive of local liberties than any had ever been known. Some said we must forgive our enemies and confine ourselves entirely to insulting our friends.[3]

Outside Germany, many fell for the blandishments of pacifism and the idea that wars would end if only, as a 1933 Oxford Union debate concluded, everyone agreed that they would, under "no circumstances fight for king and country." Chesterton referred this naive belief in an April 5, 1919 article (Ch. 7), when he wrote that pacifists thought that war was a "game between crowned heads with little national flags stuck all over a map; or it is a dark agreement to differ between wicked diplomatists who sit round a table and say 'Let us have a war,' like men proposing a game of bridge." When such men proposed a game of war, pacifists said, all people had to do was refuse to play. Many went further and, like H.G. Wells, said the way to end war was to do away with nations. Chesterton knew better.[4] Like Winston Churchill, his ideas have stood the test of time far better than those of virtually all of his contemporaries. In this chapter, we explore Chesterton's efforts to ensure that the war did not end in foolish and grand schemes that would fail to prevent an even bloodier war.

---

2. Disdain for a 'Strong Man' doesn't mean a dislike for strong leadership. During the 1930s, as Hitler, Stalin and Mussolini were pushing Europe into repression and ultimately war, Chesterton was calling on Britain's elected officials to display strong, intelligent leadership. Half a century later Ronald Reagan, Margaret Thatcher and John Paul II would demonstrate Chestertonian-like leadership, leading Eastern Europe to freedom and ending the Cold War. That's what Chesterton was calling for after WWI, and again what he called for after Nazism began its rise to power. As I write, a belief in a Saddam-like 'Strong Man' who maintains 'order' and 'stability' is common among those (living comfortably elsewhere) who think that dictatorships are the only to keep down the troubles in the Middle East. Belief in the Strong Man dies hard.

3. *The Collected Works of G. K. Chesterton*, vol. XXXV, 138. From *Illustrated London News*, August 3, 1929.

4. The idea that a few could stop wars would not die. In a May 16, 1931 article in the *Illustrated London News* Chesterton refers to his "respectful astonishment" at a recent remark by Albert Einstein: "If you can get two per cent of the population to assert in times of peace that they will not fight, you can end war." Chesterton responded: "But here the theorist asks us to believe, not merely that two men could fight a hundred men, but that a hundred men could not fight at all because two men were not fighting." Ronald W. Clark notes that Einstein tailored his own peace message to his locale, talking differently in wartime Germany than in neutral Switzerland. [*Einstein: The Life and Times* (New York: Avon, 1971), 237.]

Chesterton does not mention here an argument about the "weakest link" he published on July 20, 1907. By their disruptive political activities, pacifists weaken a nation's ability to fight and hinder the war effort of a free country far more effectively than that of a repressive one, giving a terrible advantage to the latter and tilting the flow of history in favor of dictators. (See: *The Collected Works of G.K. Chesterton*, vol. XXXV, 520–523.) Ideology can also drive some to aid the enemy, as when nuclear scientists who favored communism gave secrets about building an atomic bomb to the Soviet Union during and just after World War II.

NATIONS ARE UNIQUE

January 4, 1919

On the contrary, I believe something very valid might be done to stop such frantic rivalry, if the patriots of all countries could come together. But I am sure that nothing can be done so long as it is the cosmopolitans of all countries who come together.

EDITOR: In this first year after the war, Chesterton begins by touching on a debate over freedom of the seas that troubled post-war peace negotiations. Freedom of the seas is a principle that every nation has a right to use international waters for trade and travel. In peacetime, there was little controversy. But there was a debate over how aggressively a nation could blockade an enemy in wartime. During WWI, Britain used an extensive blockade to prevent food from *neutral* nations from reaching other *neutral* nations (such as Holland), simply because some of that food might reach Germany. This angered nations who were major food exporters, particularly the United States, and is why the second of President Wilson's "Fourteen Points" called for, "Absolute freedom of navigation upon the seas, outside territorial waters, alike in peace and in war." Here Chesterton hints that if Britain spent too much effort defending its restricted view of freedom of the seas, it could lose on a more important issue.

That issue was the size of navies. Before the war there was an extensive naval arms race, with Britain and Germany building expensive battleships that were soon obsolete. Chesterton criticized that in a March 27, 1909 article (Ch. 1), commenting: "People whisper in a panic-stricken way that Germany is building ironclads of the size of small islands.... I have my doubts about both the moral and the military value of this sort of imagination." As he often did, Chesterton balanced that by pointing out that each nation is different, that as a nautical trading nation Britain must have a larger fleet.

Nor was this debate simply about the size a nation's fleet. At that time, influential voices were calling for a powerful, militarized League of Nations. An article in the *New York Times* less than two weeks before Chesterton's took that view. The article is a poorly argued opinion piece masking as news. It claimed the new League of Nations would end the freedom of the seas distinction between war and peace, leaving the seas "open and free in time of peace and war alike."[5] Apparently even a brutally attacked nation would have no right to blockade its foe. The author went on to claim, "If the League of Nations were attacked, however, all laws would be in abeyance and the league would defend the world order, of which it would be the trustee and guardian." Note the "all laws." The new League would not be limited even by the rules that now govern warfare between nations, for instance the protection of neutral shipping and the borders of neutral nations. The "world order" the *New York Times* advocated was to be lawless, although we need not assume that it realized that.

Then comes a remark illustrating why Chesterton warns that some wanted a League of No Nations. "The principle," the *New York Times* wrote, "would be the same as that which permits a Sheriff to break down a door, although a private person may not do so." In this scheme, nations are no more than private individuals, with only the most limited rights to defend themselves and no borders ("doors") they have a right to defend. Nations would no longer be sovereign states, able to wage just and necessary

5. Charles H. Grasty, "Expect Agreement on Naval Power," *New York Times* (December 24, 1918), 2. Grasty was a war correspondent for the AP and the *New York Times*. He wrote *Flashes from the Front* (1918).

wars.[6] Only the League ("Sheriff") could do that—and do so more ruthlessly than any nation in history. The author also assumes, without saying so, that these truncated governments would have enough unbridled *internal* power to repress dissent and force their unwilling people to obey the League, pay its taxes, and die in distant League wars. The older approach, which Chesterton calls "Christendom"—built on what people actually are rather than what some think they ought to be—is easier to reconcile with democracy than newer progressive ideas about an international league that looks, on closer examination, disturbing like a global dictatorship.

The article that follows provides a look at what Chesterton meant by a nation and why he regarded it worthy of being protected from the ravages of cosmopolitans and internationalists. His remarks about each nation having a right to "its own peculiar laws" and "its own peculiar weapons"—something that implies an independent foreign policy and military—can be taken as Chesterton's commentary on today's expansive European Union, whose multiculturalism imperfectly conceals a deep-seated hostility to genuine "equality in variety." What Chesterton says about Christendom's respect for a preexisting "national soul," may also explain why those promoting this expanded EU believe *their* Europe owes nothing to Christianity. They are right. *Their* vision of Europe is a foe of the Christendom that took its cues from the Bible and respected national identities. When the Bible's last book, Revelation, describes the end of history, it mentions nations no less that 19 times. The book's (and Bible's) last chapter opens with a Eden-like "tree of life" whose "leaves are for the healing of the nations." Biblically, people will live and display their nationalities forever.

Bizarre as it may sound to those who can't see beyond how secular the current European leadership is, Islam, far more monolithic than Christianity, does fit with this all-encompassing, cosmopolitan hostility to national independence.

THE recent delicate discussions about the Navy are an illuminating instance of a principle often emphasised here. It is that the international settlement must be a national settlement. It must take account of the special character and situation of every country, including our own country. It must seek equality in variety, not equality on uniformity. **Wherever something is found which the instinct of Christendom recognises as the national soul, there the conscience of Christendom concedes to that State the right to a certain self-government and self-defence.** But it cannot possibly govern itself except by its own peculiar laws; and similarly it cannot possibly defend itself except by its own peculiar weapons. If something of this sort is not granted, nothing of any sort is really granted. It would be very silly, as I have often said, if the League of Nations turned out to mean the League of No Nations. It would be quite as silly if all the talk about the freedom of the seas ended in our losing the freedom of the lands—of the very lands that we have fought to free. And, after all, among the lands we fought to free, we cannot entirely forget our own.

Any nation is in its nature a unique thing. That is where it differs decisively from any mere official division made within any independent State at present, or within any

1919–1922

6. This resembles the idea that to be legitimate, wars must have the approval of the United Nations or of a select group of nations, such as Germany and France, whose prior judgments have not been particularly impressive.

united States of the future. A nation, like a man or a dog or any other living thing, is large or small, like us or unlike us; but it is like itself. The case of nationalism against imperialism is that you cannot turn five terriers into a mastiff. But the case of nationalism against a certain sort of internationalism is that, if every dog is to have his day, it must not only be a dog-day, but his own day. If you permit the dog to save himself, you cannot forbid the bloodhound to save himself by smelling, or the greyhound to save himself by speed. Nor, I will add, can you forbid the Newfoundland dog to save himself by swimming. And the same principle applies to certain other simple creatures, whose historical career has been hitherto upon the water.

In short, if our Navy is unique, it is because our nation is unique—which does not in the least mean that it is superior. It is as unique as the French civic equality, and its splendid result—the French democratic militarism. It is as unique as the special sort of federal freedom in America, where the United States are really States as well as united. But, touching all the talk about the right or wrong of so unique a Navy, it is yet more difficult to speak with precision, because the special case is so special that there is really nothing quite like it. A rough but not unfair comparison might be made between the position of the old English Navy and of the old Russian Army. The parallel is not, perhaps, a happy omen, though it is still a heroic memory. Fortunately, in any case, even the largest Navy is a compact and secure system compared with even the smallest army; and there is no fear that English sailors will have to fight on rafts instead of boats, as Russian soldiers had to fight with sticks instead of rifles. But the point of the parallel is this, and it is really relevant. Nobody, so far as I know, ever said that Russia was wicked simply and solely because she had the largest army in the world. Upon that point Russia's excuse or explanation would be mere common-sense. It might be stated superficially by saying, first, that she had a large army to defend her large territories; and, second, that foreign countries could not pretend that it was used, or seemed likely to be used, except to defend those territories. Russia was a State specially situated, which was by its very nature strong in numbers—just as it was by its very nature weak in various other things. If it was an advantage, it was a natural advantage, and almost an involuntary advantage—almost as involuntary as its accompanying disadvantages. To this extent there is a true parallel; and the universal admission of the Russian right to numerical preponderance is highly pertinent to our own position. Russia had the weakness of wide frontiers; and no one grudged her the special strength of a population approximately equal to its task. We have the weakness of scattered possessions, properties that are our means of life; and no one need grudge us a special seafaring tradition that has grown almost as naturally as a population. So long as there is nothing beyond this national and natural specialization, great nations can not only remain practically peaceful, but they can remain practically equal. The unnatural spirit enters when there is mere competition, for competition is mad imitation.

If the German rulers had done what some say they did, if they tried to outnumber the Russians by establishing slavery for others and polygamy for themselves—if they really started those two heathen experiments, then their population would not be a natural characteristic, but an unnatural crime. And when the German rulers did what we know they did—when they tried merely to copy the English speciality without the English excuse, the thing was not a development, but a design. I am the very reverse of a Jingo; but it is not jingoism, but justice, to say that in this perfectly impartial historical sense the British Navy was a natural thing and the German Navy an artificial thing. All prejudices apart, it remains true that our enemies wanted ships without colonies—not to mention colonies without colonists. Before any other great state enters on the mechanical madness of such a course, we can quite inoffensively ask that this historical difference between the real and unreal should be remembered. We can point out the distinction between what is unique and trying to be universal, and what is unique and trying only to be individual. England does not ask to be stronger than everybody—or, in that sense, to be stronger than anybody; but she asks to be as strong as herself.

In speaking thus of armament, I am far from meaning that it is useless for anybody to discuss any sort or degree of disarmament. **On the contrary, I believe something very valid might be done to stop such frantic rivalry, if the patriots of all countries could come together. But I am sure that nothing can be done so long as it is the cosmopolitans of all countries who come together.** Nationalists could explain to each other what was really national, and therefore really necessary. Internationalists cannot explain anything to anybody, for they cannot even explain internationalism to themselves. If they did, they would begin to realise that internationalism, in most cases, merely means international finance.[7] As against that cosmopolitan conspiracy, it is more than ever necessary that every nation should hold fast whatever it knows to be national, as the humorous democracy of America, or the splendid and spontaneous soldiering and strategy of France. What we should make clear to all our foreign friends is that we really feel our maritime tradition as a thing of nationalism and not of vulgar imperialism.

G.K. Chesterton, "Our Note-Book," *Illustrated London News* 154 (January 4, 1919), 2. US: January 4, 1919. Also published as "The Need for a National Settlement."

POLISH NATIONALISM

January 11, 1919

The enemies of Poland are not now engaged on the physical partition of Poland, but on the philosophical partition of the idea of Poland. They are talking scepticism about where one nation begins and another leaves off.

EDITOR: This article and the next are undoubtedly among the proof-texts for those who believe Chesterton was a raving anti-Semite. But Chesterton was no more anti-Semitic for these remarks than he was anti-German (as bigotry) for his

7. The fewer the legal and cultural difference between nations, the more easily a few giant corporations can dominate the marketplace. This is mostly easily seen with entertainment: music, movies, and literature.

far harsher and more common criticism of Germany. In fact, one of his criticisms of the German people—that they fail to respect the national aspirations and culture of other people—is precisely the criticism he directs at these "Anti-Polish Jews," who, as "international Anarchists," were as untypical of Jews as they were as Poles.[8] And it's precisely the same reason that, in this same paragraph, he criticizes Austria's eighteenth-century behavior toward Poland, calling it worthy of "the blackest page of European history." From Chesterton's point of view, calling a man's national symbol a "white goose" is as boorish and barbaric as calling his wife a "fat goose."[9] The particular anti-national bigotry Chesterton denounces here can be expressed in three ways.

- First, it can deny a group the right to a *geographic nation* with internationally recognized borders. That was what Poland faced after World War I and what Israel has faced throughout its history from its more militant foes.[10]
- Second, it can deny a group the right to a *cultural nation* with a specific cultural, ethnic and religious identity. Poland isn't to be Catholic and distinctly Polish. Israel isn't to be Jewish rather than Arab. But a geographic nation with no recognizable identity is like a human devoid of personality. It is a pitiful, unhealthy thing, a mere shell of a creature. There's nothing there to love, respect, or defend, either as a citizen or as a visitor. Differences are required for love as well as hate.
- Finally, in its most deceptive form it can deny a group the right to a *morally legitimate nation* by either ridiculing its patriotism (as here) or, if the situation gets nastier, by claiming that a nation's unique identity represents bigotry or racism against those who fit less well with the national identity. This approach is often taken after the first two schemes fail, as it is with present-day Israel, which can protect both its borders and its national identity quite well.[11]

8. At the end of his December 7, 1918 article (Ch. 6), Chesterton referred to "the pro-German Pole who is a Jew." During the long Prussian occupation, a few Jews assisted efforts to forcibly Germanize the Polish people.

9. At the level of neighborhoods and local customs, that is why he wrote *The Napoleon of Notting Hill* (1904).

10. There's a chilling illustration of this anti-Polish sentiment in H.G. Wells' 1933 *The Shape of Things to Come.* Writing authoritatively as if he were looking back from the distant future, Wells failed utterly as a prophet. He ridiculed Hitler as "far inferior" to Mussolini and—strange as it sounds today—claimed the new German dictator would be unable to rise "to the real constructive effort or the competent industry" of his Italian counterpart (p. 182). Ignoring Poland's extensive defense needs, he sees Poland as, a "new militant power" spending one-third of its budget on armament (p. 86). While Chesterton quite correctly believed peace depended on Britain and France supporting the small Eastern European countries against German aggression, in this foolish book, Wells sees the continued existence of those countries after WWI as an untidy nuisance.

> Not only was Poland thus put back on the map. As a result of a sedulous study of historical sentimentalities, traditions, dialects and local feelings, a whole cluster of new sovereign Powers, Czechoslovakia, Jugoslavia, Finland, Esthonia, Latvia, Lithuania, and attenuated Hungary and an enlarged Romania, was evoked to crowd and complicate the affairs of mankind by their sovereign liberties, their ambitions, hostilities, alliances, understandings, misunderstandings, open and secret treaties, tariffs, trade wars and the like. [H.G. Wells, *The Shape of Things to Come* (New York: Macmillan, 1933), 86.]

11. Those who adopt this attitude seem unable to distinguish between healthy patriotism and dangerous supremacist thinking. They bully smaller countries for simply wanting to be themselves despite a difficult geographic situation. In Chesterton's day that meant Poland and Czechoslovakia. Today it means Israel. At the same time, they ignore genuine dangers posed by powerful countries with aggressive ideologies. That included the Teutonism Chesterton so ably criticized both before and after it was incarnated in Nazi ideology. More recently, it has led them to minimize or ignore the brutal nature of Soviet communism and to downplay the dangers posed by militant Islam. That attitude can be illustrated by Jimmy Carter's *Palestine: Peace Not Apartheid,* a book which criticizes Israel, a country where all religions are legally protected and respected, but says almost nothing critical about the Arab world, where Muslim groups violently persecute one another, and where Jews and Christians are second-class citizens or worse. Perhaps the single factor that drives this inconsistency is a lack of courage. Some people can't grasp the courage that inspires Poles, Czechs and Israelis to be themselves in spite of the risk. While ordinary cowardice can include a willingness to admit, "I'm too afraid to do that, but

After World War I, Poland became a geographic and a cultural nation, so the attacks turned to the moral legitimacy of Polish patriotism, as if a few catcalls about "Down with the White Goose" could destroy a patriotism the Prussians had not be able to crush in over a century of occupation. Given what Chesterton believed and his support for Zionism, if he were around today, he would attacks that similarly absurd claims that "Zionism is Racism." Chesterton believed nations such as Poland and Israel have as much right to exist as a "philosophical" idea as a "physical" one. Like individuals, a nation is free only if it is free to be its own special self.

Contrary to those who see nationalism as an unequivocal evil, Chesterton believed that patriotism is a great benefit to the world. Notice that he points out, in an amazingly prophetic passage, that the future peace of Europe rests on the patriotism of the smaller nation-states of Eastern Europe and their ability to resist a German domination that would turn "three-quarters of Europe into a Teutonic civilisation—or rather, a Teutonic barbarism." The leaders of Britain and France would foolishly disregarded that warning, allowing Czechoslovakia, with its large armaments industry, to slip into German hands in the fall of 1938. By the time they stood up for Poland in the spring of 1939, it was too late.[12]

Europe's leaders had no excuse for their earlier complacency or their later panic. In *Mein Kampf* (1925–1926), Hitler was clear that Germany's goals should be the conquest of Eastern Europe, including "the territory east of the Elbe" (Poland) and the organization of a "new Reich" with the "Brandenburg-Prussian state as a model."[13] In a conversation in July of 1941, as German armies pushed deep into Russia, he remarked: "The reason why I'm not worrying about the struggle on the Eastern Front is that everything that happens there is developing in the way that I've always thought desirable. At the outbreak of the first World War, many people thought we ought to look towards the mineral riches of the West, the raw materials of the colonies and the gold. For my part, I always thought that having the sun in the East was the essential thing for us, and to-day I have no reason to modify my point of view."[14]

Finally, remember that Chesterton was aware that forming independent nations would not solve every problem. On December 29, 1918, he and his wife left for British-ruled Palestine. He was under contract to write a book called *The New Jerusalem,* and doctors said that his wife's health would benefit by escaping England's damp winters. On January 7 they reached Egypt and about the time this article was published, they were in Jerusalem. There Chesterton developed a forboding.

> A voice not of my reason, but rather sounding heavily in my heart, seemed to be repeating sentences like pessimistic proverbs. There is no place for the Temple of Solomon but on the ruins of the Mosque of Omar. There is no place for the nation of the Jews but in the country of the Arabs. And these whispers came to me first not

I respect the courage of those who can," these people have moved into a strange, topsy-turvy world of their own where cowardice is called bravery, as in Carter's attempts to posture himself as the victim of Jewish attacks.

12. Given that Poland did not share borders with France or Britain, the only effective way either country could aid Poland quickly was by countering the German attack on Poland with an attack on Germany's industrialized Rhineland. That would have forced Germany to withdraw from Poland to defend its western border.

13. Adolf Hitler, *Mein Kampf* (Boston: Houghton Mifflin, 1943), 647. Under the Hohenzollern dynasty, Brandenburg grew ever larger, devouring the Duchy of Prussia in 1618 and growing until after 1870 it dominated Central Europe. Hitler's "Brandenburg-Prussia state as a model" is what Chesterton calls the "The cannibal theory of a commonwealth, that it can of its nature eat other commonwealths," in his July 29, 1919 article.

14. Adolf Hitler, *Hitler's Secret Conversations* (New York: Farrar, Straus and Young, 1953), 14.

> as intellectual conclusions upon the conditions of the case... but rather as hints of something immediate and menacing and yet mysterious. I felt almost a momentary impulse to flee from the place, like one who has received an omen. For two voices had met in my ears; and within the same narrow space and in the same dark hour, electric and yet eclipsed with cloud, I had heard Islam crying from the turret and Israel wailing at the wall.[15]

....

The interesting—and, indeed, inspiring—events now occurring in Poland included an occurrence which had its comic side. It seems that a knot of some sort of international Anarchists interrupted the proceedings of the more responsible Poles by calling out with cheerful monotony "Down with the White Goose!" The remark was a reference to the White Eagle with the ancient cognisance of the great kingdom of Poland,[16] now once more the chief hope of Christendom, as on that day when the sword of Sobieski delivered Vienna from the Eastern hordes.[17] How Vienna repaid Poland for that deliverance is written in the blackest page of European history.[18] The malcontents called the eagle a goose to suggest that Polish patriots are still engaged on a wild-goose chase. It is agreed that these particularly discontented persons are non-national. These particular Poles are Polish Jews, and these particular Polish Jews are Anti-Polish Jews. But the matter which is more momentous at present is not so much who these people are, as how they are likely to attempt—and perhaps achieve their evil work. It can be stated in a fairly simple formula. The enemies of Poland are not now engaged on the physical partition of Poland, but on the philosophical partition of the idea of Poland. They are talking scepticism about where one nation begins and another leaves off; and that is why it is fortunate that they hit by accident on one image that expresses the unity of the great Polish people in the past.

I use this heraldic figure of the White Eagle because heraldry really satisfied the desire of definition in humanity. Its clear colours and shapes sharply outlined

15. Joseph Pearce, *Wisdom and Innocence* (London: Hodder & Sloughton, 1996), 251. Chesterton wrote three articles about visiting Poland starting with the June 25, 1927 *Illustrated London News. The Collected Works of G.K. Chesterton*, vol. XXXIV, 329–341. In the second he noted of the fighting just after World War I: "When the Poles defeated the Bolshevists in the field of battle, it was precisely that. It was the old chivalric tradition defeating everything that is modern, everything that is necessitarian, everything that is mechanical in method and materialistic in philosophy. It was the Marxian notion that everything is inevitable defeated by the Christian notion that nothing is inevitable—no, not even what has already happened." Chesterton believed even the past can be undone. A Poland destroyed in the eighteenth century can be reborn in the twentieth. An Israel that ceased to exist in 70 AD can spring to life again in 1948. Nothing is inevitable.

16. The White Eagle (*Orzeł Biały*) as a symbol of the Polish nation dates back at least to the thirteenth century.

17. John III Sobieski (1629–1696) was King of Poland from 1674–1696. He was a brilliant military leader best known for his victory over a much larger Turkish army at the Battle of Vienna in 1683. His arrival on September 11 (note the date) marked the turning point in the 300-year invasion of Christian Eastern Europe by the Islamic Ottoman Empire. Chesterton's "once more the chief hope of Christendom" remark alludes to early stages of fighting as the new and atheistic Soviet Union attempted expand its borders westward in what would become the Polish-Soviet War (February 1919–March 1921). Chesterton is concerned about the possibility of a Poland too small and weak to defend itself and its smaller Eastern European neighbors from either Germany's "Teutonic barbarism" or the Soviet Union's more modern, scientific barbarism.

18. Between 1772 and 1795 Polish independence was destroyed by a series of partitions in which Prussian, Russia and Austria carved territories for themselves out of Poland. Because Poland fought for Napoleon, the Congress of Vienna (1815) kept it divided and occupied. It did not win its independence until the end of World War I.

corresponded to the clear-cut convictions of the great mediaeval civilisation from which it came. In heraldry the lion could lie down with the lamb, but he could not be mixed up with the lamb or mistaken for the lamb. He could not even be evolved into the lamb. Heraldry produced monsters, but not mongrels. Moreover, most of its monsters were really as well selected and suitable as domestic pets. And whether or no a white eagle exists in actuality, it is in this case very appropriate in allegory. There could hardly be a nobler or more national emblem, for a Christian and chivalric nation like Poland, than such a shining bird with the shape of the eagle and the colour of the dove. It contains in one compact symbol, as heraldry could often do, all that combination of holiness with high defiance which seems so complex to many moderns. It might have been on the shield of St. Louis.[19]

An eagle is an eagle, just as a Pole is a Pole; but we must always be ready nowadays to find any such reality reduced to unreality by certain modern doubts about relativity and degree. A sceptic, dealing with the subject of eagles, can always get rid of it altogether by splitting hairs—or feathers. A sophist can easily ask whether the eagle would be quite himself with no feathers. A professor could pluck the eagle plume by plume till there was nothing left. Or the professors might prove that the eagle was not exactly an eagle, because he was only a bit stronger than a partridge, or rather larger than a canary, or somewhat keener on aviation than a cock. The fact remains that an eagle is an eagle; and you will soon discover, in social relations with him, that he is not a canary or a cock. If you trust to his crowing in the farmyard to wake you in the morning you are likely, at the least, to oversleep yourself. If you put the eagle in the cage of the canary, you will hardly do so without a struggle. If you serve it up for dinner instead of the partridge, you may have a severer struggle still. It is equally obvious that what applies to an eagle applies to a white eagle. **It is counted a sort of madness to say that black is white; but it is considered nowadays a natural scepticism to say that black is grey—and still more to say that white is grey.** International sophists will certainly tell us that the white eagle of Poland is grey.

Now we must not for a moment tolerate this sceptical philosophy in the settlement of Europe. It is all the more intolerable because it may seem a plausible philosophy in the settlement of Eastern Europe. It is quite true that there is a chaos of races and religions in those lands that stretch away towards Asia, and are far from the great civic centres of Europe. But it is much more true that there is in that chaos a corporate, communal, and actual thing called Poland—almost as concrete as an eagle or a cock. It is, perhaps, the one thing in those wild places that really has this ancient and accepted actuality. It lives; it must be allowed to live; it must have all that is necessary to its life. **There is a very simple reason, if there were not even better reasons—its life is necessary to our life. A free Poland is not only necessary to a free Europe, but is rather specially necessary to a free England.** Poland is not so far away from us as Egypt or India, and is far more essential to our survival.

19. Louis IX, known as Saint Louis (1215–1270), was King of France from 1226–1270. He participated in two unsuccessful crusades and was canonized by the Catholic Church in 1297, the only French king to become a saint.

If a strong Pro-Ally State does not appear in Eastern Europe, Germany may gain from defeat all that she hoped to gain from victory. The Central Empires will again be central, because all that vague and vast circumference can have no other centre. That means turning three-quarters of Europe into a Teutonic civilisation—or rather, a Teutonic barbarism. That means that the old chivalric States in the West will become merely a fringe—which the solemn fools of Teutonism will very probably describe as a Celtic fringe.

Some people simply cannot believe that what suits our ideals can also suit our interests—nay, they actually neglect their own interests because they suspect their own ideals. They might see that a strong Poland is useful; but they are embarrassed by the fact that it is just. But my purpose here is not merely to point out the danger, but to counter the controversial form it will take. Poland will be belittled in theory and diminished in practice chiefly by this argument from degrees and fine shades. It will be said that Dantzig or Posen is not Polish, although partly Polish—as if the sophist should admit that the eagle has a rather aquiline nose.[20] But you cannot deal with the Polish democracy by counting noses, especially when so many of them are Jewish noses. Compared with such statistical stuff, the old painted sign, that is merely heraldic, is far more historic. We should be wiser to look, like prophets and poets, to a merely symbolic imagery, and see the White Eagle of Poland replace the Black Eagle of Prussia, as the day dethrones the night.

G.K. Chesterton, "Our Note-Book," *Illustrated London News* 154 (January 11, 1919), 34. US: January 11, 1919. Also published as "The Partition of Poland."

POLAND AND PEACE-MONGERS

January 18, 1919

The Poles have never enjoyed that perfect social adjustment that made all the Prussian Professors write down the same sentence, as all the Prussian soldiers would make the same salute.

EDITOR: This is another article that some are likely to use as an illustration of Chesterton's alleged anti-Semitism. But readers should note that, far from being hostile to the Jews of Poland, Chesterton insists that they should be given privileges in the country, so they are "safe and secure." The one right he would deny to them was a most undemocratic right of "preventing the national existence of the Poles." That's hardly anti-Semitic. No country can retain a healthy national identity if every minority living inside its borders is given veto power over its customs, policies and practices. Far from being anti-Semitic, Chesterton saw in many Jews the same national way of looking at themselves that would permit, even after 1800 years in exile, the creation of a Jewish nation. That's why he says, "I have always held the Zionist or Jewish Nationalists' position." The Jews, he believed, had as much right to a nation of their own as the Poles. But the flip side of that is that they have no more right to crush

20. Dantzig (or Danzig) is today's Polish port city of Gdańsk. Posen is Poznań, a large city in western Poland. In 1939 Nazi Germany would use Dantzig's large German population to stir up trouble with Poland, creating the bizarre spectacle of a repressive dictatorship feigning concern about the rights of Germans under Poles.

Polish nationalism than the Germans did or, for that matter, than non-Israelis have to dictate Israel's national identity. Notice that, if he's against anyone, it's "Prussian Professors" who goose step to the ideal of Teutonic supremacy.

Chesterton was quite willing to allow Poland's Jews to continue to live as Jews, a right that many German intellectuals in the period before the war were all too eager to deny. Israeli historian Uriel Tal described the situation this way.

> The intellectual class in Germany, whose influence extended far beyond its numerical representation in the general population, was the class on which the Jews pinned their hopes for achieving full integration, and it was also the one from which they suffered their deepest disappointment. Even at the beginning of the period we are discussing, the liberal intellectuals were known to believe "that the desire of the Jews to be German was to all intents and purposes unrealistic as long as Judaism was not absorbed in it German-Christian environment by complete assimilation and dissolution by means of miscegenation."[21]

A little over a year after the Chesterton article which follows, Winston Churchill, who throughout his life also strongly supported the Jews, wrote a magazine article remarkably similar to what Chesterton says here. "There are," he wrote, "three main lines of political conception among the Jews, two of which are very helpful and hopeful to a high degree to humanity and the third absolutely destructive." Like Chesterton, he spoke highly of "national Jews" who while, "dwelling in every country throughout the world, identify themselves with that country, enter into its national life, and, while adhering faithfully to their own religion, regard themselves as citizens in the fullest sense of the State which has received them."

The second was a destructive group much like the "international Anarchists" that Chesterton had criticized, although Churchill's words were far harsher: "In violent opposition to all this sphere of Jewish effort rise the schemes of the International Jews. The adherents of this sinister confederacy are mostly men reared up among the unhappy populations of countries where Jews are persecuted on account of their race. Most, if not all, of them have forsaken the faith of their forefathers, and divorced from their minds all spiritual hopes of the next world." It was those Jews, he warned, who were attracted to Bolshevism and were helping the Soviets to terrorize the Russians.

The third group were the "very helpful" Zionists who wanted a nation of their own. Churchill described the clash "between the Zionist and Bolshevik Jews" as "a struggle for the soul of the Jewish people," and called on the national Jews to support the Zionists, "to vindicate the honour of the Jewish name." That argument was like Chesterton's belief that all healthy-minded patriots should support one another, much as a happily married man encourages another man in his marriage. Championed by both Chesterton and Churchill, it was a powerful attack on the very heart of anti-Semitic rhetoric. Jews who were patriotic Englishmen, both men said, should support their fellow Jews in the establishment of a national homeland for Jews. Doing so was not conspiratorial or in any way a violation of the duties they owed their own country. Unfortunately, as also happened with Chesterton, some English Jews, unable to see the kindness that lay behind the criticism (or perhaps to accept the fact that

21. Uriel Tal, *Christians and Jews in Germany* (Ithaca: Cornell University Press, 1975), 31–32. The quote comes from an 1880 Jewish pamphlet. Later in his book Tal notes that, "the Jews, who were determined to retain their separate status, found that they had much in common with the Christian conservatives." (p. 294)

then fashionable Bolshevism was evil) attacked Churchill for waging a "reckless and scandalous campaign."[22]

In 1930, Chesterton, responding to similar criticisms, would explain why charging him with anti-Semitism, "misrepresents me in a matter in which I do not wish to be misrepresented."[23] He linked the nonsense that there was a Teuton (here he uses Aryan), with "the great nineteenth-century blunder" that Semites exist. Jews exist, he said, as a recognizable religion (including culture). They also ought to exist, he believed, as an independent nation. But he had nothing but contempt for a "sham science" that built elaborate historical and scientific theories around meaningless terms such as Teuton, Aryan, and Semite.

> I am no more an Anti-Semite than any Zionist or detached and independent Jew who thinks that the solution of the Jewish Problem would be the separation of the races. It is perhaps doubtful whether the Jewish Problem can be solved thus. It is also doubtful whether the Jewish Problem can be solved at all. But, in answer to the charge of fanatical Anti-Semitism, I should like to add one word, and an even more emphatic one. If I were an enemy of the Jews, I should call myself an enemy of the Jews; if I were anything that could be called Anti-Jew, I should wish to be called Anti-Jew. But under no circumstances whatever would I consent to be called Anti-Semite. The word is a monstrous monument of the great nineteenth-century blunder, the habit of talking sham science in order to avoid talking real religion. There is a such thing as a Jew; he might be hated as a Jew, though I do not hate him; he might be murdered as a Jew, though I never happened to murder him. But who in the world would want to murder a Semite? The word dates from the days when even fanatics had to disguise themselves as prigs, and I trust that, whatever be the merit of my views in the matter, I am myself neither one nor the other.
>
> This last point is much more important than any book of mine or any article of anybody else's. For what determines the human part of human history is religion and not race; certainly not the pompous Victorian theories about race.... It was the whole nonsense of the nineteenth century that it talked as if we were more certain of Semites than of the existence of Jews, or as if we had more evidence that Aryans or Indo-Germanic than we have that white men are white.[24]

Although Chesterton politely smooths over it, in Mr. Armstrong's fourth point (quoted below) displays a blatant anti-Polish bigotry. He assumes the right to tell the

22. Martin Gilbert, *Churchill and the Jews: A Lifelong Friendship* (New York: Henry Holt, 2007), 39–43. The original appeared in the *Illustrated Sunday Herald* on February 8, 1920. Unfortunately, some present-day, conspiracy-ridden anti-Semitic groups use that article for evil purposes, quoting from it out of context and missing its central message. It's difficult to talk sense to such people.

23. In the 1930s, even some who may not have been anti-Semitic were ambitious enough to use it politically, talking in a coded language that allowed them to appeal to anti-Semitism, while leaving enough ambiguity for denial. Franklin Roosevelt's first inaugural address (1933) included these remarks: "Yet our distress comes from no failure of substance. We are stricken by no plague of locusts.... Primarily this is because the rulers of the exchange of mankind's goods have failed, through their own stubbornness and their own incompetence, have admitted their failure, and abdicated. Practices of the unscrupulous money changers stand indicted in the court of public opinion, rejected by the hearts and minds of men." Roosevelt did not say who those "money changers" were, but anti-Semites heard "Jew," particularly given the virulent anti-Semitic climate surrounding Hitler's rise to power one month earlier. When Chesterton wrote the 1930 remarks quoted above, he was refusing to play deceptive FDR-like games. He was not only *not* anti-Semitic, he would *not* allow himself to be "misrepresented" as one by others. When he disliked a group (such as Prussian professors), he said so clearly and unmistakably.

24. *The Collected Works of G.K. Chesterton*, vol. XXXV, 382–383, *Illustrated London News*, September 20, 1930. By denying that Semites exist and ridiculing all the then-fashionable and scientific racial theories of history, Chesterton cut the ground entirely out from under all anti-Semitism.

Poles that they were incapable of rebuilding their nation—something we now know they have achieved quite well—and suggests they could learn "organization" from the Germans without suggesting anything Germans might learn from Poles.

In today's context, Chesterton is criticizing a "multi-culturalism" that denies to any people either nationhood altogether or, failing that, the right to a nation with its own culture, language, religion, and personality. He suggests that, while minority groups should be protected and secure, they should not dictate how others behave, either by claiming to be "offended" by something the majority values or by being deliberately offensive themselves, violating the civility on which any healthy society depends. His ideas are known as "majority rules" and "minority rights." Not exactly bigotry.

Today, the nation that best illustrates the 'particularist' point of view that Chesterton championed is the modern state of Israel. With its strong Jewish identity but troublesome location surrounded by Muslim xenophobes who believe it has no right to exist, it has replaced Catholic Poland as the country some blame for the world's ills and regional wars—as well as the country they seem most willing to toss to the wolves. Were Chesterton around today, he would support Israel's right not only to exist and retain its Jewish identity (which he was already doing prospectively), but to defend itself against those who would destroy it by denying its Jewish uniqueness and moral legitimacy. Chesterton defended Zionism for the same reason that he defended the nationalism of Boers, the Irish, the Poles, and the Belgians. He was a consistent champion of the right of small nations to exist independent of foreign domination and, even more important, to be themselves.

PEACE has left the peace-mongers with a legacy of one sincere sentiment—a hatred of the great hope of the Polish people. It is natural enough that these singular democrats, who were always ready with an excuse for Prussia, should now always be ready with a depreciation of Poland. It is equally natural that the attack on Poland should be conducted in the same fashion as the apology for Prussia—not directly and defiantly, but by clouds of casual hints, misleading fancies, and more misleading facts. I could give many examples of the worst way in which the thing is done—as in that character of the candid friend which is commonly assumed by the very uncandid foe. But I prefer to take the thing at its best rather than at its worst; and I will take the case of a letter I found, a few minutes ago, in the current issue of the *Nation*—a letter from Mr. T. Percy Armstrong. I take his case as a convenience, and even as a compliment.[25] For he states in a short, lucid, and moderate fashion what others sow at random, in suggestions always scattered and generally scatter-brained. His object is to suggest that it will be very difficult for Europe to create the nation that Frederick the Great destroyed—in short, that it is doubtful whether such a thing could exist as the thing which for many centuries actually existed. As he uses most of the arguments generally used, and these very clearly and within a short compass, I will here arrange them under separate headings, and deal with them in turn.

25. Armstrong's letter appeared in the January 4, 1919 issue of the *Nation* (page 405) as "The Revival of Poland." It closes with an admission that the real heart of the Polish problem is that Germany enjoys bullying its neighbors. "An outburst of anarchy in a few years on the east of Germany might prove intolerable to her, and give her an excuse for re-kindling the flames of another war." That's a near perfect description of how WWII will begin.

First of all, he says, "No doubt it would be an admirable thing to erect a new Slav barrier to the east of Germany, but can it be done? Bismarck, no mean judge upon the point, declared that it could not." This, it will be admitted, is a rather innocent opening for the discussion. It is much as if a man were to say, "The Duke of Alva, a soldier and statesman of no little experience, put small faith in the project of turning Holland into an independent Protestant republic"; or as if he said, "Marat, a man of very vigilant logic, did not hope for much from the royalist scheme for restoring the Bourbons"; or as who should say, "Nero, a gentleman of considerable culture, was not very sanguine about the Christians succeeding in their effort for human salvation."[26] The attitude of Bismarck towards Poland and towards Russia was pretty simple and self-evident; and it certainly was not a mere detached doubt about whether any Slav could establish any State. He did not want to be the ally of Poland, because he did want to be the oppressor of Poland. But he had no objection to being the ally of Russia, on the one condition that Russia also would be the oppressor of Poland. He was not so unwilling that a Slav State should be strong, as he understood being strong, which was being brutal.

Second, Mr. Armstrong says, "The frontiers of old Poland were open to an invasion upon the east and west; there can be no real strength in a long thin kingdom stretching from the Baltic almost to the Euxine." Here it is enough to repeat the historical test already suggested. Mr. Armstrong really answers the whole of his own sentence with a single word contained in his own sentence. It is the single word "old." The very fact that the frontiers of Poland are old frontiers is a proof that these frontiers remain in the memory and revert to the power of the Poles. **The very fact that Poland is an ancient State proves that it is not an ephemeral State.** That it suffered violence and vicissitudes of fortune is true, as it is true of most ancient States; and the only moral, from the argument of Mr. Armstrong, must be that there cannot be any such things as inland States. But Poland was only murdered by a quite abnormal conspiracy quite late in a quite lengthy history. It is like trying to demonstrate the incurable disease and inevitable early death of a gentleman assassinated at the age of eighty.

Thirdly, Mr. Armstrong says that the population is not homogeneous, and that there are other races, notably the Jews, "constituting a middle class that in the past, at any rate, was not in full sympathy with national aspirations." Personally, I should say that this middle class, past and present, is not in sympathy with national aspirations because it happens to belong to another nation. Mr. Armstrong's phrase is a rather mild one for a mob of aliens who hooted the White Eagle of Poland with howls of "Down with the white goose!" At least, if ever I hear British subjects crying in the

26. Chesterton chose marvelous examples. As their ruler, the Spanish General Fernando Álvarez de Toledo, 3rd Duke of Alba (1507–1582) treated the Protestants in the Spanish Netherlands brutally, killing some 6,000 of them between 1567 and 1573. Similarly, the French scientist, Jean-Paul Marat (1743–1793), played a key role in the French Revolution's Reign of Terror. Finally, to divert attention from rumors he had set Rome on fire to have an excuse to rebuild the city, the Roman Emperor Nero (37–68 AD) brutally persecuted the Rome's Christians. Bismarck, Chesterton reminds us, displayed a similar hostility toward Poles and is no more to be trusted.

street that the British Lion is a mangy cat, my feelings will be but faintly expressed by saying that they are not in full sympathy with national aspirations. **But there is no space here to discuss the Jewish problem, on which I have always held the Zionist or Jewish Nationalists' position. Suffice it to say that I would give special and secure privileges to the Jews; but certainly not the privilege of preventing the national existence of the Poles.**

The fourth point in the letter is that "the Poles, with all their brilliant gifts, are deficient in the capacity for organisation." I wish to repeat here that I do not charge Mr. Armstrong himself with unfairness or even unfriendliness to the Poles; I use his text as a useful summary of the difficulties that are so much discussed. With this impersonal proviso, I may be permitted to say that the above argument has always struck me as a base, brutal, and microscopically mean argument. It is needless to add that it was in a special sense the German argument. If I poison my uncle, and then placard the world with the news that he drank himself to death, I really think that the second part of my action is more abominable than the first. If I steal all my friend's money, and then lock him up as a lunatic who cannot look after property, I am myself something very much lower than a thief. Poland went to pieces solely because it was knocked to pieces; the Teutonic theory that there was something anarchic in its own nature was a tardy Teutonic after-thought and a greasy German excuse. The Poles doubtless have their national faults, like other nations; but that such faults prevent them altogether from acting corporately is contradicted by the way in which they have constantly acted. Mr. Armstrong then adds, touching this matter of organisation, that it is "just here that the Germans have taught and can teach them much." Certainly there are things the Poles could not do in any case, and about which I doubt whether any German has ever taught them anything. **The Poles have never enjoyed that perfect social adjustment that made all the Prussian Professors write down the same sentence, as all the Prussian soldiers would make the same salute. The Poles are incapable of that clear organisation that makes it possible for a massacre of babies to begin at a certain signal, stop at another signal, and begin again at a third signal.**[27] Certainly they have not the German gift for organisation; and certainly the Germans might teach it, if the Poles would stoop to learn it. But there happens to be another type of organisation with more savoury associations, of which the great example in the West is France, and in the East Poland. It is that spontaneous self-organisation of free men, which need not work with an office and a uniform—which can even work against the office and against the uniform. And there never was a more splendid triumph of this true organisation than that won over the land-grabbing legislation of the Prussians by the living organisation of the Poles.

G.K. Chesterton, "Our Note-Book," *Illustrated London News* 154 (January 18, 1919), 66.
US: January 18, 1919. Also published as "On Creating Poland."

27. When you realize that perhaps the most horrifying aspect of the Jewish Holocaust was the sheer organizational efficiency that lay behind it, this remark takes on chilling prophetic overtones.

PROTECTING SMALL NATIONS

February 15, 1919

The spiritual deliverance of Europe, so far from depending on larger and vaguer things, turns more than ever on small and special things—on little nations and on lost provinces.

EDITOR: Chesterton points out that grand schemes for world peace, such as the League of Nations, will have little chance for success if the concrete problems of Europe, particularly German aggressiveness and the uncertain status of small countries, aren't dealt with practically and effectively. History has proved him right. The League of Nations will be ineffective and World War II will begin over the very country Chesterton warns would be a problem—Poland.

Chesterton is opposing what he called a "League of No Nations" in a January 4, 1919 article. Deal with the Polish problem, he says, by giving the Polish their old love, a nation of their own. Don't try to manufacture an Englishman who thinks "less of England than of Europe" or "so staggering a prodigy as an international Irishman." Focus on solving actual problems, always remembering, "There are always particular things to be purified, particular men to be punished, particular goods to be restored." People do not need to give up "old loves" to be rid of "old hates."

Chesterton had a deep-seated love for small nations and an open contempt for vast empires. In his 1936 autobiography, he explained how he'd always been more impressed by the small than the large. When his father installed the "first telephone I ever saw" between a top-floor bedroom and the back of their garden, he was "really impressed imaginatively." He was no more impressed by a telephone voice coming from "as distant as the next continent. The miracle is over." In the same way, he was more drawn to a microscope than a telescope: "I was not overwhelmed in childhood, by being told of remote stars which the sun never reached, any more than in manhood by being told of an empire on which the sun never set. I had no use for an empire that had no sunsets."[28]

WHAT chiefly puzzles a plain man, merely glancing at the papers in connection with the Peace Conference, is the order of items in the report, if not on the agenda paper. It would almost seem as if the argument were beginning with the League of Nations—a process which everyone must admit to be beginning at the other end, and some of us may suspect to be beginning at the other end of nowhere. The ordinary patriotic person will think it a plain case of putting the cart before the horse, to put the chariot of peace in front of the horses of victory. Whether such a car of triumph celebrates the true triumph—whether, in short, the League of Nations as at present pursued is even an object worth pursuing—all that may be separately considered. But at least we need not pursue it by walking backwards, by beginning the day with sunset, by reading the Bible hindforemost from the New Jerusalem, by complicating the peace before we have simplified or even concluded the war, and being reconciled to the enemy in order to consider how to be revenged

28. G.K. Chesterton, *The Autobiography of G.K. Chesterton* (New York: Sheed and Ward, 1936), 102–103. Notice how effectively Chesterton dismisses in a single sentence all the pretensions of British Imperialism.

on him. Apart from all partisan preferences, it is a point of impartial logic; and the principle of being off with the old love before you are on with the new applies as much to an old hate as to an old love. **But in truth the League of Nations, as some of its prophets are already preaching it, does really involve the abandonment of old loves as well as of old hates. It does mean that an Englishman is to think less of England than of Europe, that a Frenchman is to think less of France than of the League of Nations, that we are to behold so staggering a prodigy as an international Irishman, and are to employ all our science (if I may be allowed such levity) to depolarise the Pole.** That is an ideal of intensity and clarity for a number of sincere intellects, very near the centre of the great council of civilization. And for the democracy, the mass of mankind everywhere, it is an abomination and a blasphemy which will not be endured.

In short, if it is absurd to announce a reconciliation before studying the quarrel, it is still more absurd to announce a reconciliation to which we are not reconciled. I do not say that President Wilson, or the Prime Ministers of the Allies, have themselves abandoned the philosophy of patriotism; I am pretty sure that individually they have not. But all modern politicians have been taught the deplorable trick of trying to be practical politicians.[29] The practical politician is a man who always takes the notion that lies nearest—not because he is morally prompt, but because he is mentally lazy. One result of this is that they are surrounded by a swarm of quacks, struggling for their wandering attention, like a swarm of hotel touts struggling for a bag. Thus they are more likely to have the paper prospectuses of preposterous Utopias thrust into their hands than to have leisure to listen to the real talk even of the crowd, far less to think out the elementary logic of the question. Yet that elementary logic is surely very easy to state. Even if we are to deal first with a League of Nations, we presumably have to deal with the Nations as well as the League. **The principle of "the self-determination of all peoples" must obviously mean permitting every people to settle its own affairs—and not settling every people's affairs for it.** Yet people are talking as if national problems were not to be solved by the nations, or even by the League of Nations, but actually by the Peace Conference before it has even created the League of Nations. One thing is apparently to be settled even before the League, and that is the very thing which the League might be created to settle. For instance, there is much talk, at the time of writing about an international policy about Labour—which is always narrowed to mean manual proletarian industrial labour. Yet men labour in many other fashions, even when they are poor men—for instance, when they are free peasants. And even of the problem of proletarian industrialism there are many quite intelligent and intelligible solutions, such as Slavery, or

29. Chesterton described the practical politician in the February 28, 1925 *Illustrated London News*. "Practical men have been responsible for practically all our practical disasters.... This is the perpetual and pitiful tragedy of the practical man in practical affairs. He always begins with a flourish of contempt for what he calls theorising and what people who can do it call thinking. He will not wait for logic—that is, in the most exact sense, he will not listen to reason. It will therefore appear to him an idle and ineffective proceeding to say that there is a reason for his present failure." *The Collected Works of G.K. Chesterton*, vol. XXXIII, 509.

State Socialism, or Guild Socialism, or that better distribution of capital for which I have often expressed sympathy in these columns. It seems to me senseless to suppose that even the first steps towards a selection can be made by men of many and motley nations, each with quite variegated traditions, and difficulties—men only leagued to make war on the barbarian, and now only met together in order to make peace with him.

For, though the suggestion will now seem strange and distant, there was once a sort of idea that the Peace Conference intended to confer about Peace. Its meeting was not, perhaps, a coincidence wholly unconnected with the fact that there has just been a war. **And, having one of those simple and laborious minds which prefer to think of one thing at a time, I suggest that we decide to do something with the present war even before we prevent all possible future wars, especially by a cosmopolitan conspiracy which I should myself like to prevent.** While the war was waged, I resisted many revolutions with which I was in considerable sympathy;[30] and until the war is properly settled I certainly will not throw myself into a revolution with which I have practically no sympathy at all. I am disposed to urge, therefore, that we decide on some policy touching obscure and forgotten peoples called the Germans, to say nothing of the French, the Serbs, and the Poles, before we begin to prophesy the future feelings of the Patagonians towards the Eskimos, or speculate on how soon the Hottentots will learn to love the Laps. **In short, I suggest that we consider how to restrain our enemies and reinstate our friends before we consider how to make friends of men who have never been near enough to be enemies.**

Schemes of this colossal and almost cosmic scope are being waved in front of us to-day, in a sort of wild effort to find something larger and greater than the great war. But the great war, in its end as in its beginning, is to be judged by things inside it and not by things outside. It was only a great war, as distinct from a big butchery, by the greatness of the moral issues involved. And the moral issues within the war are still the same. **The spiritual deliverance of Europe, so far from depending on larger and vaguer things, turns more than ever on small and special things—on little nations and on lost provinces.** Posen is more important than all Siberia, for without Posen there is no Poland, and without Poland there is no dawn in the East.[31] Any Prussia that is demanding Posen is the same Prussia that divided Poland more than a hundred years ago, the same Prussia that invaded Belgium less than five years ago. And why, indeed, should it not be so, since the group of "moderate" Socialists now ruling Prussia is the very same which then warmly applauded the invasion of Belgium? **The malady that made the war was a moral malady, and must still find**

30. Chesterton used "revolution" for social changes far less radical than mobs and barricades. Irish home rule, set aside for the war but to be freely given by Britain, would probably head the list of revolutions he wanted.

31. Posen, a region in western Poland, was part of Prussia from 1848–1918. With a mixed population of Poles, Germans and Jews, the Treaty of Versailles gave areas with a Polish majority to Poland. If those areas reverted to Germany, it would raise questions about all Poland's right to exist in Germany's shadow. That's why Chesterton writes, "without Posen there is no Poland." The "dawn in the East" probably refers to Chesterton's desire to see other small nations formed or restored in Eastern Europe. Seventy years later, Poland, with its brave people and strong sense of national identity, would be a center for resistance to Soviet occupation—a "dawn in the East."

a moral cure. And every great moral story turns on what are called small things. There are always particular things to be purified, particular men to be punished, particular goods to be restored. If the makers of the peace do not right the wrongs of the war, it matters nothing what other world-wide and wonderful things they do. The conscience of Christendom will not be purged. They will be like physicians curing a corpse, from which the soul is already gone.

G.K. Chesterton, "Our Note-Book," *Illustrated London News* 154 (February 15, 1919), 202. US: February 15, 1919. Also published as "The Great Scheme of the League."

Polish Precipice

April 5, 1919

It is intolerable that they should waste so much time over a League of Nations that they have no time left for the nations—for the indisputable, national possessions of our Allies in Italy and Poland.

Editor: Almost two months later, Chesterton returned to his criticism of the League of Nations as it was then being established. He draws prophetic parallels between Soviet communism and Islam. Both were based on a "narrow simplicity that will sacrifice everything else—chivalry, charity, laughter, the family, and the flag—this remains an ideal which is in its nature an idolatry." And that's why both pose such a danger to "everything else."

In *Irish Impressions*, published this same year, Chesterton would compare the indefinable but still real essence of a nation to that of a person.

> He cannot define it, because nobody can define a person, and nobody can define a nation. He can only see it, smell it, hear it, handle it, bump into it, fall over it, kill it, be killed for it, or be damned for doing it wrong. He must be content with these mere hints of its existence; but he cannot define it, because it is like a person, and no book of logic will undertake to define Aunt Jane or Uncle William. We can only say, with more or less mournful conviction, that if Aunt Jane is not a person, there is no such thing as a person. And I say with equal conviction that if Ireland is not a nation, there is no such thing as a nation.[32]

Some time ago I noted here that pottering about with the League of Nations, before we had even finished the War of Nations, was a silly business. This truth seems now to have burst suddenly even upon those who are on the spot and in possession of all the secrets. But long before that I had ventured to suggest another neglected truth, which recent events have also brought to the surface. It concerns another fallacy in the whole philosophy of war, as commonly associated with a League of Nations. It might be stated by saying that you can abolish war, and still not abolish fighting. It could be stated more simply by saying that you could eliminate war, and still experience revolution. **What the pacifists call "war" is a certain game between crowned heads with little national flags stuck all over a map; or**

32. Quoted in Maise Ward, *Gilbert Keith Chesterton* (London: Sheed & Ward, 1944), 343–344.

it is a dark agreement to differ between wicked diplomatists who sit round a table and say "Let us have a war," like men proposing a game of bridge. But the root of war, in the real sense of fighting, is far deeper. It is that, so long as things have different values for different people, a man *may* value something more than his own life or other people's. The possibility of war is a result, right or wrong, of intellectual liberty; and the most hopeful campaign for permanent peace, right or wrong, was the old attempt to impose religious uniformity.[33] If all men gave the same moral value to the same material thing, wars might be made at least as rare as railway collisions. But one civilization may scientifically wish to exterminate as a pest a beetle, let us say, which another regards as a sacred beetle. You cannot make a man *promise* never to have a vision of a divine beetle, for that is not the nature of visions. You certainly cannot forbid him to be martyred for the beetle, for that is not the nature of martyrdom. The insect may be an institution, an ideal theory, or even an idealised personality—and, indeed, there are political personalities that can be most ideally magnified with a microscope. But even political insects may be sacred insects. And if an insane simplification of politics has appeared in Eastern Europe, Christendom will survive it as it survived the similar peril of Islam; but it will have discovered once more that the greatest wars are religious wars, and that the most incalculable wars are revolutions.[34]

Meanwhile, even politicians seem to agree that things had better be settled rapidly. But this is surely not, as some seem to fancy, a reason why they should be settled wrong. An astounding argument seems prevalent in many papers which really reverses the whole story of the war. It may be summed up somewhat thus: that the need is so urgent to impose terms on Germany that she must be allowed to impose terms on us. In other words, we cannot begin to reap the benefits of the enemy's defeat—until we agree that he has not been defeated. This, and nothing less, is involved in many hasty and hazy suggestions, which imply a certain irresponsibility about the Polish right to Danzig or the Italian rights upon the Adriatic coast.[35] If

33. It's true that wars can break out when two nations attach the same value to something. The Franco-Prussian War and WWI came in part because both France and Germany wanted the mineral resources of Alsace-Lorraine. But Chesterton is referring to a difference he calls religious, fitting with his claim that "the greatest wars are religious wars," with religion including all heart-felt beliefs. Many Germans, he notes elsewhere, can't see the religious-like value others attach to their land. For Germany, attacking France through Belgium was merely a matter of paying damages to Belgium after France was defeated (with money extorted from France). Any value the Belgians, Serbs, Poles or others attach to their country, homes, language and culture made no sense. What was for those other peoples something sacred—a "divine beetle"—was to Germans a "pest" to be eliminated. It's why the Frederick the Great kept expanding the territory under his control, and why Germany under Bismarck tried to Germanize Poles. It's why during World War I Belgians resisting the German occupation were shot and their towns burned. It's why, a generation later, Nazi Germany would see in Eastern Europe little more than a vast *lebensraum*—living space for their people. What was to Poles, Czechs, Slavs, and others their sacred homelands was to these Germans simply real estate. Wars happened because Germany viewed those lands differently from how their own people viewed them. In this article Chesterton points out that many allied leaders and journalists were making a similar mistake, treating the feelings of Poles and Italians as mere "sentimental politics." See September 17, 1910, December 31, 1910, January 14, 1911 (Ch. 1) and January 29, 1916. (Ch. 4).

34. This "insane simplification" is Soviet Communism, when he links to a "similar" insane simplification, Islam. Perhaps that's one reason why some who were attracted to the former now find the latter appealing.

35. Elsewhere, Chesterton explained the importance of the Baltic harbor at Danzig: "We know that if the Poles have a port and a powerful line of communication with the West, they will be eager to help the West. We know

Germany is really beaten down in battle, it is as easy to insist on the right things as elaborately to insist on the wrong ones. If Germany is not beaten sufficiently, why was she not beaten more, when it would certainly have been possible to do so? In any case, it is quite intolerable that our representative should fill the first few months with talking about an arrangement that is too good to be true, and then actually give that as a reason for devoting the last few days to a settlement that is too bad to be true. **It is intolerable that they should waste so much time over a League of Nations that they have no time left for the nations—for the indisputable, national possessions of our Allies in Italy and Poland.**

Moreover, the comments of the Press are curiously loose in argument. I was sorry to see that an able journalist whose work I have admired touching other matters, Mr. Sidney Dark, of the *Daily Express*, referred to the project of a strong buffer State in Poland as an experiment in sentimental politics.[36] **Certainly I have a sentimental objection to Prussia in Posen or Danzig, as I have an equally sentimental objection to Prussia in Antwerp, to say nothing of a maudlin melodramatic objection to Prussia in Kent.** And certainly the resistance to these things was an experiment, and a very dangerous experiment—an experiment that very nearly failed. But I cannot conceive anybody calling the security of Poland unnecessary, unless he calls the whole war unnecessary.

To talk of an Englishman having a sentimental attachment to Polish independence is exactly like talking about his having a sentimental attachment to his own life. If any sceptic should rebuke a Scot, let us say, for associating some high and sublime crag with the liberty of his own land, it seems to me quite rational to ask why, if it comes to that, anybody should associate a high crag with sublimity any more than with liberty. But an association of ideas equally ancient and arbitrary will lead me to avoid, if possible, being thrown from the top of a high and sublime crag to the bottom of it. And I take it to be simply self-evident that if England now stands on the edge of a precipice in danger of being hurled into the abysses of death, the name of that precipice is Poland.

For, unless Poland can be made a strong bulwark, it seems perfectly obvious that all Central and Eastern Europe will be one thing, unified by two processes. The first will be the sham Bolshevising of Germany; the second will be the real Germanising of Bolshevism. The Prussian will accept a thin veneer of the new theories of Lenin, just as he did of the new theories of Luther. And, in return, the Russian will have the benefit of all the organization and practicality of the Prussian—that is, he will learn to be more methodical in his massacres and more expert in his espionage.[37] If

that if they have no port they will have no reason to help the West and no power to help anybody." Maisie Ward, *Gilbert Keith Chesterton* (London: Sheed & Ward, 1944), 365.

36. The writings of Sidney Dark (1874–1947) are almost as numerous and diverse as Chesterton's.

37. Chesterton was right to raise the grave danger of communism operating with Prussian efficiency. Germany never went communist, except after WWII in impoverished eastern Germany. As a result, Soviet communism functioned in a vodka-induced haze with typical Russian inefficiency. That has proved one of the few strokes of good fortune in a century that would become bloodiest in human history. Although Nazism would prove equally murderous, its racial bigotry meant that groups who weren't "Aryan" or "Teutonic," did not find its core

this does not threaten England and all the West, England has never been threatened in history, and certainly not in 1914. Poland is the only possible representative of the more mellow, more humane, and more humorous ideals of the West, in a world where the ideals—and even the good ideals—will be crude and cruel. For it is not necessary even to be without sympathy with the wilder ideals of the East. **Some of the Bolshevists may have hold of a great truth in the equality of men, just as the Moslems had hold of a great truth in the unity of God. But the narrow simplicity that will sacrifice everything else—chivalry, charity, laughter, the family, and the flag—this remains an ideal which is in its nature an idolatry.** It is the worship of the sacred beetle—or, at the best, of the sacred bee; the vision of the mere swarm, clouding the clear horizons; the pitting of the soul of the hive against the soul of the home.[38]

G.K. Chesterton, "Our Note-Book," *Illustrated London News* 154 (April 5, 1919), 472.
US: April 5, 1919. Also published as "On Settling the Demands of Both Sides."

CHRISTIANITY AND WAR

April 12, 1919

In plain words, we are acting as if there was no such thing as a barbarian peril in Europe. It was an ignorant and provincial assumption even in 1914; there are no words for what it is in 1919.

EDITOR: Chesterton stresses that it was not Christianity that mistakenly thought wars could be eliminated but modern, progressive thinkers. He points out that it would be easier to do away with money than to eliminate war, "for money really is a form or fiction which varies with the contracts of different communities; whereas war is the last reality to which men revert when those contracts have broken down." In a 1930 article, Chesterton dealt those who blamed churches for wars.

> Such writers do not know what they mean by the Churches; they do not know the real historical relation between any Churches and any wars; they cannot even see the fact which they themselves make obvious; the real historical relation between modern secular science and those wars. I do not know which of the Churches is responsible for which of the chemical formulas. I do not know whether Martin Luther invented mustard gas, or George Fox manufactured tear-shells, or St. Thomas Aquinas devised a stink-bomb producing suffocation. But I should rather fancy, in my ignorant and artless way, that these things were invented by modern scientists,

ideology as appealing as communism's more easily exported class bigotry. To appeal to non-German groups, Nazism was left with little more than an ugly anti-Semitism whose chief appeal, in Eastern Europe and the Middle East, was to embittered losers who make poor allies. In contrast, communism's primary appeal was to intellectuals and academicians whose bitterness came from a feeling that their genius was not properly recognized and rewarded in a money-centered, capitalistic economy.

38. Chesterton's contrast between the hive (collectivism) and home (freedom) is healthier and more human than the usual contrast between a hive and an atom-like self seen in philosophies like than of Ayn Rand. Deprived of the strength provided by family, friends and community, few individuals can resist the might of an all-encompassing State. Hannah Arendt shared Chesterton's views when she wrote that, "It has frequently been observed that terror can rule absolutely only over men who are isolated against each other and that, therefore, one of the primary concerns of all tyrannical governments is to bring this isolation about." Hannah Arendt, *The Origins of Totalitarianism* (New York: Harcourt Brace Jovanovich, 1973), 474.

most of whom were probably modern materialists. There is no doubt at all that they were produced specially and solely in the one historical epoch given over to historical materialism.[39]

If these remarks open with a text from the *Occult Review*, the reader need not anticipate with alarm any more remarks about Spiritualism. The problem which puzzles me here is one of this world, and not the other; and, indeed, the problems of this world often seem the more puzzling of the two. As I think there are many things more spiritual than spiritualism, so I find many things very much more occult than occultism. The phenomena of spirit control are far less fantastic than those of food control or paper control. People putting their hands on a bare table and waiting for spirits to descend are no more adventurous than people putting empty plates on a bare table and waiting for prices to fall. Given our ignorance of things beyond, I can understand a man still believing in Spiritualism, although Plato has just communicated with him in bad Greek and Dr. Johnson in bad grammar.[40] If, therefore, I venture to refer here to some very fair and friendly remarks about a book of mine which have appeared in the *Occult Review*, it is not because they concern myself, but because they concern, in a rather curious fashion, the problem of the present peace and the late war in Europe.[41] What does the editor of the *Occult Review* mean—what does anybody or everybody mean—by saying that in the case of the recent war Christianity was a failure? What do they suppose that Christianity teaches about war? That it cannot happen? That it will never happen again? On the contrary, it was the opponents of Christianity—the people who thought themselves too progressive and enlightened for Christianity—who were perpetually telling us that war was an anachronism like the tournament or the gladiatorial show. Take the first hundred pure pacifists and pure secularists anywhere; there are not many of them anywhere. You will find a vast proportion of the pacifists are secularists, and a considerable proportion of the secularists are pacifists. The rationalists prophesied peace, and relegated war and Christianity together to a lumber-room of the rods and racks of the Inquisition. When they found their own progressive prophecy was false, they simply invented a Christian prophecy that was fictitious.

Any amount of nonsense has been talked in the name of Christianity, but I cannot recall any Christian theologian, orthodox or otherwise, who maintained the muddle-headed modern idea that the lapse of so many centuries would cure everybody of being angry—or, in Mr. Carnegie's phrase, that war was a thing of the past. If I had told Mr. Carnegie that money was a thing of the past, he would have been much surprised. Yet it would have been much more rational, for money really is a form or fiction which varies with the contracts of different communities;

39. *The Collected Works of G.K. Chesterton*, vol. xxxv, 348. From *Illustrated London News*, July 26, 1930. Chesterton chose leading representatives of various religious traditions: Protestant—Martin Luther (1483–1586), Quaker—George Fox (1621–1691), and Catholic—Thomas Aquinas (1225–1274).

40. Plato was Greek, and Dr. Samuel Johnson (1709–1784) was such a gifted writer, he's still quoted today.

41. Edith K. Harper reviewed *The Crimes of England* in the February 1916 issue of *Occult Review*, but this probably refers to an article entitled "The 'Orthodoxy' of Gilbert K. Chesterton" by the editors in the April 1919 issue.

whereas war is the last reality to which men revert when those contracts have broken down. There are moral reformers who propose to abolish war. There are also moral reformers, and more logical ones, who propose to abolish money. These reformers are patient and faithful people—and well they may be, for they have been waiting since the beginning of human history. Some of them have expected to abolish war at various times; and some of them may have expected to abolish war in our own time. But it is simply false to suggest that Christians, as such, have ever expected anything of the kind.

The truth is that in this case, as in so many others, the enemies of the old religious traditions of Europe do not fight fair. Their experimental science is a game of which the familiar formula begins "Heads I win."[42] While a church displays war-flags or blesses battle-ships, it is accused of seeking to inflame men to fighting. When they begin to fight, it is mocked with having failed to prevent what it had been reviled for having tried to promote. The church is first blamed for confessing itself a church militant, and then mocked because it turns out after all not to be a church triumphant.[43] The truth is that there never was a historic event that so heavily endorsed the historic philosophy of Christendom as did the late war. People do not think so, because they do not know what the historic philosophy of Christendom was. The only part of it that concerns us here is this proposition—that no scientific changes have altered the soul, and that the business of the soul is with sin. Until the autumn of 1914, thousands of thinking people in this island really did not believe that men so scientific as the Germans could be so sinful as the Germans. **There was a prevalent progressive philosophy which genuinely, though vaguely, felt that man, being now a magician who controlled the elements, could never be so black a witch as to divide the elements merely to make a gas that would poison and torture his brethren.** It has taken us four years to learn, if we are capable of learning anything, that this progressive philosophy is not only poison, but also gas.

But I have a more timely and topical reason for mentioning this old moral truism just now. It seems to me that all the discussions about the peace are full of an abrupt and absolute oblivion about the war. The disadvantage of learning lessons unwillingly is a disposition to forget them rapidly; and many seem already to have forgotten the very things they were astounded to discover. Thus men are devising war frontiers for Germany, and areas of government for Germany, with the mathematical abstraction of men making maps, for all the world as if nobody had ever noticed anything odd about German war or German government. Men blame Poland or France or Italy or Serbia for seeking particular strips of territory, as if they were children at a friendly tea-party, demanding more than their share of their friends' sweets. Men ask why

42. The full saying is, "Head I win, tails you loose." It's practiced by scientists who believe that any area "experimental science" enters is one that religion must soon exit. But when science entered very visibly on the side of eugenics in Chesterton's day, it was good that religion did not exit and allow scientists to dictate who could have children. That's why the Inkling edition of Chesterton's 1922 *Eugenics and Other Evils* added a subtitle taken from Chesterton's own words, "An Argument Against the Scientifically Organized Society."

43. "Church militant" (*Ecclesia Militans*) refers to Christians alive and engaged in spiritual struggle. The "church triumphant" (*Ecclesia Triumphans*) are believers who have died and gone to heaven, where peace reigns.

they should want more than they have got, for all the world as if we did not know quite well why they want it. Nobody could guess from all this that a few months ago all these lands were at the bottom of the sea—were under the inundation of a sea known for nearly three thousand years under the awful name of the barbarians. We do not wish to be unjust even to barbarians; but it is not unjust to men to anticipate that they may do what they have not only repeatedly done, but repeatedly defended. **In plain words, we are acting as if there was no such thing as a barbarian peril in Europe. It was an ignorant and provincial assumption even in 1914; there are no words for what it is in 1919. But one thing is certain—Nemesis will not abandon our education, and in some wild fashion or other we shall again discover the soul through its sins.**[44]

G.K. Chesterton, "Our Note-Book," *Illustrated London News* 154 (April 12, 1919), 512. US: April 12, 1919. Also published as "Enemies of Religious Traditions."

Equity for Victims

May 10, 1919

Now not only do I deny that it is wicked to win and use a victory; I strongly affirm that it is wicked to win and then not use a victory.

Editor: Using an argument built on English legal practices, Chesterton defends the justice of dictating to Germany a peace with terms that make future German aggression less likely. Equity refers a part of the English legal system called a court of equity, which judges not based on statutory law, but on the principle of fairness, showing flexibility according to the particular circumstances of a case. Chesterton is saying it's wrong (as equity) to treat a criminal and his victim the same. Take a sex offender being released from prison. Pure equality would suggest that, if a sex offender is monitored and his address is publicly available, then that same policy should be extended to his victims (or more likely, if not to the victim, then not to the criminal, who has an equal right to privacy). Equity would look at the actual situation, including the risk that the criminal would take revenge on victims who testified against him, as well as the risk he poses to others. It would rule that, since the two parties are radically different, it's unfair to treat them the same. In much the same fashion, in the postwar debate over national borders, it was a violation of equity for a large criminal nation, Germany, to be treated the same as smaller victim nations such as Belgium, Poland and Serbia. To counter the idea that a stress on equality is modern and progressive, Chesterton points to the equality of barbarian societies, where there was no counterbalancing weight (equity) on the scales to the correct for the weight (might) of a king's sword. Justice requires both equity and equality.

Modern disputes are often clashes between equality and equity. We can see that illustrated in how weapons in the hands of nations, identifiable groups, or individuals are regarded. Equality demands that all be treated alike. Peaceful nations are

44. In Greek mythology, Nemesis was the Greek goddess of retribution, punishing those who did evil, particularly those with the *hubris* (exaggerated pride) to set themselves above the moral order. In this case, Chesterton refers to those who should be restraining an evil—German barbarism—but do not. That is itself an evil.

treated as if they were as dangerous as aggressive or even demented ones. The U.S. is as dangerous as Sadaam's Iraq, and a nuclear Israel is as deadly as a nuclear Iran. Groups and individuals are also treated with this same unthinking equality. An elderly Catholic nun boarding a plane is as likely to be a bomb-carrying terrorist as a young Saudi male. An ordinary citizen with a pistol is as dangerous as a violent criminal. In contrast, balancing equality with equity would not only refuse to judge that way, it would demand precisely the opposite policies. Peaceful nations must be armed to stop aggressors. Potentially dangerous groups must be watched far more carefully than peaceful ones. Ordinary, law-abiding citizens should be armed to stop criminals who will almost always have weapons. In short, justice often requires that equity trump equality. What is different must be treated differently.

IT is not only a sin, but a self-contradiction, to create equality without equity. Equality without equity is not merely iniquity, it is also inequality. For the man who is in the wrong has already had more than his rights; and to credit and not debit the amount to him is not to balance the books, but to cook the accounts. Equality and equity involve everywhere the restoration of rights. These are exceedingly simple truths, the alphabet of all law and morality. But they seem to be entirely forgotten in the discussion about our attitude to Germany; and forgotten not only among the Germans, but among ourselves. People talk of the scales of justice hanging even; but they forget that it is exactly when scales hang uneven that they are doing the work of scales. Scales have to measure the different weights and values of things; and that is exactly what we have to do, if we would redress the balance, after the barbarian king has again thrown his sword into the scale.

Thus, I do not myself care much about the individual barbarian king now in exile among the Dutch.[45] I think he is what he was when people were hailing him as "the Lord Chief Justice of Europe," the glory of the Teutonic Race and the Royal Family—a shallow, morbid, miserable little man. Even recently somebody revived the old style of speaking about him, and called him "the once puissant and mediaeval Emperor who tried to make himself the mouthpiece of God. " In so far as he made himself the mouthpiece of God he was not mediaeval, but rather anti-mediaeval. As a matter of fact, he was about as mediaeval as the *Daily Mail*. He was a sort of perpetual special edition, and he is now a back number—that is about the most exciting thing to be said of him. I gravely doubt if he was chiefly responsible for the war, or particularly responsible for anything. But the official arguments actually offered against holding him responsible appear unconvincing. For instance, it is apparently said by the American delegation that "proceedings against him might be wise or unwise; but in any event they would be against an individual out of office, and not against an individual in office." But, after all, it does not seem so very paradoxical that a person should not be on the throne of judgment while he is also in the dock—not to mention the gallows. **The weakness of the argument, as of many modern arguments, is, of course, that it omits the universal moral idea of punishment. But, as the**

45. Wilhelm II, the Kaiser of WWI, fled to the Netherlands for political asylum the day before the war ended.

moderns still go on punishing the poor and ignorant, I have no sympathy for their fine feelings against punishing the rich and responsible. I do not think these feelings even deserve so noble a name as sentimentalism, but should rather be described as snobbishness.

In the argument itself, therefore, there is no little logical weakness; but, if it were carried out consistently, it might at least have one practical advantage. If the German Emperor was not responsible for war, or if he is anyhow now not responsible for government, the proper inference is plain enough—that we should turn our attention to those Germans who now are responsible for government, and consider how far they were formerly responsible for war. And the truth is that the men of whom Scheidemann is the type really had almost as much responsibility for war as they have since had for government.[46] It may well be maintained that their warlike spirit was worse than the Kaiser's because it was more wanton than the Kaiser's. It might be held that the War Lord was in some sense bound to lead in war; but a leader of the Socialist party was not bound to lead in the justification of war. It might be held that it was not so much William Hohenzollern as the Deutscher Kaiser who followed the armies across Belgium and waited in a white uniform at Nancy for the triumph that never came.[47] But it was certainly Herr Scheidemann, as well as a mere member of the Reichstag, who followed the armies into Belgium to whitewash with hypocritical sophistries the most wicked oppression of modern history. It was certainly not necessary for an irresponsible professor of Socialism to go entirely out of his way to excuse and eulogise the chief act of Prussianism. He was not acting as a Socialist, and he was certainly not acting as a Pacifist. But, above all, if he was really acting as a democrat, the fact is far from reassuring about the spirit and future of German democracy. If he was really representing those whom he was supposed to represent, we can only deduce that German popular feeling was then, and probably is now, as ambitious and aggressive as German autocratic or aristocratic feeling. If he does not trouble about representing anybody, it is useless to refer us to an improved popular sentiment which he is supposed to represent. The menace to mankind seems to remain the same, whether he was a democrat then or whether he is an oligarch now. But, in any case, I imagine nobody will say that Scheidemann was a mediaeval, or that he merely professed to be the voice of God. Scheidemann was a modern, and modestly professed merely to be the voice of Humanity. And the highly practical fact we have to face, if we are not to involve the world in another hideous calamity, is the very simple fact that it is just as easy to parade the one imposture and impiety

46. Philipp Scheidemann (1865–1939) was a Social Democratic party leader and, like most of his party, he supported the war. In a letter published in the *New Yorker Volkszeitung* on September 10, 1914 and republished in *New York Times Current History: The European War from the Beginning to March 1915*, Vol 1, No. 2, he wrote:

> Moreover, we Social Democrats have never ceased to be Germans, because we belong to the Socialist International. And if we in the Reichstag have unanimously approved the war credit, we have done no more after all than to carry out what has often been repeated by our greatest Socialists from the Reichstag platform.

For more criticism of Scheidemann, see the next article (May 24, 1919). Chesterton focused on him because he founded the Weimar Republic and was at that time its first Chancellor (February 13–June 20, 1919).

47. Chesterton gives the Kaiser an ordinary-sounding name, William Hohenzollern, based on his royal line.

as the other. **It is just as easy to massacre men in the name of Man as to burn churches in the name of God. It is as feasible to decree inhumanity in humanitarian language as to decree sacrilege in sacred language.** What the deeds of these men will be may remain to be seen. Since they thought such things as the invasion of Belgium consistent with Socialism in opposition, I cannot conceive why they should not think them consistent with Socialism in power.

I am astonished to find the French and Italians rebuked, in reasonable papers like the *New Statesman*, apparently for wanting a peace based on our victory. Does the *New Statesman* desire a peace based on the assumption of our defeat? Presumably not, for during the war, to do it justice, it was firm enough upon the necessity to win. **Now not only do I deny that it is wicked to win and use a victory; I strongly affirm that it is wicked to win and then not use a victory.** If you fight and do not desire victory, I can only say that you must desire butchery. If people do not deserve to be suspected in policy and restrained in power, they certainly do not deserve to be ripped in pieces with shrapnel or impaled on steel spikes.[48] I should accept the whole of the pacifist vision of war, if I had to take it along with the pacifist version of peace. War would really be as vile as they paint it, if it were as valueless as they would make it. But such ignorance of the French and Italian case comes chiefly from ignorance of something of which France and Italy are full—the real history of civilization. It can be summed up here for the moment in one sentence—that this is not the first time the barbarians have moved against civilization; and there is not, and never has been, even the adumbration of an intelligent reason for supposing that it will be the last.

G.K. Chesterton, "Our Note-Book," *Illustrated London News* 154 (May 10, 1919), 660. US: May 10, 1919. Also published as "On German Responsibility."

Unrepentant Germany

May 24, 1919

It is, in the real sense, a matter of conscience to show generosity to the defeated, so long as it is consistent with justice to the oppressed.

Editor: Chesterton is skeptical that Germany has changed its attitude toward aggressive war and points out that its current leaders supported the war when it began and still refuse to admit the nation's guilt. Notice his opening remarks that the Allies once-vivid anger at German aggression was degenerating into no more than a grumbling so vague it was as likely to focus on Poles or Serbians as on Germany. You can find similar attitudes today among those who blame Israel for the problems of the Middle East. They want to blame someone, and a small democratic country that doesn't support terrorism is the safest target for those with soft heads and weak hearts. Under pressure to act, a coward often becomes a bully.

48. Chesterton's argument is marvelous. He's saying, "If we have a right to kill Germans in wartime for invading Belgium, then we certainly have a right after the war to make them do lesser things, so they don't invade again.

There is a danger that the spirit discovered in the great war may die away on both sides in a sort of grumbling. **Grumbling is anger in solution, as sentimentalism is love in solution; and they are both much safer when they are solid—when they are vivid and not vague.** Human anger is a higher thing than what is called divine discontent. For you must be angry with something; but you can be discontented with everything. It will be well if we clear our minds a little about our position in Europe—and especially about our relations with the Germans—and the principles upon which we propose to act. We were angry with the Germans for certain things that they did; and I willingly agree it is not enough to be merely discontented with anything they do. But the question of how we stand to them necessarily depends upon how they stand to themselves. They may have risen on stepping-stones of their dead selves to higher things, though their stepping-stones hitherto have generally been the dead selves of their enemies, and not infrequently of their friends.[49] But I, for one, have far more sympathy with the desire to excuse them on the ground that they have been brought low than on the ground that they have risen high. For it is right and reasonable enough, to begin with, to deal differently with those who really wish to spare Germany because she is vanquished, as compared with those who really wished to spare her because she was victorious. **It is, in the real sense, a matter of conscience to show generosity to the defeated, so long as it is consistent with justice to the oppressed.** We had much better get this hackneyed but unaltered human ideal clear of all clouds of mere grumbling, before we go on to see how far it really applies.

It is true that many who say this have no right whatever to say it. The peace party are disqualified from pleading for a new Germany by the simple fact that they pleaded just as hard for the old Germany. It may be right to inquire whether the enemy is still criminal or is now penitent. But why should I accept the assertion of his penitence from the very people who practically denied his crime? Why should I be finally satisfied with the fall of the Kaiser, at the request of people who were almost equally satisfied with the rule of the Kaiser? Why must I believe that Germans are now horrified at things done in the cause of Germany, and believe it on the bare word of Englishmen who were not horrified at those things when done against the cause of England? Why should the Prussians execrate Prussianism, when the English Pacifists were always ready to excuse Prussianism even in the name of Pacifism? The white dove may be at war with the black eagle; but the man who tells me so is the same man who always told me that the black eagle was not so

49. Chesterton is alluding to the first stanza of one of the most powerful English poems of the nineteenth century, Alfred Lord Tennyson's "In Memoriam A.H.H," which begins: "I held it truth, with him who sings/ To one clear harp in divers tones,/ That men may rise on stepping-stones/ Of their dead selves to higher things." Tennyson wrote it in memory of a friend, Arthur Henry Hallam, who died suddenly in 1833, just before he would have married Tennyson's sister. Tennyson continued to work on it for 17 years, creating a poem that is about much more than the death of one man. It wrestles with religious, scientific, and philosophical questions that trouble us to this day, questions about the meaning of life in a world that seems filled with meaningless deaths. The poem is best known for the lines: "'Tis better to have loved and lost/ Than never to have loved at all."

black as he was painted. So far as that argument goes, the inference would seem to be simple and sinister. Prussian despotism is repudiated by the Prussian Socialist party—just about as heartily as Prussian war was repudiated by the English Peace party. It is not saying much.

For in this respect what was called the German Revolution was a very singular revolution. Indeed, it was quite unique among revolutions. The rebels have not repudiated the old régime half so much as rebels would be justified in doing, and as rebels generally do. We may not be disposed to trust Trotsky to rule the Russian people, but we can certainly trust him to denounce their original rulers. Marat might not do the best that could be done with the French Republic, but he would certainly say the worst that could be said about the French Monarchy.[50] Now we know, as a fact of common sense, that Scheidemann does not say the worst that could be said of the Prussian Monarchy. And he does not say it for an exceedingly simple reason—that he himself was one of the worst accomplices in one of the worst actions of that worst of all human governments. It was he who went, like an amateur of atrocity, into conquered Belgium, to excuse the conquest on the most enlightened modern principles.[51] There is nothing whatever to indicate that he would not excuse it again, in similar circumstances, on similar principles. The same can be said, even more strongly, of his representative in France, Count Rantzau, famous for his furious demand for the retention of Alsace and the imperial spoils of 1870.[52] The new German authorities have not rebelled against that imperialism. They do not even regret it. In their reply, they say quite plainly that they do not admit that the Kaiser's Government was chiefly responsible for the great conflict.[53] If words have any meaning at all, this must mean that the present German Government, in

50. Chesterton used a similar argument in the January 18, 1919 issue of *Illustrated London News*. He discussed the German Chancellor, Philipp Scheidemann, two weeks earlier in the May 10, 1919 issue.

51. A month after the war began, a news correspondent described what "Scheidemann, a Socialist member of the Reichstag" said at a conference with the Dutch Social Democratic Labor Party in Amsterdam, noting: "I am now informed that Herr Scheidemann defended the attitude of the German Socialists in supporting the war." "Socialist Defends War" *New York Times* (September 5, 1914), 5.

52. Ulrich von Graff Brockdorff-Rantzau (1869-1928) was Germany's Foreign Minister at the Paris Peace Conference (1919). On February 17, 1919 the *Times* (London) published an editorial denouncing a recent Weimar speech by Count von Brockdorff-Rantzau, suggesting the following: "The speech of the new Foreign Minister is the latest example of the ill-advised temper in which the Germans regard or attempt to regard the position in which they stand. He does not, indeed, pretend that the German arms have won the war. He attributes the Allies' victory to their economic and not to their military conduct of the war. All through his speech he assumes the position which President Ebert took up when he calmly proclaimed in his first address: 'The question of guilt seems to be almost trifling.'" (Friedrich Ebert (1871–1925) was the first president of the Weimar Republic.) The same issue of the *New York Times* that reported that editorial, also noted that Brockdorff-Rantzau had sent the Allied governments, "a protest against any attempt to regard the Alsace-Lorraine question as closed until it has been finally settled by the Peace Conference." The article noted that a rumor had appeared in a Berlin paper that Brockdorff-Rantzau was resigning. "Report Brockdorff Out After Protest," *New York Times* (February 18, 1919), 2. Later, and along with Scheidemann and five other members of the cabinet, he resigned rather than sign the Treaty of Versailles. "Assembly Now for Peace," *New York Times* (June 21, 1919), 1–2.

53. Hitler held this view, writing of propaganda: "It was absolutely wrong to discuss war-guilt from the standpoint that Germany alone could not be held responsible for the outbreak of the catastrophe; it would have been correct to load every bit of the blame on the shoulders of the enemy, even if this had not really corresponded to the true facts, as it actually did." *Mein Kampf* (Boston: Houghton Mifflin, 1943), 182.

similar circumstances, would suddenly invade Serbia and Belgium, and would not admit that it was provoking a war in Europe.

Now it is plain, on the same elementary ethics, that, before we are generous to people in the position of the Germans, we have to be just to people in the position of the Serbians and the Belgians. The knight-errant may spare the ogre, but he must save the captives of the ogre; if he fails to do so, he not only fails in common sense, but in knight-errantry. It is not only unreasonable, it is also unchivalrous, to spare the dragon and sacrifice the princess. It is to these eternal truisms that we must reduce our moral conduct, if we mean to judge it morally; and it can be judged entirely without virulence or vulgar swagger, as I have tried to judge it here. By the very highest and even the most fantastic standard of chivalry, it resolves itself into the question of whether German barbarism is still a danger to other States, especially small States. In other words, is it now a question of sparing the conquered, or is it still a question of taking the last steps to conquer them? What can we do in such a case but judge by their own comments on their own crimes? And what can we say of them except that they still refuse to regret those crimes, they still elect leaders who led in those crimes, and that they still threaten us with consequences which may very probably turn out to be crimes?

This is the question which we are ready to put, in an entirely sober and liberal spirit to papers like the *New Statesman* or the *New Age*, which claim to be magnanimous to the fallen, after having been militant against the foe. I do not put it to the Pacifist papers, for they would have yielded to German success; and that is not magnanimous, but mean. But I do put it to the more patriotic moderates as a serious and sincere query—How do they explain Scheidemann of Belgium or Rantzau of Alsace, if the German spirit is not still a menace to mankind?

G.K. Chesterton, "Our Note-Book," *Illustrated London News* 154 (May 24, 1919), 738.
US: May 24, 1919. Also published as "On Being Generous to the Germans."

CRIMINAL GERMANY

May 31, 1919

I do not even think that a cosmopolitan contempt for patriotism is merely a matter of opinion, any more than I think that a Nietzcheite contempt for compassion is merely a matter of opinion.

1919–1922

EDITOR: Unlike the Boer war, which he opposed, in this particular war Chesterton finds ample reasons to be a hardliner. He believes Germany needs punishment rather than sympathy. His foe is the *Nation*, a liberal magazine trying to feel Germany's pain. The issue he raises is the most important one imaginable. In a little over twenty years Europe will be plunged into the horrors of the Second World War precisely because, as Chesterton puts it, neither "any prominent person responsible for the New Germany" nor "the average German" thinks the nation did anything wrong. Sins left unconfessed are often repeated.

I have been in many minorities and have received many controversial challenges from the majority, which I have done my best to answer. Now that I happen to be on the side of the majority, at least on one important matter, I should think it very unworthy not to accept any plausible challenge from any reputable representative of the minority. I am convinced that the pacifist and semi-pacifist apologies for Germany are not only anti-national, but anti-normal. **I do not even think that a cosmopolitan contempt for patriotism is merely a matter of opinion, any more than I think that a Nietzcheite contempt for compassion is merely a matter of opinion.[54] I think they are both heresies so horrible that their treatment must not be so much mental as moral, when it is not simply medical.** Men are not always dead of a disease and men are not always damned by a delusion; but so far as they are touched by it they are destroyed by it. But I would always treat an eccentric as an equal, unless I could literally treat him as a lunatic. It is quite clear to me that, if he has a claim to a hearing, he has a claim to an answer. So long as he has a right to talk, he has a right to be talked to. And when a paper of the serious status and standards of the *Nation* puts a clear challenge to those Englishmen who approve of the present Allied policy towards Germany, I most certainly think such a question should be answered; and I will proceed to answer it.

The writer in the *Nation* asks us, in effect, to imagine ourselves in the shoes of the Germans. He asks whether we, as English, would accept such terms, even if "our fault were like midnight" and our cause wrong in every item. It would considerably simplify this part of the argument if the *Nation* could kindly point out any prominent person responsible for the New Germany who does admit that his fault is like midnight, or even like the tenderest twilight. We could see our way clearer, if we could find any particular indications that the average German does think he was wrong in every item, or in any item. But this is a parenthesis; it is an important parenthesis, because it makes all the difference in the world to the wisdom of clemency whether the barbarians are morally in a mood of regret or not. So far as I can make out, in the moral sense, they not only regret nothing in the new Germany, but do not regret much in the old Germany. But the particular point raised by the *Nation* is not what they actually do feel, but what we should feel in their place. Of course it is possible to get into a wild metaphysical maze and tangle to the old tune of "Supposing I were you," for if an Englishman were in the German's place he would be a German. But I accept the challenge to the imagination on the broad lines of the brotherhood of men; and I will put the most obvious answer first. It is the most obvious point about this test that it is never applied to the most obvious examples. It is not applied to the pick-pocket in the street or the burglar in the back garden; and if it were it would destroy the whole of that system of police protection under which comfortable men like the editor of the *Nation* and myself walk the world in safety. It may puzzle the

54. The German philosopher Friedrich Nietzsche's (1844–1900) hated compassion and pity, which he regarded as signs of weakness, particularly in *The Antichrist* (1888). Chesterton was right to consider him a horrible heretic, and it isn't surprising that, aided by his sister, Nazism promoted some of his nastier ideas.

respectable pacifist to hear it, but I have many moods in which I wish that police system could be destroyed. Strange as it may seem to the internationalist, I really do feel for burglars and pick-pockets the same sort of half-sympathy which he only feels for foreign princes and cosmopolitan capitalists.[55] And even where it is hardest to have sympathy, it is possible to have imagination. I can easily conceive that Scheidemann, who helped to trample on Belgium, has nevertheless an intolerable sense of surprise that somebody is trampling on him.

Therefore, on the actual admission of the *Nation* there is an obvious answer to the *Nation*. There is no question here of some of the defences offered for Germany. Some have maintained that the German Government was not to blame for doing things which its own spokesman barely excused or explained away. And some have maintained that the German people did not approve of things for which they circulated medals and sang songs. But here the *Nation* assumes the guilt not only of the German Government, but of the German people; and only asks us to imagine a similar guilt in the English people. But if it assumes guilt, and admits the idea of punishment which generally accompanies guilt, I cannot see how it alters the case to imagine the attempt to escape which generally accompanies punishment. The justice of it, if disputed at all, should be disputed on the ground that a nation cannot be criminal, or that a nation cannot be punished by nations. I myself believe that a nation can be criminal, and can be punished for crime. I believe it because I am a nationalist, and still more because I am a democrat—or, if the phrase be more exact, a republican. That is, I believe a commonwealth has a common will, a corporate spirit which can be loved, and which therefore can be blamed. Those who say that a democratic Germany cannot deserve punishment are denying the first dogma of democracy. But the *Nation*, to do it justice, does not deny that Germans might deserve punishment, or that we in a similar case should deserve punishment. It only suggests that we should try to avoid punishment—which is exceedingly probable, but not morally final.

That is the logic of the case; but a more living and sympathetic understanding of it will ultimately lead the same way. The editor of the *Nation* knows very well that I am not a flatterer of British institutions; that on many matters we have been in revolt together; that on some matters I am more in revolt than he. But I do seriously think there is a difference here between British abuses and German abuses, which is a reality, beyond all likes and dislikes. In short, when he asked us to imagine ourselves German, I think he was still only asking us to imagine ourselves English. Heavy as has been the weight of our own corruptions, I can conceive that the English have it in them to act very much as the *Nation* imagines them acting. I fancy they might really both repent and resist.[56] It may be a paradox; but I think they would really

55. Chesterton wants even-handed justice. Today he would blast his opponents for their odd sympathy for criminals and terrorists in both high and low stations, from Iraq's genocidal Saddam Hussein to the meanest suicide bomber killing Israeli children. Each is a "sympathy" that makes it hard for others to walk in safety.

56. In a February 26, 1916 article (Ch. 4), Chesterton wrote, "there never was an English wrong without an English protest." Germany's most deep-seated problem was that there were so few German protests.

resist if they could really repent. But there have not been any true signs of Germany repenting, or as yet even of her resisting. And if all observers will study this strange situation patiently, **I think they will gradually find growing a strong and rather strange impression, about the thing they have hitherto called "Germany." In fact, it has not behaved like a normal nation either in victory or defeat. It was *less* bitter than a normal nation in defeat, as it had been more brutal than a normal nation in victory. I throw out, by way of a possible explanation, the proposition that it is not a normal nation, or a nation at all. It was a horde of tribes held together by the promise of the sack of Rome—that is, of all the cities of the Roman tradition.** So it is possible to have a sympathy with Germans; but it is the same sort of sympathy I have for all the criminal classes, when they are caught.

G.K. Chesterton, "Our Note-Book," *Illustrated London News* 154 (May 31, 1919), 776.
US: May 31, 1919. Also published as "The Mood of the Barbarians."

Barbaric Germany

June 14, 1919

In short, he says in substance that he expects to suffer because he is beaten, but he does not see why he should suffer because he deserves to be beaten. That is Prussian philosophy and Prussian history and Prussian peace and war in one sentence.

Editor: Chesterton uses remarks made two weeks earlier by Germany's Foreign Minister to show that the nation's leaders refuse to accept guilt for the war. Chesterton does not believe victors, simply because they have won, can dictate any terms they want. If this had been "a fair fight between free nations" over some technical difference, "heavy indemnities or large rectifications of frontier" would not be right. Harsh demands are only justified because what Germany did wrong and must be punished. In this article, perhaps more than any other, Chesterton wrestles with what to do with a Germany that refuses to admit error and change: "If they will not confess that they are criminals, they shall at least confess that we regard them as criminals."

Count Rantzau recently made a remark which exactly measures the real abyss—not yet bridged—between the barbarians and the city of civilization which they lately besieged.[57] It sums up the whole cross-purposes of the Peace

57. Germany was given until June 25 to accept Allied demands. Here is a quote of Rantzau's reply to those demands in a slightly different translation. Note the revealing slip when Rantzau doesn't merely refuse to accept what his nation's accusers are saying, but rejects any "avowal of its sins." Note too the belief that Germany will only "make sacrifices" (implying giving up more than necessary) because it has been "vanquished." Asked whether he considered unbridgeable the gulf between allied demands and German offers, the Count replied:

> This question itself is based on a controversy of principles, on which no agreement can be reached. It is possible to be of different opinion about the resources of Germany, but there exists no agreement about the question whether this nation is to do penance as a criminal or to fulfil its obligation as a party to the treaty.
>
> If, in October, 1918, an avowal of its sins had been laid before the German nation for its acceptance instead of a preliminary treaty regarding the foundation of peace, it would have continued to fight. At present Germany cannot fight any more, but she can still say 'No.'

After declaring that if he were in the position of President Wilson, Premier Clemenceau or Premier Lloyd George he would be afraid of "assuming an equality with God," Count von Brockdorff-Rantzau continued:

Conference. And it has that invariable mark of a man in the middle of such a misunderstanding—that precisely what he thinks hard is easy, and precisely what he thinks easy is hard. What he said was this—"At the moment when the moral cloak of penal justice is removed from the peace document it becomes bearable for Germany to a certain extent. That we, as the vanquished, must make sacrifices in power and goods we realise. We decline, however, to agree like criminals to our removal into a second-class position amongst nations."

In short, he says in substance that he expects to suffer because he is beaten, but he does not see why he should suffer because he deserves to be beaten. That is Prussian philosophy and Prussian history and Prussian peace and war in one sentence. They understand the idea of *Væ Vicis*, but there is no such thing as a correct German translation of *debellare superbos.*[58] Now I can say for myself, and I believe for most Englishmen along with me, that we disagree with the Count upon every point—even upon the point in our favour. I would not take the advantage which he concedes as reasonable. But I would insist on the attitude which he resents as intolerable. I would not have the Germans crushed merely because they were conquered. The Germans did it to the French in 1871, but I would not do it to the Germans even in 1919.[59] The truth is that, if we did not take the moral view which Rantzau disapproves, we should not make even the material demands which Rantzau expects. We should be quite content, after a fair fight between free nations, with securing one or two definite points in dispute; and we might well do without heavy indemnities or large rectifications of frontier. We are forcing the Prussian power to pay not for having lost the war, but for having waged the war. Or rather, to put it more correctly still, they are to pay not so much for having waged war, as for having waged Prussian war. That is our defence for our demands; and without it we should make infinitely milder demands—or, perhaps, no demands. **In short, we are asked to treat the Germans as the conquered, but not as the criminals. But, in fact, it is only because we do regard them as the criminals that we would even consent to treat them as the conquered.** It is not a pleasant business to have to treat them as either, and I hope it will soon be over. I for one am glad to be on the right side, but I often find it almost humiliating to be on the winning side. What reconciles me to it is not the triumph which Rantzau tolerates, but the justice which Rantzau denies. That justice must and shall be vindicated, either by penitence or by punishment. If the Germans will not see it as what they would call subjective, they shall see it as something which even they will be bound to call objective. Or, to talk a more human

At the moment when the moral cloak of penal justice is removed from the peace document, it becomes bearable for Germany to a certain extent that we, as the vanquished, must make sacrifices in power and goods. We realize this, but we decline to agree like criminals to our removal into a second-class position among the nations. [Quotations from: "Big Four Discuss German Proposal," *New York Times* (June 3, 1919), 2.]

58. *Væ Vicis* is Latin for "woe to the vanquished," and *debellare superbos* means "to conquer the proud."

59. The Germans treated the French harshly at the end of the Franco-Prussian War (1870–1871). With Paris under siege and its population starving, France yielded the city. Victorious, Germany annexed Alsace-Lorraine and continued to occupy France until it was paid an indemnity of five billion gold francs. In terms of its national GDP, France paid Germany roughly $200 billion in today's money (2005).

tongue, if they will not feel it in their consciences, they shall see it with their eyes, and glare at it through their goggles as if at a comet. **If they will not confess that they are criminals, they shall at least confess that we regard them as criminals.** They shall realise that by the end of the war, especially the submarine war, the great mass of mankind had come to regard them as criminals. If they do not know that the things they have done are horrible, they shall know that they are horrifying.

Hence we cannot accede to Count Rantzau's rather complicated request that a moral cloak of penal justice should be removed from a peace document.[60] For us there is no question of a penal cloak for a peace document; the document itself is penal, like the documents upon which we are daily putting crowds of much poorer and more hardly tempted people in jail. We would not even make it painful, if we did not have to make it penal. We would not trample on the barbarians merely because we had triumphed over them, though we do not need Rantzau's hint to tell us that this is exactly what they would have done if they had triumphed over us. We cannot simply enjoy the sack of Cologne, as he and his Prussians would have enjoyed the sack of Paris. We do not even enjoy the occupation of Cologne, it being in the abstract an uncomfortable matter to be in another man's country—let alone it being still more uncomfortable to be so long away from one's own. Our men are there, still loaded with packs and weapons, because, unless certain things are settled, the barbarians will forget all about it and immediately begin to do it again.

In the course of the same protest, the Prussian nobleman makes another curious remark. He says that the leaders of the Allies ought not to claim to act in the name of God. There is something decidedly quaint about an old supporter of the Kaiser complaining of the unfortunate habit of invoking God. But, while the men whose theocracy Rantzau rebukes really claim far less theocracy than the man whom Rantzau served and reverenced, it is true that they do act in the name of God in the very real sense of acting in the name of the image of God—of the human standard which preserves the human stature as something erect above the beasts. **For nobody can understand the recent eruption of Teutonism who does not realise that the most ancient and the most modern things, being equally crude and cruel, combined to destroy the humour and humanity of a more mellow and historic culture.[61] They combined the bestial beginnings with the evolutionary endings of**

60. What Rantzau cannot accept is what he sees as the Allied effort to conceal naked use of force that behind "a moral cloak of penal justice." It isn't merely that he and his fellow Prussians believe that might makes right. It's that they can't imagine any other way of thinking. The logical extension of the Count's attitude is that Germany retains the right to wage yet another violent and aggressive war as long as she makes sure she wins.

61. Historian Daniel Gasman described Germany's transformation this way:

> One should bear in mind in discussing the history of liberalism in the nineteenth century that a relatively powerful middle class came into political prominence in such western countries as England and France where a strong state structure and a sense of national and historical identity were already in existence. Jealous of its own political prerogatives, liberalism in western Europe proclaimed a belief that that government is best which governs least professed an attachment to the natural and inalienable rights of man. In Germany, on the other hand, the middle class was comparatively weak and a stable state structure was non-existent. As a consequence, and particularly after 1848, and even more so after Bismarkian unification in the 1860's, liberalism in Germany, aware of its own weakness, looked increasingly to the advantages which a strong state could offer for the realization of its own program. For the German liberals, the organization of the national state

man. Therefore they used the newest instruments to produce the oldest tortures. Therefore they used the newest arguments to defend the oldest tyrannies.[62] By thus telescoping history, the Teutonists crushed out of it the part that really stands for humanity. Some of their professors openly made man a mere link, and almost a missing link, between the monkey and the superman.[63] Those who fought this tendency, whether or not they acted by the authority of God, could be said with strict truth to act by the authority of man. And in the mass they did act by the authority of man, in the practical sense of mankind. Count Rantzau talks of the Allies judging the whole world; but in plain fact it was Germany that was judged by the whole world. As neutral after neutral went to war against the new piracy, a judgment was delivered more solidly human than any recorded in history. The Allies might be wrong about many things in the future; they might think each other wrong about many things in the future. The one thing on which they were not doubtful, the one thing in which they were not divided, was the moral condemnation of Germany; for that belongs to the past.

G.K. Chesterton, "Our Note-Book," *Illustrated London News* 154 (June 14, 1919), 854. US: June 14, 1919. Also published as "Judgment for the Germans."

Civilization Leads

June 21, 1919

We do not necessarily object even to the savage being tolerated as a savage, but we do object to the savage being worshipped as a noble savage.

Editor: Chesterton believes that nationalities, cultures, and, to the extent that racial differences exist, races should be allowed to be themselves without imitating others or setting themselves above the rest. He mocks German attempts to claim that their culture is so superior that it can run roughshod over everyone else. But that did not mean that he is a modern cultural relativist or a diversity fanatic, seeing (or pretending to see) all societies as equal. He makes a strong distinction between civilized and barbaric societies, placing Germany among the latter.

There isn't space here to go into the distinctions Chesterton saw between civilization and barbarism, but many center on concepts of chivalry that include protecting

appeared to be much more important than freedom of all men, and revealingly enough they called themselves National Liberals. Abandoning in practice many of the political principles to which they were abstractly committed, they were able to throw virtually unqualified support to the authoritarian Bismarkian state. [Daniel Gasman, *The Scientific Origins of National Socialism* (London: MacDonald, 1971) xv–xvi.]

62. Gasman noted the impact of Darwinism: "It may be said that in no other country of Europe, or for that matter even in the United States, did the ideas of Darwinism develop as seriously as a total explanation of the world as in Germany. But Darwinism in Germany was a system of thought that was often transformed almost beyond recognition." Daniel Gasman, *The Scientific Origins of National Socialism* (London: MacDonald, 1971) xiii.

63. Ernst Haeckel, perhaps Germany's leading biologist, wrote: "Intelligent dogs not only discriminate between individual men, cats, etc., according as they are sympathetic or the reverse, but they have a general idea of man or cat, and behave very differently towards the two. On the other hand, the power of forming concepts is still so slight in uncivilized races that it rises but little above the mind of dogs, horses, etc.; the mental interval between them and civilized man is extremely wide." Ernst Haeckel, *The Wonders of Life*, transl. Joseph McCabe. (New York: Harper and Brothers, 1904), 316. For more on Haeckel, see the introduction to Chapter 4.

non-combatants in war and not abusing captured foes. One marvelous example came during Israel's 1948 War of Independence. After a desperate struggle, the Jews defending the Jewish quarter of the Old City of Jerusalem were forced to surrender, and the British-trained Jordanian Legion promised them safe conduct to Israeli lines. To keep the disarmed Jews from being shot from a rooftop, Jordanian soldiers marched to their outside, using their own bodies to shield the very people they had been fighting only hours before. Chesterton would have praised the behavior of those Jordanian soldiers as civilized and condemn that of those on the rooftops and their modern, bomb-carrying, terrorist counterparts as barbaric. Civilized behavior, even in opponents, is to be praised, while barbaric behavior, whatever its source, is to be condemned and punished. As Chesterton notes in closing, civilization should lead and direct barbarism, telling it how to behave, and not vice-versa.

The wildest writer cannot make this world out wilder than it is. I, for one, have written tales in my time which were barely tolerable as nonsensical nightmares; but the silliest part of them has always come true. To take an idle instance, I introduced into a nonsense novel an Oriental crank who proved the Moslem origin of civilization from the word Crescent in a name like Denmark Crescent.[64] Long afterwards, I heard with my own ears an Anglo-Israelite, or student of the Lost Ten Tribes, saying quite calmly that Denmark Crescent proved that Englishmen were descended from the tribe of Dan. That is much more nonsensical than my nonsense, for my man was an alien talking of things he had never seen, and the crescent is, after all, a symbol in universal use. But the other was a solid, educated Englishman; and what he had done with the whole kingdom of Denmark, or how he explained it away, I cannot imagine. I can also recall, in an equally egotistic vein, that I once wrote some journalistic sketches or stories which turned upon queer trades.[65] I have forgotten what they were, I am happy to say; but I am pretty sure I should not find in those lost tales any trade so extraordinary as one which I have just noted in an ordinary newspaper. An American lady has recently died, generally respected and lamented, whose whole art, science, and profession consisted in uncurling the hair of negroes.[66] That is the sort of thing one could not hit with a hundred guesses. It helps to prove that the world is not only so full of a number of things, but of a number of impossible things. For even on the face of it there are many mysteries in the matter. If the object is to obliterate the distinction, the selection is somewhat puzzling. It would appear difficult for a gentleman with a conspicuously black face to conceal himself behind his attenuated hair; the distinction seems a fine one, and such straightening of hair is suggestive of the splitting of hairs. But what I understand even less is why

64. This is in the first chapter of his 1914 *The Flying Inn*. Later Chesterton wrote of actually hearing a "crank so cranky as that." *The Works of G.K. Chesterton*, XXXIII, 546. From *Illustrated London News*, May 2, 1925.

65. His 1905 *The Club of Queer Trades*.

66. This appeared in the American press: "Mrs. C.J. Walker, known as New York's wealthiest negress, having accumulated a fortune from the sale of so-called anti-kink hair tonic and from real estate investments in the last fourteen years, died yesterday morning at her country estate.... Her death recalled the unusual story of how she rose in twelve years from a washerwoman making only $1.50 a day to a position of wealth and influence among members of her race." "Wealthiest Negress Dead," *New York Times* (May 26, 1919), 15.

the negro should wish to make his curly hair straight, especially as so many white people take the trouble to make their straight hair curly. It is said that the negroes regard it as a sign of a servile status; but I cannot imagine why. It would seem more natural to regard straight, limp hair as drooping in captivity, or hair that lies flat on the head as lying prostrate before the conqueror. It would seem more reasonable for them to regard their own strong, erect, tenacious hair as constituting a sort of cap of liberty.

For, though there is a moral to this rather mad episode, I do not mention it in derision of the negro. The negro has many valuable qualities, and has infused many valuable elements into our general culture, such as the fantastic folk-lore of Uncle Remus.[67] But I do mention it by way of a parable, in order to ask what would have happened if some professors had started the theory that the only true culture was negro culture, just as they did in the case of German culture. Suppose they took seriously what I have suggested fancifully, and argued that the white man should always copy the black man and not the black man the white. The first thing to note, as in every case of raving nonsense, is that it is ratified by remarkable coincidences. This very example of hair is one of them. It would be easy for the professors to prove that the praise given by all poets and lovers to curly hair was praise of any approximation to nigger hair. It would be easy for the professors, after the German fashion, to abound in books and charts, with diagrams of straight lines compared with spirals and volutes.[68] But not only have the negroes stronger hair, they have also stronger heads. They are hard-headed in a sense beyond that of the Scots; they are men of iron in a manner more literal than the Prussians. The triumphant negro pugilist would tower above the controversy, and the knockout blow of Mr. Jack Johnson would have the same historic significance as the sudden and successful stroke of Prussia in 1870.[69] The trick would be quite easy to work, if the negroes chose to work it as the Germans did. It is only the trifling business of falsifying the whole world's history to give a larger space to your own. They would only have to suggest that, since Toussaint L'Ouverture struggled with Napoleon, he was more important than Napoleon.[70] They would only have to talk about Booker Washington as greater than George Washington. Both these negro men of genius have their proper claim to respect; all that is wanted is to magnify them ten million times larger than life. That is what the Germans did, and it was very successful—for a time.

It is needless to give all the examples of how to erect a great racial theory. Briefly, a vast philosophy of history would be established in all the schools, which would in plain truth be merely poisonous trash. It is not that we do not like the barbarian to

67. Uncle Remus was an elderly slave invented by Joel Chandler Harris (1848–1908) to tell animal stories (similar to *Aesop's Fables*) based, he claimed, on African oral traditions and the folk tales of Southern slaves.

68. German biologist Ernst Haeckel displayed this obsession with hair in his *The History of Creation* (Ch. 28), making it a major factor in his classification of the different human races. See the introduction to Ch. 4.

69. Jack Johnson (1878–1946) was the first black Heavyweight Champion of the World, 1908-1915. Chesterton mentions him when he ridicules Teutonism in the September 5, 1914 issue of *Illustrated London News* (Ch. 2).

70. Toussaint L'Overture led the successful Haitian slave revolt against some of Napoleon's best officers. His biography is in John R. Beard, *The Life of Toussaint L'Overture* (Seattle: Inkling Books, 2002).

be civilised; it is not necessary that we do not like him even when he is uncivilised. What we cannot and will not tolerate is that the barbarian should civilise other people. We know that the moment the barbarian begins to civilise he begins to barbarise.

Without pretending to any precise parallel between European and Ethiopian races, we may take this as the general truth about the northern barbarism which has boiled up so often in history. It is not a question of liking or disliking the barbarians, of destroying or preserving them; it is a question of basing all our action on the fundamental fact that they are the barbarians, as compared with the civilised people. **We do not necessarily object even to the savage being tolerated as a savage, but we do object to the savage being worshipped as a noble savage.**[71] **We have to restore the conditions in which Rome and not Berlin is the magnet of mankind.** We have to depolarise the North Pole of Prussia. It is something more than a pun to say we can only do it by the real Pole of Poland. We have to treat the Prussian as a barbarian because he is so stupid that nothing else will prevent him from treating Paderewski as a barbarian.[72] We object to Germans spreading culture among Europeans, especially Eastern Europeans, just as we should object to black men spreading cannibalism among white men. We object to the Germans, by any process, dominating the Poles, Roumanians, and Russians, because it is like a donkey riding on a man. We do not even necessarily dislike a donkey; but we do distrust him. At any rate, we distrust him in that equestrian posture. Or, to return to the original figure, we may imitate the savage's curly hair while he imitates our straight hair; but we will not imitate his crooked thoughts when he ought to imitate our straight thoughts. It is the question of who shall lead and who shall follow; and on that there can be no compromise.[73]

G.K. Chesterton, "Our Note-Book," *Illustrated London News* 154 (June 21, 1919), 886.
US: June 21, 1919. Also published as "The Worthlessness of Racial Theories."

False Teutonic History

June 28, 1919

Germany increased in power and wealth; and in a train of more or less servile fashions, from spiked helmets to kindergartens, there came a fashion of false history which exaggerated the pirate settlements of the Dark Ages into the total Teutonising of Britain.

71. Those believing in a "noble savage" thought human nature was good, so primitive tribes unencumbered by civilization should be superior. A German novelist name Karl May (1842–1912) popularized its ideas.

72. Ignacy Jan Paderewski (1860–1941) was Poland's Prime Minister (1919), as well as a talented composer and a world-class pianist. He represented Poland at the Paris Peace Conference and signed the Treaty of Versailles. His many accomplishments explain why Chesterston enjoys suggesting Germans consider him a barbarian.

73. In his ground-breaking 1936 lecture, "Beowulf: The Monsters and the Critics," J.R.R. Tolkien described how the deeply Christian compiler of *Beowulf* drew from pagan and Christian sources to create his masterpiece. From Northern pagans, he took an "unyielding" courage that fights "on the right side, though it is not the side that wins, The winning side is Chaos and Unreason." Yet it fights believing "that defeat is no refutation." In *Beowulf*, he said, "a Heroic age more wild and primitive than that of Greece is brought into touch with Christendom, with the Sermon on the Mount, with Catholic theology and the ideas of Heaven and Hell." J.R.R. Tolkien, *Beowulf: The Monsters and the Critics* (Folcraft: Folcraft, PA, 1936, 1972), 17–19.

EDITOR: Chesterton argues that in recent decades the English people have been taught a false view of their history, one with too much stress on the nation's Germanic roots and too little on the influence of the Roman Empire and Christianity. Notice his blunt comment on the academic political correctness of that era: "Teutonism was the fashion; and those who followed the fashion obtained the fame. Those who did not follow the fashion, even when their fame could not be denied in other ways, were simply denied the dignity of scholars."

A VERY interesting criticism of some remarks in this column has appeared in the form of a letter to the *New Witness*. I hope I may be allowed for the moment to reply to them in the paper that contained the article, rather than in the paper that contained the letter.[74] Mr. G.H. Powell protested, forcibly but fairly, against what he regarded as my anti-Teutonic bias in tracing our history to a Roman rather than a German root.[75] He agrees that we were all horrified at recent German brutalities, but suggests that we were more horrified because we were surprised. And he argues ingeniously that the very surprise was a testimony to a truer German tradition. To this there is at least one obvious answer. The horror may have been a novelty to those who admired the Germans, but it was not a novelty to those who knew the Germans. We may be the German's cousins; and the German's cousins may have been surprised. But the German's neighbours were not surprised. The French, the Poles, the Northern Italians, would have told the same tale of twenty wars with the barbarians. If the Prussians had been chivalrous and tender until the day before yesterday, a Frenchman or a Pole would not have felt as he always did about the Prussians. Indeed, it was the chief problem of the Pro-German Pacifists that their internationalism was not even international, but merely insular. But my original article dealt rather with culture and tradition than politics, and I willingly transfer the combat to that rather less trampled ground.

Mr. Powell reveals the fallacy of a mere fashion by asking me whether any historical authority attacked Teutonism before the war. I answer, to begin with, that not a single historical authority ever heard of Teutonism until a comparatively short time before the war. Neither Alfred nor Guthrum nor Canute had ever heard of the Teutons.[76] The whole thing would have been nonsense to them, and nonsense to their children, and their children's children; and so on for a trifling interval of something like a thousand years. That thousand years is crammed with civilisation, with complexity, with learning, with varied adventure. And nobody ever heard of the German theory, not even the Germans. **It happened that, in the eighteenth century, the ambition of Prussia and the adventurous policy of the English aristocracy**

74. As an editor for the *New Witness*, Chesterton's "be allowed" has more to do with finding the time to write a reply than with getting permission. *The New Witness* (1914–1923) later became *G.K.'s Weekly* (1925–1936). Chesterton had written on the Roman versus Germanic issue many times before, but the Powell letter seems to have been triggered by his *Illustrated London News* article two weeks earlier on June 14, 1919 (Ch. 7).

75. This is apparently George Herbert Powell (1856–1924), author of the 1889 *Pocket Guide to Croquet*.

76. Anglo-Saxon Alfred the Great defeated the Danish Viking Guthrum at the Battle of Edington in 878. Canute the Great (c. 995–1035) was King of England and much of Scandinavia at the height of Danish power.

combined against the dominance of France, and so gave a lead by which all the Germans benefited. Germany increased in power and wealth; and in a train of more or less servile fashions, from spiked helmets to kindergartens, there came a fashion of false history which exaggerated the pirate settlements of the Dark Ages into the total Teutonising of Britain. None of the generations nearer to the event remembered that we owed all to the pirates—least of all those who knew the pirates, and quite as little even the pirates themselves.

But about the Victorian time it became the fashion; and it illustrates what I mean by the fallacy of a fashion. Mr. Powell feels that we could not easily find in Victorian England a famous historian who was not Teutonist. Possibly not—because a famous historian means a fashionable historian. **Teutonism was the fashion; and those who followed the fashion obtained the fame. Those who did not follow the fashion, even when their fame could not be denied in other ways, were simply denied the dignity of scholars.** But Mr. Powell is quite wrong in supposing that they did not exist, or that they were not scholarly. For instance, of thousands who have enjoyed the generous romances of Sir Arthur Quiller Couch, few probably know that he fought the Teutonic fallacy in the field of literary history long before the war.[77] Of the thousands who admire Mr. Belloc's satiric prose and verse, few have any notion of the detail of his historical research, or of the heavy artillery of facts with which he has bombarded Teutonism for decades before the war.[78] As a fact, Mr. Belloc is a more industrious historian than Carlyle; and "Q" a far more traditional disciple of culture than Kingsley.[79] But there is a simple test to show that such Teutonism is a

77. Sir Arthur Thomas Quiller-Couch (1863–1944), who also wrote under the pseudonym "Q," was a prolific author and a professor of English at Cambridge. In Chapter IX of *On the Art of Writing* (1916) he wrote:

> Dane, Norman, Frisian, French Huguenot—they all come in. And will you refuse a hearing when I claim that the Roman came in too? Bethink you how deeply Rome engraved itself on this island and its features.... I see a people which for four hundred years was permeated by Rome. If you insist on its being a Teutonic people (which I flatly deny) then you have one which alone of Teutonic peoples has inherited the Roman gift of consolidating conquest, of colonising in the wake of its armies; of driving the road, bridging the ford, bringing the lawless under its sense of law. I see that this nation of ours concurrently, when it seeks back to what alone can inspire and glorify these activities, seeks back, not to any supposed native North, but south to the Middle Sea of our civilisation and steadily to Italy, which we understand far more easily than France—though France has helped us times and again.... I hazard that the most important thing in our blood is that purple drop of the imperial murex we derive from Rome.

In a November 6, 1918 lecture republished in *On the Art of Reading* (1920) he said:

> There was, as we have seen, a time in Europe, extending over many centuries, when mankind dwelt under the preoccupation of making literature, and still making more of it.... There follows an age which interrupts this hive-like labour with sudden and insensate destruction. German tribes from the north, Turkish from the east, break in upon the granaries and send up literature in flames.

78. In *Europe and the Faith* (1920) Hilaire Belloc wrote: "That is what history has to say of the early Church in the Roman Empire.... It is history indefinitely better proved, and therefore indefinitely more certain than, let us say, modern guesswork on imaginary 'Teutonic Institutions' before the eighth century or the still more imaginary 'Aryan' origins of the European race, or any other of the pseudo-scientific hypotheses which still try to pass for historical truth."

79. In the *Illustrated London News* on December 15, 1917 (Ch. 5), Chesterton wrote, "with [Thomas] Carlyle the ancient tide has turned, the new flood has come; and it is a flood of flattery for barbarians, flattery for Germans, and especially of flattery for Frederick the Great." An English novelist and the Regius Professor of Modern History at Cambridge, Charles Kingsley (1819–1875) was the author of *The Roman and the Teuton* (1864), which, as Max Müller would note in an introduction to an 1889 edition, "produced a permanent impression on many a young mind." But by the end of the century, just Chesterton beginning his career, the tide in scholarship had be-

fad and not a fact. And, curiously enough, it is the very test that Mr. Powell invokes in favour of Teutonism that I should here invoke against Teutonism. He appeals to the "cosmopolitan" authority of historians like Ranke but by appealing to the authority he loses all the unanimity.[80] Nobody can pretend that before the war there were only Teutonist historians in Europe, whatever may be true of England. Fustel de Coulanges was a far greater historian than Freeman or Green.[81] **So small a thing was the Teutonic theory, limited both in time and space. Germanism never really spread beyond Germany, and England, and such colonies as copy England. Germanism is not really old even in Germany, and we may doubt if it will live to be old even in Germany. In all the other places named it is very recent, and it is already dead.**

Without hesitation, therefore, I should reply that *real* historical scholarship was Anti-Teutonic even just before the war. Only it was not the mode in Victorian society, nor (I will add) the Victorian Court. Therefore, a mere picturesque amateur like Kingsley was made a professor, while a historical student like Belloc would still only be treated as a picturesque amateur.[82] But it was not my original intention to urge against Teutonism the argument of real historical scholarship, because I myself, unfortunately, am not a real historical scholar. It was my intention to urge the popular or traditional argument, which I can myself value, but which is strangely undervalued. I say that if our society had a purely Saxon origin there would be far more Saxon evidences known not to the learned, but to the ignorant. **National tradition is tested, not even by what the village school-master can learn, but by what the village idiot cannot help learning.** Proverbs, rhymes, romances, ritual, dates, would all refer to our Teutonic origins; in fact they nearly all refer to our Roman origins. They refer at least to the legend of the Mediterranean, to the romance coming from the South. The child sang "How far is it to Babylon?" not "How far is it to Berlin?" We say that all roads lead to Rome, and not to Rugen. Our national emblem is not an elk or a walrus rampant; it is the lion from the South, and none of the wild beasts from the North. But the Red Lion on a public-house sign is a popular testimony quite as plain as the red lion of the shield of Scotland;

---

gan to shift. One writer explained the change, placing an emphasis on inherited racial characteristics of groups that Chesterton would ascribe to learned culture.

> This "Aryan theory" has entered deep into our literature. Charles Kingsley, for example, has drawn a striking picture of the Aryan invasion in his famous novel *Alton Locke*. We are constantly reminded of it in books and articles in the magazines and newspapers. Few authors and journalists even now are aware that of late years it has been quite discredited in science, not only by anthropologists but by philologists themselves. Max Müller, its chief exponent in England, seems to hold by it with the tenacious love of a parent, or, at all events, a foster father. [John Munro, *The Story of the British Race* (New York: D. Appleton, 1899), 19.]

80. Leopold von Ranke (1795–1886) founded the scientific study of history with its emphasis on primary sources. His first book was *History of the Latin and Teutonic Nations from 1494 to 1514* (German, 1824; English, 1887).

81. Numa Denis Fustel de Coulanges (1830–1889) was a French historian who opposed the influence German universities then had on the study of history, including racial views of history then becoming fashionable. Edward A. Freeman (1823–1892) was an English historian best known for his *History of the Norman Conquest* (1867–1876). John R. Green (1837–1883) was also an English historian. His *Short History of the English People* (1874) was one of the first to focus on the historical progress of one people.

82. Hilaire Belloc (1870–1953) was a personal friend of Chesterton, a fellow Catholic, and a gifted debater.

and the signs over the shops would have been quite as full of the South as the crests towering above the tournament. The three balls above a pawnbroker's come from Lombardy, and not from Lubeck or Lüneburg. It is the poor girl in the popular song who sings "If I were King of France, or still better Pope of Rome." It would only be a highly exclusive and even solitary gentleman who would sing "If I were a prince of Mecklenburg-Strelitz, or still better a professor of theology at Göttingen." In short, it is a question of a vast tide of significant trifles, flowing from the south to the northern provinces of the Roman Empire. Mr. Powell suggests that such cases are coincidences; but the truth is just the other way. My case is so true that I cannot show it to be true without showing it to be trivial—or, worse still, interminable. It is the Teutonists who pick out a few coincidences that can be put shortly in a school history. If I gave my list I should go on for ever.

G.K. Chesterton, "Our Note-Book," *Illustrated London News* 154 (June 28. 1919), 924.
US: June 28, 1919. Also published as "History from the Teutonist's Perspective."

HINDENBERG AND GERMAN GUILT

July 19, 1919

I suspect that the financial, scientific, and educational elements in Germany had all the bellicose vices of the Junker, and perhaps less of his bellicose virtues.

EDITOR: Chesterton hammers on a key issue being debated at that time: Has Germany really changed? If it has, there's room for leniency. If it hasn't, then yet more pressure is needed. Behind that debate is a point Chesterton stresses here. In speeches and deeds *after* the abdication of the Kaiser and the end of the war, Germany had not demonstrated any "proof that the brutality has been broken in practice." Sadly, history would prove him right. In July of 1930, Chesterton would warn that the eighty-two-year-old Paul von Hindenburg had one last, dreadful deed to do.

> When we are told that the ancient Marshall Hindenburg is now Dictator of Germany we suspect a note of exaggeration.... Hindenburg never was the dictator of anything and never will be. He is, however, the man who keeps the seat warm for a Dictator to come. Hindenburg has led us back to Frederick the Great.[83]

Germany would get the dictator that many Germans wanted. On January 30, 1933, President Hindenburg would appoint Hitler as Germany's Chancellor, a position that Hitler would use to become "Dictator to come." It should come as no great surprise that Hitler was a fervent admirer of Frederick the Great, referring to him in *Mein Kampf* as a "heroic genius."[84]

83. Maisie Ward, *Gilbert Keith Chesterton* (London: Sheed & Ward, 1944), 537.

84. Adolf Hitler, *Mein Kampf*, Ralph Manheim, transl. (Boston: Houghton Mifflin, 1943), 238. Those who think Chesterton goes too far when he blames many of Germany's ills on Frederick the Great, should keep in mind how eager politicians (including dictators) are to copy their successful predecessors. Frederick didn't need to write books arguing for Prussian expansion. All he had to do was successfully conquer his neighbors and be widely praised for it. After that, those who aspired to be "Great" like him—Bismarck, Kaiser Wilhelm II, and Hitler—would follow his example. You see something similar, although not necessarily in a bad sense, every four years as Presidential candidates try to convince the American public that they're like FDR, JFK or Reagan.

THERE is one aspect of all the talk about the trial of the Kaiser which seems to be strangely overlooked—at least, by most of the talkers.[85] It may be put shortly by saying that to deal with him as the devil of Germany does definitely imply that the devil has been cast out. Even Pacifists generally admit that Germany did behave at certain times as if possessed of a devil.[86] But it ought to be the Pacifists who pursue the Kaiser with special vengeance, since it was the Pacifists who specialized in the explanation that the evil was only in the Kaiserdom. Probably the Pacifists will not be consistent in this, or in many other things. But the most extreme opponents of the Pacifists are hardly more consistent. For they can hardly hold, as they do, that there was an equally evil movement in the whole German democracy, and then condemn the Kaiser for having imposed it like a despot. Anyhow, if the Emperor was the evil, it can hardly be denied that Germany has purged herself of that evil. **Whether a whole people can really get rid of its past by sending one egotistical old gentleman to live in Holland may be another question. That he is responsible for some wicked things is most probable; that he is responsible for many silly things is certain.** If I mean to speak of him as a scapegoat, I am not denying that he played the goat. But if we fall into the habit of talking as if he were responsible for everything, we certainly do so far relieve the Germans of responsibility. And when we reach that point we are met by an extraordinary fact.

For certain of the Germans in Germany step forward and accept responsibility. The first of them, the famous soldier Hindenburg, distinctly says that he did what was done by Prussian militarism, and presumably what was denounced as Prussian militarism. Hindenburg was not driven out of Germany; Hindenburg was not exiled to Holland; Hindenburg was not even deprived of his power, far less of his influence. He is, to say the least of it, tolerated by the new Germany; and he publicly identifies himself with the old Germany. I am not judging the old General's action; he may be acting generously. He may not be so black as he is painted by himself. I merely point out that in our view he is painting himself black, and it is all the blacker if in his own view he is painting himself white. In any case, the black and white are as plain as they are on a Prussian post. He says quite simply, in so many words, that the man responsible for the campaign which civilization condemns is not the man who has been deposed, but the man who has not been deposed. The man we have disarmed was innocent; the man still in arms was guilty. This is surely a very remarkable and arresting statement; and it is astonishing that so many fail to see it.[87]

---

85. For the "talk" about trying the Kaiser and others as war criminals, see: "Germans Who Face International Tribunal," *New York Times* (July 13, 1919), SM4. That article notes, "the melodramatic offer of the two younger sons of William Hohenzollern to stand trial in London in his stead." It mentions others in more detail, including the Baron Oscar von der Lancken, "a member of one of the oldest houses in Pomerania," who "is held partly accountable for the murders of Edith Cavell and Captain Fryatt." In the case of Edith Cavell, he not only refused to intercede on her behalf, "he prevented appeals from being sent over his head to higher authorities."

86. Chesterton used this same theme of a devil or demon-possessed Germany in G.K. Chesterton, "The Triumph of the Degenerate," *Everyman: Special Belgian Relief Number,* Charles Sarolea, ed. (November 1914), 10.

87. On Friday, July 4, a little over two weeks before this article was published, General Paul von Hindenburg telegraphed German President Ebert: "The signing of the Peace Treaty gives me occasion for declaring that I was responsible for the decisions and acts of Main Headquarters since Aug. 29, 1916, and also that all proclama-

Now it is a far more practical problem for the future whether we can trust what is now the German Republic than whether we can trust one particular man who is no longer the German Emperor. And that problem is very practically affected by the fact that a man can boast of having commanded the military methods now brought to judgment not only while he is still in Germany, but apparently without arousing any particular surprise or repudiation in Germany. If the Germans removed Hohenzollern and retained Hindenburg, what is their attitude when Hindenburg avows all the actions of Hohenzollern? Their attitude to the General must be a measure of their real moral change; and we can only say that, if they were so moral and so much changed as some suggest to us, they would probably tear the General in pieces. I do not want him torn in pieces particularly; but that is because I do not believe that they are much less responsible than he is. **I suspect that the financial, scientific, and educational elements in Germany had all the bellicose vices of the Junker, and perhaps less of his bellicose virtues.** I have always insisted that the moral disease was something highly modern—was not (as innocent people say) merely militaristic; and most certainly was not (as idiotic people say) merely mediaeval. What were called the new ideas were by far the most dangerous; and for me, therefore, the difficulty is not finally met when the new ideas have themselves produced a new Government.

Prussianism was full of that typically modern combination of moral anarchy with mechanical order. Not only in military, but in mercantile and other social things, Prussia made herself the authority and awful example of this general modern evil. For instance, no modern capitalists made more ruthless use of the low trade tricks of underselling and freezing out than did the German Jews who carried German trade round the world. This commercial practice is not mediaeval. A man was often hanged in the Middle Ages if he attempted it.[88]

---

tions and orders of his Majesty, the Emperor and King, concerning the waging of warfare were issued upon my advice and upon responsibility. I beg you, therefore, to inform the German people and the allied Governments of this declaration." "Hindenburg Says 'Try Me,'" *New York Times* (July 6, 1919), 6. It's easy to suspect that the general, having lost the war at an enormous cost in human lives, is trying to play the hero—and succeeding.

88. "Underselling and freezing out" meant that product was sold below cost to eliminate competitors, then prices were raised. Chesterton should have pointed out that these "German Jews" were usually employees of others. For centuries wealthy Europeans used a few Jews to do their dirty work. When a public outcry developed, rage was turned on Jews in general, who had to flee, conveniently allowing the wealthy to get out of their debts to Jewish moneylenders. That's why nineteenth-century reformers regarded anti-Semitism as foolish—it directed anger at the wrong people. Imitating the Czars, Stalin put a few Jewish misfits over his repressive machinery, turning anger that should have be directed at him on Jews. These 'bait and hate' tricks illustrate why Jews were often blamed for the evils wrought by both monopoly capitalism and communism, illogical as that sounds. Historically, anti-Semitism has been of limited political use in the United States. Because there was no group with a centuries-old stranglehold on power like the European nobility, there was no need for a scapegoat. But unable to end the Great Depression, Franklin Roosevelt—whose family was perhaps the closest the United States has had to a nobility—did direct public anger at financiers in ways that hinted of anti-Semitism, as noted in a footnote to the January 18, 1919 article. But desperately needing the Jewish vote, he did not dare blame Jews by name. Only recently have some in American politics begun to blame Jews for problems in the Middle East that existed for centuries before modern Israel came into existence, including the many centuries when Middle Eastern Jews were a small and ill-treated minority. Islam's xenophobia, its demeaning treatment of non-Muslims ,and its ready recourse to violence date back to its founder and are only incidentally related anything its Jewish and Christian victims might do.

When people say that Germany is no longer militaristic, what do they mean? That Hindenburg would not treat the Poles as Bissing treated the Belgians?[89] Hindenburg himself does not leave us with that impression. And the Poles are the permanent test in the matter, for, if Germans were repentant about anything, it must be about Poland. When people say that Germany is now Socialistic, what exactly do they mean? Do they mean that a German firm would not now use any of these corruptions of capitalism against any rival? Does it mean what I always meant by Socialism when I was a Socialist—that the very existence of profits in this sense has ceased; that there are neither rich nor poor in Germany, but only fairly paid servants of the State? The German commercial utterances themselves do not leave us with that impression. I am far from saying that Germany may not be the better for what has happened; and I am at the opposite pole from saying that Europe will not be the better for it. But the guarantee, for the present, lies in the proof that the brutality has been broken in practice, not in any proof that it has been dropped in theory.[90] There is only one good thing in all this vast scientific religion of success, and that is its failure.

G.K. Chesterton, "Our Note-Book," *Illustrated London News* 155 (July 19, 1919), 80. US: July 19, 1919. Also published as "Purging Germany's Evil."

CANNIBAL THEORY

July 26, 1919

Prussia was not, like the Christian States, tempted to do this or that injustice, and cover it with this or that sophistry. Prussia proclaimed a theory of continuous growth, by which a State was decaying if it was not expanding at the expense of others; in other words, that a State must always live upon other States.

EDITOR: Chesterton takes on a well-known socialist writer who has attacked his belief that there was something exceptional in the modern culture, history, and ideological roots of Prussia that set it off from historic Christendom. There is an important distinction, he says, between the practice of some evil, and the presence of a theory that justifies and even demands evil doing.

I SHOULD never dream of defending my books, well knowing them to be utterly indefensible. But I shall always take every opportunity of defending my opinions, well knowing them to be entirely correct; which is the only possible meaning of having any opinions.[91] If, therefore, I take the opportunity to say a word for some of my

89. General Moritz von Bissing (1844–1917) was military governor of occupied Belgium from 1915 to 1917. He signed the death warrant for nurse Edith Cavell. See the October 30, 1915 *Illustrated London News* (Ch. 3).

90. For the critical distinction Chesterton makes between practice and theory, see the third paragraph of the next (July 26, 1919) article. His point is that any nation weakened by defeat can, for a time, abandon a *practice* like aggressive war. The real issue is whether they've abandoned the *theory* that justifies that aggression. Had Germany's recent failure in war caused it to abandon its "vast scientific religion of success?" Making fun of his books as usual, Chesterton's "rambling pamphlet" is his *A Short History of England* (1917).

91. In *Orthodoxy*, Chesterton explained this distinction when he contrasted the old and new humility: "The old humility man made a man doubtful about his efforts, which might make him work harder. But the new humility makes a man doubtful about his aims, which will make him stop working altogether." Writing was his effort.

historical views, it is but an accident that those views were expressed in a rambling pamphlet of my own, which I was reluctantly persuaded to call a history. In answering this particular critic, who is one of the ablest and most suggestive critics of our time, there is hardly any danger, as it happens, of my reply being referred to literary vanity or irritation. For Mr. Robert Lynd, in his recent and brilliant book of essays, writes in far too generous a fashion about the literary accomplishment, and differs in the main merely with the theoretical aim.[92] And my theoretical aim is a thing I would always justify; it is the only thing about me that I think particularly justifiable. Mr. Lynd expresses a scientific wish to cut me in two; a sentiment familiar to many of my fellow-citizens in tubes and trams. "One half of him I should like to challenge to mortal combat as an enemy of the human race." That half of him has very great pleasure in accepting the challenge, even of Mr. Lynd, a gentleman of much more active and graceful figure. The other half of me will be only too delighted to remain in some remote tavern, writing unconvincing romances and nursery rhymes, to refresh Mr. Lynd after his well-earned triumph. I say that what I justify are convictions and not creations; but I must begin with another distinction which may seem to dissipate this one. I do care quite enough for my convictions to state them rather more exactly and even cautiously than Mr. Lynd supposes. In the case of several remarks of which he complains, as if they were wild exaggerations, it is really only necessary to look again at the remarks themselves, to see that they state their own logical limitations.

Thus I said that "the case for despotism is democratic," which is not at all the same thing, as he almost seems to fancy, as saying that a despotism is always a democracy. It only means that men have trusted a strong central Government not for its own sake, but for the sake of certain good effects on the whole people; and when Mr. Lynd says that those good effects are "not to be found among the facts of history," I can only say that, with my own exceedingly limited historical knowledge, I believe I could bury him in examples. An even clearer example of what I mean can be found in a phrase I used about the rise of Prussia: "The cannibal theory of a commonwealth, that it can of its nature eat other commonwealths, had entered Christendom."[93] He passes, with a graceful compliment, to the contradiction of

---

He needed to doubt it in order to write better. Opinions were his "aims." They needed to be defended as true or abandoned altogether, since truthfulness is the only reason to hold them. In that same passage he wrote: "A man was meant to be doubtful about himself, but undoubting about the truth." Perhaps this distinction between a fallible self and infallible beliefs is why Chesterton could keep the friendship of people, such as Shaw and Wells, whose beliefs he strongly criticized. Making truth objective removes the troublesome issues of personality. This paragraph also demonstrates Cheserton's marvelous ability not to take himself too seriously.

92. Robert Wilson Lynd (1879–1949) was a journalist and a fierce Irish nationalist who had a notable column in the *New Statesman* from 1913 to 1945. Chesterton is referring to Lynd's essay on "The Two Mr. Chestertons" in his *Old and New Masters* (London: T. Fisher Unwin, 1919). It's easy to suspect that Lynd attacked the "doctrinaire" half of Chesterton as an "enemy of the human race," because Chesterton was as effective a critic of the socialism of the *New Statesman* as he was of monopoly capitalism. Lynd preferred a politically harmless Chesterton who was little more than a clever "poet who juggles with stars and can keep seven of them in the air at a time."

93. Lynd was quoting from Chesterton's *A Short History of England*: "What was paganism in Chatham was atheism in Frederick the Great. And what was in the first patriotism was in the second something with no name but

this, referring to the aggressions of ancient Greece, Rome, and Israel, and then of "Christian Spain, Christian France, and Christian England."[94]

Now, honestly, I had never realised how exact and free of exaggeration my own statement was, until I read Mr. Lynd's criticism of it. I discovered, with considerable surprise, that what I had written was precise to the verge of pedantry; certainly much more precise, in this particular case, than Mr. Lynd's writing, or even Mr. Lynd's reading. I never dreamed of denying that Christian nations had *committed* injustices; that is why I said "the cannibal theory" and not "the cannibal practice." But I take it to be a solid fact of scholarship that in the Middle Ages, for instance, there was a thing accepted in theory by all Christian nations; it may be called "legitimacy"; that various princes, bishops, and republics had a right to their territory by a code common to Europe. The very exaggerations of it were the admission of it; the later development of the divine right of kings, for instance. It is a fact that Prussia came from outside this fixed framework; and it is a fact that Prussia preached, in theory and not merely in practice, a vision of modern mutability and incessant struggle for life, which denied that there could exist for long any fixed framework. I say "incessant"; and this is the point of another perfectly correct detail in my original description; that the thing is "of its nature" cannibal. **Prussia was not, like the Christian States, tempted to do this or that injustice, and cover it with this or that sophistry. Prussia proclaimed a theory of continuous growth, by which a State was decaying if it was not expanding at the expense of others; in other words, that a State must always live upon other States.**[95] Finally, I have never denied that something more like this collision of tribes without boundaries may have occurred, though in a much healthier form, before there were any Christian States at all, or outside their influence—in Asia or Africa. Therefore, I wrote, again with almost priggish exactitude, "had entered Christendom," and not "had entered the world." Mr. Lynd pays a most generous tribute to the truth in many of my other statements; but I hope he will allow me also to thank him for having so flatteringly drawn my attention to the complete reliability of the remark which he denies.

If I differ from Mr. Lynd's criticisms about the past, I differ still more from his criticisms about the present. He strikes me as having a very insufficient sense of the modern malady of England; which is surely a regrettable piece of absence of mind, in a gentleman coming from Ireland. Thus, he asserts, as something self-evident, that

Prussianism. The cannibal theory of a commonwealth, that it can of its nature eat other commonwealths, had entered Christiandom." (London: Chatto and Windus, 1917), 194.

94. Here's Lynd's argument: "How finely said! But, alas! the cannibal theory of a commonwealth existed long before Chatham and Frederick the Great. The instinct to exploit is one of the most venerable instincts of the human race, whether in individual men or in nations of men; and ancient Hebrew and ancient Greek and ancient Roman had exhausted the passion of centuries in obedience to it before the language spoken either by Chatham or by Frederick was born. Christian Spain, Christian France, and Christian England had not in this matter disowned the example of their Jewish and Pagan forerunners."

95. As Hitler put it: "For Germany, consequently, the only possibility for carrying out a healthy territorial policy lay in the acquisition of new land in Europe itself." *Mein Kampf* (Boston: Houghton Mifflin, 1943), 139.

I can only talk of a governing class if I admit that it has continually grown larger.[96] I admit nothing of the sort; and I affirm the exact contrary. If he had said that the governing class has grown looser, I might agree with him.

In almost any department of power, it can be shown that the limitation has largely remained stationary; but where it has altered, has actually narrowed. In land it has mostly remained stationary; that is, England is still a country of great landlords. If anything it is a country of greater landlords—that is, of fewer landlords; anyhow, it is certainly not one of more freeholders. In commerce, there was a time when England might be called a nation of shopkeepers, in the sense that many small shops made up the working force of the whole society. It is now a nation of a few big shops. In politics there was a time when considerable decision and discretion belonged to all the Commons in Parliament assembled; when it was worth while to persuade them personally with eloquence or privately with bribes. It was so down to the nineteenth-century Parliaments where the Governments of Palmerston or Gladstone could be overthrown by their own supporters.[97] Power passed from the Parliament to the Government. It narrowed from the Government to the Cabinet. It narrowed from the Cabinet to the War Cabinet. And he tells me, with the intellectual courage of his race, that I shall at least agree that a governing class has grown larger and freer.

G.K. Chesterton, "Our Note-Book," *Illustrated London News* 155 (July 26, 1919), 128.
US: July 26, 1919. Also published as "Defending My Historical Views."

LUDENDORFF'S FRANCS-TIREURS

September 13, 1919

The root of this, as of all other realities involved, is in one fundamental fact: that Prussia really came from outside Europe, just as Turkey really came from outside Europe. She has not been inside our civilisation from the first; she was a thing of ancient barbarism modernised in a hurry.

EDITOR: Since this article focuses on the fiercely debated role of the Belgian *franc-tireur* (plural *francs-tireurs*) in World War I, it might be good to understand the meaning and history of the term. In its oldest meaning *Franc* referred to the Franks, who were a Germanic tribe that conquered parts of northern France as the Roman Empire collapsed. Because they were a free people ruling over a subjected population, it acquired a sense of being free. In addition, because many of the Franks were warriors, it carried a military flavor. Finally when the Franks fought in the Crusades, it became

96. Robert Lynd: "This theory of history, as being largely the story of the evolution of the 'governing class,' is an extremely interesting and even 'fruitful' theory. But it is purely fantastic unless we bear in mind that the governing class has been continually compelled to enlarge itself, and that its tendency is reluctantly to go on doing so until in the end it will be coterminous with the 'governed class.'" Lynd argued that the "governing class" was larger in the sense that the doors of power were now open to more groups. For Chesterton, that merely meant that "the governing class has grown looser." Power was no longer confined to a landed aristocracy, so a Cockney could own a large chain of fish and chips shops or sit in the Cabinet. But Chesterton stresses that fewer people now own farms or shops. They have become employees rather than "freeholders." In government, power had become so concentrated that fewer people could shape policy "personally with eloquence or privately with bribes."

97. Henry Temple, 3rd Viscount Palmerston (1784–1865), was forced to step down in 1858 when his own party did not support him in a bill widening the franchise. William Gladstone (1809–1898) had to step down from his third term as Prime Minister because his party split over an 1886 bill giving home rule to Ireland.

a synonym for Crusader, meaning someone who fights for a great cause. *Tireur,* which refers to someone who carries a gun, fit well with *Franc*, giving a combined meaning of someone who has freely taken up arms, fighting for something he believes in, as opposed to a professional soldier, who obeys orders, or a mercenary, who fights for money. It roughly corresponds to the *militia* in the U.S. Bill of Rights, that is someone who carries arms in defense of his home and community. As you might expect, Chesterton's liking for *francs-tireurs* would be as strong as a Prussian's loathing.

During the wars following the French Revolution, the *francs-tireurs* were a light infantry organized outside the regular army. The fact that the related Spanish *francotirador* and Portuguese *franco-atirador* mean sharpshooter suggest that some units may have had special skills much like England's long bow archers in past centuries.

The *francs-tieurs* who created the controversy did not arise until late 1860s when rifle clubs with that name began to form in eastern France, inspired by the recent aggressive behavior of Prussia. They practiced shooting with rifles, elected their own officers, and resisted all efforts to merge them into the regular army, creating the same tensions that surround independent militias in the United States.

The Franco-Prussian War of 1870 demonstrated that their fears were justified. During the war, the French tried to merge the *franc-tieurs* into their regular army, but met with resistance, because these men preferred to operate on their own in small units close to their homes. Their existence infuriated the Germans, who invoked the letter of the laws of war, executing those they caught armed and without uniforms, much as they would do in World War I. The actual harm *francs-tiers* did was small, under a thousand casualties, and they did not prevent a single German victory. But because they could attack anywhere, even far behind German lines, they tied down a much larger force. It is also easy to suspect that the Prussians, with their love for uniforms, order and discipline, did not like soldiers who displayed none of those traits.

The Belgian *francs-tiers* under German occupation in World War I were like their French neighbors, and the Germans were responding just as harshly as they had before. When Chesterton suggests that the Germans may not have learned anything about right and wrong from World War I, he could have also pointed out that they had learned nothing from the Franco-Prussian War.

As an editorial comment, it might help to suggest that the wider context of the fighting is perhaps the best way to determine if *francs-tieurs* are legitimate soldiers entitled to the same treatment as prisoners of war, or whether they can shot as the Germans did. Chesterton describes the context that makes them a soldier in this article: "a free man, who fights to defend his own farm or family against foreign aggressors, but who does not happen to possess certain badges and articles of clothing."[98] Such a solder is not fighting in ways that increase civilian casualties. Those civilians are his family, friends and neighbors—the very people he is defending. That contrasts dramatically with situations where the tactics or lack of a uniform are deliberately intended to target or draw fire on innocent civilians, either to hamper a more ethical enemy or to generate unfavorable coverage in a press that's often clueless about these darker motivations. In such situations, the combatants are most emphatically not *francs-tieurs* and not only can legitimately be dealt with harshly, they should and must be treated that way rather than as legitimate prisoners of war. Rather than protecting civilians,

98. Chesterton mentioned this uniformless fighting in the early stages of the war on September 12, 1914 (Ch. 2).

they deliberately use them as targets or shields. They aren't *francs-tireurs*. They aren't militia. They aren't even militants, whatever that means. They're terrorists and should be treated as such.

Ludendorff has written a book to explain that he took the field "with chivalrous and humane conceptions of warfare"; and that he was largely responsible for the unrestricted submarine warfare against small and neutral boats.[99] Those two facts will be sufficient food for any mind approaching it merely with an appetite for humour. But there is one detail in his declaration which has a certain serious historical interest. The passage about his humane and chivalrous feelings occurs, of all places in the world, in the account of the invasion of Belgium. And I am delighted to say that what shocked Ludendorff's humanity and chivalry was the conduct of the Belgians in being invaded. In the face of the facts, attested ten times over, about the crowds of Belgians shot down practically without inquiry, he repeats his lesson to the effect that only men found shooting were shot. And being shot by Belgians was the only thing in Belgium that shocked his chivalric humanitarianism. "This *franc-tireur* warfare was bound to disgust any soldier. My soldierly spirit suffered bitter disillusion."

It is astounding how clumsy Prussians are at this sort of thing. Ludendorff cannot be a fool, at any rate, at his own trade; for his military measures were often very effective. But without being a fool when he effects his measures, he becomes a most lurid and lamentable fool when he justifies them. For in fact he could not have chosen a more unfortunate example. A *franc-tireur* is emphatically *not* a person whose warfare is bound to disgust any soldier. He is emphatically not a type about which a general soldierly spirit feels any bitterness. He is not a perfidious or barbarous or fantastically fiendish foe. On the contrary, a *franc-tireur* is generally a man for whom any generous soldier would be sorry, as he would for an honourable prisoner of war. What is a *franc-tireur*? A *franc-tireur* is a free man, who fights to defend his own farm or family against foreign aggressors, but who does not happen to possess certain badges and articles of clothing catalogued by Prussia in 1870. In other words, a *franc-tireur* is you or I or any other healthy man who found himself, when attacked, in accidental possession of a gun or pistol, and not in accidental possession of a particular cap or a particular pair of trousers. The distinction is not a moral distinction at all, but a crude and recent official distinction made by the militarism of Potsdam. If Ludendorff had said that he was forced to carry it out because it was imposed by

99. General Erich Ludendorff (1865–1937) was Germany's chief military strategist and its commander-in-chief on the Western Front at the end of the war. Chesterton refers to his 1919, two-volume *Meine Kriegserinnerungen, 1914-1918*, which was translated that same year and published in London by Hutchinson as *My War Memories, 1914–1918* and in New York by Harper as *Ludendorff's Own Story, August 1914–November 1918*. Undisturbed by the enormous casualties of a war he had led and lost, Ludendorff scrambled to profit from the book's sales overseas, and was quoted saying: "Well, I have fought the world for four years on a much more serious matter; so I can easily hold out for a while against it till it comes to my terms in this instance." He won that particular war of greed. English-language sales alone earned him 2.5 million marks, and sales in other countries earned another million marks. George Renwick, "German War Lords Get Rich by Writing," *New York Times* (December 31, 1919), 2. It's unlikely that Chesterton was surprised when Ludendorff supported Hitler in his rise to power.

the militarism of Potsdam, he would be perfectly right, and entitled to respect as a soldier doing his duty. When he says that his soldierly spirit suffered bitter disillusion, he is manifestly a sniveling humbug. If that was his disillusion, what was his illusion? Had he lived in the happy dream that Belgians would enjoy being invaded? Had he believed in his innocence that a peasantry could have no temptations to resist the license of a soldiery? Even if Prussians could think it wholly right to behave as they behaved to Belgium, they could not possibly think it horribly wrong for the Belgians to resent it. On all that side there is nothing but a hideous humour about the German general's hypocrisy. He goes through a country in which babies were spitted on bayonets and children found bleeding to death with their hands cut off; until at last he catches sight, in the crowd, of a Belgian carrying a gun without a uniform; and his soldierly spirit suffers bitter disillusion.

This is funny; but this is not the interesting point in history and psychology. The real point is not his attempt to deceive, but his inability to deceive. Having been told to contort his wooden Prussian face into a fine expression of sensitive and sympathetic indignation, he has not the least notion of how to do it. If he had said the Belgians tortured his soldiers, or betrayed their own soldiers, there would be some meaning in the phrase about things bound to disgust any soldier.

For the plain truth is that Ludendorff has not the most shadowy notion of what anybody means by talking about chivalrous and humane conceptions of warfare. They are all dead words to him which he thinks it convenient to adopt, and does not think it possible to understand. He uses civilised terms, but does not know how to use them rightly. It is as if a cannibal thought that our disgust was a matter of taste in cookery, and showed his culture by a few French words out of a menu. His soldierly spirit can produce a disillusion as bitter over a man without a helmet as over a child without a head. In short, the whole thing is a dull, elaborate lie; but the interesting part of it is not that the Prussian can lie, but that the Prussian cannot deceive. And he cannot deceive because he does not even understand what he is pretending to be.

There is nothing new or odd about this to anybody who knows anything about German history. **The root of this, as of all other realities involved, is in one fundamental fact: that Prussia really came from outside Europe, just as Turkey really came from outside Europe. She has not been inside our civilisation from the first; she was a thing of ancient barbarism modernised in a hurry. As the North Germans were never enough within the Roman system to absorb the true idea of citizenship, so they were never enough within the mediaeval system to absorb the true idea of knighthood.** Hence, while there may be great stories of Prussian valour, and certainly of Prussian victory, there are literally no great stories of Prussian chivalry. There are no legends about the great Prussian soldiers like the legends about Bruce or the Black Prince, let alone about Bayard or St. Louis.[100] Frederick

100. Robert the Bruce (1274–1379) was King of Scotland from 1306 to 1329 and led his nation during the Wars of Scottish Independence. He is mentioned on April 25, 1908 (Ch. 1), October 10, 1914 (Ch. 2) and November 3, 1918 (Ch. 6). Edward the Black Prince (1330–1376) fought effectively against the French. Bayard was a magical horse in *Chanson de Renaud de Montauban*. Saint Louis (1215–1270) was the only French king to become a saint.

the Great was certainly a fine soldier. Moltke was certainly a fine soldier.[101] But even those wriggling sophists who tried to pretend that they were just, never pretended that they were generous. Ludendorff may be a fine soldier, but he is certainly a Prussian soldier. And his capacity for any generous emotion may be exactly measured by his evident incapacity to simulate even a generous anger. In future it will be well for the pro-Prussian apologists, now more active than ever, to keep their propaganda in the hands of the more intelligent traitors of England, France, and America. If they are wise, they will tell the Prussians themselves to be silent.

G.K. Chesterton, "Our Note-Book," *Illustrated London News* 155 (September 13, 1919), 380. US: September 13, 1919. Also published as "Ludendorff and Other Prussian Apologists."

Civilisation as a Choice

July 10, 1920

The pessimists believe that the cosmos is a clock that is running down; the progressives believe it is a clock that they themselves are winding up. But I happen to believe that the world is what we choose to make it, and that we are what we choose to make ourselves; and that our renascence or our ruin will alike, ultimately and equally, testify with a trumpet to our liberty.

Editor: Chesterton has a knack for noticing that political groups most people regarded as radically different are actually quite similar in some important way. Militarism and pacifism, he points out, both believe that might made right, meaning that the strong should triumph over the weak. In this article he suggests that, "The optimist and the pessimist are brothers, one might even say twins.... However much they differ, they agree on one point, and it is much the most important point. They agree that man's course is marked out for him, and that man has very little to do with it." The usual name for that is fatalism, and Chesterton was not a fatalist.

A German professor has written a book to prove that the whole of civilisation is now in decay.[102] The recent struggle was once represented as the war that will end war; and it is now represented as the war that will end everything. Doubtless

101. German militarism sometimes ran in families. Chesterton means either Helmuth von Moltke the Elder (1800–1891), who was Chief of the Prussian and later German General Staff from 1857–1888, or (more likely) Helmuth von Moltke the Younger (1848–1916), Chief of the German General Staff from 1906–1914, and thus involved in the planning that lead to WWI. To the family's credit, there was a third Helmuth von Moltke (1907–1945), a great-grand-nephew of the elder, who was part of a failed plot to assassinate Hitler. In an August 26, 1941 letter to his wife, he spoke words much like what Chesterton had been saying a generation earlier.

> What will happen when the nation as a whole realises that this war is lost, and lost differently from the last one? With a blood-guilt that cannot be atoned for in our lifetime and can never be forgotten, with an economy that is completely ruined? Will men arise capable of distilling contrition and penance from this punishment, and so, gradually, a new strength to live. Or will everything go under in chaos? [Helmut James von Molke, *Letters to Freya: 1939–1945* (New York: Random House, 1990), 156.]

102. Oswald Spengler (1880–1936) published the first volume of his *The Decline of the West* in the summer of 1918 (revised in 1922) and the second volume in 1923. Although had begun to write the book in the more optimistic years before the war and the first volume was completed by 1914, when it was published it became an enormous success because it anticipated the post-war pessimism, particularly in Germany. His 1920 book, *Prussianism and Socialism*, offered as a partial solution for Europe's woes a blend of socialism and authoritarian government that Nazism would typify. He initially supported Nazism, but became disillusioned with the party and with Hitler, criticizing them in *The Hour of Decision* (1934), a book that sold well until banned by the Nazis.

something must be allowed for bias in a book coming from Germany. A defeated State will be glad to maintain that it has dragged down everything else in its fall. And when the professor says that the most civilised nations will collapse first, it is possibly not without a recollection that the most cultured, philosophical and real-world-politik-scientifically-studying nation has considerably collapsed already. Nevertheless, the professor and his thesis are not to be dismissed; or, rather, we could not dismiss the thesis, even if we could dismiss the professor. There is a disinterested and dispassionate case for his apparently dismal conclusion. And whether or no the notion is right, the neglect of it is very wrong. It is one of the possibilities that ought to have been faced, and perhaps avoided, long ago; and it would have been, if the mind of man had really been free. But the mind of man was chained to the chariot-wheels of a blind and brainless modernism: like a poor man running behind a cab. **The mind is not free till it is free from fashion as well as from tradition; and therefore free from the future as well as the past.**

For a reason that may be mentioned in a moment, I do not believe that our civilisation is doomed to go downhill. But I think it very probable that it will be forced to reverse its engines. More especially I think it may be forced to reverse its judgments. I have already remarked on this recently, and I am surprised that everybody else has not realised it long before. Half our history has been an explanation of our success. We were perpetually being told that mutton chops, or mutton-chop whiskers, or some such things, were the secret of England's greatness. We were constantly informed that the white man's billycock explained his success in bearing the white man's burden.[103] But if our progress ends in destruction, or even in any very difficult and dangerous experience, it will not be a triumph for men to explain, but a defeat they will explain away. We shall look at the mutton-chop whisker of the Early Victorian with a colder and even a more suspicious eye, free from the glamour of Early Victorian optimistic and progressive romances. We shall gaze on the billycock of the Late Victorian with something less of the sentiment due to a crown or a heroic helmet; seeking in it no longer the secret of England's greatness, but even, perhaps, some hints of the beginning of England's weakness. But, however this may be, I have two reasons for doubting this doom: first, because Christendom has gone through such dark ages before, and always shown a power of recovery; and second, because I do not believe in doom at all. **All this talk about optimism and pessimism is itself a dismal fall from the old talk about right and wrong. Our fathers said that a nation had sinned and suffered like a man. We say it has decayed, like a cheese.**

The optimist and the pessimist are brothers, one might even say twins. Certainly they are not opposites; the real opposite to both of them is something so opposite that they never even think of it. However much they differ, they agree on one point, and it is much the most important point. They agree that man's course is marked out for him, and that man has very little to do with it. They both believe that man is a machine, being started uphill or being started downhill. They both believe, in that

103. A billycock is a felt hat with a rounded top like a bowler or derby hat.

sense, that man is a motor-car. Or rather, to speak more strictly, they believe that man is the car but not the motor.[104] They do not believe that man is, in the literal sense, an automobile. The progressive always uses the fatalistic argument, even against the reactionary: he always says it is vain to regret the good old times and vain to resist the way the world is going. The reactionary always uses the fatalistic argument even against the progressive: he says it is vain to think of curing the modern disease of degeneration, and especially vain to think of curing it with the quack remedy of a Utopia. Thus the optimist and the pessimist do indeed differ from each other, but they agree on the fundamental matter of fatalism. They agree on what we may call the shape of the world, which they conceive as a wheel; or on the nature of the world, which they conceive as a fatalistic system. **In short, they may really believe very different things, but they disbelieve in the same thing. They disbelieve in the great dogma that "man is man and master of his fate."**

Most modern people probably do assume that we must be either progressing or retrograding, or so fixed as to be unable to do either. Most do take for granted that the life of mankind is thus, as it were, made good or bad beforehand. Yet this view becomes manifest nonsense if we simply transfer it from the life of mankind to the life of a man. It would instantly seem absurd to take a man at thirty, and ask whether he was fated to be better or worse when he was forty. Everybody would see the fallacy, if one school of thought said that young Mr. Robinson would certainly be a saint when he was middle-aged, and another school of sages proved equally lucidly that he would have to be a sinner.[105] Mr. Robinson, however young, might possibly venture to interrupt their learned controversy by asking where he came in. It might occur, even to his callow and undeveloped judgment, that his own decision might have something to do with his own destiny. And we all know, as a matter of mere common-sense, that nobody can predict whether Mr. Robinson will be nicer or nastier when we meet him twenty years hence. Certainly there is nothing in the mere passage of time to make him either nastier or nicer. Certainly there is nothing holy and heroic, and certainly there is nothing decadent and corrupt, about the mere fact of being forty-five. There is a comparatively short period of physical growth at the beginning, and there is a much shorter period of physical death at the end. But if these things correspond to anything in the history of humanity, it is to the earliest appearance of man on the planet, about which hardly anything is known, and his ultimate disappearance from it, about which nothing is known. I am aware that these statements would sweep away large libraries of evolutionary treatises and futurist novels; but these statements are none the less true, and indeed, self-evident

104. Hitler held this mechanistic view of history, writing: "To 'learn' history means to seek and find the forces which are the causes leading to those events which we will subsequently perceive as historical events." *Mein Kampf* (Boston: Houghton Mifflin, 1943), 14.

105. Chesterton may be alluding to a poem called "What Mr. Robinson Thinks" by James Russell Lowell (1819–1891). But the Mr. Robinson that's humorously mocked in that poem is so conventional, he hardly seems to think: "Fer John P./ Robinson he/ Sez the world 'll go right, ef he hollers out Gee!" It's more likely he's using Robinson as the name of an ordinary man, much like another author might use Smith. That's precisely what he does in a June 4, 1921 *Illustrated London News* article, where Robinson and Brown are two typical businessmen.

and unanswerable. So far as the practical changes in human history are concerned, they are like the changes in the history of any human being. The key to them is not in biology, but in biography. When the life, letters and table-talk of young Mr. Robinson are given to a gratified public, they may or may not tell the whole truth either about his secret drinking or his secret alms-giving. It may be very difficult to tell whether he was on the whole better when he was forty than when he was thirty. But one thing is certain: we shall not find the wisest uncle or the most omniscient aunt predicting with certainty, when he is thirty, what will be the difference when he is forty. And remember that even this parallel is an understatement. There are some physical laws modifying the life of a man; but we know nothing about any such laws there may be modifying that of a race. There may be a physical significance in the sixth or the sixteenth year; there is nothing but a number in the sixth or the sixteenth century. **When these men say the world is dying, they mean the world is dead. And they mean it is only dead because it has never been alive. The pessimists believe that the cosmos is a clock that is running down; the progressives believe it is a clock that they themselves are winding up. But I happen to believe that the world is what we choose to make it, and that we are what we choose to make ourselves; and that our renascence or our ruin will alike, ultimately and equally, testify with a trumpet to our liberty.**

G.K. Chesterton, "Our Note-Book," *Illustrated London News* 157 (July 10, 1920), 46.
US: July 10, 1920. Also published as "The Decay of Civilisation and Men."

War to End All Pacifisms

July 31, 1920

The Barbarian is very little affected by the flag under which he marches to slay and spoil. For practical purposes the Barbarian is the man who does not believe in chivalry in war or charity in peace; and, above all, who does not believe in modesty in anything.

Editor: Chesterton believes pacifism and internationalism are torn by internal contradictions. They oppose war in general, but often fail to denounce a specific war, as when "internationalism could condemn any aggression against anybody, but could not condemn Austrian aggression against Serbia." He warns that, "The Barbarian is little affected by the flag under which he marches to slay and spoil." Driven by pride and a ready recourse to violence, they convert easily to any cause that rationalizes their aggression. Communists become Nazis as Hitler rises to power, and with the fall of Soviet tyranny, Marxists become more favorably disposed to radical Islam.

During the war there were moods and moments when one felt it would be one of the blessings of the beginning of peace that it might be the end of pacifism. As it seems to be doubtful whether the peace has begun, it may be unreasonable to expect the peace-mongers to have finished. But as a matter of fact, the very serious condition in which the world is left reveals even more clearly a curious contradiction in all their pacifist propaganda, old and new. Now that the world does really wish for repose, and has some right to expect it upon a worthier basis, it only becomes the more apparent that those who were most eager to give it are least able to get it. And the reason is that they claim to bridge the deepest divisions of mankind, while there is a deeper division even in their own minds. They were not quite sure what they wanted; but as a matter of fact they wanted two incompatible things. They are not the less contrary because they can both be called peace.

The case is clearer and more admitted in the position and policy of America than in the position and policy of England. But the case is somewhat the same in both. **The point in each is that the power can be insular or it can be international: but it cannot be both. In other words, it can remain at peace or it can work for peace: but the two peaceful attitudes are antagonistic to each other. If it remains at peace it must tolerate war: and if it works for peace it must risk war.** But it cannot have the neutrality of the North Pole without being as remote as the North Pole, and we may add as cold as the North Pole. And it cannot impose a *Pax Romana* without fighting like the Romans. The Swiss were content with peace for themselves and the Bolshevists would probably like to impose their own peace on everybody else; but the Swiss Bolshevist, if so awful a being exists, must have a soul considerably torn asunder. This simple truth, as I say, has more or less been recognized as a simple truth in the policies of America. There were two possible attitudes—the attitude of the old American policy of isolation, and the attitude of President Wilson and his policy of Internationalism. We might say that it set the Monroe Doctrine against the League of Nations. But the English pacifists seem to be far less clear in their heads than the American pacifists; and seem to want at once to keep the peace without spreading it, and to spread it without defending it.

Thus we hear the same Labour leaders or liberal idealists generally, who cry aloud day and night for a universal law imposed by the League of Nations, somewhat inconsistently shriek aloud in horror at a hint of restraining Bolsehvist [Bolshevist] ambition, or even of driving Bolshevism back to its own borders. Just as they used to say, in the war, that internationalism could condemn any aggression against anybody, but could not condemn Austrian aggression against Serbia; so they say now, in the peace, that internationalism can define and defend all the frontiers of the world, but must not define or defend the frontiers of Poland.[106] Those who think they can prevent a new war from beginning might naturally have their attention drawn to a part of the world where the old war never stopped. Those who firmly believe in the

106. Chesterton is referring to the Polish-Soviet War, which lasted in all its phases from February 1919 to March 1921. The Treaty of Versailles had failed to define Poland's eastern borders and, even if it had, neither side would have regarded them as final. In an offensive begun in the spring of 1920, Soviet forces advanced on Warsaw. At the time Chesterton was writing this article, the city seemed likely to fall, an event that might have triggered a communist revolution in Germany and, as Chesterton suggests, given Prussian barbarism a dangerous new ideology. That's why Chesterton is so critical of "Labour leaders" and "liberal idealists," who call for a League of Nations to keep the peace in an abstract sense but "shriek aloud in horror at a hint of restraining" Soviet aggression. This shows that the attitude of appeasement that would do so much harm in the mid-1930s was already present in 1920. Fortunately, in the Battle of Warsaw, fought from August 13 to 25, 1920, Polish troops drove the Soviets back, forcing them to call for a cease fire in October. The Peace of Riga ended the war on March 18, 1921.

expedient of a League of Nations might naturally be supposed to feel an interest in the region where there are any number of nations and no league. If they cannot induce even the new nations to be international, what chance have they with the deep division and hardened memories of the old nations? If the nations born in the war have no sense of the horrors of war, what chance is there for the nations whose very patriotism is associated with long and prosperous periods of peace? If Ukrainia springs fully armed out of somebody's brain or out of nowhere, how can France be expected to put off the armour of St. Louis and of Joan of Arc? If Jugo-Slavia is born bellicose, how can Italy of the Caesars be expected to be pacifist? If the new Poland would strangle serpents in its cradle, what about the weary Hercules, the wandering Englishman, with his twelve-labours in the four quarters of the world?[107]

If we can no longer be content with our insularity, there can be no real doubt about the nature of our intervention. Here, again, the controversy is but a continuation of one of the vital controversies of the war. Poland is our only possible bulwark, not especially against Bolshevism, about which we can have what opinions we like; but against Barbarism, about which we have not an opinion but a living and everlasting experience. Bolshevism has exchanged atrocities with some remote Russian reactionaries, about whom we know and care nothing; but Barbarism has tortured our own brothers and friends with poisoned gas and deceived them with poisoned water. Bolshevism has done all sorts of things in the newspapers; but Barbarism has done them in the streets, even in the streets made sacred by the very offices of the newspapers. Bolshevism may be a storm muttering in the distance; but Barbarism has left its thunderbolts lying about in Piccadilly and the Strand. **In a word, Bolshevism may be one of the forms of Barbarism; it may be the most dangerous form of Barbarism; it may be the newest; but it is not the nearest.** It is not the form with which we are the most familiar or the side of the thing that has come closest to us. Nor is it the essence of the thing—the eternal element behind all the forms of it. It is no way bound up with a few Jewish demagogues any more than with a few German despots. Barbarism did not enter with the disappearance of the Tsar; nor did Barbarism disappear with the disappearance of the Kaiser.

The Barbarian is very little affected by the flag under which he marches to slay and spoil. For practical purposes the Barbarian is the man who does not believe in chivalry in war or charity in peace; and, above all, who does not believe in modesty in anything. Whatever he does, he over does, like the arrogance of a negro; and it is true that if you give him an inch, he will take an ell, or (as the famous illiterate truly observed) a hell.[108] That is the thing against which the long breakwater of Poland could alone protect us. And if Poland fails, the wall of the world has fallen.

107. As a punishment, the Greek god Apollo ordered Hercules to perform twelve seemingly impossible labors. Perhaps the best known was the fifth—to clean out the Augean stables in a single day, Hercules diverted two rivers to do that. Chesterton is drawing a parallel to how Britain labors to keep order "in the four quarters of the world." Since WWII, the U.S. has taken on Britain's role of maintaining order and promoting democracy.

108. Chesterton is referring to *A Narrative of the Life of Frederick Douglass, an American Slave* (1845) by Frederick Douglass (1818–1895), who was famous both for his escape from slavery and for learning to read. But there Doug-

G.K. Chesterton, "Our Note-Book," *Illustrated London News* (July 31, 1920), 476. US: July 31, 1920. Also published as "On Insularity and Intervention."

H.G. Wells and Nationalism

June 4, 1921

We can only turn hate to love by understanding what are the things that men have loved; nor is it necessary to ask men to hate their loves in order to love one another.

Editor: Chesterton offers a more practical way to avoid wars than the cosmopolitan World State of H.G. Wells. In an article in the spring of 1932, he will go even further in his stress on the need to learn sympathy with the patriotism of others, writing: "Real Pacifism will appear for the first time when the Pro-German forces himself to understand the cause of France, or the admirer of Bolshevist Russia realises the case for Christian Poland. Until that happens, it is merely turning the White Flag into something as provocative as the Red."[109]

Certain casual considerations have crossed my mind in the pleasure of reading the last book by Mr. H.G. Wells. It is called *The Salvaging of Civilisation*, but it might well be called *The World-State*, being largely a plan for avoiding wars by a cosmopolitan commonwealth. I do not pretend to review the book here, or indeed anywhere. It is the glory of Mr. Wells's work that it would always need a book to review the book. But I would suggest one criticism: that Mr. Wells is hardly enough of a nationalist to reconcile the nations. Such a peacemaker tends inevitably to talk to them too much as if they were savage tribes being told to bury the hatchet. Now,

---

lass reverses the adage of his slave owner. Giving a black man an inch—the ability to read—is a "great good," he says, because it reveals to him the barbarism of slavery, even as it creates a 'hell' between master and slave.

> Very soon after I went to live with Mr. and Mrs. Auld, she very kindly commenced to teach me the A, B, C. After I had learned this, she assisted me in learning to spell words of three or four letters. Just at this point of my progress, Mr. Auld found out what was going on, and at once forbade Mrs. Auld to instruct me further, telling her, among other things, that it was unlawful, as well as unsafe, to teach a slave to read. To use his own words, further, he said, "If you give a nigger an inch, he will take an ell. A nigger should know nothing but to obey his master—to do as he is told to do. Learning would *spoil* the best nigger in the world. Now," said he, "if you teach that nigger (speaking of myself) how to read, there would be no keeping him. It would forever unfit him to be a slave. He would at once become unmanageable, and of no value to his master. As to himself, it could do him no good, but a great deal of harm. It would make him discontented and unhappy." These words sank deep into my heart, stirred up sentiments within that lay slumbering, and called into existence an entirely new train of thought.... That which to him was a great evil, to be carefully shunned, was to me a great good, to be diligently sought; and the argument which he so warmly urged, against my learning to read, only served to inspire me with a desire and determination to learn. In learning to read, I owe almost as much to the bitter opposition of my master, as to the kindly aid of my mistress. I acknowledge the benefit of both.

Douglass visited Europe (including England) in 1886–1887, when Chesterton was a London schoolboy (12-13 years old), so his attitude may reflect what he was taught in school. Chesterton's mention of "arrogance" refers to a belief that a person, group, or nation who is new to wealth, power, or prominence may behaved arrogantly, lacking either the forced humility of those in lesser stations (such as slaves) or the more confident but subdued attitudes of those who have held power for many generations (such as plantation owners or the English nobility). Chesterton believed some of Germany's 'barbarisms' were the result of its new status as a military and economic power. It had not learned the more balanced, civilized views that develop over many generations.

109. G.K. Chesterton, "Our Note-Book," *Illustrated London News* 180:2 (June 25, 1932), 1034. The white flag of pacifist surrender, he says, creates as much trouble in the world by refusing to sympathize with what the French and Poles believe, as the red flag of Bolshevik revolution does by threatening to take away all they own.

if savages can bury the hatchet, it is because it is something like a stone hatchet. It is primitive and brutal; but it is another matter to ask a nation to bury the sword, which heroes and judges have borne, not in vain. A man might fling it away in a mystical moment, as Sir Bedivere flung Excalibur.[110] But even Sir Bedivere hesitated thrice, and the nation may hesitate longer. But suppose, while he was hesitating, a critic came and told him that the magic gems were all paste, and the Round Table all rubbish. I think he would not throw it away, but hit the critic a great swipe with it. **Now, all this international idealism tends inevitably to the depreciation of nations. To avert national quarrels, men minimise national memories. It almost amounts to insulting a man in order to make him feel more friendly.**

The truth is that all this is a misunderstanding of the very nature of friendship, and especially of reconciliation. If two business men, Mr. Brown and Mr. Robinson, are rivals who hate each other, you do not unite them by merely mentioning an imaginary firm of Robinson and Brown. Still less do you do it by inventing a new portmanteau word, and calling them both Brobinson. It is useless to press upon them eagerly all sorts of printed handbills and prospectuses, in which the names of Brown and Robinson figure in a sort of monogram, interwreathed with decorative hearts and flowers. Even this will not remove all irritation. In short, in the case of any two men thus disunited, it is bad psychology to thrust in their faces an arbitrary prophecy that they will both be partners in a Utopian business that does not exist. If you really wish to bend yourself to the heroic and saintly task of reconciling two men who had a genuine and bitter quarrel, you would be wiser to begin at the very opposite end. It would be well to begin, for instance, with the fact that each man has a family, and that even his public irregularities are sometimes directed by his private affections. The only palliation of the pettifogging pedantry which is so regrettable in Robinson is to be found in the unconscious faces of the nine little Robinsons. The only excuse for the gambling recklessness which we all lament in Mr. Brown is the persuasive charm which we all recognise in Mrs. Brown. These are the things which might conceivably and truly make men forgive their enemies. **We can only turn hate to love by understanding what are the things that men have loved; nor is it necessary to ask men to hate their loves in order to love one another.**[111]

---

110. Sir Bedivere was one of the first knights to join King Arthur's Round Table and one of the last still alive. In Thomas Mallory's *Le Mort d'Arthur*, a dying King Arthur's commands him to throw the sword Excalibur into the lake. Twice Sir Bedivere hides the beautiful sword and attempts to lie to Arthur. On the third occasion Arthur's warns him, "But now go again lightly, for thy long tarrying putteth me in great jeopardy of my life, for I have taken cold. And but if thou do now as I bid thee, if ever I may see thee, I shall slay thee with mine own hands; for thou wouldst for my rich sword see me dead." Only then does Sir Bedivere cast the sword into the lake.

111. Chesterton's reasoning in this article resembles the "little platoon" argument in Edmund Burke's *Reflections on the Revolution in France*. In that 1790 book, Burke predicted how a few individuals would manipulate the mass of ordinary people and pervert the French Revolution.

> To squander away the objects which made the happiness of their fellows, would be to them no sacrifice at all. Turbulent, discontented men of quality, in proportion as they are puffed up with personal pride and arrogance, generally despise their own order. One of the first symptoms they discover of a selfish and mischievous ambition is a profligate disregard of a dignity which they partake with others. **To be attached to the subdivision, to love the little platoon we belong to in society, is the first principle (the germ as it were) of public affections. It is the first link in the series by which we proceed toward a love to our country and to mankind.** The interest

1919–1922

And just as two grocers are most likely to be reconciled when they remember for a moment that they are two fathers, so two nationals are most likely to be reconciled when they remember (if only for a moment) that they are two patriots. Just as Mr. Robinson can plead a sense in which he was a good father when he was a bad citizen, so at many a time during the past centuries the same Mr. Robinson would have had to plead that he was a good Englishman though he was a bad European. I do not at all under-rate the necessity or desirability of turning Mr. Robinson into a good European. I have dedicated a good many odes, addresses, petitions, invocations, and hymns of supplication to Mr. Robinson, in the patient hope of persuading him to be a good European. But I am sure it cannot be done by ignoring his feelings as a good Englishman, or the reasons for his strong internal conviction that a good Englishman is a good thing. **On the contrary, I believe we must see the intrinsic value of the nation before we see its international value to other nations.** We must see the man as lovable in his loneliness, as all the more individual for being insular. Before we see Robinson, as in a vision, in any haloed and transfigured form of Brobinson, we must have learned to see Robinson as Robinson Crusoe.

For we cannot in commonsense expect to succeed by bustling about with negative novelties, and telling the English that Nelson is all nonsense, or the Scots that Wallace is a myth, or the French that Jeanne d'Arc is dead and done for, or the Americans that Bunker's Hill is not worth bothering about, and, by thus insulting every nation, arrive at the mutual love of nations.[112] Whether or no the thing can be done at all, it cannot be done like that. Whether or no we are to have a world-state, it is certain that we shall never get it so long as its exponents despise the deepest sentiments of the most democratic States in the world. History will never deny that republics have been even excessively patriotic; and, whatever can be said against patriotism, no one will deny that it is popular. Chauvinism was a charge brought as much against ancient Athens as against modern France; and Mr. Hannibal Chollop

of that portion of social arrangement is a trust in the hands of all those who compose it; and as none but bad men would justify it in abuse, none but traitors would barter it away for their own personal advantage.

Today, this abusing and despising of the little loves that make for "the happiness of their fellows" by a "selfish and mischievous ambition" centers on marriage and family, the local community or (in Chesterton's example) the nation. But the alleged ideal—typically human progress, socialism, environmental agendas, or world peace—is often perverted by the means. For only in the "little platoons" of family, community and nation, can people learn to understand and respect the similar loves that others have for their family, community and nation. That may explain why some of the self-promoting champions of great causes have such sordid personal lives. They behave despicably at the national or international level, because they never learned love and respect in small communities.

112. Notice that Chesterton chose heroes from all sides. The victory of Admiral Horatio Nelson (1758–1805) over the *French* and his death in the Battle of Trafalgar (1805) made him *England's* greatest naval hero. William Wallace (c. 1270–1305) led *Scottish* resistance to *English* occupation of during the Wars of Scottish Independence. Jeanne d'Arc (c. 1412 –1431) inspired *French* resistance to *English* domination late in the Hundred Years' War. The Battle of Bunker Hill (June 17, 1775) played a key role in the American Revolution, demonstrating that *Americans* could engage in pitched battle with *British* infantry and inflict heavy loses.

was by no means too proud to fight.[113] The cock can crow with a red cap as well as a red crest; and the imperial eagle is not the only sort of spread eagle.[114]

That this narrow national bragging is dangerous I do not deny; but I do not think that the cure is to read the internationalist literature. I think it is to read the nationalist literature—of other people. If I wanted to teach English people to be friends with the French, I would teach them to read Rostand and not Rolland. It would be far better for an English boy to learn to understand *L'Aiglon*, and follow the sad flight of the eaglet in the track of the great eagle, rather than to follow that very dismal dove of peace which migrated to the Alps in order to say it was "above the mêlée."[115] A boy ought not to be above the mêlée but in the mêlée; only it might be of a more chivalric sort worthy of the tradition of its mediaeval name. It might be a mêlée in which the men calling on St. George had some notion of what was meant by the other men calling on St. Denis.[116] Now, men had this understanding, more or less, in mediaeval war; they have only lost it in modern war. No French knight denied that St. George's cross was a cross, or set lance in rest against it in exactly the same spirit as if it had been a crescent. No English archer actually wished to turn St. Denis into St. Sebastian. That narrowness has come with what is called the wider emancipation; with journalism and its free lances, not to mention its long bows. **And it will generally be found, I think, that modern wars have been ruthless in proportion as they have been rationalistic. It was not a love of Germany that excited the Germans to aggression; it was a universal scientific theory of the anthropological value of Teutons, and the economic necessity of empires.** In our efforts to get a world-state, we are only too likely to get half-a-dozen world-states, with half-a-dozen world-philosophies. It would really be more practical to have a comprehension and recognition of nationalism; or, in the only sane sense, a league of nations.

G.K. Chesterton, "Our Note-Book," *Illustrated London News* 158 (June 4, 1921), 738.
US: June 4, 1921. Also published as "The Intrinsic Value of the Nation."

113. Hannibal Chollop is an American in Charles Dicken's *Martin Chuzzlewit* and is described colorfully.
Mr Chollop was a man of a roving disposition; and, in any less advanced community, might have been mistaken for a violent vagabond. But his fine qualities being perfectly understood and appreciated in those regions where his lot was cast, and where he had many kindred spirits to consort with, he may be regarded as having been born under a fortunate star, which is not always the case with a man so much before the age in which he lives. Preferring, with a view to the gratification of his tickling and ripping fancies, to dwell upon the outskirts of society, and in the more remote towns and cities, he was in the habit of emigrating from place to place, and establishing in each some business—usually a newspaper—which he presently sold; for the most part closing the bargain by challenging, stabbing, pistoling, or gouging the new editor, before he had quite taken possession of the property.

114. Chesterton claims that people's attitudes are remarkably similar throughout history. Roman soldiers wore a decorative "red crest" on their helmets, while freed Roman slaves wore a red hat, which was later a symbol of the French Revolution. The same can be said of eagles, which can symbolize many causes, imperial or democratic.

115. There are several allusions. Edmond Rostand (1868–1918), a French poet and playwright, wrote *L'Aiglon* (1900) about the life of Napoleon II (1811–1832), who is the eaglet (he was called the Bald Eagle) and the ill-fated son of Napoleon (the eagle). Romain Rolland (1866–1944) was a Nobel Prize winning French writer and a famous pacifist who wrote *Above the Battle* (1916) and lived in Switzerland.

116. Saint George (c. 275/280–303) was a Roman soldier martyred as a Christian and the patron saint of several countries, including England. Saint Denis, who died about 250 AD, was Christian martyr and the patron saint of France. In 287 AD. Saint Sebastian, the patron saint of soldiers, died a Christian martyr pierced with arrows.

ARMAMENT DEBATES

November 26, 1921

There are a great many good arguments on all sides of these questions; and I think that in using arguments, as in using armaments, we should examine our weapons, and see, first, that they are honourable, and second, that they are effective.

EDITOR: Chesterton stresses that good arguments should not introduce extraneous issues. A debate about building battleships has nothing to do with whether building them creates jobs. The following week balances what he says this week.

I STRONGLY object to the wrong arguments on the right side. I think I object to them more than to the wrong arguments on the wrong side. I am afraid that this taste for intellectual justice is not universally understood. Most people have a moral sense, and therefore wish to be on the right side; but many do not seem to care whether they are wrong on the right side or right on the right side. Any sophistry will serve their turn, even if it destroys all their other sophistries.

For instance, I think Prohibition a piece of low, provincial persecution of the dirtiest and most dismal sort. I defy anybody to say what are the rights of a citizen, if they do not include the control of his own diet in relation to his own health. I know that, while it is servile in theory, it is simply snobbish in practice. I can testify by my own experience that even the persecution is only a persecution of the poor. Prohibition is a provision by which a lord may be as drunk as a lord, so long as the hall-porter and the cabman are kept artificially sober to look after him. It began with some colonial trick for cheating niggers; and it ends by treating the majority of white men as if they were niggers.[117] If it spreads we shall know that barbarism is returning.

Well, that is what I think about Prohibition. But when, for example, people use the argument against it that it increases the efficiency of criminals, I can see that such an argument is indefensible; as indefensible as the tyranny it attacks. It is argued by some opponents of Prohibition that the measure has produced a crop of successful crimes, a campaign of burglary and murder, because the criminals who used to be fuddled and inefficient are now lucid and alert. It is obvious that this sort of argument will not do. We cannot actually defend a beverage on the ground that it is bad for people. We cannot preserve a deleterious drug simply because it is deleterious. **It is an intolerable proposition that we should consciously keep a part of the population partially poisoned so that in their paralytic condition they are less likely to do harm.** Moreover, in trying to score a small point, it simply surrenders the great essential point. The case for wine and beer and cider and the rest is that they are good things, great and generous gifts of God, only liable to abuse like all other gifts. We cannot preach at once that wine makes glad the heart of man and that it makes weak the heart of murderers; that it inspires poets and depresses pickpockets. It is an unjust argument in favour of justice; it is an illiberal

117. This seems to be an allusion to British efforts to enforce alcohol prohibition in their African colonies.

argument in favour of liberty; it is an untrue argument in favour of truth; and such an argument I will never use.

But this attitude leads to much bewilderment. There is a somewhat similar case in the current dispute about the reduction of armaments, arising out of the naval proposals of Mr. Harding and Mr. Hughes.[118] It is objected that the scrapping of any sort of armament would involve an intensification of the tragedy of unemployment; and that therefore no such change must be attempted at any time or in any degree. Now, as it happens, my sympathies contain and combine, more than do most people's, the case for Labour and the case for Armament. I am what most Bolshevists would call a Jingo in foreign policy. I am what most Jingoes would call a Bolshevist in domestic policy. I have never believed in internationalism or cosmopolitan pacificism [pacifism], as do so many with whom I agree in supporting strong trades unions. I have never agreed with imperialism or capitalism, as do so many with whom I agree in supporting strong naval defences for England. I am sure that unless the country has sufficient ships we shall perish; and that unless the working class has sufficient wages we shall perish. I am by accident at the very angle of opinion from which to see these points simultaneously. I am in a position to see at once all the horror of unemployment and all the danger of disarmament. Unfortunately, I cannot help seeing also that the argument above-mentioned is a fallacy.

For if armaments were what their opponent assumes, mere instruments of torture or engines of hell, he would not be fairly answered by being told that the production of them was a cause of employment. I do not know whether any wood-cutters were thrown out of work when people abandoned the practice of burning witches; but it is clear that people could not go on burning witches merely to give employment to wood-cutters. I do not know whether there was a convulsion in the market when the manufacturers of racks ceased to have orders from the Government; but it is clear that the Government could not put some people on the rack merely to avoid putting other people on the rates. I do not know if the thumbscrew factories presented a forsaken and desolate appearance when all their bright and busy machinery had been abandoned; but it is clear that we could not in logic maintain the Spanish Inquisition merely because it gave employment to a large number of industrious torturers and deserving executioners. The argument for the Spanish Inquisition is tenable enough;

118. At this time, Warren G. Harding (1865–1923) was the U.S. President and Charles E. Hughes (1862–1948) was his Secretary of State. Chesterton would have found amusing how naively the better class of church pulpits in New York City responded to Hughes's call for a "naval holiday of ten years." At the [Episcopal] Cathedral of St. John the Divine, for instance, Bishop William Manning was engaged in extraordinary leaps of thought. "The peoples of the world," he said, were behind the proposal and "the very boldness of it is its assurance of success." He went on to commend the "courage" of the proposal and the "leadership" of those advancing it. In his extraordinary gush of praise, he failed to explain how it could be a bold display of leadership to propose an scheme that was both assured of success and adored by the entire world. Nor does he seem to be aware of a critical factor—that millions of Germans and Japanese did not agree with the scheme. "Hughes Arms Plan Praised in the Pulpits," *New York Times*, (November 14, 1921), 4. During this era, the *New York Times* often regarded the sermons of the city's liberal Episcopal clergy as if they were the voice of God. In this article, Episcopalian bishops were given some 14 column inches compared to less than an inch each to remarks by Catholic and Methodist leaders.

but it is the argument for it as defending a faith, not as providing a wage.[119] The argument for the British Navy is tenable enough; but it is the argument for it as defending a nation, not as distributing wages. I personally do not think the argument arises; because I do not think that a battle-ship is a thing as monstrous and exceptional as a torture-engine. But if a man does think it so, he is justified in wishing to destroy it. And whatever else such men do, it is their duty to distinguish their ideas clearly and to state them honestly. If a man wishes to provide employment, he should say he wishes to provide employment, and not take cover under the excuse that we have to build battle-ships. If he wishes to provide battle-ships, he should say so, and not take cover under the excuse that he wishes to provide employment.

I have taken these examples against myself, to illustrate this vital need for logical loyalty and responsibility. They are against myself, in the sense of being against my own side, or at least against certain arguments on my own side. In the one case, I am perhaps more hostile than anybody to Prohibition; not so much because it prohibits poor men from drinking their beer, as because it prohibits poor men from choosing their drinks. In the other case, I believe I am one of the few people who have been opposed with equal emphasis to the cutting down of ships and to the cutting down of wages. But I do not like the moderate drinker being muddled with sophistries to show that he is not muddled with beer; I do not like the navalist to fight unfairly with the enemies of navalism that he may fight fairly with the enemies of England; and I do not like the social reformer to leave his mind unemployed when he is seeking a cure for unemployment. There are a great many good arguments on all sides of these questions; and I think that in using arguments, as in using armaments, we should examine our weapons, and see, first, that they are honourable, and second, that they are effective.

G.K. Chesterton, "Our Note-Book," *Illustrated London News* 159 (November 26, 1921), 710. US: November 26, 1921. Also published as "Prohibition and Disarmament: An Analogy."

Agreeing to War

December 3, 1921

Peace-makers persist in talking as if war were a thing to be judged on its own merits; as if it were a question of what everybody should do, instead of a question of what somebody should do when confronted with the very annoying fact of the existence of somebody else.

Editor: Chesterton corrects a "false impression" left by his previous week's article and explains why pacifist dreams are unlikely to ever be fulfilled. Notice his telling comparison of war with burglary: "We can lump the theft and the thief and the thief-taker and the cry of 'Stop Thief!' all together, if we choose, and cover the whole tangle of contradictions with the one word, 'War.' But calling it by a single word does not make it a simple thing."

119. Chesterton isn't agreeing with the torture of the Spanish Inquisition, since two sentences later he calls it "monstrous." He's merely pointing out that arguments for "defending a faith" or "defending a nation" are "tenable"—meaning can be defended—without bringing up issues such as jobs.

People are professing nowadays that it is perfectly easy to love their enemies, so long as they are not asked to be just even to their friends. Love, of which the great mystics made a most divine and even terrible secret, has become a most dreary and vulgar platitude. But justice, especially intellectual justice, is still as unfashionable as any virtue could wish to be. In a recent article I tried the experiment of an exercise in equity; by giving a case of an unfair argument against people I heartily dislike, the cosmopolitan pacifists, and in favour of people with whom I warmly sympathise, the discontented proletariat. But the very fancy of thus arguing against oneself is so unfamiliar to myself and most modern people that it is very difficult to do without being misunderstood. On re-reading what I wrote, I fear I may have given a false impression of what I think both about disarmament and unemployment. I think something could be done in naval disarmament; but I think that to do it hastily and sweepingly would be equally unjust to national defence and native labour; that is, to England and to Englishmen. But then I do not think defence is indefensible. I only said that those who think armaments indefensible could not be expected to maintain them as merely artificial means of providing employment. And, for the rest, I think we shall not get the good of disarmament until we have thought a little more clearly about the nature of arms.

The present problem of war is that men do not deal with the difficulty because they do not see it. When they talk about war, and especially when they talk against war, they still talk of it as if it were an institution, and even a co-operative institution. They talk as if it were the product of agreement, instead of being the product of disagreement. **They talk as if several nations agreed to have war. The truth is that, if they could agree to have war, they could probably agree to have peace.** The trouble is that they do not always agree about either. The fundamental fact is something like this: that there are certain operations of which our whole conception assumes the presence of a single consistent will: as when we discuss what laws shall be framed for a whole community. But there are other operations the whole point of which is to assume the actual existence of alien or antagonistic wills; as when we speculate on how often the laws are likely to be broken. Legislators do not meet to decide how many murders shall occur in the country. Lawyers do not meet to draw up a code about how many burglaries shall take place in the town. By legal hypothesis they are agreed on what they want; but these things, if they occur at all, will occur in spite of what they want. Murder is not an immoral institution which they have mistaken for a moral one. Burglary is not a bad thing which they have supposed, in their superstition, to be a good thing. It is simply the other side of the truth; that there can be other wills besides the will which we are ourselves, by hypothesis, formulating or directing. The law says that nobody shall burgle; that is, it conceives the vision of a world without burglars. If there are burglars, they come from outside that world and that conception. The general will not only does not want a burglar, but it does not want a policeman chasing a burglar. It is no longer a question of what the general will wants, but of what happens when something else happens to frustrate what it wants. It only wants the chase in the sense that it did not want the theft. **We can lump the theft and the thief and the thief-taker and the cry of "Stop Thief!" all together, if we choose, and cover the whole tangle of contradictions with the one word, "War." But calling it by a single word does not make it a simple thing. It is in its nature a complexity, because it is in its nature a contradiction.**

Peace-makers persist in talking as if war were a thing to be judged on its own merits; as if it were a question of what everybody should do, instead of a question of what somebody should do when confronted with the very annoying fact of the existence of somebody else. In other words, they will persist in reading history on the assumption that several people came together and said: "Let us have a war." If society as a whole says anything about war or burglary, of course it can only say that there should be none. But the individual, as distinct from the society, must have some morality about what he ought to do when another individual is in fact a burglar. And the case is exactly the same between an individual nation and the society of nations.

Now, it is perfectly rational to say on this basis that the society of nations could impose peace on individual nations. It could; at least to the extent to which it is imposed on individual citizens, especially burglars. Whether such a World State would be as democratic as the free nations, whether such a peace might not be a slavery worse than war, is another problem altogether. Peace could be thus imposed; only unfortunately the peace-makers are the very last people who would consent to impose it. It is the idealistic internationalists, more than anybody else, who refuse the only method by which it would be possible to establish this international ideal. It is the pacifists, more than anybody else, who would prevent the only working plan of peace. And the cause of this is surely clear enough. The idealists who insist on peace also insist on pardon. Their desire for pardon and for peace are doubtless both founded on the same moral spirit; and it is doubtless a perfectly sincere and humane moral spirit. But in the light of their own comparison with law and order, their peace and pardon are not a consistent policy. Their peace and pardon are almost a contradiction in terms. Nothing is more certain than that the rule which prevents burglary and murder is not founded on pardon. Nothing is more certain than that law and order are founded on what they call vindictiveness. When they call the French, for instance, vindictive against Prussia, they seem to forget that their own World State, on their own assumptions and admissions, would have to be vindictive against Prussia.

A multitude of people are marking time by repeating the phrase "We no longer settle our private quarrels by duels." Apparently they cannot go on to ask themselves what we do instead. We do not let bygones be bygones: we set detectives to trace them back as far as possible into the days gone by. We do not let sleeping dogs lie: we set judges and executioners to give the dog a bad name and hang him. **If a private person had done England a thousandth part of what the Prussian did in Europe,**

there would be no talk of pardon or even of release from penal servitude. The international idealist may answer that there is no comparison between a person and a whole people. Possibly not; but it is his comparison, not mine. If he may compare a public war to a private duel, why may not I compare a public aggression to a private crime? All that their comparison shows is what hardly needs showing. It is that a man will be protected, either by the axe of his country's law or by the sword at his side. He will not consent to blunt the axe and break the sword, at the same time and for the same reason.

G.K. Chesterton, "Our Note-Book," *Illustrated London News* 159 (December 3, 1921), 746. US: December 3, 1921. Also published as "Some Thoughts on War and Armaments."

A Boy's Bow

January 7, 1922

For the modern mind seems quite incapable of distinguishing between the means and the end, between the organ and the disease, between the use and the abuse; and would doubtless break the boy along with the bow, as it empties out the baby with the bath.

Editor: In this delightful article defending a boy's right to own a toy bow, Chesterton explains how little boys ought to be protected and suggests that modern pacifist rhetoric could lead quite logically to the destruction of much of the world's greatest art and literature, as much of it is as war-like as a boy's play.

The arguments Chesterton uses here about a boy's weapons apply equally to recent efforts to prohibit some forms of 'hate speech,' while pointedly neglecting others. Why are Nazi writings, speeches and paraphernalia banned but not those of much more murderous Communism? In his biography of Robert Browning, Chesterton spoke of the importance of free speech, even when it seemed dangerous.

> It is not by any means self-evident upon the face of it that an institution like the liberty of speech is right or just. It is not natural or obvious to let a man utter follies and abominations which you believe to be bad for mankind any more than it is natural or obvious to let a man dig up a part of the public road, or infect half a town with typhoid fever. The theory of free speech, that truth is so much larger and stranger and more many-sided than we know of, that it is very much better at all costs to hear every one's account of it, is a theory which has been justified upon the whole by experiment, but which remains a very daring and even a very surprising theory. It is really one of the great discoveries of the modern time; but once admitted, it is a principle that does not merely affect politics, but philosophy, ethics, and finally, poetry.[120]

As with dangerous toys, Chesterton would have us fight dangerous words with healthy influences: "You trust to your private relation with the boy, and not to your public relation with the stone."[121]

120. Republished as the May 9 reading in G.K. Chesterton, *Chesterton Day by Day* (Seattle: Inkling, 2002), 47.

121. As a young boy, I carried a pocket knife to school, untroubled by any thought that it might be against the rules. It wasn't for protection, since none of my classmates would think of using a knife to threaten someone. As Chesterton suggests here, adults had taught their kids well. Knives were for a hundred boyish purposes, from cutting string to whittling a stick. But notice how some modern school authorities have gone down the very

It would be too high and hopeful a compliment to say that the world is becoming absolutely babyish. For its chief weak-mindedness is an inability to appreciate the intelligence of babies. On every side we hear whispers and warnings that would have appeared half-witted to the Wise Men of Gotham.[122] Only this Christmas I was told in a toy-shop that not so many bows and arrows were being made for little boys; because they were considered dangerous. It might in some circumstances be dangerous to have a little bow. It is always dangerous to have a little boy. But no other society, claiming to be sane, would have dreamed of supposing that you could abolish all bows unless you could abolish all boys. With the merits of the latter reform I will not deal here. There is a great deal to be said for such a course; and perhaps we shall soon have an opportunity of considering it. **For the modern mind seems quite incapable of distinguishing between the means and the end, between the organ and the disease, between the use and the abuse; and would doubtless break the boy along with the bow, as it empties out the baby with the bath.**

But let us, by way of a little study in this mournful state of things, consider this case of the dangerous toy. Now the first and most self-evident truth is that, of all the things a child sees and touches, the most dangerous toy is about the least dangerous thing. There is hardly a single domestic utensil that is not much more dangerous than a little bow and arrows. He can burn himself in the fire, he can boil himself in the bath, he can cut his throat with the carving-knife, he can scald himself with the kettle, he can choke himself with anything small enough, he can break his neck off anything high enough. **He moves all day long amid a murderous machinery, as capable of killing and maiming as the wheels of the most frightful factory. He plays all day in a house fitted up with engines of torture like the Spanish Inquisition. And while he thus dances in the shadow of death, he is to be saved from all the perils of possessing a piece of string, tied to a bent bough or twig.** When he is a little boy it generally takes him some time even to learn how to hold the bow. When he does hold it, he is delighted if the arrow flutters for a few yards like a feather or an autumn leaf. But even if he grows a little older and more skilful, and has yet not learned to despise arrows in favour of aeroplanes, the amount of damage he could conceivably do with his little arrows would be about one hundredth part of the damage that he could always in any case have done by simply picking up a stone in the garden.

path Chesterton describes, trying to ban a thing and representations of it. They punish children for bringing toy soldiers (with almost microscopic toy guns) to school as a part of 'zero tolerance' policies. If Chesterton were around, he would point out that to be really consistent these people must ban all pictures of weapons from books in the school library and any literature about war. Consistency is the "hobgoblin of little minds."

122. The English village of Gotham is said to have came up with a clever ploy to keep King John from building a road through their town or a lodge near it—the tales differ. In either case, the result would have been the same, burdensome taxes . When the king's men arrived, villagers feigned the most foolish of behaviors, such as standing around a tree to keep a bird from escaping. After the king's men left, shaking their heads, the project was abandoned. The villagers are said to have remarked: "We ween there are more fools pass through Gotham than remain in it." Others claim that tales of the "Wise Men of Gotham" really do describe a village of fools.

Now you do not keep a little boy from throwing stones by preventing him from ever seeing stones. You do not do it by locking up all the stones in the Geological Museum, and only issuing tickets of admission to adults. You do not do it by trying to pick up all the pebbles on the beach, for fear he should practice throwing them into the sea. You do not even adopt so obvious and even pressing a social reform as forbidding roads to be made of anything but asphalt, or directing that all gardens shall be made on clay and none on gravel. You neglect all these great opportunities opening before you; you neglect all these inspiring vistas of social science and enlightenment. **When you want to prevent a child from throwing stones, you fall back on the stalest and most sentimental and even most superstitious methods. You do it by trying to preserve some reasonable authority and influence over the child. You trust to your private relation with the boy, and not to your public relation with the stone.** And what is true of the natural missile is just as true, of course, of the artificial missile; especially as it is a very much more ineffectual and therefore innocuous missile. A man could be really killed, like St. Stephen, with the stones in the road. I doubt if he could be really killed, like St. Sebastian, with the arrows in the toy-shop.[123] But anyhow the very plain principle is the same. If you can teach a child not to throw a stone, you can teach him when to shoot an arrow; if you cannot teach him anything, he will always have something to throw. If he can be persuaded not to smash the Archdeacon's hat with a heavy flint, it will probably be possible to dissuade him from transfixing that head-dress with a toy arrow. If his training deters him from heaving half a brick at the postman, it will probably also warn him against constantly loosening shafts of death against the policeman. But the notion that the child depends upon particular implements, labelled dangerous, in order to be a danger to himself and other people, is a notion so nonsensical that it is hard to see how any human mind can entertain it for a moment. The truth is that all sorts of faddism, both official and theoretical, have broken down the natural authority of the domestic institution, especially among the poor; and the faddists are now casting about desperately for a substitute for the thing they have themselves destroyed. The normal thing is for the parents to prevent a boy from doing more than a reasonable amount of damage with his bow and arrow; and for the rest, to leave him to a reasonable enjoyment of them. Officialism cannot thus follow the life of the individual boy, as can the individual guardian. **You cannot appoint a particular policeman for each boy, to pursue him when he climbs trees or falls into ponds. So the modern spirit has descended to the indescribable mental degradation of trying to abolish the abuse of things by abolishing the things themselves; which is as if it were to abolish ponds or abolish trees.** Perhaps it will have a try at that before long. Thus we have all heard of savages who try a tomahawk for murder, or burn a wooden club for the damage it has done to society. To such intellectual levels may the world return.

123. Stephen, one of the leaders in the early church, was stoned to death in Acts 7. Saint Sebastian is said to have died, shot with arrows, when the Roman emperor Diocletian persecuted Christians.

There are indeed yet lower levels. There is a story from America about a little boy who gave up his toy cannon to assist the disarmament of the world. I do not know if it is true, but on the whole I prefer to think so; for it is perhaps more tolerable to imagine one small monster who could do such a thing than many more mature monsters who could invent or admire it. There were some doubtless who neither invented nor admired. It is one of the peculiarities of the Americans that they combine a power of producing what they satirise as "sob-stuff" with a parallel power of satirising it. And of the two American tall stories, it is sometimes hard to say which is the story and which the satire. But it seems clear that some people did really repeat this story in a reverential spirit. And it marks, as I have said, another stage of cerebral decay. You can (with luck) break a window with a toy arrow; but you can hardly bombard a town with a toy gun. **If people object to the mere model of a cannon, they must equally object to the picture of a cannon, and so to every picture in the world that depicts a sword or a spear. There would be a splendid clearance of all the great art-galleries of the world. But it would be nothing to the destruction of all the great libraries of the world, if we logically extended the principle to all the literary masterpieces that admit the glory of arms.** When this progress had gone on for a century or two, it might begin to dawn on people that there was something wrong with their moral principle. What is wrong with their moral principle is that it is immoral. Arms, like every other adventure or art of man, have two sides according as they are invoked for the infliction or the defiance of wrong. They have also an element of real poetry and an element of realistic and therefore repulsive prose. The child's symbolic sword and bow are simply the poetry without the prose; the good without the evil. The toy sword is the abstraction and emanation of the heroic, apart from all its horrible accidents. It is the soul of the sword, that will never be stained with blood.

G.K. Chesterton, "Our Note-Book," *Illustrated London News* 160 (January 7, 1922), 2.
US: January 7, 1922. Also published as "On Dangerous Toys."

WEARY OF WAR

May 6, 1922

The abhorrence of everything military is as abnormal as militarism. War-weariness is at least as deceptive as war-fever; both are delusions, and distort the reality of things.

EDITOR: Chesterton fears that a weariness about the long war, while understandable, would mean that the British people would quit thinking about the possibility of another war, preferring illusions to a less-pleasant reality. His fear is so acute, he calls for others to, "take up what position he thinks best, so long as he does not sleep at his post." Chesterton biographer, Maisie Ward, wrote of his attitude at this time.

> If all Englishmen had kept the same unwavering gaze at reality as Chesterton much of what he called "the rather feeble-minded reaction" that followed the war might have been avoided and with it the advent of Hitler. Particularly he opposed

> the tendency to call "Kaiserism what is now called "Hitlerism" and should be called "Prussianism." While agreeing that care should be taken not to write of German atrocities that could not be substantiated he insisted that there was no ground for forgetting or ignoring the findings of the American enquiry in Belgium which had established more than enough. These horrors, the bombing of civilians, shelling of open towns and sinking of passenger ships culminating with the *Lusitania*, were in the main what brought America into the war.... Here, as with England, Chesterton did not admit as primary what has since been so exclusively stressed—the economic motive.[124]

In the end, the Americans and British would be seduced by comforting rhetoric blaming the war on militarism in general and munitions makers in particular. That allowed pacifist groups to 'heroically' champion world peace by bashing a few harmless generals, admirals, financiers, and industrialists. It also left people unprepared for what would happen when Hitler gained control of a nation that still believed in racial superiority, military aggression, and 'might makes right.'

In a 1923 article, Chesterton would give another reason why so many became disillusioned after the war—they had too great a faith in the inevitability of progress.

> The disappointment after the war, including the disappointment of Mr. Masterman, seems to me to have been due to the very fact that the world went into it with a false notion of *progress*. We thought a man could fight to *improve* things; and especially to improve his own position. We forgot that a man may fight not to improve things, but to rescue them. He may fight, not to improve his position, but to save his life. It is not fantastically quixotic to say that he may sometimes even fight to save somebody else's life.... But it is unreasonable to expect them to be intrinsically improved only by being nearly destroyed.[125]

CERTAIN old buffers, not very distinguishable from old bullies, are fond of talking to the young about the illusions of enthusiasm.[126] They and others rather fail to allow for the illusions of boredom. **It is not merely a question of being too fond of a thing to see it impartially. There is also such a thing as being too bored with a thing to see it at all.** But the thing is none the less solid because it is not seen. A man is none the less shutting his eyes to the truth because he shuts them in unaffected slumber.

Now England is in this very perilous position touching peace and war and a number of international things. But the logical point, which seems oddly neglected, could be as easily illustrated from trivialities as from tragedies. A young fool falls in love, and almost immediately falls out again; and very probably has a reaction against his late romance. He does not wish to think about the girl at all, still less to be reminded of the sonnet that he wrote to her eyebrow, or the time when he treasured a lock of her raven hair. But he will be a greater fool than ever if he proceeds to imagine

124. Maisie Ward, *Gilbert Keith Chesterton* (London: Sheed & Ward, 1944), 344–345.

125. *The Collected Works of G.K. Chesterton*, vol. XXXIII, 92. From the *Illustrated London News*, May 5, 1923. C.F.G. Masterman (1873–1927) wrote *England After the War* (London: Hodder and Stoughton, 1922).

126. In the *Oxford English Dictionary* the most likely meaning for "buffer" is "a foolish fellow." In this case, their folly lay in a one-sided fear of 'enthusiasm'—a term that at that time was used like we use 'fanaticism' today.

that the girl no longer exists, or that she has not got any eyebrows, or that her hair is not really black but red, or possibly green. Because he is tired of contemplating her existence, it does not follow that she is tired of existing; or that she immediately ceases to exist. It is still a fact that she is black-haired, and very probably still a fact that she is beautiful; and these facts will operate without reference to his feelings. In other words, his indifference is quite as much of a delusion as his infatuation.

Now what he would be feeling about love most of us are feeling about war. There is a reaction against it as a romance; but that does not dispose of it as a reality. That we are sick of the subject does not make it merely subjective. **Men would be monsters either of heartlessness or heroism, if they felt at the end of those five infernal years exactly what they felt when the first volunteers were roused by the outrage upon Belgium. But though the feelings of men naturally change, they will still suffer if they imagine that facts change with feelings.** The facts would remain hard facts, even if the feelings were entirely healthy feelings. And it is not possible even for the healthiest men to be quite healthy in their recoil from such a strain. In fact, our phrase for such fatigue is quite correct. We may well say that men are sick of war; for this also is a sickness. **The abhorrence of everything military is as abnormal as militarism. War-weariness is at least as deceptive as war-fever; both are delusions, and distort the reality of things.** And that distortion just now is so mortally dangerous to England and Europe that, even in these idle jottings, I cannot refrain from setting it down as a thing as serious as it really is.

The newspapers are talking nonsense of the most deadly sort. For they are saying at once that England can forbid everything and cannot fight for anything. They imply that never again, whatever happens, will we go to war; being moved in this not even by any honest lunacy of Tolstoyan ethics, but by the mere emotional ebb-tide or natural reaction of which I have spoken. And at the same time they lecture the French about the dreadful danger of their losing the invaluable English friendship, and incurring the terrible English enmity. The French will not unnaturally answer that they can hardly be permanently restrained by a friendship which will always refuse to support them, and an enmity which will always refuse to fight them. What on earth can we do with the French, if we are paralysed at once by pacificism [pacifism] and by separatism? How can we influence the French, if we must always have a conscientious objection to any co-operation with their plans and to any war on behalf of our own? How are we to be the dictators of Europe when we begin to bully by promising never to fight? How can we forbid the French to act alone, if we forbid ourselves to act at all?

The French have had the advantage in the matter of never having been moved by mood or emotion, but having seen the facts of Europe in their solid sameness. Of course, they have felt the fatigue and the disgust as we have; but they have not acted on them.[127] They have acted on the facts and in the light of reason and their own interests. It is not so much fun to shout that France is in danger at the end of a war as at the beginning of a war. But it may be just as much of a fact that has to be shouted; nor is it by any means true that everything is over except the shouting. And the case against the pacifism of the papers, now they are in an anti-military mood, is still the same simple case which they themselves urged against the pacifists for five years when they were in a military mood. It is still every bit as true, as when we first told it to Morel or Norman Angell,[128] that we cannot always at once preserve peace and preserve justice, that whether we are peaceful depends on whether others are provocative, that we can never arbitrate if we always refuse to act, that if something is to be rescued it can only be done by militant energy and not by neutrality and nonentity, and that even that neutrality may not protect us from those who hold themselves at liberty to attack neutrals. All this is still true, though we did say it ourselves incessantly for five mortal years.

The English are a very moody people; which is one reason why they have produced so many great poets. **They are at present in a very comprehensible mood of being tired of war and disgusted with politics. It is very defensible; because war is very tiring, and politics are very disgusting. But this is a moment when it is very dangerous to trust to the mood instead of the mind.** Objective things outside us take no notice of our natural emotional reactions. Objective things are often objectionable things. But it will be very unlucky if they make themselves objectionable, at the exact moment when we are too bored with them even to object. Politics are a very wearisome thing, and politicians are very wearisome people; but this is the worst possible moment for them to do the wrong thing, merely because the world is too weary of them even to watch them. This is a very deadly and determining crisis in the diplomatic history of the world; and it is as essential that rulers of great nations should be right about it as ever it was in 1914. It is dangerous that they should be trusted if they are not trustworthy. It is more dangerous that they should be tolerated if they are not trusted. If, after making the effort of examination and vigilance, we come to the conclusion that they are trusted and trustworthy, by all means let us make whatever compromise they suggest. But just now it is sheer suicide to make the compromise because we cannot make the effort. It will be none the less destructive because we shall not be rushing on destruction in our fury, but rather relapsing into destruction in our fatigue. Therefore I do most earnestly think it the duty of any Englishman at this moment to resist, and ask his countrymen to resist, the natural reaction of indifference. I do not ask him necessarily to agree with me about the problem; nor am I expounding my own solution of it here. I have

127. Chesterton had a high regard for the French, which some ascribe to the half-French Hilaire Belloc. But during the 1930s, the French were at least as unwilling to resist Hitler's aggression as the English. They lost the Battle of France in six weeks (May 10–June 25, 1940), yielding to German occupation while Britain fought on.

128. During the war, Edward D. Morel (1873–1924) was a leader in the pacifist Union of Democratic Control. Chesterton mentions him in a December 11, 1915 article in the *Illustrated London News* (Ch. 3). Norman Angell (1872–1967) was a Labour Party politician and one of the founders of the Union of Democratic Control. He is mentioned by Chesterton on June 21, 1913 (Ch. 1) and May 11, 1918 (Ch. 6). For his views, see Appendix C.

always held, and still hold, that a strong alliance with France and Poland would give real peace to Europe, and gain real concessions for England. But apart from my own position, it is possible to warn a man not to allow his own to be determined by sub-conscious tedium. Let him take up what position he thinks best, so long as he does not sleep at his post.

G.K. Chesterton, "Our Note-Book," *Illustrated London News* 160 (May 6, 1922), 652. US: May 6, 1922. Also published as "The Present Anti-Military Mood."

IMPERIALISTIC INTERNATIONALISM

June 17, 1922 (excerpt)

What is the matter with internationalism is that it is imperialism. It is the imposition of one ideal of one sect on the vital varieties of men.

EDITOR: If the "honest Indian gentleman" mentioned in the first sentence is the famous Mahatma Gandhi, at that time in a British prison in India, then his mention in this article is particularly apt. For in an September 18, 1909 article in the *Illustrated London News*, Chesterton had written: "The principal weakness of Indian Nationalism seems to be that it is not very Indian and not very national." He went on to add: "But the Indian Nationalists whose works I have read simply say with ever-increasing excitability, 'Give me a ballot-box. Provide me with a Ministerial dispatch-box. Hand me over the Lord Chancellor's wig. I have a natural right to be Prime Minister. I have a heaven-born claim to introduce a Budget. My soul is starved if I am excluded from the Editorship of the *Daily Mail*,' or words to that effect." In this article, Chesterton gave his test for a true democracy.

> The test of a democracy is not whether the people vote, but whether the people rule. The essence of a democracy is that the national tone and spirit of the typical citizen is apparent and striking in the actions of the State, that France is governed in a French way, or Germany in a German way, or Spain in a Spanish way. Votes may be the most convenient way of achieving this effect; but votes are quite vain if they do not achieve it.

Indian Nationalists, Chesterton was pointing out, were acting as imperialists, undemocratically forcing British culture and traditions on the Indian people. Gandhi took that criticism seriously, publicly crediting Chesterton with his change of heart. In what appears to be the January 8, 1910 issue of *Indian Opinion*, along with a translation of Chesterton's article, Gandhi wrote:

> Indians must reflect over these views of Mr. Chesterton and consider what they should rightly demand. What is the way to make the Indian people happy? May it not be that we seek to advance our own interests in the name of the Indian people? Or, that we have been endeavouring to destroy what the Indian people have carefully nurtured through thousands of years? I, for one, was led by Mr. Chesterton's article to all these reflections and I place them before readers of *Indian Opinion*.[129]

As a result, Gandhi developed an Indian nationalism that was home-grown, although its exaggerated stress on *khadi* (homespun cloth), perhaps goes too far in

129. Mahatama Gandhi, *The Collected Works of Mahatama Gandhi*, vol. 10, p. 109.

the other direction, imposing a passing fad of Gandhi's on the national culture. Today, the primitive loom used to make that cloth is incorporated into India's flag, but its citizens sensibly wear clothes made on modern looms. (The rest of the article that follows discussed H.G. Wells' history of Napoleon and isn't relevant to this book.)

For an example of what may have been in the pamphlet that Chesterton refers to here, see the extract from Gandhi's writings in Appendix F at the back of this book.

I recently received a pamphlet from an honest Indian gentleman who has a new religion that will establish universal peace. I confess that the impression produced on my mind by the excellent Hindu humanitarian was that he might very well unite all human beings, if only all human beings were Hindus. But I hasten to add that this humanitarian illusion is very far from being confined to Hindus. It seems to me that exactly the same error is made by the most energetic and scientific humanitarians of the West—as by Mr. Wells and the upholders of a World State. **What is the matter with internationalism is that it is imperialism. It is the imposition of one ideal of one sect on the vital varieties of men.** But it is worse than the imposition of ideals. It is actually the imposition of indifference. If the internationalist were really the interpreter or reconciler of nations, he would find himself expounding and excusing the very things he is now denouncing and deriding, the militarism of France or the fanaticism of Ireland. To teach internationalism he must talk nationalism. He must throw himself into other people's enthusiasm; as it is, he is only saddling other people with his own indifference. Moreover, this philosophy always fails, because the peacemaker not only wishes that the special love and loyalty did not exist, but assumes that it does not exist. He ignores it, and his whole attitude becomes one of ignorance. His attitude can truly be called indifference, because he does not know the difference....

G.K. Chesterton, "Our Note-Book," *Illustrated London News* 160 (June 17, 1922), 890.
US: June 17, 1922. Also published as "Napoleon and the Family."

King Arthur's Legacy

December 16, 1922

Much of the dulness of modern history came from the idea of progress. For history must be progress reversed. If things have always automatically grown brighter and better, then to trace things backwards is to go further and further not only into darkness but into dulness.

1919–1922

Editor: In a 1950 letter, J.R.R. Tolkien said that he wrote *The Lord of the Rings* "to restore to the English an epic tradition and present them with a mythology of their own."[130] He was concerned because England's most ancient myths, a speciality of his, were only represented by a few literary fragments such as *Beowulf*, everything else having been lost in various conquests. Chesterton sensed that same lack, but blamed it on a different cause, the more recent loss of folk tales traditionally passed down from father to son.

130. J.R.R. Tolkien, *The Letters of J.R.R. Tolkien* (Boston: Houghton Mifflin, 1981), 231.

And all this fabulous and magical business about Merlin [and King Arthur] is important for a reason that has, perhaps, fallen too much out of sight. It is the profoundly romantic and mysterious element in the real tradition of Britain. It was familiar to our fathers, but it was largely lost to us by two evils: the Puritan industrial movement and the Teutonic theory of history. The first is obvious enough; and few will maintain that a group of Manchester merchants were in the habit of murmuring and crooning to each other in the twilight the cryptic rhymes and riddles of Merlin. But the other influence was really far more fatal. It killed English folk-lore by insisting that it must be German folk-lore; and, for whatever reason, the Germanic pirates who invaded the eastern coast did not really found much folk-lore in England. Perhaps there is no particular reason why savages from the coasts of Frisia should bring with them anything resembling the fairy-tales found long afterwards in the forest of Bavaria. But all these were lumped together by the learned under the name of Teutonic; and the upshot of it was that Britain lost her old fairy tales and got no new ones. The Victorian popular writers, like Carlyle and Kingsley, told us that our fathers worshipped Odin and Thor. And as we could not find in anything our fathers had handed down the faintest reference to Odin or Thor, we lost all interest in the way in which such things are handed down. The Victorian writers told us that the founders of our nation had been Hengist and Horsa; and as there were obviously no popular legends about Hengist and Horsa, we gave up looking for popular legends about anybody. It would have been very different if we had looked for popular legends about Arthur and Merlin. There we should have touched a living tradition that lingered down to the latest times like the legends of Oisin or St. Patrick. At heart England was quite as mystic as Ireland. For those who care for such terms, England was quite as Celtic as Ireland. For centuries there was a real tradition that Arthur would return; I never heard of anybody who wanted Hengist to return. But anyhow the moral is that there is a soul of England buried somewhere in England, though its burial-place be as nameless and mysterious as the grave of King Arthur at Glastonbury.[131]

Like Tolkien, Chesterton set about replacing this loss by retelling those ancient tales through more modern poems such as his book-length *The Ballad of the White Horse* (1911)[132] and "The Ballad of St. Barbara" (1922). And we close this chapter with what he said about the history that became the legend of King Arthur.

SOMEBODY recently asked me what I meant by a reference to the myth of Arthur; or, rather, a reference to the myth of the myth of Arthur. For in my opinion it is only a modern myth that he is only an ancient one. The chief difference between ancient and modern times seems to be that formerly legends grew very slowly, and now they grow very fast. See how fast the fable that all English things were German, and all German things were superior, spread in the nineteenth century, when it had been spun out of nothing by a few professors. See how rapidly the images of those two imaginary beings, the Missing Link and the Primitive Man, have become idols of the market-place. The old legends generally grew more slowly and always had more

131. *The Collected Works of G.K. Chesterton*, vol. XXXIII, 173–174. From the *Illustrated London News*, September 8, 1923. Oisin (or Ossian) was a heroic Gaellic warrior and poet described in the epics *Fingal* and *Temora*.

132. Included in *G.K Chesterton's Early Poetry* (Seattle: Inkling Books, 2004).

historical basis; and it seems to me overwhelmingly probable that the story of King Arthur had a very solid historical basis. This must in a sense be mere guesswork, for I am not competent to judge of the details; but I think I am as competent as anyone else to judge of the theories, in the sense of seeing whether they hang together and are inherently probable and consistent. Now the theory that treats Arthur entirely as a fairy-tale seems to me more fantastic than any fairy-tale. It sometimes takes the form of saying that there was some prehistoric Celtic god or other, who afterwards came to be described in more detail as a king in Camelot. I have never been very clear, by the way, about how this vague transition from divinity to humanity is supposed to present itself to human nature. A particular story of an incarnate god or a fallen angel one can imagine easily enough. But I am a little confused about how the mere act of the Pimlico populace continually calling upon heaven, in their human difficulties, would of itself become a story that a Mr. Heaven had lived in a particular street in Pimlico.[133] It seems rather more likely that a simple people would exaggerate a hero into a god, rather than deliberately diminish a god into a hero. But this is something of a side issue, and I do not insist on it. Anyhow, they say there must have been a Celtic god, and doubtless there was; doubtless there were many Celtic gods—too many Celtic gods for a fastidious monotheistic taste. I might respectfully inquire what had become of all the others; and why they have not all turned into Christian kings with orders of chivalry? And then the critics complete the confusion by saying, as a sort of after-thought, that Arthur may also have been the name of a king, but implying that this can have nothing to do with the idea of King Arthur.

Now all this seems to me mythical in the worst sense; that it is concentrated on myths and wholly careless of history. If we are studying a historical problem, it would be well to begin with the historical part of it; and if we want to know more, it is best to grasp what we know already. Now we do know as a historical fact that the beginning of the Dark Ages was a time when the north-west corner of the Roman Empire was ruined by barbarian invasions. We do know that those who successfully defended civilization everywhere became great legendary yet historic heroes; and that in this respect the story of Arthur is just like the story of Alfred. There was certainly a legendary Alfred as well as a historical Alfred; and every common-sense comparison would lead one to think there was a historical Arthur as well as a legendary Arthur. But the question is one of proportion; and the saving of Christendom by the heroes of the Dark Ages does seem to me a sufficient cause for so huge a legend: the last trickle of tradition from some lost Welsh polytheism does not seem to me a sufficient cause. There are a dozen parallel cases of Christian heroes; there are not a dozen parallel cases of Welsh gods.

Then we come to the old suggestion that Arthur was not Arthur, but another person of the same name. Here again people seem to forget that a legend requires a story as well as a name. A legend is *about* something; it is not started by a word, but by some true or false event. A professor centuries hence might be puzzled by the

133. Pimlico is a residential area in central London that includes Victoria Station in the north.

mere word "Wilson" in a record of our time; and be doubtful whether it meant Sir Henry Wilson the General or Mr. Woodrow Wilson the President.[134] But only the professor would be puzzled about the name; the populace would have been thinking about the thing. If the Americans degenerated into a sort of American Indians, but still kept in their wigwams some tradition about a Wilson, it would not be about a Wilson who was shot by wild Irishmen in Eaton Place. It would be about a sort of Hiawatha who inscribed Fourteen Points in picture-writing on the bark of a birch-tree. If Belfast ever becomes a romantic ruin, where the last Orangemen lament the losses of Ulster, Wilson will be the name of a man martyred by Fenians, and not by American Republicans voting for Mr. Harding and Normalcy. The stories of the two men would be some sort of traditions or travesties of what they did. And the very earliest historical references to Arthur are references to what he did. What he did was to defend Britain, as a Christian and civilised State, against the heathen invasions. The very first references to him deal with stories like that of the Battle of Mount Badon, in which Arthur drove the heathen before him and carried a holy image, some say on his shield and some on his shoulders.[135] If I remember right, William of Malmesbury, soon after the Norman Conquest, refers to Arthur not as a wild Welsh demigod or even a doubtful Welsh saint, but as a solid historical character whose name needs to be cleared from the *later* accretions of Welsh fancy.[136] Now there is no doubt at all that battles similar to the Battle of Mount Badon did in all sorts of countries stem or turn the tide of barbarism. There is no doubt whatever that, when they did, they left an enormous impression on the imaginations of men, like a story of the Deluge or the Day of Judgment. If the result was a myth, it was like some myth about a man who had saved the sun and stars.

But there is another historical truth that is here forgotten. **Many doubts about the Court of Camelot are founded on the notion that anything so far back in time must itself have been barbaric.[137] The truth is that, if it was far enough back, it would almost certainly have been civilised. It would have been in the last phase of the old Roman civilization.** The fallacy is like that of a man who should say at daybreak that if it was darker four hours before, it must have been darker still fourteen hours before. He would forget that fourteen hours might bring him back into the previous day. And the fascination of this study of the Dark Ages is precisely that the darkness does hide a buried day; the last lost daylight of the great culture of antiquity.

134. Woodrow Wilson, President during WWI, was followed by Warren Harding, a Republican who advocated a "Return to Normalcy" after Wilson's costly internationalism. Henry Wilson (1864–1922) was a British field marshal assassinated by Irish radicals as he returned to his home on Eaton Square. Chesterton's point is that, while myths may get details wrong, they often accurately preserve a name and what he did that mattered.

135. In the Battle of Mount Badon around 500 AD Romanized British and Celts defeated invading Anglo-Saxons. The ninth century *Historia Brittonum* refers to older traditions that King Arthur led the victorious army.

136. William of Malmesbury (*c.* 1080/1095–*c.* 1143) was a monk and an English historian who, about 1120 AD, wrote *Gesta regum anglorum—Deeds of the English kings (449-1127)*, one of the best early histories of England.

137. In some of the ancient tales, King Arthur's capital is in Camelot with the knights of the Round Table.

Much of the dulness of modern history came from the idea of progress. For history must be progress reversed. If things have always automatically grown brighter and better, then to trace things backwards is to go further and further not only into darkness but into dulness. It is to go from gold to lead and from lead to mud; from beautiful novelties to dreary negations. But, as a fact, these beautiful novelties have never appeared except when this negative theory of the past was itself negatived. They have come when people were quarrying in an older civilisation, because it was more civilised than their own civilization. That is obviously what happened at the Renascence; but it happened in many cases where it is less obvious. **I believe that the peculiar magic and mastery still belonging to the Arthurian story is largely due to the long period during which men looked back to Roman Britain as something more rich and subtle and artistic than the barbarous centuries that succeeded it.** They were not wrong in believing that Arthur and Lancelot were more courtly and cultured then [than] Hengist and Horsa.[138] If Arthur and Lancelot existed at all, they almost certainly were. The same has been true, of course, ever since people began to study the mediaeval civilization with any intelligence. Some sentimentalists in the eighteenth century may have begun by thinking ruined abbeys (especially by moonlight) merely interesting as rugged and barbaric, "with shapeless sculpture decked."[139] But since we have begun to search out the scheme and science of mediaeval architecture, we have realised that it is the very reverse of barbaric, that it is especially organised and orderly. We have recognised that Gothic architecture was certainly not made by Goths; and that the shapeless sculpture was anything but shapeless, and had a very deliberate shape. But we do not remember that, as we have groped for an understanding of the mediaeval system, so the men of the Dark Ages may well have groped for an understanding of the old Roman system. And it is natural that the last monuments of it should have appeared enormous in the twilight; and one of these monuments was the memory of Arthur.

G.K. Chesterton, "Our Note-Book," *Illustrated London News* 161 (December 16, 1922), 980. US: December 16, 1922. Also published as "King Arthur: Myth and History."

138. Hengest and Hengist were brothers in legends which claim that they led to a large wave of immigration to England by Germanic tribes. They are mentioned in an October 21, 1911 (Ch. 1) article on a similar theme.

139. Thomas Grey (1716–1771) used this phrase in his once famous "Elegy Written in a Country Churchyard" (1751), which begins: "The curfew tolls the knell of parting day;/ The lowing herd wind slowly o'er the lea;/ The ploughman homeward plods his weary way,/ And leaves the world to darkness and to me." And includes: "Far from the madding crowd's ignoble strife/ Their sober wishes never learned to stray;/ Along the cool sequestered vale of life/ They kept the noiseless tenor of their way./ Yet ev'n these bones, from insult to protect,/ Some frail memorial still erected nigh,/ With uncouth rhymes and shapeless sculpture decked,/ Implores the passing tribute of a sigh."

Appendices

Differing Views—Editor

In these appendices we offer seven differing views about war. We start with Saint Thomas Aquinas, someone with whom Chesterton had substantial agreement and about whom he wrote a popular biography. We then move to six of Chesterton's contemporaries: Winston Churchill, Norman Angell, Bernard Shaw, Bertrand Russell, Mahatma Gandhi, and H.G. Wells. With the exception of Churchill, Chesterton disagreed with what these men wrote about war, so including a sample of what they were saying allows us to evaluate how well each argued his point of view, as well as how history has judged what he wrote.

A. Is It Always a Sin to Go to War?

Thomas Aquinas, 1265–1274

Editor: This short excerpt from the *Summa Theologica* of St. Thomas Aquinas, written between 1265 and 1274, illustrates what Chesterton meant when he wrote about how Christendom had dealt with war. Notice that there are no utopian schemes and no efforts to impress us with how clever the author is. Instead, there is a somber recognition that all human efforts, however well-intended, are likely to go astray unless carefully restrained. Wars are right and necessary in some circumstances because there is no other way to reestablish justice after a wrong has been done. But wars are also likely to lead to excesses of revenge and ferocity which must be prevented.

R[esponse]. There are three requisites for a war to be just. The first thing is the authority of the prince by whose command the war is to be waged. It does not belong to a private person to start a war, for he can prosecute his claim in the court of his superior. In like manner the mustering of the people, that has to be done in wars, does not belong to a private person. But since the care of the commonwealth is entrusted to princes, to them belongs the protection of the common weal of the city, kingdom, or province subject to them. And as they lawfully defend it with the material sword against inward disturbances by punishing malefactors, so it belongs to them also to protect the commonwealth from enemies without by the sword of war. The second requisite is a just cause, so that they who are assailed should deserve to be assailed for some fault that they have committed. Hence Augustine says: "Just wars are usually defined as those which avenge injuries, in cases where a nation or city has to be chastised for having either neglected to punish the wicked doings of its people, or neglected to restore what has been wrongfully taken away." The third thing requisite is a right intention of promoting good or avoiding evil. For

Augustine says: "Eagerness to hurt, bloodthirsty desire of revenge, an untamed and unforgiving temper, ferocity in renewing the struggle, lust of empire—these and the like excesses are justly blamed in war."

1. To the objection from the text that "all that take the sword shall perish with the sword," [Matt. 26:52] it is to be said, as Augustine says, that "he takes the sword, who without either command or grant of any superior or lawful authority, arms himself to shed the blood of another." But he who uses the sword by the authority of a prince or judge (if he is a private person), or out of zeal for justice, and by the authority of God (if he is a public person), does not take the sword of himself, but uses it as committed to him by another.
2. To the objection from the text, "I say to you not to resist evil," [Matt. 5:39] it is to be said, as Augustine says, that such precepts are always to be observed "in readiness of heart," so that a man be ever ready not to resist, if there be occasion for non-resistance. But sometimes he must take another course in view of the common good, or even in view of those with whom he fights. Hence Augustine says: "He is the better for being overcome, from whom the license of wrong-doing is snatched away: for there is no greater unhappiness than the happiness of sinners, the nourishment of an impunity which is only granted as a punishment, and the strengthening of that domestic foe, an evil will."

Thomas Aquinas, *Aquinas Ethicus,* vol. I, Joseph Rickaby , trans. (London: Burns and Oates Ltd, 1896), 407–409. This text is from *Summa Theologica*. Other editions of this section note that some of the quotes, which Aquinas probably quoted from memory, cite the wrong source.

B. The Balkan Situation
Winston Churchill, 1912

Editor: On October 20, 1912, Winston Churchill, then First Lord of the Admiralty, delivered the speech excerpted here in Sheffield. At that time Europeans were afraid war in Europe would break out in the Balkans, a region with a confusing mixture of different nationalities (with historic ties to major European powers) that were struggling to break free of a corrupt Ottoman Empire.

The First Balkan War had begun some two weeks earlier on October 8. The people of Bulgaria, Serbia, Greece and Montenegro had created a temporary alliance to win their freedom. Near the start of his speech, Churchill expressed delight at what was happening across Europe: "So far we see all the Governments, without exception, honestly striving to adjust their differences, to preserve their amity, and to bring their combined influence to bear to make an end of a long and fierce quarrel." Churchill went on to criticize the pacifists of his day for their theories about how wars began. He points out that none of their theories applied to the fighting in the Balkans. Those they blamed for war had either labored to prevent it (diplomats) or shown no interest in it (press and public). This was a war inspired by legitimate and deep-seated desires for national independence. Declaring it evil would perpetuate an injustice.

Soon after, the *Review of Reviews* praised this speech, pointing out what it did to "Mr. Norman Angell's theory," whose unfortunate impact had been "to enable the citizens of this country to sleep quietly, and to lull into false security the citizens of all great countries." The magazine said Angell's popular book, *The Great Illusion,* was itself a "great delusion," and that Churchill was more realistic.

Preventing war, Churchill warned, required more than keeping an eye on pacifism's short list of alleged evil-doers. War could "burst upon us with all the forces of a spontaneous explosion"— war based not on the intrigues of a few but on a distant people's "intense realisation of their wrongs and of their duty." In such a situation, who could "suppose that the long antagonisms of history and of time can in all circumstances be adjusted and compacted by the smooth and superficial conventions of politicians and ambassadors?"[1] Churchill had just predicted with astonishing accuracy how war in Europe would break out two years later.

THESE are not satisfactory considerations, but there is another aspect of this war which awakens grave reflections. We have sometimes been assured by the persons who profess to know that the danger of war has become an illusion, and that in the modern days the danger would not exist at all but for the machinations of statesmen and diplomatists, but for the intrigues of financiers aided by the groundless suspicion of generals and admirals—formented by the sensationalism of the press—and all directed upon the ignorance and credulity of the people. Well, here is a war which has risen from none of these causes, and here is a war which has broken out in spite of all that rulers and diplomatists could do to prevent it, and a war in which the press had no part, a war in which the whole force of the money power has been subtly and steadfastly directed to prevent it, directed to prevent a war which has come upon us not through the ignorance or credulity of people, but, on the contrary, from their knowledge of their history and of their destiny and from their intense realisation of their wrongs and of their duty, as they conceive them. A war which from all these causes has burst upon us with all the forces of a spontaneous explosion, and which within the limits in which it is operating has carried all before it in destruction and in strive—face to face with such a manifestation, who is the man who is bold enough to say, for instance, that force is never a remedy? Who is the man who is foolish enough to say that martial virtues do not play a vital part in the health and honour of every people? Who is the man who is vain enough to suppose that the long antagonisms of history and of time can in all circumstances be adjusted and compacted by the smooth and superficial conventions of politicians and ambassadors?

Winston Churchill, "Balkan Situation and Defence Preparedness," Cutlers' Feast, Sheffield, October 30, 1912. In *Winston S. Churchill: His Complete Speeches, 1897–1963*. vol. II, Robert Rhodes James, ed. (New York: Chelsea House, 1974), 2030. Audience responses removed.

1. Norman Angell quoted from the *Review of Reviews* article in a 1913 edition of his *The Great Illusion* and tried to answer the problems Churchill had raised. But he was forced to step back some sixty years to the Crimean War (1853–1856), and the unlikely conjecture that, had Britain listened to pacifists of that day, the current troubles in the Balkans would not exist. Norman Angell, *The Great Illusion* (New York: G.P. Putnam's Sons, 1913), 386–387.

C. The Great Illusion
Norman Angell, 1913

Editor: While Chesterton was widely read, it's interesting to speculate just how different history might have been if what he had written about war and its prevention had received as much attention and praise as that given to his contemporary, Norman Angell (1872–1967), who was born only two years before him.

On the topic of war, the two men differed greatly. Chesterton believed war was often necessary and felt that in certain circumstances fighting should be "merry." He had no patience with those who believed WWI was a "war to end of war." For him that war, like every war, had a much more limited and practical goal. It should punish German aggression and perhaps teach the nation not to make war again. He warned that there existed a Prussian mind-set which drove Germany to war that, if not forcibly corrected, would lead to still more horrible wars. Like Churchill's 1912 speech, it's one of the most chillingly accurate predictions in modern history.

In contrast, Angell was one of the foremost pacifists of the twentieth century. It'd be wrong to say he thought war would simply disappear, shoved aside by the winds of progress. His views more radical than that. He believed the world was now so structured that no modern country could benefit economically from any war. His 1910 book championing that, *The Great Illusion*, was translated into twenty-five languages and sold over two-million copies over the next two decades.

On the eve of WWI, Angell found little about Prussia of concern. He saw history driven by economic forces rather than human choices, national cultures, or ideologies. Economics, he believed, was making Germany peaceful. After remarking on how the poverty of the deserts had driven the Beduin to plunder, he turned to Prussia.

> The same may have been to some extent the case in Prussia before the era of coal and iron; but the fact that to-day 99 per cent of the population is normally engaged in trade and industry, and 1 per cent only in military preparation, and some fraction too small to be properly estimated engaged in actual war, shows how far she has outgrown such a state—shows, incidentally, what little chance the ideal and tradition represented by 1 per cent. or some fractional percentage has against the interests and activities represented by 99 per cent.[2]

A few pages later, Angell commented what some were calling Prussia's dangerous sense of military superiority, sneering at the idea "as purely non-existent as the phantom German war-balloon to which the British press devoted serious columns." He goes on to claim: "Despite the hypnotism which German 'progress' seems to exercise on the minds of English Jingoes, the German people themselves, as distinct from the small group of Prussian Junkers, are not in the least enamored with it, as is proved by the unparalleled growth of the social-democratic element, which is the negation of military imperialism."[3] Tragically, given his great influence, Angell had failed to grasp just how deeply militarism was ingrained into the German psyche.

2. Norman Angell, *The Great Illusion* (New York: G.P. Putnam's Sons, 1913), 246. Just after the war began, he attempted a hasty correction with *Shall this War End German Militarism* (London: Union of Democratic Control, 1914). But altering schemes to fit new events as substantial as this suggests the schemes themselves are flawed.

3. Norman Angell, *The Great Illusion* (New York: G.P. Putnam's Sons, 1913), 253–54. The "German war-balloon was a dirigible, not a formidable weapon in WWI, but in the 1930s the bomber that replaced it would terrify many.

Angell's arguments have other flaws. Chesterton mentioned two in his June 21, 1913 article (Ch. 1). First, for Angell's ideas to make sense, Chesterton said, Europe would have to have "grown pure and sweet enough to believe in his gospel of peace." Yet how could they do that when all they were hearing from him was that for "purely selfish reasons" war isn't profitable. Second, if they become peaceful merely for selfish reasons, won't they selfishly take what's not theirs when the gain is certain?

Events would soon prove that a nation that behaves badly doesn't necessarily suffer economically in world trade, as Angell will claim below. Only the British fleet kept the rest of the world from trading as usual with Germany during the war. If executing civilians, burning towns, and sinking ocean liners didn't make countries take their business elsewhere, then confiscating property and giving it to Germans would have made no difference. The same profit motive that Angell was depending on to end war, would make at least some wars profitable.

As we see later with Gandhi and Wells, Angell had a scheme for world peace that he thought everyone should accept whose motives weren't perverse. Gandhi found his truth through religion and Wells through science. For Angell, truth came through what he calls reason. In his autobiography, he less than modestly quoted a 1926 magazine article: "Many people whose minds are closed to reason are exasperated by *The Great Illusion*, a masterpiece of political argument so cogent that if you do not agree with it there is nothing left for you to do but lose your temper."[4] That's odd, since Chesterton had no problem disagreeing without loosing his temper.

In that same 1952 book, looking back over his life, Angell criticized Presidents Woodrow Wilson and Franklin Roosevelt for failing to promise, through the League of Nations, to defend France from Germany. If peace is your supreme objective, that may seem reasonable. But aren't other objectives just as reasonable? After WWI, Americans preferred "normalcy" to another murderous European war. Was that unreasonable? During the 1930s they wanted to deal with the more pressing problem of hunger at home rather than pay the enormous costs of stationing a half-million-man army in France for an uncertain number of years—about the only action that might have kept Hitler from overrunning France. Nor would American troops in France have prevented a war that began in the East when Germany attacked Poland. Was the U.S. to send large numbers of troops to every country in Eastern Europe? That's absurd. In the real world, *pure reason* doesn't exist, only *reasons* that point in many directions and suggest differing priorities. In that context, Angell's remark about Roosevelt having, "all the authority of the United States behind him," seems extraordinarily naive. Roosevelt was not a dictator. Even if he had wanted, he could not have single-handed sent enough American military forces to Europe to deter a Hitler bent on war.

Finally, keep in mind that at this time Great Britain was the premier economic and military power in the world and had been so within living memory. What Angell assumes will be the behavior of Europe's dominant power was relatively benign British behavior. Britain had not driven "Swiss and Belgian merchants" from the "British Colonial market," nor had it used the Royal Navy to limit competition from Norwegian merchant ships. Instead, world trade took place in greater safety under the protection

Chesterton held a more accurate view of German social democrats, noting that during the war, most socialists supported the war effort and that after the war they refused to criticize their nation's role in starting the war.

4. Norman Angell, *After All* (New York: Farrar, Straus and Young, 1952), 300. Quoting from *The Nation*, July 17, 1926. His remarks about Wilson and Roosevelt are on pages 144–145.

of Britain. Angell assumes any modern conqueror would behave like that, respecting property and national feelings. But British restraint, which Chesterton calls "civilization," did not mean the world had reached a "stage" where it was "impossible for one nation to seize by force the wealth or trade of another." If a nation were ruthless enough, war remained as profitable as ever. Nazi Germany did not profit from World War II because it *lost* the war. Had it won, what was being done to the Jews would have also been done to the Slavs, and within a few generations, all the wealth of Eastern Europe would have passed into German hands. If the Nazis had continued to carry out their Darwinian agenda, over the next few centuries most of Europe would have become Germanic. At no point in that long and grisly process would the nations of the world have refused to do business with Germany.

This appendix is a synopsis of Angell's theory from a popular edition of his *The Great Illusion*, published on the eve of war in 1913. For that and other activities, Angell was awarded the 1933 Nobel Peace Prize. For comforting people in their illusions and leaving Europe woefully unprepared for the horrors of Hitler, he received the fame he sought. For telling people unpleasant truths and wisely seeking to prevent the next war, Chesterton would receive no Nobel Prize and much unfair criticism. As a measure of genuine accomplishment, the Noble Peace Prize may mean little or nothing.

WHAT are the fundamental motives that explain the present rivalry of armaments in Europe, notably the Anglo-German? Each nation pleads the need for defense; but this implies that someone is likely to attack, and has therefore presumed interest in so doing. What are the motives which each State thus fears its neighbors may obey?

They are based on the universal assumption that a nation, in order to find outlets for expanding population and increasing industry, or simply to ensure the best conditions possible for its people, is necessarily pushed to territorial expansion and the exercise of political force against others (German naval competition is assumed to be the expression of the growing need of an expanding population for a larger place in the world, a need which will find a realization in the conquest of English colonies or trade, unless these are defended); it is assumed, therefore, that a nation's relative prosperity is broadly determined by its political power; that nations being competing units, advantage, in the last resort, goes to the possessor of preponderant military force, the weaker going to the wall, as in the other forms of the struggle for life.

The author challenges this whole doctrine. He attempts to show that it belongs to a stage of development out of which we have passed; that the commerce and industry of a people no longer depend upon the expansion of its political frontiers; that a nation's political and economic frontiers do not now necessarily coincide; that military power is socially and economically futile, and can have no relation to the prosperity of the people exercising it; that it is impossible for one nation to seize by force the wealth or trade of another—to enrich itself by subjugating or imposing its will by force on another; that, in short, war, even when victorious, can no longer achieve those aims for which people strive.

He establishes this apparent paradox, in so far as the economic problem is concerned, by showing that wealth in the economically civilized world is founded upon credit and commercial contract (these being the outgrowth of an economic interdependence due to the increasing division of labor and greatly developed communication). If credit and commercial contract are tampered with in an attempt at confiscation, the credit-dependent wealth is undermined, and its collapse involves that of the conqueror; so that if conquest is not to be self-injurious it must respect the enemy's property, in which case it becomes economically futile. Thus the wealth of conquered territory remains in the hands of the population of such territory. When Germany annexed Alsatia, no individual German secured a single mark's worth of Alsatian property as the spoils of war. Conquest in the modern world is a process of multiplying by x, and then obtaining the original figure by dividing by x. For a modern nation to add to its territory no more adds to the wealth of the people of such nation than it would add to the wealth of Londoners if the City of London were to annex the county of Hertford.

The author also shows that international finance has become so interdependent and so interwoven with trade and industry that the intangibility of an enemy's property extends to his trade. It results that political and military power can in reality do nothing for trade; the individual merchants and manufacturers of small nations, exercising no such power, compete successfully with those of the great. Swiss and Belgian merchants drive English from the British Colonial market; Norway has, relatively to the population, a greater mercantile marine than Great Britain; the public credit (as a rough-and-ready indication, among others, of security and wealth) of small States possessing no political power often stands higher than that of the Great Powers of Europe, Belgian Three per Cents, standing at 96, and German at 82; Norwegian Three and a Half per Cents at 102, and Russian Three and a Half per Cents at 81.

The forces which have brought about the economic futility of military power have also rendered it futile as a means of enforcing a nation's moral ideals or imposing social institutions upon a conquered people. Germany could not turn Canada or Australia into German colonies—*i.e.*, stamp out their language, law, literature, traditions, etc.—by "capturing" them. The necessary security in their material possessions enjoyed by the inhabitants of such conquered provinces, quick inter-communication by a cheap press, widely-read literature, enable even small communities to become articulate and effectively to defend their special social or moral possessions, even when military conquest has been complete. The fight for ideals can no longer take the form of fight between nations, because the lines of division on moral questions are within the nations themselves and intersect the political frontiers. There is no modern State which is completely Catholic or Protestant, or liberal or autocratic, or aristocratic or democratic, or socialist or individualist; the moral and spiritual struggles of the modern world go on between citizens of the same State in unconscious intellectual co-operation with corresponding groups in other States, not between the public powers of rival States.

This classification by strata involves necessarily a redirection of human pugnacity, based rather on the rivalry of classes and interests than on State divisions. War has no longer the justification that it makes for the survival of the fittest; it involves the survival of the less fit. The idea that the struggle between nations is a part of the evolutionary law of man's advance involves a profound misreading of the biological analogy.

The warlike nations do not inherit the earth; they represent the decaying human element. The diminishing role of physical force in all spheres of human activity carries with it profound psychological modifications.

These tendencies, mainly the outcome of purely modern conditions (*e.g.* rapidity of communication), have rendered the problems of modern international politics profoundly and essentially different from the ancient; yet our ideas are still dominated by the principles and axioms, images and terminology of the bygone days.

The author urges that these little-recognized facts may be utilized for the solution of the armament difficulty on at present untried lines—by such modification of opinion in Europe that much of the present motive to aggression will cease to be operative, and by thus diminishing the risk of attack, diminishing to the same extent the need for defence. He shows how such a political reformation is within the scope of practical politics, and the methods which should be employed to bring it about.

Norman Angell, *The Great Illusion* (New York: G.P. Putnam's Sons, 1913), ix–xiii.

D. Common Sense about the War
Bernard Shaw, 1914

Editor: Three months after the war began, Bernard Shaw published a book-length critique. His cynicism about war and those fighting or supporting it does not mean he was a pacifist. In the first of seven points at the end, he claimed, "The War should be pushed vigorously, not with a view to a final crushing of the German army between the Anglo-French combination and the Russian millions, but to the establishment of a decisive military superiority by the Anglo-French combination alone." That illustrates the shallowness of Shaw's oft-professed concern for British soldiers. Until the 1917 Russian Revolution, progressives disliked fighting alongside Russia's 'reactionary' Czar. Shaw wanted the English and French to marshal a "decisive military superiority," so they would win without Russia's help. That could only be done by having more English and French soldiers die. His personal disdain for fighting alongside a reactionary regime was a sufficient motive for a rushed and costlier war.[5]

Despite Shaw's claim to be horrified by the killing, in his article he seems more interested in convincing readers how much more bravely and clearly he thinks than the average "thoughtless" English citizen or soldier. Aquinas does not mention himself

5. The left displayed no such disdain for fighting alongside "Uncle Joe" Stalin in WWII. Despite the millions of people Stalin murdered during the 1930s, he was seen as a member of the vanguard of progress.

a single time Appendix A. In the same amount of space here, Shaw refers to himself with words such as "I" and "me" some thirteen times. People who actual risk their lives to save others often downplay what they've done, calling it "nothing." Others talk constantly about their "courage," when all they've done is promote an opinion popular among their particular clique. That posturing is so common among pacifists that, although Shaw isn't one, people often think he is. He sounds like pacifists, especially those described in Chesterton's May 11, 1918 article.[6]

Shaw differed from Chesterton primarily in his effort to blame both sides for the war. His arguments were erratic and inconsistent, but it's easy to suspect that they generated the public outrage so necessary for his continuing success as a playwright. Finally, keep in mind that WWII, which came after Britain and France made numerous concessions in an effort to maintain the peace (appeasement), suggests that the blame for both wars rests squarely on the peculiarities of Germanic thinking as described by Chesterton. Germany started two wars in succession because it believed it had the right as a superior race to benefit from conquest.

The time has now come to pluck up courage and begin to talk and write soberly about the war. At first the mere horror of it stunned the more thoughtful of us; and even now only those who are not in actual contact with or bereaved relation to its heartbreaking wreckage can think sanely about it, or endure to hear others discuss it coolly. As to the thoughtless, well, not for a moment dare I suggest that for the first few weeks they were all scared out of their wits; for I know too well that the British civilian does not allow his perfect courage to be questioned: only experienced soldiers and foreigners are allowed the infirmity of fear. But they certainly were—shall I say a little upset? They felt in that solemn hour that England was lost if only one single traitor in their midst let slip the truth about anything in the universe. It was a perilous time for me. I do not hold my tongue easily; and my inborn dramatic faculty and professional habit as a playwright prevent me from taking a one-sided view even when the most probable result of taking a many-sided one is prompt lynching....

And first, I do not see this war as one which has welded Governments and peoples into complete and sympathetic solidarity as against a common enemy. I see the people of England united in a fierce detestation and defiance of the views and acts of Prussian Junkerism. And I see the German people stirred to the depths by a similar antipathy to English Junkerism, and anger at the apparent treachery and duplicity of the attack made on them by us in their extremist peril from France and Russia. I see both nations duped, but alas! not quite unwillingly duped, by their Junkers and Militarists into wreaking on one another the wrath they should have spent in destroying Junkerism and Militarism in their own country. And I see the Junkers and Militarists of England and Germany jumping at the chance they have

6. Shaw liked to taunt, knowing people would usually react so angrily, few would notice weaknesses in his arguments. But that meant that people were more likely to remember his sneers and their anger at what he said than what he had actually said. In an effort to clear his record, in 1932 he published a collection of his wartime writings (including this one) as *What I Really Wrote about the War.*

longed for in vain for many years of smashing one another and establishing their own oligarchy as the dominant military power in the world. **No doubt the heroic remedy for this tragic misunderstanding is that both armies should shoot their officers and go home to gather in their harvests in the villages and make revolution in the towns;** and though this is not at present a practical solution, it must be frankly mentioned, because it or something like it is always a possibility in a defeated conscript army if its commanders push it beyond human endurance when its eyes are opening to the fact that in murdering its neighbours it is biting off its nose to vex its face, besides riveting the intolerable yoke of Militarism and Junkerism more tightly than ever on its own neck. But there is no chance—or, as our Junkers would put it, no danger—of our soldiers yielding to such an ecstasy of common sense.[7] They have enlisted voluntarily; they are not defeated nor likely to be; their communications are intact and their meals reasonably punctual; they are as pugnacious as their officers; and in fighting Prussia they are fighting a more deliberate, conscious, tyrannical, personally insolent, and dangerous Militarism than their own.... [8]

Now that we know what a Junker is, let us have a look at the Militarists. A Militarist is a person who believes that all real power is the power to kill, and that Providence is on the side of the big battalions. The most famous Militarist at present thanks to the zeal with which we have bought and quoted his book, is General Friedrich Von Bernhardi.[9] But we cannot allow the General to take precedence of our own writers as Militarist propagandist. I am old enough to remember the beginning of the anti-German phrase of that very ancient propaganda in England. The Franco-Prussian war of 1870–1871 left Europe very much taken aback. Up to that date nobody was afraid of Prussia, though everyone was a little afraid of France; and we were keeping "buffer States" between ourselves and Russia in the east.... Suddenly Germany beat France right down into the dust, by the exercise of an organized efficiency in war of which nobody up until then had any conception. There was not a State in Europe that did not say to itself, "Good Heavens! what would happen if she attacked *us*?" We in England thought of our old-fash-

7. English soldiers never revolted against this "intolerable yoke of Militarism," and yet that yoke did not grow "more tightly," because it never existed. This folly of moral equivalence, an inability to distinguish English non-militarism from German militarism would leave the nation cynical and ill-prepared for the next war.

8. Shaw then translates definitions of "Junker" from a German dictionary and uses them to label almost everyone of importance in the British government a Junker. But his sleigh of hand fails. How a German dictionary defines Junker, a "young nobleman" or a "country gentleman," isn't what the English mean when they talk of German Junkers and isn't even the pejorative meaning many Germans attach to "Junker." Despite Shaw's claims, there's no moral equivalence between the German and English nobility or between Germany's large, conscription army, trained to fight a quick and aggressive two-front war, and Britain's small professional army, trained to maintain order in a far-flung empire. Chesterton described those differences in an October 6, 1906 *Illustrated London News article* (Ch. 1). His assessment is much more honest and accurate than Shaw's rant.

9. Friedrich von Bernhardi (1849–1930) was the author of *Germany and the Next War* (1912), which praised war in Darwinian terms. The ever flexible Charles Darwin can be cited in favor of pacifism (men have evolved beyond war) or militarism (war being a useful struggle to determine who is fittest).

ioned army, and our old-fashioned commander George Ranger (of Cambridge),[10] and our War Office with its Crimean tradition of imbecility; and we shook in our shoes....[11]

Now, please observe that I do not say that the agitation was unreasonable. I myself steadily advocated the formation of a formidable armament, and ridiculed the notion that we, who are wasting hundreds of millions annually on idlers and wasters, could not easily afford double, treble, quadruple, our military and naval expenditure. I advocated the compulsion of every man to serve his country, both in war and in peace. The idlers and wasters, perceiving dimly that I meant the cost to come out of their pockets, and meant to use the admission that riches should not exempt a man from military service as an illustration of how absurd it is to allow them to exempt him from civil service, did not embrace my advocacy with enthusiasm; so I must affirm it now lest it should be supposed that I am condemning those whose proceedings I am describing....[12]

Well, there is no obscurity about that problem. Those Germans who took but an instant to kill had taken the travail of a woman for three-quarters of a year to breed, and eighteen years to ripen for the slaughter. All we have to do is to kill, say 75 per cent of all the women in Germany under 60. Then we may leave Germany her fleet and her money, and say "Much good may they do you." Why not, if you are really going in to be what you, never having read "this Neech they talk of," called a Nietzschean Superman? War is not an affair of sentiment.... Now it is not more cowardly to kill a woman than to kill a wounded man. And there is only one reason why it is a greater crime to kill a woman than a man, and why women have to be spared and protected when men are exposed and sacrificed.[13] That reason is that the destruction of the women is the destruction of the community. Men are

10. Prince George, Duke of Cambridge (1819–1904), was commander-in-chief of the British Army almost forty years (1856–1895). He was a stubborn and controversial figure, often resisting politically inspired army reforms. The "Ranger" may come from his title as Ranger of Hyde Park, St. James Park, and Richmond Park.

11. Not so, protected by the Royal Navy, the English knew they had little to fear from a land-bound Germany until the late 1890s, when Germany began to enlarge its Navy and raise the possibility that it could become powerful enough in the North Sea to invade England. Even then, English worries grew slowly, as Chesterton's own writings demonstrate. The rest of Europe had good cause to fear Germany. From the 1860s on, its size, industrial might, demonstrated competence in war, and willingness to wage aggressive war were facts to be reckoned with and not "propaganda." Two major wars in the next century demonstrate the correctness of those fears.

12. These "idlers and wasters" were those who inherited land and wealth. Shaw says he is willing to spend any sum on the military, however wasteful, to impoverish them and to create a larger-than-necessary army merely to draft them into its ranks. Shaw may be worse than a militarist. A militarist claims a large military is necessary for the nation's defense, something that may be true. Shaw wants a large military merely to destroy those whose only crime is being born richer than he. He envies and hates them so much, he is willing to encourage an arms race with Germany that may lead to war. (Shaw also forgets the many servants this old-monied class employs.) At least that's what he says here. Shaw often writes outrageously to attract attention.

13. There are many reasons why women, children, and other non-combatants should not be killed in wartime, reasons rooted in long-held ideas about decency and human rights that Chesterton calls "Christendom" and "chivalry." But Shaw's views are modern and dogmatically Darwinian. Its only over-arching value is survival, so any means to achieve that is permitted. For Shaw and those like him, the 'race' that exterminates the other is the one that wins. That contrasts with Chesterton, who thought scientific talk about race was nonsense. He wanted no German women or children killed, but did want Germany to be punished harshly enough to learn the cost of aggression. See the closing paragraph of his June 19, 1915 article (Ch. 3).

comparatively of no account: kill 90 per cent of the German men, and the remaining 10 per cent can repeople her. But kill the women, and *Delenda est Cathago.*[14] Now this is exactly what our Militarists want to happen to Germany. Therefore the objection to killing women becomes in this case the reason for doing it. Why not? No reply is possible from the Militarist, disable-your-enemy point of view. If disablement is your will, there is your way, and the only effectual way....[15]

Bernard Shaw, "Common Sense about the War" *The New Statesman* IV:84 (Nov. 14, 1914), 3-5, 18.

E. THE ETHICS OF WAR
Bertrand Russell, 1915

EDITOR: Today's pacifists often claim British philosopher Bertrand Russell as one of their own. But his celebrated 1915 essay, "The Ethics of War," defends genocidal invasions that replace an existing population with a new population claiming to represent a superior civilization.[16] But keep in mind what Chesterton pointed out at the end of WWI. Unlike their Quaker predecessors, modern pacifists have little interest in the war as a concrete injustice committed against living people, whether they live in a Belgium destroyed by occupation or a reborn Poland. Pacifists were willing to brush aside war crimes Germany had committed because it wasn't the *wrongs* of war that bothered them, but war as an *abstraction*, a blot on the world as they thought it should be. For such people, abstractions really are more important than human realities. Russell shared their point of view, writing in his 1915 essay the following.

> Of the evils of war to the non-combatant population in the regions where fighting occurs, the recent misfortunes of Belgium have afforded an example upon which it is not necessary to enlarge. It is necessary, however, to point out that the misfortunes of Belgium do not, as is commonly believed in England, afford a reason in favor of war. Hatred, by a tragic delusion, perpetuates the very evils from which it springs. The sufferings of Belgium are attributed to the Germans and not to war; and thus the very horrors of war are used to stimulate the desire to increase their area and intensity. Even assuming the utmost humanity compatible with the conduct of military operations, it cannot be doubted that, if the troops of the Allies penetrate into the industrial regions of Germany, the German population will have to suffer a great part of the misfortunes which Germany has inflicted upon Belgium. To men under the influence of hate this thought is a cause of rejoicing, but to men in whom humane feeling is not extinct it shows that our sympathy with Belgium should make us hate war rather than Germany.

Russell was wrong. War did not cause the Belgian atrocities. Invaders typically treat civilians better than that. That's why German behavior created such outrage. Love rather than "hatred" caused people to be angered by the burning of the Louvain library, the execution of the Edith Cavell, and the sinking of the *Lusitania*. It was Rus-

14. "Carthage must be destroyed" was a slogan that the Romans used during the Punic Wars.

15. Having goals does not force someone to use any means to pursue them. A community, for instance, can reduce speeding on a highway without hanging everyone caught driving over the limit. It's rhetoric like Shaw's that Chesterton is opposing when he criticizes those who want to fight evil with evil.

16. This is precisely why Chesterton opposed the Boer War.

sell and those like him who were afflicted with the worse of hatreds—a cold, smug indifference to the sufferings of others . As subsequent history demonstrated, the fault did rest with Germans. After WWI, the Allies occupied "the industrial regions of Germany" without burning towns, executing nurses, or shooting hostages. By blaming an abstraction, Russell helped those who wanted Germany to get off scot-free and denigrated those who were trying to stop the evil Germany was doing.[17]

This arrogance flows from an elitism that spreads down to followers. They regard the most of humanity, not with the measured but genuine respect Chesterton accorded them, but with utter contempt. They see most people "under the influence of hate," while seeing themselves as "men in whom humane feeling is not extinct."[18] For Russell, pointing out that wars often have good reasons was encouraging hatred by the rabble. The best illustration that the opposite is true, that evil is more likely in a progressive elite, lies in Section III of Russell's essay, excerpted for this appendix. Notice that Russell is doubly wrong. He is wrong *ethically* when he commends wars of genocide, and he is wrong *factually* when it claims genocidal "wars of colonization" are no longer possible now that all the temperate climates have been "acquired for European civilization." Russell knew Western Europe considered itself more civilized than Eastern Europe, and that Germans claimed to be the pinnacle of European civilization. The same Darwinian beliefs that rank white over black and brown, defended here by Russell, also provide justification for the war between 'superior' and 'inferior' European races that Germany would wage in WWII. Accept that the Teuton is superior to the Jew and Slav, as many educated people then did, and Russell's 1915 essay becomes a justification for Nazi-like genocide.

Russell not only finds much to praise in the very sort of war that most ordinary people find abhorrent, he goes on in Section V to attack wars of self-defense. There his views bear the same bizarre quality found in Gandhi's non-resistance.

> I think, however, that, even as a matter of practical politics, the principle of non-resistance contains an immense measure of wisdom if only men would have the courage to carry it out.... What one civilized nation can achieve against another by means of conquest is very much less than is commonly supposed.... We cannot destroy Germany even by a complete military victory, nor conversely, could Germany destroy England even if our Navy were sunk and London occupied by the Prussians. English civilization, the English language, English manufactures would still exist, and as a matter of practical politics it would be totally impossible for Germany to establish a tyranny in this country. If the Germans, instead of being resisted by force of arms, had been passively permitted to establish themselves wherever they pleased, the halo of glory and courage surrounding the brutality of military success would have been absent, and public opinion in Germany itself would have rendered any oppression impossible. The history of our own dealings with our colonies affords abundant examples to show that under such circumstances the refusal of self-government is not possible.

History has demonstrated the folly of those remarks. The fact that *England* displayed restrain in dealing with its colonies says nothing about whether *Germany*

17. Chesterton deals with Russell's argument in a September 28, 1918 article, replacing war with fire (Ch. 6).
18. If you believe, as Russell did, that evolution is working in man to "Move upward, working out the beast, And let the ape and tiger die" (a line from Tennyson's "In Memoriam"), then ordinary people represent the 'ape and tiger,' while the chosen few are those "working out the beast." Strong emotions are symptoms of "the beast."

would display similar restraint, as the Belgians discovered between 1914 and 1918, and as many Europeans discovered between 1939 and 1945.[19] Russell, who viciously attacks the English and French for their alleged "hatred" of Germany, seems to regard Germans as the most gentle of conquerors. Strange to say the least.

Chesterton was more realistic, stressing that German culture is not English culture and that some English flaws come from learning bad lessons from Germans. Their violence wasn't because their invasion was met with a "force of arms" rather than roads strewn with flowers. For these Teutonic barbarians, weakness only generated more contempt. European Jews had no weapons and no means to fight, but they were destroyed in the millions, with no protest raised by "public opinion in Germany." Had Nazi Germany won the war and applied the policies they had planned, the Slavic peoples and cultures of Eastern Europe would have ceased to exist just as surely as aboriginal tribes and cultures had been exterminated a century earlier.

A decade and a half before Chesterton criticized the Germans in WWI, he had attacked Britain's Boer War. Unlike Russell, he did not believe that civilized, industrialized societies have a right to take land from those less advanced. Nor did he believe that civilized societies are exempt from destruction by barbarians, whether they were as primitive as the Huns or as technologically advanced as Germany. Chesterton knew his history well. All Russell had was Charles Darwin, a most pitiful substitute.

In the excerpt that follows, Russell opposes WWI because it pits members of a superior European "civilization" against one another rather than against dark-skinned people. In Darwinian terms, he believed Western Europeans had a right to conquer and populate all comfortable climates. It is not out of place to note that Nazism would use similar arguments to justify its struggle for "living space" in Eastern Europe.

Are there any wars which achieve so much for the good of mankind as to outweigh all the evils we have been considering? I think there have been such wars in the past, but they are not wars of the sort with which our diplomatists are concerned, for which our armies and navies have been prepared, and which are exemplified by the present conflict. For the purposes of classification we may roughly distinguish four kinds of wars, though of course in any given case a war is not likely to be quite clearly of any one of the four kinds. With this proviso we may distinguish: (1) Wars of Colonization; (2) Wars of Principle; (3) Wars of Self-defence; (4) Wars of Prestige. Of these four kinds I should say that the first and second are fairly often justified; the third seldom, except against an adversary of inferior civilization, and the fourth, which is the sort to which the present war belongs, never. Let us consider these four kinds of war in succession.

19. There is method to Russell's madness. Russell regarded Darwin's "survival of the fittest" as the supreme law, never failing and applicable in all circumstances. Because he saw British society as highly civilized and hence "fit," he could not grasp how it could become extinct, particularly at the hands of another civilized society. He failed to realize that there is no progressive content to Darwinian fitness. Survival results from a complex interaction of numerous factors, including utter ruthlessness, a trait Nazism displayed in abundance. Notice also that Russell, while claiming German rule over England would be benign, made no effort to move to occupied Belgium, where he could experience the Germans first hand. He resembles Cold War intellectuals who saw a 'moral equivalence' between the U.S. and the Soviet Union, but remained on the side of the Iron Curtain where free speech was respected. Such people admit nothing into their lives that might challenge their cherished dogmas.

By a war of colonization I mean a war whose purpose is to drive out the whole population of some territory and replace it by an invading population of a different race. Ancient wars were very largely of this kind, of which we have a good example in the Book of Joshua.[20] In modern times the conflicts of Europeans with American-Indians, Maories, and other aborigines in temperate regions, have been of this kind. Such wars are totally devoid of technical justification, and are apt to be more ruthless than any other war. Nevertheless, if we are to judge by results, we cannot regret that such wars have taken place. **They have the merit, often quite fallaciously claimed for all wars, of leading in the main to the survival of the fittest, and it is chiefly through such wars that the civilized portion of the world has been extended from the neighborhood of the Mediterranean to the greater part of the earth's surface.** The eighteenth century, which liked to praise the virtues of the savage and contrast them with the gilded corruption of courts, nevertheless had no scruple in thrusting the noble savage out from his North American hunting grounds. And we cannot at this date bring ourselves to condemn the process by which the American continent has been acquired for European civilization. In order that such wars may be justified, it is necessary that there should be a very great and undeniable difference between the civilization of the colonizers and that of the dispossessed natives. It is necessary also that the climate should be one in which the invading race can flourish. When these conditions are satisfied the conquest becomes justified, though the actual fighting against the dispossessed inhabitants ought, of course, to be avoided as far as is compatible with colonizing. **Many humane people will object in theory to the justification of this form of robbery, but I do not think that any practical or effective objection is likely to be made.**

Such wars, however, belong now to the past. The regions where the white men can live are all allotted, either to white races or to yellow races to whom the white man is not clearly superior, and whom, in any case, he is not strong enough to expel.[21] Apart from small punitive expeditions, wars of colonization, in the true sense, are no longer possible. What are nowadays called colonial wars do not aim at the complete occupation of a country by a conquering race; they aim only at securing certain governmental and trading advantages. They belong, in fact, rather with what I call wars of prestige, than with wars of colonization in the old sense. There are, it is true, a few rare exceptions. The Greeks in the second Balkan war conducted a war of colonization against the Bulgarians; throughout a certain territory which they intended to occupy, they killed all the men, and carried off all the women. But in

---

20. With people, Darwinians often use 'race' as a substitute for species, developing racial theories to explain history and making victory in war a racial "survival of the fittest." But that strained analysis cannot be forced on to the past, when people thought differently and justified their wars in other ways. The Israelis knew they differed little racially from their Philistine opponents and justified their actions with religion rather than race.

21. Darwinians grudgingly conceded that it wasn't easy to rank Europe as "clearly superior" to China and Japan, whose civilizations predate those in Northern Europe. They fretted that Asians, whose populations were limited by food availability, would immigrate to the land-rich U.S. and multiply faster those of European extraction. See Chapters VII and XXIV of *The Pivot of Civilization in Historical Perspective* (Seattle: Inkling Books, 2001).

such cases, the only possible justification fails, since there is no evidence of superior civilization on the side of the conquerors.

In spite, however, of the fact that wars of colonization belong to the past, men's feelings and beliefs about war are still those appropriate to the extinct conditions which rendered such wars possible. When the present war began, many people in England imagined that if the Allies were victorious Germany would cease to exist; Germany was to be destroyed or smashed, and since these phrases sounded vigorous and cheering, people failed to see that they were totally devoid of meaning. There are some seventy million Germans; with great good fortune, we might, in a successful war, succeed in killing two millions of them. There would then still be sixty-eight million Germans, and in a few years the loss of population due to the war would be made good. Germany is not merely a State, but a nation bound together by a common language, common traditions, and common ideals. Whatever the outcome of the war, this nation will still exist at the end of it, and its strength cannot be permanently impaired. But the imagination in what pertains to war is still dominated by Homer and the Old Testament; men who cannot see that circumstances have changed since those works were composed are called practical men and are said to be free from illusions. Those, on the other hand, who have some understanding of the modern world, and some capacity for freeing their minds from the influence of phrases, are called dreamy idealists, Utopians, traitors, and friends of every country but their own. If the facts were understood, wars amongst civilized nations would case, owing to their inherent absurdity. Men's passions always lag behind their political organizations, and facts which leave no outlet for passions are not readily admitted. In order that hatred, pride, and violence may find an outlet, men unconsciously blind themselves to the plainest facts of politics and economics, and modern war continues to be waged with the phrases and theories invented by simpler men in a simpler age.

Bertrand Russell, "The Ethics of War," *International Journal of Ethics* 25:2 (January, 1915). 127–142.

F. Soul-Force and Tapasya

Mahatma Gandhi, 1917

Editor: In his June 17, 1922 *Illustrated London News* article (Ch. 7), Chesterton mentions getting a "pamphlet from an honest Indian gentleman who has a new religion that will establish universal peace." Today, it's hard to discover what that pamphlet may have been or if its author was the world famous Mahatma Gandhi, at that time serving a well-publicized sentence in a British prison in India. But a search of Gandhi's writings and consultation with Gandhi scholars turned up the article excerpted here, "Soul-Force and Tapasya," dated in September 1917. What Chesterton received seems to have been either this or something similar.

Like H.G. Wells, the Indian author Chesterton criticizes here wanted to solve the problem of war with what Chesterton terms "the imposition of one ideal of one sect on the vital varieties of men." For Wells that "one ideal" was an all-powerful World State.

For Gandhi it was a particular variety of Hinduism he claimed to have originated "in South Africa in 1908." The two differed primarily in the kind of force they intended to apply. Wells put his trust in a powerful military that would intimidate any country tempted to assert its independence. He imagined a world populated with people much like himself—comfort-loving, devoid of nationalistic feelings, and willing to let their lives be run by experts.

In contrast, Gandhi assumed a "pure soul-force" that "is not physical force." He wanted a military that did too little to protect people rather than one powerful enough to crush them. His problems lay in a different misunderstanding of human nature. He assumed a world like that he saw in South Africa and India, a world where political power rested in the hands of guilt-ridden British colonizers who lacked the will to apply 'might makes right' doctrine. That's why it will seem so ludicrous when he later recommends his 'soul-force' to Eastern European Jews being murdered in the millions by Nazis. It's easy to suspect that, given Gandhi's vanity, he was willing for all those Jews to die if their deaths could somehow prove the 'truth' of his ideas. Keep in mind that, with his world-wide fame, Gandhi never had to face the risks those nameless Jews had to face. The British, however irritated, did not dare to kill Gandhi. The Nazis could kill Jews by the millions, knowing what they were doing would only merit a small-type, back-page story in the *New York Times.*[22]

Angell, Wells and Gandhi placed a great emphasis on 'truth.' Angell thought truth lay in his peculiar variety of reasoning. Wells thought all truth was modern and scientific, while Gandhi thought it ancient and spiritual, but none of the three took into account a critical truth Chesterton stressed—the enormous "varieties of men" and the fact that what *they* believe must be part of any practical scheme. The solution to the world's ills cannot began with, "First, assume everyone thinks like me."

The force denoted by the term 'passive resistance' and translated into Hindi as *nishkiya pratirodha* is not very accurately described either by the original English phrase or by its Hindi rendering. It's correct description is '*satyagraha.*' *Satyagraha* was born in South Africa in 1908. There was no word in any Indian language denoting the power which our countrymen in South Africa invoked for the redress of their grievances. There was an English equivalent, namely, 'passive resistance,' and we carried on with it. However, the need for a word to describe this unique power came to be increasingly felt, and it was decided to award a prize to anyone who could think of an appropriate term. A Gujarati-speaking gentleman submitted the word '*satyagraha,*' and it was adjudged the best.[23]

'Passive resistance' conveyed the idea of the Suffragette Movement in England. Burning of houses by these women was called 'passive resistance' and so also their fasting in prison. All such acts might very well be 'passive resistance' but they were not '*satyagraha.*' It is said of 'passive resistance' that it is the weapon of the weak, but the power which is the subject of this article can be used only by the strong. This power is not 'passive' resistance; indeed it calls for intense activity. The movement

22. For how the U.S. press covered the plight of European Jews, see Deborah E. Lipstadt's *Beyond Belief: The American Press and the Coming of the Holocaust, 1933-1945* (1993).

23. Gujarati is a language derived from Sanskrit that is spoken in the Indian state of Gujarati near Pakistan.

in South Africa was not passive but active. The Indians of South Africa believed that Truth was their object, that Truth ever triumphs, and with this definiteness of purpose they persistently held on to Truth. They put up with all the suffering that this persistence implied. With the conviction that Truth is not to be renounced even unto death, they shed the fear of death. In the cause of Truth, the prison was a palace to them and its doors the gateway to freedom.

Satyagraha is not physical force. A *satyagrahi* does not inflict pain on the adversary; he does not seek his destruction. A *satyagrahi* never resorts to firearms. In the use of *satyagraha*, there is no ill-will whatever.

Satyagraha is pure soul-force. Truth is the very substance of the soul. That is why this force is called *satyagraha*. The soul is informed with knowledge. It burns with the flame of love. If someone gives us pain through ignorance, we shall win him through love. 'Non-violence is the supreme *dharma*' is the proof of this power of love. Non-violence is a dormant state. In the waking state, it is love. Ruled by love, the world goes on. In English there is a saying, 'Might is Right.' Then there is the doctrine of the survival of the fittest. Both these ideas are contradictory to the above principle. Neither is wholly true. If ill-will were the chief motive-force, the world would have been destroyed long ago; and neither would I have had the opportunity to write this article nor would the hopes of the readers be fulfilled. We are alive solely because of love. We are all ourselves the proof of this. Deluded by modern western civilization, we have forgotten our ancient civilization and worship the might of arms.

We forget the principle of non-violence, which is the essence of all religions.[24] The doctrine of arms stands for irreligion. It is due to the sway of that doctrine that a sanguinary war is raging in Europe.

In India we also find the worship of arms. We see it even in that great work of Tulsidas.[25] But it is seen in all the books that soul-force is the supreme power.

Rama stands for the soul and Ravan for the non-soul. The immense physical might of Ravana is as nothing compared to the soul-force of Rama. Ravana's ten heads are as straw to Rama. Roma is a *yogi*, he has conquered self and pride. He is 'placid equally in affluence and adversity,' he has 'neither attachment, nor greed nor the intoxication of status.' This represents the ultimate in *satyagraha*. The banner of *satyagraha* can again fly in the Indian sky and it is our duty to raise it. If we take recourse to *satyagraha*, we can conquer our conquerors the English, make them

24. Of course, non-violence is not "the essence of all religions." Pagan religions often gloried war, and Islam spread primarily through military conquest. As Gandhi no doubt knew, until it was eliminated by the British, India's Thugee sect worshiped the Hindu god Kali through carefully planned murders and robberies. Although less violent, in the Bible both the Old and New Testaments find qualities in soldiers to praise. Gandhi is less interested in the actual truth than in the peculiar sort of "Truth" he claims as his own.

25. Gosvāmī Tulsīdās (1532–1623) is considered one of the greatest Hindi poets. His "Ramacharitamanas" tells of the exploits of Rama, an incarnation of the god Vishnu, in a epic poem that retells the Sanskrit tale "Ramayana." In that tale, Ravana is the powerful, ten-headed, twenty-armed King of Lanka. When Ravana begins to destroy the world and disturb the Brahmins. Rama is born and defeats him in a fierce one-on-one battle. In the next paragraph Gandhi struggles to make a tale about warriors allegorically champion non-violent 'soul-force.'

bow before our tremendous soul-force, and the issue will be of benefit to the whole world....

Mahatma Gandhi, "Soul-Force and Tapasya," in *The Moral and Political Writings of Mahatma Gandhi: Non-Violent Resistance and Social Transformation,* vol 3, Raghavan Iver, ed. (Oxford: Clerendon Press, 1987), 44–46. *Tapasya* refers to the renunciation that allows someone to live a pure life and endure suffering. Originally published in September 1917.

G. In the Fourth Year

H.G. Wells, 1918

Editor: When Chesterton criticized those who trusted a League of Nations to keep the peace, books such as H.G. Wells' *In the Fourth Year: Anticipations of a World Peace* (1918) were typical of schemes he found unrealistic or dangerous. At the start of the third chapter, Wells states that the peace he has in mind will be kept by force.

> If this League of Free Nations is really to be an effectual thing for the preservation of the peace of the world it must possess power and exercise power, powers must be delegated to it. Otherwise it will only help, with all other half-hearted good resolutions, to pave the road of mankind to hell. Nothing in all the world so strengthens evil as the half-hearted attempts of good to make good.[26]

That was the dilemma Wells and those who thought like him faced. Make the League half-heartedly weak, like the League of Nations actually became, and it could not stop a newly aggressive Germany. But a League strong enough to keep peace is also strong enough to crush freedom. When Wells suggests (below) that this "war of ideas" was a "war against the idea of imperialism," he's not just criticizing European colonies. Germany waged war quite effectively with almost no colonies. He's talking about an 'imperial' mind set that says the English should rule *themselves* and defend *their* freedoms and customs from *outside* aggressors with their *own* military forces. He wants none of that. His World State, which he promoted in numerous books from 1901 on, is the ultimate imperialism, concentrating all power in its hands and treating all the countries of the world as its colonies. In the third chapter Wells writes:

> I am suggesting here that the League of Free Nations shall practically control the army, navy, air forces, and armament industry of every nation in the world. What is the alternative to that? To do as we please? No, the alternative is that any malignant country will be free to force upon all the rest just the maximum amount of armament it chooses to adopt.[27]

Wells' mistake is common among those who concoct utopian solutions. They promise to deal with one problem, a costly armament race triggered by a single "malignant

26. H.G. Wells, *In the Fourth Year: Anticipations of a World Peace* (New York: Macmillan, 1918), 27. Wells' reasoning is flawed. This would not be a League of *Free* Nations. If it is to be the supreme power in the world, able to prevent any country from going to war, its power is not "delegated." The weaker doesn't delegate to the stronger.

27. H.G. Wells, *In the Fourth Year* (New York: Macmillan, 1918), 34–35. We can also approach the problems with Wells' idea from a different angle. The League has no territory of its own, so where will its armament industry be located? What nations will build its cannons, planes, tanks and ships, and where will they be based? What nations are going to provide the expertise and man its war machine? In practice, only a few nations would provide the bulk of the League's military power and, since all other nations would be disarmed, those few will have even more power than they do today. That's precisely what Wells advocated in his 1901 *Anticipations*—a world under the domination of English-speaking people.

country" such as Germany, while saying nothing about the greater ills that would result if the world were ruled by a single power. To maintain power, the World State must spend more on arms than is now spent in a world of generally amiable nations. Its foes would not be a single rogue state. They would be any possible alliance of countries seeking to break free from its domination. It would have to tax the entire world heavily to maintain that large a force and draft millions to serve in its military.

In other books, Wells went even further, revealing just how monolithic and monochromic his future World State would be. The remarks that follow are the last sentences in the closing chapter, "The Modern State in Control of Life," of Wells' *The Shape of Things to Come* (1933). It isn't too far off the mark to suggest that these controllers real interest doesn't lie in ending human suffering, but in using major crises, either real (such as WWI) or contrived (the 'Population Bomb' hysteria[28] of the 1960s), to gradually impose their "pattern of living upon our race."

> Plainly the thesis is that history must now continue to be a string of accidents with an increasingly disastrous trend until a comprehensive faith in the modernized World-State, socialistic, cosmopolitan and creative, takes hold of the human imagination. When the existing governments and ruling theories of life, the decaying religions and the decaying political forms of to-day, have sufficiently lost prestige through failure and catastrophe, then and then only will world-wide reconstruction be possible. And it must needs be the work, first of all, of an aggressive order of religiously devoted men and women who will try out and establish and impose a new pattern of living upon our race.[29]

The result is hardly surprising. It would be a world so heavily indoctrinated by those aggressively "devoted men and women," that only writers who thought like Wells would treated with respect. If a Dr. Samuel Johnson, were to appear, witty and urbane, he would, Wells said, be regarded as "an ill-mannered, offensive, inadaptable and tiresome old gentleman" and "hustled off to meet Mr. G.K. Chesterton," who'd be regarded as antiquated and out of touch. For thousands of years, humanity has communicated across the generations through great literature that touches our common humanity. All that would end. Like Aldous Huxley's *Brave New World*, published the year before, in Wells' brave new World-State, humanity would loose its past for what even Wells admitted would seem an "inhuman humanitarianism" and a "cruel rationality."[30] That is a heavy price to pay even if, as Wells claimed, this new World State really could create a world without war and still more horrible if it couldn't.

We only include the preface to Wells' *In the Fourth Year* here, but the entire book is worth reading with Chesterton's telling arguments in mind. The issues Chesterton and Wells debated remain as important today as they were in 1918.

---

28. Of population control, Wells wrote: "The workers often resented Modern State methods almost as much as their immediate employers. Men have always been difficult to educate and reluctant to submit themselves to discipline, and there was a curious suggestion of the schoolmaster about these fellows of the Modern State nuclei. Dislike of what was at hand helped to conjure up fears of what might lie beyond. Once freedom of business had gone, what rules and regulations might not presently enmesh the wilful individual under the thumb of this one world employer? For instance, the Modern State centres were talking of a control of population; it was easy to see in that a hideous invasion of the most private moments in life. Weights and measures and money to-day, and wives and parentage to-morrow!" H.G. Wells, *The Shape of Things to Come* (New York: Macmillan, 1933), 304.

29. H.G. Wells, *The Shape of Things to Come* (New York: Macmillan, 1933), 430–431. Note that "democratic" isn't part of the World State's description. It must be among the "decaying political forms of to-day."

30. H.G. Wells, *The Shape of Things to Come* (New York: Macmillan, 1933), 345.

In the latter half of 1914 a few of us were writing that this war was a "War of Ideas." A phrase, "The War to end War," got into circulation, amidst much sceptical comment. It was a phrase powerful enough to sway many men, essentially pacifists, towards taking an active part in the war against German imperialism, but it was a phrase whose chief content was its aspiration. People were already writing in those early days of disarmament and of the abolition of the armament industry throughout the world; they realized fully the element of industrial belligerency behind the shining armour of imperialism, and they denounced the "Krupp-Kaiser" alliance.[31] But against such writing and such thought we had to count, in those days, great and powerful realities. Even to those who expressed these ideas there lay visibly upon them the shadow of impracticability; they were very "advanced" ideas in 1914, very Utopian. Against them was an unbroken mass of mental habit and public tradition. While we talked of this "war to end war," the diplomatists of the Powers allied against Germany were busily spinning a disastrous web of greedy secret treaties, were answering aggression by schemes of aggression, were seeing in the treacherous violence of Germany only the justification for countervailing evil acts. To them it was only another war for "ascendancy." That was three years and a half ago, and since then this "war of ideas" has gone on to a phase few of us had dared hope for in those opening days. The Russian revolution put a match to that pile of secret treaties and indeed to all the imperialist plans of the Allies; in the end it will burn them all. The greatest of the Western Allies is now the United States of America, and the Americans have come into this war simply for an idea. Three years and a half ago a few of us were saying this was a war against the idea of imperialism, not German imperialism merely, but British and French and Russian imperialism, and we were saying this not because it was so, but because we hoped to see it become so. To-day we can say so, because now it is so.

In those days, moreover, we said this is the "war to end war," and we still did not know clearly how. We thought in terms of treaties and alliances. It is largely the detachment and practical genius of the great English-speaking nation across the Atlantic that has carried the world on beyond and replaced that phrase by the phrase, "The League of Nations," a phrase suggesting plainly the organization of a sufficient instrument by which war may be ended for ever.[32] In 1913 talk of a World League of Nations would have seemed, to the extremest pitch, "Utopian." To-day the project

31. Krupp was Germany's largest steel-maker, and before WWI the Kaiser ruled an only partially democratized Germany. The term "Krupp-Kaiser alliance" is roughly the equivalent of the term "military-industrial complex" used by President Eisenhower in his farewell address to the nation on January 17, 1961.

32. As Chesterton points out, "League of Nations" is vague enough to be a foundation for radically different schemes, depending on whether the stress is placed on the 'League' or 'Nations' as the basic building block. Wells liked this ambiguity. "A phrase suggesting plainly" what Wells intended would bear an unappealing title like the "World State for Crushing Independent Nations." It could never be the means by which "war may be ended for ever," and would be torn by more civil wars than our present world is troubled by wars between nations. To maintain its monopoly on military force, it would have to intervene inside countries, crushing anyone criticizing the established order and fomenting rebellion. Since any rebellion against it would be considered treason, crimes against civilians would be far more common than that in traditional wars, where invading armies typically recognize that people in other countries have a right to place their loyalty elsewhere.

has an air not only of being so practicable, but of being so urgent and necessary and so manifestly the sane thing before mankind that not to be busied upon it, not to be making it more widely known and better understood, not to be working out its problems and bringing it about, is to be living outside of the contemporary life of the world. For a book upon any other subject at the present time some apology may be necessary, but a book upon this subject is as natural a thing to produce now as a pair of skates in winter when the ice begins to bear.

All we writers find ourselves engaged perforce in some part or other of a world-wide propaganda of this the most creative and hopeful of political ideas that has ever dawned upon the consciousness of mankind. With no concerted plan we feel called upon to serve it. And in no connection would one so like to think oneself un-original as in this connection. It would be a dismaying thing to realize that one were writing anything here which was not the possible thought of great multitudes of other people, and capable of becoming the common thought of mankind. One writes in such a book as this not to express oneself but to swell a chorus. The idea of the League of Nations is so great a one that it may well override the pretensions and command the allegiance of kings; much more does it claim the self-subjugation of the journalistic writer. Our innumerable books upon this great edifice of a World Peace do not constitute a scramble for attention, but an attempt to express in every variety of phrase and aspect this one system of ideas which now possesses us all. In the same way the elementary facts and ideas of the science of chemistry might conceivably be put completely and fully into one text-book, but, as a matter of fact, it is far more convenient to tell that same story over in a thousand different forms, in a text-book for boys here, for a different sort or class of boy there, for adult students, for reference, for people expert in mathematics, for people unused to the scientific method, and so on. For the last year the writer has been doing what he can—and a number of other writers have been doing what they can—to bring about a united declaration of all the Atlantic Allies in favour of a League of Nations, and to define the necessary nature of that League. He has, in the course of this work, written a series of articles upon the League and upon *the necessary sacrifices of preconceptions* that the idea involves in the London press. He has also been trying to clear his own mind upon the real meaning of that ambiguous word "democracy," for which the League is to make the world "safe." The bulk of this book is made up of these discussions. For a very considerable number of readers, it may be well to admit here, it can have no possible interest; they will have come at these questions themselves from different angles and they will have long since got to their own conclusions. But there may be others whose angle of approach may be similar to the writer's, who may have asked some or most of the questions he has had to ask, and who may be actively interested in the answers and the working out of the answers he has made to these questions. For them this book is printed.

H.G. Wells, *In the Fourth Year: Anticipations of a World Peace* (New York: Macmillan, 1918), v–ix.

Index

N

Printed in the United States
202213BV00003B/1-18/P

9 781587 420610